GW00503792

The
Making of Milwaukee

By John Gurda

Milwaukee County Historical Society

To Sonja,
and to our children,
Nikolai, Kjerstin, and Anders

— true Milwaukeeans all

Take away the multitudes of people who inhabit the city and what have you? A barren conglomeration of unkept structures not unlike an abandoned cemetery. It is the people, the men and women who toil with brain and brawn, who keep the wheels of industry whirling, who stimulate the life-blood of commerce and trade, and support the structure of government as an instrumentality for their mutual well-being: these men and women make a city.

A city then, in the broader sense, is a community of people, who band themselves together to secure for themselves the things that are vital to a happy, productive, orderly existence.

– Mayor Daniel W. Hoan, 1931

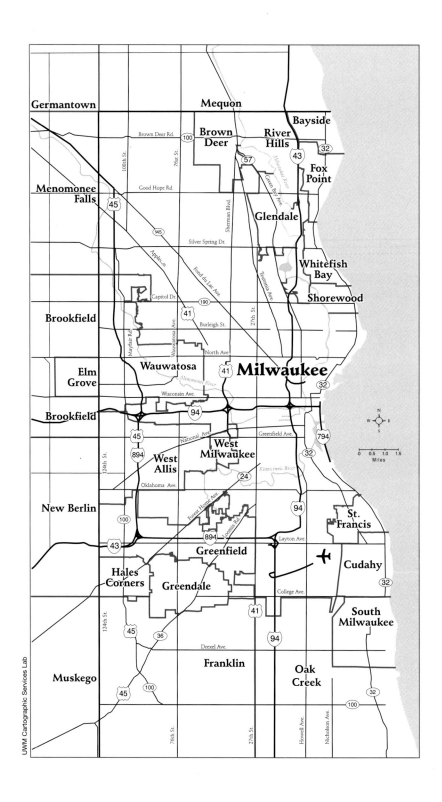

Foreword

"All history is local history," wrote Wisconsin scholar William Best Hesseltine. He was exaggerating, of course; the fighting at Gettysburg had an impact far beyond the bloody fields of rural Pennsylvania, and the stock market crash of 1929 affected more than a relative handful of brokers in Manhattan. But Hesseltine was exaggerating to make a point: It is on the local level that history comes to life. No single event – no technological advance, no economic trend, no social shift – is truly historic until it touches and transforms the lives of individuals in their home communities.

The Making of Milwaukee describes history coming to life in one home community, from its obscure beginnings as an Indian settlement through its hopeful days as a booming Great Lakes port, its rise as a stronghold of industries and immigrants, its bold experiments with municipal government, and its gradual (but never complete) immersion in national and global affairs. By the early twentieth century, Milwaukee had developed a national reputation based on three related hallmarks: Germanism, Socialism, and beer. All three have faded in importance, but the Milwaukee area retains, in the early years of another century, a thoroughly distinctive sense of place. Choice and circumstance have combined to produce a community that is unique in all the world, one whose character reflects influences as diverse as Harley-Davidson and Pabst Blue Ribbon, Golda Meir and Father Groppi, the German revolutionaries of 1848 and the Milwaukee Braves of 1957.

The approach I've taken in telling Milwaukee's rich story is, for lack of a better term, structural. The operative question throughout the book is "Why?" Why did promoters pick this location and not another? Why, with Chicago only ninety miles away, did a genuine metropolis emerge? Why such a heady mix of immigrants? Why such late-blooming racial discord? In digging through nearly two centuries of accumulated change, I have tried to uncover Milwaukee's civic bedrock – the shifting foundation on which individuals have built their lives and the community has constructed its identity.

There is no doubt that the deepest layer of that bedrock is economic. In every age, people have chosen to live in urban areas not because of their climates or landmarks or cultural attractions, but because they offer jobs. For black sharecroppers in the twentieth century no less than for European peasants in the nineteenth, it was economic opportunity that brought people to Milwaukee, and it is economic opportunity that keeps them there. I define cities as concentrations of people animated by concentrations of capital. More simply put, money is the root of all cities.

Despite this emphasis on foundations, *The Making of Milwaukee* is not an economic history. Just as geology literally supports biology on the surface of our planet, the urban economy provides the soil for human culture in our cities. Once people have gathered in a particular place to make a living, everything else follows: political machines, symphony orchestras, young ladies' sodalities, bowling leagues, saloons and, of course, conflict. With full knowledge of the omissions and abridgments in this particular account, I have tried to do at least primitive justice to the broad range of human creations that constitute the Milwaukee community.

This book would not have been possible without major support from the Lynde and Harry Bradley Foundation and the Jane B. Pettit Foundation. Crucial late-inning assistance was provided by the Northwestern Mutual Life Insurance Foundation and the Brady Corporation. The Metropolitan Milwaukee Association of Commerce (MMAC), through its Community Support Foundation, acted as the grant administrator. Publication of the book was underwritten by the Greater Milwaukee Foundation (and its Dr. Abraham B. and Irma F. Schwartz Fund), the Bradley Foundation, and the Pettit Foundation. The third edition was made possible by grants from the Bradley Foundation and the David and Julia Uihlein Charitable Foundation, with assistance from the Luedke-Smith and the Harry and Mary Franke Idea Funds of the Greater Milwaukee Foundation. I am grateful to all these institutions for their commitment to bringing history to life.

The manuscript was reviewed for accuracy by a distinguished group of Milwaukee experts: Harry Anderson, Steven Avella, Nancy Lurie (Chapter 1), Frederick Olson, and Frank Zeidler. Alan Borsuk offered editorial counsel that was unfailingly gentle but always on target. Graphic designer Jim Price (with Kate Hawley's help) has once again made my words look good. Mary Ellen Powers of the MMAC served as the project's fiscal agent with grace and good humor. Sarah Johnson was an indispensable guide to the treasures of the *Milwaukee Journal Sentinel* photo library, and Steve Daily played the same vital role at the Milwaukee County Historical Society. I am also indebted to the entire staff of Milwaukee's Central Library and particularly its Humanities Room – my research home away from home.

At times when the sheer volume of information began to seem overwhelming, I was sustained by two things: my native interest in all things Milwaukee and my belief in the usefulness of history. I am firmly convinced that, as the velocity of change increases, it is increasingly important to rebuild our connections with the past, whether that past involves our families, our home communities, or our entire society. We do so not for comfort but for context, not to feed a misplaced sense of nostalgia but to broaden our understanding of the world around us. History, at its root, is why things are the way they are. It is my fervent hope that *The Making of Milwaukee* will add a useful historical dimension to the ongoing conversation about Milwaukee in particular and American cities in general. We look back to look ahead; the deepest value of the past is to help the present shape its future.

John Gurda

The Making of Milwaukee
Contents

Chapter 1

Native Milwaukee

I t's one o'clock on a Wednesday afternoon, and the parking lots at Potawatomi Bingo are already full. Inside the cavernous hall, nearly 2,000 people are hunched over their cards, daubers poised to blot out the first numbers. The musical drone of the nearby slot machines is the only sound that breaks the pre-game silence. The mood is earnest, expectant. Hope abounds.

It takes the caller nearly three hours to exhaust the afternoon's line-up of games, an assortment that has players scanning their sheets for Six Packs, Picture Frames, Crazy Kites, Cloverleaves, Sputniks, and a dozen other patterns not generally found in nature. Expectations thin as the session wears on; disappointment, for all but a few, is palpable. When the last game – something called G-Ball Coverall – ends with an exultant cry of "Bingo!" in a far corner of the room, hope evaporates.

The ebb and flow of hope have produced a land-office business for Potawatomi Bingo. The casino regularly outdraws the Milwaukee Brewers and outearns some of the city's largest banks. Its success is both highly controversial and supremely ironic. The facility is, first of all, the property of the Forest County Potawatomi, a community of roughly 1,000 people planted in the woodlands of northern Wisconsin. The group's ancestors were once the dominant tribe in Milwaukee, paddling their canoes and erecting their wigwams in the heart of the future metropolis.

They were evicted in the 1830s, beginning a diaspora that left the tribe without a Milwaukee foothold until the opening of the casino in 1991. Potawatomi Bingo marks the return of the natives, under vastly changed circumstances, to an ancient homeland.

There is a deeper irony in the casino's location. It lies near the center of the Menomonee Valley, between a malodorous slaughterhouse and the steel shanks of the Sixteenth Street viaduct. The valley is rarely listed among Milwaukee's scenic wonders, but it was, in its original form, a critically important resource for Milwaukee's natives. Until white settlers buried it under tons of gravel and garbage, the Menomonee Valley was a sprawling marsh that provided the early Potawatomi and their neighbors with an abundance of fish, waterfowl, and wild rice. ("Menomonee" is an Indian word for wild rice.) In a land known for its native bounty, the valley was a more bountiful place than most.

The modern Potawatomi have found a new source of riches in the Menomonee Valley, and there is a crowning irony, a symmetry bordering on the poetic, in the casino's success. Before their eviction in the nineteenth century, Milwaukee's natives were systematically separated from their wealth: the millions of acres of land they controlled. Imported vices, particularly alcohol, hastened the process. Employing another vice, today's Indians are systematically reclaiming their wealth – one gambler at a time.

Before History

Although their ties to the land are incontestable, the Potawatomi were not the first Milwaukeeans. That distinction belongs to scattered bands of hunters who followed mastodons and musk oxen to the present site of the city. (Anthropologists call them Paleo-Indians; what they called themselves is a mystery.) They arrived at least 12,000 years ago, when the chill scent of retreating glaciers still lingered over southern Wisconsin, and human settlement has been more or less continuous since that time. As the hunters added gathering and then gardening to their repertoire of skills, nomadic bands gradually gave way to semi-permanent villages established on the most fertile corn ground. Each group in the slow procession of cultures left scattered evidence of its tenure: spear points, fluted axes, beads and, after 1000 B.C., pottery.

Some early residents left more imposing signs of their presence. Milwaukee County was once dotted with more than 200 earthen mounds that persisted as mute testaments of an earlier culture. Built between 800 B.C. and 1200 A.D., most of the mounds were simple cones and ovals, but there were also dozens of effigies. Southern Wisconsin was the center of Effigy Mound culture in North America, and Milwaukee County had a menagerie of birds, panthers (or water spirits), and turtles, some more than 250 feet long. Each contained tons of earth, all of it excavated with stone tools and deposited one laborious basketful at a time.

The greatest concentration of mounds was on the South Side, near the present site of Forest Home Cemetery. Indian Fields, as the early white settlers called the area, boasted more than sixty earthworks, one of them a rare panther intaglio, a cat-shaped crater painstakingly carved into the surface of the soil. Obliterated in the mid-1800s, the panther's old outline now encloses the graves of Laackes, Kieckhefers, Hokansons, and dozens of other more recent Milwaukeeans.

The meaning of the effigies vanished with their builders. Many contained burials, but by no means all. The earthworks may have been clan totems, territorial markers,

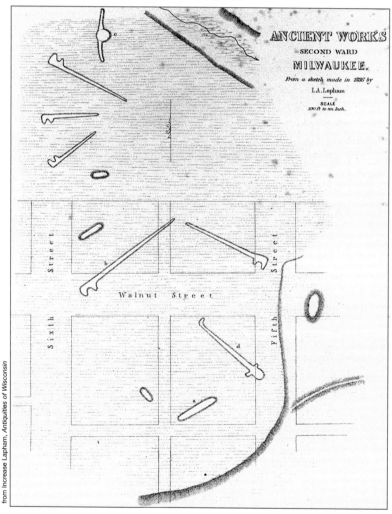

ANCIENT WORKS
SECOND WARD
MILWAUKEE.
From a sketch made in 1836 by
I.A. Lapham
SCALE
100 ft to an Inch.

Walnut Street

Sixth Street

Fifth Street

or simply places for communities to gather after the winter hunt. Given the labor required to build them, it is clear that the mounds had special significance for their creators. It is equally clear that they had no lasting significance for the white settlers who found them on their property. Although isolated examples remain – a modest berm in Lake Park, a gumdrop on the State Fair grounds – nearly all the rest were leveled for farmland and building sites in the nineteenth century. The region's outstanding collection is preserved at Lizard Mound County Park, near West Bend, but the work of Milwaukee's mound-builders has all but disappeared.

Who followed them is a matter of spirited debate. Two modern tribes – the Ho-Chunk (Winnebago) and the Menominee – probably developed from cultures present in the region many centuries ago, but their connections to the mound-builders are imperfectly understood. It is likely that residents of the 1500s, on the eve of European contact, already viewed the effigies as ancient wonders.

Milwaukee was Ho-Chunk territory, loosely defined, at the time of contact. Related by language to Sioux tribes living west of the Mississippi, the Ho-Chunk dominated an area stretching from Door County to northern Illinois. The Fox Valley-Green Bay area, including the shores of Lake Winnebago, was their particular stronghold. To the northwest were (and are) the Menominee, whose largest village was at the mouth of the Menominee River near Marinette. The boundary between the two tribes was fluid and easily crossed.

Practically nothing is known about Milwaukee during the years just before contact. The natives never organized an Old Settlers' Club, and they didn't attach plaques to their most ancient wigwams. The only clear evidence, most of it literally fragmentary, is archaeological. What is known, beyond the possibility of doubt, is that the 1600s were a cataclysmic century for the Ho-Chunk and their neighbors, an abrupt break with a past that survives only in legend. The cause of that break was a new force rising in the east: a colony planted by France and built on a foundation of furs. After millennia of relative isolation, the tribes of the upper Great Lakes came under its influence, and purely parochial concerns, in Milwaukee and elsewhere, were overshadowed by international developments. The local picture must be viewed in its global frame.

The story that flows from European contact is hopelessly one-sided, simply because the written record begins with white recorders. The explorers, missionaries, traders, and other uninvited guests who reached the interior tended to view the natives as resident aliens, and the chronicle they produced is a quagmire of garbled tribal names, nebulous geography, and casual stereotypes. The story is complicated by the fact that European influences arrived long before Europeans themselves. The region's natives had been trading with distant tribes for centuries; Wisconsin burials from the time of Christ contain obsidian from Wyoming, turquoise from Arizona, and shells from the Gulf of Mexico. The old networks were filled with the goods of New France after 1600. Jean Nicolet made a spectacular first landing on the shores of Green Bay in 1634, wearing "a grand robe of China damask" and firing his pistols in the air. Although Nicolet was probably the first European to appear in person, it is almost certain that brass kettles and glass beads preceded him to Wisconsin.

The native trading networks transported much more than kettles and beads. European diseases – smallpox, cholera, measles, typhoid, scarlet fever, and influenza – spread like wildfire across the continent, savaging a population with no immunity to alien bacteria. Estimates of overall mortality in North America range from a low of 30 percent to a high of 95 percent. Wisconsin's Ho-Chunk were among the hardest-hit. In the thirty years following Nicolet's surprise visit of 1634, the tribe's population plummeted from thousands to hundreds. Contamination marks the beginning of white-Indian relations in Wisconsin, and it continues, in one form or another, throughout the story that follows.

Iroquois aggression pushed numerous tribes from homelands farther east. By 1768 – the year of this map – the Potawatomi had dominated the western shore of Lake Michigan for over a century.

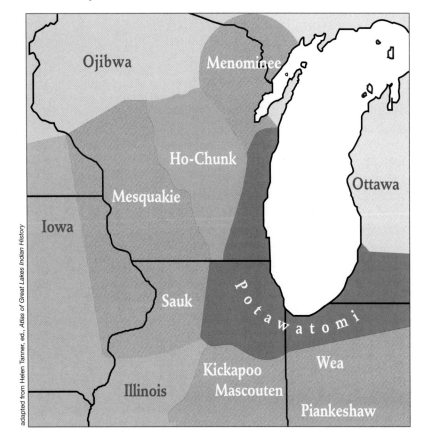

adapted from Helen Tanner, ed., *Atlas of Great Lakes Indian History*

The newcomers disrupted tribal settlement patterns nearly as profoundly as they disturbed tribal health. Through the 1600s and well into the 1700s, the North American fur trade had two competing power centers: Montreal for the French, and Albany for the Dutch and (after 1664) the English. Montreal tapped the rich "furshed" of the St. Lawrence Valley and the upper Great Lakes, a region populated by a bewildering variety of tribes. Albany's principal suppliers were the confederated Iroquois nations who controlled what is now upstate New York. The border between French and Dutch-English interests was indefinite but hotly contested.

By 1640, only twenty years after the Pilgrims landed at Plymouth Rock, the Iroquois had nearly wiped out the most valuable fur animals in their home country. The beaver, whose water-repellent fur yielded a felt that was hugely popular among European hatmakers, was in particularly short supply. Determined to expand their hunting grounds and, not incidentally, to divert French sources of supply, the Iroquois mounted a full-scale offensive against the tribes of the interior. War parties carried the campaign as far west as Illinois and Upper Michigan. Armed with muskets supplied by the Dutch and later the English, these fervent expansionists were practically invincible. Some tribes, including the Huron, were nearly exterminated; others fled for their lives like sheep before a wolf.

They fled, more often than not, to eastern Wisconsin. The Iroquois menace created what historian Richard White called a "shatter zone," a broad, largely depopulated area covering much of modern-day Ontario, Michigan, Indiana, and Ohio. In one of the great but virtually untracked migrations in American history, thousands of shatter-zone residents poured into Wisconsin, seeking refuge behind the barrier of Lake Michigan. Most entered from the north. The vacuum created by the Ho-Chunk s' demographic disaster was quickly filled, and the nearby Menominee were forced to accommodate new neighbors. They included Potawatomi, Ojibwe (Chippewa), Ottawa, Fox, Sauk, Kickapoo, Mascouten, and the tattered remnants of the Huron people.

There was no Red Cross to welcome the refugees, but they found what they needed in Wisconsin: fish and game for their families, birchbark for their canoes, and respite from the depredations of the Iroquois. The various tribes were as different from each other as Poles from Italians or Germans from Scots, but they soon discovered common ties. All but the Huron spoke Algonquian dialects, and some had long histories of intertribal cooperation. The Potawatomi, Ojibwe , and Ottawa, for instance, were linked in legend as the "Three Fires." Although conflicts would erupt in the next century, the most serious involving the Fox, the newcomers gradually developed a common-fate mentality. Perhaps a dozen new villages cropped up along the shores of Green Bay and northern Lake Michigan. Reflecting durable native traditions of hospitality and egalitarianism, most housed members of several tribes.

Tribal identities began to blur, but they never disappeared. In the new land of equals, the Potawatomi were more equal than most. Pushed from the lower peninsula of Michigan in the 1640s, they quickly emerged as the most influential tribe in eastern Wisconsin. The Potawatomi were present in Door County as early as 1648, and they had spread as far south as Milwaukee by the late 1600s, always in the company of other tribes.

European traders, the ultimate cause of the exodus, followed the Algonquians west.

Visitors had been few since Nicolet's 1634 expedition, but in 1671, during a lull in the Iroquois wars, a small armada of French officials paddled out from Montreal for an elaborate annexation ceremony at Sault Ste. Marie. With the typical European blend of naiveté and arrogance, they claimed the western two-thirds of North America for France.

This sprawling empire was already occupied, of course, but Frenchmen were soon probing its interior. In 1673 explorer Louis Joliet, accompanied by Father Jacques Marquette, embarked on a journey that would bring glory to both crown and cross. Beginning at a Jesuit mission on the Straits of Mackinac, the link between Lakes Michigan and Huron, their party of seven followed the

Joliet and Marquette pioneered a circle route that became one of the principal "highways" of the fur trade.

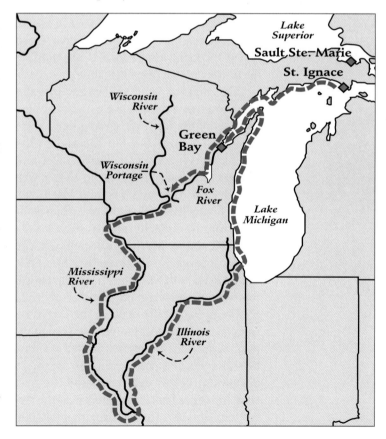

Michigan shoreline to Green Bay and then ascended the Fox River to its headwaters in today's Columbia County. An easy portage brought the wayfarers to the Wisconsin River, which carried them, one month after their departure, to the broad waters of the Mississippi. "Discover" is too strong a word – natives had been using the river for millennia – but Joliet and Marquette were probably the first Europeans to see the upper Mississippi.

After floating downstream to Arkansas, where rumors of hostile Spaniards convinced them to turn around, the group paddled back to a bend above St. Louis and ascended the Illinois River. A portage at Chicago brought them to Lake Michigan again, and the weather-beaten travelers finally beached their canoes at Green Bay in late September, more than four months after their 2,500-mile voyage began. (Marquette camped at Milwaukee on a return trip in 1674, providing a local connection for the university that bears his name.)

The elliptical canoe trail blazed by Joliet and Marquette soon became a main-traveled highway of the fur trade, giving rise to settlements like Green Bay, Portage, and Prairie du Chien in Wisconsin and Peoria, Joliet, and Chicago in Illinois. The gateway to this vast territory was the French post at Mackinac, which flourished as the point of exchange for furs from the interior and traders' goods from Montreal. Mackinac was easily the largest European settlement on the upper Great Lakes, with a summertime population that swelled to several thousand.

Green Bay, at the head of the Fox-Wisconsin waterway, became a major secondary post. The first French traders arrived at Green Bay in 1668, the first Jesuit missionaries began to preach a year later, and the first French soldiers built a crude fort near the river mouth in 1717. There were perhaps 10,000 Indians in the vicinity at the time. The European newcomers and their native suppliers quickly developed a mutual dependence that would last for more than a century.

"Good Land" on the Lakefront

Milwaukee, it will be noticed, was barely in the loop. The location of the future metropolis had no strategic value, and its rivers led to nowhere in particular. For the traders and missionaries who followed the great circle route down the Fox-Wisconsin waterway to the Mississippi and back again on the Illinois River and Lake Michigan, Milwaukee was little more than a convenient campsite. It was, nonetheless, a native settlement of some importance. The earliest mention of the community dates from 1679, when Father Zenobius Membre visited a village of Fox and Mascoutens at the mouth of the "Melleoki" River – the present site of Jones Island. There was evidently a population explosion in the decades that followed. Later visitors described mixed settlements of Potawatomi, Sauk, Ottawa, Ojibwe , and Menominee families in Milwaukee, their numbers and tribal affiliations shifting from year to year. The Potawatomi were the senior partners in the local alliance of tribes, a position they held until white settlement began in earnest.

With the exception of the Menominee, all of these early Milwaukeeans had entered the state as refugees. The Iroquois were finally pacified in 1701, taking their place as a neutral nation between the English and the French farther east. In the half-century of relative peace that followed, the refugees became semi-permanent residents, establishing at least nine villages in the Milwaukee area.

Nearly all were perched on high ground within easy reach of the nearest river. The village at the river mouth itself, commanding the entrance to Milwaukee, was probably built on the fire circles of much older settlements. Other villages crowned the bluffs overlooking the wetlands of central Milwaukee: in today's Mitchell Park, at Twenty-third and Clybourn, at Fifth and Wisconsin, on Walker's Point, and in northern Bay View.

Population estimates for each village range from 200 to 1,200, with the average certainly below 500. Each was a compact cluster of wigwams – simple domes with roofs of bark and walls of woven reeds – as well as a self-contained social unit, with its own clan networks, storytellers, and political leaders. The names of those leaders – Siggenauk, Onaugesa, Naskewoin, Pauschkena, Kenozhaykum, Oseebwaisum – typified the ancient music of the Algonquian dialects.

Few, if any, of the villagers were year-round residents. When the leaves fell each autumn, extended family groups dispersed for the winter hunt, an arduous trek that often took them hundreds of miles from home. In late winter they returned to the region's maple groves, arriving in time to tap the trees and turn their sap into maple sugar. With the start of the growing season in April or May, the Indians regrouped in Milwaukee, filling their villages with the smell of woodsmoke and the sound of barking dogs.

It was probably these early villagers who gave Milwaukee its name. That name, however, at least in its original form, was lost as soon as Europeans tried to pronounce it. By the same linguistic legerdemain that turned "Ojibwe" into "Chippewa," Milwaukee was variously known as Mahnawauk, Melleoki, Milouakik, Meneawkee, Milowages, Meolaki, Minnawack, and (a personal favorite) Milwacky. It was not until the early 1800s that the name settled down to its present pronunciation, and an alternate spelling – Milwaukie –lingered into the 1860s. The meaning of the name is just as elusive. There is no "l" in the Potawatomi language, and native speakers throw up their hands when asked for the English translation of "Milwaukee." The name has been variously rendered as "good land," "gathering place," "wet land," a medicinal plant, and even "stinking river" – a possibility with modern connotations.

"Good land," the most common translation, is also the most appropriate. Milwaukee may have lacked the strategic location of a

Indian villages and mound sites in central Milwaukee. (Parentheses on this and later maps denote modern street names.)

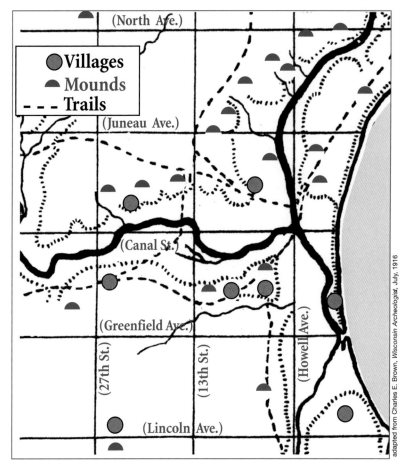

adapted from Charles E. Brown, *Wisconsin Archeologist*, July, 1916

7

Green Bay or a Chicago, but it had abundant resources of its own. Most of the present county was covered with a towering forest of sugar maples, basswoods and, near the lakeshore, beech trees. The virgin canopy was so dense that, to exaggerate only slightly, a traveler could walk from Milwaukee to Waukesha on a bright summer day without seeing the sun. Elk, black bear, deer, and smaller game animals were plentiful in the forest, and its floor was a carpet of mayapple, trillium, bloodroot, and hundreds of other native flowers each spring. In the southwestern reaches of the county, maples gave way to oaks, and the oaks thinned out to pure prairie, a northern tongue of the tallgrass sea that swept south across Illinois. Buffalo roamed the oak savannas and grasslands of Milwaukee County before white settlement; they were reported as far north as Green Bay in the 1650s.

Three rivers –the Milwaukee, the Menomonee, and the Kinnickinnic – converged near the lake. They would play a pivotal role in Milwaukee's early development, sparking rivalries, creating neighborhoods and, in the Menomonee's case, dividing the county into two sections, north and south, of roughly equal size. Milwaukee is still a bivalve community, forever hinged at the Menomonee Valley.

The rivers also created wetlands. Although forests and prairies covered more ground, Milwaukee's defining feature was a sprawling marsh that soaked what is now the heart of the city. The original wetland covered large sections of downtown, the Third Ward, Jones Island, Walker's Point, and even Bay View. A broad finger of the central marsh reached into the interior, filling the Menomonee Valley as far west as Forty-third Street (and inundating the site of Potawatomi Bingo). On the west side of today's downtown, around the Grand Avenue shopping mall, the open marsh hardened to a swamp, a thicket of tamaracks and cedars extending north past Juneau Avenue. Steep bluffs, some more than 100 feet high, ringed the central wetlands. Punctuated by ravines and dotted with coldwater springs, they were favored building sites for both the Indian villagers and the white settlers who replaced them.

The wetlands were indispensable to Milwaukee's natives. The rivers themselves provided both canoe trails and an abundance of fish. No one went hungry during the annual spawning runs – bass and sturgeon in spring, trout and whitefish in fall. Skilled spearmen worked throughout the summer, patrolling the Milwaukee River at a time when the bottom was visible to a depth of eighteen feet. The riverine marshes teemed with waterfowl, particularly during migrations. In October, 1698, a group of visiting missionaries reported feasting for two days on "ducks and teal" taken from Milwaukee's wetlands. Water-loving plants were another gift of the marsh: reeds and rushes for mats and bags, and that perennial staple, wild rice. There were drawbacks to life on the marsh – swarms of mosquitoes and the occasional wet moccasin – but the advantages were obvious.

Local resources supported a significant population, but there was plenty of elbow room in native Milwaukee. One student of Indian culture (Publius Lawson) guessed that there were 4,000 people in the Milwaukee area by the late 1700s. Another scholar (Helen Tanner) estimates that in 1768 there were 60,000 natives living in the entire Great Lakes basin – a region stretching from Montreal to Minnesota. Although settlement was sparse, the natives' impact on the land should not be underestimated. Indians trod lightly on the soil, but Milwaukee was hardly the "trackless waste" conjured up by white pioneers. There were the effigy mounds, of course, which the Potawatomi and their neighbors continued to use for burials. Every village occupied several acres of cleared ground, and all the native settlements were linked by an extensive network of Indian trails. The Green Bay trail, which roughly paralleled today's Green Bay Avenue, was so popular that it was worn to a depth of nearly two feet.

Native agriculture was another sign of human impact. Local residents grew a variety of exotic plants – corn, beans, squash, melons, and perhaps tobacco – that had been carried north, centuries earlier, from their native habitats in Mexico or the tropics. Sizable garden beds were a feature of every Milwaukee village, and one community specialized in the production of corn. At Indian Fields, the old effigy mound site near Forest Home Cemetery, corn hills covered most of a square mile of land – as much acreage as a modern Wisconsin dairy farm. The adjoining village, near the present corner of Forest Home and Lincoln Avenues, was headed by a chief whose English name was, appropriately, Cornstalk. Corn grown at Indian Fields and elsewhere became a vitally important commodity in trade with the Europeans. In 1778 a fur trader at Mackinac wrote a revealing letter to his supplier in Montreal: "I shall send a Young Brother in law of mine to take his place at Millwakee, as much on account of the Corn to be got there as the Peltry."

Milwaukee's natives shaped the land as the land shaped them, a process that later generations would call "symbiotic." The region was a relative paradise of natural resources – wetland, woodland, and grassland – that served its residents as larder and

medicine chest, playground and place of worship. Life was never easy in the native communities; life expectancies were short, hunger common, and the winters long. But there is clear evidence that Milwaukee fully deserved its designation as "good land."

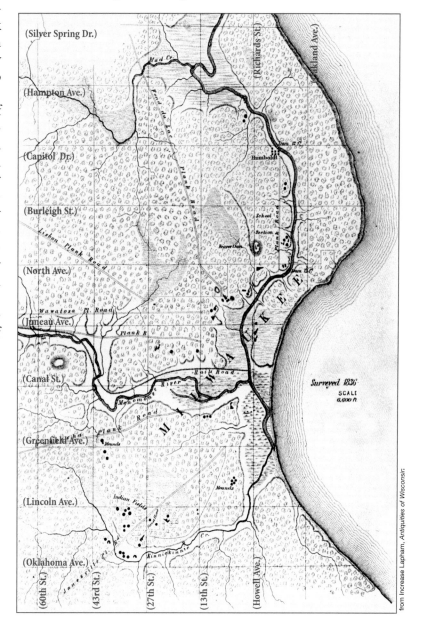

The woodlands, wetlands, and mound sites of native Milwaukee were mapped by Increase Lapham between 1836 and 1852.

from Increase Lapham, *Antiquities of Wisconsin.*

A Calamitous Partnership

The temptation to romanticize Milwaukee's natives is almost overpowering. There is an appealing simplicity to living on the land, to living off the land, and it becomes more appealing as modern life becomes more complex. We look back wistfully to a time of virgin forests and clean water, when people had an abiding spiritual relationship with the earth, untainted by the artifice and anxieties of civilization.

The fact is that no record of such a life exists, and that such a life was practically impossible after 1650. The influence of Europe, of civilization, was inescapable: in the European diseases that plagued the Ho-Chunk, in the trade-based Iroquois wars that drove the Algonquian tribes from their homelands, and in the resettlement of Milwaukee by mixed bands of refugees. Natives entered a relationship with the pale-skinned newcomers, some more willingly than others, and the price of that relationship was pervasive change.

The primary engine of change was, of course, the fur trade. Milwaukee's Indians exchanged the bounty of their land, beginning with beaver pelts, for a long shopping list of imported goods: muskets and traps, hoes and kettles, beads and blankets. Although they were hardly westernized, the natives gradually became dependent on European material culture. Trade goods began to appear in Wisconsin burials in the 1650s; within a century they had virtually replaced native artifacts.

The price the Indians paid for these fabulous articles was counted in more than furs. It is telling that the first recorded mention of a trader in Milwaukee is also a report of alcohol abuse. In 1741 the governor of New France noted a complaint of the Indians at "Meolaki," who felt that "they could never pacify their young men, as long as these Frenchmen kept coming so near to Them with Brandy." French brandy, followed by English rum and then American whiskey, was one of the fur trade's most important lubricants, and its impact on local tribes was devastating.

The fur trade also affected the natives' spiritual world. As furs became a commodity, there were no longer ritual apologies to the spirits of the beaver and bear whose pelts were hauled to the nearest trading post each spring. People no longer listened for voices in the woods. Historian Calvin Martin argues that the animals lost their tongues when they became a medium of exchange, and with them the trees and stones grew silent. One tangible result was reckless overhunting. Beaver were nearly extinct around Mackinac in the early 1700s; by 1800 they were scarce in eastern Wisconsin as well.

The fur trade was corrosive enough in peacetime, but its pressures were overpowering during periods of armed conflict. Appealing to the warrior tradition in native society, as well as to their self-interest as trading partners, colonial officials called upon the Indians to risk their lives, and frequently to lose them, in conflict with common enemies. "Friendly" tribes helped the French quell a series of insurrections by the Fox nation in the early 1700s, but intertribal fighting was the least of it. Acting as allies in some cases and as mercenaries in others, thousands of Great Lakes warriors became the armed instruments of policies set in the capitals of Europe. As one power replaced another, the conflicts came to resemble a bloody game of musical chairs. In the end, it was the Indians who had nowhere to sit.

In the mid-1700s, after fifty years of relative quiet, the Milwaukee area's tribes were drawn into a series of conflicts that would, in barely three decades, transform the political geography of North America not once but twice, with disastrous consequences for the natives. In 1754 French forces captured a fort being built by British colonists in western Pennsylvania – the first major engagement of the French and Indian War. When the British counterattacked in 1755, Milwaukee's Potawatomi joined the force that hastened to the defense. Near Fort Duquesne (the present site of Pittsburgh), they met and defeated an army whose leaders included a young colonel named George Washington. According to tribal legend, the Potawatomi returned to Wisconsin on British horses taken as booty during the battle. (Whether George's mount was among them is unrecorded.) Horses soon replaced canoes as the favored means of transport; the local herd grew so large that Milwaukee's Indians had to fence their gardens with poles and brush.

Horses were a welcome change, but the outcome of the war was not. When Montreal fell in 1760, New France ceased to exist, and England reigned supreme over eastern North America. The victors quickly asserted their claim to the interior. In 1761, two years before the final peace treaty was signed, British soldiers occupied the old French forts at Mackinac and Green Bay. After nearly a century under the French flag, Milwaukee was nominally British territory.

Although Indian support for the French had been overwhelming, there were no British reprisals after the war. In 1762 Lt. James Gorrell, the new commander at Green Bay, chided visiting warriors for "imprudently" backing the French, but he added, "I light also a fire of pure friendship and concord." The fur trade was crucial to the colonial economy, and punitive action against its sole suppliers would have been impolitic.

No sooner had the British stabilized their hold on the Great Lakes than they faced trouble farther east. Years of colonial restiveness burst into open rebellion in 1775, and British authorities found themselves at war with their own subjects. Most Great Lakes Indians sided with their British trading partners during the American Revolution. One of the lone holdouts was a Milwaukee chief of Potawatomi-Ottawa ancestry named Siggenauk, or Blackbird. In 1778 George Rogers Clark pushed a small British force out of Illinois and appealed to the natives for support. Siggenauk was among the chiefs who visited Clark at the ancient settlement of Cahokia, opposite modern St. Louis. He decided to cast his lot with the Americans, and Clark sent him back to Milwaukee with two pack horses laden with gifts. Siggenauk rendered valuable service to the colonials, frustrating British attempts to recruit warriors and staging occasional raids on British outposts.

Col. Arent De Peyster, the British commander at Mackinac, was outraged. Addressing a group of native allies in northern Michigan, he blasted "those runegates of Milwakie – a horrid set of refractory Indians." A thousand miles from the real action, De Peyster did what he could to respond. In 1779 he dispatched the sloop *Felicity* to Milwaukee to arrest the rebel chief "either by fair or forced method." (The *Felicity* was in all likelihood the first European-designed ship to call on Milwaukee.) Fearing a chilly reception, the soldiers declined to row ashore, but a small delegation of natives did visit the sloop. Although they freely accepted British gifts of rum and tobacco, the Indians showed no inclination to turn over their chief. The crew sailed back to Mackinac empty-handed, and Siggenauk remained a thorn in the British side until the war ended.

Artifacts on this and following pages are from the Milwaukee Public Museum collection.

In 1795 Jacques Vieau established a trading post on a bluff overlooking the Menomonee Valley. The site is now part of Mitchell Park.

With American victory secured in the peace of 1783, the present Midwest changed hands for the second time in twenty years. The new nation's hold on its wilderness zone was tenuous at best. The army established a modest presence, taking over Mackinac Island in 1796 and building Fort Dearborn on the Chicago portage in 1803, but the Great Lakes region became a sort of free trade zone. Canadian interests, using British capital and French labor, continued to dominate the fur trade; the relatively few Americans who started ed posts were strangers in their own country.

It was during the American period that Milwaukee emerged from its relative obscurity as a trading post. Names like St. Pierre, Marin, and Laframboise began to appear on the fur-company rosters, and in 1795 Milwaukee's natives met a trader who would outlast them all: Jacques Vieau. Like most of his counterparts, Vieau had begun his career as a *voyageur,* paddling between Montreal and the upper Great Lakes. He eventually settled in Green Bay and worked his way into the ranks of management. Vieau also met and married Angeline Roy, a trader's daughter of French and Menominee ancestry. In 1795 Vieau was engaged by the North West Company, the dominant Canadian firm, to open new posts along the western shore of Lake Michigan, at Kewaunee, Manitowoc, Sheboygan, and Milwaukee. Milwaukee anchored the chain of posts. Vieau built a cabin on top of the bluff in today's Mitchell Park, providing his family with a panoramic view of the Menomonee Valley. (A tablet erected by the Old Settlers Club in 1925 still marks the site.) The post bordered a sizable native village and practically straddled the trail between Milwaukee and Mukwonago.

Jacques Vieau did not have the local market to himself. At least one earlier trader, Alexander Laframboise, continued to visit Milwaukee, and a steady procession of French (and a few British) Canadians established posts after 1795. The newcomers included Jean Mirandeau, Thomas Anderson, Antoine Le Clair, Joseph La Croix, Jean Beaubien, and the settlement's first "Stash," Stanislaus Chappeau. Like their native suppliers, all set up housekeeping on the banks of Milwaukee's rivers. They were independents, as a rule, and some probably worked in the tradition of the *coureurs du bois* ("woods cruisers"), an unlicensed and generally unscrupulous bunch who caused headaches for generations of colonial officials. Jacques Vieau was a notable exception to the general pattern. Not only was he a licensed agent of the North West Company, but he also showed remarkable staying power. Although he was never a permanent resident, Vieau traded in Milwaukee from 1795 to the mid-1830s – a tenure of nearly forty years.

As a French Canadian working for British interests on American soil, Jacques Vieau had somewhat divided loyalties, but events in the larger world forced a resolution. Continuing tensions between the British and the Americans erupted into armed conflict in the War of 1812, a struggle that severely tested the young republic's control of the Great Lakes region. The vast majority of natives, including, this time, those in Milwaukee, sided with their British partners. British-Indian forces recaptured Detroit, Mackinac, and Green Bay, and in 1812 a group of 400 to 600 Potawatomi warriors, including many from Milwaukee, killed more than 50 Americans who were trying to flee Fort Dearborn. The incident was Milwaukee's only decisive victory in a one-sided rivalry with Chicago that lingers to the present day.

The War of 1812 was a rematch of the Revolution, and the outcome was the same: total victory for the United States. Like the British before them, the Americans took no action against their native adversaries, but they did cement their hold on the region. In 1816 military crews rebuilt Fort Dearborn and added two outposts in Wisconsin: Fort Howard in Green Bay and Fort Crawford in Prairie du Chien. French Canadians like Vieau continued to run the fur posts, but natives who had grown up with French and then English goods found themselves trading for American merchandise.

The fur trade entered its final phase with passage of the Exclusion Act in 1816, a measure that barred British subjects (i.e., Canadian citizens) from commerce with the Indians. Established traders were frequently exempted, but the new policy provided an opening for America's first millionaire: John Jacob Astor. A long-standing partnership with Canadian firms had already made him the dominant American in the trade; Astor collected furs in New York City and shipped them as far as China. With passage of the Exclusion Act, he began to dream of monopoly. Astor's American Fur Company went into high gear, establishing new posts, manipulating government officials, and hounding independent traders. Wisconsin was soon American Fur country. In 1824 John Lawe, a Green Bay independent (and probably Wisconsin's first Jewish resident) conceded defeat: "The old times is no more.... That pleasant reign is over and never to return any more." Jacques Vieau saw the handwriting on the wall; by 1821 the French Canadian had joined the American Fur Company and become a United States citizen.

Solomon Juneau and his wife, the former Josette Vieau, were the last (and longest-remembered) of the French-speaking families who settled in Milwaukee during the fur trade era.

The Last Trader

It was Jacques Vieau who brought a considerably more famous French Canadian to Milwaukee: Laurent Solomon Juneau. Widely considered the founder of the city, Juneau was a latecomer to the fur trade, but his career followed the traditional pattern step for step. Milwaukee's first mayor was born in 1793 in Repentigny, a small farming village near Montreal. For well over a century before Juneau's birth, Montreal had been the undisputed capital of the Great Lakes fur trade, serving as both its financial center and its primary labor market. Like thousands of young Montrealers before him, Juneau entered the trade as soon as he was old enough to handle a paddle. In about 1808, at the age of fifteen or sixteen, he signed on as

Milwaukee Public Library

Milwaukee Public Museum

a *voyageur* and took his place in one of the legendary Montreal trading canoes headed west. (Each craft was nearly 40 feet long, providing room for a crew of at least 8 men and 4 tons of cargo.) Juneau's canoe presumably followed the classic Canadian route to the interior: up the Ottawa and Mattawa Rivers to Lake Nipissing, down the French River to Lake Huron, and along Huron's northern shore to Mackinac. The voyage covered 900 miles and took a month to complete.

The *voyageurs'* daily routine was bone-grinding. Juneau and his compatriots paddled fourteen hours a day in summer, singing as they went to the rhythm of the paddles. On portages, which were numerous and long, each man was expected to carry at least two bales of furs or trade goods – a total weight of 160 to 180 pounds. (A modern backpacker might shoulder 50 pounds for a week in the woods.) It is little wonder that Juneau complained of "the confound rheumatism" in his middle years. The *voyageurs* typically slept under their canoes, but they also acted as manservants for the clerks and traders on board, carrying them to shore, pitching their tents, and preparing their food. Meals consisted of pea soup or corn chowder, seasoned with lard and often served with bannock, a primitive substitute for bread. There was little glamour and still less leisure in the wilderness life, but there was certainly color. Hard-working, hard-drinking, and relentlessly cheerful, the *voyageur* became as much a fixture in Canadian folklore as the cowboy has in the United States.

When his term of service (usually three years) came to an end, the typical *voyageur* returned to Montreal with a lifetime of memories. Some, however, developed a taste for the backwoods and an abiding fondness for the fur trade. Solomon Juneau was among those who stayed. His early career is impos-sible to reconstruct, but Juneau apparently worked for others in the region between Mackinac and the Mississippi. (He was reported at Prairie du Chien in 1817.) In about 1818, perhaps on Mackinac Island, Juneau met Jacques Vieau. More than thirty years Juneau's senior, Vieau was nearing the quarter-century mark as the mainstay of the Milwaukee trade.

In 1818 Juneau came to Milwaukee as Vieau's clerk and protégé, taking up residence in the little log cabin above the Menomonee Valley. He soon became his mentor's son-in-law as well. Jacques Vieau had at least twelve children, including a daughter named Josette. After what must have been a closely watched courtship, given the family's cramped quarters, Solomon and Josette were married in 1820. He was twenty-seven; she was seventeen. Josette's father was already "an ancient of days" and ready for a less demanding pace. As Juneau gained experience, Vieau entrusted more and more of the American Fur agency's business to his son-in-law.

The old trader maintained a string of outlying posts in southeastern Wisconsin, and Juneau and his bride apparently moved to one of them after their 1820 marriage. In 1821 both Juneau and Vieau were absent from Milwaukee, for the local American Fur agency was in the hands of James Kinzie, a Chicago resident whose brother, John H., would become that settlement's first village president. The young Chicagoan quickly established himself as a scalawag. Flouting American Fur's regulations, Kinzie smuggled whiskey into Milwaukee and used it to separate the local Indians from everything they owned, including their ponies. "I arrived at Milwalka on the 17th [of July]," reported a visiting Army lieutenant in 1822, "and found the Indians too much intoxicated to assist me in crossing the River."

When the authorities learned of his misdeeds, Kinzie was summarily exiled to Chicago, leaving Milwaukee's natives without a trading post of their own. "The Indians from that place," reported the federal Indian agent in Green Bay, "represented to me that they would be badly off for a trader, should Mr. Kinzie leave them." Solomon Juneau was apparently occupied elsewhere, because the Green Bay official lured Jacques Vieau, a trader "well known here for his integrity," out of semi-retirement to fill the gap. Vieau worked for the government for nearly three years and

Like their native suppliers, the Juneau and Vieau families lived on the edge of Milwaukee's central swamp. This homespun map was drawn in 1833 by Morgan Martin, who would soon become Solomon Juneau's business partner.

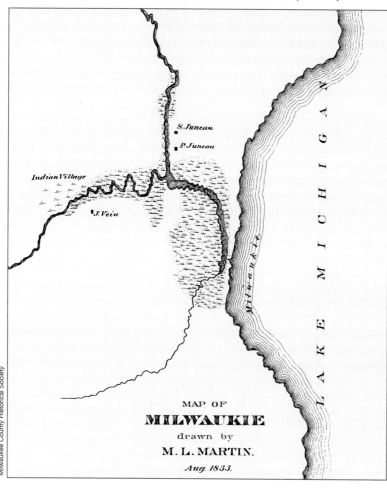

Milwaukee County Historical Society

MAP OF
MILWAUKIE
drawn by
M. L. MARTIN.
Aug. 1833.

then, in 1824, returned to American Fur's employ as head of the "Milwaukie outfit."

An old competitor, Jean Beaubien, was soon making life difficult for the Milwaukee veteran. In December, 1824, Jean Baptiste Jacobs, one of Vieau's employees, wrote a plaintive letter to a friend in Green Bay:

Hell, and every thing goes bad here – onley 3 packs [of furs] at this time. Last Winter about this time he [Vieau] had 20 packs and i believe we are going to starve. We onley have 4 bushels of Corn to pass the Winter and cannot get more. We arived so Late that Mr. Beaubien got all the Corn and all the good Indians of this Plase.... I believe we are to get the Rifrafts, those which are good for knowthing.

Vieau's band did survive the winter, and Jacobs (who had, surprisingly, once worked as a teacher) went home to Canada.

In 1825 Solomon Juneau returned to Milwaukee, working, like his father-in-law, for American Fur. (It was not unknown for the company to employ two traders in the same territory.) Solomon and Josette moved into a post of their own on what is now the corner of N. Water Street and E. Wisconsin Avenue. Juneau's brother, Pierre, one of the post's retainers, lived in a crude cabin immediately south. The site offered the first dependably dry ground above the mouth of the Milwaukee River.

Juneau was, by all accounts, an accomplished trader. An American Fur agency in the 1820s was like a Ford automobile dealership in the 1920s: a virtual guarantee of success for those with intelligence and drive. Juneau made the most of his opportunities. He developed a solid relationship with the local tribes, learning to speak Potawatomi and Menominee fluently. Juneau stood at least six feet tall in his moccasins and had a wrestler's physique. When the occasion demanded, he could be firm with the Indians, sometimes to the point of physical violence, but he also earned a reputation for fair dealing and human concern.

Although he had their earnest respect, Juneau maintained a scrupulous distance from his suppliers. He and Josette sent some of their children (of whom at least thirteen survived infancy) to boarding schools in Green Bay and Detroit as soon as they were old enough to travel. "One tries in vain," Solomon wrote to a friend in 1830, "to raise children very politely among Indians." In an 1838 letter to her daughters in Detroit (dictated to and translated by a family friend), Josette made it clear that she was considerably more French than Indian:

> The French language, if you can learn gramatically, will please me above all other branch of education and I live in hopes that you will be able in a few months to write me a letter in the French language, as you know very well I do not understand the English.

Josette closed the letter with a touching sentiment that any modern parent will recognize: "This is what I and your father wishes to see, all of you dear children well educated, which is the best Fortune we can leave you all after we are dead and gone."

It should be noted that Juneau, Vieau, and their occasional competitors were not full-time, permanent residents of Milwaukee. Green Bay was their metropolis, particularly a ragtag French settlement called Shantytown, which lay one mile upriver from the present city limits. Milwaukee, by contrast, was a seasonal outpost. Both Andrew Vieau, Juneau's brother-in-law, and Morgan Martin, later his business partner, state categorically that the trader made his home in Green Bay until the mid-1830s. He may have wintered in Milwaukee, but Juneau headed to "La Baye" when the springtime furs came in – an early instance of Milwaukee's vital connection with "up north."

Juneau and Vieau shared the Milwaukee trade for nearly a decade, working as either collaborators or friendly competitors. There was enough business to sustain both families for a time, but the pair soon faced the rigors of a declining market. Beaver were nearly extinct in the

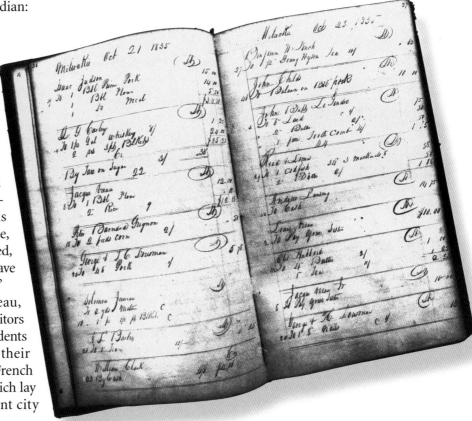

A page from Juneau's ledger

region by the 1820s; the staples of the trade were raccoon, deer, and muskrat pelts. With its abundant wetlands, Milwaukee was still, in an earlier trader's words, "a great place for muskrats," but changes in the fashion industry depressed prices for furs of any kind. The silk top hat had replaced the beaver hat in European high society by 1830, and expensive furs were gradually giving way to machine-produced clothing. In 1828 and again in 1832, the U.S. Congress declared that the American fur trade was "in a state of great depression."

A local disaster aggravated the traders' problems. In the winter of 1831-32, during the natives' normal hunting season, a smallpox epidemic swept through Milwaukee. Juneau described the calamity in a December letter to Green Bay:

> *All my children are sick with smallpox, as well as dear Mr. Viau.... All the Indians are afraid of dying. They say it was Mr. Viau's man who brought this sickness from the Bay or in the merchandise that they brought from the Bay.*

Jacques Vieau and his grandchildren pulled through, but many of the natives did not. In another letter to Green Bay in April, 1832, Juneau wrote, "There aren't any Indians who are completely recovered.... 85 Indians have died, among whom there were 25 good hunters." Vieau's suppliers apparently suffered the most. In an earlier time, the natives would have sent their dead to the hereafter with traditional ceremonies, but the work of grave-digging fell to Vieau and his men in 1832. The trader's son, Andrew, provided a graphic account of the epidemic's unceremonious end: "With a crooked stick inserted under a dead Indian's chin they would haul the infected corpse into a shallow pit dug for its reception and give it a hasty burial."

Jacques Vieau's problems snowballed. Throughout fur country, Indians bought their supplies on credit in fall and hoped for a successful hunt to repay their debts in spring. With so many of his customers under the ground, Vieau faced a mountain of uncollectible debts. "This winter ruined my father almost completely," recalled Andrew Vieau. After trying for three or four years, without success, to recoup his losses, the old French Canadian retired to his farm outside Green Bay, where he died in poverty at the age of at least ninety.

Juneau must have suffered losses of his own, but retirement, at the age of thirty-nine, was out of the question, and a move to more promising country had little appeal. Impelled by hope, stubbornness, or simple inertia, he decided to stay in Milwaukee. There he remained in the 1830s, the only trader in a land on the threshold of absolute change.

A Curtain Falls, a Curtain Rises

Smallpox, overhunting, and a declining market were hardly the most potent threats to Solomon Juneau's future as a fur trader. Since the earliest years of the Republic, a wave of American settlers had been gathering to the south and east. With the opening of the Northwest Territory in 1787, that wave of humanity broke across the Ohio River. It swelled westward each year, washing over Ohio, Indiana, and Illinois and finally rippling north into Michigan and Wisconsin.

The western wilderness soon became the American frontier, and there was a sea change in the prevailing attitude toward the land and its occupants. Solomon Juneau and his native suppliers needed the land to stay as it was; the pioneers needed to reshape it in their own image. Juneau's livelihood depended on the Indians; the settlers' economy depended on their removal. The contest between these radically opposed viewpoints was, to say the least, unequal. The middle ground shared by the Indians and traders soon gave way, and a much older ground – a partnership with the earth that had persisted for 12,000 years – disappeared completely.

It didn't take the Great Lakes tribes long to sense the coming change. During the colonial period, they had enjoyed substantial leverage. The region's natives were valued as suppliers by English and French fur traders, and they were courted as military allies by both powers. When the opportunity arose, they could play one side against the other with impressive dexterity. That leverage vanished in the American period. With the fur trade in decline and the British confined to Canada, the region's natives were increasingly expendable, and they knew it.

Armed resistance was one option. Marauding war parties made life on the frontier hazardous for white settlers, but more ambitious uprisings were put down with brutal efficiency by American troops, first in Ohio and then in Indiana. As the pioneers (and the soldiers) edged closer to Wisconsin, the future of the resident tribes began to take shape. In 1825 the United States convened a grand council of chiefs and band leaders at Prairie du Chien. The nominal purpose of the conference was to settle intertribal disputes along the Mississippi, but its tangible result was a map assigning specific borders to each tribe in the region. The borders were meaningless in practice and often laughably inaccurate. Eastern Wisconsin, for instance, was identified as Menominee land as far south as the mouth of the Milwaukee River – more than 100 miles from the tribe's true homeland. The territory west of the river was assigned to the Potawatomi, Ojibwe , and Ottawa. (The "Three Fires" were to go out together.) The present site of downtown Milwaukee, in other words, was divided at the river between two tribal groups, even though the villages on both sides were thoroughly polyglot. Whatever its shortcomings, the 1825 map served admirably as a prelude to eviction; its rigid borders provided the framework for land cessions that were dictated only a few years later.

By 1830 the wave of pioneers was poised to break over Wisconsin. Black Hawk, a Sauk leader, offered brief resistance in 1832, but he lost heart when neighboring tribes reneged on promises of aid. Militia commanders either ignored or misunderstood Black Hawk's attempts to surrender. His band was hounded through southern Wisconsin and finally butchered on the banks of the Mississippi, near the site of a town that was later named, with misplaced bravado, Victory. Black Hawk's resistance was a notable exception. Most tribes in the region were quiescent before his uprising, and the Sauk warrior's crushing defeat convinced those who wavered that the warpath led to extinction. Tribal leaders stalled for time and bargained for the best terms possible, but they accepted the inevitable.

Solomon Juneau himself acceded to the new regime. In 1831, after years of operating as an illegal alien, Juneau became an

American citizen and began to teach himself English. His native suppliers faced a significantly more perilous future. Their days of self-sufficiency were already ancient history; bows and arrows were curiosities by the 1830s, and the pottery prized by modern collectors was found only under old burial mounds. As the frontier edged closer, Milwaukee's natives were a dispirited lot, and some individuals were practically denatured. A chief named Onautissah presided over the village at the river mouth in the 1830s. Known as "king of the Potawatomis," Onautissah had a four-poster bed in his wigwam and levied a weekly tax of several gallons of whiskey on the early whites.

The condition of Milwaukee's natives fell rapidly from dispirited to dispossessed. In 1831, bowing to federal pressure, the Menominee ceded their lands north and east of the Milwaukee River to the United States. In 1833, after a lengthy treaty conference in Chicago, "the united nation of Chippewa, Ottawa, and Potawatomie" gave up five million acres on the other side of the river, a tract that sprawled west to the present sites of Watertown and Janesville. Indian title to the land was, in the apt metaphor of the day, "extinguished."

The natives were not, technically speaking, homeless. The Milwaukee area's Potawatomi, for instance, were granted five million acres in western Iowa and northwestern Missouri as compensation for their Wisconsin lands. The Potawatomi had wangled a three-year grace period from the date their treaty was ratified by the Senate in 1835. They remained in Milwaukee during the interim, racing their ponies on the sand flats along the lake, hunting in the surrounding forests, and bringing their furs to Solomon Juneau's post.

In 1838 their time was up. At the beginning of the corn-planting season, federal contractors gathered the natives at Indian Fields, the ancient burial ground on the South Side, and began the long, arduous trek to lands west of the Mississippi. It was Milwaukee's own Trail of Tears. The Potawatomi trudged west for more than a month, and there were undoubtedly deaths along the way. Even before they arrived, it was clear that the terms of the original treaty had been written in disappearing ink. When Missouri refused to harbor the Indians, their reservation in western Iowa was enlarged. When settlers wanted their lands in Iowa, the Potawatomi were pushed west again to Kansas. There, on the treeless plains outside Topeka, the descendants of this woodland people remain to the present day.

The story does not end in Kansas. Perhaps half the Potawatomi, and an unknown number of their neighbors, simply ignored their marching orders, and the government lacked either the will or the resources to evict them forcibly. Those who stayed in Milwaukee proper became the city's first minority group. Solomon Juneau continued to trade with them, even as their numbers dwindled. He described his "little trade with the Indians" as "tolerable fair" in 1839, a year after their supposed removal. (The American Fur Company continued to pay much higher prices for "prime Indian handled" pelts than for those trapped by white settlers for extra cash.) In 1842, however, Juneau was forced to confess that "the fur trade is of no consequence in this place, being but very few Indians here." Some of his old suppliers had been reduced to panhandling. In periodic accounts that appeared well into the 1850s, the *Milwaukee Sentinel* described "ridiculous" Indians dancing on the street corners "almost in a state of nudity" for pennies that were "speedily exchanged for whiskey." For the hordes of immigrants newly arrived from Europe, the spectacle was, reported the newspaper, "a source of unspeakable wonder."

A much larger group of natives wanted no part of the emerging city. At least 2,000 Potawatomi left their homes in the Milwaukee area for the forests of northern Wisconsin, Upper Michigan, and Ontario. Those who tarried in Wisconsin stayed one step ahead of white settlement for generations, moving so often that they were dubbed "the strolling Potawatomi." In 1913, finally, the federal government purchased 14,439 acres scattered across Forest County as a reservation for these wanderers. It is their grandchildren who brought Potawatomi Bingo to Milwaukee in 1991. The descendants of ancestral Milwaukeeans are among those selling bingo sheets and servicing slot machines in the Menomonee Valley hall.

With the advent of Indian gaming, we come, to borrow an ancient Indian symbol,

full circle. For two centuries, from the 1630s to the 1830s, Milwaukee's natives were engaged in a dramatic struggle for balance: between divergent tribal interests, between the conflicting claims of European powers, between the demands of the fur trade and the tug of tradition. With the advent of white settlement, that state of balance, never fully achieved, was finally and irrevocably lost.

The two centuries after European contact were a period of drastic change, for both the natives and their land, but change had barely begun by the time the Indians departed. The region was on the verge of a transformation. A swarm of ambitious newcomers, pursuing dreams that no Indian would recognize, was about to plant a city in the wilderness. That city would grow with astounding speed, stripping away all signs of an earlier presence until, in the end, nothing remained but the names: Milwaukee, Menomonee, Muskego, Kinnickinnic, Wauwatosa, Waukesha, Mukwonago, Ozaukee, ... "Bingo!"

Chapter 2

City on the Swamp, 1835 – 1846

An old portrait of Solomon Juneau hangs in a quiet corner of Milwaukee's Central Library. Rarely noticed, even by librarians, it shows Juneau in a formal pose, seated in a red damask chair and wearing a black coat, silk vest, and stiff white collar. A quill pen and inkwell lie at his side, as if he had just put the finishing touches on the map of Milwaukee that rests in his lap. Gazing directly at the viewer, Juneau looks alert, determined, positively senatorial. The artist's brush has transformed a rough-hewn backwoods trader into an august man of affairs.

None of his old cronies could have guessed that Solomon Juneau would one day sit for an official portrait. No one at Green Bay or Mackinac had the faintest idea that his log cabin would anchor an aspiring metropolis, or that Juneau himself would serve as its first mayor. Founding a city was the last thing on his mind; the fur trade and a growing family had always been Juneau's primary concerns. But the old *voyageur*, more by accident than design, became a charter member of the crew that built a city on the swamp. In the mid-1830s, Juneau took his place among a group of newcomers who had every intention of turning his homesite into a townsite. They included Morgan

Solomon Juneau, the fur trader who stayed to win and lose a fortune in urban real estate. This pairing of portrait and photograph, like those that follow, offers an instructive contrast.

Milwaukee Public Library

Wisconsin Historical Society

Martin, a well-born New York lawyer who became Juneau's business partner; Byron Kilbourn, a combative Connecticut-born Yankee; and George Walker, a genial son of Virginia. Separated by background, temperament, and moral standards, these rival promoters had only one thing in common: a firm belief that they could turn a mudhole into a metropolis.

Their belief was rooted in the region's geography. To borrow an old line from the real estate trade, Milwaukee had three advantages: location, location, and location. It was, first of all, part of the territory "north and west of the Ohio River," the region that played the role of the Sunbelt in post-Revolutionary America. The Northwest Territory lay directly in the path of the new nation's expansion in the first half of the 1800s, and people and capital poured in from older sections of the country. Ohio became a state in 1803, Indiana followed in 1816, and Illinois joined the Union two years later. Michigan, Iowa, and Wisconsin were next in line.

A novel public works project stimulated the westward flow and altered its course: the Erie Canal. Early settlement of the Northwest Territory had proceeded from the south, along the Ohio and Mississippi Rivers. (Lead miners, many with Southern roots, were the first whites to people Wisconsin, following the Mississippi to the state's southwestern corner in the 1820s.) The Erie Canal opened an alternate route. Completed in 1825, it was the engineering marvel of its age. Forty feet wide and four feet deep, the canal provided a continuous 363-mile watercourse from the Hudson River at Albany to Lake Erie at Buffalo.

Buffalo blossomed as a transfer point. Passengers bound for the Northwest left their horse-drawn canal boats on Buffalo's waterfront and proceeded to one of the lake ships tied up at the docks. Those ships carried emigrants across Lake Erie, up the Detroit River to Lake Huron, and finally through the Straits of Mackinac to Lake Michigan. Three-masted schooners were the conveyance of choice in the early years, but steamboats – all wood-hulled, wood-burning side-wheelers – dominated the passenger trade by the late 1830s. (Sailing vessels persisted as the freight trains of the lakes, carrying lumber, grain, and other bulk commodities.) The entire trip from the East Coast frequently took a month – not much less than the canoe voyage from Montreal to Mackinac.

Finishing the Erie Canal was like opening a dam. A flood of newcomers washed west across the Great Lakes, most of them either New England Yankees or upstate New Yorkers, who were typically Yankees once removed. Uniformly young and uniformly British in origin, these "Yankee-Yorkers" were seeking opportunities that seemed extinct in the settled East. Established farmers coveted the virgin farmland of the Northwest Territory. Younger sons with no hope of inheritance came west to start farms of their own. Speculators, merchants, and adventurers sought their fortunes on the urban frontier. In 1837 the *Wisconsin Democrat*, a Green Bay paper, rolled out the welcome mat for newcomers of all classes:

> *Let the farmer forsake his barren hills and "stony ground," where he but starves to live, and lives to starve; let the mechanic – yes, let all branches that form the great working class in our country, who are discontented, or do not succeed in their reasonable expectations at the East – scatter themselves throughout our wide domain that yet remains to be cultivated and settled – and nothing will be wanting but industry and economy to build up an abiding prosperity.*

As the exodus accelerated, fears of depopulation gripped parts of the East. In the mid-1800s, New York State gave up three residents for every one it gained from other states; only a high birth rate and massive European immigration kept New York from losing ground.

The Northwest's appeal was obvious, but why Milwaukee in particular? The answer, again, is location. In an age when everyone and everything traveled by water, it was obvious that the future belonged to settlements with superior harbors. Chicago, perched on the portage between Lake Michigan and the Illinois River, enjoyed an early advantage, but Chicago was near the southern tip of the lake – a dead end, relatively speaking. Other sites seemed more promising. All along Wisconsin's eastern shore, promoters dreamed of urban grandeur wherever a river reached the lake: the Pike at Kenosha, the Root at Racine, and even Sauk Creek at Port Washington, to name only a few. Milwaukee had two resources that its rivals lacked: the largest bay and the deepest river on the western shore of Lake Michigan, Chicago not excepted. Milwaukee Bay was six miles long and three miles wide, providing at least marginal protection for vessels in stormy weather. The Milwaukee River was considerably more important. Fed by the Menomonee and the Kinnickinnic in its lower reaches, the stream was twelve to eighteen feet deep near its mouth – more than enough to float the largest ships on the lakes.

The fact that most of central Milwaukee was underwater was irrelevant. For a civilization that could thread a canal across 363 miles of upstate New York, filling a few square miles of marshland held no particular terrors. The sandbar at the river mouth,

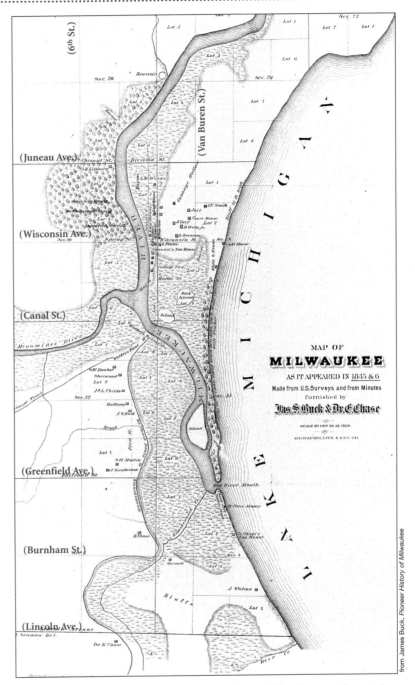

Most of central Milwaukee was underwater, but the site's harbor potential made it a magnet for townsite promoters in the 1830s.

from James Buck, *Pioneer History of Milwaukee*

25

which blocked vessels drawing more than five feet of water, was viewed as another problem with an easy engineering solution. The landscape could be reshaped to suit its new inhabitants; what mattered was Milwaukee's natural potential as a port.

That extraordinary potential attracted a small army of urban aspirants. Morgan Martin arrived in 1833, Byron Kilbourn and George Walker in 1834 – just ahead of the deluge. Kilbourn described the migration of early 1835 as "a flood," bringing perhaps 200 people to the embryonic city and forcing the *Green Bay Intelligencer,* Wisconsin's first newspaper, to take notice. "Land speculators are circumambulating it," reported the paper, "and Milwauky is all the rage."

The speculative rage soon mushroomed into a full-blown frenzy. One chronicler described Milwaukee in the mid-1830s as "an unenclosed lunatic asylum," with some lots changing hands twice or three times in a single day and prices rising with perilous speed. One speculator bought a parcel west of the Milwaukee River for $350 and sold half of it a year later for $19,500. The wilderness outpost came to resemble an open-air Monopoly board, with every player observing the first rule of the game: Grab all the property you can, and worry about improvements later. By August of 1835, soon after the first public land sale opened at Green Bay, every acre within two miles of Juneau's cabin had been claimed.

The settlement would have prospered in any case. Milwaukee's riverine geography and its location on the lake made the site an obvious choice for urban development. The identities of the men credited with founding the city are, therefore, largely immaterial; if Juneau, Martin, Kilbourn, and Walker had never existed, other individuals would

certainly have stepped into their roles. The true "founder" of the city was the westering impulse of the American people.

But individuals always make a difference. Milwaukee's leading promoters took divergent paths in exploiting the site's natural advantages. As development began in earnest, they worked at cross purposes and sometimes in open conflict, sparking a rivalry that had a permanent impact on Milwaukee's landscape. The chronicle of the city's founding is therefore not one story but three.

Solomon, Morgan, Byron, and George

Morgan Martin is the least celebrated of Milwaukee's founders. When he merits mention at all, it is in a secondary role, as the fourth member of a trio. Despite his low profile, Martin was a pivotal figure in the community's early years. He was the man responsible for the transformation evident in Solomon Juneau's official portrait; it was he who led the veteran trader to exchange his buckskins and calico for a black coat and stiff collar. The two men formed an unlikely alliance that produced a fortune for both, however fleeting, and a considerably more durable friendship.

Martin was much like the other Easterners seeking their futures on the frontier. Descended from solid colonial stock, he was born in 1805 in Martinsburg, New York, an upstate crossroads founded by his father. In 1827, when he was barely in his twenties, Martin moved to Green Bay and set up a law practice among the settlement's French Canadians, a people he described as "free-and-easy, good-hearted and hospitable." He remained a Green Bay resident for the rest of his life, taking a prominent part in local affairs, but Martin was constantly on the lookout for opportunities elsewhere.

Milwaukee proved to be the paramount opportunity in eastern Wisconsin. "I first visited Milwaukee and spent there the 4th of July, 1833," Martin recalled decades later. "My visit was one of exploration ... with a view of laying out a town at the point where Milwaukee now stands." Solomon Juneau, the site's apparent proprietor, was away at the time, attending the Chicago treaty session that would extinguish the last Indian claims in southeastern Wisconsin. Martin caught up with Juneau in October and proposed a business partnership. He was familiar with the intricacies of real estate, and Juneau had occupied the east side of the river long enough to claim sole possession under the prevailing laws. Together,

Martin argued, they could turn the Milwaukee wilderness into a thriving city. Juneau's first reaction, reported the New Yorker, was disbelief:

> *His first hint of the prospective value of his location at Milwaukee came from me, and he was so incredulous that it was sometimes difficult to prevent his sacrificing his interest to the sharks who soon gathered about him. Himself the soul of honor, and unaccustomed to the wiles of speculators, without a friend to caution him he would have been an easy prey of designing individuals.*

With returns from the fur trade diminishing by the year, Juneau quickly decided that a joint venture made sense. In October, 1833, Martin purchased from Juneau "one undivided half of all his possession at Milwaukie River" for $500 – one of the great bargains in the history of Milwaukee real estate.

Morgan Martin, Juneau's partner and fourth member of the trio that founded Milwaukee

Wisconsin Historical Society

Neville Public Museum, Green Bay

The partnership between the shrewd Yankee lawyer and the open-handed French Canadian was practically without precedent. Martin was entirely typical of his generation: ambitious, hard-working, and full of grandiose schemes. His business judgment was erratic, as later events would demonstrate, but Martin was as skilled as any promoter and more honest than most. Juneau was the anomaly. Most fur traders were, in historian Louise Phelps Kellogg's apt phrase, "pioneers of the pioneers," and they generally left as soon as speculators appeared. Juneau was an obvious departure from the pattern. He moved with relative ease from one stage of development to the next, staying in Milwaukee to win and then lose a fortune in frontier real estate. He was, in the end, a transitional figure, but Juneau played a crucial role in the city's early development.

Some of his Yankee contemporaries harbored an image of Juneau as a rustic, a child of the forest who never adjusted to the ways of civilization. In surviving accounts, they describe him as "one of Nature's noblemen," but their praise is tempered by terms like "trusting," "impulsive," and "too yielding." Juneau may have lacked the educational advantages of his new neighbors, but he knew retail. The veteran merchant had outlasted his competitors to make a decent living in the declining years of the fur trade, and he found little basic difference between selling blankets and selling land. Juneau also displayed obvious native intelligence, learning enough English to write passable letters of his own by 1837. The fact that he was less grasping than his Yankee counterparts need not be construed as a fault.

Once he could visualize a future in real estate, Juneau entered the game with alacrity. The official government survey was the essential first step, if only to prevent claim-jumping. In December, 1834, Albert Fowler, Juneau's bookkeeper, wrote to Martin that his boss had been forced to defend the Milwaukee claim physically:

> *Those young men that were building on the Lake Shore when you were here attempted to make a claim on his location and near his inclosure. He gave them notice that if they did not remove the house peaceable that he would remove it forceably for them. They did not remove it and he consequently threw it down on the day following. They laid up the logs again and insisted that they have as good a right to a claim as Mr. Juneau had. He tells me to inform you that he will hold possession at the peril of his life until he has a voice from you.*

Juneau believed that "those young men" were acting for James Kinzie, the same Chicagoan who had been drummed out of Milwaukee for selling whiskey to the Indians in the early 1820s. With a little prodding from Martin, federal crews surveyed central Milwaukee in January, 1835, fixing property lines permanently.

(The federal survey followed the grid pattern typical of the entire Midwest. The land was divided into sections of 640 acres, or one square mile, and further subdivided by individual developers. The original section lines persist as major arterials, including Juneau Avenue, North Avenue, Burleigh Street, and Capitol Drive on the North Side; Greenfield, Lincoln, and Oklahoma Avenues on the South Side; and Twenty-seventh Street from one end of the county to the other.)

With the survey completed, Juneau and Martin divided their holdings into lots and began to sell them to all comers. The land was not yet theirs to sell but, as a long-time (if seasonal) resident of Milwaukee, Juneau had a pre-emptive right to his claim. He exercised that right at eastern Wisconsin's first public land sale, a well-attended affair that convened at Green Bay in July, 1835. Juneau purchased 133 acres bordered roughly, in modern coordinates, by Broadway, Sixth Street, Wisconsin Avenue, and Juneau Avenue – the heart of Milwaukee's downtown. At the minimum price of $1.25 an acre, he paid the magnificent sum of $165.81 for the parcel. (Even in those pre-inflationary times, $1.25 was dirt-cheap, or cheap dirt, and it still guaranteed the government a profit; the average price paid for Indian land was only ten cents an acre.) Juneau's brother, Pierre, exercised his pre-emption on another 157 acres in what is now the Historic Third Ward.

That parcel, and others nearby, soon became part of the Juneau-Martin holdings.

With their titles secure, Juneau and Martin worked to make sure that their side of the river remained the center of the infant metropolis. Wisconsin was part of Michigan Territory at the time, and James Doty, a leading light in territorial politics, happened to be Martin's first cousin. In 1835, probably with assistance from Doty, Juneau became Milwaukee's first postmaster. The appointment helped to make his trading post the single most important gathering place in the settlement. In 1836 Juneau and Martin built Milwaukee County (organized the year before) its first courthouse, a pleasant little Greek Revival structure on

Hoping to attract settlers, Juneau and Martin donated land and built a courthouse on what is now Cathedral Square in 1836.

Milwaukee Public Library

29

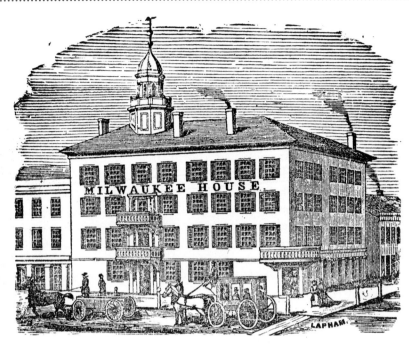

The Milwaukee House, another Juneau-Martin project, was the finest hotel in frontier Milwaukee. It originally stood on the corner of Broadway and Wisconsin Avenue.

present corner of Water Street and E. Wisconsin Avenue – the site of Juneau's trading post – became Milwaukee's commercial crossroads, and the streets that intersected there were the first to be graded. In 1836 Nelson Olin, a New Yorker whom Juneau hired away from a job in Green Bay, agreed to grade Wisconsin Avenue from the river to the lake for $3,000. After a trip back to New York for oxen, scrapers, shovels, and pickaxes, Olin went to work in June. He recalled the project as a definite challenge:

> *A harder job never was done in Milwaukee for the same money. There was a hollow midway between East Water and Main [Broadway] streets forty feet deep that took nearly two weeks of hard work to fill up. Van Buren Street also contained a terrible gulf to fill up. There was heavy timber from there to the lake. Some large trees had to be grubbed out, all of which came into play in filling up the hollows, which were very numerous at that early day.*

Just as much effort was required to level the bluffs that ringed the east side, including the precipitous bank that rose just north of Michigan Street. James Buck, who arrived in 1837, estimated that a crew of laborers cut away at least fifty feet of the bluff to soften its grade. The "borrowed" soil was used to fill in a portion of the adjoining Third Ward marsh.

Morgan Martin calculated that he and his partner spent $100,000 on townsite improvements – roughly $1.5 million in current dollars. Money was no problem for the partners, at least in the early years. Milwaukee was a genuine boom town, its fortunes fueled by pure speculation. The settlement's population swelled to more than 1,000 in 1836, and the greatest number of

the north end of what is now Cathedral Square. In the same year, they erected the Milwaukee (or Bellevue) House, a four-story hotel complete with an ornate cupola. Located on the corner of Wisconsin Avenue and Broadway, it became the premier hostelry of the pioneer period. As settlers poured into Milwaukee, the community qualified for a land office of its own, and that, too, became an east side plum. In a letter to Martin on September 20, 1836, Juneau hinted at bribery: "I have had some little difficulty to have the land office located on our side of the River. I had to make some little sacrifice as you know that it is of great importance to have it on our side."

Courthouses and hotels were certainly important, but streets were even more essential to the settlement's future. Downtown Milwaukee was quite literally a wilderness, and the work of cutting streets through the forest was back-breaking. The newcomers bought lots from Juneau and Martin. Housing was so scarce that many were forced to camp on the beach until a rough-and-ready crew of carpenters could throw up houses for them. In 1836, when Juneau brought a boatload of lumber down from Green Bay, the entire shipment was sold before his men had time to unload it. As the speculative fever mounted, Juneau himself succumbed, paying thousands of dollars for lots he had sold for hundreds only the year before.

Morgan Martin remained in Green Bay for the duration. He resisted Juneau's entreaties to move his law practice to Milwaukee, betting that Wisconsin's oldest settlement would also remain its largest. His sentiment was widely shared, at least in Green Bay. In 1837 the local *Wisconsin Democrat* dismissed Milwaukee and Chicago with a wave of its editorial hand: "Both of their towns are but *experiments –* ephemera of a summer's day, and may vanish before a summer's wind." Martin and the *Democrat* were mistaken, of course. Their community languished in the cul-de-sac of the bay, well off the main-traveled water route. It was not until the 1890s, when industrialization began in earnest, that Green Bay's population passed the 10,000 mark. Milwaukee, by that time, had more than 200,000 people.

With Martin's participation limited to frequent letters and occasional visits, Juneau shouldered most of the workload. His pace in the 1830s must have been frenetic. Not only did he continue to trade with the Indians during their last days in Milwaukee, but he also enlarged his post to supply the Yankees with everything from bags of clover seed to barrels of nails. (In 1838, according to his register, the trader sold a hymnal and a quart of gin to the same settlers.) Although Juneau remained active in the retail business, his real stock in trade was city lots. As the resident partner on the east side of the river, Juneau served as a one-man hospitality committee, welcoming visitors, loaning them horses, and dispensing both jobs and advice to any number of newcomers. Land sales, street improvements, and building projects were all part of his daily round.

Josette Juneau was just as busy. In 1835 her family moved to a new home, one of Milwaukee's first frame dwellings, on the corner of Water and Michigan Streets. There were eight children under the roof by then, with more to come, but Josette frequently lent a hand as midwife, nurse, and hostess for the growing number of women in the settlement. Morgan Martin remembered her with affection: "Mrs. Juneau was a most amiable and excellent woman, and many of the first settlers around Milwaukee will no doubt bear ample testimony to the deeds of charity by which she was distinguished."

A lesser man might have resented Martin's protracted absences, but nothing threatened Juneau's friendship with his partner. Despite their geographic separation, despite radical differences in their backgrounds and temperaments, the east side's impresarios developed an absolute and abiding trust in each other. In 1835 Juneau informed Martin that "a company of messrs. wealthy merchants" had offered to buy out his claim. "I referred them to you," he wrote, "and told them that you would decide for our common interest." Martin returned the favor in 1838, writing to Juneau, "In every thing, taxes &c., act for me as you would for yourself and I am satisfied." The pair routinely floated each other loans, discounted each other's notes, and invested jointly in other fledgling Wisconsin communities. There were times when the partners had so many transactions going on at once, both separately and together, that they literally did not know what they owned, but there was never a hint of friction. "At the close," Martin recalled, "accounts between us were adjusted and property valued at hundreds of thousands of dollars divided, with as little difficulty as you would settle a trifling store bill."

The fruits of their labors were apparent to all. At the peak of the real estate boom, Juneau was reported to be worth at least $100,000, more than enough to make him a millionaire in modern dollars, and Martin's assets were probably even greater. But the more obvious fruit of their partnership was the city taking shape around Juneau's old trading post. On June 27, 1837, the *Milwaukee Sentinel,* a promotional organ launched with Juneau's backing, expressed wonder at the settlement's progress:

Byron Kilbourn was easily the most aggressive of Milwaukee's founding fathers – and the least scrupulous.

MILWAUKEE *has risen as by enchantment,* enterprize *being the "magic wand" by which a city has been made so suddenly to spring into a vigorous and prosperous existence – inviting, by its unrivalled commercial and other advantages, merchants, mechanics and traders of every class, from the old settled portions of the country, to better their condition by locating and pursuing a more lucrative business, within its bounds.*

★★★★★

Much of the "enterprize" in pioneer Milwaukee was supplied by Byron Kilbourn. There are no soft edges in surviving portraits of the west side's founder; the man who gazes from the frame is dour, daunting, and clearly determined to have his way. Kilbourn was the temperamental opposite of his rivals across the river. He was in all things a tireless, even ruthless, competitor, and there was little room for compromise in his make-up. Kilbourn summed up his business philosophy in a rare 1835 letter to Morgan Martin: "My 'sense of justice' in the

Wisconsin Historical Society

Wisconsin Historical Society

fulfilment of a contract, is to comply strictly with its terms. Liberality, generosity and suchlike sentiments, I discard from business affairs." Ambitious to the point of avarice, Kilbourn probably made more enemies than Juneau, Martin, and George Walker combined. But this schemer was also a dreamer. Byron Kilbourn was willing to risk everything, including his good name, in the effort to bring a great city into being on the west bank of the Milwaukee River.

Kilbourn was born in Connecticut in 1801, but he was raised in Ohio, where his father founded Worthington, now a suburb of Columbus. A reversal of the family's fortunes prompted the young man to leave home at sixteen. Kilbourn found his first calling as a surveyor, hauling chains and setting posts for various canal projects in Ohio. His work brought him to the attention of Micajah Williams, the surveyor general of the entire Northwest Territory. Throughout the frontier period, surveyors and speculators were often the same people. They generally had both the first look at the land and the first chance to claim it. In 1834 Williams sent Kilbourn to Wisconsin as a district surveyor. Kilbourn's official task was to survey the public lands around Manitowoc, but Williams had become the younger man's partner as well as his patron. Kilbourn was instructed to find the best harbor site north of Chicago and, with money forwarded from Ohio, to buy it at the earliest opportunity.

After a detailed exploration of the lakeshore, Byron Kilbourn, like Morgan Martin, chose Milwaukee, a site whose natural advantages were unequaled. Finding the east bank of the river already occupied in 1834, he staked his future on the west side. Kilbourn soon built a home for his wife and two young daughters near what is now the corner of Third Street and Juneau Avenue. The site offered the first solid ground on the west bank, and it provided clear access to the interior. From the very beginning, Kilbourn was acutely conscious of Milwaukee's promise as a trading center for the farmers who were sure to people its hinterland. He described the community's "commercial advantages" in an 1835 letter:

> *Where there are inhabitants there must be business; and if business, it must be done somewhere. Chicago is eighty miles distant, and Green Bay about one hundred; it is therefore clear that the business of this region can not be done at either of those places.... Green Bay, Milwaukee, and Chicago, each has its own appropriate country; and that* naturally *united to Milwaukee by common interest, is at least equal in extent and fertility, and I hesitate not to add, will sustain a more dense population than either of the others.*

Kilbourn was determined that Milwaukee's business would be done on his side of the river. He was, however, at a decided disadvantage in the early stages of his competition with Juneau and Martin. Their land, as part of the Menominee cession, had been the property of the United States since 1831, but the west bank, by terms of the 1833 Chicago treaty, belonged to the Potawatomi, Ojibwe, and Ottawa until 1838. It was not, technically speaking, for sale. Kilbourn had a gift for evading technicalities, and this case was no exception. Micajah Williams, his patron and partner, was still surveyor general of the Northwest Territory. Citing "the peculiar situation and wants of that section of country, and the public advantage which would flow from that tract being brought into market as soon as possible," Kilbourn persuaded

Williams to include the west side in the 1835 federal survey – the necessary prelude to public sale.

Milwaukee's Indians returned from their 1835 winter hunt to find surveyor's stakes and claim shacks on their west-bank land. Some were outraged by this blatant violation of the treaty they had signed, and they grew angrier as white encroachment continued. In October, 1835, when most of the community's white males were reportedly attending the land sale in Green Bay, a group of local firebrands made tentative plans to massacre the remaining settlers. Josette Juneau, who presumably knew them all by name, got wind of the plot. While her children slept, she patrolled the primitive streets of Milwaukee all night, making it clear that no violence would be tolerated. The threat passed almost without notice.

Byron Kilbourn had no claim of his own to pursue at the Green Bay land sale. The federal pre-emption law applied only to settlers who had made improvements before 1834, a proviso that guaranteed Juneau's claim and left Kilbourn in the cold. Again, he viewed the apparent setback as a technicality. In the interest of simple fairness, the federal law assigned "floating rights" to settlers who claimed the same quarter-section (160 acres) of public land. Each received eighty acres of the original claim and the right to buy another eighty anywhere in the same land district. The system was subject to flagrant abuse. "Floats" were practically legal tender on the frontier, and speculators often used them to secure the most desirable properties. Kilbourn prevailed upon some friendly French Canadians to file claims for the same quarter-sections near Green Bay. (The claims were in Kilbourn's handwriting.)

He then bought their floating rights and applied them to land he wanted in Milwaukee, evicting a handful of earlier white settlers in the process. Kilbourn did not stop there. Fully aware that he was treading somewhat shaky ground, he made the arduous journey to Washington, D.C., in late 1835 to secure a federal patent on his lands. For the minimum government price of $1.25 an acre, Kilbourn became the owner of more than a mile of prime riverfront property.

Rivers rarely follow section lines. The rigid coordinates of the federal survey had placed part of Juneau's claim on the west bank of the Milwaukee and part of Kilbourn's on the east side. In the early months of 1835, before the land sale, Juneau and Martin had proposed merging their interests with the west side's, an arrangement that would have spared the young settlement endless controversy. Kilbourn, characteristically, declined. The non-conforming parcels were swapped after the sale, and the river became the border between competing domains.

Kilbourn had taken several shortcuts in his attempt to catch up with Juneau and Martin. Once his title was secured by patent, he tried diligently to overtake them. With financial backing from Micajah Williams, Archibald Clybourn of Chicago, and other capitalists, Kilbourn went to work on his own list of townsite improvements. His homestead on Chestnut Street (which was, ironically, renamed Juneau Avenue a century later) anchored Milwaukee's second commercial nexus. At its heart were a "general land office," a general store, and a warehouse, and nearby was the American House, the west side's leading hotel. To the north, near Cherry Street, was a site Kilbourn had reserved for the county courthouse – a plum that soon fell to the east side. (Court Street immortalizes the founder's intentions.) Although he lost the battle for the courthouse, Kilbourn fired the first shot in the newspaper war. In 1836 he launched the *Milwaukee Advertiser,* an aptly named weekly designed to trumpet the virtues of Milwaukee in general and its west side in particular. Solomon Juneau founded the *Sentinel* in 1837 to tell the other side of the story.

Kilbourn probably spent even more on street-grading and landfill projects than Juneau and Martin, simply because he had more to fill. The *Sentinel* described central Milwaukee as "a species of cove" – a broad bowl of flat land rimmed by steep bluffs. Most of the flat land was wet, and most of it was on the west side. The bluff line was a long curve that swept west from the Milwaukee River at today's Cherry Street to the Menomonee Valley near Eighth Street, and it enclosed dense stands of water-loving tamaracks and cedars. (State Street was originally Tamarack, and Kilbourn Avenue was Cedar.) "We had to be careful," recalled one early west sider, "to keep on the bogs or roots of trees to prevent from getting into the water and mire." The trees were eventually taken for timber, and the wetlands of the west side disappeared under eight to twenty feet of fill, all of it taken from the surrounding bluffs. Frontier Milwaukee recalled Isaiah's prophecy for Israel: "Every valley shall be exalted, and every mountain and hill made low."

All of Kilbourn's projects, from launching newspapers to filling in swamps, had one overriding goal: to swell the west side's fortunes at the expense of the hopeful little settlements across the rivers. There was no

personal enmity in his scheming; Kilbourn availed himself of Morgan Martin's legal services and recruited Solomon Juneau for the board of a canal company he had formed. Townsite promotion was, in his view, strictly a business affair. In pursuing his goals, however, Kilbourn found it hard to identify the boundary between business rivalry and all-out war.

The result was a competitive zeal that verged on nastiness. In 1836 Kilbourn built Milwaukee's first bridge, a crude span across the Menomonee River near today's Second Street. Its sole purpose was to divert overland traffic from Walker's Point, Milwaukee's original south side, to Kilbourn's community on the west side. In the same year, he published a map of the "City of Milwaukee" that showed all 1,113 lots for sale on the west side of the river but left

Kilbourn's 1836 map of the "City of Milwaukee" showed the thriving settlement on Juneau's side of the river as a complete blank.

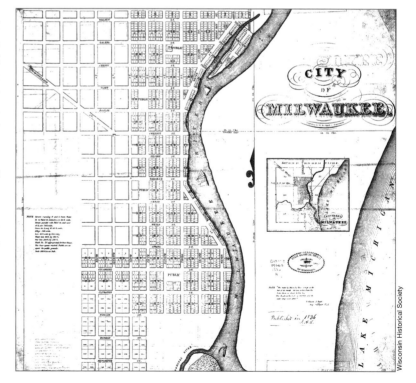

Juneau's east side absolutely blank. In 1837 Kilbourn launched the *Badger,* a steam-powered lighter whose mission, reported the *Advertiser,* was to land passengers "from the large steam boats which do not come over the bar" at the river mouth. The *Badger* called exclusively at the west side's docks. The steamboat *Detroit,* a Kilbourn vessel that connected Milwaukee with the stagecoach terminal at Michigan City, Indiana, observed the same policy.

Byron Kilbourn was hardly reticent about his determination to rule the fledgling metropolis. In an 1837 letter to Micajah Williams, his chief financial backer, Kilbourn described his plans in some detail:

> *... by next fall, if you will make us a visit, I feel sanguine in demonstrating to you that the business of Milwaukee is to be done on the West Side. My bridge over the Menomonee marsh will*

give Walker's Point a cooler, as all agree who look at its bearing on the business of the place – and as to a bridge over the [Milwaukee] river, I consider it out of the question; but if they [Juneau and Martin] should succeed, contrary to all expectations, in erecting it, I will take good care that they shall have no use of it – for we can construct a couple of small steamboats for harbor use, and pass them through the bridge so frequently that it can never be closed. It will cost us less to do this than it will them to build the bridge, and the bridge will be of less use to them than a ferry. It wants a strong pull, &c., and the story is told.

Although he never really caught up with the east side, Byron Kilbourn made significant progress toward his goals. The lasting outcome of his one-sided campaign was geographic. There might have been rivalries in any case, but Kilbourn undoubtedly

Lacking development capital and beset by claim-jumpers, George Walker finished a distant third in the race to dominate pioneer Milwaukee.

aggravated Milwaukee's sectionalism. In his attempts to isolate and impoverish his rivals, he did not even lay out his streets in conformance with the east side's. Under the influence of Kilbourn's intense parochialism, the east and west sides of the river became the East and West Sides or, in popular parlance, Juneautown and Kilbourntown. To this day, the bridges between the two sides cross the river at an angle.

✶✶✶✶✶

George Walker finished a distant third in the contest for pioneer supremacy in Milwaukee. His poor showing was not for lack of distinctive character. Walker was Milwaukee's own Falstaff, in both dimensions and demeanor. He tipped the scales at 350 pounds, and a contemporary described the city's fourth founder as "the very personification of jollity and good humor." Despite his girth, Walker was said to be the finest dancer in the territory and a skater of unusual grace – when the ice was thick enough.

The father of Milwaukee's South Side was, appropriately, a Southerner. Born in Lynchburg, Virginia, in 1811, Walker had moved to the southern tip of Illinois with his family at the age of fourteen. Four years later he was on his own, pursuing the Indian trade in the Chicago area. In March, 1834, Walker came to Milwaukee and began a new career as a townsite developer. Betting that a location nearer the river mouth would be the first to attract settlers, he built his cabin on a narrow finger of land in the central marsh, near the southern end of today's Water Street bridge. Walker's Point, as the site came to be called, was a minor peninsula, 12 feet high and perhaps 300 yards long, that had been carved between old channels of the Milwaukee and Menomonee Rivers. The point

Milwaukee County Register of Deeds

quickly became the nucleus of settlement on Milwaukee's South Side.

George Walker labored under multiple handicaps in the effort to make his point the center of Milwaukee. Youth was the first; Walker trailed Martin by seven years, Kilbourn by eleven, and Juneau by nineteen. Unlike his older counterparts, Walker had no powerful friends, and his access to Eastern capital was severely limited. As the "personification of jollity," he was also something less than a barracuda in business dealings.

With no senior partners to promote and protect his interests, the young Virginian was vulnerable, and disaster struck early. At the first public land sale in 1835, his claim on Walker's Point was "floated" by a trio of Green Bay residents. The claim was jumped, in other words, by earlier settlers who had transferable rights to land anywhere in eastern Wisconsin. It is possible that the trio was

Walker's Point began as a minor peninsula reaching into the marsh near S. First and S. Water Streets. The original point was soon "borrowed" for landfill.

acting on behalf of Martin and Juneau; Martin had had earlier dealings with one of the claim-jumpers, and Juneau periodically mentioned "our interest on Walker's Point" in letters to his partner. Whatever the case, Walker was forced to give up his log cabin and other "valuable improvements" on the point that bore his name.

The "float party" allowed Walker to claim another quarter-section southwest of today's Sixth and Pierce Streets. He platted the parcel as "Walker's Point Addition" and reserved one block as a public park (the present Walker Square), but the land was somewhat off the beaten path in 1835. Hoping to stay in the real estate game, Walker bought back a portion of his original claim for $1,500 an acre – a rather substantial advance on the government price of $1.25.

George Walker was off to a dismal start, and things soon got worse. In 1838, after months of rumors, the federal government disallowed all claims on Walker's Point. The problem, officials declared, was that all land south and west of the Milwaukee River belonged to the Indians until 1838, rendering the 1835 sale invalid. It was a curious ruling, all the more so since Byron Kilbourn's claim had the same defect. But Kilbourn had secured a federal patent for his land, a detail the South Siders had overlooked. One suspects that political enemies or commercial rivals, perhaps even Kilbourn himself, had a hand in the decision.

The outcome of the ruling was complete chaos. There were now three parties contesting for primacy on Walker's Point: George Walker, the Green Bay claim-jumpers, and the settlers who had actually purchased lots from one or the other. Walker's Point became a no-man's-land. Ownership descended into a legal limbo, and there it remained for years.

George Walker's multiple problems had a profound impact on Milwaukee's social and economic geography. Under different management, under more favorable conditions, his claim might well have become the city's downtown. Milwaukee's front door during the pioneer period was, of course, the river mouth. Juneautown and Kilbourntown developed well upstream, reflecting their founders' aversions to wetland. Kilbourn's homestead was fully two miles north of the river mouth, and Juneau's was only a half-mile closer. Walker's Point was more accessible than either. It was, moreover, the terminus of the major overland trails from the south, and its access to the interior was at least as good as Kilbourntown's. Whether viewed by land or by lake, the South Side's geographic advantages were obvious. The subdivision directly opposite the river mouth was called, quite logically, "Milwaukee Proper."

Geographic common sense ultimately made less difference than the aims and advantages of the individual founders. It was Kilbourn and Juneau who determined the business district's location as well as its east-west axis; their rivalry gave Milwaukee a downtown that followed the bluff line away from the lake. Had George Walker been Milwaukee's dominant developer, the city might have grown up around the river mouth – the pattern observed in Racine, Sheboygan or, for that matter, Chicago. City Hall might have sprouted at Sixth and National, and the Grand Avenue shopping mall might occupy the site of the Allen-Bradley clock tower. In the histories of cities, as in the lives of individuals, nothing is inevitable.

From Boom to Bust and Back Again

Milwaukee's founders formed an unlikely quartet. There was little similarity between the homespun virtues of a Juneau and the Yankee gentility of a Martin, even less between the cunning of a Kilbourn and the bumbling of a Walker. The most tangible quality the founding fathers shared was their bald-faced boosterism. Struggling to be noticed in the competition for settlers, they touted the virtues of their settlements with all the subtlety of carnival barkers. Whether starting newspapers or courting investors, hiring press agents or building boats, each used every means at hand to attract attention. As Walker's problems demonstrated, their efforts met with varying degrees of success, but the founders seemed to believe that they could simply promote a city into existence.

Their bubble burst in 1837. A national depression stopped Milwaukee in its tracks, and dreams of urban prosperity gave way to genuine privation. The root cause of the Panic of 1837 was America's unsettled monetary policy. The United States had no paper money supply in 1836; the vast majority of notes in circulation were issued by state-chartered banks, a famously haphazard set of institutions. State banks, particularly those in the West, were often of uncertain ancestry and even more dubious solvency. These "wildcat" banks flooded the market with notes backed by gold and silver worth a small fraction of their face values. Wisconsin became a separate territory in 1836, on the eve of Michigan's statehood, and its territorial banks were, if anything, even less reliable. The inevitable results were runaway inflation and rampant speculation. In the twilight of his presidency, Andrew Jackson decided to restore the dominion of "hard money." Under the terms of his Specie Circular, all land claimants were required to make their purchases in gold or silver after August 15, 1836. Almost instantly, the money supply tightened and speculation came to a grinding halt. "I have nothing to inform you," wrote Solomon Juneau to Morgan Martin in November, 1836, "only that money is dam scarce. I cannot get any money for our land property."

Milwaukee was a paper city that had turned a handsome paper profit for its promoters. As the currency crisis blossomed into a full-scale depression, speculators were caught short. Demand plummeted, banks failed, and paper profits turned into real losses. Lots that had sold for thousands of dollars could be had for as little as a barrel of flour or a good pair of boots. One Easterner had put $15,000 down on $60,000 of Milwaukee real estate in 1836. He invested every penny he had, to the point of having to borrow money for the trip home. When the young man returned to Milwaukee in 1837, the market had collapsed. He was forced to

sell his holdings for $5,000, and he was still on the hook for the mortgage money he'd borrowed. Edward Holton saw no improvement a year later: "Surely a more desolate, down-to-the-heel, slip-shod looking place could scarcely be found than was Milwaukee in October 1838." Hans Crocker, an Irish-born lawyer, put the situation more succinctly: "Everything went to smash."

Milwaukee's founders felt the impact of the crash differently. George Walker, still struggling to get started, had little to lose. Byron Kilbourn had a great deal at stake, but he weathered the crisis without surrendering his fortune. Morgan Martin and Solomon Juneau, who had just begun to enjoy the fruits of their efforts, were hit the hardest. In 1837 Martin was completing Hazelwood, a Greek Revival mansion he intended as a dream home for his bride, Elizabeth. Perched on the east bank of the Fox River in Green Bay, the house featured hardwood moldings, ornate plasterwork, and decorative hardware shipped all the way from New York. Hazelwood (now a popular house museum) was a frontier showplace, but its builder, unfortunately, was a principal in the Bank of Wisconsin, Green Bay's first financial institution. The bank floundered in 1837 and failed in 1839, taking a sizable piece of Martin's fortune with it.

Although he had no mansion to pay for, Solomon Juneau was just as hard-pressed as his partner in 1837. "The times are the hardest kind," he wrote to Martin in December. The pair's townsite venture was crippled by high overhead and falling revenue, and Juneau's problems were compounded by the fact that he was still paying for lots he had bought back at the height of the frenzy. The old trader had also poured thousands of dollars into the steamboat *Milwaukie,* which proved to be a very large hole in the water. Launched at Buffalo in 1838, the ship ran aground off Milwaukee in 1841; she was dismantled without earning a nickel of profit.

Hazelwood, Morgan Martin's frontier showplace on the Fox River

Neville Public Museum, Green Bay

Juneau and Martin did not let their financial distress affect their friendship. As Milwaukee's postmaster, Juneau was periodically behind in his accounts with the authorities in Washington. The partners had engaged in reciprocal borrowing for years; at the end of 1837, it was Juneau who needed $2,000. Martin's reply indicated that their relationship could weather any crisis:

I am ready at all times to accommodate you in every way in my power. If a draft is made on you from the P.O. Dept. you may come here and we will manage the matter in some shape. I want to see your face my friend once more, but in the mean time do not suffer care to trace wrinkles on it.

Juneau, Martin, and the settlement's other promoters came to see their problems as a simple matter of timing. Frontier Milwaukee was, to a marked extent, a colony of speculators surrounded by nothing at all. Its leaders were merchants without a sustaining market, purveyors of dreams that only genuine settlers could bring to life. In a letter to a recent visitor in September, 1839, Byron Kilbourn analyzed Milwaukee's collapse as a case of premature expectations:

When here you must have considered our place very dull, as it really is and has been since the first revulsion in money matters. Our country was then too recently settled to afford any surplus for export, and having all to purchase, without any thing to sell, relying only on migration to preserve our circulating medium, we had necessarily to retrench in every thing until the products of our own country could bring us out. This we shall in some measure realize this season, and still more so in the next, and we have no fears but business in every branch will revive. <u>Our natural advantages & resources are such that we cannot long remain prostrate.</u>

Milwaukee was in no danger of becoming a ghost town, but the Panic of 1837 demonstrated that the community could not build its future on a foundation of hope alone. Prosperity depended absolutely on the growth of an agricultural hinterland. Milwaukee's boom would resume when the panic eased, but the fledgling city would thereafter grow in tandem with the country; urban commerce would expand in balance with rural customers.

Those customers continued to arrive even in the depths of the depression. Claim by claim, Milwaukee County was dotted with the shanties of Yankee-Yorkers who hoped to make farms on the frontier. Their work was substantially more productive than speculation in city lots, but it was infinitely more arduous. The settlers' first obstacle was trees – hundreds of thousands of trees. The Milwaukee area's uplands were covered with towering maples, beeches, and basswoods, providing a wood supply that was, in Wisconsin historian Joseph Schafer's choice phrase, "oppressively plentiful." Although they must have looked longingly at the open prairies to the south and west, local farmers went at the forest with a vengeance, turning the trees into raw material for ships and shops, wharves and wagons, and an ever-growing number of houses. The demand for lumber grew steadily, but most of the region's trees ended up as firewood – in homes, shops and, not least of all, steamboats. In 1838 Byron Kilbourn published this notice in the *Milwaukee Advertiser:*

We respectfully call the attention of the commanders of Steam-Boats to the fact that we have on hand TWO THOUSAND CORDS of good STEAM-BOAT WOOD, which we have made arrangements to have delivered at a moment's notice.

This small mountain of fuel consisted of indiscriminately mixed hardwoods: virgin oak, maple, cherry, walnut, and beech that some woodworkers would kill for today. Americans who rail against the ongoing destruction of tropical rain forests would do well to remember that our own country was clear-cut first.

Once the land had been stripped of its native vegetation, imported plants quickly filled the vacuum. Wheat was the cash crop of choice, just as it had been back East. The first winter wheat was sown in 1837, reported the *Advertiser,* marking "the dawn of that day when we shall no longer be dependent upon distant states for the staff of life." Although wheat would anchor local agriculture for the next generation, there was plenty of room for other crops. At the end of the 1837 growing season, members of the Milwaukee County Agricultural Society – whose founding president was Byron Kilbourn – showed off plants that had grown to championship size in the virgin soil, including four-pound beets, eighteen-pound cabbages, and rutabagas the size of pumpkins.

Some settlers looked beneath the soil for buried treasure. In September, 1835, the Olin brothers, Nelson and Thomas, opened a clay pit near the lakeshore and built a 25,000-brick kiln – apparently the first in Milwaukee. To their intense disappointment, the brick they produced was pale yellow in color, not the familiar red material they had known in New York State. It became apparent, on further investigation, that Milwaukee brick was a unique commodity with a ready market. At least six kilns were in operation by 1845, and their output was sold throughout the Great Lakes region. Milwaukee has been known as the Cream City ever since.

As the pioneers dug and drained, chopped and trapped, the land was, in a word, domesticated. Native wildflowers were plowed under, and some native mammals were nearly exterminated; in 1840 Milwaukee County paid out $166 in bounties for wolf skins. The process of domestication was outrageously destructive, but it was also agonizingly slow. In June, 1838, only 4,820 of the 525,000 acres within the present borders of Milwaukee and Waukesha Counties were under cultivation – less than one percent of the total. A farmer considered himself fortunate to clear and cultivate a few acres each year.

The patience of the pioneers seems all the more remarkable in light of the fact that they did not own their land. The federal pre-emption law had lapsed in 1836, making the newcomers nothing more than squatters. They organized an association in 1837 to record their claims and to defend them – by force, if necessary – against all interlopers, but it was not until 1839 that they had a chance to buy their prospective farms. With a new pre-emption law on the books, the public domain in southeastern Wisconsin went on sale for the first time since 1835, and the government was soon literally doing a land-office business. In March the register of claims wrote that he had "been busy counting money night and day for the last four weeks," taking in more than $600,000.

The outcome of the 1839 sale was clear: permanent agricultural settlement. Between 1836 and 1840 – the worst years of the depression – the population of Milwaukee and Waukesha Counties nearly doubled, climbing from 2,893 to 5,605, and would-be farmers outnumbered villagers by a margin of at least three to one. The total population was minuscule by modern standards but, after the reckless speculation of the pre-1837 years, evidence of solid growth was encouraging. The success of the land sale was a clear sign of a new and healthy beginning. "After the sale," wrote historian Joseph Schafer, "Wisconsin was no longer an experiment."

Small groups of Indians continued to reside near Milwaukee after 1839, and others returned for seasonal visits. Their reaction to the changes in their hometown can only be imagined. Older residents of every period have felt a mingled sense of wonder and loss at the disappearance of childhood landmarks, but no one could have been more surprised, or dismayed, than Milwaukee's natives, who saw their wilderness cut, split, and stacked to make room for a city.

A Place at the Center

Milwaukee's founders firmly believed that their settlement, straddling a deep river that emptied into a broad bay, was intended by nature to become a great city. Geography alone, however, was not enough to assure its success. As the surrounding townships filled in with farm families, the community's leaders worked overtime to exploit their natural advantages and to create new ones. Their goal was to make Milwaukee the undisputed center – commercial, political, and cultural – of the entire region.

The cross-river rivalries, paradoxically, aided the whole community's cause. They raised the local energy level markedly, making Milwaukee an obvious center of attention. Competition gave rise to resources that might otherwise have emerged much later: two newspapers, a commodious courthouse, good hotels, and crude but serviceable street systems, all before 1840. These wilderness amenities helped to make Milwaukee a destination, a focal point for new arrivals from the East as well as aspiring farmers from the countryside.

Other centralizing forces emerged in the first years of settlement, including an enterprise that would play a crucial role in the growth of both city and country: the Wisconsin Marine and Fire Insurance Company. Established in 1839 by one Scotsman, George Smith, and managed by another, Alexander Mitchell, it was a bank in all but name. Although its charter specifically excluded banking privileges, the Wisconsin Marine issued "certificates of deposit" in convenient denominations of one, three, and five dollars. Backed by Scottish capital and the fiscal acumen of Smith and Mitchell, those certificates became the most trusted currency on the shores of Lake Michigan. In sharp contrast to notes issued by wildcat banks, "George Smith's money" was practically as good as gold.

The importance of a strong financial institution on the frontier was incalculable. The "insurance company," now Chase Bank Milwaukee, furnished a reliable medium of exchange for local commerce and, just as importantly, a source of credit for the region's fledgling farmers, merchants, millers, brewers, and manufacturers. Even the territorial legislature, a group with no love for banks or bankers, borrowed money from the company (at 12-percent interest). The Wisconsin Marine survived runs, recessions, and endless political antagonism to become the most important bank in the territory and then the state. It also provided a home base for Alexander Mitchell, whose illustrious (and spectacularly successful) business career is charted in subsequent chapters.

43

The Wisconsin Marine helped to cement Milwaukee's position as the region's financial center. Efforts to make it the transportation center were even more important. At the top of the list was the Milwaukee and Rock River Canal, a Byron Kilbourn enterprise. The Erie Canal had touched off an epidemic of "canal fever" in the Northwest Territory, and even the scrawniest port community dreamed of becoming another Buffalo. With ten years of experience on Ohio's canals, Kilbourn believed that he could make it happen for Milwaukee. He envisioned a serpentine canal following the Menomonee River northwest into today's Waukesha County, traversing the lake district around Oconomowoc, and finally joining the Rock River near Fort Atkinson.

Kilbourn's immediate goal was to connect Milwaukee's west side with the fertile farmland of the Rock River basin, a region that his *Advertiser* described as "uniting in itself all the natural advantages of soil, climate, water power, and commercial facilities, which can be desired." His ultimate goal was considerably more grandiose: a connection with the Mississippi River at Rock Island, Illinois. Kilbourn envisioned Milwaukee and Buffalo as twin terminals, joined across the lakes as the dominant collectors of traffic from both east and west. The *Advertiser* ballyhooed the Milwaukee and Rock River Canal as "the last connecting link between the Hudson and the Mississippi ... the *Grand Western Canal*."

The Milwaukee and Rock River Canal, a Kilbourn enterprise, was promoted as "the last connecting link between the Hudson and the Mississippi."

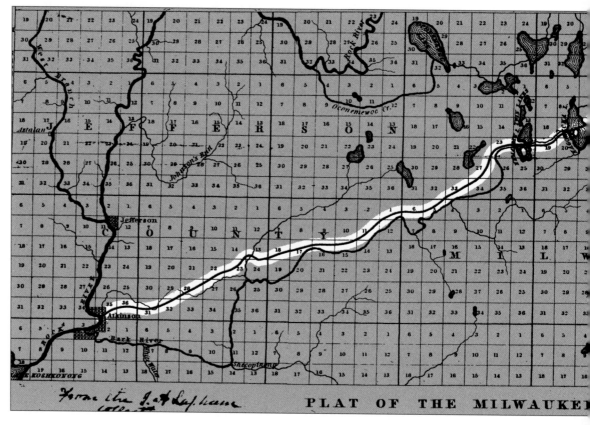

PLAT OF THE MILWAUKE[E]

By the autumn of 1840, Kilbourn had a crew of perhaps fifty men at work on the Milwaukee end of the waterway. They dug an oversized ditch on the west bank of the Milwaukee River that stretched 1.25 miles from today's McKinley Avenue to a lock and dam just south of North Avenue. The dam resembled the work of oversized beavers; whole trees were stacked with their butt-ends downstream and then covered with 100,000 cubic yards of gravel. The structure raised the upstream water level twelve feet, producing ample hydraulic power and a dependable year-round flow for the first leg of Kilbourn's canal.

The Milwaukee and Rock River Canal was in trouble even before the dam-builders had finished their work. Other settlements, including Juneautown, resented the government aid Kilbourn had wangled, but his real nemesis was James Doty, a towering figure in territorial politics. Doty, a resident of Green Bay, favored the Fox-Wisconsin waterway, not the Milwaukee-Rock project, as the main route to the interior. (It was an interest he shared with first cousin Morgan Martin.) When Doty became governor in 1841, he stripped Kilbourn of his power to sell canal bonds. The legislature, whose support for the enterprise had never been robust, soon repudiated the bonds already sold. Without a source of capital, the company quickly starved to death.

The canal's demise left an assortment of clouded titles, bruised egos, and unpaid

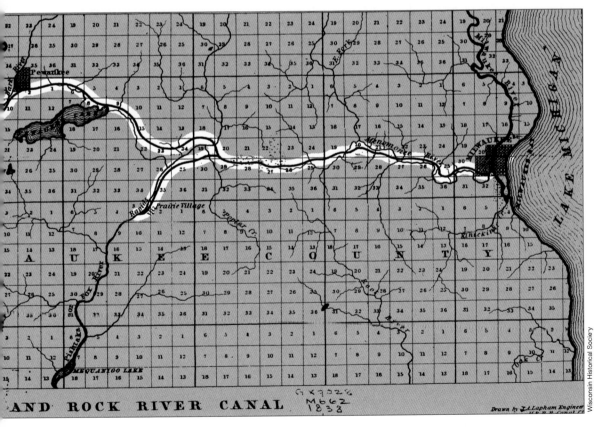

... AND ROCK RIVER CANAL

Drawn by J. J. Lapham Engineer

bills, but the most tangible legacy of Kilbourn's dream was the 1.25-mile ditch on the west side of the Milwaukee River. It was not a monument to failure; the truncated canal became a millrace that supported the first industrial district in a community later known as an industrial giant. Within a few years of the dam's completion in 1843, "the Water Power" was lined with sawmills, flour mills, woodworking plants, and other businesses that contributed materially to Milwaukee's regional dominance. Buried under tons of landfill in 1885, the old millrace is navigable today as N. Commerce Street.

The termination of Kilbourn's canal gave other internal improvement projects a new sense of urgency. It was obvious that Milwaukee's welfare depended on the welfare of the rural townships surrounding it, and there was rabid interest in improvements that would connect village and country.

Roads were an obvious requirement, as they had been since the dawn of white settlement. In 1838 Congress appropriated $15,000 for a road from Green Bay through Milwaukee to Chicago, and another $10,000 for a highway from Milwaukee to Madison, a vacant dot on the map that had been named Wisconsin's capital two years earlier. Even those turnpikes were little more than scratches on the face of the wilderness. In 1839 one of Morgan Martin's associates described the "road" from Green Bay to Milwaukee as a hodgepodge of "quagmires, marshes, landslides, ditches, Brooks, rivers, mud, creeks, swamps, Indian trails, gutters, ravines, upon hills and down hills, Woods and Wilderness."

Links to the interior, both roads and railroads, would dominate the local agenda in years to come, but Milwaukeeans were even more concerned about their ties to the outside world. They looked across the lakes to the settled East and found their own port facilities wanting. As the number of ships arriving each year soared from 82 in 1835 to nearly 1,000 in 1845, Milwaukee's deficiencies as a harbor became painfully obvious. Despite the *Sentinel's* 1837 assertion that Milwaukee Bay could shelter 300 vessels "with ease and safety," the bay afforded scant protection when storm winds blew from the east. In April, 1840, two sailing ships were driven ashore near the river mouth. "We know not the amount of damage," wrote the *Sentinel*, "but they now lay high upon the beach a striking and forcible illustration of the necessity of an appropriation for the improvement of our harbor."

The obvious solution was to breach the sandbar at the river mouth and dredge a channel to the deep water that lay just inside. Until that feat was accomplished, passengers and freight had to be lightered

Hoping to shorten the route upriver, promoters suggested opening a new mouth ("Present Harbor Inlet") across the sandbar.

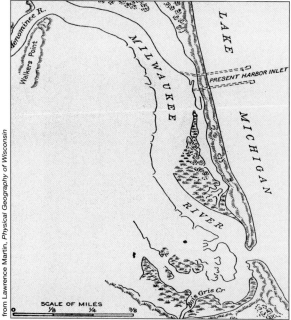

from Lawrence Martin, *Physical Geography of Wisconsin*

SCALE OF MILES

from ship to shore, a task that could be downright hazardous when heavy seas were running. In October, 1839, four crewmen drowned when waves capsized the yawl they were rowing back to their ship after a night on the town. The drownings strengthened the community's resolve to build a first-class harbor. Milwaukeeans could have taxed themselves to finance the project – a tack tried, with limited success, in Racine – but most felt that it was a federal responsibility. Local leaders declared that it was high time for the federal government to return some of its land-sale revenue in the form of improvements. Even Chicagoans, not normally boosters of any project benefiting their northern rivals, agreed that the harbor grant made sense. The *Chicago Democrat* editorialized:

> *After September, it is almost impossible to get boats to agree to land merchandize at Milwaukee at any price, such is the danger of laying off that town in an ordinary gale and sending freight on shore in small boats.... There is quite an amount of merchandize now in our city because it could not be left there.*

Support for the project came from as far away as Buffalo, the major terminal for all western ports. In January, 1840, Buffalonians sent a petition to Congress filled with forty-eight feet of signatures requesting a harbor appropriation for Milwaukee.

It was not until 1843 that the federal government authorized $30,000 for harbor improvements – in the wrong place. The Milwaukee River was separated from the lake by a narrow, wooded peninsula in its last mile. At its slenderest point (the site of the present harbor entrance) the peninsula tapered to a width of less than 100 yards, and most Milwaukeeans had come to

believe that the Army engineers would punch an outlet through the sandbar at that point – the so-called "straight cut." To the general public's dismay, the engineers dredged a channel and built piers at the existing river mouth instead. The decision added an unnecessary mile of meandering river channel to the upstream voyage – a challenge for steamships and, in the days before tugboats, a near-impossibility for sailing vessels. Editorial writers ranted and local businessmen raved, to no avail. It was widely believed that South Siders who owned land opposite the river mouth had influenced the engineers' decision.

By the time the first steamboat cleared the new entrance, in the autumn of 1843, private enterprise had developed an alternative closer to the settled portion of Milwaukee. Several months earlier, a group of entrepreneurs had completed a lake pier at the foot of Huron (now Clybourn) Street. Nearly a quarter-mile long, it enabled visiting ships to dock in deep water and discharge passengers and cargo – for a fee. Although the pier was

Milwaukee had the look and feel of a typical western boom town in 1844. This engraving shows the west side of Water Street near Wisconsin Avenue, now the site of Chase Bank Milwaukee.

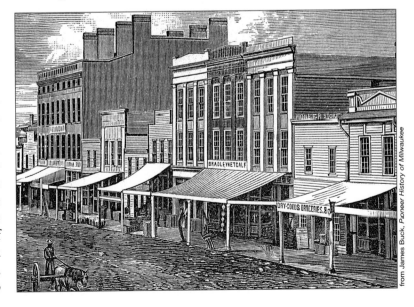

from James Buck, *Pioneer History of Milwaukee*

useless in rough weather, it became a lucrative alternative to the river route, so lucrative that three more piers were built nearby in the next four years. Huron Street blossomed as Milwaukee's point of entry. "The march of improvement on Huron street," wrote a local reporter in 1843, "is a cause of astonishment to the oldest inhabitant." There were forty-five buildings on the street, including what must have been the greatest concentration of hotels in Wisconsin. Each employed "runners," a noisome bunch who practically assaulted new arrivals with pitches for their respective hostelries.

The piers served as Milwaukee's front door for more than a decade. Much to Byron Kilbourn's chagrin, they strengthened the East Side's hold on the settlement's commercial life and reinforced the east-west orientation of the future city's downtown. Although the river had been the site's premier attraction, its role, for the time being, was distinctly secondary.

Milwaukee continued to grow while the various internal improvement projects were discussed, delayed, and occasionally completed. Even the Panic of 1837 and the ensuing depression could not keep settlers away. Milwaukee's population reached roughly 1,700 in 1840, an increase of more than 50 percent since 1836, and its growth accelerated with the return of better times. On May 1, 1841, the *Milwaukee Courier,* which had just succeeded the *Advertiser,* described a boom in progress:

> *Milwaukee has at no period since 1836 given such substantial evidence of prosperity as at the present time.... There is not a comfortable dwelling that can be rented in the town; everything in the shape of a house is full, and more are needed.*

The demand was so great that several buildings in Sheboygan, a town whose time had not yet come, were dismantled and put up again in Milwaukee. Still there was a shortage of housing. On August 19, 1843, more than two years after the *Courier* report, a *Milwaukie Sentinel* correspondent described feverish activity:

> *I never saw so much building going on in my life. They are building houses and stores in all directions. Being here is just like living in a carpenter's shop – the sound of the hammers heard continually.*

Milwaukee's population mushroomed to more than 6,000 in 1843 – one of the greatest proportional gains in the community's history. Southeastern Wisconsin edged out the lead region as the most populous in the territory, and Milwaukeeans saw no reason they couldn't overtake Chicago, whose population stood at roughly 7,500.

At Home on the Edge of the World

Commerce was Milwaukee's reason for being. All the money and energy expended on lake piers, an improved river mouth, new roads, and Kilbourn's abortive canal had a single object: to stimulate the flow of goods and people to and through the hopeful little community. But Milwaukee did not live by trade alone. A genuine village – or, more accurately, villages – emerged on the lakeshore, and local residents developed the full range of human institutions – political, religious, and cultural – that constituted a life as well as a living.

The settlement was shaped decisively by the common Yankee ancestry of its pioneers. Lawyers advertised references from Boston,

Albany, and Montpelier as a matter of course. Pioneer schoolmasters, who were holding classes as early as 1836, drilled their students in lessons they had learned in Pennsylvania or New York. The major religious faiths, with the exception of Catholicism, could have been found in any New England village. Even the first names – Hiram, Abigail, Enoch, Eliza, Uriel, Eliphalet, Priscilla, and Zebiah – were reminiscent of upstate New York and New England.

So were the local instruments of self-government: county, town, and finally village. When Wisconsin became a territory in 1836, its powers included the authority to incorporate settlements of at least 300 people. Milwaukeeans were first in line. In 1837 a pair of rival villages came into existence: the Town of Milwaukee and – a backwoods mouthful – the Town of Milwaukee on the West Side of the River. To no one's surprise, their first presidents were, respectively, Solomon Juneau and Byron Kilbourn. Walker's Point was too small to incorporate, but George Walker himself played an active role in territorial politics, becoming speaker of the assembly in 1843. Byron Kilbourn served several terms in the legislature, and Morgan Martin went to Washington as Wisconsin's territorial delegate in 1845.

In 1839, after two years of legal independence, Juneautown and Kilbourntown joined forces as the Town of Milwaukee. (Walker's Point was still mired in title problems.) The new structure suggested a grudging acknowledgment on both sides that, despite obvious differences, they had much in common. As later events would demonstrate, the merger was a marriage of economic convenience, not a true union. The East and West Sides, now reclassified as wards, cut their administrative overheads by uniting, but each retained absolute control of its own treasury.

Walker's Point finally joined the party. In 1842, after passing the hat for a trip to the land office in Washington, George Walker gained a clear title to his original claim on the South Side. That eliminated the land sharks who had jumped his claim, but Walker was still at odds with some of the settlers who had bought lots from him. Several had filed large claims of their own during the long legal impasse. "They appropriated nearly all the dry ground," Walker complained in an 1844 letter to the *Sentinel,* "leaving the marsh to me." Although he made no attempt to evict the settlers, Walker did reserve the top two feet of their soil for use as landfill. It took at least three years of negotiation and compromise to resolve the dispute.

Walker's Point never truly recovered from its slow start. Despite its favored geographic position, the South Side remained by far the smallest of the three pioneer settlements, a fact of continuing relevance. But clearing up its legal mess gave the community a green light for growth, and the resumption of good times brought an abundance of new settlers. By 1845 Walker's Point was large enough to join its sisters across the rivers as the South Ward of the Town of Milwaukee.

Residents of all three sections found it relatively easy to set up civic housekeeping: They simply transplanted the institutions they had known back East. Adapting an older legal framework to frontier conditions, however, produced a body of ordinances seldom encountered in New York or New England. In 1840 the village board voted "to prevent Hogs from going at large within the corporate limits of the Town of Milwaukee," and in the same year, probably as a concession to local prudery, the town banned bathing in the Milwaukee River "between sunrise and nine o'clock in the evening." There were also mandatory fines for scofflaws who indulged in games of chance, operated "houses of ill fame," or sold liquor to "any Indian or Indians, male or female."

Such controls were undoubtedly necessary. Yeoman farmers and sturdy artisans trekking west in search of opportunity – the figures of frontier legend – certainly flocked to Milwaukee, but the settlement also attracted its share of outlaws who flourished on the fringes of civilization. They made

First Presbyterian Church was the stronghold of a particularly aggressive form of Yankee Puritanism. The church stood on the corner of Mason and Milwaukee Streets.

Milwaukee Public Library

vice one of the community's earliest imports, with a particular emphasis on alcohol. There were corner saloons in Milwaukee almost as soon as there were corners. Pioneer historian James Buck recorded 138 "rum holes" in 1843 – an astronomical average of one for every forty residents.

Milwaukee's first murder followed a dispute between two liquor dealers and an Indian customer. Solomon Juneau recounted the crime in a letter to Morgan Martin on July 21, 1836:

> *One of our Milwaukie Indians has been murdered by 2 white men Saturday last about ten o'clock at night in the street between my house and Brown's store. The murderers were detected on the spot and we have got them secured now and we are now building a gaol back of the public square for their reception.*

Milwaukee's first jail, like frontier justice itself, was improvised; the murderers escaped before their trial. One was reportedly hanged for a similar offense in Indiana a year later.

At the other extreme were settlers who were upright to the point of rigidity. There was a strong puritanical streak in Milwaukee's Yankee community, and no groups were more strait-laced than the Presbyterians and Congregationalists, both of whom traced their lineage to John Calvin. Every member of First (now Immanuel) Presbyterian Church, which was organized in 1837, pledged "total abstinence from all intoxicating drinks, and strenuously to avoid all sinful amusements and associating with the wicked." The faithful of First Congregational (now Plymouth) Church, established in 1841, made a similar promise: "We will keep the Sabbath holy; we will not conform to the world in its fashions and follies, such as gaming, dress unbecoming of godliness, balls, dances, and theaters, and all scenes of dissipation." Members who strayed beyond the bounds of either Calvinist covenant – by "Sabbath profanation," "habitual neglect of the means of grace," or "mingling with vicious company" – were brought to trial before church elders and, if found guilty, were "excluded from fellowship."

The Calvinists showed just as much interest in the failings of their fellow citizens. One visiting preacher, Abel Barber, described Milwaukee in the mid-1830s as fertile ground for missionary work:

> We have coarse and clamorous infidelity, petty grog shops becoming numerous, much profane swearing, contempt of the Sabbath and of all religious institutions, and most determined irreligion.... A strong, sweeping current of worldly enterprise, a rush and scramble after wealth, is general as a matter of course.

Even fellow Protestants were suspect. Another missionary, Stephen Peet, noted in 1839, "The Episcopalian Society is taking a large class of fashionable, ball-going and card-playing folks."

These latter-day Puritans did not monopolize moral discourse in Milwaukee. Other Anglo-American creeds, including Episcopalian, Methodist, and Baptist, were established by 1840, and Catholics, Lutherans, and Jews – the immigrant faiths – were inching toward organization. The first Catholic Mass was said in Solomon Juneau's home in 1835, and the first Catholic church, St. Peter's, was completed four years later on lots donated by Juneau. An 1842 observer recorded a melange of ministers in Milwaukee: "two Roman Catholic priests, one Episcopalian, one Presbyterian, one Congregational, one Episcopal Methodist, one Universalist, one Unitarian, and a few Nothingarians."

The life of the mind was as important to some pioneers as the welfare of the soul. It might be said that higher civilization reached Milwaukee in the person of one man: Increase A. Lapham. He was born in upstate New York, the son of a Quaker contractor employed on the Erie Canal. That canal provided Lapham with a practical apprenticeship in surveying, stone-cutting, and civil engineering. He brought his skills to Milwaukee in July, 1836, when he was recruited by Byron Kilbourn to work on the Rock River Canal and other engineering projects. The guileless Quaker and the scheming Yankee were an unusual pair, but they remained lifelong friends; Lapham ultimately served as the executor of Kilbourn's will.

Increase Lapham was a surveyor by trade but a scientist by instinct. Within two years of his arrival, he had prepared a catalogue of all the plants and shells in the Milwaukee area. Lapham went on to publish definitive studies of every known effigy mound in Wisconsin, every known

Increase Lapham was a scientist, surveyor, and one of the most original minds ever to grace the Milwaukee scene.

Wisconsin Historical Society

grass in the United States, and every known meteorite that had landed in North America. Other projects included a study of the minuscule lunar tides on Lake Michigan and an herbarium that eventually contained 24,000 plants of 8,000 species. When the telegraph transformed long-distance communication, Lapham lobbied long and hard for its use in weather forecasting, an effort that led to the creation of the U.S. Weather Service.

A number of his neighbors shared Lapham's encyclopedic range of interests. In 1839 local savants established the Milwaukee Lyceum "for the sake of the higher advancement of general knowledge, literature, and science." The group's projects included a lecture series, periodic debates, and a natural science collection. Lapham, naturally, was a luminary of the Lyceum. By 1842 there were enough kindred spirits in town to support the community's first circulating library (a service of Philetus Hale's bookstore) and enough theatergoers to fill the house for Milwaukee's first play – *The Merchant of Venice*, staged in a third-floor hall near Byron Kilbourn's home.

Shakespeare's arrival was heartening, but no one would have mistaken Milwaukee for Amherst or Albany. In the 1830s and '40s, the town was perched on the edge of the world – a fact that became brutally apparent each winter. When ice closed the Great Lakes shipping lanes, usually in November, Milwaukee was beyond the reach of civilization until the following April. News was scarce, mail service was exceedingly slow, and settlers had only each other to stare at for the next four or five months.

The enforced idleness must have been maddening for Milwaukee's more restless souls, but there were compensations. Some residents kept their hands in one of the continuous euchre games under way at local hotels. In 1836 two music-starved settlers recruited a Chicago fiddler to play for a series of winter "cotillion parties." Despite a critical shortage of women, the events were pronounced "a great success." Other Milwaukeeans spent the winter on the ice. The central marsh served as a vast outdoor skating rink, and the Milwaukee River was both a major thoroughfare and an informal race track. Increase Lapham described the river in an 1836 letter to his brother: "Sleighs, cutters and jumpers are flying about in every direction. The river is frozen solid as a rock, affording the most smooth and level road imaginable."

A House Divided

The Milwaukee River did not always support smooth sledding. Despite long winters shared by the fireside, despite the growth of interest in higher culture, despite the generally satisfactory conduct of local government, frontier Milwaukee's salient characteristic was its sectionalism. The river lacked the grandeur of the Colorado, but it formed a canyon between Kilbourntown and Juneautown, and the rising tide of settlement in the 1840s failed to submerge the rivalries of the early years. Demonstrating, perhaps, the native human appetite for conflict, new arrivals embraced, and in some cases magnified, the sectional prejudices of their established neighbors. The East and West Sides were like conjoined twins fused at the spine: inseparable, but congenitally unable to see things from the same perspective.

Milwaukee's founding fathers were involved in the intramural dispute to varying degrees. Byron Kilbourn, ever the competitor, was a fierce partisan, but George Walker remained generally neutral – a politic course for someone still struggling to get started. Beset by more urgent concerns, Solomon Juneau was practically a noncombatant. Neither the fur trade nor the real estate business could lift him out of the hole he had fallen into when the first, false boom of the 1830s collapsed. In 1844 Juneau notified the American Fur Company that his debts exceeded his assets by $20,000 – more than $300,000 in current dollars.

There was no shortage of other protagonists to carry the rivalry forward. The dispute between Juneautown and Kilbourntown turned on the issue of bridges, or the absence thereof. Pinched between the river and the lake, East Siders wanted access to the outside world, and West Siders, led by Kilbourn, were determined to deny them that access. Kilbourn's strategy amounted to a slow, passive siege: If the East Side could be effectively isolated, it might some day become a satellite of the West Side. The strategy had obvious flaws. West Siders crossed east to the courthouse, the post office, and the churches of Juneautown at least as often as East Siders crossed west. A well-placed bridge or two might even have pulled some of the East Side's burgeoning pier traffic over to the West Side. In the 1840s, however, each side found it easy to believe that any blow to its rival was a boost to its own fortunes.

Crossing the river had been a concern since the earliest days of Yankee settlement. The first arrivals made the passage in a pair of row-it-yourself scows, which were replaced by private ferry service in 1837 and a county-operated shuttle two years later. The makeshift ferries were inadequate to

the needs of a growing community. In 1840 the Wisconsin legislature required Milwaukee County to build "a good and substantial drawbridge" at Chestnut Street (Juneau Avenue). The *Milwaukee Advertiser,* no doubt reflecting Byron Kilbourn's sentiments, pronounced the measure a slap in the face to residents of the West Side:

We have never heard of a more high-handed act of injustice perpetrated against the undoubted right of the people – the right of deciding upon the fact whether they themselves shall be taxed for a local improvement.

Even though it promised to make their lives easier, West Siders considered the bridge a sop to their rivals on the East Side, an improvement paid for by all for the benefit of a few. (Some critics said the same about Byron Kilbourn's canal.) The fact that Kilbourn could see the humble span from his own front door must have been doubly galling. He used the columns of the *Advertiser* (September 26, 1840) to air his own objections:

From '36 up to last winter, I had to contend single handed against the property holders, on the east side of the river, and succeeded in staving [the bridge bill] off.... In every manner in my power did I combat this measure, until I found, that to continue the contest single handed, against a majority of our members in the Legislature was more than I could do, and therefore I determined to cease my opposition, and let those members who were so anxious to have a bridge, take their own way for it, and account to the people for the abuse of power placed in their hands.

"The history of this *bridge squabble*," added Kilbourn, "gives the political history of Milwaukee." The Chestnut Street bridge was indeed a major issue in the 1840 territorial election. Two residents of Juneautown were candidates for seats in the legislature, and the *Advertiser* warned, in no uncertain terms, that their election would submit Milwaukee County to "THE DICTATION OF LAWYERS, EAST SIDERS OR FAG-ENDS." The warning was to no avail. Backed by the superior numbers on their side of the river, the East Side candidates won, and Kilbourn was stuck with a bridge in his own backyard.

One bridge proved so convenient that three more were built. The Milwaukee River was spanned at Spring Street (Wisconsin Avenue) in 1842, Oneida (Wells) Street in 1844, and Walker's Point (Water Street) in the same year. None of the structure would have impressed a visiting engineer; teams using the float bridge at Spring Street were advised to get a running start or risk sinking at either end. The bridge at Chestnut was the only one supported by tax revenues; all others were built and main-

tained by private subscription, with East Siders footing most of the bills.

More bridges meant more aggravations for the West Side. Some of the ward's more vocal partisans, including, apparently, Byron Kilbourn himself, considered them a clear menace to the West Side's natural monopoly on traffic with the interior, and they took what they viewed as appropriate action. In March, 1842, the *Courier* reported that "several citizens of the West Side" had opened the draw on the Chestnut Street bridge "and thus cut off communication with the East Ward." Such acts of vandalism were relatively rare until 1845. Walker's Point joined the Town of Milwaukee in that year, altering the balance of power on the village board. The shift may have emboldened the West Side's trustees to press for closure on the bridge issue.

Matters reached a head at the board meeting of May 7, the first one attended by delegates from the South Side and, as it

In 1845 the bridge at Chestnut Street (now Juneau Avenue) sparked a small-scale civil war that left a number of Milwaukeeans bruised, bloody, and finally convinced that their cross-river rivalry had gone far enough.

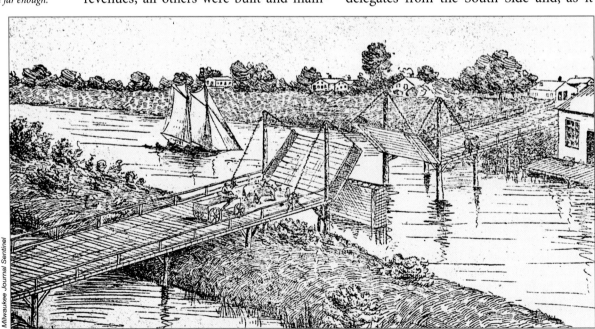

Milwaukee Journal Sentinel

turned out, the first skirmish in a series of comic-opera episodes that have come down through history as the Bridge War of 1845. The meeting's flash point was a resolution offered by Byron Kilbourn himself. The measure would have authorized the West Ward "to remove out of Chestnut street so much of the old county Bridge and all appendages thereto as occupy any part of said street west of the Milwaukie river," i.e., to sever the end of the bridge that encroached on Kilbourntown. Trustees from the other wards refused to even vote on such an irregular proposal.

The West Siders took a rather extreme view of their own sovereignty, and they were undeterred by the official rebuff of May 7. On the morning after the meeting, Milwaukeeans awoke to find that the west end of the Chestnut Street bridge had been dropped into the river. As the news raced through the East Side, a crowd gathered at the scene of the crime. The mob's mood shifted quickly from shock to outrage to a desire for revenge, but speeches by "several respectable citizens," reported the *Sentinel*, temporarily averted a brawl. The village board reconvened in the evening, minus a quorum from the West Side. Without directly addressing the previous night's vandalism, the trustees made it illegal to "cut, remove or damage" any of the town's bridges, under penalty of a $50 fine and five days in jail. Although they had done their share to foster sectionalism in earlier years, both newspapers went on record against mob rule. "One act of violence generally leads to others," declared the *Sentinel*, "just as the first wine cup leads to the long revel."

The dispute continued at a low boil for the next week or two. On May 15 the village board decided to repair the Chestnut Street span; even Byron Kilbourn voted with the majority. Four days later, however, the conflict erupted into violence. On May 19 a mob of East Side vigilantes destroyed the Spring Street span and took their axes to the Menomonee River bridge, which linked the West Side with the Chicago road. Their actions were apparently an attempt, however myopic, to cut off Kilbourntown from both the south and the east. The West Siders offered more than token resistance. "Many of the mob at the Menomonee bridge," reported the *Sentinel*, "were armed with pistols and guns, and one or two individuals were considerably injured, though not dangerously."

Bloodshed tends to have a sobering impact. When Milwaukeeans realized that they were on the verge of killing each other, most began to have second thoughts about life in a house divided. Residents of both sides concluded that violence offered few inducements to new settlers; strangers passing through on May 19 must have thought that the community had lost its collective mind. As both sides nursed their wounds, it became increasingly obvious that Milwaukee needed more access, not less; more settlers, not fewer; more cooperation, not open warfare.

The Bridge War of 1845 ended in a truce, and a city. Although sectional tensions would never disappear completely, powerful forces of union were at work. On December 2, after months of periodic run-ins and attempts at resolution, a group of leading citizens issued a call for an open meeting to discuss "a number of important projects." Cross-river collaboration was high on the list. In publicizing the meeting, the *Sentinel* gave an understated description of one of Milwaukee's most serious flaws:

There has been but little concert of action among our citizens, and but very seldom any united and intelligent efforts to improve the advantages we enjoy. In the strife of local or individual competition the good of the whole has been too often neglected or overlooked. The jealousies and rivalries incident to a new and growing settlement have at times jeoparded the general interest, and, on one memorable occasion, at least, threatened to disturb the public peace.

But let bygones be bygones. Let us forget that there were ever any differences of opinion among us as to where this road should be opened or that bridge built. Let us counsel together upon matters affecting the general interest and welfare. Let us one and all resolve to put our shoulders to the wheel, and, knowing neither party, sect nor ward, *unite in a common effort to advance the common weal.*

Those who attended the December 3 meeting formed committees to tackle a variety of projects, including railroad promotion, fire prevention, public education, and mail service. The most important committee, in retrospect, was one that met "to draft a City Charter," a compact that would unite Juneautown, Kilbourntown, and Walker's Point under a single urban umbrella.

Milwaukee's ascension to cityhood was surprisingly swift. The charter committee submitted its first draft to the village board on December 27, and the trustees referred the document to voters in early January. Most East Siders voted against the charter, probably because it required them to pay the lion's share of bridge costs, but solid support from the West and South Sides resulted in a landslide victory. The territorial legislature was inclined to pass the measure. As the price of their cooperation, however, representatives of Milwaukee County's western townships demanded legal independence. The result was Waukesha County. With that detail settled, the legislature approved the charter, and on January 31, 1846 – more than two years before Wisconsin became a state – the city of Milwaukee came into existence.

The community's first mayor was Laurent Solomon Juneau. He had not sought the office, which carried no salary, and he left most of its duties to John B. Smith, an East Side alderman who served as "acting mayor." In his inaugural address, penned by another Yankee neighbor, Juneau made no pretense to the skills of statecraft: "I feel conscious that my burden is light, knowing as I do that those with whom I am to cooperate are well versed in all matters pertaining to our welfare."

Despite his reluctance to govern, Juneau was an obvious choice for the mayor's post. Although he was generally known as a Democrat, the trader had avoided the vituperative partisanship of his neighbors. More important, he was lionized by the growing hordes of newcomers. Between 1840 and 1846, the population of Milwaukee County (present borders) swelled from 3,345 to 15,599, and more than 9,500 lived in the city proper. Like modern suburbanites who reverently preserve the log cabins of long-vanished pioneers, the newcomers looked to Juneau as the only history they had. He was their sole link to a past that was becoming more romantic with the passage of time.

Mayor Juneau served most effectively as a symbol of how far Milwaukee had come. The years between 1835 and 1846 were, like all beginnings, eventful. The community had gone from boom to bust to boom again. Its residential base had grown from Solomon Juneau's immediate family to an increasingly diverse populace of nearly 10,000. Its citizens had fought and settled a small-scale civil war. The cross-river rivalry had been good for Milwaukee, in a backhanded sort of way. Its excesses were obvious – the presence of two competing newspapers as early as 1837 was nothing short of hilarious – but the rivalry was a stimulus, a goad to greater efforts on both sides. Milwaukee, as a result, evolved quickly from a backwoods trading post to a small city that had every intention of becoming a large city.

The transition from pipe dream to genuine community had been made with relative ease, but the settlement's future was by no means guaranteed. As the city on the swamp took its first, tentative steps to urban independence, Milwaukeeans found themselves with other, more formidable bridges to cross.

Chapter 3

Here Come the Germans, 1846 – 1865

On May 23, 1996, near the midpoint of the city's 150th-anniversary year, President Bill Clinton and Chancellor Helmut Kohl of Germany paid a state visit to Milwaukee. The pair had no particular business to transact, no epoch-making accords to sign. Their meeting was largely symbolic, an attempt to broaden the chancellor's view of America and, not incidentally, to shore up Clinton's re-election prospects in the heartland. Thousands of people waited in a light rain all morning for the leaders to arrive at Pere Marquette Park, a riverfront green space located squarely between the sites of Solomon Juneau's log cabin and Byron Kilbourn's homestead. As the skies lifted, the crowd heard Clinton extol Milwaukee as a place where Kohl "could get some really great bratwurst, where everywhere he turns around there's a sign with a German name on it, and where he could feel at home in America's most German-American city."

Clinton was not indulging in election-year hyperbole. In 1990 a stunning 48 percent of the Milwaukee area's residents claimed at least some German heritage. That topped 44 percent for Cincinnati and 41 percent for St. Louis – two other German-American capitals – and doesn't begin to reflect the depth of the Teutonic influence on Milwaukee. Where else does a card game called *Schafskopf* (sheepshead) still enjoy such widespread popularity? Where else do residents order a *Schneck* (sweet roll) with their morning coffee? Who else goes dip-netting in early spring for a fish spelled "smelt" but invariably pronounced "schmelt"? And what other American phone book boasts forty-three pages of names beginning with "Sch-," from Schaab down to Schwulst, and including five pages of Schmidts? Helmut Kohl had steak and ribs during his 1996 visit, not bratwurst, but there is no mistaking the role that immigrants from his nation have played in Milwaukee's history.

The *Deutsch-Athen* of America

Milwaukee's German community is older than the city itself. The first notable group of newcomers arrived in the fall of 1839, when a number of "Old Lutherans" fled a royal attempt to meld them with Reformed Protestants in a Prussian state church. Perhaps a thousand dissenters made the crossing, and nearly half settled in Buffalo. Their less impoverished comrades pushed on to Milwaukee, where they split again, most heading north to found the Freistadt ("Free Town") community in today's Mequon and the rest remaining in the village proper. The urbanites clustered near Third and Chestnut, in the heart of Kilbourntown, where one of their members promptly built a half-timbered house that doubled as a place of worship. The choice of location was fateful. Although Germans settled in nearly every section of Milwaukee, the areas north and west of the original Kilbourntown became their particular stronghold.

Milwaukee in 1854.
The view is from
"Comstock Hill," near
Third and Walnut
Streets.

The trickle of the 1830s became a flood in the 1840s. Crop failures, economic distress, and political unrest gave the Germans ample reason to leave, and America provided an obvious alternative. Letters from the New World were quickly "read to shreds" in the German states, and a growing number of guidebooks channeled the flow of immigration to Wisconsin. As the German *Auswanderung* accelerated, Milwaukee began to take on a definite Teutonic tone. When Solomon Juneau became the city's first mayor in 1846, a thousand copies of his inaugural address were printed – 500 in English and 500 in German. The community's growth after incorporation was even more dramatic. The number of German-born residents more than doubled during the 1850s, and by 1860 German immigrants and their American-born children constituted a comfortable majority in Milwaukee.

Why Milwaukee? The influx was a case of timing, pure and simple: The beginning of mass emigration from Europe coincided precisely with the opening of Milwaukee and Wisconsin to settlement. In 1825, when Solomon and Josette Juneau established their riverside trading post, a paltry 8,500 Europeans immigrated to the United States. In 1835, when Juneau and Morgan Martin registered their land claim, the number rose to 42,000. In 1845, the year of Milwaukee's Bridge War, the tally exceeded 100,000 for the first time. Then came the deluge. Immigration rose steadily each year, reaching a peak of 405,000 in 1854. In the single decade after 1845, nearly 3 million Europeans settled in the United States, a record that would stand until the 1880s.

The vast majority of the decade's immigrants – 79 percent – were either Irish or German. Carrying poverty with them like a weight, Irish families tended to settle wherever they landed, creating huge Celtic enclaves in Boston, New York, and other coastal towns. The Germans, who were in marginally better financial shape, headed directly for the frontier: today's upper Midwest. Drawn by cheap land, fluid social conditions, and the security of their own numbers, German immigrants reshaped the demographic face of the region. As a well-advertised boom town, Milwaukee would have attracted its share of newcomers in any case; for reasons almost entirely circumstantial, it became the most German city in the most German state in the Union.

The Germans were not like other immigrants. What made them unique in Milwaukee, and perhaps in urban America, was their extraordinary internal diversity. To speak of the city's German "community" is, in some respects, a misnomer. Its members came, first of all, from every section of a country that did not exist, in a legal sense, until 1871, when it was unified under Prussian auspices. Leaving homelands spread from Pomerania on the Baltic Sea to Bavaria in the Alps, the immigrants were strangers to each other as well as to the people they met in America.

Economic differences were even more obvious. Some newcomers arrived with little more than the clothes on their backs; emigration, for them, was an alternative to starvation. Others saw America as a new field for careers that had already shown considerable promise in Europe. Frederick Miller, for instance, arrived in 1855 with $9,000 in gold coin, more than enough to launch a brewing company that has since become the second-largest in the United States.

Religion was a third point of departure. Catholics were the largest group, constituting perhaps a third of Milwaukee's German

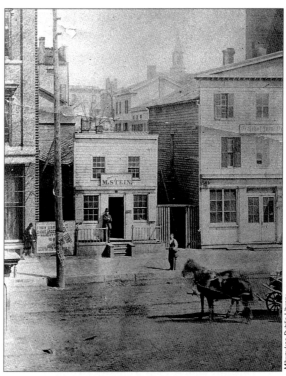

A small German neighborhood developed on the east bank of the Milwaukee River. One of its anchors was the Water Street gun shop of Matthias Stein, who arrived in the 1830s.

Milwaukee Public Library

population. With the appointment of John Martin Henni, a German-speaking Swiss, as Milwaukee's bishop in 1843, the city became a national center of German Catholicism. In 1847 Henni began construction of St. John's Cathedral, whose original steeple was a pure specimen of the German Baroque. Sharing a public square with the courthouse erected by Solomon Juneau in 1836, St. John's was an emphatic statement of the Catholic presence. Lutheran steeples were nearly as obvious. Subject to sharp disagreements on theological fine points, members of Milwaukee's second-largest denomination split regularly along synodical lines. Reformed, Methodist, and even Baptist believers rounded out the Christian roster, and German Jews, who began to arrive in 1844, numbered at least 200 families (and three congregations) by 1856.

And then there were the Forty-Eighters, a group as celebrated in the history of German America as the *Mayflower's* passengers were in colonial New England – and probably just as overcounted. In 1848 a wave of revolutions swept through Europe, convulsing the German states in particular. The uprisings were crushed by royal forces of reaction, forcing many of the movement's leaders to seek refuge in America. The Forty-Eighters included journalists and judges, students and professors, and a variety of other free-thinking intellectuals who, as one of their number put it, "had learned every possible thing, except what they could use in America."

The Forty-Eighters were never a large group – only a few thousand, at most, crossed to the New World – but Milwaukee became one of their strongholds. Compulsive and capable organizers, they launched new groups that added a distinctive layer to an already vital community life. One of the best-known was the Milwaukee Musical Society, formed in 1850 under the baton of Hans Balatka, a German-speaking Czech. When it was barely a year old, the Society staged a full-dress performance of Haydn's *Creation*, featuring an orchestra of 30 and a chorus of nearly 100. Balatka himself was declared a musical genius. When the Musical Society lost most of its sheet music in an 1852 fire, the director transcribed the notes to Handel's *Messiah* from memory.

Education was another Forty-Eighter passion. In 1851 some of Milwaukee's more progressive Germans founded the German-English Academy as "a new school for our modern times which will educate men for *this world*." Its guiding light for more than two decades was Peter Engelmann, a staunch believer in hands-on learning. His personal collection of fossils, minerals, and plants later became the nucleus of the Milwaukee Public Museum's natural history collection, and his German-English Academy evolved, with two other institutions, into the present University School of Milwaukee.

A less cerebral institution has achieved similar longevity: the Milwaukee Turners. Organized in 1853, the *Turnverein* encouraged the development of "a sound mind in a sound body," with particular emphasis on gymnastics and calisthenics. The group's clubhouse on Fourth Street also served as a social and cultural center for the Forty-Eighters and like-minded immigrants. In 1857 they hosted a Turnfest that drew more than 7,000 delegates from throughout the Midwest.

The uprisings of 1848 also brought Milwaukee its first feminist: Mathilde Anneke. In 1852, three years after her arrival in the city, Anneke launched a monthly newspaper called *Die Frauen Zeitung* ("Woman's

St. John's Cathedral, dedicated in 1853, was a benchmark in the growth of Milwaukee's Catholic community, the city's largest denomination both then and now.

Milwaukee County Historical Society

Times"). Her stated goal was "the complete emancipation of women," and she started in the composing room. The firebrand hired German-speaking women to set the *Zeitung's* type, a move that sparked the formation of an all-male union to keep the typographer's trade safe for men. Although such stout resistance killed her newspaper after only seven issues, Mathilde Anneke remained an influential writer, speaker, teacher, and suffragist until her death in 1884.

Milwaukee's Germans, women as well as men, suffered from an embarrassment of organizational riches. The average citizen could select from a crammed menu of *Turnvereine,* militia units, temperance clubs, singing societies, volunteer fire companies, political groups, mutual aid societies, theater troupes, debating societies, fraternal lodges, and fishing clubs – not to mention a wide variety of religious congregations. German Milwaukee's robust organizational life, particularly the ambitious cultural efforts of the Forty-Eighters, gave the city an international reputation as the *Deutsch-Athen* of the United States.

The beverage of choice in the German Athens, and one of its key social lubricants, was beer. Milwaukee's first brewery, technically, was organized by a group of Welshmen in 1840, but its product found few takers in the German community. "Of course their brew could hardly be considered beer in its German sense," sniffed Rudolf Koss, Milwaukee's pioneer German historian, "but to the Americans this somewhat murky, sweet, and ale-like drink was satisfactory." Help arrived in 1841, when Hermann Reutelshöter (spelled variously) began to produce lager beer in his Walker's Point establishment. By 1856 there were more than two dozen breweries in Milwaukee, nearly all of

Milwaukee Public Library

Turner Hall was a particular stronghold of the Forty-Eighter movement. It became a popular center for gymnastics, social life, and a free-thinking political philosophy.

Milwaukee County Historical Society

Mathilde Anneke, the feminist Forty-Eighter who hired women to set her newspaper's type

Milwaukee County Historical Society

The Best (later Pabst) brewery at Ninth and Juneau in about 1859

them owned by Germans, operated by Germans, and oriented to German customers. The foundations of fortunes later associated with the Miller, Pabst, Schlitz, and Blatz families were all in place well before the Civil War.

Breweries were not the only German landmarks associated with beer. From the time Louis Trayser opened his *Zum Deutschen* Little Tavern on State and Water Streets in 1837, the *Bierstube* was a focus of fellowship and an anchor of neighborhood. Beer halls were nearly as common as bakeries and butcher shops in some sections of Milwaukee. The scene shifted outdoors during the summer months. The city's first beer garden, featuring "extensive promenades,

rustic bowers, and a beautiful view from Tivoli Hill," opened on the banks of the Milwaukee River (near Cherry Street) in 1844, and others soon followed. In the days before public parks, the beer gardens were immensely popular retreats, particularly on Sunday afternoons, when immigrant families gathered for German beer, German music, and German fellowship.

There was quite literally something for everyone in the German community. From beer halls to masked balls to Turn halls, the range of social and cultural outlets was virtually complete, creating a breadth of choices no other ethnic group could match. Kathleen Conzen, whose *Immigrant Milwaukee, 1836-1860* remains the classic study of the early Germans, argues persuasively that they created a parallel social universe, separate from but at least equal to the networks established by the dominant Yankees. "It was an ethnic and not a class community," wrote Conzen, one that "ensured the cultural security and institutional variety which meant that few would feel it either necessary or satisfying to leave the community completely."

Milwaukee's image as the German Athens was not the retrospective creation of romantics looking back on a vanished Golden Age. Even the early arrivals knew they had something special. In an 1850 letter to an old friend in Reutlingen, John Kerler, Jr. described the collective impact of German immigrants on his new hometown:

> *Milwaukee is the only place in which I found that the Americans concern themselves with learning German, and where the German language and German ways are bold enough to take a foothold. You will find inns, beer cellars and billiard and bowling alleys, as well as German beer, something you do not find much of in this country. The Dutchman (the Americans call the Germans this name by way of derision) plays a more independent role – has balls, concerts and theaters – naturally not to be compared to those in Germany, and has even managed to get laws printed in German. His vote carries a heavy weight at election time. You will find no other place in which so much has been given the Germans, and if you value this, you may safely prefer Wisconsin, and especially Milwaukee, to other places.*

Nearly 150 years after Kerler sang Milwaukee's praises, the German influence is far from extinct. The city's continuing identification with beer and bratwurst is only the most obvious hand-me-down from its Teutonic ancestors. On a more subtle, even subliminal, level, it can be argued that the Germans made Milwaukee safe for ethnicity. The simple fact that a non-English-speaking group was the city's largest made it easier, relatively speaking, for later arrivals to resist the melting pot. Pressures to assimilate were always present, but they may have been weaker in Milwaukee than in cities with larger Anglo-Saxon populations. The Yankees were outnumbered; it was acceptable to be something else. Several generations later, ethnic food, ethnic dance, and ethnic festivals exert an attraction that often surprises newcomers. Milwaukee's lakefront festivals in particular – African, American Indian, Arabian, Asian, German, Irish, Italian, Mexican, Polish – are convincing displays of continuing ethnic vitality, together drawing nearly 600,000 patrons each summer.

Ethnic festivals are just one expression of a civic personality trait, a Milwaukee earmark, that seems rooted in the expectations of the early Germans. For all their supposed obsession with *Ordnung*, the immigrants were, in some respects, a good deal less rigid and more relaxed than the Yankee element. Many brought with them a taste for simple things: the quiet comforts of the family circle, the camaraderie of a *Schafskopf* game with old friends, the sense of well-being that blossoms in the presence of good food, good friends, and good beer. The Teutonic newcomers transplanted a taste for small-scale pleasures that Milwaukeeans of many backgrounds still sum up in a single word: *Gemütlichkeit*. Expressed in everything from festivals to fish fries to flower gardens, it has proven to be one of the most durable legacies of the early German community.

65

Strength in Numbers

The Germans were hardly the only immigrants in early Milwaukee. Although no single group approached them in size or social complexity, the city attracted thousands of other newcomers from northern and western Europe. Natives of Ireland were a rather distant second, their relative strength peaking at 15 percent of the city's population in 1848. In contrast to the Germans, the Irish were Catholic to the core; Milwaukee's first resident priest was Rev. Patrick O'Kelley, an 1839 arrival, and the church he built, St. Peter's, housed a largely Irish congregation. O'Kelley's parishioners were distressingly poor. Whether they came as dispossessed peasants in the early 1840s or as refugees from famine a few years later, the immigrants sailed with little and settled with even less. Their occupational choices began and ended at the entry level.

It was, in fact, the promise of work in a booming frontier town that brought the first Irish families to Milwaukee. Many hop-scotched to the region from jobs farther east, coming as they were needed to dig Kilbourn's canal, fill in swampland, grade new streets, and lay railroad track. The sheer number of Germans gave those immigrants an edge in the job market – Kathleen Conzen noted that "The average Milwaukee ditchdigger was 'Dutchman' and not 'Paddy'" – but a higher proportion of Irish newcomers worked with their backs and hands. In 1850, 55 percent of Milwaukee's Irish breadwinners were unskilled laborers – more than twice the proportion of Germans. Even their primary neighborhood was a construction zone. The greatest number of Irish families settled in the Third Ward, south of the Michigan Street bluff between the river and the lake. Most of it was a former swamp reclaimed, one wagonload of dirt at a time, by the same immigrants who built houses there as soon as the muck dried.

Their descendants would scale the social and economic heights, but the early Irish clearly showed the effects of grinding poverty and marginal social status. Whiskey-fueled altercations were so common that the Third Ward was known as "the Bloody Third." Of the 627 lawbreakers who spent time in the county jail in 1858, fully 258 (41 percent) were natives of Ireland – five times their share of the general population.

British immigrants – natives of England, Scotland, and Wales – made up more than 7 percent of Milwaukee's residents in 1850. Scots were curling on the ice of the Milwaukee River as early as 1845, and there were enough Englishmen in the city to start a cricket club not many years after. In contrast to the troublesome Irish, the British were "model immigrants," more than happy to adopt American ways. They showed a strong affinity for Yankee neighborhoods, Yankee churches, and Yankee institutions – which were, in many cases, ultimately British in origin. Acceptance was rarely a problem. Those with a modicum of talent and money to invest did very well in Milwaukee, and some did extraordinarily well. Alexander Mitchell, the Scottish banker who arrived in 1839, ended his days as the wealthiest Wisconsinite of his generation.

There were perhaps a dozen other groups, each making up less than 2 percent of the city's population at mid-century. Norwegian immigrants gravitated to Walker's Point, where they lived within walking distance of their jobs as seamen, shipbuilders, and captains on Milwaukee's developing waterfront. Devoutly (and dividedly)

Lutheran, they organized a succession of churches on the South Side. Dutch families settled on the North Side, particularly in a section known as *Hollandsche Berg* ("Dutch Hill") near Tenth and Galena Streets. Austrian and Swiss newcomers tended to settle in German-speaking neighborhoods, just as Swedes and Danes found homes among the Norwegians. Bohemians (Czechs) were the first of thousands to arrive from the Slavic nations of eastern Europe, and the roots of the African American community date to the city's earliest years. Joe Oliver, who had sailed the Great Lakes as a ship's cook, came ashore to work for Solomon Juneau in 1835. Although Wisconsin Territory would soon deny the vote to "people of color, paupers, idiots and lunatics," Oliver cast his ballot in Milwaukee's first election. By 1850 there were nearly 100 blacks in the city, including 14 barbers, 7 cooks, 6 whitewashers, 3 masons, and a single farmer.

The influx of newcomers, particularly European newcomers, took older residents by surprise. Milwaukee had begun as a village of transplanted Yankees who shared a common language, a common political vocabulary, and a common range of Protestant faiths. Although the Yankees relinquished none of their power, they watched

Wooden shoes and windmills: In 1856 John Grootemaat, a Dutch immigrant, built a traditional mill on the Green Bay road (now King Drive) near Burleigh Street.

Milwaukee Public Library

67

the cultural underpinnings of the early community vanish before their very eyes. "The public houses and streets are filled with new comers," remarked the *Milwaukee Courier* in 1843, "and our old citizens are almost strangers in their own town." The erosion continued as immigration accelerated. In 1850 a Boston newspaper correspondent described the city's population as "of a mixed and motley character," and the federal census for that year confirmed his observation. Milwaukee's Yankees were astounded to learn that 64 percent of their city's 1850 population was foreign-born.

Although they were newcomers themselves and outnumbered by a margin of two to one, the Yankees viewed themselves as the hosts in the relationship. Their official response was a warm welcome, if only because the immigrants were a source of fresh cash. The *Milwaukee Sentinel* (September 10, 1839) greeted an early contingent of Germans with open arms:

> *The German families, indeed, have bags of gold, some of them having $20,000 and upwards. We understand that there are 500 more families expected from Germany during the fall and spring ensuing. They are hardy and intelligent, and will be a great acquisition to the wealth and industry of the country.*

Hospitality, however, had its limits. Although they were more than happy to do business with the newcomers, most Yankees had no interest in living with them. As the tide of newcomers rose, more and more of the "American" element headed for the high ground between the river and the lake on Milwaukee's East Side. There, literally looking down on a German community to the west and the Irish Third Ward to the south, they developed the most prestigious neighborhood in pioneer Milwaukee: Yankee Hill.

Simple separation was not enough for some Yankees. A vocal minority viewed the influx of immigrants, especially Catholic immigrants, as an onslaught, and their preference for "native" institutions hardened into a hateful nativism. In 1844 Rev. John Miter, pastor of First Congregational (now Plymouth) Church, preached a Thanksgiving Day sermon that was notably lacking in ecumenical spirit. Miter roasted "Popery" as "the most pestilential of all evils" and Catholic immigrants as "the great Roman torrent swelling in our own fair West, and threatening us with a desolating flood." The pastor seriously proposed denying these "passive subjects of a foreign hierarchy" the right to vote. Other nativists agreed. Within a decade, anti-immigrant, anti-Catholic sentiment crystallized in the Know Nothing party, whose local leaders launched the *Daily American* in 1855. Using rhetoric that could fall easily from the lips of any "English First" activist today, the newspaper spoke out in favor of "Americans ruling America" and urged public officials to "keep *down* the newly arrived flood of emigration until they understand our language and our laws."

Some European habits became particular lightning rods for Yankee wrath. Milwaukee's bluenoses, especially those who attended the Presbyterian and Congregational churches, were horrified by the behavior of the city's Germans. Not only did these burghers show a definite fondness for beer, but they filled the beer gardens to overflowing on Sunday – an instance of "Sabbath profanation" that scandalized some Yankees. Where the Germans saw wholesome family recreation, Milwaukeeans of Puritan lineage saw only "dens of vice" frequented by "the vile and abandoned." Determined to keep the body politic pure in practice, if not in spirit, this influential minority campaigned for strict temperance legislation.

Not surprisingly, most immigrants –Irish and Bohemian as well as German – viewed the Puritan prohibition campaign as a threat to their way of life: a regressive, repressive crusade that sought to impose one group's values on everyone in the community. Conflict, in this highly charged atmosphere, was inevitable. In 1849 the state legislature, bowing to what historian Rudolf Koss called "a temporary Presbyterian majority," made saloonkeepers post bond for the behavior of their customers. The measure was a far cry from true prohibition, but Milwaukee's immigrants were outraged. A mob of several hundred Germans stormed the home of Sen. John B. Smith, one of the law's leading supporters, and did considerable damage to his windows and furniture.

Immigrants were more likely to use votes than violence in their efforts to shape public policy. Politics, in fact, became their favorite route to recognition in the mid-1800s, and the electoral process, both nationally and locally, assumed an ethnic dimension it would never lose. Even moderate members of Milwaukee's Yankee community were alarmed. In 1843, when immigrants campaigned for instant and universal suffrage, the *Sentinel's* editor, New York-born Elisha Starr, declared that they had crossed a line:

> *There are many foreigners of intelligence now in Wisconsin – men whom we would cheerfully vote for, if opportunity offered for any office – but is it not going a little too far, to make a law that will enable such individuals as have loaded down many a scow during the past summer to vote the moment they land upon our shores? Is it not asking too much?*

Milwaukee in 1854: The city was not quite the chaste New England village that appears in this drawing.

Wisconsin's residency requirement for "free white males" was fixed at three months in 1844, and one year later, after howls of protest from the nativist camp, raised to six months. The Yankees' message was clear: Help yourself, but don't take too much.

The battle lines became clearer as immigration gathered momentum. A majority of "Americans" supported the Whig and, after 1854, the Republican Party, which was heavily Yankee, heavily Protestant, and heavily oriented to the interests of business. Democrats appealed, and in some cases practically pandered, to "the laborers, the producers – the hard-fisted and true-hearted sons of humanity," as one leader described his constituency in 1847. Needless to say, the vast majority of laborers and producers were immigrants, and the flood of newcomers was like manna from heaven for Milwaukee's Democrats. Wisconsin shifted steadily to the Republican column after 1855, but Milwaukee remained a Democratic stronghold for decades.

Irish immigrants, nearly all of them Democrats, were proportionately more visible in local politics than other newcomers. Thomas Gilbert, a native of Ireland, served as president of Milwaukee's village board in 1844, and the city's first Irish-born mayor, a lawyer and businessman with the unlikely name of Hans Crocker, took office in 1852. Lacking command of the English language, German immigrants were somewhat slower to find their niche. The group's acknowledged civic leader was Dr. Franz Huebschmann, a physician whose prescription for the German community's health was political involvement. Huebschmann practically abandoned medicine for his new calling as a politician. He helped launch Milwaukee's first German newspaper, the Democratic *Banner,* in 1844, and served variously as a

school board member, alderman, county supervisor, and state senator. The doctor's tireless activism helped to keep Milwaukee's Germans solidly in the Democratic fold.

The immigrants had a more tangible reason to vote Democratic: patronage jobs. As long as their party remained in power, Democrats faced no shortage of work in the public sector. The pattern was obvious even before Milwaukee became a city. On December 20, 1844, the *Milwaukie Sentinel* expressed frustration at the immigrants' hammerlock on public works jobs:

Who is your street Commissioner and Supervisor of highways of this city, and who are the persons in his employ? Who by combination and political intrigue "rout out" and drive native citizens from all employment in the grading and filling up of streets, and other labor, the pay for which comes out of the Treasury of the Corporation, and to replenish which the native citizens pay nine-tenths of all the taxes? Foreigners–foreigners and hardly any but foreigners, nine-tenths of whom vote the Locofoco [Democratic] ticket.

Patronage rose to new heights with the ascendancy of "Boss" Jackson Hadley. Although the immigrant communities produced notable leaders of their own, it was Hadley, a dyed-in-the-wool Yankee, who ran the local Democratic Party. A native New Yorker and one-time high school principal, he was Milwaukee's leading political figure at mid-century, serving multiple terms in the state legislature and the city council – often at the same time. Hadley created a genuine machine in the 1850s, propelled by German and Irish votes and fueled largely by patronage. His cause was aided, ironically, by the sectional jealousies that had developed in Milwaukee's frontier period. The city charter preserved those jealousies intact, creating a pattern of ward autonomy that bordered on the absurd. Each of the city's five wards acted as its own district for school purposes, its own township for county functions, and its own contractor for public improvements. The aldermen were practically kings in their own wards, with enormous power to award public works contracts, and it was "Boss" Hadley who coordinated the division of spoils.

No one denied that Milwaukee's landscape needed an enormous amount of grading and filling, but the public works system controlled by Hadley was a morass of double-billing, kickbacks, and other species of graft. Reformers howled, attacking the boss as "king of the Tax-Eaters" and accusing his aldermanic allies of "waste, extravagance, carelessness and corruption." The *Sentinel* blasted Hadley's ability to "muster his little army of graders, officered by his contractors, and march them to Democratic caucuses to receive his nomination, or to the polls to carry his election." But Jackson Hadley's critics were impotent; he weathered every electoral challenge and every attempt to reform the system, keeping Milwaukee and its immigrant voter base safe for the Democrats. More than 150 years later, the abuses have largely disappeared, but the custom of aldermanic privilege is still honored on issues ranging from tavern licenses to zoning changes.

Neighbors and Strangers

Tensions between natives and newcomers were obvious in the political arena. Yankees resented the immigrants' involvement in Hadley's machine, and the hottest discussions of the day – on such topics as temperance, suffrage, and Sabbath laws – generally found "Americans" on one side and transplanted Europeans on the other. It should not be inferred, however, that the foreign-born were one big, happy family. Nativist pressures may have driven them into each other's arms at election time, but Milwaukee's immigrants were hardly a community of interest. The major groups were barely aware of each other in Europe, and they did not always develop closer ties in America.

German and Irish immigrants, the two largest groups, found accommodation difficult even when they had religion in common. Milwaukee's pioneer Catholic church was St. Peter's, on the corner of State and Jackson Streets. Its early congregants were a mixture of German, Irish, and French-speaking Catholics, but St. Peter's soon became so strongly identified with the Irish that in 1846 – the year of Milwaukee's incorporation – German members moved four blocks west and began to build St. Mary's Church, a landmark that still stands on Broadway at Kilbourn Avenue. (St. Peter's

St. Mary's Church, now "Old" St. Mary's, was built in 1846 by German Catholics who wanted some distance from their Irish counterparts.

Milwaukee Public Library

71

is now a focal point of the Crossroads Village at Old World Wisconsin, the outdoor ethnic museum west of Milwaukee.)

Nor could a common allegiance to the Democratic Party prevent conflict. In 1848 and again in 1854, German and Irish voters who were backing different candidates clashed physically at the polls. "Blood flowed freely from the wounds inflicted," reported the *Sentinel* in 1854, adding wryly, "To call out the military (all Germans and Irish) would not perhaps have been wise." In the same year, a German section gang working on the railroad line to La Crosse struck for better pay and, reported the *Sentinel*,

Milwaukee's Flugblaetter *(Dec. 3, 1853) pictured Catholic prelates living grandly on the pennies of the poor. Anticlerical in the extreme, most German freethinkers were nearly as scornful of other faiths.*

Ein Bild aus dem Leben.

Ernsten Betrachtungen gewidmet.

Für die Kirche.

"drove off the Irish laborers who were willing to work at the present prices paid by the contractors."

The occasional discord between German and Irish Milwaukeeans paled in comparison with the divisions afflicting the German "community." Religious, regional, and economic differences were self-evident, but the most serious split developed between the Forty-Eighters and their more conservative neighbors. The exiled revolutionaries were justly praised for their cultural leadership, but their personal views were decidedly at odds with those of the German majority. Not only did the Forty-Eighters uniformly vote Republican, but they were also devout freethinkers – rationalists who espoused a general anticlericalism and a fierce anti-Catholicism. Reason alone, they contended, could lead mankind to the harmony intended by nature, if only believers would throw off the intellectual shackles of organized religion. The Forty-Eighters were, in modern terms, "secular humanists" of a rather bellicose variety. Many longed for the day when, as one picturesquely put it, "the last priest has been hung with the intestines of the last prince."

The freethinkers did their best to provide fresh alternatives to the established Christian churches. In 1851 they established the *Freie Gemeinde* ("Free Congregation"), a vaguely Unitarian society that met to ponder "the great teachings of nature and history." It was followed in 1853 by the *Verein Freier Männer* ("Society of Free Men"), which convened weekly to discuss topics ranging from the souls of animals to the relative merits of Thomas Paine and George Washington. Quite intentionally, the society's sessions were held on Sunday mornings – in a beer hall. Even the Milwaukee *Turnverein,* a group better known for its gymnastic prowess, was rooted in the republican, rationalist tradition. The Turner constitution was a rather strident statement of radical principles:

> *This* Turnverein *declares itself expressly and with right for the Red Flag of Socialism, and shall become the army of the future which shall be of the greatest significance in the opposition against the secret Order of jesuits and of the political Reaction.... The Turner halls are the direct adversaries of the monasteries of monks; they spread health and life and make man conscious of his power and independence.*

Vocal and often vitriolic, the Forty-Eighters kept Milwaukee's believers on the defensive. Catholics, their principal targets, did not take the abuse lying down. When the Milwaukee Musical Society sought permission to hold a concert in St. John's Cathedral, Bishop John Henni took one look at the number of professed atheists on its membership list and barred the doors. When the Sons of Hermann, a secret fraternal order, began a membership drive, Henni let it be known that any Catholic who joined would be denied a church burial. By 1852 Milwaukee's Catholics were sufficiently aroused to start their own newspaper, *Der Seebote* ("The Lake Messenger"), which ably championed the Roman cause. Some Protestants were just as indignant as the Catholics; a Lutheran churchman complained in the 1850s that "one could not drink a glass of beer in the saloons without being angered by anti-Christian remarks or raillery against preachers."

Conflict was commonplace in early Milwaukee – within ethnic groups, between ethnic groups, and between new Americans and their Yankee "hosts." The city was not,

however, an armed camp. The tensions of the 1845 Bridge War, largely a Yankee affair, were not revisited as Milwaukee became a confederation of cultures. There were even glimpses, however occasional, of a fundamental unity underlying the city's diversity. When the Hibernian Society staged a St. Patrick's Day Ball in 1852, Valentine Hess and his German band provided the music. Individual businesses were models of ethnic cooperation, not to mention canny cross-ethnic marketing. O'Neill and Schultz operated a coalyard on Wells Street in the 1850s; Yankee Winfield Smith and German Edward Salomon (later Wisconsin's governor) shared a law partnership; and the Wolf & Davidson shipyard, jointly owned by a German and a Scot, became Milwaukee's largest in the late 1860s. Some neighborhoods, too, were admirably mixed, particularly Walker's Point. The South Side community was still feeling the effects of the slow start occasioned by George Walker's title problems (its 1855 population was less than 13 percent of the city's), but the neighborhood housed a generous assortment of Yankee, German, Irish, Norwegian, and Bohemian residents.

There were more ambitious attempts to build bridges of understanding between the groups who called Milwaukee home. In 1852 some of the city's Germans invited "their fellow citizens at large" to greet the arrival of spring with a traditional May Fest. The result was Milwaukee's first ethnic festival. Held on "Spring street hill" (near Tenth and Wisconsin), the event drew at least 10,000 people for a full day of outdoor games, dancing, shooting exhibitions, singing and, of course, May wine. The *Sentinel* (June 1, 1852) judged the day "an entire success":

It was a pleasure to see with how much spirit our German fellow-citizens entered into the celebration, and with what hearty good-will those not of German birth participated in the festivities. It was an additional pleasure to note the genial brotherly feeling which pervaded all classes and disposed one and all to bid "all hail the May!"

Pioneer historian James Buck, who had little sympathy for immigrants of any description, saw the event differently, calling it "a complete failure." "How it must elevate the mind," Buck scoffed, "to climb a greased pole, chase a greased hog, and jump tied up to the neck in a bag!"

Milwaukee was a city of neighbors and strangers at mid-century. Newcomers from Europe had to withstand the gibes of nativists like Buck and weather the antagonisms that seem endemic to a pluralistic society, but few, in the end, were sorry they had made the trip. John Diederichs, an 1847 arrival, spoke for thousands in a letter to his loved ones in Germany: "I thank the Lord that I am here, and regret that I did not come sooner."

Commerce by Lake ...

Milwaukeeans of all backgrounds faced a common task. Whether they were natives or newcomers, Yankees or Europeans, local residents shared a vision of their community's future as the commercial capital of Wisconsin. Milwaukee's founders had always dreamed of their embryonic city as a point of exchange, a middleman, a center for collection and distribution. It was, after all, the site's harbor potential, not its minerals or timber or water power, that had attracted developers like Byron Kilbourn and Morgan Martin. Destiny, in their view, had singled out Milwaukee as a classic port city, one that would trade the surplus of its hinterland for the goods of the wider world. In the two decades after incorporation in 1846, that is precisely what happened.

Two things were necessary for the city to realize its commercial destiny: settlers to trade with, and dependable channels of trade. Milwaukee's success, in other words, was a matter of population and transportation. Population was the easy part. Wisconsin joined the Union in 1848, and its appeal to newcomers was practically magnetic. Whether they were migrating from the East or emigrating from Europe, thousands were drawn to the Badger State at mid-century. Wisconsin's population mushroomed from 30,945 in 1840 to 305,390 in 1850 and 775,881 in 1860, a round of triple-digit increases that drew international attention.

Before and after: A popular guide to Wisconsin led German immigrants to expect dramatic progress in improving their farms.

from Increase Lapham, *Wisconsin*

𝕰𝕴𝕹𝕰𝖘 𝕵𝖆𝖗𝖒𝖊𝖗𝖘 𝕳𝖆𝖚𝖘 𝖚𝖓𝖉 𝕳𝖔𝖋 𝖎𝖓 𝖂𝖎𝖘𝖈𝖔𝖓𝖘𝖎𝖓 𝖛𝖔𝖗 10 𝕵𝖆𝖍𝖗𝖊𝖓.

𝕯𝖊𝖘𝖘𝖊𝖑𝖇𝖊𝖓 𝕵𝖆𝖗𝖒𝖊𝖗𝖘 𝕳𝖆𝖚𝖘 𝖚𝖓𝖉 𝕳𝖔𝖋 𝖎𝖓 𝖉𝖊𝖗 𝖏𝖊𝖙𝖟𝖎𝖌𝖊𝖓 𝖅𝖊𝖎𝖙.

The vast majority of new residents settled in the southern half of the state, and they came to farm the land. Wisconsin added roughly 5,000 farms a year in the 1850s, including a surprising number in Milwaukee County. The original city proper took in just over seven square miles, bordered by Lake Michigan, Twenty-seventh Street, North Avenue (dropping to Walnut Street west of Sixth), and Greenfield Avenue. The rest of Milwaukee County – all 236 square miles of it – was a wilderness fast becoming farmland. By 1860 two-thirds of the county's acreage was owned by farmers, and more than half their land was under the plow. The average Milwaukee County farm covered only sixty-five acres – testimony to the back-breaking labor involved in clearing the virgin forest. Farmsteads on the open prairies of Racine and Kenosha Counties were nearly twice as large, and they were cleared more than twice as fast.

Wherever they settled, nearly all Wisconsin farmers planted wheat, the undisputed king of frontier agriculture. Durable, portable, and adapted to cool climates, it was practically the only crop grown on the majority of farms. Wisconsin's rise as a center of wheat culture was meteoric. In 1850, only two years after graduating from territorial status, the state ranked ninth among America's wheat-producers; by 1860 it had risen to second place. Milwaukee County contributed its share to the mountain of grain. In 1850 the state's most urban county produced 373,805 bushels, good for fourth place among Wisconsin's thirty-two counties.

The city of Milwaukee's interests lay in shipping grain, not growing it. From the day in 1841 when the first boatload of wheat cleared Milwaukee harbor, local entrepreneurs sought to capture the flow of Wisconsin grain and the business of its producers.

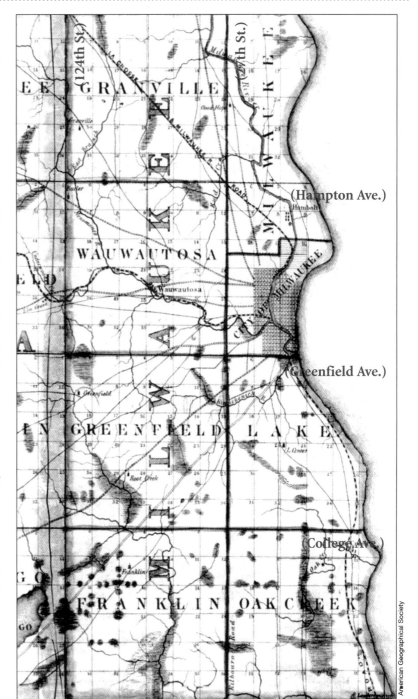

Milwaukee County developed as a compact urban core surrounded by seven unincorporated rural towns. Several of the town names on this 1855 map persist in modern suburbs.

American Geographical Society

Wisconsin Marine Historical Society

In 1856 the Dean Richmond *became the first ship to carry wheat directly from Milwaukee to Europe. It docked in Liverpool after a voyage of seventy-seven days.*

Sidewheel steamboats like the Nile *steadily replaced schooners on the Great Lakes, particularly in the passenger trade.*

They did so in the face of stiff competition. Chicago was an ever-present threat to the south, and the completion of its canal to the Illinois River (and thereby the Mississippi) in 1848 gave that city a fresh burst of energy. Racine and Kenosha provided competition much closer to home. Both had built oversized piers to attract lake commerce, and both were lobbying diligently for federal funds to improve their harbors and roads. Racine won its city charter in 1848 and Kenosha followed in 1850 – only a few years behind Milwaukee. To the north, Sheboygan and even Port Washington continued to nurse dreams every bit as grandiose as Milwaukee's.

Just as the cross-river rivalry had spurred the East and West Sides to greater heights than either might have reached on its own, competition with other would-be giants stirred Milwaukee's leaders to concerted action. Exploiting every natural asset and creating any number of new ones, they tried to make their community the obvious place to do business in the region. What that meant, in practical terms, was better transportation. All the banks, stores, warehouses, and grain elevators in the Northwest were useless unless customers could get to them with an absolute minimum of inconvenience.

Providing better transportation proved a good deal thornier than the population "problem." Milwaukee's premier natural advantage had always been its potential as a harbor, but much of that potential was still implicit in the early years of cityhood. Visiting ships generally used the lake piers near the foot of Huron (Clybourn) Street. Although they had handled huge volumes of passengers and cargo since their construction in the mid-1840s, the piers were unsafe in rough weather and unsuited to the shipment of bulk commodities like wheat. Grain merchants sought instead the safe anchorage of the Milwaukee River, and they built elevators on its banks as far north as today's Juneau Avenue.

Schooners and steamships entered the river at its original mouth, which had been dredged and reinforced by U.S. Army engineers in 1843. As river traffic increased, so did agitation for the "straight cut," a new harbor entrance a half-mile north of the original opening. The idea of breaching the peninsula at its narrowest point had been circulating since the first days of white settlement. Promoters argued that it would move the city's front door considerably closer to its business district and, not incidentally, spare ship captains a mile of tortuous river channel. Despite the straight cut's obvious benefits, Milwaukee

did virtually nothing for years. The reluctance of Congress to part with harbor improvement funds explains part of the delay, but the project's proponents also faced entrenched resistance from South Siders. The businessmen of Walker's Point and points south were determined to retain their favored position near Milwaukee's front door, even if the city's economic center had settled farther upstream. When the state legislature passed a measure allowing Milwaukee to tax its citizens for the straight cut, one South Side assemblyman resigned in protest.

The continuing growth of marine traffic gave the project a new sense of urgency. As the number of vessel arrivals soared from roughly 1,000 in 1846 to 2,680 in 1854, backers of the straight cut were increasingly frustrated by government's inability to act. Byron Kilbourn, characteristically, took matters into his own hands. In 1848, during his first term as Milwaukee's mayor, Kilbourn assembled a crew of laborers to dig a ditch across the sandbar. He hoped that the crude cut would encourage nature to take its course and carve a new outlet. Nature chose instead to obliterate the opening during the very next storm, and the Milwaukee River continued to enter the lake through its old mouth.

The straight cut's supporters finally prevailed. In 1854, with no assurance of federal help and over the heartfelt objections of South Side aldermen, the city of Milwaukee hired private contractors to finish the job. They dredged a channel 12 feet deep and 260 feet wide at the present harbor entrance, reinforcing it with stone-filled wooden piers that reached 1,120 feet into the lake. The new channel wasn't cheap: Milwaukee ultimately invested nearly $450,000 in the project, and the federal government chipped in another

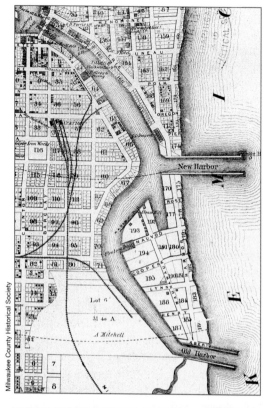

After years of discussion, the straight cut ("New Harbor") was finally completed in 1857. The streets on the resulting island were a figment of the mapmaker's imagination.

Capt. James M. Jones, shown with his wife, opened a successful but short-lived shipyard near the river mouth in 1854. The peninsula is still known as Jones Island.

$84,000. But the city was all smiles when the straight cut was completed, after four seasons of work, in 1857. "The Harbor thus constructed by the liberal and enlightened enterprize of our own people, is undoubtedly the best on the Lakes," declared the *Sentinel.* "[It is] the safest, most accessible and roomiest Harbor on all these inland seas."

The area most immediately affected by the project was, of course, the peninsula that separated the river from the lake. In 1854 a former lake captain named James Monroe Jones had opened a shipyard on the river side of the peninsula, just south of the proposed straight cut. The heart of his yard was a piece of reclaimed marsh that came to be known as Jones Island. Captain Jones built at least two dozen vessels on the "island," but his prosperity was all too fleeting; in 1857 a financial panic nearly ruined him, and in 1858 a northeast storm practically obliterated his shipyard. For a time the windswept site of his old works was a genuine island, isolated between the old and new harbor entrances, but storm waves eventually plugged the original mouth with sand. A peninsula re-emerged at the river mouth, this time pointing north rather than south. Jones Island, as the site is still known, thus became perhaps the only parcel of land in Milwaukee's history to change political representatives without a formal redistricting.

The straight cut had a broader and more salutary impact on Milwaukee's economy. The new entrance improved access to the river, which offered, in the *Sentinel's* words, "room and water enough for all the vessels in our Lake." The old lake piers were instantly obsolete. As they lapsed into disrepair, a genuine inner harbor developed, and the Milwaukee River was described as "a forest of masts" from its new mouth up to the North Avenue dam. Land-based traffic suffered accordingly. Bridges were opened with annoying frequency, and wagons and carriages were sometimes backed up for an hour or more. Few Milwaukeeans did more than grumble. Water, they knew, was the city's lifeblood, and the traffic it carried was an important measure of their collective vitality.

... and Commerce by Land

Land-based transportation was, of course, every bit as vital as lake traffic. Like all port cities, Milwaukee looked in two directions at once: west to its developing hinterland and east to the older states and Europe. The community's leaders wanted to occupy, in other words, the strategic midpoint between the nation's breadbasket and its major markets. Their efforts to forge better links with the interior required, if anything, even more energy and enterprise than their campaign to improve the city's harbor.

The public roads radiating outward from Milwaukee at mid-century were an embarrassment. Most were little more than wagon ruts in the wilderness, peppered with stumps and subject to regular flooding. Bone-jarring in good weather

It was not unusual, in the mid-1800s, to see a schooner under full sail in the heart of downtown Milwaukee. The view is west on Michigan Street from Broadway.

Milwaukee County Historical Society

Milwaukee quickly became the region's hub, and most of the "spokes" radiating outward in 1858 were plank roads.

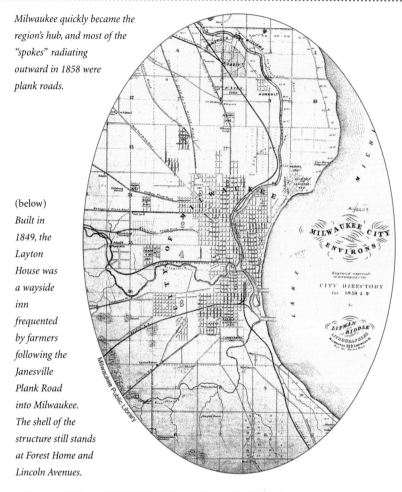

Milwaukee Public Library

(below) *Built in 1849, the Layton House was a wayside inn frequented by farmers following the Janesville Plank Road into Milwaukee. The shell of the structure still stands at Forest Home and Lincoln Avenues.*

Wisconsin Historical Society

and impassable in bad, they attracted frequent notice in the local press. On April 2, 1849, for instance, the *Sentinel* printed the complaint of "A Farmer" who had encountered slow going on his way through the South Side:

> *Directly in front of the residence of George H. Walker ... there is no road, but a slough hole, through, over, or under which it is impossible for a loaded team to pass, and in which, for the last week, at least six teams per day are engulphed, sometimes six at a time.*

Plank roads emerged as a short-term alternative to the area's "slough holes." They were, in essence, overgrown boardwalks, composed of oak planks, generally three inches wide and eight feet long, laid on oak stringers buried in the earth. Ditches on both sides of the roadway promoted drainage, and periodic turnouts allowed impatient teamsters to pass their slower neighbors. Work on the first highway, the Watertown Plank Road, began in 1848 and was finished from Milwaukee to Watertown, a distance of 58 miles, in 1853. It was an expensive proposition for its promoters, costing more than $110,000, but the road quickly turned a profit. The new turnpike cut the travel time to Watertown from three days during wet periods to a day and a half in all weather, and it attracted droves of farmers, peddlers, and aspiring settlers. At the rate of a penny per mile for every horse and carriage (and two cents for each animal pulling a freight wagon), the road brought in as much as $1,300 a week.

The success of the Watertown Plank Road, coupled with the continuing need for better transportation, spawned a host of other toll highways. The Wisconsin legislature chartered 135 turnpike and plank road companies before the fever broke, authorizing 32 in 1852 alone. All were strictly private affairs, organized with profit in mind. Milwaukee became the system's hub; plank roads converged on the city like wooden spokes from every direction but east, connecting the budding metropolis to Janesville, Mukwonago, Waukesha, Lisbon, Appleton, Fond du Lac, and Green Bay as well as Watertown. With a few exceptions, the old plank-road corridors are still in use, many under their original names, and they lend some diagonal relief to the otherwise rigid geometry of Milwaukee's street network.

For all their virtues, plank roads were something less than a permanent solution to the region's transportation problems. The oak planks had a disturbing tendency to float away during heavy rains, and they usually rotted after a few years in constant contact with the soil. Even without those drawbacks, the roads were only as fast as the oxen or horses that used them. A fresh alternative – the steam railroad – was already revolutionizing transit in the East, and a growing number of Wisconsinites came to view trains as the key to their state's future. Chief among them was a familiar figure: Byron Kilbourn. Although he had been the driving force behind the Milwaukee and Rock River Canal, Kilbourn was never married to a single technology. When political rivals scuttled his canal, the pioneer switched easily to rails. In 1847, one year before statehood, he prevailed upon the territorial legislature to charter Wisconsin's first railroad – the Milwaukee & Waukesha – and installed himself as its first president.

Ever the competitor, Kilbourn came to view steam trains as the difference between success and failure in the race for regional pre-eminence. Although his antagonism toward the East Side and Walker's Point had diminished somewhat since incorporation, the West Side's founder had discovered another enemy. Elected mayor in 1848, Kilbourn used his inaugural address as a call to arms:

> *Milwaukee has her rivals, or rather, perhaps, her competitors, who in a spirit of generous emulation are entering with her upon the race for greatness and supremacy. If New York has her Boston, so Milwaukee has her Chicago, in competition for the rich prize which nature awarded and designed to be hers. Boston enterprize has compelled New York to build her New York and Erie Railroad. Will not Chicago enterprize compel Milwaukee to build her Mississippi railroad? Unless we are content to see the business of the finest region of country, wrested from our grasp, we must do it, and that without delay.*

The fact that Milwaukee could still see itself as the region's New York underlines the fluidity of the urban frontier. Kilbourn's comments also indicate that current local attitudes toward "Flatlanders" have venerable roots.

Work on the Milwaukee & Waukesha's roadbed began in the autumn of 1849, and Kilbourn's crews spiked the first rails into place on September 12, 1850. The railroad's name had been changed to the Milwaukee & Mississippi by that time, a title more in keeping with its ultimate destination. The first of several maiden runs took place on November 20, 1850, when the locomotive *Wisconsin* carried two cars and fifty passengers up the Menomonee Valley to Wauwatosa. Traveling at the breathtaking speed of thirty miles per hour, the train completed the trip in just twelve minutes. Solomon Juneau was among the dignitaries aboard. "Mr. Juneau expressed much astonishment," noted the

Milwaukee's first locomotive arrived by schooner in September, 1850.

Milwaukee Sentinel, "as well he might, as he looked back to sixteen years ago, when he was alone, the only white settler upon that very spot." A reporter from the *Washington County Blade* took a more philosophical view: "These are things to be wondered at. Here are great events in human progress the accomplishment of which fill up the life time of many, compressed into a few short years of others."

Other celebrations followed in short order. On February 25, 1851, when the M&M made its first trip to Waukesha, hundreds of farm families lined the tracks, and

The city's first passenger depot was built in 1851 at Second Street and St. Paul Avenue, not far from the present Amtrak station.

a brass band serenaded nearly 500 diners gathered in the company's Waukesha car house. (The one-way fare to Waukesha was set at seventy-five cents.) By the end of 1852, as the railroad continued its westward progress, similar ceremonies had been held in Eagle, Palmyra, Whitewater, and Milton. All journeys began on Kilbourn's West Side; the railroad depot stood at Second Street and St. Paul Avenue, barely three blocks from the present Amtrak station.

Byron Kilbourn's presidency was derailed even before the first train reached Eagle. Unhappy, for some reason, with his fellow Milwaukee & Mississippi board members, Kilbourn decided to replace them – even though he lacked voting control of the company. As the railroad's principal stock agent, the promoter sold an "immense" number of shares to friendly parties at one mill on the dollar, thereby garnering enough votes to unseat his adversaries on the board. The sales were clearly fraudulent, and the company's other directors were outraged when their leader's scheme was exposed. The board meeting of January 7, 1852, turned into a showdown. Kilbourn offered neither explanation nor apology for his actions. He sat at the head of the table, silent as a stone, for twenty minutes and then left, practically daring the board to fire him. They did just that, and installed John Catlin of Madison as the M&M Railroad's new president.

The stock-fraud affair enhanced Kilbourn's reputation for skullduggery, but it did not keep him from railroads for long. In April, 1852, barely three months after his firing, Kilbourn prevailed upon a pliant member of the state legislature to sponsor a bill incorporating the La Crosse & Milwaukee Railroad. The would-be rail czar kept his involvement a secret, hoping that lawmakers would consider the bill, in his words, "purely a La Crosse measure – a little, distant, out of the way hamlet that a few hardly heard of." Kilbourn's own reputation made the subterfuge necessary. "Such was the prejudice of members," he admitted, "that nothing was to be said about Kilbourn or Milwaukee or the bill would be knocked skyward." Unaware of the deception until it was too late, the legislature approved the La Crosse & Milwaukee's charter. Byron Kilbourn had another train to ride – one that was, he boasted, "worth a dozen" of the Milwaukee & Mississippi.

The new line's eastern terminus was on the west bank of the Milwaukee River at Chestnut Street (now Juneau Avenue), in the original heart of Kilbourntown. Its planned route followed the river north for a few miles and then angled northwest through Hartford, Horicon, Beaver Dam, and Portage. The railroad was projected to cross the Wisconsin River at a new settlement named, with typical panache, Kilbourn City – today's Wisconsin Dells. Although construction proceeded at a snail's pace, the La Crosse & Milwaukee advertised itself as "the Great Northern Route," promising the most direct connection, by river and rail, with St. Paul and, some day, the Pacific.

The two lines started by Kilbourn had plenty of competitors. In the 1850s, as railroad fever reached epidemic proportions, Wisconsin's legislature chartered more than 100 companies, including one that planned, apparently in all seriousness, to lay tracks to the Bering Strait. The state made absolutely no attempt to coordinate or control rail development, and the result, not surprisingly, was a competitive free-for-all. The lines that showed tangible progress (a clear minority) practically tripped over each other in their efforts to secure the best routes, the juiciest political favors, and the most affluent investors. "There has been a lack of concert among these companies," Byron Kilbourn complained in 1854, "and in some instances, a spirit of hostility indulged in, greatly detrimental to the best interests of the City."

Competition for capital was especially keen. After pouring huge sums into wildcat banks and canals to nowhere, eastern investors had lost much of their taste for frontier finance, forcing railroad promoters to find their money closer to home. Most targeted the group most likely to benefit from rail service: Wisconsin's farmers. By 1857 nearly 6,000 farmers had purchased $5 million of stock in a long list of state railroads. Such diffuse ownership, crowed Byron Kilbourn, "approaches more nearly to an organized democracy than any corporate body within our knowledge, and is entirely destitute of every feature of monopoly." The system was less benign than Kilbourn claimed. Cash-poor, as always, most farmers mortgaged their land and buildings to purchase stock. Railroad

Both of Milwaukee's pioneer railroads were featured prominently in city directories of the 1850s.

companies, in turn, frequently sold the mortgages to raise cash from the same "foreign capitalists" they lambasted in their stock promotions. As later events would demonstrate, the practice exposed thousands of farmers to ruin.

Municipal financing was another popular tool. In 1853 the city of Milwaukee began to issue bonds for its resident railroads, accepting their securities as collateral. The municipality, in other words, borrowed money on behalf of private corporations – a rather dramatic sign of Milwaukee's determination to win the regional railroad wars. Rail lines were considered as essential as schools or firehouses, and voters gave nearly every bond issue overwhelming support. "No city in the Union," bragged the *Milwaukee Sentinel* in 1854, "has done as much in proportion to its means and population, towards opening avenues of trade and travel with the interior, as the city of Milwaukee." The community's "liberal and judicious investments" in steam lines soon strayed beyond the bounds of reason. By 1855 Milwaukee had issued $823,000 in railroad bonds, and in 1858 the total topped $1.6 million–more than one-fourth the city's $6 million assessed valuation. Towns and villages in the interior were just as eager to support the railroads. The Milwaukee & Mississippi followed a connect-the-dots route to Madison, stopping in nearly every settlement that was willing to pledge its credit on the railroad's behalf. The M&M's hunger for funds thus stretched an eighty-mile journey to ninety-six miles.

With creative sources of financing, a soaring population, and a growing demand for their services, the railroads converging on Milwaukee showed genuine progress. In 1857 the M&M became the first line in the state to reach the Mississippi, winding its way down the Wisconsin River valley to Prairie du Chien. In 1858 Kilbourn's La Crosse & Milwaukee touched the riverbank at La Crosse, sixty miles upstream. Both railroads established connections with steamboat companies that plied the big river as far north as St. Paul, the limit of navigation. Their success seemed assured. Wheat was by far the most important cargo, and the volume of wheat shipped on the Milwaukee & Mississippi soared from 237,000 bushels in 1852 to 1,678,000 in 1857. With profits approaching 22 percent as early as 1855, the company promised a stock dividend of at least 10 percent "under all circumstances and at all times."

Milwaukee did not, of course, have the only railroad terminals in the state. A delicate tracery of iron rails criss-crossed southern Wisconsin, covering 750 miles by 1857. Nearly a dozen companies offered regular service, but Milwaukee, as the home of the only two cross-state lines, was the uncontested hub of rail traffic. Fueled by the commerce of its hinterland, the lakeshore city gained ground on its nearest rivals in Wisconsin. By 1860 Milwaukee had more people than Racine, Janesville, Madison, Oshkosh, Fond du Lac, Sheboygan, and Kenosha *combined.*

Milwaukee's real contest was with Chicago. Although the Illinois city had an earlier start, the two settlements were serious rivals at mid-century, engaged in a lively struggle for commerce, capital, and settlers. In 1847, near the beginning of the railroad era, Milwaukee's population was 14,067, hard on the heels of Chicago's 16,859. Promoters like Byron Kilbourn

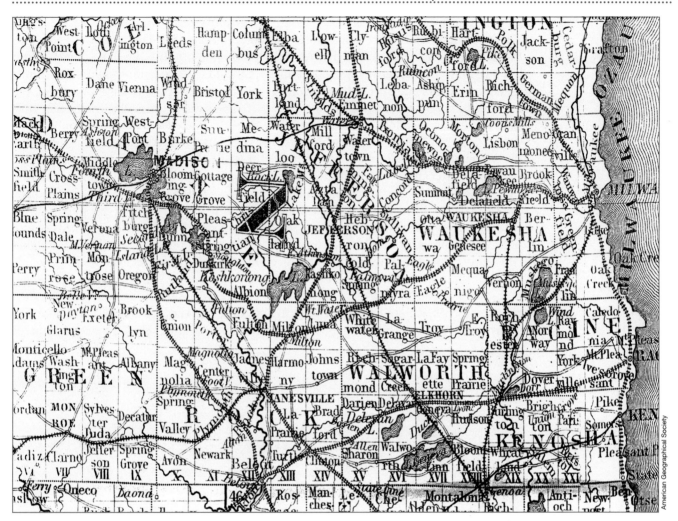

By 1858 railroad lines crisscrossed southern Wisconsin, with the greatest number converging on Milwaukee.

were confident that home-grown railroads would close the gap. Chicago, however, was fast becoming the center of a parallel but significantly larger rail system. Like Milwaukee, the Windy City had reached west first, hoping to tap the agricultural riches of outstate Illinois and Iowa; its rail network reached the Mississippi (at Rock Island) in 1854, three years before Milwaukee completed its link to the river. But the region's geography had given Chicago an even greater advantage, one that Milwaukee could never hope to duplicate: a direct land connection with all points east. Cross-country traffic was naturally funneled around the southern end of Lake Michigan, and Chicago, as the largest settlement in the vicinity, was ideally positioned to capture it. In 1852 the Michigan Southern became the first railroad to enter Chicago from the east. Only four years later, the city at the foot of the lake was the terminus of ten trunk lines and the largest railroad hub in the world.

85

The challenge to Milwaukee was obvious. The community was ninety miles closer to the eastern seaboard than Chicago by water, but it lay ninety miles farther away by land; a marginal advantage during the schooner era became a serious handicap in the railroad age. It was, therefore, with some trepidation that Milwaukee's leaders observed the completion of a rail line from Chicago. On May 19, 1855, Mayor James Cross traveled to Kenosha for the formal opening of the Green Bay, Milwaukee & Chicago Railroad, commonly known as the Lake Shore line. After expressing ritual hopes that the two cities would be united "by bonds stronger than iron," Mayor Cross drove home the last spike "as if he were used to it," reported the *Milwaukee Sentinel*. The ceremony was officially a celebration, but there

was ample cause for concern. Many shared Byron Kilbourn's fear that Chicago's railroads would pull Milwaukee into the orbit of its old rival, transforming the city from a budding metropolis to a minor satellite.

There was no immediate danger. By 1858 the Lake Shore line had a depot on Walker's Point, but it lacked a connection with either of Milwaukee's railroads. The gap was quite intentional. Neither the Milwaukee & Mississippi nor the La Crosse & Milwaukee had any desire to divert their grain shipments to Chicago; if the Lake Shore wanted to ship Wisconsin products, it would have to build its own Wisconsin tracks. The city's leaders, in the meantime, sought a more permanent alternative to the Chicago connection. When George Walker, the South Side's founder, became mayor in 1853, he beat the drum for

A Lake Shore train from Chicago chugged across the inner harbor in 1860. Later absorbed by the Chicago & North Western, the line had its first Milwaukee depot in Bay View.

cross-lake ferry service between Milwaukee and a railhead at Grand Haven, Michigan. "This route," he wishfully proclaimed, "is destined to become the great thoroughfare – for trade, travel and emigration between the East and the West." Four years later, on the eve of a national depression, the ferry project was still very much alive.

The outcome of the contest was never in serious doubt. As Chicago grew into its role as "Freight Handler to the Nation," the city's population skyrocketed, rising from 29,963 in 1850 to 112,172 in 1860 and 298,977 a decade later. Milwaukee had kept pace through the 1840s, but it was substantially less than half Chicago's size by 1860, and not even one-fourth in 1870. The old portage stopover was well on its way to becoming America's "Second City."

Entering the Top Twenty

Any disappointment Milwaukeeans felt was purely relative. Their community's growth was only slightly less explosive than Chicago's, and observers continued to comment on the "magical" progress of Wisconsin's "town-wonder." (One visitor was so impressed that he carried a variant of the name with him to the Pacific Coast, founding what he hoped would be another boom town: Milwaukie, Oregon, now a suburb of Portland.) Milwaukee, Wisconsin, may have lost the race for regional dominance (a fact that no one was willing to concede for years), but it was destined to play much more than a supporting role. With a better harbor, better rail connections, more aggressive promotion, and superior access

to capital, Milwaukee rose head and shoulders above its state rivals to become Wisconsin's commercial capital. The dollar value of goods passing through the city, in both directions, soared from $1.2 million in 1840 to roughly $36 million in 1855 – a volume that no other community in the state could match.

Population was an obvious yardstick of progress. Swelled by European immigration, the city's head count climbed from 9,508 at incorporation in 1846 to 20,061 in 1850 – a gain of more than 100 percent in just four years! By 1860, despite the rigors of a national depression, the city's population had more than doubled again, reaching 45,246. Triple-digit increases were practically taken for granted, and they carried Milwaukee into the upper ranks of urban America. The census of 1860 showed the community in twentieth place, just behind Detroit and just ahead of Cleveland. In little more than a quarter-century, Milwaukee had emerged from literally nowhere to become one of the top twenty cities in the United States.

The community's growth was, within certain limits, almost self-generating. Milwaukee attracted newcomers, especially European newcomers, on the basis of reputation alone, and each settler arrived with something the city could use: a pair of hands, a set of skills, or perhaps only a need for goods and services. With retail and wholesale trade as its foundation, the local economy expanded at a gallop and, as the economy expanded, Milwaukee's work force diversified. There was room for city-builders of all sorts: brewers and barristers, carpenters and capitalists, even portrait-painters and piano-tuners. Milwaukee became a center of trades as well as a center

of trade, giving settlers more reasons to settle and rural residents more reasons to do business in the city. As long as people could find productive outlets for their energies, the spiral soared ever upward.

As the economy continued its climb, Milwaukee did begin to put on urban airs. By 1853 its citizens could choose from no fewer than seven daily newspapers, four printed in English and three in German. In 1857 they marveled at the newly completed Newhall House, an elegant hotel that crowned the corner of Michigan Street and Broadway. Built by wheat magnate Daniel Newhall for a reported $275,000, it featured halls of "tesselated marble" and more than 300 guest rooms. In the same year the city opened its first public high school, offering a three-year program for students who could pass a demanding entrance exam. Milwaukee also kept pace with the latest technological breakthroughs. The first telegraph crackled to life in 1848, the first gaslights flickered on in 1852, and the first horse-drawn streetcars (a George Walker project) began to run on East Water Street in 1860. These were all wonders of the age, but urban growth had its less savory side. Child mortality rates reached appalling levels, fish die-offs in the Milwaukee River revealed a serious pollution problem, and crime of all types flourished. By 1851 the county jail had hosted 1,000 inmates (some for such antique offenses as bastardy and buggery), and the number of imprisonments grew with the city.

Of all the milestones, positive and negative, that marked Milwaukee's emergence as an urban center, perhaps the most telling was the death of Solomon Juneau in 1856. The old trader had not stayed around to witness the startling progress of the settlement he had helped to found. In 1848, with little to show for his fifteen years in urban real estate, Juneau had decided to start over in the country. He purchased a piece of land in Dodge County, where the Fond du Lac road crossed the Rock River, and founded the settlement of Theresa, a name shared by his mother and oldest daughter. There, in the rolling hills of the Kettle Moraine, the one-time mayor spent the rest of his life. Juneau opened a grist mill and a general store, grinding the settlers' wheat and selling them cloth by the yard and seed by the pound. He also kept his hand in the fur trade, stocking ear bobs and blankets to exchange with his native suppliers. (Due in part to Juneau's presence, Theresa remained a center of Indian settlement until 1851, when the federal government gathered more than 600 natives near the Rock River mill and herded them west to Kansas.)

In 1856 Juneau left home for the annual Indian payment on the Menominee reservation, always a major sales opportunity for traders. It was there, in the woods of northern Wisconsin, that he suffered an attack of undetermined nature and died on November 14. After brief interment on the reservation, Juneau's remains were transported to Milwaukee, where his old friends gathered at St. John's Cathedral for the largest funeral the city had ever witnessed. It took nearly thirty minutes for all the carriages to pass beneath the *Sentinel's* windows. The founder's body was buried in the Catholic cemetery near Twenty-second Street and Wisconsin Avenue, and later, when urban development claimed that site, moved to Calvary Cemetery.

Juneau had packed an enormous amount of living into his sixty-three years, much of

Wisconsin Historical Society

Wisconsin Historical Society

(above)

Completed in 1857, the Newhall House rivaled the best big-city accommodations...

(left)

... but Solomon Juneau's death in 1856 was a more convincing sign that the frontier had passed. Samuel M. Brookes finished this portrait in the trader's last year.

it the hardest kind. In 1833 he and his family had been practically the only white residents in southeastern Wisconsin. By the time of his death, the site of Juneau's old trading post had become the commercial heart of a city of 40,000. With Solomon Juneau was buried, for all practical purposes, the frontier. Milwaukee's childhood was most definitely over, and the community had entered the tumultuous, sometimes troubled years of urban adolescence.

Scandal on the Tracks

Another Milwaukee founder, in the meantime, was experiencing troubles of his own. Byron Kilbourn was caught short by the Panic of 1857. Coming precisely twenty years after the collapse of 1837, the panic ushered in a nationwide depression that brought Milwaukee's growth to a screeching halt. As unemployment soared, Milwaukee County's poor farm – the nucleus of

the present County Institutions in Wauwatosa – was filled beyond capacity, and the Milwaukee Relief Society fed nearly 1,000 people during the harsh winter of 1859-60. The city of Milwaukee, teetering on the brink of bankruptcy, halted most public works projects, closed its two high schools, and laid off many of its teachers, even though the student-teacher ratio was already a whopping 61 to 1.

Wisconsin's railroads, including Kilbourn's La Crosse & Milwaukee, were literally stopped in their tracks. Bankruptcy claimed even the most reputable companies, and thousands of farmers who owned stock in the lines sank with them. The mortgages they had exchanged for shares of stock reverted to eastern capitalists when the railroads failed, and the ultimate result, for many farmers, was foreclosure and eviction. Long considered the foundation of agricultural prosperity, railroads were increasingly seen as agents of ruin.

A bird's-eye view of Milwaukee in 1858

Milwaukee Public Library

Kilbourn's problems went well beyond financial distress. In 1856, shortly before the economy collapsed, Congress had authorized two land grants to support railroad construction in undeveloped sections of Wisconsin. It was the state legislature's privilege to select the two companies that would receive the grants. The La Crosse & Milwaukee went after the larger of the pair, a parcel totaling thousands of square miles worth an estimated $17.35 million. It quickly became the focus of one of the juiciest political scandals in Wisconsin's history.

Byron Kilbourn was blessed with a cast-iron conscience. Whether he was fabricating claims to prime Milwaukee real estate or undercutting his political and economic rivals, the West Side's impresario had always shown an impressive absence of scruples. In his efforts to win the 1856 land grant, Kilbourn outdid himself. Leaving nothing to chance, he let it be known that a vote in favor of the La Crosse & Milwaukee would be liberally rewarded. A small coterie of henchmen, among them "Boss" Jackson Hadley, offered $5,000 in railroad bonds for each vote in the Assembly and $10,000 for each in the state Senate. They found an amazingly large number of takers. Kilbourn ultimately distributed more than $500,000 in bonds to seventy-two legislators, leaving a minuscule caucus of six who were honest enough to turn him down. He did not stop at the legislature. Gov. Coles Bashford, a Republican, accepted $50,000 in bonds, which he promptly (and wisely, it turned out) exchanged for $15,000 in cash. Another $246,000 in bonds ended up in the hands of opinion leaders like Rufus King, editor of the *Milwaukee Sentinel*, and business magnate Alexander Mitchell.

With the wheels so lavishly greased, the outcome of the vote was never in question. To Kilbourn's dismay, however, rumors of wholesale bribery began to swirl as soon as the grant was awarded. The promoter dismissed the allegations as "a loose fabrication" at first, but he also emphasized that the La Crosse & Milwaukee had been locked in a titanic struggle with Chicago interests for the land grant. In a long letter to the *Sentinel* (June 3, 1857), Kilbourn declared that a desperate situation had called for desperate measures:

> *Chicago has always looked upon our prosperity and progress, with a sinister eye, and she cannot bear to see us hold such equal success with her in the contest for supremacy. She therefore devised a well planned scheme through means of a grant of land to prostrate us at one blow, and give her supreme control of all those resources, which of right belong to us and which if succeeded would have had the desired effect.... The emergency was upon us, and required the most prompt and energetic action to meet, and for one I was not disposed to shirk or shrink from any effort or responsibility in my power to secure a favorable result.*

Kilbourn highlighted his civic credentials, describing himself as "one who has spent the prime of his life in the cause of Milwaukee and her interests – the founder of one half of the city and the oldest inhabitant in it." (Walker's Point apparently did not figure in his definition of the city.) The promoter viewed himself as a public servant, protecting Wisconsin's interests against the predatory intentions of Chicago bandits.

Kilbourn's fellow Wisconsinites viewed him as a crook. Even in an age known for its fast dealing and easy virtue, the land-grant bribes went far beyond the accepted limits of propriety. By 1858 rumors of corruption had grown so general that the state legislature was compelled to launch an investigation. As the inquiry was beginning, Kilbourn announced plans to endow a Milwaukee university for needy young men, complete with "an Astronomical Observatory of the first class." Certain that the offer was only a public-relations ruse, the legislature refused to issue a charter for "Kilbourn University" and forced its would-be founder to the witness stand. Without a hint of embarrassment, Kilbourn argued that his

Byron Kilbourn's wholesale bribery of the Wisconsin legislature drew the satirical attention of Harper's Weekly (June 12, 1858).

gifts of railroad bonds were simply tokens of appreciation for public-spirited legislators:

> If they, in securing a great public good, should incidentally confer a great benefit on the La Crosse company, instead of some other company, that company could well afford to acknowledge the favor by a reciprocal act of liberality, by setting off, or granting to those conferring a favor, a small share of the benefits so conferred. Whether such an argument would bear the strictest test of morality, was not for me to determine, [but] I saw nothing in it legally offensive....

When investigators asked why, in his opinion, Gov. Bashford had taken the bribe proffered by the railroad, Kilbourn's reply was a model of candor: "I believe he accepted it for the reason that he thought the company could well afford to make such a donation without doing it any material damage, while to him the sum was large enough to confer a real benefit." The railroad could afford it, in other words, and Bashford could use it; ethics had no place in the equation.

The committee's final report was damning. The investigators concluded that the La Crosse & Milwaukee's managers, led by Byron Kilbourn, were "guilty of numerous and unparalleled acts of mismanagement, gross violations of duty, fraud and plunder." There were, however, no trials and no convictions. Much like foxes investigating a henhouse break-in, the legislators declined to recommend charges against their peers, and existing laws were insufficient to jail Kilbourn. The real losers were the people of Wisconsin. As the land-grant scandal made headlines across the nation, the Badger State was widely viewed as a sinkhole of political depravity. In 1859 businessman Lemuel Weeks lamented that "the fair fame of our State has been so tarnished by corruption, ... a whole legislative

POLITICAL MARKET.

CONSCIENTIOUS RAIL-ROAD PRESIDENT to DEALER. "Ah! let me see. I think I'll take this bunch of Legislators at $5000 a head. The Senators, at—what price did you say?"

DEALER. "Can't afford 'em less than $10,000 each."

R. R. P. "Well, hand them over. I suppose I'll have to take the lot."

DEALER. "Any thing else to-day. I have a Lot of Editors, at various prices, from a Thousand down to Fifty Cents."

R. R. P. "No, nothing in that way, to-day. But I want a Governor very much indeed, and will stand $50,000 for him. Get me a Wisconsin one, if possible!"

body has been bought up, and the dishonor has gone broadcast throughout the land."

Although he avoided prison, Byron Kilbourn paid a steep personal price for his misdeeds. Weighed down by legal as well as financial problems, his railroad sank into bankruptcy in 1858. Its well-traveled bonds were worthless, its infamous land grant was ultimately forfeited, and its management passed into the hands of New York creditors. Thanks to extensive real estate holdings, Kilbourn remained a wealthy man even after losing the La Crosse & Milwaukee, but he lost something far less expendable: his good name. Disgraced and discredited, the promoter saw his career as a public figure come to a rather inglorious end. Kilbourn finished his days in Nixonesque isolation. Troubled by chronic rheumatism, he left Wisconsin for Hot Springs, Arkansas, in 1868 and finally settled in Jacksonville, Florida. On December 16, 1870, a few months after his sixty-ninth birthday, Kilbourn lay down for an after-dinner nap and never woke up. The entrepreneur was buried in Jacksonville, and there he remained until 1998, when Historic Milwaukee Inc., a local preservation group, brought his body north again. Byron Kilbourn finally came to rest in the city he had, with more energy than integrity, helped to transform from a wilderness outpost to a Midwestern metropolis.

War for the Union

Purely local news, even news as riveting as the Kilbourn scandal, was distinctly secondary to the national headlines by the late 1850s. Americans on both sides of the Mason-Dixon Line watched in horrified fascination as regional tensions pulled their country apart. Although Milwaukee was miles removed from the fault lines and

later the battle lines, the prevailing pressures were sharply felt in the young city; burning issues in Washington and Richmond generated heat in Milwaukee as well.

The most obvious point of regional contention – slavery – was creating shock waves on the local scene long before the earth shook at Fort Sumter. Although no Wisconsinite could legally own slaves and few were willing to defend the practice, there was ample room for discord. The issue of abolition, in fact, played the same role that abortion would in the late twentieth century. The most ardent abolitionists were filled with all the passionate conviction and righteous anger of modern anti-abortion activists, and they were just as apt to see the world in terms of a single issue. Some Milwaukeeans resented their shrill rhetoric. In 1847, under pressure from radicals in the congregation, the elders of First (now Immanuel) Presbyterian Church declared that slavery was "fraught with sin against God," but they had equally harsh words for anti-slavery agitators who spoke "the language of bitter denunciation ... dogmatic intolerance ... and sweeping condemnation." The abolitionists knew when they weren't wanted. Led by businessman Edward Holton, they left their "weak-backed" brethren at First Presbyterian to form the Grand Avenue Congregational Church.

The radicals soon had a newspaper to buttress their views: the *Milwaukee Free Democrat,* edited by a one-time New York schoolteacher named Sherman Booth. Booth's activism made him a national celebrity. In 1850 Congress passed the Fugitive Slave Act, a measure that helped slaveowners recover their runaways on Northern soil. Abolitionists throughout the region were outraged, and many planned open

Sherman Booth, the abolitionist editor whose defiance of the Fugitive Slave Act sparked a confrontation between Wisconsin and the federal government

Wisconsin Historical Society

Joshua Glover, the Missouri fugitive at the heart of the dispute

Wisconsin Historical Society

resistance. Wisconsin's radicals got their chance in 1854, when Joshua Glover, a fugitive from Missouri, was captured in Racine, beaten, and carted off to jail in Milwaukee. Working his horse to a lather, Sherman Booth rallied nearly 5,000 citizens, both black and white, to an indignation meeting in the courthouse square. After a series of incendiary speeches, some of the crowd's brawnier members borrowed a timber from the construction site of St. John's Cathedral and reduced the jailhouse door to splinters. Free at last, Joshua Glover was escorted to Waukesha, an abolitionist stronghold, and finally spirited across the border to Canada.

Sherman Booth was arrested and imprisoned for his role in the rescue, giving the editor a highly visible forum for continued attacks on the Fugitive Slave Act. He had impressive local support. Soon after his arrest, Wisconsin's Supreme Court set Booth free, ruling that the law was unconstitutional. A state court, in other words, voided an act that had been passed by both houses of Congress and signed by the president! The judges based their ruling on the same appeal to states' rights that the South was using in defense of slavery, and federal courts were quick to strike it down as seditious. Booth was the object of a tug-of-war between state and federal authorities for the next seven years, shuttling in and out of jail with every shift in jurisdiction. The fiery editor was a prominent martyr for the abolitionist cause until 1859, when he was indicted for indiscretions with a teen-aged babysitter. Although the seduction case tarnished his image, Booth lost none of his zeal. In 1861, one month before the outbreak of the Civil War, he won a pardon from President James Buchanan and resumed his anti-slavery crusade.

The same tensions that produced a dramatic rescue were responsible for a tragic shipwreck. In 1857, cementing the state's reputation as a hotbed of anti-slavery sentiment, Wisconsin voters made Alexander Randall, a fire-breathing abolitionist, their governor. During an impasse in the Booth case, Randall called on the state's volunteer militia units to stand behind him in case of a confrontation with federal forces. That appeal sparked a confrontation with his own constituents. Garret Barry, commander of Milwaukee's Union Guard, stated that, if forced to choose between his state and his nation, he was sworn to uphold the laws of the nation. That was enough for Randall, who promptly disbanded and disarmed Barry's troops.

The case had clear political overtones. Most of Milwaukee's militiamen were Irish and German immigrants, who generally voted Democratic. The Union Guard, for instance, was the pride of Milwaukee's Irish community, and Garret Barry was the Democratic county treasurer. Most abolitionists, by contrast, were Republicans, and Republicans tended to be both nativists and prohibitionists, qualities that put them instantly at odds with the immigrants. Barry and his men were not about to meekly accept the edict of someone with motives as suspect as Gov. Randall's. Determined to regroup and rearm, they planned a fundraising excursion to hear Stephen Douglas, the Democratic presidential candidate, in Chicago. Their party left on September 7, 1860, aboard the side-wheel steamship *Lady Elgin*, one of the finest vessels on the Great Lakes. After a full day of pomp and parades, the Union Guard boarded the steamer for the return voyage to Milwaukee. In the early morning hours of September 8, the *Elgin* collided with a lumber schooner just off Winnetka. Buffeted by storm waves, the vessel sank within thirty minutes. Nearly three-fourths of the approximately 400 passengers on board lost their lives.

The waves played no favorites; the dead included German militiamen, Milwaukee

The wreck of the Lady Elgin *off Winnetka, Illinois, September 8, 1860*

from Leslie's Illustrated Newspaper

firefighters, and a visiting member of the British Parliament. But it was the families of the Irish Third Ward – the Murphys and Monahans, Coughlins and Connollys – who suffered the heaviest losses. The *Milwaukee Sentinel* (September 10, 1860) described the pall that settled over the Irish community as the news sank in:

> It would be utterly impossible to convey any idea, to those who did not visit the Third Ward, of the scene presented there. It seemed as though sounds of moaning proceeded from every third house. Little crowds of women were congregated along the walks, some giving free expression to their grief, others offering condolence. Never before has our city been stricken with such a calamity.

Seven months later, the nation was stricken with an even greater calamity: the onset of the Civil War. In April, 1861, Confederate forces attacked Fort Sumter and forced its garrison to surrender; decades of smoke finally erupted into flame. Milwaukee's loyalty to the Union was unquestionable. The Glover rescue had demonstrated the presence of a strong anti-slavery element, and even native Southerners like George Walker were virulently anti-Confederate. The war itself, however, was greeted with resounding ambivalence.

On the one hand, thousands answered Abraham Lincoln's call to arms. The *Daily News* (August 15, 1862) described the feverish pace of early recruiting activities:

> Drums beat, fifes play, bands parade the streets in full blast, gathering crowds at every corner, and literally blocking the streets and crossings. The city is one complete hive of busy men and boys, and to the outward eye nothing is left undone to secure recruits. Placards garnish every street, and flaming handbills setting forth the advantages of enlisting in this or that company meet the eye at every turn. Little boys run after and hail you; ... men already enlisted swarm around public places urging old comrades to join them, and the ladies lend the sanction of their presence and efforts at every suitable opportunity.

Before the summer of 1862 had ended, brewers and publishers were short-handed, women were working as typesetters and farm laborers, and the Newhall House had been forced to hire boys as waiters. Rufus King, after years of publishing the news in the *Milwaukee Sentinel*, became a full participant, leading Wisconsin's famed Iron Brigade as a brigadier general. One of his counterparts in the German press was just as eager to fight. In 1862 Bernhard Domschke, an exiled revolutionary who edited the *Milwaukee Herold*, led a column of his employees into the ranks of a German-speaking regiment, forcing the paper to suspend publication for a time. Pledged to the ideal of liberty for all, Forty-Eighters like Domschke found the lure of military service practically irresistible.

Other immigrants were openly skeptical. Although patriots were never difficult to find, most newcomers had experienced their fill of government edicts and armed conflict in Europe, and they had little interest in risking their lives – or their sons' lives – for a country that still considered them strangers. In 1861 the enlistment rate for immigrants in Wisconsin was only one-third the rate for native-born Americans. It didn't help that the war was being prosecuted by a Republican administration. Although Abraham Lincoln carried Wisconsin in 1860 and again in 1864, the voters of Milwaukee, most of them immigrants, returned large majorities for his Democratic opponents in both elections. Abner Kirby, a Democrat who became the city's mayor in 1864, pronounced Lincoln "the weakest man on the whole list of presidents" and blamed him for allowing "a few fanatics" to drag the country into "this bloody and unholy strife."

A major source of immigrant discontent was the military draft. In the late months of 1862, with the war going badly for the North and enlistments waning, Congress passed the nation's first draft law, a measure whose enforcement was shrewdly left to the individual states. The system that emerged was anything but democratic; a prospective draftee could escape service by either hiring a substitute or buying his way out for $300. Those with insufficient means faced quick conscription, and the result, in some communities, was bedlam. Draft protesters, most of them Germans and Luxembourgers, took to the streets of Port Washington in November, 1862, burning draft records and vandalizing the homes of prominent Republicans. A crowd of Germans threatened violence in West Bend, and only a show of force by the military prevented trouble in Milwaukee. Successive drafts were no more popular. In an odd foreshadowing of a later generation's behavior, many draftees fled to Canada, and others sought deferments on specious medical grounds. Although the heroism and sacrifices of the "Badger boys in blue" – from Antietam to Gettysburg – should never be discounted, it was obvious that many Milwaukeeans, particularly those from abroad, were determined to sit out a conflict in which they felt no direct involvement.

Rufus King, Sentinel editor and one-time school superintendent, left Milwaukee to lead Wisconsin's famed Iron Brigade in the first years of the Civil War.

(below)
At least forty members of a Milwaukee Turner Schutzbund (shooting club) entered the Union Army as sharpshooters. Such avid support was anything but universal among Milwaukee's immigrants.

A regiment of soldiers bivouacked on the lawn of the Milwaukee County Courthouse, now Cathedral Square

As the Civil War dragged on, more and more casualties of the conflict limped home to Wisconsin. Soldiers disabled in combat (or in camp) were generally discharged after rudimentary medical treatment and left to their own devices. For those without family or friends to support them, the result was often destitution, and the figure of the tramp veteran was all too common in the North. The women of Milwaukee – the Yankee Protestant women of Milwaukee – decided to do something about it. Their leaders included Henrietta (Byron) Kilbourn, Martha (Alexander) Mitchell, Caroline (George) Walker, and other pillars of pioneer society. In 1864, after years of wrapping bandages and knitting mittens, they opened the Milwaukee Soldiers' Home in a row of storefronts on the west bank of the Milwaukee River. The Home provided, in the words of its state charter, "a temporary place of rest and refreshment for the soldiers of the Federal army, and a permanent home for such Wisconsin soldiers as had

no homes and, disabled by wounds or sickness, were unable to support themselves." In its first year of operation, the Soldiers' Home served more than 2,500 veterans.

In the aftermath of Robert E. Lee's surrender on April 9, 1865, a river of returning soldiers threatened to overwhelm the modest West Side facility. Determined to serve anyone who showed up, the women of Milwaukee organized a state fair to raise funds for more commodious quarters. Their "Great Fair" of 1865, held in a huge temporary hall on Broadway at Clybourn Street, featured everything from art exhibits to farm machinery, and it netted more than $100,000 for the cause. The ladies' labors were rewarded in 1866, when the United States made Milwaukee one of four sites in its network of "national asylums" for disabled soldiers. (George Walker, in his last effort as a civic leader, lobbied diligently for Milwaukee's selection. The South Side's founder died on September 20, 1866, shortly after a trip to Washington.) With a major

Milwaukee Public Library

boost from funds raised by the women, federal officials purchased a wooded, rolling tract just west of the city and erected a cluster of Cream City brick buildings. The first opened in May, 1867, and the National Soldiers' Home – a scenic, self-contained community with its own theater, post office, and even swan ponds – became a must-see attraction for Milwaukee visitors. The original buildings, their graceful slate roofs still intact, are the focal point of the present Veterans Administration Center.

The Fortunes of War

The residents of the Soldiers' Home, many of them "maimed, crippled, and helpless for life," embodied the staggering human costs of the war. The economic benefits of the struggle, however unintended, were much more apparent in Milwaukee. Like most conflicts fought largely on enemy soil, the Civil War was good for business. It closed the lower Mississippi River to all

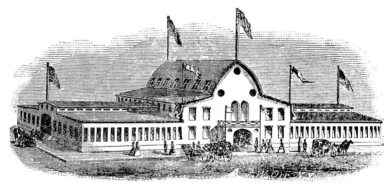

State Historical Society of Wisconsin

With proceeds from a "Great Fair" held in a temporary hall on Broadway (above), local women guaranteed Milwaukee's selection as the site of a "national asylum" for disabled Civil War veterans. The Soldiers' Home (top) is now part of the Veterans Administration complex.

99

commercial traffic, diverting an enormous amount of business to northern shipping routes, including the river-to-lake routes in Wisconsin. The volume of eastbound freight on the state's two leading railroads, both terminating in Milwaukee, soared from less than 40,000 tons in 1860 to almost 250,000 in 1865. Nearly derailed by the Panic of 1857, Wisconsin's trains were once again whistling along on the high track.

Although the Civil War revived the railroad business, it did not bring back the competitive chaos of the 1850s. The trend, in fact, was toward consolidation. Marginal branch lines were pruned, trunk lines were reinforced, and large companies grew at the expense of the small. In 1863 the La Crosse & Milwaukee, minus Byron Kilbourn, was reborn as the Milwaukee & St. Paul Railroad.

Alexander Mitchell, the Scottish-born banker who knitted Wisconsin's bankrupt railroads into a coherent regional system in the 1860s

Milwaukee Public Library

Under the guidance of Alexander Mitchell, who became the road's president in 1865, the Milwaukee & St. Paul developed a ravenous appetite for competing lines. In 1866, after gobbling up a host of smaller firms, Mitchell's railroad devoured its chief rival in the state: the Milwaukee & Prairie du Chien, a successor of the pioneer Milwaukee & Waukesha line launched by Kilbourn back in 1847. Already Wisconsin's leading banker, Alexander Mitchell became its railroad magnate as well. Competing head-to-head with the Chicago & North Western for regional supremacy, he developed a system that would evolve into one of America's great rail empires: the Milwaukee Road.

It was wheat that filled the trains during the war. Bumper crops pushed Wisconsin into second place among the nation's wheat-producing states (behind Illinois) in the early 1860s, and grain shipments made up nearly three-fourths of the tonnage carried by Wisconsin's railroads: some for the Army, more for export, and nearly all heading east through Milwaukee. "Wheat is king," crowed the *Milwaukee Sentinel* in 1861, "and Wisconsin is the center of the Empire." As wartime inflation lifted the price per bushel from a meager 65 cents in 1860 to $2.26 in 1864, Milwaukee became the funnel for tons of high-priced grain pouring in from the fields of Wisconsin, Minnesota, and northern Iowa. The phalanx of grain elevators rising from the riverbanks – and the nearby flour mills they supplied – were the most conspicuous landmarks on the city's skyline, and the tonnage of vessels calling to carry the kernels away nearly doubled between 1858 and 1862. In the latter year, Milwaukee outdistanced Chicago to become the largest shipper of wheat on the planet, a title the two cities passed back and forth for the next decade.

Milwaukee Public Library

Other businesses benefited even more directly from the Civil War. As the Union Army demanded ever-increasing quantities of pork and beef, meat-packing became an important industry; Milwaukee's pioneer packing plants more than doubled the number of hogs they processed during the war years. The city's tanners, most of them German immigrants, turned the hides of Wisconsin farm animals, principally cattle, into Army boots, cartridge belts, and leather harnesses. The number of tanneries in the city jumped from thirteen in 1860 to thirty in 1870. Even the breweries felt the stimulus of war. Whiskey, widely available at fifteen cents a gallon before Fort Sumter, had long been Milwaukee's drink of choice. When the government imposed a stiff "war tax" on hard liquors, the price of a stiff drink skyrocketed, and even Yankees developed a taste for the beverage that would one day make Milwaukee famous.

The effect of all this activity was electric. Milwaukee's population jumped from 45,246 in 1860 to 55,641 in 1865 – a gain of 23 percent in just five years and twice Wisconsin's rate of increase. Growth at the top of the economic ladder was even more impressive. The number of city residents whose annual incomes exceeded $10,000 (roughly $120,000 in current dollars) almost doubled in a single

Wheat was the foundation of Milwaukee's economy in the Civil War decade, and grain elevators, not smokestacks, dominated the city's skyline.

year, rising from 44 in 1863 to 83 in 1864. Meat-packer John Plankinton topped the list at $104,400, more than enough to make him a millionaire in modern terms. Plankinton was a towering exception – most workers earned less than $600 annually – but jobs were plentiful and prosperity was general.

It was obvious, by war's end, that Milwaukee was realizing the future its founders had planned for it. By schooner and steamship from the lake, by road and rail from the land, the channels of commerce converged in the young city. Between 1846 and 1865, Milwaukee became Wisconsin's business emporium, the state's single most important place to buy

and sell, ship and receive, gather and distribute. That was the dream that had stirred men like Byron Kilbourn and Morgan Martin in the first place. They had envisioned Milwaukee as a classic port city and, given its harbor potential, there was a certain determinism at work in the early years. But the city's success was anything but automatic; like most pioneers, Milwaukeeans willed their future. They picked a reasonable role – capital of commerce – and then proceeded, despite discord, depression, and stiff competition, to make it their own.

The results were tangible. In the two decades after 1846, Milwaukee grew from a hopeful frontier town of fewer than 10,000

Milwaukee's status as a rail hub in the late 1860s ensured the city's prosperity even as nearby Chicago became America's transportation center.

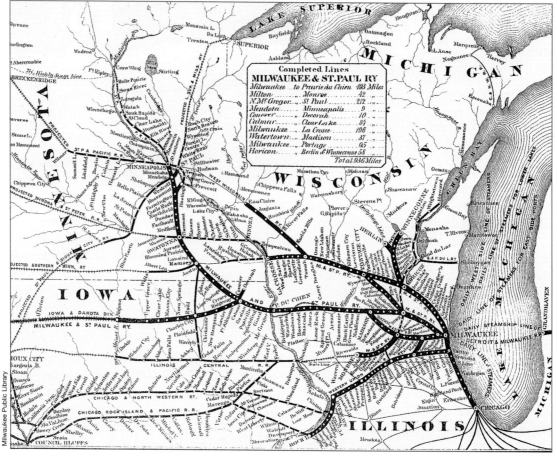

people to an aspiring metropolis of more than 55,000. It moved from infancy to urban adolescence. It became the greatest shipper of wheat on earth, one of the top twenty cities in America, and a leading source of products ranging from harness leather to lager beer. Milwaukee also developed unique patterns of human diversity. Yankees kept a firm grip on the economic reins during the first generation of cityhood; with the exception of stars like Alexander Mitchell, a proud Scot, immigrants played at most a supporting role. But the numbers, and increasingly the influence, belonged to newcomers from Europe. The size and vitality of the German community was Milwaukee's single most striking characteristic, and other groups – Irish, British, Scandinavian, Bohemian – were having a profound impact on neighborhood life, patterns of leisure and, above all, politics. Milwaukee was poised to make a sharp turn in 1865, one that would introduce new industries and new immigrants, but its base, both human and economic, was secure.

Of all the assets that combined to form that base, railroads were probably the most important. Milwaukee's success depended on its locational advantages, a superior harbor, ample political clout, and access to capital, but the presence of two major rail lines spanning the entire state was decisive. In the last half of the nineteenth century (and well into the twentieth), virtually all travel of any length was done by rail; trains were like automobiles, trucks, and planes rolled into a single transportation system. Just as current maps of the United States feature the interstate highway network, maps of the 1800s highlighted the nation's railroads. As settlement in Wisconsin progressed, the rail lines were like iron arteries pumping the state's wealth into Milwaukee. Offering high-speed, high-volume, all-weather access to the interior, they assured the city an enduring place as an economic center. Even as Chicago widened its regional lead, the railroads made Milwaukee a genuine alternative.

The major lines – the La Crosse & Milwaukee and the Milwaukee & Mississippi – formed the core of the rail empire established by Alexander Mitchell in the 1860s. Both of those pioneer railroads, interestingly, were creations of Byron Kilbourn. He may have been a combative curmudgeon with an undernourished sense of ethics, but Kilbourn was also an irrepressible dreamer, a man whose taste for risks had a galvanizing impact on his city. In an 1883 banquet speech, Alexander Mitchell looked back on what might have been. Without mentioning Kilbourn by name, he paid oblique tribute to the man who preceded him as Wisconsin's railroad czar:

> *If the citizens of Milwaukee had remained passive and had done nothing to command the trade of the great region north and west of us, then she would have missed her opportunity and would have been relegated to the position of a quiet country village. But the business men of Milwaukee were equal to the occasion.... The location of Chicago at the head of Lake Michigan forced greatness upon her. The citizens of Chicago, individually or in their corporate capacity, did comparatively nothing for the first railroads which entered that city, while, if it had not been for the enterprise and public spirit and liberality of the citizens of Milwaukee, both individually and collectively, Milwaukee to-day might have been no larger than Manitowoc or Sheboygan.*

Chapter 4

Wheat, Iron, Beer, and Bloodshed, 1865 – 1886

From its footings on the southern edge of downtown, the Daniel Hoan Bridge rises in a graceful arc over Milwaukee's harbor, descends the entire length of Jones Island, and finally comes to rest again on the foundations of Milwaukee industry. There are no structures to mark the site, no relict sheds or crumbling smokestacks, but the Bay View end of the bridge lies squarely on the buried ruins of a pioneer iron mill. For nearly sixty years, its gigantic blast furnaces lit the nighttime sky over the southern lakeshore with a fiery red glow. Those furnaces fed a phalanx of long, narrow mill buildings that rolled the red-hot iron into everything from rails to nails. The rest of the thirty-acre complex was a soot-blackened maze of machine shops, warehouses, engine rooms, and ore docks. Chartered by the state legislature in March, 1866, the Milwaukee Iron Company was the region's

The Milwaukee Iron Company was the first heavy industry in a community that became famous for manufacturing.

Milwaukee Journal Sentinel

first heavy industry and, in a longer view, the fulcrum on which Milwaukee turned from commerce to manufacturing as the foundation of its economy.

A humbler institution was founded in March, 1866: St. Stanislaus Catholic Church. Polish immigrants had been trickling into Milwaukee for years, but it was not until 1866 that they were numerous enough to organize a parish. Thirty families strong, the Poles bought a small brick church on Fifth and Mineral Streets, in the Walker's Point neighborhood, from a German Lutheran congregation that had moved to larger quarters. Raising the $4,000 purchase price required genuine sacrifice (one member raffled off a cherished gold watch for $225), but the effort made history: St. Stanislaus Church was the first Polish congregation in urban America. Its members were among the earliest immigrants to arrive during the industrial period and, within a generation, they and the Poles who followed were challenging their Yankee, German, and Irish neighbors for a fair share of political power and economic clout.

The Milwaukee Iron Company and St. Stanislaus Church neatly symbolize two pillars of the post-Civil War years: industries and immigrants. They were opposite sides of the same coin, mutually dependent outcomes of two radical and related shifts, one technological and the other social. The first was driven by the steam engine, which emerged as a new source of cheap, portable power and thereby speeded the mechanization of tasks formerly done by hand. During the same period, overpopulation and social unrest helped to create a new source of cheap, portable labor in Europe, particularly in the southern and eastern portions of the continent. The two trends intersected in the cities of North America, remaking their neighborhoods and reshaping their economies. Milwaukee's transition was gradual, but the final result, for industrialists and industrial immigrants alike, was a paradoxical blend of new economic opportunities and, by the period's end, murderous conflict.

Milwaukee County Historical Society

King Wheat and Emperor Alexander

The shift in the local economy was apparent only in hindsight. Before Milwaukee gained its modern reputation for industrial prowess, there was a lengthy period of overlap with the city's first claim to fame: the wheat trade. Receipts of the amber grain actually rose during the post-Civil War period, climbing from 12 million bushels in 1865 to an all-time high of 28.5 million in 1873 – seven years *after* the Milwaukee Iron Company incorporated. Even later, in 1879, financial titan Alexander Mitchell offered a straightforward assessment of Milwaukee's economic base. "The carrying trade, including produce exchanges," he proclaimed, "[is] paramount in importance to the others, ... first in point of fact, and on it the others in a great measure depend." The city eventually lost its title as the world's largest wheat market, falling behind Chicago, St. Louis, and even Toledo in some years, but King Wheat remained Milwaukee's monarch for nearly a decade after the war.

No one did more to prolong the reign of wheat than Alexander Mitchell himself. As president of the Marine Bank, long Wisconsin's largest, he controlled the flow of capital that could nourish or starve aspiring businesses. Although he was a leading local investor in the Bay View iron mill, Mitchell had shown, over the years, a definite preference for the grain trade. James Seville, a founder of the company that became Allis-Chalmers, recalled how difficult it was for would-be industrialists to find financial backing:

> All new enterprises were supposed to have their own capital, for if they had not, the chances were small for accommodation at the banks,

Downtown Milwaukee in 1870. The bridges still crossed the river at an angle.

Milwaukee Journal Sentinel

(below)
The Age of Sail was not yet over. Graceful schooners like this one tied up near the Grand Avenue bridge helped keep Milwaukee's wheat trade afloat into the late 1800s.

Milwaukee Public Library

because all the capital the banks had was required by those handling the products of the country at large. The commercial interests were the paramount objects in view by the banks then in existence, and anyone having sufficient "nerve" to go into manufacturing must do it on his own resources or "bust."

Alexander Mitchell's role as a railroad executive was even more crucial to the health of Milwaukee's economy, particularly its grain trade. The Milwaukee & St. Paul Railroad was Wisconsin's largest when he assumed the presidency in 1865, and the system grew at a gallop after the Civil War. Working with and through Sherburn S. Merrill, his dexterous general manager, Mitchell directed an expansion campaign that kept pace with the westward progress

The lion in winter: Alexander Mitchell, Wisconsin's emperor of capital, sat for this portrait in 1884, his sixty-seventh year.

Milwaukee Club

of America's agricultural frontier. In 1867 the line reached St. Paul and continued to push west across the prairies. Five years later the company opened a new corridor to Chicago, which led, in 1874, to the adoption of a new name: the Chicago, Milwaukee & St. Paul Railroad. The CM&StP had 1,399 miles of track at the time, and its network included the lines of no fewer than thirty-six corporate ancestors. Still the westward push continued. As the railroad crossed into what is now South Dakota, its Milwaukee connections were practically burned into the map. Mitchell, whose fabled Corn Palace draws almost 600,000 tourists annually, was named for Alexander himself, and Aberdeen, in the northern tier of counties, borrowed the name of the financier's hometown in Scotland. By 1886 the Chicago, Milwaukee & St. Paul system covered 5,200 miles of track in the heartland of North America.

The railroad served all paying customers, of course, including manufacturers, but the fact that one of America's leading lines made its home in Milwaukee was an enormous comfort to commodity traders whose faith in King Wheat was being tested. In 1878 Oren Britt, one of the city's leading grain merchants, cited the CM&StP Railroad as a major reason for continued confidence:

I am no believer in the idea that we have reached the climax of our grain trade. The wheat-growing area is constantly enlarging. It is true that it is being pushed farther from us. But the territory is immediately occupied by the railways having their interests centered here.

The Chicago & North Western Railroad was Mitchell's, and Milwaukee's, most formidable competitor. Organized in 1859, it was, like the CM&StP itself, a conglomeration of older lines that had failed in the Panic of 1857. The North Western pushed steadily into Wisconsin from its Chicago base, concentrating on north-south lines that threatened to divert traffic from the Mitchell railroad's east-west routes. Milwaukeeans were always quick to suspect the motives of Windy City businessmen, but the executives of both lines were pragmatists who put business concerns ahead of civic pride. They practiced a policy of open collusion whenever possible, sharing profits and even leaders in some years; Alexander Mitchell served briefly as the president of both railroads in 1869-70. At other times the fragile alliance dissolved in a round of rate wars that offered rural shippers at least sporadic relief from freight charges that often bordered on the extortionate. Railroads, observed historian Robert Nesbit, were "shamelessly courted where they did not exist and cordially hated where they did."

Mitchell himself was sometimes described as "Alexander the Great" in the years following the Civil War. As railroad magnate, banker, and backer of the grain trade, the Scotsman was indeed a sovereign power in postwar Wisconsin, an emperor of capital whose authority was beyond question. Nothing mirrored Mitchell's rise to greatness more faithfully than his own residence. It was, in its first incarnation, a relatively modest brick house on the west side of Ninth Street between Spring (now Wisconsin Avenue) and Wells Streets. As the financier's fortune grew, so did his estate. Mitchell bought out his neighbors, one by one, demolished their homes, and then surrounded virtually the entire square block with a wrought iron fence that cost a reported $20,000. The original house was enlarged

and remodeled several times during the same years, but the real transformation took place in 1876, when Edward Townsend Mix, Milwaukee's leading architect, added a mansard roof and an ornate tower. The interior of the mansion that emerged was a designer's delight, a showcase for the finest in hand-tooled leather, stained glass, marble work, and ornamental wood-carving. Mitchell's family was among the first in a procession of affluent Milwaukeeans who migrated to the high ground of the West Side. In 1876, accordingly, Spring Street was renamed Grand Avenue.

The grounds of Mitchell's mansion were every bit as grand as his home. An octagonal gazebo, literally covered with wooden scrollwork, dominated one corner of the property, and a nearby fountain was stocked with 200

The Union Depot on S. Second Street was the terminal for all trains entering Milwaukee from the south.

Milwaukee Public Library

The Mitchell estate on Grand Avenue featured a stunning mansion and one of the most complete horticultural conservatories in the region.

brook trout. But it was plants that made the estate famous. Anticipating the aptly named Mitchell Park Domes by almost a century, the banker developed one of the finest horticultural conservatories in the West. His gardeners tended nearly 9,000 specimens protected by 15,000 square feet of glass, with an emphasis on the exotic: banana and pineapple plants; peach, apricot, and fig trees; an assortment of 800 rose bushes; and the full range of tropical and temperate flowers. (Mitchell sported a fresh carnation in his lapel every day.) There was even a dark chamber that produced mushrooms for the family's dinner table. A Minnesota reporter was awestruck after an 1870 visit to the conservatory:

I could but feel inwardly thankful that it had pleased an overruling Father to give wealth to men who possessed the taste and culture necessary to the production of such a panorama of floral wonders as may be seen in Mr. Mitchell's garden.

True to the stereotype of the tight-fisted Scot, the laird of the manor shared his wealth sparingly, but local churches came to expect lilies, azaleas, and roses from the Grand Avenue greenhouses every Easter Sunday. Although the conservatory is long gone, the Mitchell home is still very much in use as the Wisconsin Club.

The mistress of the mansion was no shrinking violet herself. Martha Reed Mitchell, a pioneer's daughter who married

her husband in 1841, was widely known for her interest in art, historic preservation, and the advancement of women. In 1876 she hosted the inaugural meeting of the Woman's Club of Wisconsin, a group whose stated purpose was "to elevate and purify our civilization" by sponsoring activities that would "excite women to intellectual and moral culture." The meeting's keynote speaker was Mary Mortimer, first president of the Milwaukee Female College. Her remarks were a Victorian declaration of independence:

> We have heard, to weariness, of the "Sphere of Woman,"... a modest, retired one, hidden from the evil world by the fireside, where, with quiet, beautiful patience, she shall rear her children and obey and please her lord. Under this situation we have grown not only weary, but rebellious, and have come out in this Nineteenth Century to declare that we have as much right to dwell in the sunlight and make a noise as our brother man.

Martha Mitchell was the Woman's Club's first president. Her genteel sisterhood made an unmistakable noise in 1886, when the group formed the nation's first stock company composed entirely of women and began to build an elegant clubhouse on Yankee Hill.

The Mitchells were a determined, even willful, couple who liked to do things in the grand style, and that preference carried over to Alexander's business enterprises. In addition to heading the state's largest bank and largest railroad, he ran the largest marine and fire insurance firm west of Buffalo: Northwestern National Insurance, founded in 1869. All three of his businesses prospered, and in 1876 Mitchell decided to bring them together under one magnificent roof. Working again with architect E.T. Mix, he built a

temple to business that remains one of Milwaukee's most admired landmarks. Located at Water and Michigan Streets, on the site of Solomon Juneau's second home, the Mitchell Building is an exuberant statement of commercial confidence, six stories of stone carved in picturesque variations on French themes. (A hint of Mitchell's Scottish heritage persists in the pillars of Aberdeen granite flanking the entrance.) Completed in 1878, the building won instant praise. Pioneer historian James Buck pronounced it the ideal marriage of money and taste:

> This magnificent structure, the pride of Milwaukee, as well as the whole northwest, was erected at a cost of nearly four hundred thousand

The Mitchell Building on E. Michigan Street took commercial architecture in Milwaukee to new heights.

Milwaukee Public Library

dollars, and in architectural beauty and grace it stands as a monument of what the genius of man can accomplish, when unlimited means are at his command.

A lot of money, in other words, goes a long way.

The Mitchell Building soon had an equally distinguished neighbor. Its proprietor had always been a power in the Chamber of Commerce, Milwaukee's leading business organization. In 1879, fully aware that the group was unhappy in the cramped building next to his, Mitchell offered to tear it down, put up a new structure, and lease it to the Chamber on a long-term basis. The result, completed in 1880, was another E.T. Mix creation, this one only slightly less elaborate than the edifice next-door. The Chamber of Commerce Building's focal point was a three-story trading room that was among the most lavishly decorated public spaces in the region. It was in the trading room's "pit" that the price of wheat was set, and it was there that fortunes were made or lost on the turn of a trade. Restored to its original glory in 1983, the Grain Exchange is Milwaukee's single most tangible reminder of its heyday as the world's center of wheat commerce.

A Future Cast in Iron

Even before the Chamber of Commerce occupied its elegant new quarters, some inexorable forces were both pushing and pulling Milwaukee away from its dependence on wheat. The push factors were most obvious. Wheat was literally wearing out its welcome on Wisconsin soil; declining fertility and a growing number of pests reduced yields dramatically. (Similar problems had brought an earlier generation of wheat-growers from New York to Wisconsin.) With persistent prodding from visionaries like William Dempster Hoard, the state's farmers shifted steadily to diversified agriculture and finally to dairying. By the 1880s, Wisconsin was well on its way to becoming America's Dairyland, and the wheat belt continued its westerly migration into Minnesota and the Dakotas.

Milwaukee's grain traders were not unduly concerned – at first. The city's merchants had long considered the sprawling territory to the north and west their "natural" hinterland, and the steady expansion of the Chicago, Milwaukee & St. Paul Railroad seemed to ensure a growing supply of both grain and customers. The rise of Minneapolis

Milwaukee-area farms, including the Alvin Swan homestead in rural Wauwatosa, shifted steadily from wheat to dairying after the Civil War.

from *Illustrated Historical Atlas,* 1876

and St. Paul altered that perception permanently. As the farming frontier pushed west across the Great Plains, the Twin Cities began to play the same role Milwaukee had a few decades earlier. St. Paul blossomed as a transportation and wholesale trade center, attracting customers Milwaukee merchants had long considered theirs. Minneapolis, rising beside the most important water-power site on the entire Mississippi, developed a specialty in flour. In the early 1880s, with St. Anthony Falls providing the muscle, Minneapolis became the leading flour-producer (and wheat-buyer) in America; the foundations of modern giants like Pillsbury and General Mills were firmly in place.

As the Twin Cities chipped away at Milwaukee's hinterland, and as farmers closer to home switched to other crops, the community watched its wheat trade go into free fall. From the all-time high of 28.5 million bushels in 1873, receipts of the grain plunged to 18.2 million bushels in 1876 and a mere 8.1 million in 1882. Some dealers refused to see the handwriting on the wall. In 1881 a Chamber of Commerce official shrugged off the decline as the natural result of short crops, and he blithely predicted that "the trade in this commodity will attain a greater magnitude in the future than has ever been known." Such optimism was soon dismissed as wishful thinking, if not outright denial. In the Chamber's report for 1886, President Charles Chapin made a quiet concession: "We ... realize the fact and we may accept it gracefully, that Milwaukee's prominence as the famous wheat market of the world is a thing of the past."

An alternative future, one based on industry, had been emerging for at least twenty years by the time Chapin filed his report. Just as market forces pushed Milwaukee away from wheat, the approach of

urban maturity was pulling the city in the direction of manufacturing. With a growing population, a growing corps of skilled workers, and a growing market for finished products, Milwaukee was ready to do more than buy, sell, and trade the farm products of its hinterland. Some leaders came to believe that the city was squandering golden opportunities. In 1871 Milwaukee's *Journal of Commerce* put the case plainly:

> At present, we are sending our hard lumber east to get it back as furniture and agricultural implements; we ship ores to St. Louis and New York to pay the cost of bringing it back in shot, type, pipe, sheet lead, white lead, paint, etc.; we ship away our wool crop and import cloths, carpets, blankets and other fabrics; we give rags for paper, and hides for boots and harness, and iron ore for stoves – and our consumers all the while are paying the double costs of this unnecessary transportation.

The concept of value added was nothing new. Although they were generally lost in the shadow of the grain trade, manufacturers had been at work in Milwaukee since the frontier period. Their presence was another expression of the mutual dependence that had always existed between city and country. Farmers relied on Milwaukee for a broad range of goods and services, of course, but the products of the country also shaped the business of the city. Urban merchants viewed farm products as commodities to be bought and sold, while manufacturers saw them as raw materials to be processed into something else: wheat into flour, hogs into hams, cowhides into leather, barley into beer, and ore into iron. In the years following the Civil War, the balance between those viewpoints finally tipped in favor of manufacturing.

Eber Brock Ward, the one-man conglomerate who chose Milwaukee as the site for his newest iron mill in 1866

The Milwaukee Iron Company marked the dawn of the new era. It was launched in 1866 by Eber Brock Ward, a Detroit capitalist who was among the most visionary business leaders of his generation. Beginning as a cabin boy on one of his uncle's schooners, Ward became, in his early forties, skipper of the largest commercial fleet on the Great Lakes. With marine revenue as his foundation, the captain branched out aggressively, becoming, in time, a one-man conglomerate. When trains began to divert traffic from his shipping lanes, Ward adjusted easily, buying an interest in several Michigan railroads. When iron-ore mining began in Upper Michigan, he saw even more opportunities, both for ship cargoes and for an entirely new activity: manufacturing. Eber Ward became a pioneer in the American iron and steel industry, establishing works near Detroit in 1853, at Chicago in 1857 and, after a break for the Civil War, just outside Milwaukee in 1866.

Milwaukee was, in hindsight, an obvious choice for an iron mill. Its real estate was relatively cheap, and the Bay View site could easily accommodate boatloads of ore from Michigan and coal from Pennsylvania. The fact that a growing regional railroad was based in Milwaukee played an even larger role. Like its sisters, the Bay View mill specialized in rails, and Eber Ward wanted the Milwaukee & St. Paul's business. Alexander Mitchell welcomed a source of supply so close to home; he gladly accepted Ward's invitation to become a board member as well as a major investor in the mill. But there was an even more compelling reason for Milwaukee's selection: the presence of iron ore deposits in nearby Dodge County. Located just north of the hamlet of Iron Ridge, the beds contained an ore that, when mixed with softer Lake Superior varieties, yielded an iron of unusual strength. Mining activities had started in the 1840s (the ubiquitous Byron Kilbourn was an early promoter), but it was not until the Ward interests took over in 1869 that large-scale extraction began. In the decades that followed, the "inexhaustible" Iron Ridge deposits yielded nearly three million tons of high-grade ore. Most of it was hauled to Milwaukee – less than fifty miles away by Mr. Mitchell's railroad. The principal underground mine (at Neda) operated for sixty-five years before closing in 1914. Its current "residents" have earned the site a measure of notoriety: The mine houses one of the largest wintering colonies of bats in North America.

The iron mill that devoured so much Dodge County ore dwarfed any previous manufacturing enterprise in Milwaukee or, for that matter, Wisconsin. After a lengthy construction period, the Bay View mill began production on April 8, 1868, with a total of 185 employees. Just four years later, it was the second-largest manufacturer of rails in the country, and its labor force exceeded 1,000 – a payroll larger than Falk's or Ladish's in the early 2000s. At a time when the average shop had only a handful of employees, the Milwaukee Iron Company represented a different order of magnitude. It was so large, in fact, that a company town developed just outside the plant gates. Bay View lay a mile or two beyond the limits of urban settlement in the 1860s, and the mill's managers tried diligently to establish a resident work force. Milwaukee Iron built cottages and boarding houses for "agents and servants of the company," donated land for churches, and sold lots on easy terms to workers who wanted to build their own homes. The *Milwaukee Sentinel* (March 13, 1868) reported the birth of a community even before the first rail had been rolled:

As the region's largest employer, Ward's mill (left) literally put Bay View on the map. The bird's-eye view below shows the fledgling village in 1879.

Milwaukee Public Library

> *The village of Bay View has sprung up within a year. There have already been 25 buildings erected, including a store and a large boarding house, and 10 more are contracted for. They are mostly small cottages, costing about $500 each, but are exceedingly neat in appearance, and very comfortably furnished. The Methodist denomination has succeeded, with help from the company, in erecting a neat little church, which has been beautifully finished. A school will shortly be established, so that, it will be seen, the religious and educational wants of the inhabitants of the village will not be neglected. Within two months the village will contain 700 or 800 inhabitants, all of whom will derive their support from the rolling mill. It is beautifully situated on an eminence overlooking the lake, and will be, ere many years, one of the most thriving manufacturing towns in the northwest.*

As the plant supporting the village grew ever larger, local newspapers reported the latest developments in breathless detail. In 1871 the *Sentinel* described the installation of two mammoth engines that supplied the "blast" for the mill's blast furnaces. Both of these mechanical bellows were painted

Milwaukee Journal Sentinel

115

"wine-color, with gold decorations," and they bore "life-like likenesses" of Eber Ward and Alexander Mitchell. Housed in a building with wainscoted walls and two chandeliers "of artistic design," the behemoths were described as "the most beautifully decorated blast-engines in the world."

Milwaukee's business leaders were well aware that the iron mill represented a new epoch in their community's history. In 1872 the Chamber of Commerce made J.J. Hagerman, the mill's superintendent, one of its vice-presidents. He was quick to see the gesture for precisely what it was. "I am not so vain as to consider it a personal compliment," the ironmaker said in his acceptance speech, "but just what you intended it to be, a recognition of the growing importance of our manufacturing interests." Hagerman, a former purser on Capt. Ward's steamship line, could not resist tweaking the Chamber for what he considered its fixation on farm products:

> *I trust the day is not distant when the products of the plow, the loom, and the anvil, will be worthy of equal representation on this floor; when pigs of iron will be no less familiar than pigs of another kind. When made up for use, they will not be half so apt to "sour" while waiting for a market.*

Milwaukee's progress toward the industrial future envisioned by J.J. Hagerman was temporarily halted by the Panic of 1873. In the nationwide depression that followed – the first since 1857– fledgling industries like the Milwaukee Iron Company were hit particularly hard. As the nation's railroads slowed their expansion efforts, the market for rails evaporated, leaving the Milwaukee Iron Company with little to do. The mill's output sagged alarmingly, and

Eber Ward's death in 1875 only aggravated the company's problems. In 1876, as Ward's empire crumbled, Milwaukee Iron was forced into bankruptcy. Receivers operated the mill on a part-time basis, but jobs were anything but secure. As layoffs mounted, Bay View's boarding houses were nearly vacant, families lost their homes, and hundreds left the company town for more promising locales.

Better times returned in March, 1878, when the Bay View plant opened again as part of the North Chicago Rolling Mill Company, a reorganized Ward property. With the addition of a merchant mill that produced iron bars and plates in standard sizes, Bay View's output climbed steadily, and the work force soared to a new high of 1,500 hands. In 1879, as if to confirm the return of prosperity, local residents voted overwhelmingly to make their little community an incorporated village. Bay View thus became Milwaukee's first suburb, taking in 2,592 people and 892 acres of land.

Acorns and Oaks

The Bay View iron mill was only the most conspicuous sign of Milwaukee's turn to manufacturing. Evidence of the shift was everywhere after the Civil War, and its scope frequently surprised residents accustomed to simpler times. In 1871 the *Journal of Commerce* took a fresh look at the local landscape:

> *Within the last five years, it is true, a great change has been inaugurated. One has only to walk on the portion of Ninth Street over-looking the city, and see the smoke of the foundries, mills, tanneries and other manufactories which are springing up along our splendid water-front, and observe the throngs of laborers going to and*

from their various daily industries, to compre-
hend the destiny that is awaiting this favored
place and to feel that the onward strides are
already begun.

The *Evening Wisconsin* took up the refrain in 1881, predicting that Milwaukee would become "*the* manufacturing metropolis of the West."

The emergence of that metropolis was apparent in federal census returns. In 1859 the census-takers found a total of 558 manufacturing establishments in Milwaukee County; by 1889 the number had mushroomed to 2,879 in the city alone. During the same thirty-year period, the value of products manufactured in the county showed triple-digit increases every decade, rising from $6,659,070 in 1859 to $18,798,122 in 1869, $44,494,549 in 1879,

and $98,598,451 in 1889. A less obvious measure revealed the same trend. As steam engines enabled manufacturers to shed their reliance on water power, receipts of the coal required to run those engines showed phenomenal growth, climbing from 92,992 tons in 1868 to 350,840 in 1879 and 759,681 in 1886. In earlier years, wheat had been Milwaukee's most important cargo, and coal had arrived as ballast in the holds of returning ships. In the 1880s, that relationship was substantially reversed.

With the exception of the Milwaukee Iron Company, the community's leading postwar industries had been around since the pioneer period: flour-milling, meat-packing, tanning, and brewing. They remained dependent on the products of the surrounding farm country, but every branch of business assumed a scale that few

Central Milwaukee in 1879. The presence of industry along the rivers was increasingly obvious.

Milwaukee Public Library

117

Milwaukeeans could have imagined before the Civil War. The postwar industries also reflected an important ethnic shift: As Germans took control of several leading concerns, the traditional Yankee monopoly on economic power was finally broken.

Flour-milling was one of Milwaukee's most venerable industries. In 1843, when Byron Kilbourn dammed the Milwaukee River for his abortive canal, millers were among the first to take advantage of the resulting water power. When a pair of floods in 1866 and 1867 made life on the millrace a little too exciting for most flour companies, several moved downstream and switched to steam power. The two largest mills of the 1870s, both perched on the west bank of the river near today's Vliet Street, were the Eagle (owned by Bavarian-born John Kern) and the Phoenix (run by Yankee Edward Sanderson). Subject to the vagaries of weather and the rise and fall of distant markets, flour-milling was an unpredictable business in the best of times. The city's output fluctuated wildly, rising from 624,930 barrels in 1868 to 1,225,941 the following year, then crashing to 555,049 barrels in 1878 and rising again to 1,346,509 in 1882. Milwaukee never caught up to its principal rivals – St. Louis and then Minneapolis – but milling remained an important industry long after the wheat belt had passed to lands west of the Mississippi.

The meat-packing business showed much steadier growth. On the local level, the industry's acknowledged patriarch was John Plankinton, a native of Delaware who had come to Milwaukee in 1844. Within a year of his arrival, Plankinton owned the largest butcher shop in the county, and he had begun to cure and pack meat for shipment to more distant customers. As the number of farms around Milwaukee multiplied, a growing surplus of hogs and cattle attracted others to the packing business, including John Layton and his son, Frederick. The Laytons were English immigrants who owned a butcher shop downtown and a farm near what is now the intersection of Lincoln and Forest Home Avenues – an area known to early white settlers as Indian Fields and to more recent residents as the Layton Park neighborhood. In 1852 John Plankinton and Frederick Layton established a partnership. The pair opened a packing house on what is now Plankinton Avenue and began to process large numbers of hogs and cattle, including some, no doubt, fattened on the Layton family's farm. A few years later, with the business growing nicely, the partners broke ground (or, more accurately, swamp) for an even larger complex in the Menomonee Valley.

The Daisy flour mill was one of several lining the banks of the Milwaukee River in the 1870s and '80s.

from James Buck, *Milwaukee under the Charter*

Frederick Layton left to form his own company in 1863, becoming, over the years, one of Milwaukee's wealthiest citizens and a leading philanthropist as well. John Plankinton operated on his own for a brief period, but in 1864 he entered a partnership with a man twelve years his junior: Philip Armour. Their company became one of the nation's largest, specializing in pork, and their Valley complex grew to cover an area of fourteen acres. Much of the credit belonged to the pair's general manager, a young Irishman named Patrick Cudahy. In 1885, when Armour left to pursue interests in Chicago, Plankinton made Cudahy his partner – the third in an illustrious series of associates.

Plankinton and company mastered the art of using, in hog-packer's parlance, "everything but the squeal." Meat was their principal product, of course, and Milwaukee shipped tons of pork (and smaller quantities of beef) to the British navy, the northern pineries, and even the West Indies. But packing also supported a host of ancillary industries; meat scraps were turned into sausage, fat into lard, feet into glue, bristles into brushes, and bones and blood into fertilizer. It all added up to an enormous business. The number of hogs disassembled in Milwaukee soared from 88,853 in 1866 to 225,598 in 1876 and 553,077 in 1886. (John Plankinton's firms had the lion's share of the meat business.) In the 1870s and '80s, Milwaukee was generally the fourth- or fifth-largest packing center in America, and in 1879 meat was (by value of product) the city's most important industry.

Tanning was another enterprise that relied on the resources of the surrounding countryside: cowhides, above all, but also hemlock trees, an abundant species in northern Wisconsin. Before synthetic agents

Milwaukee Journal Sentinel

John Plankinton was Milwaukee's dominant packer at a time when meat was the city's most important product.

became available, prodigious quantities of hemlock bark were chipped and stewed to produce tannin, the chemical compound that turns hides to leather. Milwaukee tanneries consumed more than 30,000 cords of tanbark in a good year, and schooners piled high with hemlock slabs were a common sight on the city's waterfront.

Although Yankees were involved in the business, tanning became a distinctly German stronghold. Leading the immigrant wave were Guido Pfister and Frederick Vogel, two Württembergers who came to Milwaukee in 1847 after brief sojourns in Buffalo. Pfister established a retail store, Vogel a tannery, and in 1853 they joined forces as the Pfister & Vogel Leather Company. By the mid-1880s, the partners owned three plants whose combined output made them the leading tanners in the city. Later arrivals

Milwaukee County Historical Society

*The Milwaukee &
St. Paul Railroad's
stockyard in the
Menomoneee Valley
supplied local packers
with a steady stream
of hogs and cattle.*

included Albert Trostel and August Gallun, immigrants who established a partnership of their own in 1858. Trostel and Gallun eventually parted company, operating separate Milwaukee tanneries that lasted into the late twentieth century.

With German-trained craftsmen leading the way, the city's tanning industry showed remarkable growth. A rash of consolidations reduced the number of plants from 30 in 1872 to 15 in 1886, but fewer tanneries produced more leather. Milwaukee's output climbed from 102,570 hides in 1865 to 265,548 in 1880 and 533,357 in 1886. Some of that output was consumed locally; Bradley & Metcalf, a firm established by two Yankee newcomers in 1843, became one of the largest boot and shoe manufacturers in the Northwest, and other firms turned out everything from horse collars to chaps and saddles. The

greatest demand, however, came from the sprawling shoe factories of New England. By 1890, with orders from Eastern customers on the rise, Milwaukee was the largest producer of plain tanned leather in the world.

If German immigrants were the leading figures in the tanning trade, they were practically the only figures in Milwaukee's most celebrated industry: brewing. From the day the first lager brewery opened in 1841, Germans had dominated the city's beer business, and some firms reached far beyond the local market after the Civil War. The most expansive company was established by Jacob Best and his sons on the "Chestnut Street hill" (near Ninth Street and Juneau Avenue) in 1844. The Bests did quite well in their early years, but the brewery's real success began when the flamboyant Frederick Pabst took charge. A former

Leather was another leading Milwaukee industry. Mountains of tanbark rose alongside the Pfister & Vogel tannery in the Menomonee Valley.

Milwaukee Public Library

lake captain (and one-time cabin boy for Eber Brock Ward), Pabst became Phillip Best's son-in-law in 1862 and his business partner two years later. With a nose for quality and a flair for promotion, Captain Pabst pushed the Best brewery to the front of the pack: It was Milwaukee's largest producer in 1868 and America's largest in 1874. With the retirement of the Best trademark in 1889, the company was Pabst's in name as well as in fact.

The captain's closest local competitor in the 1870s was Joseph Schlitz, a bookkeeper by training. In 1875, when Schlitz was lost at sea during a trip back to Germany, control of his firm passed to the Uihlein brothers. Milwaukee's third-largest brewer at the time was Valentine Blatz, a Bavarian-trained brewmaster who, like Joseph Schlitz, had entered the ranks of senior management by marrying his boss's

Trostel and Gallun were two more German immigrants who found success in the tanning business.

Milwaukee Journal Sentinel

widow. The number of local breweries plummeted from 26 in 1856 to 18 in 1876 and only 9 in 1885 but, as in the tanning business, fewer plants meant greater volume. With Pabst, Schlitz, and Blatz leading the way, Milwaukee's growth as a brewing center was nothing short of astounding. The city produced 58,666 barrels of beer in 1865, 279,286 barrels in 1875, and 1,117,256 in 1885 – a nineteen-fold increase in twenty years! The Chicago fire of 1871 is often cited as a major reason for Milwaukee's success, but such sustained growth clearly indicated both a superior product and a resolve to reach consumers in distant markets. Taking full advantage of technological breakthroughs like bottling plants and refrigerated railcars, Milwaukee's nineteenth-century brewers planted the seeds of their city's reputation as "the beer capital of the world."

The brewers, tanners, packers, and millers of the post-1865 period showed, in one respect and in one respect only, a surprising resemblance to the area's early Indian tribes: They built an economy based on the natural resources around them. The level of complexity was much higher in the late 1800s, of course, but Milwaukee's industries depended absolutely on the products of nearby farms, forests and, in the case of the Milwaukee Iron Company, the earth itself. Even the climate was enlisted as a resource; ice cut on the area's rivers

Frederick Pabst was Milwaukee's (and America's) leading brewer by the mid-1870s.

Capt. Pabst's beer wagons paused for the camera before rolling out on their morning runs.

Milwaukee County Historical Society

In 1855 Fred Miller bought a small brewery on the Watertown Plank Road from a member of the Best family. The company he founded is now the second-largest brewer in America, and still doing business on the original site.

and lakes was indispensable to local brewers, and it helped make meat-packing a year-round business.

During the same period, some manufacturers were exploring a field with virtually no direct ties to the land: machinery. Products like rails and pig iron were relatively crude; their added value was largely a change in physical properties. Machines, because of their high engineering content, embodied intellectual property as well. Although the move to machinery would not peak until later in the century, Milwaukee of the 1860s was already dotted with small machine shops whose proprietors had large ideas.

Edward P. Allis led the list. He was neither an inventor nor a mechanic, but rather one of the purest exemplars of the entrepreneurial spirit Milwaukee has ever known. It was Allis, more than any other individual, who made the city's name synonymous with machinery. Born in Cazenovia, New York, he came west in 1846 as a twenty-one-year-old college graduate in search of

opportunities. Allis was engaged in the tanning business at first, but in 1861 he bought the Reliance Works, a bankrupt machine shop on the Milwaukee River near Wells Street. The aspiring manufacturer broadened the company's product line, enlarged its work force, and soon had more orders than the riverfront shop could handle.

In 1867 Allis moved the Reliance Works to a twenty-acre site in Walker's Point, near First and Florida Streets. The new shop turned out flour-milling equipment, small steam engines, and heating plants, but Allis was certain that his crews could build anything. He was so confident, in fact, that when Milwaukee announced plans for a municipal water works in 1871, he decided to bid on both the pipes and the pumps. The fact that the Reliance Works had never manufactured either product was immaterial. Allis built the necessary facilities, hired the necessary experts and, with contract in hand, proceeded to turn out equipment that exceeded the city's expectations.

The leap of faith was entirely typical of E.P. Allis, and just as suggestive of his business philosophy. The capitalist's formula for success was simple: Find a promising market, hire the best engineers available, and get out of their way. Between 1873 and 1877, Allis assembled an engineering team that took his company to the forefront of three barely related fields. George Hinkley developed state-of-the-art sawmill equipment, with an emphasis on band saws; William Gray perfected a system of rollers that replaced grindstones in the flour industry; and the legendary Edwin Reynolds designed some of the largest, most efficient steam engines in the world. Success was never guaranteed – the company sank into bankruptcy for a time in 1876 – but Allis clearly had superb instincts. Under his guidance, sales rose steadily in all lines, and the work force mushroomed from 200 hands in 1871 to 400 in 1875, 600 in 1880, and 800 in 1883. By 1889 the Reliance Works employed nearly 1,500 men – as many as the Bay View iron mill.

There was sweet irony in Edward Allis's success. Milwaukee had entered the post-1865 period as a world center of the wheat trade and a leading miller of flour. Those laurels passed to Minneapolis, but manufacturing had its compensations: By the 1890s, nearly eighty-five percent of the milling machinery used in the Twin Cities was supplied by E.P. Allis and Company.

Edward P. Allis, the fearless entrepreneur who helped make Milwaukee a machinery capital

The Reliance Works, Allis's plant in Walker's Point, turned out everything from steam engines to sawmill equipment.

124

Room in the Valley

Whether it took the form of machine shops or slaughterhouses, breweries or tanneries, industrial expansion had an enormous impact on Milwaukee's landscape. Every new (or newly enlarged) business had to locate somewhere, and the range of possibilities was limited. Access to rail lines was a given; it was, after all, trains that brought the hordes of hogs into Milwaukee's packing plants, and it was trains that carried the products of Milwaukee's breweries away to a national market. River frontage was nearly as essential; access to the Great Lakes shipping fleet was one of the city's major advantages. Manufacturers, then, gravitated to sites served by both rail and river.

The truncated canal below Byron Kilbourn's dam supported a number of pioneer industries, and the upper Milwaukee River remained the city's flour mill and tannery district long after the advent of steam power. Industries that needed larger tracts of land were forced to locate downstream. The Milwaukee Iron Company found a lakefront site on the south end of the Jones Island peninsula, and E.P. Allis chose Walker's Point for his Reliance Works. (Milwaukee's landscape was still fluid at the time, often literally so: Allis had to fill in a swamp before his site was ready.) By the late 1860s, as landfill continued, space on the urban end of the Milwaukee River was at a premium, and would-be industrialists had to look elsewhere for room to grow.

Where they looked, more often than not, was the Menomonee Valley. What had been a prime natural resource for the early Indian tribes became a prime industrial

Milwaukee Public Library

resource for their acquisitive successors – after a few improvements were made. In the early 1860s, the Valley was what it had been for centuries: a waterlogged wilderness visited by only the adventurous. The *Milwaukee Sentinel* (August 12, 1861) described "the windings and sinuosities" of the river as a liquid maze:

> When you fancy yourself sailing up the stream, the chances are that you are only being lured into a cul de sac of wild rice, and when you fondly imagine you are miles away from the city, some sudden turn will bring you up before a great brewery or ship yard, where several hundred employees stare at you ironically.

The *Sentinel* went on to recount the exploits of two recent visitors:

> They were gone all night, and some anxiety was felt for their safety. A deputation of friends found them in the morning wildly shooting about amid the wild rice ..., both completely worn out, having rowed some eighteen or twenty miles without getting out of the bayou.

The Menomonee Valley in a state of nature was a sprawling marsh filled with cattails and wild rice. This view is southeast from Thirtieth and Park Hill in the Merrill Park neighborhood.

Such adventures were practically impossible after 1869, when a group of business leaders launched the Menomonee Improvements. Their plan, endorsed by public authorities and aided by other private efforts, was to dredge a network of canals and slips in the heart of the Valley and create dry land in the spaces between. The project required colossal quantities of fill, including dredge spoil, gravel "borrowed" from adjoining bluffs, and even garbage. In 1886 the *Sentinel* described the mess behind one "Free Dump" sign: "rotten potatoes and fruit, the contents of paunches and entrails of animals, the refuse of meat shops, and all sorts of filth [under] a thin covering of ashes and dirt." The landfill project took years to finish – maps of the late 1890s still pictured large areas labeled "Swamp" – but the result was the most valuable industrial real estate in the region. The Menomonee Valley offered hundreds of acres of developable land, six miles of dock frontage, and superlative rail

service – everything, in short, that an industrialist could desire.

Lumber yards, coal yards, and sash and door factories sprouted in the eastern end of the Valley even before the muck was dry. They were soon joined by some nationally significant neighbors. Pfister & Vogel began to develop a tannery complex at what is now the south end of the Sixth Street viaduct in the 1870s; it quickly became the largest in a city known for leather. Adjoining P&V to the west was the old Melms brewery, once Milwaukee's leading producer. Frederick Pabst purchased the facility in 1870 and built his company's first bottling plant on the site five years later. Farther west was the city's meatpacking district. In 1869 the Milwaukee & St. Paul Railroad opened a large stockyard in the Valley, just north of today's Mitchell Park Domes. Attracted by this central source of supply (and the site's distance from residential districts), magnates like

"Shallow Water": The Valley was still a work in progress when this bird's-eye view was published in 1886.

from *Die Stadt Milwaukee, 1886*

John Plankinton and Frederick Layton built some of the nation's largest packing houses on nearby Muskego Avenue. Still farther west was a complex that dwarfed them all: the main shops of the Chicago, Milwaukee, & St. Paul Railroad. The first buildings opened in 1880, on a 160-acre site west of today's Thirty-fifth Street viaduct. Under the guidance of general manager Sherburn S. Merrill, the "West Milwaukee" shops made and repaired all the rolling stock for a railroad that owned 5,000 miles of track. By the mid-1880s, the complex employed nearly 1,800 workers – more than either the Bay View iron mill or E.P. Allis's Reliance Works.

The Menomonee Valley provided building materials as well as building sites. The region's largest brickyard was located on the south rim of the Valley, near today's Thirteenth Street. Operated by George Burnham, a native of upstate New York, it furnished jobs for 200 men in 1880, when the yard's output of pale yellow bricks topped 15 million. Thousands were used in nearby industrial plants, reinforcing Milwaukee's image as the Cream City, and thousands more were shipped to eager customers as far away as Europe.

Local observers were suitably impressed by the all the activity in the Valley. The *Sentinel* (August 18, 1882) described its ongoing transformation as evidence of the community's progress:

The CM&StP Railroad shops, complete with locomotive roundhouse (top photo), were the Valley's crowning glory. They were the city's largest employer in the 1880s and served the Milwaukee Road for more than a century.

Milwaukee Public Library

Milwaukee County Historical Society

Nothing, perhaps, more strikingly exhibits the rapidity and solidity of Milwaukee's growth than the march of improvement in the Menomonee Valley. The bogs and marshes in that locality are being converted into firm ground, and the waters which formerly spread themselves thinly out over a large surface are being confined to an artificial channel and made navigable for great ships. The vast tract, which but a few years ago was the home of the wild duck and the resort of the sportsman with his gun, is now partially converted, and will soon be entirely so, to the seat of manufacturing and commercial enterprises, which take rank among the first of their kind in the entire Northwest.

The *Sentinel* reporter was not exaggerating the Menomonee Valley's importance. It was hardly the city's scenic high point, but the Valley's impact on Milwaukee, both geographic and social, was immeasurable. By providing a platform for industrial expansion at the very heart of the city, it allowed Milwaukee to remain a compact, high-density community; with so many jobs so close at hand, there was little need to spread out. The Valley's influence on adjoining neighborhoods was even more profound. As the most formidable geographic barrier in the city, it made the South Side, in effect, a separate settlement, a self-contained community with an enduringly distinctive sense of place.

The Valley also had a decisive impact on local employment patterns. Its overwhelmingly industrial character encouraged blue-collar workers to settle on the adjoining high ground. To the north, for instance, between Thirtieth and Thirty-fifth Streets, lay the estate of Sherburn S. Merrill. As his CM&StP shop complex developed, hundreds of Irish families moved west from the Third Ward and other Celtic strongholds in search of jobs. Merrill, ever the enterprising Yankee, sold them lots, and the result was Merrill Park – the Irish neighborhood of most sainted memory in all the city's history.

Industries and Immigrants

Milwaukee's industrial growth reflected the influence of several forces: the rise of steam technology, the advent of a national rail network, the steady maturation of the region's markets, easy access to raw materials, and the presence of entrepreneurs with the desire and the capital to pursue opportunities. It also depended absolutely on a stable and steadily growing force of industrial workers. For every Pabst or Plankinton, every Allis or Vogel in Milwaukee, there were thousands of workers whose names have been lost to history. For every new mill or tannery, every business block or bank building, there were thousands of modest cottages built for wage-earners. Their numbers exploded after the Civil War, rising from 8,433 in 1869 to 20,886 in 1879 and 38,850 in 1889 – an increase of 360 percent in just twenty years and double the rate of growth for the city as a whole. Such dramatic expansion permanently altered the demographic face of Milwaukee. By 1880 industrial workers made up 44.6 percent of the local labor force – the sixth-highest concentration in urban America. A specialist in wheat only one or two decades before, Milwaukee had become a national center of industry.

Industrial workers were, on one level, a welcome resource, and contemporary reports are filled with references to Milwaukee as a congenial place for the laboring classes. Frank Flower, whose *History of Milwaukee* remains a standard reference, described the community as "a workingman's city" in his 1881 book, a place that offered even the poorest newcomer "good air, good water, cheap living, and a chance to found a home of his own." The *Milwaukee Sentinel* (February 15, 1870) also praised the "remarkably healthy" local climate and pronounced it vastly superior to a nearby rival's: "We cannot doubt that the laborer in Milwaukee is considerably more efficient than his brother who inhales the nephitic odors of Chicago." The resident work force, in turn, was hailed as a competitive advantage for local industries. Few promotional booklets failed to mention the good work habits and modest

Even small machine shops could make history. In 1867 Charles Kleinsteuber's shop on Third and State produced the world's first practical typewriter from the designs of Milwaukeean C. L. Sholes.

Frederick J. Miller (in white hat) and his workers, most of them presumably Germans, posed for a "mug" shot in about 1880.

Milwaukee Journal Sentinel

Miller Brewing

wage demands that were said to characterize Milwaukee's workers. An 1871 account in the *Journal of Commerce* lapsed into caricature:

> *Labor, common and skilled, is fifteen per cent.*
> *cheaper in Milwaukee than it is in Chicago. The*
> *ruling price for ordinary labor there is eleven dol-*
> *lars a week; here, it is nine. A large proportion of*
> *the population of Milwaukee is composed of*
> *thrifty, frugal, industrious, productive Germans,*
> *each of whom owns a little land about his house,*
> *and sports a pig or two, and sends his troop of*
> *children to school, and lays up money on nine*
> *dollars a week. Here is the basis of manufacturing*
> *enterprises. Here are thousands of men waiting*
> *for some productive employment, with an*
> *exhaustless and perennial supply where these*
> *came from. Here is the muscle and the material.*
> *All that is needed is capital, pluck and brains.*

And who were the thousands supplying "the muscle and the material" in this editor-ial cartoon? Milwaukee's industrial workers, early and late, were overwhelmingly immigrants. In 1869, a year after it opened, only 22 of the 300 men employed at the Bay View iron mill were "Americans"; the other 93 percent came from Europe. Twenty-one years later, after plenty of time for the melting pot to work its supposed magic, the mill's work force, enlarged to 1,522 men, was still 76 percent foreign-born. In other industries, particularly those on the lower end of the skills continuum, the ratio was even higher.

The patterns in the workplace reflected patterns in the city as a whole. The proportion of American-born residents in Milwaukee climbed steadily, rising from 49.5 percent of the population in 1860 to 61.1 percent in 1890, but those numbers simply reflected the huge numbers of children being born to immigrants. Milwaukee remained a notably European city, and its German accent was unmistakable. More Germans, in fact, entered the city after the

The corner of Third and North was the heart of a thoroughly German neighborhood in 1880. It would soon become the neighborhood's commercial crossroads as well.

Milwaukee Journal Sentinel

Civil War than during the mid-1800s, the period usually associated with their immigration. The ranks of the German-born swelled from 15,981 in 1860 to 31,483 in 1880 and a new peak of 54,776 in 1890. Milwaukee was an increasingly cosmopolitan community, but natives of Germany made up 27 percent of its population in 1880, the highest concentration of a single immigrant group in any American city.

The constant infusion of new faces further complicated an ethnic group that was already Milwaukee's most complex. German newcomers gravitated to industrial jobs, both skilled and unskilled, simply because those were the jobs available. By the time they learned to count change and ask for directions in English, some of their countrymen had been in America for a full generation, and a significant few had risen to positions of leadership. German capitalists were a significant factor in the flour-milling industry, the dominant force in tanning, and practically the only group in the beer business. The result was increasing social stratification within the German community. As the years passed, men like Frederick Pabst and Guido Pfister found that they had less and less in common with the Adolfs and Ottos on their bottling lines and tannery floors.

Their real peers were other industrialists of all ethnic backgrounds, and Milwaukee's power structure began to shed its exclusively Yankee cast. By historian Robert Nesbit's count, the number of Germans belonging to the Chamber of Commerce rose from 19 percent of the membership in 1872 to 26 percent in 1883 and 37 percent in 1892. Intermarriage was the next step. By the late 1800s, it was no longer *verboten* for a Pabst to marry a Goodrich or a Carpenter to enter

Leslie's Illustrated (Feb. 6, 1886)

wedded life with a Falk. There were comparable cracks in the political establishment. In 1884 Emil Wallber, a Berlin-born lawyer, became Milwaukee's first German mayor. "He is prominently identified with the Musical Society," wrote a contemporary, "and is one of the leading Turners in the country." Although social integration was never complete, Milwaukee's Germans had clearly made remarkable strides.

On all social and economic levels, the Teutonic imprint on Milwaukee was unmistakable. Whether new or old, wealthy or working-class, Germans were everywhere after the Civil War. In 1876 half of Milwaukee's ten daily newspapers were published in German, and the German papers had significantly more readers. Beer gardens, including several adjacent to German breweries, were thronged on Sunday afternoons.

Milwaukee Germans supported a Turner training school that drew aspiring gymnastics teachers from across the country.

Milwaukee County Historical Society

Emil Wallber, Milwaukee's first German-born mayor

131

Milwaukee Journal Sentinel

The Schlitz beer garden, near
Eighth and Walnut Streets, was
an immensely popular retreat
that offered everything from
opera music by the Bach-
Luening Orchestra (above) to
exhibitions by championship
Turner teams (below).

Milwaukee Public Library

Milwaukee County Historical Society

Bilingualism was accepted, even expected. Patrick Cudahy, an Irishman who worked for Yankees, found it necessary to learn German early in his career, and attendants at the Public Museum were required to speak German as well as English. German plays and German concerts remained pinnacles of cultural accomplishment in the city. One of the largest gatherings in nineteenth-century Milwaukee was the 1886 *Saengerfest*, a singing festival attended by German choral societies from throughout the Midwest. The highlight of the gathering was the opening concert, which featured a mind-boggling mass of 3,000 singers, backed by a 102-piece orchestra, giving a spirited rendition of Wagner's *Hymn to Art*.

The *Saengerfest* attracted national press coverage, reinforcing Milwaukee's image as the *Deutsch-Athen* of America. Other visitors took a broader view of the city, but practically all commented on its Teutonic flavor. This account from *Peculiarities of American Cities*, a travel book published in 1884, is typical:

> No one who visits Milwaukee can fail to be struck with the semi-foreign appearance of the city. Breweries are multiplied throughout its streets, lager beer saloons abound, beer gardens, with their flowers and music and tree or arbor-shaded tables, attract the tired and thirsty in various quarters. German music halls, gasthausen, and restaurants are found everywhere, and German signs are manifest over many doors. One hears German spoken upon the streets quite as often as English, and Teuton influence upon the political and social life of the city is everywhere seen and felt. Germans constitute nearly one-half the entire population of Milwaukee, and have impressed their character upon the people and the city itself in other ways than socially. Steady-going plodders, with their love for music and flowers, they have yet no keen taste for display, and every time choose the substantial rather than the ornamental.

A preference for substance over ornament remains a cornerstone of the Milwaukee character; some traits, even stereotypical traits, are apparently indelible.

Although their presence was overwhelming, Germans did not have the city to themselves after the Civil War. Yankees from New York and New England exerted an influence beyond their numbers, and a host of European nations were represented in the population. None of the Europeans, however, posed a significant challenge to German primacy – none, that is, until the Poles arrived. Their movement was rooted in the familiar combination of push and pull. Economic motives were uppermost; the vast majority of Poles were impoverished peasants emigrating *za chlebem* – for bread. But the newcomers also felt a strong push from political forces at home. Their state had ceased to exist in 1795, when it

Polish immigrants, many with large families, became Milwaukee's second-largest ethnic group in the 1880s.

courtesy Jim Borzych

was divided among Prussia, Austria, and Russia. Conditions in the Prussian, or western, partition were especially conducive to emigration. Under Otto von Bismarck, the "Iron Chancellor," young men were forced to serve in the German military, and the Polish language and culture were brutally suppressed. There was intense resistance, much of it centered in the Catholic Church, but hundreds of thousands chose to emigrate. A significant number found their way to Milwaukee. The overwhelming majority of the city's Poles – as many as 88 percent – came from the German partition.

Given the prevailing tensions in Europe, their choice of German Milwaukee might seem surprising, but it made perfect economic sense. For a group with few urban skills and little money, the developing industries of the urban Midwest offered an abundance of entry-level jobs. The fact that many Poles spoke reasonably fluent German was probably a contributing factor. In company with Chicago, Detroit, Cleveland, and Buffalo, Milwaukee became one of the largest centers of Polish settlement in America.

St. Stanislaus Church was the group's Milwaukee beachhead. In 1872, six years after buying its first, hand-me-down home in Walker's Point, the congregation moved south to Mitchell Street and built an imposing new church. Its twin spires, later capped with gold leaf, became one of Milwaukee's most familiar landmarks. Within ten years of its move, the parish boasted nearly a thousand families, all of them young; in 1883 alone, St. Stanislaus recorded an astounding 602 baptisms – an average of nearly a dozen every week. Anchored by "St. Stan's," Mitchell Street blossomed as a commercial district dubbed the "Polish Grand Avenue," and the adjoining blocks filled in with immigrants' homes. As the South Side *Polonia* (Polish-American community) pushed south and west, new churches rose as benchmarks of its growth: St. Hyacinth in 1882, St. Vincent de Paul and St. Josaphat in 1888, and a steady procession of others. All were offshoots of St. Stanislaus.

Mitchell Street, known in some quarters as the "Polish Grand Avenue," became the South Side's downtown.

Milwaukee Journal Sentinel

A second *Polonia* developed in the Brady Street area of the East Side, literally in the shadow of St. Hedwig's, a church built for the city's second Polish congregation (1871). The East Side's appeal was obvious: easy access to jobs in the tanneries and mills on the nearby Milwaukee River. The city's third Polish settlement, and certainly its most unusual, developed on Jones Island. Immigrants from the Kaszuby region on the Baltic seacoast colonized the wind-swept peninsula in the 1870s. Joined by German-speaking Pomeranians and a scattering of other groups, the Kaszubs made Jones Island the center of commercial fishing in southeastern Wisconsin. Their village, whose population ultimately peaked at nearly 1,600, was a picturesque jumble of homes, saloons, fish sheds, and net reels linked by a street system that might best be described as improvised. The community was unique in Milwaukee, and perhaps in America. While their counterparts on the mainland took places in the industrial rank and file, Jones Islanders continued the semi-rural, village-oriented way of life they had known for centuries in the homeland. For the Kaszubs, that way of life included a strong attachment to the Catholic Church; once each week, other Milwaukeeans were treated to the picturesque sight of immigrant families rowing across the Kinnickinnic River to St. Stanislaus in their Sunday best.

In the national context, Milwaukee's *Polonia* was notable for its early start. Not only did the immigrants make St. Stanislaus the first Polish church in urban America, but they also established the country's first Polish Catholic school (1868), the first Polish military company (Kosciuszko Guard, 1874), and the first successful Polish daily newspaper (*Kuryer Polski*, 1888). In 1878 August Rudzinski became the first Polish American in the country to hold municipal office, winning a seat on the county board. (A saloon-keeper by trade, Rudzinski was also an early president of St. Stanislaus Parish and the first captain of the Kosciuszko Guard.) Politically ambitious

Dominated by immigrants from the Kaszuby region on Poland's Baltic seacoast, the Jones Island fishing village was one of the most unusual urban settlements in America.

Milwaukee County Historical Society

and uniformly Democratic, the Poles quickly became a potent factor in local politics. Although they were never numerous enough to govern alone, Polish voters had sufficient strength to tip the balance of power with regularity.

It took some time for other Milwaukeeans to notice their new neighbors. On November 30, 1874, eight years after the immigrants founded their first parish, the *Milwaukee Sentinel* published a lengthy profile of "The Polacks." The story was laden with the casual caricatures of the time:

> As a class the poorer Poles, and it is of such this article treats, are remarkably clannish; they settle in little communities and live in themselves. They make small effort to learn the English tongue, being generally satisfied when they say "work," "dollar," "yes" and "no." One reason for their settling so close together is their very strong attachment to their church. They are almost all Catholics, and no nation with, perhaps, the exception of the Irish, has clung with such remarkable tenacity to its faith under most trying circumstances....
>
> [T]he houses are generally very small; very frequently one of these little cabins has three or four families crowded into it. Usually the first money they can call their own is put into the purchase of a lot, or part of a lot, on which they mean to erect a house as soon as possible. They have a strong prejudice against paying rent.

Largely of peasant stock, the immigrants persisted in the Old World belief that property, not labor, was their key to security. The results were extremely high population densities in Milwaukee's Polish neighborhoods and, considering their dire financial straits, amazingly high rates of home-ownership.

It was generally agreed that the Poles were a substantial addition to the community, but no one knew precisely how substantial. The fact that Poland had been erased from the map made census figures meaningless; immigrants from the German partition of Poland were technically German. The *Sentinel* article quoted above placed the community's population at 7,000 in 1874, up from perhaps 150 in 1866. By the late 1880s, Milwaukee's *Polonia* had grown to roughly 30,000 – well behind the 50,000-plus immigrants from Germany, but large enough for a strong second place in the city.

The rise of the Polish community was not the only ethnic news in post-Civil War Milwaukee. Some long-established groups, including the Irish, the Czechs, and the Dutch, were relatively static, relying on natural increase rather than new immigration to maintain their numbers. Others – German, Scandinavian, and British – showed impressive growth. Continued British immigration was a clear response to industrial demand. When the Milwaukee Iron Company opened in 1868, its managers were practically forced to import skilled workers from the iron industry's center: Great Britain. In 1869 the mill's workers were described as a mixture of "English, Welsh, Germans, and a few Irish." The flow of emigrants from the United Kingdom made Bay View the most British community in the Milwaukee area.

The most notable ethnic trend of the postwar period was a gradual shift in the source regions of immigration, both nationally and locally. As peasant-based European economies crumbled and despots relaxed their restrictions on emigration, the tide shifted away from the northern and western sections of the continent and toward its southern and eastern quadrants. Polish immigrants were the most obvious sign of the emerging trend, but they were joined by other Slavic and, later, Mediterranean groups. Slovaks, who began to arrive in about 1880, were among the most numerous. Like the Poles, they were Catholics by faith, farmers by occupation, and industrial workers by fate. Most Slovaks settled among their Czech cousins in the older sections of Kilbourntown until they could establish institutions of their own.

The shift in origins created special problems for an older Milwaukee ethnic group. Most of the city's early Jewish residents were German-born, and proudly so. Rabbi Elias Eppstein made the point emphatically at an 1873 gathering of the Sons of Hermann:

> *We are Germans by tongue; Germans by will of reasoning our way onwards; ... Germans by the desire to seek knowledge and wisdom, and foster them; Germans by uniting in social life; and Germans by assisting each other in times of need.... We are Americans, but German Americans....*

In the early 1880s, uprooted by a toxic blend of poverty and pogroms, the first wave of Russian Jews arrived in Milwaukee. As described by Rabbi Louis Swichkow in his *History of the Jews in Milwaukee*, their German brethren responded generously at first, helping the newcomers find jobs and housing, but cultural differences were painfully apparent. As Jewish emigration from eastern Europe accelerated, the gap within the community grew even wider.

One more group registered important gains after the Civil War. The African-American population, a presence in Milwaukee since the 1830s, increased from 106 in 1860 to 176 in 1870, 304 in 1880, and 449 in 1890. Blacks constituted less than 1 percent of the city's population during the period, but they were soon numerous enough to organize a church. In 1869, only three years after Polish immigrants founded St. Stanislaus, black Milwaukeeans established St. Mark African Methodist Episcopal (AME) Church and moved into a German congregation's old home on the corner of Fourth Street and Kilbourn Avenue. Now located on Atkinson Avenue at Sixteenth Street, St. Mark AME remains one of the largest and most influential congregations in Milwaukee's African-American community.

St. Mark AME Church on Fourth and Kilbourn was the African-American community's first house of worship. Founded in 1869, it predated some well-known European congregations by several decades.

Milwaukee Public Library

Growing Pleasures, Growing Pains

A fairly simple formula describes life in Milwaukee after the Civil War: Industries plus immigrants equaled growth. The city's population more than quadrupled in thirty years, rising from 45,246 in 1860 to 204,468 in 1890. Milwaukee climbed through the ranks of America's cities from twentieth place to sixteenth, lagging Detroit but leading Newark by a comfortable margin. As the city got bigger, it also got busier. The number of trains departing on an average day exploded from 12 in 1866 to 123 in 1886, and those trains moved more people more quickly than ever before. By the early 1880s, coal had replaced wood in the boilers, steel had replaced iron on the tracks, and the average passenger speed had risen from twenty-five to fifty miles per hour. As the entire community moved forward "with railroad velocity," old-timers found it difficult to keep pace.

The city's swelling sense of importance produced a host of new landmarks. Railroad depots were the grand entrances to America's cities during the Victorian era, and Milwaukee had a pair of beauties. In 1886, after years in the cramped Union Depot in Walker's Point, the Chicago, Milwaukee & St. Paul Railroad built a new terminal downtown, bordering the small park (now Zeidler Union Square) on Michigan between Third and Fourth Streets. Designed by the ubiquitous Edward Townsend Mix, it was an elaborate composition of red brick and sandstone, capped by an ornate clock tower. Not to be outdone, the Chicago & North Western built an even more imposing depot on the lake bluff three years later. Its graceful

Two grand railroad stations served as bookends for Milwaukee's downtown in the 1880s. The Milwaukee Road depot stood on W. Michigan Street ...

Milwaukee County Historical Society

Romanesque tower anchored the eastern end of Wisconsin Avenue for more than seventy-five years.

The train depots served as bookends for Milwaukee's developing central business district. Since the pioneer period, East Water Street had been the city's commercial center, with a smaller concentration of businesses across the river on West Water (now Plankinton Avenue). In 1877, after T.A. Chapman moved his department store up the hill from East Water to Milwaukee Street – a distance of two blocks – the merchant was praised for his "broad idea of spreading out rather than confining the retail business of the city to narrow limits." As the population boomed and new buildings went up east of the river, Solomon Juneau's old claim cemented its reputation as Milwaukee's center of finance, publishing, and the carriage trade.

The East Side lost an old landmark in January, 1883, when the Newhall House, once Milwaukee's leading hotel, burned to the ground. At least seventy-five people perished, some incinerated in their rooms, others leaping to their deaths from upper-story windows. (Among the rescued was America's shortest celebrity: two-foot-tall Tom Thumb.) The *Milwaukee Journal*, launched barely two months earlier, attacked the Newhall's owners with a vengeance, charging that they had let the hotel become a firetrap with inadequate fire escapes, a defective chimney, and fire hoses so old they cracked when unrolled. No charges were filed, but the *Journal's* incendiary reporting helped make the new paper's reputation. The Newhall tragedy had the broader effect of making fire safety a much higher priority in the central business district.

... and the North Western depot towered over the city's lakefront.

Milwaukee County Historical Society

Harper's Weekly (January 30, 1883)

The Newhall House fire claimed scores of lives in 1883.

Three years after the blaze, a new landmark rose from the charred bricks on Broadway: the home office of Northwestern Mutual Life Insurance. Founded in Janesville in 1857, the company had moved to Milwaukee two years later and found its fortune. By the mid-1880s, Northwestern was the seventh-largest life insurance firm in the country – a definite sign that manufacturing was not Milwaukee's only growth industry. The new home office was a conspicuous symbol of success, with six stories of carved stone, an elaborate array of arches, and a magnificent covered atrium. Critics agreed that it was a neighbor worthy of the masterpieces across the street: the Chamber of Commerce and the Mitchell Building.

A new seat of government emerged a few blocks north, on what is now Cathedral Square. Milwaukee had long since outgrown the chaste little courthouse put there in 1836 by Solomon Juneau and Morgan Martin. In 1873 the county replaced it with a towering neoclassical edifice built of Lake Superior brownstone. The new courthouse was so big that there were not enough county offices to fill it at first. The city of Milwaukee, it so happened, was running out of room in its official home, a converted market hall at Wells and Water Streets. In a rare instance of intergovernmental cooperation, city officials moved up the hill and into the east wing of the county courthouse, where they stayed for the next twenty-three years.

The West Side was not entirely bypassed in the post-Civil War building boom. In 1878 the Milwaukee Public Library was chartered as "a branch of the educational department of the City of Milwaukee." After two years in makeshift quarters, the library moved into a neoclassical building erected by John Plankinton at Fourth and Grand. The reading rooms were open to "all well-behaved persons," but "home use" of the system's 17,000 books was restricted to "actual residents of the city proper." Another embryonic giant was coming to life not far from the Library Block. In 1881 Milwaukee's Jesuits completed a four-story brick building on the crest of the hill at Tenth and State Streets. Marquette College, as they called their creation, opened with five professors and thirty-five students. The college grew slowly until 1907, when Marquette moved to its present Wisconsin Avenue campus, opened schools of law and medicine, and became a university.

Milwaukee Journal Sentinel

A more durable landmark rose from the rubble three years later: the home office of Northwestern Mutual Life Insurance.

A more imposing landmark emerged just down the hill from Marquette's first site. After a spirited bidding war with residents east of the river, the West Side landed one of the most ornate public structures ever erected in Milwaukee: the Industrial Exposition Building. Many cities of the Victorian period sponsored annual trade shows to highlight their industrial products and cultural achievements. In 1878 a group of business leaders decided that Milwaukee was ready for an exposition of its own. They formed an association, raised a stock fund, and hired Edward Townsend Mix to design a building. His creation, completed in 1881, was a brick-and-glass palace that covered the entire square block bordered by State Street and Kilbourn Avenue between Fifth and Sixth – the present site of the Milwaukee Theatre. The hall's focal point was a "grand polygonal dome" that towered over a baroque assemblage of parapets, porticoes, arches, and dormers.

The Exposition Building's reason for being was an annual fair, generally running for forty days each autumn, that showcased the latest word in "Manufactures, Inventions, Industrial Products, Art, Education, Natural History and Music." During the long non-Exposition season,

Milwaukee County Historical Society

A new courthouse filled the north half of Cathedral Square in 1873.

141

Completed in 1881, the Industrial Exposition Building was an architectural confection in the grandest Victorian style and Milwaukee's temple to industry.

Milwaukee Public Library

Marquette College opened its first building a few blocks west in the same year.

Milwaukee Public Library

the building served as a convention center, concert hall, ice-skating rink, state fish hatchery, roller rink, bicycle racetrack, and even the Public Museum. By the time it burned down in 1905, the Exposition Building had become Milwaukee's ultimate multi-purpose structure, but it continued to occupy an honored place as the city's temple to industry.

Like citizens of every generation, Milwaukeeans of the post-Civil War period were astonished by the changes taking place in the city around them. "One by one the old landmarks have passed away," wrote booster Charles Harger in 1877, "until now there remain but few of those once-prominent structures." Long-time residents began to feel, many for the first time, a sensation of distance from their roots, an awareness of the city's passage from a straightforward past to a most complicated present. In 1869, before the way back was lost entirely, the Old Settlers' Club was organized. In its first incarnation, the club was open only to men who had settled in Milwaukee County before 1839 – an obvious organizational death sentence. In 1881, with their ranks thinning rapidly, the group decided to admit the *sons* of anyone who had arrived before 1843. The Old Settlers' Club served as the local nucleus of nostalgia for another two generations. Its members organized dinners, collected artifacts, installed plaques, and generally congratulated themselves on the rags-to-riches rise of their community. Milwaukee was finally old enough to have a history, and its oldest residents looked back with parental pride.

Any smugness the Old Settlers might have felt was tempered by the proximity of Chicago. In the 1880s, that city became the second-largest in the United States, with a population of more than a million. Milwaukee's success was self-evident, but Chicago was more than five times larger. The fact that Wisconsin's metropolis had been dwarfed by its old rival tended to diminish a sense of civic accomplishment. In 1872 John Johnston, a Marine Bank executive, offered a statement of local attitudes that might have been written yesterday:

> There is one thing we are deficient in here. We have not the necessary blow and brag. Not only have we not that, but we daily see men standing with their hands in their pockets whining about Milwaukee being a one-horse town, and such like talk. Such men are not worthy to live here. Milwaukee is not Chicago, but there are few cities like Chicago. Still, if Milwaukee be not Chicago, Milwaukee has grown at a rate surpassed by but a very limited number of cities in this whole Union. Instead of grumbling and whining, let us have some city pride, some "esprit du corps," and let us not listen to any citizen of Milwaukee trying to make us believe he has traveled far and seen great cities, by crying down this the handsomest and healthiest and happiest city in the West. Let us cultivate the talent of brag, and whether at home or abroad, let us boast of Milwaukee, her beauty, her order, her growing trade, commerce and manufactures.

Civic meekness was always a temptation with Chicago only ninety miles away, but Milwaukee had other reasons to curb its collective ego. Local residents were forced to conclude that growth was not an unmixed blessing, particularly as it affected the physical environment. Early settlers had consumed natural resources with prodigal abandon, but the days of perceived abundance began to end after the Civil War. In

1867 Increase Lapham, the first in a distinguished line of Wisconsin environmentalists, warned that the wholesale destruction of forests was already causing problems: With fewer trees to retard run-off, floods on the Milwaukee and Menomonee Rivers were growing in suddenness and severity. Lapham's pleas for reforestation fell on deaf ears in a country so recently covered with virgin timber. Complaints about air quality were just as easily ignored. As coal consumption soared, a permanent pall of smoke settled over Milwaukee's freight-yards and factory districts, but most resi-

The North Point Water Tower was an improbable but highly popular addition to Milwaukee's skyline.

Milwaukee County Historical Society

dents seemed willing to accept air pollution as a by-product of progress. In 1873 *Leslie's Illustrated* described the Bay View iron mills – approvingly – as the equivalent of a home-grown volcano: "The smoke from their chimneys rises across the beautiful harbor, so that travelers have said that it has the picturesque effect of Vesuvius on the Bay of Naples."

Problems with water quality were more difficult to swallow. As unchecked population growth fouled Milwaukee's ground water, city officials turned instinctively to the region's pre-eminent natural resource: Lake Michigan. In 1874 an E.P. Allis-equipped pumphouse at the foot of North Avenue began to draw untreated lake water through an offshore intake and into a mammoth reservoir in Kilbourn Park, one mile west of the lake. From the reservoir it flowed by gravity to the city's homes and businesses. A cast-iron standpipe was erected atop the lake bluff to absorb the rhythmic pulsing of water from the Allis pumps and create a constant pressure, thereby saving wear and tear on the water mains. In an unprecedented fit of municipal whimsy, officials decided to surround the pipe with a fairy-tale stone tower worthy of the Brothers Grimm. The standpipe was capped decades ago, but the North Point Water Tower, minus Rapunzel, remains one of the East Side's most cherished landmarks.

Although it was a popular alternative to polluted wells and cloudy springs, the new system did not end Milwaukee's water woes. As the city grew, so did concerns about urban waste: domestic, industrial, and animal. In the heyday of horse-drawn transportation, tons of manure landed on the city's streets every day, producing "streams of liquid filth" after each rain. It was partly in response to the manure problem that Milwaukee began work on a municipal sewer system in 1869. The system's purpose, however, was not treatment but diversion; the new sewers simply ran to the nearest river and discharged their loads. The result was a pollution problem of epic proportions. The *Milwaukee Sentinel* (August 13, 1878) printed a graphic description of the city's principal river in late summer:

> *Not a citizen of Milwaukee possessing a nose to smell, or a stomach to endure, but is already prepared to unanimously denounce the filthy, villainous, unhealthy, plague-breeding condition of the river. In its palmiest days, the Chicago river, which has been for years the scorn of vain-glorious Milwaukee, could never boast of a fouler collection of the seeds of death than now floats upon the odorous tide that passes through the heart of this city. In a day when an east wind prevents the sluggish current from setting outward, as was the case yesterday, life in the vicinity of East and West Water streets is simply unendurable.*

Like most up-and-coming cities, Milwaukee craved national publicity, but the results were not always welcome. In an otherwise positive article about the community, *Harper's Monthly* (April, 1881) treated the whole country to another colorful account of the Milwaukee River:

> *It is a narrow, tortuous stream, hemmed in by the unsightly rear ends of street buildings and all sorts of waste places; it is a currentless and yellowish murky stream, with water like oil, and an odor combined of the effluvia of a hundred sewers. Nothing could better illustrate the contaminations of city life than the terrible change its*

waters undergo in a mile from their sparkling and rural cleanliness, up above, into this vile and noxious compound here among the wharves.

The lower Menomonee River, fed by tanneries, packing plants, and distilleries, was, if possible, even more loathsome.

Intercepting sewers were promoted as the answer to what local officials delicately described as "the river nuisance." Beginning in 1880, new pipes intercepted liquid waste before it could reach the rivers and conveyed it to a station on Jones Island, from which it was pumped into Lake

A pair of ornate landmarks dominated the dusty corner of Water and Wells Streets: the Grand Opera House (center) and the original City Hall (right).

Milwaukee County Historical Society

Milwaukee Journal Sentinel

Michigan. When that expedient failed to sweeten the rivers, Milwaukee was desperate. In 1888 city crews bored a tunnel through the East Side's bedrock from the lakefront (near today's McKinley Marina) to the Milwaukee River (just below the North Avenue dam). On the lake end of the tunnel, they installed the largest water pump in the world, an Allis-built behemoth that could move 40,000 cubic feet every minute. The pump literally flushed the river, replacing the cesspool below the dam with cold, clear lake water. The problem, of course, was that the filth in the river was simply transferred to the lake, and the lake was the source of Milwaukee's drinking water. Decades before local residents could spell "cryptosporidium," the city suffered periodic outbreaks of typhoid fever and "intestinal flu."

"Eight Hours for What We Will"

If problems in the physical environment seemed intractable at times, they were relatively straightforward in comparison with the social ills that accompanied industrialization. One of the less salutary aspects of big-city status was a growing cleavage along class lines, a cleavage that led more and more often to open conflict. Milwaukee had hardly been a community of interest before the Civil War; discord within and between wards, ethnic groups, and political factions was painfully obvious. But the postwar lines of demarcation were more vividly drawn, the prospects for reconciliation more remote, and the stakes quite literally a matter of life and death.

In the trades-based economy of the 1850s and '60s, a rough equality had prevailed. Conditions were far from idyllic, but shops were generally small, and the gap between owners and workers did not always seem unbridgeable. The rise of the factory system altered the very nature of work in some of Milwaukee's leading industries. In a context of increasing mechanization and increasing scale, hard-earned skills were devalued, and the relationship between employer and employee was stripped down to its economic core: the exchange of labor for wages. The *Milwaukee Sentinel* (April 15, 1869) described a telling interview with a foreman at Bradley & Metcalf, the city's leading boot and shoe manufacturer:

The simple fact proved to be that the division of labor – one single and simple operation being assigned to each class of workmen – and the introduction of machinery, had enabled the manufacturers to substitute unskilled for skilled labor. In the course of conversation Mr. Shaw remarked that he could take an unskilled laborer from the street and in two days time teach him to do some portions of the work as well as a man who had spent years in learning the shoemaker's trade. And he added further that of the 450 men now employed in the establishment, perhaps not more than ten were sufficiently skilled to have been of any service ten or fifteen years ago.

Like all technological advances, the division of labor and the triumph of machinery seemed inevitable and desirable – from the industrialist's viewpoint, at least – but the human costs were incalculable. Emil Seidel, Milwaukee's first Socialist mayor, spent part of his early career as a woodcarver in a North Side furniture factory. Seidel described a poignant scene that was played out repeatedly in his small shop:

Every time a machine was installed to do what machines had never done before, the cabinet makers and carvers came, singly or in twos, to see the work it did, untiringly, as fast as the hand fed it – "oh, so much faster than at the bench." They took a piece to see better and feel of it – "how smooth, through knots and everything." The machine-hand grinned, proud of his work, with eyes sparkling. With the victory of the machine he was coming up. Quietly, the others slunk back to their benches. They were licked.

As machines did more work and the proportion of unskilled hands edged steadily upward, labor costs per unit of production dropped sharply. In the 1880s, workers on the lowest (and broadest) rungs of the economic ladder generally put in at least ten hours a day, six days a week, for no more than $1.25 a day. That translates to roughly $2.15 per hour in modern dollars – without benefits. Displaced farm workers from Europe found even those meager wages preferable to starvation at home; immigrants lined up for the available jobs.

Most soon found that long hours and low wages were not the only drawbacks of the new factory system; working conditions were, by modern standards, nothing short of barbarous. With the advent of steam power, individual machines in most shops and mills were connected to a central drive shaft by open belts that posed a constant threat of injury. Flour mill employees frequently coughed their way home after spending ten hours in thick clouds of grain dust. Laborers on the killing floors of Milwaukee's packing houses spent their working lives up to their elbows in hog entrails. Tannery hands, particularly those who scraped the hair and flesh from putrefying cowhides, had some of the foulest-smelling jobs in American industry. Ironworkers had some of the hottest. Temperatures around the Bay View furnaces regularly topped 160 degrees, and a reporter visiting in the summer of 1873 expressed surprise that the men didn't melt.

Brewery work was perhaps the single bright spot. It took considerable brawn to manipulate foaming barrels of Milwaukee's finest, but the job had a unique fringe benefit: free beer. In 1886 a manager at the Schlitz brewery reported that each of his men drank an average of forty short glasses a day, and the plant champion managed to put down 100 – more than three gallons.

Brewing, unfortunately, accounted for barely five percent of Milwaukee's industrial employment in 1885. The rest of the city's blue-collar workers, stuck in jobs that were too hard, too hot, or too hazardous, toiled under conditions that would be considered criminal today.

They did not accept their plight without protest. The struggle for better wages and working conditions began in Milwaukee's infancy, and it has been more or less continuous ever since. In 1842, four years before the city was chartered, a motley crew of tradesmen formed the Mechanic's Protection Society to ensure fair and prompt payment for their services. In 1847 an assembly of masons struck for an increase in their daily wage to $1.75, and one year later a group of ship carpenters won their demands for better pay and a reduction in working hours from twelve to ten hours a day. Local efforts mirrored

The blast furnaces at the Bay View iron mill were hell on earth in the summer months....

Milwaukee County Historical Society

larger trends; in 1859 the city's typographers became the first trade to organize as a local unit of an international union.

The Civil War gave fresh impetus to organizing efforts. As a vicious bout of wartime inflation pushed wages below the subsistence level, workers struck for higher pay, often successfully, and their campaign continued after the war. By 1867, according to labor historian Thomas Gavett, sixteen unions were active in Milwaukee, one of which achieved national prominence. In March, 1867, the city's skilled shoemakers organized the Knights of St. Crispin to combat the erosion of their status in an increasingly mechanized business. When their movement spread to industry centers in the East, membership soared to 50,000, making the Knights, for a brief period, the largest union in America. The Panic of 1873 virtually killed the organization, but other Milwaukee unions survived the hard

times. They included the Sons of Vulcan, established in 1869 by skilled ironworkers at the Bay View rolling mill. In about 1872 they built a headquarters called Puddlers Hall on St. Clair Street, just south of the mill. Still in use as a tavern, Puddlers Hall is among the oldest landmarks of organized labor in the Midwest.

Although the labor movement made important progress before 1880, it was by no means a power on the American scene. The movement's first steps were halting and uncertain, hindered by the stubborn resistance of employers and, even more frequently, by downturns in the economy. The fact that most early unions served skilled workers in particular trades also limited their appeal; some, in fact, tried hard to keep unskilled workers out of their industries. Before it could claim genuine relevance, the labor movement needed at least two things: an organization open to

Milwaukee Public Library

The mill's puddlers regularly worked in temperatures exceeding 160 degrees. Not surprisingly, they were among the first Milwaukee workers to organize, forming the Sons of Vulcan in 1869.

workers on all levels, and an issue that could spur them to collective action. That organization was the Knights of Labor, and that issue was the eight-hour day.

The Noble and Holy Order of the Knights of Labor was founded by a group of Philadelphia garment workers in 1869. Certain that unchecked capitalism would lead to "the hopeless degradation of the toiling masses," they developed a complete platform of political and social reforms designed "to secure to the workers the full enjoyment of the wealth they create." Seeking the broadest possible base for its program, the Knights of Labor followed a policy of aggressive inclusiveness. Local assemblies were organized along the lines of trade, industry, ethnic origin, geography, and even gender; women ultimately formed nearly 200 assemblies of their own. It was a generous policy, but inclusiveness had its limits: The doors were closed to bankers, stockbrokers, saloonkeepers, and lawyers.

Wisconsin became a Knights of Labor stronghold largely through the efforts of one man: Robert Schilling. Born in Germany and raised in St. Louis, Schilling began his working years as a cooper, but he proved more adept at organizing workers than making barrels. The young man served for several years as an executive of the national cooper's union and then embarked on a full-time career as an apostle for social change. Schilling moved to Milwaukee in 1880, with his wife and six children in tow, to

Leaders of the fight for the eight-hour day: Robert Schilling (left) had enormous success as an organizer for the Knights of Labor, while his rival, Paul Grottkau, (right) kept up steady pressure from the left.

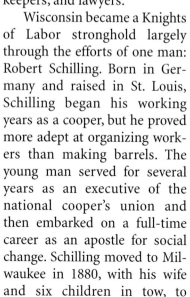

Wisconsin Historical Society

launch *Der Reformer*, a German-language political paper. Two years later, he revived a dormant Knights of Labor assembly in the city and took over a labor daily, the *Volksblatt* ("People's Paper"). An articulate proselytizer in two languages, Schilling entered 1885 as the Knights of Labor's lead organizer in Wisconsin.

After years of relative quiescence, the national organization was on the verge of a breakthrough. In 1884 the Knights of Labor endorsed another union's call for the eight-hour day and proceeded to make the issue its own. The campaign was hardly new (Wisconsin had passed a watered-down eight-hour law in 1867), but organizers of the mid-1880s were aided by a rare constellation of forces: industrial prosperity, the stirrings of group consciousness among unskilled workers, and an issue that cut across every conceivable demographic line. Bolstered by a stunning victory in a Southern railroad strike, the Knights of Labor's national membership shot up from 50,000 in 1884 to 700,000 in 1886, and Milwaukee alone accounted for 16,000 of the faithful – roughly half the city's blue-collar work force.

Robert Schilling staked out a position somewhat in advance of the national organization's. The union's top leadership believed in "mutual concession and agreement" as the answer to labor-management disputes; strikes and boycotts were sanctioned only as last resorts. Schilling was less apt to compromise than his superiors, and he was pushed still farther left by a new group in town: the Central Labor Union. Its leader was Paul Grottkau, another German immigrant and another newspaper editor. Grottkau moved from Chicago to Milwaukee in 1886 to take over a paper he renamed the *Arbeiter Zeitung* ("Worker's Times"). A gifted orator and a devout Socialist, he organized the Central Labor Union as an ideological alternative to the Knights of Labor. Both organizations played key roles in the newly formed Eight-Hour League, but Grottkau's influence gave the group a more aggressive posture than Schilling might have preferred.

Over the heartfelt objections of the national Knights of Labor, May 1, 1886, was set as the deadline for adoption of the eight-hour day in Wisconsin. The city of Milwaukee extended the benefit to municipal laborers in March, and a number of private employers followed suit. As one success led to another, the campaign for a shorter workday developed an irresistible momentum. "The agitation permeated our entire social atmosphere....," wrote Frank Flower, Wisconsin's labor commissioner. "It was <u>the</u> topic of conversation in the shop, on the street, at the family table, at the bar, in the counting room, and the subject of numerous able sermons from the pulpit." Robert Schilling found that Knights of Labor assemblies were forming spontaneously; he enrolled 618 Polish laborers at E.P. Allis's Reliance Works in a single day. Milwaukee and Chicago became the epicenters of the eight-hour movement in the entire country.

Milwaukee Public Library

Most Milwaukee employers resisted the demand for a shorter day, particularly without a cut in pay, and the result was a spate of strikes and lockouts. When the May 1 deadline arrived, at least 6,000 Milwaukeeans were out of work. The *Sentinel* reported a "Sabbath silence" settling over the city's breweries, and the *Evening Wisconsin* described a body of more than 700 sewer workers who simply "shouldered their picks and spades and marched away." On May 2, a Sunday, the Central Labor Union sponsored a parade that drew 3,000 marchers, 20,000 spectators, and every band in the city. Paul Grottkau rode in front, smoking a cigar, and the workmen behind him carried a variety of colorful banners. One summed up the movement's principal aim: "Eight hours for work, Eight hours for rest, Eight hours for what we will."

Events quickly assumed a life of their own. On May 3, an unplanned, unanticipated general strike brought the entire city to a standstill. Roughly 15,000 men were out of work – nearly half the total in Milwaukee. Seized by an epidemic of "labor fever," even newsboys deserted their posts, and one joker claimed that the police had posted a guard to keep a downtown jeweler's clock from striking. On the morning of May 3, a wave of factory hands swept through the Menomonee Valley, intent on shutting down any plants that were still open. Their first target was the shop complex of the Chicago, Milwaukee & St. Paul Railroad, which they managed to close by

Milwaukee County Historical Society

(top)

Gov. Jeremiah Rusk called out the militia when he found events spinning out of control.

One detachment of soldiers guarded Edward Allis's Reliance Works in Walker's Point.

Milwaukee Journal Sentinel

152

midday. The crowd then marched east to the Reliance Works in Walker's Point. The Polish members of the Knights assembly had already walked out, but some of their co-workers greeted the strikers with water hoses. The first wave of demonstrators was repulsed but, when it became clear that continued operation would be hazardous, Edward Allis shut the plant down.

That left one major business still running: the Bay View rolling mill. In the early morning hours of May 4, a group of perhaps 1,000 Polish strikers met at St. Stanislaus Church to march on the lakeshore plant. The mill's laborers, most of them Polish, walked out gladly when the marchers arrived, but the skilled workers, who had recently ended a long strike, stayed on the job. When the company's managers showed no inclination to close the plant, the crowd sent a delegation (headed by Robert Schilling) inside to confer. Gov. Jeremiah Rusk, in the meantime, had arrived in Milwaukee on the night train, and Gov. Rusk called out the militia. Men who had been grocers, clerks, and saloonkeepers an hour or two earlier threw on their uniforms and rushed down to Bay View to preserve order. The striking Poles were angry when the first trains arrived, and they were incensed when the Kosciuszko Guard – their countrymen, neighbors, and fellow parishioners – appeared in full regalia. As the soldiers made their way inside the plant gates, the crowd showered them with sticks, stones, and dead fowl. The mill's managers finally shut down the plant, defusing tensions for the moment, but the marchers made it clear that they intended to return.

Shortly after sunrise on May 5, the Poles regrouped at St. Stanislaus, the church established in 1866, to resume their

The calm before the storm: state militia troops at the Bay View rolling mill

courtesy Bert Sjostrom

march on the iron mill established in 1866. Nearly 1,500 strong, they walked four abreast, first down Mitchell Street, then along Kinnickinnic Avenue and Bay Street, behind a red, white, and blue banner bearing a clockface set to eight and the legend "Eight Hours." The atmosphere must have been unbearably tense. On the evening of May 4, just hours earlier, a crowd of Chicago strikers had gathered at Haymarket Square to protest the shootings of several demonstrators the day before. As the meeting was ending, someone threw a bomb into a group of policemen, killing eight and wounding many others. Reports of "howling mobs of anarchists" committing mayhem on Chicago's streets traveled like lightning through the nation's telegraph wires, leading some citizens to fear that a reign of terror was imminent. The militia companies gathered at Bay View were primed for trouble, and so was Jeremiah Rusk. When the governor was informed by telephone that a large crowd was headed to Bay View, he reportedly said, "Very well, sir. Fire on them." The captain of the Sheridan Guard, a heavily Irish militia company, gave his soldiers a more specific command: "Pick out your man, and kill him."

As the strikers turned south on Bay Street, Maj. George Traeumer, a German immigrant and former county clerk, ordered them to halt. At a distance of 200 yards, it is unlikely that the marchers could see the major, much less hear him above their own noise. When they continued to advance, Traeumer ordered his troops to open fire. The *Milwaukee Journal* described the reaction:

> As if by a common impulse the crowd fell
> headlong to the ground and for a minute it

appeared as though nearly all had been killed or wounded by the first discharge. When the troops ceased firing, all who were uninjured turned and ran pell mell back to the city, leaving six dead or dying in the dusty roadway.

The precise number of fatalities remains in doubt. County death certificates confirm five, but published estimates place the number as high as nine. Not all the victims were strikers; the dead included a thirteen-year-old schoolboy who was evidently playing hooky and a retired laborer who was watching from his backyard on Bay Street. Some accounts of the carnage resembled dispatches from a war zone, including this *Sentinel* description of the injuries to Casimir Dudek:

> Two bullets had carried away his lower jaw, and two others had passed through the upper part of his left arm.... At 10 o'clock he was still reclining in the arms of a fellow countryman on the slope of the street embankment, his lifeblood imparting a crimson tint to the tall green grass. Father Gulski, of St. Hyacinth's, was standing near him, and a crowd closed in upon the scene from all sides.... Pieces of his jaw and several teeth were gathered by bystanders....

As the confrontation in Bay View reached its fiery climax, another tinderbox was about to explode on the North Side. A crowd of nearly 2,000 strikers, most of them Germans and many allied with Paul Grottkau, assembled at the Milwaukee Garden, a beer garden on Fourteenth and State Streets, later in the morning hours of May 5. Determined to break up the gathering, the Milwaukee police, backed by National Guardsmen, waded into the crowd with their nightsticks raised and ready. The clubs saw heavy use, reported the *Evening Wisconsin*: "The dull and sickening thud of the rosewood billies as they crashed down upon the heads of the luckless idlers could be heard at a distance of a hundred feet or more." Shots were fired before the crowd finally dispersed. Had any of the bullets found their mark, the German incident at the Milwaukee Garden might have ended as tragically as the Polish march on Bay View.

Although they were overshadowed in the national press by Chicago's Haymarket affair, the events of May 5, 1886, constituted the bloodiest labor disturbance in Wisconsin's history. In its aftermath, workers slowly returned to their jobs, generally at their old wages and hours, and the citizen soldiers of the National Guard resumed their civilian lives. Public reaction to the turmoil was still running high months and even years later. Business leaders roundly applauded Gov. Rusk for his decisive handling of the crisis; "Uncle Jerry," a celebrated Civil War veteran, modestly replied that he was "performing a plain duty." The city's English-language newspapers wasted no time in demonizing the demonstrators, particularly the Poles. The *Sunday Telegraph* called them "a vicious, lawless mob, bent on blood, robbery and destruction." The *Journal* rationalized that most were "unskilled laborers who are ... the ignorant and easy instruments of crazy and vagabond demagogues." The immigrants also faced economic reprisals. In the wake of the May 5 disturbance, one manufacturer placed an ad for workers that warned, "Polanders and drunkards need not apply." A grand jury

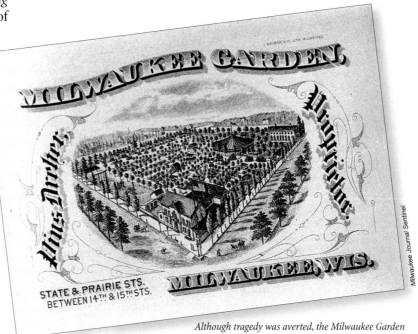

Milwaukee Journal Sentinel

Although tragedy was averted, the Milwaukee Garden was the scene of another tense confrontation between workers and civil authorities on May 5.

"Shot in a mob": the death certificate of laborer Michael Ruchalski, May 5, 1886

ultimately handed down nearly fifty indictments against the demonstrators, most for rioting or unlawful assembly, and several, including Paul Grottkau, spent time in jail.

Reaction from the workers' camp was just as intense. St. Stanislaus Church was filled to overflowing for the funerals of the shooting victims, and members of the Kosciuszko Guard found their businesses subjected to a withering boycott. Grottkau's Central Labor Union denounced the militia's action in Bay View as "over-zealous, unjustifiable and damnable," and Robert Schilling went even further. "To say it in plain German," he wrote, "it was cowardly, premeditated murder." Schilling's sympathies were plain, but a large number of less radical Milwaukeeans viewed the shootings as chilling evidence that industrial property was valued more highly than industrial workers.

★★★★★

Milwaukee underwent a sea change in the two decades after the Civil War. The city entered the period as a commercial capital with a definite Yankee-German flavor, and it ended as an industrial stronghold with an increasingly diverse ethnic mix. The old foundations were not completely erased. Milwaukee, in fact, illustrated the tendency of cities to grow by accretion, to add new layers without obliterating the old. The chronicle of the postwar period is a story of manufacturing *and* commerce, of Poles *and* Germans. By period's end, however, the community had moved materially away from the simpler dynamics of mid-century.

Milwaukee had grown larger, more sophisticated, and more diverse, but there was more room for concern than congratulation in 1886. Not since the Bridge War of 1845 had Milwaukeeans raised their fists against each other. Not since the Civil War had armed soldiers marched through the city's streets. Never before in the community's history had one group of citizens leveled deadly fire at another. The precedent was profoundly troubling. If the price of industrial growth was industrial conflict, if the social cost of immigration was social strife, some residents wondered just how much their community had gained. An easy, nearly universal belief in progress gave way to a radical question: Progress for whom? There was disagreement about the root causes of industrial conflict – a truly unjust system, or just unruly workers – but the Bay View shootings forced Milwaukeeans on all sides of the struggle to conclude that something was horribly, terribly wrong.

Chapter 5

Triumph of the Workingman, 1886 – 1910

City Hall rises to a point 350 feet (and 8 million bricks) above the streets of downtown Milwaukee. It is one of the tallest masonry structures in the world, but size is not the building's most conspicuous feature. City Hall is as painstakingly assembled as a wedding cake; one tier of columns and arches rests atop another, each broken by panels of ornate terra cotta and all crowned by a lovingly detailed clock tower. Inside the "cake," a graceful atrium soars a full eight stories, ringed by ornamental copper work and marble columns on every floor. City Hall is Milwaukee's signature building, a cultural icon that may be the best-loved landmark on the local skyline. Its image has graced everything from the opening credits of *Laverne and Shirley* to souvenir sweatshirts, and it is widely considered one of the most beautiful municipal halls in America.

City Hall: towering landmark and symbol of a new stage in Milwaukee's political evolution

Milwaukee Journal Sentinel

City Hall is also a symbol. When it was dedicated in 1895, local residents realized that the building was more than a seat of government. City Hall was widely viewed as a statement, and it embodied several messages that serve as major themes of the 1886-1910 period. The first was Milwaukee's emergence as an American metropolis. Fueled by the steady expansion of its industries and a constant infusion of immigrants, the community's population more than doubled during the period, and the new City Hall was a towering statement of civic pride. During the dedication ceremonies, William Rauschenberger, a leading alderman and future mayor, declared that Milwaukee deserved no less:

> The building in which the business of the city
> is to be transacted should in all respects
> correspond with the magnitude, beauty and
> importance of Wisconsin's metropolis, and that
> such is the case you will all agree with me who
> inspect this building.

The new building corresponded just as closely to Milwaukee's ethnic self-image. City Hall contains elements of several styles, but its steep gables and copper-clad turrets have an unmistakably Germanic ambience. The structure was built from the plans of a German-born architect, Henry Koch, working under a German-born mayor, John Koch, during a time when more than half the city's population traced its ancestry to Germany. City Hall represents a deep bow to the community's Teutonic roots, and it may be the single most enduring expression of the Germanism that lies at the foundation of modern Milwaukee.

On the last and probably most important level, the structure marked a new stage in the evolution of local government. After years in cramped rental quarters, city officials took over the largest, most lavishly appointed building in town. City Hall assumed a dominant place on the local skyline, and those inside asserted their desire to lead, not follow, the course of local development. Agreement on the city's direction, however, proved almost impossible to find. The 1886-1910 period was perhaps the most volatile in Milwaukee's political history, highlighted by a long-running struggle between forces that were generally described in terms of extremes: order vs. anarchy, corruption vs. reform, a safe status quo vs. a hazardous social experiment. City Hall was first prize in a pitched political battle that virtually defined the period. By the time it ended in 1910, the community was famous for something more than beer and bricks. In the single most important turning point in its political history, Milwaukee became the first large city in America to be governed by Socialists.

The People's Party

The opening shots in the battle for City Hall were the same shots fired in Bay View on May 5, 1886. The militia volley that morning was supposed to have killed the eight-hour crusade and crippled the labor movement, but it soon became apparent that the post-mortems were premature. Even as the champions of law and order – business leaders, the English-language press, and Gov. Jeremiah Rusk – were exulting in their victory at the rolling mill, another viewpoint was gaining currency. As soon as the initial shock wore off, the city's laboring classes condemned the shootings with a single voice. On May 23, nearly 5,000 workers, including a sizable group of Poles who had marched in Bay View, turned out for a parade sponsored by the Knights of Labor. Described as "most quiet and orderly" by the *Evening Wisconsin*, they tramped for five miles through the streets of central Milwaukee and ended their march with a picnic at the Milwaukee Garden – the precise spot where club-wielding policemen had cracked the heads of strikers not three weeks before. The parade was an act of peaceful defiance, a signal that workers would not be cowed even after the bloodshed of May 5.

Robert Schilling remained the Knights of Labor's most visible leader, and he used the Bay View incident as a figurative call to arms. In Schilling's view, the only proper response to the shootings was concerted political action:

> *The poor victims are dead and buried. They shall be revenged. Not by making blood flow; not through force. The intelligent citizens have a weapon mightier than the ball or the bayonet – the ballot.*

The discontent of Milwaukee's workers crystallized in the People's Party of Wisconsin, a movement organized by Schilling in the summer of 1886. Like other Populist efforts of the time, the party advocated a series of liberal reforms intended to make American society more humane, more equitable, and more responsive to the will of the people. Specific planks in the group's platform called for a graduated income tax, restrictions on child labor, a more flexible money supply, arbitration of labor disputes, and referendum and recall provisions. Their rhetoric was shrill at times, but the party's leaders were reformers at heart,

not revolutionaries. Milwaukee Socialists, including political rival Paul Grottkau, frequently derided Schilling and his allies as naive apologists for a corrupt system or, worse yet, as crass opportunists. For the time being, however, the Socialists joined the effort to make the People's Party a real alternative to the entrenched Democrats and Republicans.

In the fall elections of 1886, the Populist coalition filled an entire ticket with candidates, including millwright Henry Smith for Congress. Galvanized by the Bay View shootings, droves of workers went to the polls, and they handed the People's Party a resounding win. Populists took most county offices, half of Milwaukee's state assembly seats, and a place in Congress: Mr. Smith went to Washington. It was the most stunning labor victory in the entire country that autumn. Jeremiah Rusk won his third statewide race for governor but lost decisively in Milwaukee – an obvious comment on his role in the May shootings.

Labor's triumph was short-lived. The People's Party added a number of aldermanic seats in the elections of April, 1887, but its

Henry Smith, the millwright who went to Congress on the People's Party ticket in 1886

Milwaukee County Historical Society

159

engine soon ran out of steam. Paul Grottkau bolted with a small but significant bloc of Socialist voters and, much more ominously, the Democrats and Republicans joined forces against the Populists. Citing the dangers of "class rule" by "communists and anarchists," the newly formed Fusion Committee declared in 1887 that "a sense of present, imminent danger has caused the conservative citizens of Milwaukee to throw aside party ties and bind themselves together for the common good." Robert Schilling ridiculed the fusion ticket as "a matrimonial contract between a horse and an ass," but its mayoral candidate, Thomas Brown, narrowly beat his in the spring contest of 1888. The Populists' descent thereafter was rapid. Although Schilling remained active in reform politics for another decade, the city's blue-collar voters turned to other leaders.

There were some obvious lessons in the brief career of the People's Party. Its rapid rise and fall illustrated the resilience of the old-line parties and the inherent fragility of third-party movements. Its short life also demonstrated that Robert Schilling was more gifted as an orator than an organizer; long-term success at the polls would depend on the patient cultivation of grassroots support, not a fevered reaction to a civic tragedy. But the Populist victories, however fleeting, were more than flukes. Milwaukee's workers, mobilized by a sense of outrage, discovered a common voice and asserted their collective power. It would take time for their latent energy to find mature political expression, but the campaigns of 1886 and 1887 were important conditioning steps. Victory in those contests provided a solid foundation for the more durable working-class victory of 1910.

Machine Shop of the World

As political tensions subsided, for at least the time being, Milwaukee resumed the task that had absorbed its energies before 1886: industrialization. It is significant that the turmoil of the time had virtually no impact on the city's developing economy. Industry continued to expand as if Milwaukee were in the grip of blind destiny. Commerce never disappeared – the grain trade, in fact, showed impressive growth in some areas – but industry assumed an almost unshakable position at the base of Milwaukee's economy. Even death couldn't slow its expansion. The community lost a number of financial giants during the period – Alexander Mitchell in 1887, Frederick Miller in 1888, Edward Allis in 1889, John Plankinton in 1891, and Frederick Pabst in 1904 – but their successors managed, in most cases, to move forward without missing a beat.

All of what might be termed Milwaukee's traditional industries – milling, tanning, meat-packing, brewing, and iron production – continued their historic patterns of growth. Flour-milling, one of the city's oldest economic activities, reached a new peak of 2,117,009 barrels in 1892 – more than triple the figure of 1880. Milwaukee was the nation's second- or third-largest producer of flour during the period, but it was never more than a distant second: Minneapolis millers turned out four or five times more barrels in an average year.

The city retained its laurels as the leading producer of leather on the planet. Production of hides passed the 500,000 mark in 1886, reached the 1 million level in 1897, and exceeded 2 million in 1907. As sales

The Daisy flour mill and the Pfister & Vogel tanneries, both pictured in 1892, typified Milwaukee's "traditional" industries.

from Milwaukee's Great Industries

Patrick Cudahy, the Irish immigrant's son who became Milwaukee's leading meat-packer

Milwaukee Journal Sentinel

soared, Wisconsin farmers couldn't begin to meet the demand for raw materials. Carloads of cowhides came in from the great packing houses of Chicago, Kansas City, and Omaha, and calfskins arrived from as far away as Europe.

The meat-packing industry was considerably more erratic. After reaching a new record of 701,809 in 1890, the number of hogs butchered in Milwaukee crashed to 325,820 in 1893, rebounded to 1,002,044 in 1897, and dropped again to 553,723 in 1902. John Plankinton had been the region's dominant packer since the pioneer period. In 1888, after negotiating the peaks and valleys of the business for more than forty years, Plankinton sold out to his long-time general manager, Patrick Cudahy. The new proprietor kept the old Menomonee Valley plant open for a few more years, but in 1893, pressed for space and tired of complaints about foul

odors, Cudahy decided to move. "I got a county map," he recalled, "looked it over, and selected a site located about two miles south of the south limits of Milwaukee on the Chicago & North Western Railroad." The result was the village of Cudahy, which was incorporated in 1895. Although other packers turned down invitations to follow him south, Patrick Cudahy's suburb, known unofficially as "Porkopolis," gave the meat industry a new center in the region.

Brewing, Milwaukee's best-known industry, enjoyed a brief reign as its most important. In 1890, for the first and only time in the community's history, the federal census ranked beer first (by value) on the list of local products. The beverage's runaway success reflected its growing acceptance in the national market. Once spurned as a foreigner's drink, beer came to be considered as American as, well, pretzels and frankfurters. In an 1892 article, Gustav Pabst, Capt. Frederick's oldest son and eventual successor, described it as the ideal tonic for harried moderns:

The irresistible momentum with which civilization is advancing in this nineteenth century, the rapidity with which we live, crowding as we do into a life of thirty years the work which was formerly completed at three-score and ten, pushing each other in the struggle for supremacy in every field of action, has made the need of some soothing strength-giver imperative. The mild and beneficial effects of malt beverages containing hops are becoming more and more recognized, and ... those who have tasted malt beverages recognize their value and use them instinctively.

Milwaukee produced much more than its share of this "soothing strength-giver." By 1895 the city claimed three of the nation's top ten brewers: Pabst, Schlitz, and Blatz. Milwaukee outdistanced old rivals like New York and St. Louis, and still its output climbed – from 1,203,879 barrels in 1886 to 2,500,462 in 1900 and 3,724,937 in 1910. The leading companies spared no expense in promoting the ties between place and product. Two famous slogans appeared in ads of the 1890s: "Schlitz, the Beer that Made Milwaukee Famous" and "Milwaukee Beer Is Famous – Pabst Has Made It So." Schlitz, whose sales volume finally exceeded Pabst's in 1902, had the winning catch phrase, but the effect was

Milwaukee Journal Sentinel

Looking every inch the beer baron, Capt. Frederick Pabst remained in active charge of the family brewery until a few years before his death in 1904.

The Pabst bottling house was largely a female domain in the 1890s.

Milwaukee County Historical Society

the same in either case: Non-stop advertising made Milwaukee synonymous with beer. The identification was so complete that in 1900 the leading local firms had to sue New York brewers who were selling their own products as "Milwaukee Beer." More than a century later, despite the loss of all but one major producer, Milwaukee's image as a beer capital still has enormous power.

The city remained an iron capital as well, at least through the early 1900s. The Bay View rolling mill, which reopened immediately after the 1886 shootings, provided work for at least 1,500 men in most years, with employment climbing to 2,000 during seasonal peaks. The mill specialized in iron rails until 1883, when America's railroads turned exclusively to longer-lasting steel tracks. After a brief experiment with nails, the plant found its niche as a producer of "merchant" metal: standard-sized bars, bands, angles, channels, and billets that were used as raw materials in other industries. The complex changed owners as often as it changed products during the

period. The Bay View mill had been a unit of the North Chicago Rolling Mill Company since 1878, but North Chicago was absorbed by the Illinois Steel Company in 1889, which was swallowed by Federal Steel in 1898, which merged with the Carnegie interests to form United States Steel in 1901. Once a cornerstone of the country's first iron and steel empire, Capt. Eber Ward's old mill became a relatively minor holding of the largest corporation in the world.

All of Milwaukee's traditional industries, the mill included, were expanding fast enough after 1886 to sustain the city's long-term momentum. The remarkable fact is that another industry was growing even faster: metal fabrication. The value of "durable goods" turned out by the city's machine shops, foundries, and forges soared from $5,568,445 in the 1890 census to $14,495,362 in 1900, replacing beer as the leading local industry. The rise of metal-bending marked a new stage in the evolution of Milwaukee's economy. All of the traditional industries had their roots in

The Bay View iron mill remained an important local employer even after being absorbed by United States Steel in 1901.

Milwaukee Public Library

the natural resources of the surrounding region; none could have survived, much less prospered, without abundant and accessible supplies of wheat, cowhides, tanbark, hogs, barley, hops, and ore. Durable goods, by contrast, were manufactured, not processed; they were less dependent on natural resources than on expert engineering. Milwaukee's economy was liberated, in a sense, from its regional constraints, and entrepreneurs were free to produce practically anything for practically any market. Local boosters were quick to trumpet this large step forward in industrial maturity. Once celebrated as the largest wheat market on earth, Milwaukee courted new fame as the "Machine Shop of the World."

Although the city's factories turned out everything from milk pails to bicycles, machinery became Milwaukee's specialty. The move was, to some degree, predictable. Steam engines had done America's heavy lifting through most of the nineteenth century, but a trio of new prime movers – the electric motor, the gasoline engine, and the steam turbine – all crossed the commercial threshold between roughly 1885 and 1900. They provided cheap, reliable energy for tasks that ranged from drilling teeth to drilling for oil, and the result was an explosion in the demand for machinery of every type. Milwaukee was well-positioned to take advantage of that demand. The city had developed some impressive strengths in the previous generation or two: superb transportation facilities, an abundance of both skilled and unskilled labor, easy access to natural resources, a growing pool of venture capital, and an established tradition of making things. The turn of the century was a fertile time for mechanical ingenuity, and Milwaukee was particularly fertile ground.

The Edward P. Allis Company continued to plow the deepest furrow. The massive plant in Walker's Point remained one of the nation's leading manufacturers of flour mill equipment, sawmill machinery and, above all, steam engines. With Allis's death in 1889, control passed to his wife, his oldest sons, and his chief engineer, Edwin Reynolds, who functioned as the "practical head" of the firm. None had more than a fraction of the founder's business acumen, but they kept the enterprise growing. By 1900 Allis engines were hoisting rock in South African diamond mines, reducing ore to iron in Austrian blast furnaces, running flour mills in China, and supplying the motive power for New York City's transit system. The New York engines, which peaked at 12,000 horsepower, were the largest steam engines ever built.

In 1900, with its Walker's Point plant filled to capacity, the company purchased 100 acres of open land near what is now the intersection of Greenfield Avenue and S. Seventieth Street. Close enough to attract Milwaukee workers and well-served by major railroads, the site had obvious potential for industrial development. Located four miles due west of the original Allis works, the incipient suburb was called, naturally, West Allis. It became an incorporated village in 1902, the same year the first factory buildings were occupied.

The business went through a sweeping reorganization while the new plant was under construction. In 1901, a record year for American merger activity, the Edward P. Allis Company combined with two Chicago firms and one Pennsylvania concern to form the Allis-Chalmers Company. The merger was not without headaches, both financial and organizational, but it resulted in a much broader product line. In 1904, with a comprehensive range of engines, turbines, and generators pouring out of its shops, the company adopted a new slogan: "Ours the Four Powers: Steam, Gas, Water, Electricity." Allis-Chalmers never achieved the dominance in any of those fields that Allis alone had enjoyed as a maker of steam engines, but the company became one of the largest manufacturers of heavy machinery in the world.

Allis-Chalmers served as a shining role model for literally hundreds of would-be industrialists. A small army of tinkerers was at work in Milwaukee, all of them hoping to scale the same heights that Edward Allis and his successors had climbed. A remarkable number of those tinkerers were Germans, and a remarkable number of them set up shop in the Walker's Point neighborhood. Walker's Point, in fact, functioned as Milwaukee's industrial incubator through the turn of the century, a place brimming with new ideas and the talent to turn them into realities.

Henry Harnischfeger was a typical resident. In 1884 the German-born Harnischfeger and Chicago native Alonzo Pawling opened a small machine and pattern shop on S. First and Florida Streets. It was a standard job shop, repairing broken machinery for some customers and fabricating new machines from the drawings of others. One of the pair's most frequent visitors was Bruno Nordberg, a Finnish-born engineer who hired Pawling & Harnischfeger to build a steam-engine governor he had designed. Another regular was Christopher Levalley, who brought in plans for an endless chain of metal links that he hoped would replace the leather belting on heavy machinery. Encouraged by their initial

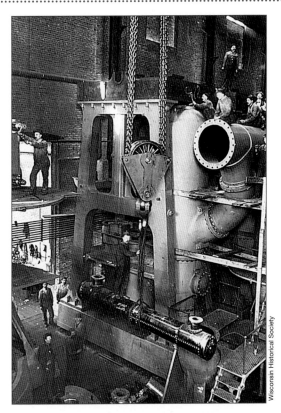

A mammoth steam pump neared completion at the E.P. Allis Reliance Works in 1894.

Wisconsin Historical Society

Organized in 1901, the Allis-Chalmers Company carried the Allis reputation for heavy machinery to new heights in a new home: West Allis.

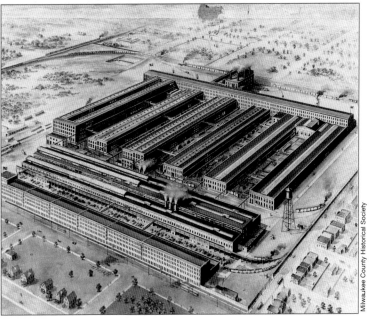

Milwaukee County Historical Society

165

results, both men soon opened shops of their own in the immediate neighborhood. Thus were born Nordberg Manufacturing and the Chain Belt Company, two firms that rose from roots in Walker's Point to become giants in American industry.

Henry Harnischfeger was glad to help his customers succeed, but the immigrant wanted a product that he and Pawling could call their own. The chance came in 1887, when a rope-driven overhead crane collapsed and killed a worker in the E.P. Allis plant, which was literally across the street from the P&H shop. An Allis engineer,

Robert Shaw, soon designed an electric overhead crane that was safer and more powerful than anything on the market. When Allis executives turned down the chance to manufacture the device, Shaw came to work for Pawling & Harnischfeger, who made electric cranes their specialty. The company quickly became a world leader in the material-handling field, turning out more than 30,000 cranes before selling the division in 1998.

Some of Harnischfeger's neighbors were just as successful. Two blocks north of P&H's first building, a pair of tinkerers named Edward Kearney and Theodore Trecker opened a tiny shop in 1898 and began to produce milling machines of their own design. Two blocks south and one year later, Arthur O. Smith built America's first pressed-steel automobile frame in his family's old bicycle factory. Just down the block from P&H on Florida Street, a high-school dropout named Lynde Bradley rented shop space in 1902. With substantial help from his brother Harry and financial backing from Dr. Stanton Allen, the young man tried to perfect his designs for a new type of electric motor controller. All of these fledgling industries, from Harnischfeger to Allen-Bradley, achieved global stature, and all came to life within a two-block radius of First and Florida Streets between 1884 and 1902 – a remarkable burst of energy in such a concentrated space and time.

After testing their wings in the marketplace, the most successful firms generally flew off to larger plants on the city's edge. Allen-Bradley (industrial controls) is still a fixture in Walker's Point, but Nordberg (mining equipment, diesel engines) moved south to Bay View, A.O. Smith (car and

Henry Harnischfeger was typical of the entrepreneurs who began giant businesses in Walker's Point. His first machine shop was a modest establishment on First and Florida Streets.

truck frames) headed north to Capitol Drive, and Kearney & Trecker (still machine tools) relocated to West Allis. Other "graduates" of Walker's Point, including Harnischfeger and Chain Belt, built spacious new homes in the area perennially identified with Milwaukee industry: the Menomonee Valley. There they joined older, resource-based businesses, including tanneries and packing plants, as well as newer machine shops that produced everything from locomotives to farm equipment.

One of the Valley's largest firms, the Falk Company, straddled both stages in the region's economic development. In 1856 Franz Falk, a Bavarian immigrant, opened a brewery on the south side of the Menomonee Valley near Thirtieth Street. It became the fourth-largest in Milwaukee, trailing only Pabst, Schlitz, and Blatz, but the founder's sons, disheartened after a pair of disastrous fires, sold out to Pabst in 1892. One of the younger Falks, Herman, soon opened a general-purpose machine shop in the ruins of the old brewery. It evolved, by the usual fits and starts, into one of the leading foundries in the region and then the largest manufacturer of precision industrial gears in the country. More than a century later, Falk is still based in the Valley. The story's broader significance lies in the fact that the Falk family, like Milwaukee itself, moved from beer to gears, from malt to machinery, in a single generation.

Another German named Herman — this one Herman Ladish — kept his feet in both worlds. As general manager of a Walker's Point malting plant, Ladish had chronic problems with an engine crankshaft. In about 1905, he took it to a blacksmith shop down the street, where the proprietors hammered out a part so perfect that Herman was moved to invest in the business. He eventually took it over, and in 1913 the capitalist moved his new company to Cudahy, where Ladish Drop Forge became the largest forge shop in America. Herman was just as involved in the grain trade, parlaying his small stake in a Jefferson County malting firm into a controlling interest. Ladish Malt, selling sprouted barley to America's brewers, became the largest malting plant in the world.

German craftsmen had no monopoly on business skills, nor did every successful firm trace its roots to Walker's Point or the Menomonee Valley. In about 1901, two benchmates at a North Milwaukee bicycle factory, William Harley and Arthur Davidson, began to work on plans for a motorized bicycle. Two of Arthur's brothers took an interest, and in 1903 the Davidsons' father, a cabinetmaker by trade, built a ten-by-fifteen-foot shed behind the family's home at Thirty-Eighth Street and Highland

The Falk Company, one of the Menomonee Valley's largest industries, moved from beer to gears in a single generation.

Falk Corporation

Avenue. The young men finished three motorcycles during their first full year in business. By 1917 they had moved into a state-of-the-art factory complex just down the hill on Juneau Avenue, and the Harley-Davidson Motor Company was turning out 18,000 cycles a year.

From machine tools to motorcycles, Milwaukee-made products carried the city's name throughout the world, but the transition to manufacturing was never complete. The local economy continued to expand by the familiar process of accretion; just as processing industries grew up alongside the grain trade after the Civil War, metal fabrication joined milling, tanning, meat-packing, and brewing at the turn of the century. Milwaukee was engaged in manufacturing *and* processing, in producing durable goods *and* perishable commodities. Metal-working establishments gained a lead they have never lost, but it should be understood that Milwaukee's prosperity depended on industry of all kinds.

It should be equally clear that the city's road to industrial prosperity was anything but smooth. Between the peaks of production, there were some deep valleys, and the deepest by far was the Panic of 1893. Beginning as a credit crisis during the summer months, the panic blossomed into one of the longest and most severe depressions of the nineteenth century. Milwaukee was especially hard-hit. Five banks failed (including the venerable Marine), dozens of employers shut down for the duration, and those who stayed open did so only by cutting both their work forces and their wage rates. When the books closed on 1894, the city's machinery manufacturers reported an average decline of 40 percent in output and 41 percent in employment. Conditions were not much better even three years later. Meat-packer Patrick Cudahy offered a sober assessment of his firm's record for 1897: "We made enough to keep the wolf from the door, but nothing to boast

Creators of a legend: Arthur Davidson, Walter Davidson, William Harley, and William Davidson posed outside their new West Side motorcycle plant in 1910.

Harley-Davidson, Inc.

of. We have been acting the part of the philanthropist, feeding the hungry with meat at cost, and furnishing employment to the needy." Even the brewing industry, long considered recession-proof, posted four straight years of production declines between 1893 and 1897.

Although the panic had lasting political repercussions, the city's economic recovery was virtually complete by 1898. Milwaukee was soon making up for lost time. The Chamber of Commerce reported that local plants were "taxed beyond their capacity" in 1899, and that the region had "practically no available vacant factory buildings" three years later. By 1906 the area's largest employers faced a two-year order backlog. The *Milwaukee Sentinel's* annual industrial survey quantified the prevailing trends. The survey charted a rise in the area's industrial output from $106.3 million in 1890 to $174.4 million in 1900 – a whopping 64-percent increase during a depres-

sion decade. Production rose even faster in the new century, climbing 89 percent (to $329.5 million) between 1900 and 1910. The metal-bending industries consistently led the way. In 1907 the *Sentinel* boasted that the sun never set on Milwaukee-made equipment: "The hum and roar of her monster engines and massive machinery is heard in every civilized land."

Double-digit increases in annual production were impressive, but the numbers don't begin to indicate how thoroughly industry came to dominate the local economy. The federal census for 1910 reported that 56.9 percent of Milwaukee's adult males were industrial workers – the second-highest concentration in the country. Only Detroit, the nation's emerging automotive center, had a higher proportion. Already known for its industrial prowess, Milwaukee developed an image as a blue-collar town that has persisted for generations.

Workers at the Meiselbach bicycle factory in North Milwaukee. Child labor was a definite fact of life in the late 1800s.

Milwaukee County Historical Society

A City of Nations

As in earlier years, the people who wore those blue collars were generally Europeans once or twice removed. It was the promise of industrial jobs that brought newcomers to the city, and it was the reality of those jobs that made them stay. In 1890 immigrants and their children made up an astonishing 86.4 percent of the community's population, earning Milwaukee a designation as the most "foreign" city in America. (The national average was only 33 percent at the time.) By 1910 the proportion of foreign stock had fallen only slightly, to 78.6 percent – still high enough to tie Milwaukee for first place among cities with more than 200,000 residents.

Germans, to no one's surprise, continued their demographic dominance. "Milwaukee is the most German city in the United States," the *Sentinel* declared in 1895, with no serious fear of contradiction. In 1910, years after the peak of immigration, first- and second-generation Germans still made up 53.5 percent of the city's residents – a clear majority. A local booster wrote in 1905 that "a visit to Milwaukee is almost like a visit to one of the cities of the Rhine," and

Edna Ferber, a *Milwaukee Journal* reporter from 1906 to 1909, looked back on a community that was "as German as Germany." Those statements were certainly exaggerations, but the Teutonic presence in Milwaukee was inescapable. Germans dominated the city's brewing, tanning, and milling industries, and they were nearly as prominent in the metal trades. German-language newspapers had more readers than the English dailies in the late 1800s, and George Brumder ran the nation's largest German publishing house from the monumental Germania Building on Wells Street. In a symbolic act of ethnic ascendancy, the Deutscher Club took over Alexander Mitchell's mansion after the Scottish tycoon's death and made it a leading center of *Gemütlichkeit.*

The Teutonic influence may have been most pronounced in the area of leisure-time pursuits. The typical German's fondness for beer gardens made Milwaukee one of the most pleasant places in America to spend a Sunday afternoon, whether patrons were taking in light opera at Schlitz Park, watching horse races at National Park, or enjoying the lake breezes at Pabst's Whitefish Bay Resort. The Musical Society, a pillar of community culture since 1850, maintained an admirably high standard of professionalism over the years, and Milwaukee was nearly overrun with lesser-known choral groups, from the *Sozialist Liedertafel* to the *Gemütlichkeit Mannerchor.* The Pabst Theater, built in 1895 on the ruins of an earlier opera house, won praise as the leading German-language stage west of New York or, some might have argued, Berlin. Nor were the visual arts forgotten. In the 1880s and '90s, German artists made Milwaukee a national center

The bookbinding department at Germania Publishing on Wells Street, the largest German-language publishing house in the country

Milwaukee Journal Sentinel

of panorama painting, a genre featuring colossal re-creations of historical scenes.

The German community was identified, for better or worse, as the wellspring of Milwaukee's deepest character traits. Local observers pointed to the thousands of duplexes popping up in the northwestern wards as solid evidence of Germanic thrift; even the humblest machinist, it was argued, could afford a pleasant home if he had a tenant to help with the mortgage. Others felt that Teutonic frugality could be carried too far. *Harper's Weekly* (July 18, 1891) declared that the city's aversion to risk doomed Milwaukee to second-class status: "Conservatism and caution are too strongly intrenched in her counting-rooms and factories for her to hope to enter into active competition with the proverbial dash and enterprise of Chicago." The article's author claimed to know precisely where the problem lay. "Milwaukee's conservatism," wrote W.W. Howard, "is due to its German population almost entirely." *The*

Book of Milwaukee, a 1901 promotional tabloid, returned the salvo, giving local Germans credit for a standard of civic housekeeping that still turns visitors' heads:

> *The Germans that form so large a proportion of the population couple closely their ideas of thrift with cleanliness, and the result is that the streets and alleys are always kept free from dirt and litter, and anyone coming here for the first time from a city like Chicago, where dirt abounds, and has abounded for so long that the residents have come to regard it as a necessity, exclaim with surprise at the cleanliness of the streets.*

The city of Milwaukee, clean streets and all, was clearly a proud citadel of Germanism at the turn of the century. German-speaking residents had the numbers, the confidence, and the institutional strength to impress their habits and values on the city as a whole. But the century's turn may have been the community's swan song as well. Historian Kathleen Conzen argues that Milwaukee's early Germans created a

The Pabst Theater was nationally known for its German-language stage productions in the years before World War I.

Milwaukee County Historical Society

Milwaukee Journal Sentinel

Panorama painting became a German specialty. Anticipating the motion picture, these huge canvases were scrolled across specially constructed stages for the entertainment of a mass audience.

Milwaukee Public Library

Ein Prosit! *Patrons at Pabst's Whitefish Bay Resort toasted their health even as Milwaukee's German culture entered a long period of decline.*

self-contained society, one parallel to but separate from the English-speaking social networks. By 1900 the separate societies had begun to merge, particularly at the higher income levels. As wealthy families moved north along the lake bluff, from Yankee Hill to Prospect Avenue and then on to North Point and Prospect Hill, Germans were more and more conspicuous in the migration. When the Milwaukee Country Club opened in what is now Shorewood in 1895, its members included five Falks, two Pabsts, and two Vogels. Franz Falk, the pioneer brewer, had spent his years in America as a Catholic and a Democrat; his younger sons developed a preference for the Episcopal Church and the Republican Party. Even Milwaukeeans of less abundant means began to shed their German associations after two or three generations. At its fiftieth-anniversary concert in 1900, the Milwaukee Musical Society presented works like *In the Sunny South* and closed with *The Star-Spangled Banner*. Ten years later, a majority of local residents, Germans included, were reading their news in English. If Milwaukee's reign as the nation's *Deutsch-Athen* was not yet over, its peak had certainly passed.

The city's Polish community was growing in both numbers and self-assurance during the same years. Emigration from Poland actually accelerated through the turn of the century – a clear response to the abundance of industrial jobs in Milwaukee. Although partitioned Poland still lacked its own column in the federal census tables, local estimates placed the population of the city's *Polonia* at 30,000 in the late 1880s, 40,000 in 1895, and 70,000 in 1910, giving the community a firm hold on second place throughout the period.

As the largest of the "new" immigrant groups and as highly visible participants in the labor disturbances of 1886, the Poles were viewed with suspicion by some of their fellow citizens. In 1895 Michael Kruszka, founding editor of the *Kuryer Polski*, wrote that "the Polanders experienced here more prejudice from different sources than any other nationality." Even neutral observers tended to emphasize the group's foreignness. Charles King, Rufus King's son and an author of some renown, described the neighborhood surrounding St. Stanislaus Church in an 1891 *Cosmopolitan* article:

> The twin towers of the Polish church stand
> like double sentries high in air, and all around
> them, in that far-away section, hundreds of
> comfortable little homes are grouped where one
> might wander for a week and hear no language
> but that of Kosciusko.

King wasn't exaggerating when he depicted the houses around St. Stanislaus as "little." In the late 1800s, Polish immigrants covered hundreds of square blocks with undersized homes on undersized lots, particularly in the district south of Mitchell Street. The Fourteenth Ward – the heart of the South Side *Polonia* – was Milwaukee's most densely settled neighborhood at the turn of the century, and a novel building practice soon made it even denser. As time passed and finances permitted, thousands of homeowners jacked up their original cottages and bricked in half-basement living units on the ground floor. The result was a house type universally known as the "Polish flat," a clever and certainly a cost-effective means of adding space without incurring the expense of new construction. By 1910 the Polish flat was as common on the South Side as frame duplexes were on the German North Side.

Not everyone welcomed the Polish version of "additive architecture." A 1910 housing survey reported dismal living conditions in the Fourteenth Ward: "On each side of every street or avenue is an almost continuous line of basements, miles and miles of gloomy, poorly lighted, damp, unventilated, overcrowded rooms." Another observer described the neighborhood's residents as "modern cave-dwellers." When the Polish flat was combined with the alley house – another Milwaukee institution – densities approached European levels; it was not uncommon for four or even five families, each with several children, to share the same thirty-foot lot.

Polish flats, or raised basement duplexes, gave immigrant families more room and a new source of income as well as enormous pride in ownership.

UWM Urban Archives

Public health officials worried that such extreme congestion would encourage the spread of disease. The South Side's mortality rate was, in fact, the city's highest in 1910, but there was no denying that the Polish flat met a deeply felt need. The immigrants brought with them the same land-hunger, the same passion for property, that had animated their peasant ancestors.

Thousands of Polish Milwaukeeans turned out for the dedication of Gen. Tadeusz Kosciuszko's statue in 1905.

Milwaukee County Historical Society

The drawbacks of the resulting "basement duplex" were obvious, but so were the benefits: a welcome source of rental income, extra space for growing families, and enhanced self-esteem. When they erected a single-story cottage on its narrow lot, the immigrants were landowners. When they converted it to a Polish flat, they became land*lords* as well.

In virtually every Polish neighborhood, there was a startling contrast between the modest scale of the newcomers' homes and the majesty of their churches. As new Catholic parishes were organized to serve the expanding population, the South Side's skyline was studded with steeples. Each marked an attempt, however unconscious, to re-create the primary associations of the Old World village. The church was the focal point of community, the hub around which life revolved, and parishes were generally synonymous with their neighborhoods. It is still not uncommon for local residents, even non-Catholics, to speak of growing up in "St. Vincent's" or "St. Hedwig's."

Of all the grand churches that rose from Milwaukee's *Polonia*, the grandest by far was St. Josaphat's, on Sixth and Lincoln. At the turn of the century, the parish had at least 12,000 members, making it, in all likelihood, the largest congregation of any faith in the state. When his parishioners outgrew one building, St. Josaphat's pastor, Father Wilhelm Grutza, engaged architect Erhard Brielmaier to design a more commodious church. Brielmaier's plans, finished in 1895, specified a brick and terra-cotta structure that was, in essence, a scaled-down version of St. Peter's in Rome. The architect was soon called upon to make a few changes. According to parish legend, Father Grutza was on a brick-buying trip to Chicago when he learned that the federal post office there was slated for demolition. Spying a bargain, the pastor bought the entire building and had it shipped, stone by stone and pillar by pillar, to Milwaukee. Brielmaier revised his plans and went to work. The result, completed in 1901, was the largest church in Milwaukee and one of the largest domed structures in the world.

St. Josaphat's Church was also one of the most expensive buildings in the city. The parish moved into its new home with a debt exceeding $7 million in current dollars – an amount well beyond the means of poorly paid industrial workers. As the community fell behind in its payments, rumors spread that St. Josaphat's creditors planned to turn the grand church into an opera house. There was an even more immediate danger. Roughly one-third of the debt was held by parishioners who had taken out second mortgages on their homes and loaned the proceeds to the building fund. If the institutional lenders had foreclosed, hundreds of families would literally have lost the roofs over their heads. It would be hard to find more compelling evidence of the importance that virtually every immigrant community attached to its places of worship.

Disaster was averted in 1910. At the urgent request of Archbishop Sebastian

Messmer, a group of Franciscan friars assumed responsibility for St. Josaphat's, and Milwaukee's other Catholic parishes assumed a third of the congregation's debt. Even with a rescue plan in place, the struggle was far from over. It took fifteen years (and a heroic round of picnics, plays, pageants, and penny drives) for the parish to retire its share of the debt, and only then did decoration of the cavernous interior begin. In 1929, more than thirty years after ground was broken, the work was finished and St. Josaphat's Church was declared a basilica – the ecclesiastical equivalent of all-star status.

Although none approached the Poles in size, Milwaukee was flooded with other "new" immigrant groups – Italians, Greeks, Serbs, Slovenes, Croats, and eastern European Jews – who had come to the city in search of work. It seemed there was always someone willing to take the entry-level jobs in Milwaukee's booming industrial economy. Those jobs were frequently dirty, demanding, and dangerous, not to mention poorly compensated, but they provided a welcome alternative to hopeless poverty in the homeland. The industrial immigrants did not, however, follow identical settlement patterns. All of Milwaukee's Polish neighborhoods, including St. Josaphat's parish, developed on the city's fringe, a geographic expression of the typical Pole's fervent desire to own a home – be it ever so humble. Other immigrants obeyed one of the great unwritten rules of urban life: The newest groups get the oldest houses. The majority of Milwaukee's newcomers lived within a mile of downtown, in hand-me-down neighborhoods left behind as earlier residents moved out to greener pastures.

The Italians were the largest group to settle in one of the old receiver neighborhoods. Beginning in the 1890s, they laid claim to the city's Third Ward, the area lying between the river and the lake south of downtown. The "Bloody Third" was the cradle of Irish civilization in Milwaukee, but its first residents had begun to move out in the 1870s and '80s, most of them to West Side

St. Josaphat's Church, shown under construction in 1897 and in its completed state, was a towering symbol of arrival for Milwaukee's Poles. Declared a basilica in 1929, it remains the largest church in the city.

Archdiocese of Milwaukee

Milwaukee Public Library

from *Milwaukee after the Fire*

A disastrous 1892 fire reduced much of the Third Ward to rubble.

Milwaukee Public Library

Sicilian immigrants rebuilt the neighborhood. The Blessed Virgin of Pompeii Church on Jackson Street was their spiritual anchor and the center of activity at festa *time.*

neighborhoods like Tory Hill and Merrill Park. Their flight was hastened by a catastrophic 1892 fire that destroyed twenty square blocks in the Ward and left perhaps 2,000 people homeless. The Italians, nearly all of them Sicilians, followed the Irish, establishing a community that rivaled or even exceeded the Polish South Side in population density and ethnic homogeneity. To the south, in Bay View, a smaller colony of northern and central Italians developed within walking distance of the rolling mill. Both communities grew rapidly through the turn of the century; the number of Italian-born Milwaukeeans climbed from a few hundred in 1890 to 1,740 in 1900 and 4,788 in 1910.

Like the Irish before them, the Third Ward Italians generally worked as laborers, earning some of the lowest wages in the city, but several took an interest in the fresh fruit and vegetable business. They typically began with small, cumbersome pushcarts, and the most successful graduated to wholesale houses of their own on a stretch of Broadway long known as Commission Row. Like their Irish predecessors, the Italians were also reflexively Catholic. In 1905 they dedicated Blessed Virgin of Pompeii Church on Jackson Street near Clybourn. Fondly remembered as "the little pink church," it was a painfully small but lushly decorated building with room for perhaps 200 worshipers. The congregation's architect was none other than Erhard Brielmaier, the same man who had designed St. Josaphat's with a seating capacity of 2,500. *Madonna di Pompeii* was the focal point of the festivals that were inseparable from summer in the Italian Third Ward. Each *festa* was sponsored by one of several religious societies whose members came from the same Sicilian village and venerated the same patron saint; all featured food, music, processions, and ear-splitting fireworks. Festa Italiana, the oldest and largest of Milwaukee's lakefront ethnic festivals, is rooted squarely in the old Third Ward tradition.

Greek immigrants tended to settle on the northern edge of downtown, both east and west of the Milwaukee River. Less numerous than the Italians (1,122 in 1910) and somewhat later to arrive (most coming after 1900), the Greeks did not fit the stereotype of the family-centered newcomer. The overwhelming majority were young, single males who had every intention of returning to Greece after they had made their fortunes in America. Industrial jobs, particularly in Milwaukee's tanneries, were the most popular route to prosperity, loosely defined. Small businesses – candy stores, short-order restaurants, saloons, and grocery stores – provided another avenue for those who could afford the start-up costs. The street trades offered opportunities at the most basic level. African Americans, who had controlled the city's shoeshine trade for years, howled when the Greeks (and a few Italians) cut the price of a shine from ten cents to a nickel in 1905. Their protests were futile; within a decade or two, most of Milwaukee's shoeshine parlors were run by Greeks.

Whatever their original intentions, most of the young men came to regard their American exile as more than temporary. Visions of a triumphant return to the village lost their glamour after a few years of steady work and growing social ties. Stanley Stacy, a pillar of the Greek community until his death in 1984, remembered an immigrant who lived above the Stacy family's tobacco store on Juneau Avenue:

courtesy Anthony T. Machi

This man, our tenant, was working as a cook in a place on Wisconsin Avenue. He had come over here with the same idea as the others: to make some money and go back. He had two daughters who were babies in Greece. When he would get ready to go back, he would buy a couple pair of shoes for a two- and a three-year-old. Well, something would happen and he would stay. The following year, he would buy shoes for a three- and a four-year-old. Something would happen again, and he would stay. This went on for years. The girls were in their twenties when he brought them to this country. When we finally cleaned out his apartment, there was a big trunk full of shoes.

The street trades, particularly the fresh fruit and vegetable business, provided many Sicilians with a living. Tony Machi posed with horse and wagon in 1912.

Signs of permanence multiplied as the years passed. The most important by far was the organization of Annunciation Greek Orthodox Church in 1906. The community's bachelors worshiped in rented quarters until 1914, when they built a thoroughly Byzantine structure on the corner of Broadway and Knapp. The church provided concrete evidence that the Greeks were in Milwaukee to stay.

Churches served as anchors of community for a variety of other Balkan immigrants, most of whom arrived somewhat later than the Greeks. Serbs began to settle in Walker's Point before 1900, attracted by the abundance of industrial jobs in the area, and they were numerous enough by 1912 to establish St. Sava Serbian Orthodox Church. The congregation held its first services in a private home but soon moved into more dignified quarters on Third Street near National Avenue. Slovenes lived in the same blocks and held similar jobs, but they were predominantly Catholic. Many worshiped at Holy Trinity, an old German parish, until 1916, when the Slovenes organized St. John the Evangelist Church and built a home of their own on Ninth and Mineral Streets. Croats, in the meantime, were establishing a foothold on the North Side, near the Schlitz brewery. In 1917 they formed Sacred Heart Catholic Church and began to worship in a second-hand building on Seventh and Galena Streets. Lumped together as "Yugoslavs" when their homelands confederated in 1918, Milwaukee's Serbs, Slovenes, and Croats kept a careful distance from each other.

Jewish immigrants were somewhat more concentrated than their Balkan counterparts.

Annunciation Greek Orthodox Church, "the church that bachelors built," stood on the northern edge of downtown.

The church was the backdrop for this funeral photograph of immigrant mother Gregoria Karides. Such photos were usually intended for relatives in the old country.

Milwaukee County Historical Society

courtesy Gregoria Karides Suchy

178

By 1910 there were roughly 10,000 Jews in the city, most of them recent arrivals from Russia, Ukraine, Lithuania, Poland, and other states of eastern Europe. Their principal community was bordered roughly by Third and Thirteenth Streets between Juneau and North Avenues – once the very heart of German Milwaukee. The new residents organized nearly a dozen synagogues in the neighborhood, all of them Orthodox, between 1882 and 1914. One of the newcomers was an eight-year-old Russian emigrant named Goldie Mabowehz, whose family moved into a Walnut Street apartment in 1906. An early shopping trip to Schuster's Department Store on Third Street made a lasting impression:

> *... I was delighted by my pretty new clothes, by the soda pop and ice cream and by the excitement of being in a real skyscraper, the first five-story building I had ever seen. In general, I thought Milwaukee was wonderful. Everything looked so colorful and fresh, as though it had just been created, and I stood for hours staring at the traffic and the people.... I spent the first days in Milwaukee in a kind of trance.*

Years later, as prime minister of Israel, Golda Meir became perhaps the most famous ex-Milwaukeean in the world.

Some Jewish immigrants were tradesmen like Golda's father (a carpenter in the Milwaukee Road shops); others were shopkeepers like Golda's mother (a grocer). Virtually all were struggling to make ends meet. Jews who had arrived earlier, most of them German by background and Reform by practice, overcame their native distaste and organized a number of social welfare programs for the newcomers. One of the most fondly remembered was the Milwaukee

St. Sava Serbian Orthodox Cathedral

Serbs settled on the South Side. The first St. Sava Serbian Orthodox Church was a modest chapel on S. Third Street.

Jewish Museum Milwaukee

Eastern European Jews settled on the North Side. Harry Forman posed at his bar mitzvah in about 1910.

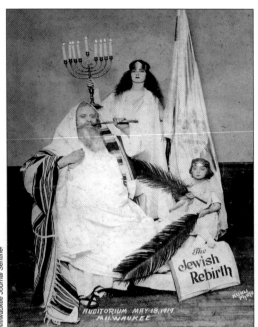

Milwaukee Journal Sentinel

Milwaukee County Historical Society

Jewish Settlement, which opened in a house on Fifth Street in 1900. The Settlement served roughly 1,300 people each week with a broad array of activities: children's clubs, sewing and cooking classes, an evening English-language school, athletic programs, literary circles, discussion groups, and a Sabbath school. The cooking classes were the province of a legendary figure named Lizzie Kander, who in 1901 published her favorite recipes in an easy-to-use guide she called *The Settlement Cookbook.* Thirty-four printings and 2 million copies later, Mrs. Kander's cookbook is still a reliable font of recipes for cooks of all backgrounds and a welcome source of revenue for Jewish charities.

Although the broad ethnic patterns were obvious even to casual observers, few sections of Milwaukee belonged exclusively, or even largely, to members of a single group. North Side Jews, for instance, shared "their" neighborhood with holdover Germans as well as Hungarians, Italians, Greeks, Croats, and African Americans, whose population neared the 1,000 mark in 1910. East Side Greeks had Italian, Irish, and German families for neighbors. Serbs and Slovenes shared Walker's Point, historically Milwaukee's most diverse neighborhood, with Germans, Norwegians, Czechs, Ukrainians, Greeks, and Bulgarians, among others. The Tory Hill community, later obliterated by the Marquette University campus, contained a liberal admixture of Croatian, Irish, German, and other European groups.

Yankees, in the meantime, continued to dominate Yankee Hill and adjacent sections of the East Side. They had been vastly outnumbered for decades, but the sons and daughters of the pioneers were still over-represented at the top of Milwaukee's social pyramid. The most prosperous had long since shed the harsher habits of their forebears. Those of Puritan lineage – the Presbyterians and Congregationalists – had outgrown their penchant for church trials and all-day services. Churches like Immanuel Presbyterian and St. Paul's Episcopal had become bastions of a tasteful, even genteel, Christianity that generally minded its own business. Some natives, however, viewed the proliferation of languages and cultures around them with alarm. On rare occasions, their contempt for Milwaukee's creeping Europeanism broke into the open. In 1891 Rev. Theodore Clifton preached a deliciously immoderate sermon on "City Evangelization" at Calvary Presbyterian Church:

> The cities are the cesspools where every form of wickedness concentrates, festers and propagates itself. Here the rich grow richer and the poor grow poorer, and the bitterness between them is intensified a hundred fold. Here the capitalist and the laborer are brought into the sharpest antagonism.... Here is the richest soil for communism, socialism, nihilism and anarchy, with all their untold miseries and horrors.
>
> We must remember that here are the headquarters of the beer-brewing interests of the West. Bacchus is worshipped at more than 1,000 saloons, yes, at about 1,300 of them – 100 altars erected to the worship of God and 1,300 of them to the worship of the devil! During the summer season beer gardens in every part of the city are thronged by men, women and children on the Sabbath day....
>
> The foreign population, with all that means of European scepticism and Sabbath breaking, is much larger proportionally than in many other societies. Every peril is here intensified – the perils of wealth, the perils of poverty, the perils of socialism, the perils of intemperance, the perils growing out of foreign immigration, the perils of ignorance and the perils of Romanism. No city in the land furnishes a richer soil for all the evils of our modern civilization which I have named, than Milwaukee. Looking upon her temples, her palaces and her hovels, Christ wept over Jerusalem. Were He back in the flesh, and were He to approach our city by lake or land, or walk through our streets, He would weep again.

Clifton's dim view of city life had its adherents, but others found much to praise in the continuing flow of immigrants. A few genuinely liked the cosmopolitan flavor contributed by the newcomers, while others cited more practical advantages. Immigrants provided a source of labor, particularly unskilled labor, that was vital to the city's booming industries. They multiplied the market for goods and services, from shingles to shoe repair. Perhaps most importantly, immigrants both old and new fueled Milwaukee's continuing ascent through the ranks of America's cities. The community's population climbed from 204,468 in 1890 to 285,315 in 1900 and 373,857 in 1910 – an 83-percent gain in twenty years. The increase of the latter decade alone exceeded the city's entire population in 1880. Milwaukee surged past Washington, Newark, New Orleans, and Cincinnati between 1890 and 1910, rising from sixteenth to fourteenth to twelfth place in the rankings. The city's steady progress was gleefully reported in the local media, and many found it easy to believe that Milwaukee was on the threshold of greatness.

Milwaukee at play: At the turn of the twentieth century, thousands of residents spent their few leisure hours in, on, or near the water.

(right)
A day at McKinley Beach

Milwaukee Journal Sentinel

(left)
A family of Bay View sailors in their Sunday best

(right)
Canoeists on the Milwaukee River, above the North Avenue dam

courtesy Meta Lawrie

Milwaukee Public Museum

(left)
Wonderland Amusement Park, now Hubbard Park in Shorewood

(right)
Ice-skaters on the upper Milwaukee River

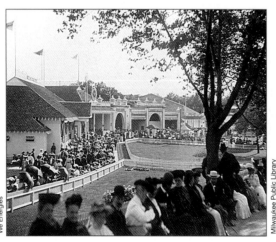

We Energies

Milwaukee Public Library

Greater Milwaukee

The city of Milwaukee couldn't hold all its residents at the turn of the century. As immigrants poured into the community, old neighborhoods were quickly overcrowded and new neighborhoods filled in as fast as houses could be built. The city's borders, practically frozen for years, were extended more than once to accommodate the growth. By 1900 Milwaukee's landward boundaries reached north to Keefe Avenue, west to roughly Thirty-Fifth Street, and south to Cleveland Avenue. Despite the annexations, Milwaukee remained one of the most densely settled communities in the country. In 1902 the city claimed America's third-highest number of persons per acre, trailing only Boston and Baltimore.

New suburbs relieved some of the congestion. Between 1892 and 1906, no fewer than eight suburbs came into being within the corporate limits of Milwaukee County. The flurry of incorporations was encouraged by more liberal state laws, but other forces played even more decisive roles. Industrial suburbs embodied the desire of employers for more land and more control. Residential suburbs embodied the desire of homeowners, most of them affluent, to choose their own tax rates and service levels. In both cases, suburban growth was aided immeasurably by electrification of the area's street railways – a story told later in this chapter.

Milwaukee's first suburb, ironically, surrendered its charter a few years before its younger siblings launched their careers. Bay View had once been beyond the pale of urban settlement, but Milwaukee reached its northern border, Lincoln Avenue, in the 1880s. As the city installed streetlights, sewers, and running water, residents on the Bay View side of Lincoln were increasingly unhappy with their kerosene lamps, backyard privies, and municipal wells. Most were quite willing to pay city taxes for city services, and in 1887 they voted overwhelmingly to join Milwaukee. After eight years of legal autonomy, a suburb became a neighborhood. The shift was accomplished with no loss of community identity; Bay View, in fact, resembled a woman who chose to marry without changing her name. Its 4,000 residents constituted the new Seventeenth Ward of Milwaukee, but "Bay View" still applied. More than a century later, the neighborhood remains one of the strongest in the city.

Turn-of-the-Century Milwaukee Suburbs			
Suburb	Year incorporated	1900 population	1910 population
Wauwatosa	1892	2,842	3,346
South Milwaukee	1892	3,392	6,092
Whitefish Bay	1892	512	542
Cudahy	1895	1,366	3,691
North Milwaukee	1897	1,049	1,860
East Milwaukee (Shorewood)	1900	—	707
West Allis	1902	—	6,645
West Milwaukee	1906	—	1,458

The old company town created the mold for suburbs farther south. Cudahy, its nearest neighbor, was nearly as dependent on Patrick Cudahy's giant meat-packing plant as Bay View was on its lakefront iron mill. Cudahy himself paid the village's incorporation fee in 1895, and his company provided local water service. Although he took paternal pride in the community's ultimate success, the Irish entrepreneur found its first years nerve-racking. "Whenever I saw

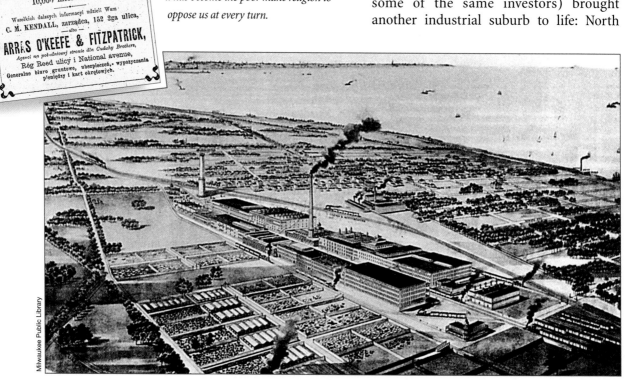

a cottage going up," Cudahy wrote in his 1912 memoirs, "I felt just that much more of a load on my back." Fully aware that seasonal layoffs would create hardships and hard feelings, he implored other industrialists to follow him south. They did so in impressive numbers, but even then Cudahy found that his role as the community's creator was no guarantee of respect:

Although the city is named Cudahy, and principally through my efforts it was built, I have the least to say about its politics of any other man living. If I attempt to favor the election of a candidate for a city office he is sure to be defeated, or if I ask for ever so small a favor from the common council, I am sure to be turned down. So well has the cheap politician succeeded in prejudicing the poor man against the rich man in Cudahy that it has become the poor man's religion to oppose us at every turn.

Still farther south, near the mouth of Oak Creek, the suburb of South Milwaukee was promoted into existence by a group of Milwaukee businessmen. Although its backers envisioned "a pleasant residence suburb, permanent and for summer months," the community's destiny was, like Bay View's and Cudahy's, industrial. Using time-honored incentives – free land and cash subsidies – the townsite's promoters labored diligently to lure manufacturers to their converted cow pasture. Their biggest catch by far was the Bucyrus Steam Shovel and Dredge Company (later Bucyrus-Erie), an enterprise that moved from Ohio in 1892. Other transplanted firms made everything from horseshoes to kitchen knives.

On the other side of the county, near the present intersection of Thirty-Fifth Street and Villard Avenue, the same dynamic (and some of the same investors) brought another industrial suburb to life: North

Milwaukee. The site's chief asset was its strategic location at the junction of two major railroad lines, one leading to Iron Mountain, the other to La Crosse. With trackside property increasingly scarce in Milwaukee, industrialists were quick to see the property's potential. Two large firms moved out from Milwaukee in the mid-1890s, one manufacturing bridges and the other bicycles, and dozens of smaller plants followed. By 1902 North Milwaukee was a bustling community with its own newspaper, three hotels, and a picturesque village hall that remains a prominent local landmark.

West Allis, the home of Wisconsin's largest manufacturer, became Milwaukee's largest industrial satellite. Allis-Chalmers acted like a magnet, pulling scores of employers (and thousands of their employees) west from the city. Most of the firms were, like Allis-Chalmers itself, involved in the metal trades, manufacturing every-

thing from steel tanks to steel springs, and one newcomer, Kearney & Trecker, produced machine tools that the others used to bend their metal. In 1904, underlining the close ties between the suburb and its industries, Theodore Trecker was elected village president.

West Milwaukee, sandwiched between West Allis and Milwaukee, was the youngest and smallest of the five industrial suburbs. Its dominant employer was the Pawling & Harnischfeger Company, which moved west from Walker's Point in 1905 after a disastrous fire at its original plant. (Henry Harnischfeger called the blaze "a blessing in disguise.") The community's excellent rail connections attracted other firms, including plants that produced malt (germinated barley) for local breweries. As West Milwaukee developed, the smokestacks and grain silos on its skyline contrasted sharply with the sylvan setting of

Villard Avenue was the main street of North Milwaukee, another industrial suburb on the northern end of the county.

the suburb's next-door neighbor, the National Soldiers' Home.

Two of Milwaukee's first residential suburbs – Whitefish Bay and East Milwaukee – developed miles from the nearest industry, a circumstance that was anything but accidental. Both were located along a scenic turnpike (now Lake Drive) that was hugely popular for Sunday carriage rides, and both began as summertime retreats for city-dwellers. In 1889 Capt. Frederick Pabst opened the Whitefish Bay Resort at what is now the foot of Henry Clay Street. His resort's band concerts, planked whitefish dinners, Ferris-wheel rides, and free-flowing beer attracted droves of pleasure-seekers – as many as 15,000 on a typical Sunday afternoon. Some came out from the city by bicycle or steam train, while the more adventurous paid a quarter to ride the *Bloomer Girl*, "a dainty little excursion steamer," from her downtown dock to the foot of the lake bluff in Whitefish Bay.

Only one mile south, in the future suburb of East Milwaukee, members of the Milwaukee Country Club gathered in 1895 to lay out a six-hole golf course on the west side of Lake Drive, just north of Edgewood Avenue. Soon enlarged to nine holes, the course provided a place for Milwaukee's upper crust to indulge their newfound passion for "pasture pool." Members who avoided the golf bug's bite could take part in tennis, lawn bowling, and trapshooting, as well as dinner and dancing in the sumptuously appointed clubhouse on the east side of the turnpike.

The country club and the summer resort were increasingly vulnerable as affluent home-seekers edged up the lake bluff from Milwaukee. The newcomers launched incorporation drives, and in 1892 Whitefish Bay, even though it was the more distant of the two settlements, was the first to become a village. The move was, in retrospect,

Whitefish Bay's best-known attraction was a resort developed on the lake bluff by the Pabst brewery.

premature. Although East Milwaukee was not incorporated until 1900, it quickly outpaced Whitefish Bay in population growth. Both suburbs eventually lost their original institutions; the Milwaukee Country Club moved to what is now River Hills in 1911, and the Pabst Whitefish Bay Resort closed in 1914. Suburban development continued in earnest, with only a brief pause for a name change. The symmetry represented by the suburbs of North, South, East, and West Milwaukee was ruined for all time in 1917, when East Milwaukee decided to call itself Shorewood.

Of the eight Milwaukee suburbs formed at the turn of the century, whether residential or industrial, Wauwatosa was the only one that had an appreciable history as a community. The water power of the Menomonee River had attracted Yankee settlers as early as 1837, giving rise to a crossroads hamlet known originally as Hart's Mills. Excellent transportation service, provided first by the Watertown Plank Road and then by the Milwaukee & Mississippi Railroad, kept the community growing; Wauwatosa prospered as a rural trading center that would not have looked entirely out of place in New England. It was not until the 1880s that Milwaukee commuters, drawn by Wauwatosa's first-rate rail connections, began to think of the settlement as a bedroom suburb. *Yenowine's News* (July 10, 1887) reported a transformation: "The old, quiet country village, a veritable 'Sleepy Hollow,' has awakened, and is throbbing with new life, infused by the bustling, tireless workers from the neighboring city." Incorporation followed in 1892, and Wauwatosa instantly became one of the largest as well as the least "artificial" of all the satellite communities.

Whatever their origins, Milwaukee's early suburbs developed at radically different rates of speed. Two of the earliest ran straight into the Panic of 1893; Whitefish Bay's pulse was barely detectable for a quarter-century, and South Milwaukee paused while the Bucyrus Company, its largest employer, went through receivership. West Allis and Cudahy, by contrast, expanded with only minor interruptions.

(top)
In 1895 the Milwaukee Country Club dedicated a lavish clubhouse on what is now Lake Drive in Shorewood.

(bottom)
The club's golfers took turns at "pasture pool" on the west side of the turnpike. The view is east from the present corner of Downer Avenue and Shorewood Boulevard.

Milwaukee Country Club

Milwaukee Country Club

From village to suburb: Downtown Wauwatosa in the 1890s

Prospect Avenue, and Yankee Hill. Ethnic patterns showed similar persistence through time and space: North Milwaukee shared the Germanism of Milwaukee's North Side, while Cudahy inherited much of the South Side's Polish flavor.

The suburbs may have been the city once removed, but they were also alternatives to the city; each hastened the movement of people and capital beyond municipal borders. No one at City Hall was unduly alarmed; the eight newly minted suburbs had a combined total of only 24,341 residents in 1910, less than 7 percent of Milwaukee's population. But the emergence of viable suburbs provided a solid platform for more incorporations and feverish growth later in the twentieth century.

As Milwaukee grew outward, it also grew upward. The community's rapid expansion, on both the urban and the suburban fronts, gave rise to a city center large enough to serve an emerging metropolis. Milwaukee never developed a central business district truly commensurate with its size, in part because Chicago tended to capture regional headquarters and in part because the city's neighborhoods spawned "downtowns" of their own, like Third Street on the North Side or Mitchell Street on the South Side. But the turn-of-the-century building boom was impressive nonetheless. Remade more than once by earlier generations, downtown was remade again, and a surprising number of the period's landmarks remained part of the local skyline at the turn of the next century.

Some of the most substantial new buildings reflected the success of homegrown entrepreneurs. With more than enough capital to keep their businesses growing, well-heeled brewers, tanners, and

Differences in ethnicity, income, and employment were even more pronounced. What the suburbs had in common was a formative connection with the city they left behind. Urban areas tend to grow centrifugally; they expand in predictable directions from a common center, and new districts generally take their identities from older districts one step closer to town. Thus industrial Bay View served as a model for industrial Cudahy and South Milwaukee, even though both new suburbs had lakefront sites every bit as stunning as the North Shore's. On the opposite side of the bay, the affluence of Shorewood and Whitefish Bay could be traced back to upper-income enclaves on North Point,

Downtown Milwaukee in the 1880s, on the verge of a building boom. The view is west on Grand (W. Wisconsin) Avenue.

Milwaukee Public Library

meat-packers invested the surplus in landmarks that paid civic as well as financial dividends. The elegant Pfister Hotel (1893) quickly became Milwaukee's premier hostelry, competing with other downtown hotels that bore the names of local business leaders: the Plankinton, the Pabst (or St. Charles), the Blatz, and the Schlitz. The Cudahy Tower Apartments (1909), originally the Buena Vista Flats, afforded their lucky residents a "good view" of Milwaukee Bay. The Pabst Theater (1895) staged the best in both German and English drama, and the Schlitz Palm Garden (1896), with its magnificent arched ceiling, was renowned for the finest in beer, food, and music. Of all the private structures that rose during the period, the most imposing was the thirteen-story Pabst Building (1892), which crowned the corner of Water Street and Wisconsin Avenue. The Pabst was a fitting symbol of the enormous changes that had taken place in the previous fifty years: On the very site of Solomon Juneau's humble trading post, a German-born brewer erected Milwaukee's "first skyscraper."

Hotels, office buildings, and beer gardens were built with profit as well as prestige in mind. One industrialist, Frederick Layton, created another landmark as an outright gift. Although he never achieved the same level of success as John Plankinton (his former partner) or Patrick Cudahy,

(left)

Completed in 1893, the Pfister Hotel set a new standard for elegance in downtown hostelries.

(right)

The Schlitz Palm Garden stood on what is now the site of the Grand Avenue retail mall.

meat-packing had made Layton a wealthy man. In 1888 the English immigrant decided to share his passion for art with other Milwaukeeans, erecting a spacious gallery on Jefferson Street, filling it with his own collection, and providing an endowment for its operation. The gift was valued at $290,000 – more than $5 million in current dollars and easily the largest act of philanthropy in nineteenth-century Milwaukee.

The Layton Art Gallery helped to put Milwaukee on the cultural map, and public spending furthered the cause. The Public Library and Museum (1898) united two of the city's most important cultural resources in a single neoclassical edifice at Ninth and Wisconsin. It was not an easy marriage, particularly as both institutions grew, but the library and museum managed to share quarters without bloodshed until the mid-1960s, when the museum moved to a striking new home across the

street. Another tax-funded landmark graced the eastern end of downtown: the Federal Building (1899), whose massive granite tower served as counterpoint to the clock tower of the nearby North Western Railroad depot. One more public building of note rose on the West Side: the Auditorium (1909), a stately convention hall that took the place of the old Industrial Exposition Building on the same site.

Of all the buildings that emerged on the local skyline at the turn of the century, either public or private, none was more prominent than City Hall (1895). It was the period's crowning glory: the tallest structure in town, its first million-dollar building, and an affirmation of Milwaukee's right to be recognized as a major American city. But the building, for all its merits, was less significant than what transpired inside. It is on the axis of City Hall that this narrative turns finally to politics.

Landmarks for a new century (clockwise from top): the Public Library and Museum, the Milwaukee Auditorium, the Layton Art Gallery (with founder Frederick Layton), and the Pabst Building, Milwaukee's "first skyscraper."

Governing in the Gilded Age

Milwaukee was more than the sum of its parts. The budding metropolis was more than a collection of industries, ethnic groups, geographic enclaves, and civic landmarks. Those were the elements of the community's chemistry; they created Milwaukee's underlying structure and supported the daily routines of its residents. They did not, however, constitute a common life. It was in the political arena that the various elements met and mixed. It was in the continuing act of self-government that diverse and often opposed interests converged and reacted, sometimes with explosive results.

Two great facts shaped Milwaukee's political climate in the later 1800s: the city's overwhelming Europeanism, and its thoroughly industrial character. Those were the dual constants, but they had different impacts at different times. The community had been a Democratic stronghold in the frontier period, simply because Democrats were the party of immigrants and Milwaukee was a city of immigrants. A genuine balance of power developed after the Civil War. Republicans had led the North to victory, boosting their prestige enormously, and upwardly mobile immigrants found much to like in the party's platforms. Milwaukee became a truly bipartisan city; between 1870 and 1910, local voters elected eight Democratic and five Republican mayors, and the two sides served roughly equal periods in office.

There were clear differences between the parties after the Civil War, but they were a matter of demographics rather than dogma. The Democrats had predictable bases of ethnic support: always the Irish, usually the Poles, sometimes the Germans. The Republicans continued to attract natives, especially Yankee natives, and businessmen of all backgrounds. What the parties shared was probably more important than what kept them apart. Both were thoroughly immersed in the values and the vices of the Gilded Age. The term was coined by Mark Twain to describe the extremes of a period between roughly 1865 and 1900, a time of rapid economic expansion, dizzying material progress, and easy political virtue. The buoyancy of the era encouraged everyone to grab for a piece of the pie. Robber barons and political bosses vied for space on the front page, and venality, not morality, seemed to govern both public and corporate life. A strong countercurrent of reform was never far beneath the surface, in Milwaukee and elsewhere. It welled up most memorably in the labor victories of 1886 and 1887, but the ease with which the old-line parties closed ranks to end that revolt clearly demonstrated who was in charge.

The representative figure of the Gilded Age in Milwaukee was John Hinsey, and the representative issue was electricity. Hinsey arrived in 1865 to take a job as claims agent for the Milwaukee & St. Paul Railroad, but his real calling was politics. By 1876 Hinsey was a prominent alderman and the Democratic Party's county chairman; by 1885 he was president of the Common Council and undisputed master of the party's local machine. The Republican *Milwaukee Sentinel* (March 19, 1885) blasted Hinsey as

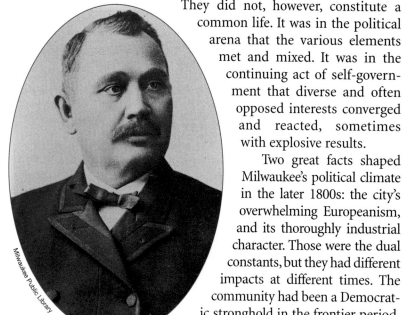

"Boss" John Hinsey, a politician of easy virtue and considerable influence

"an irresponsible and incompetent political boss" who acted as "supreme authority in matters of legislation affecting the interests of 150,000 people."

Electricity, in the meantime, had crossed the threshold from the inventor's laboratory to the real world of applications. The lights went on in Milwaukee in the early 1880s, and two of the city's brightest spots, fittingly, were the Schlitz beer garden and the Pabst brewery. All of the early installations were private systems powered by private generators; Milwaukee had no central-station service years after much smaller cities had developed public systems. The deficiency was not technical but political. Because they had to use city streets and city sidewalks, aspiring utilities needed city franchises, and the Common Council had locked the door to all comers. It was widely believed that the Milwaukee Gas Light Company owned the key. Hoping to preserve their company's street-lighting monopoly, gas lobbyists pounced whenever an electrical applicant appeared at City Hall, and they controlled enough votes to keep Milwaukee unplugged indefinitely.

It should be remembered that local aldermen were unpaid, part-time officials who had the power to award enormously lucrative contracts. They were, as a group, easily tempted, and "boodling" (taking bribes) became an accepted feature of doing business with the city. In the heat of a particularly spirited franchise debate, one Council member scorched another with the ultimate Gilded Age insult: "Alderman Richards is of so little importance that he is not worth a cent to anybody to buy him." In such a transparently corrupt atmosphere, public policy was often set by the highest bidder, and street-lighting was no

exception. In 1885 the Milwaukee Gas Light Company was apparently outbid by Sheridan S. Badger, a Chicago-based "electric light broker." Badger had enlisted the help of "Boss" John Hinsey, who pushed the lighting franchise through a suddenly pliant Common Council by a margin of twenty-six to six. In a related development, Hinsey became part-owner of the Badger Illuminating Company.

The boss's self-dealing was even more obvious in the transit field. It was generally acknowledged that Milwaukee's three horse-car companies were inadequate to the needs of a growing city; the animals simply generated too much manure and not enough speed. There was intense debate, however, about which technology should replace them – cable, steam, or electricity – and an equally spirited struggle for a municipal franchise. The winner, announced in 1887,

The Industrial Exposition Building was among the first Milwaukee landmarks to be lighted with electricity.

We Energies

The West Side Street Railway, Milwaukee's smallest horsecar company, won the city's electrification derby in 1890.

We Energies

was the Milwaukee Cable Railway Company, whose resident manager was none other than John Hinsey. The politician's lobbying on behalf of his own company was one of the most bald-faced conflicts of interest in the city's history, but few citizens seemed to mind. They did mind, however, when Hinsey sat on his franchise for nearly two years without laying a single section of track. Apparently hoping to sell out to serious developers at a profit, the boss flounced from the underground cable system to storage batteries to overhead wires without actually starting construction. The

frustrated *Sentinel* (August 8, 1889) predicted that he would request a franchise "for the use of hydraulic or balloon or some other power." "We imagine," groused the newspaper, "that wind alone will be used for Mr. Hinsey's line."

An increasingly restive Common Council, prodded by laborites elected in the wake of the Bay View shootings, finally broke ranks with Hinsey. In the autumn of 1889, over their president's deeply felt objections, members of the Council opened the door to practically any firm that wanted to use electricity, whether for lighting or for transit. The result was a furious race to electrify. The victor, on the transit side, was the West Side Street Railway, long Milwaukee's smallest horsecar line. On April 3, 1890, a West Side electric car whizzed down Wells Street like "lightning on roller skates." Other companies (including Hinsey's) followed shortly, and a *Sentinel* headline recorded the passing of an era: "Horses Sold Cheap."

The short-term result was competitive chaos. New firms practically tripped over each other in the effort to bring power and light to the masses, and the local utility scene dissolved into a maze of crossed wires and mismatched tracks. Boss Hinsey's influence ended in 1894, when he left the scene of his crimes for new adventures in Chicago. That left a Gilded-Age odd couple to break up the free-for-all and bring a semblance of order to the process of electrification. The senior member of the pair was Henry Villard, a New York City tycoon who already headed two giants – the Northern Pacific Railroad and the Edison General Electric Company. Villard wanted to develop a national utility empire as well, and he decided to start in Milwaukee. His junior partner was the Cream City's own Henry Clay Payne, a Yankee who had failed as a shopkeeper but found spectacular success as chairman of Wisconsin's Republican Party. Villard's capital and Payne's organizational skills were an unbeatable combination. In 1890 the two Henrys formed the Milwaukee Street Railway Company and proceeded to buy up every lighting and transit firm in the area. With substantial effort, they melded the loose ends into the first integrated utility in America – the first, in other words, to produce energy for lighting, traction, and power under a single management. That utility is still doing business as We Energies.

The return of order did not mean the end of dubious political entanglements. Villard and Payne wanted multiple franchises, light-handed regulation, and sympathetic officials, and they did their best to build (or buy) a receptive Common Council. It was no accident that Edward Wall, chairman of Wisconsin's Democratic Party, became a Street Railway executive, with full responsibility for the lighting side of the business. Wall, the Democratic boss, worked with Payne, the Republican boss, to create an integrated utility. They were strange bedfellows by modern standards, but the pair illustrated perfectly the unholy fusion of profits and politics that typified the Gilded Age.

As Villard, Payne, and Wall were assembling their model utility, two unexpected developments radically altered the local political climate. The first was the Bennett Law controversy. In 1889, hoping to raise the state's educational standards and halt the growth of child labor, the Republican-controlled legislature passed a measure making school attendance mandatory for children between the ages of seven and fourteen. One feature of the Bennett Law was little-noticed at first: a requirement that all schools, including parochial schools, teach their students "reading, writing, arithmetic and

Two Henrys dominated Milwaukee's utility scene, often to the detriment of local politics. Henry Payne (left) supplied the organizational skills, and Henry Villard (below) provided the money.

We Energies

*Scenes from a new era in
public transit (clockwise
from top left):*

Milady alighting from
a downtown car

Early automobiles
jostled with streetcars on
E. Wisconsin Avenue.

The Wells Street viaduct:
not for the faint of heart

Milwaukee's streetcar
system in 1897

Major lines converged at
Plankinton and Wisconsin
Avenues.

STREET
RAILWAY
MAP
— OF THE —
CITY OF MILWAUKEE.
PUBLISHED BY
EVAN EVANS,
1897.
Copyright applied for.

196

United States history, in the English language." No faith is so pure as when it's threatened. Wisconsin's Catholics and Lutherans – the immigrant religions – read the language provision as a frontal assault on their collective way of life. Germans, Poles, Irishmen, and other Europeans rose up as one and threw the Republicans out of office. Democrat George Peck, a journalist who had won national renown as the creator of *Peck's Bad Boy*, became Milwaukee's mayor in the spring of 1890 and advanced to the governor's office in fall. The Bennett Law sparked one of the most dramatic routs in Wisconsin's political history, and it helped to mobilize voters, particularly immigrant voters, who had once been content to sit on the sidelines. They learned firsthand that people of widely varied, even antagonistic, backgrounds could wield enormous power when roused to fight a common foe.

The second watershed event was the Panic of 1893. In the depression that followed, the suffering of the urban industrial class was acute. With unemployment running as high as forty percent and relief efforts pathetically disjointed, Milwaukee's jobless residents finally took to the streets. On the morning of August 22, 1893, a crowd of 1,500, most of them South Side Poles, gathered in Courthouse Square and called Mayor John Koch out of his office. One of the group's leaders, speaking in German, stated the facts simply: "Our wives and children are starving. We must have bread." When Koch could promise no relief, the crowd staged an impromptu parade through the streets of downtown. The only casualties, reported the *Milwaukee Journal*, were some unlucky Italian fruit-peddlers:

If there were any doubt in the minds of the spectators as to the truth of the statement that the men were really hungry, it passed away quickly as the Italians pushing carts loaded with bananas came up the street. In a moment they were surrounded by the crowd, their carts tipped over and the fruit taken. Some of the men in their eagerness never stopped to remove the skins from the fruit but ate it as they picked it from the street.

George Peck, the humorist who became mayor and then governor in the Democratic landslide of 1890

A determined stand by the police prevented more serious trouble, but the workers' dissatisfaction was apparent. They shared a growing belief, common since the Bay View incident, that the economic and political system was in dire need of basic reform, and they were ready to consider alternatives far more sweeping than the nostrums offered by the old-line parties. The Bennett Law flap tended to politicize ethnic voters; the Panic of 1893 helped to radicalize them.

The beginnings of a new order were apparent in the sparks that flew between the public and the Milwaukee Street Railway Company. The fledgling utility had slipped into bankruptcy during the hard times, only to rise from the ashes in early 1896 with the same management and a different name: The Milwaukee Electric Railway and Light Company. TMER&L's leaders found themselves operating in a changed political climate after the depression. The Gilded Age was ending, and support for laissez-faire capitalism was fading fast. Post-panic Milwaukeeans found their hometown utility suspect on several counts. It was, first of all, a private company that controlled a public necessity. Local residents had grown accustomed to bright nights and "rapid transit"; streetcar lines were literally lifelines for developing neighborhoods as well as new suburbs. The wisdom of trusting such an important resource to the tender mercies of a monopoly was increasingly open to question. It didn't help that the company was controlled by New York millionaires; Henry Villard and his Wall Street cronies were anything but sympathetic figures on the streets of Milwaukee. There was, finally, the matter of Henry Payne himself: a monopolist, a political boss, and a suspected corrupter of lawmakers on every level. Resentful of power, tired of privilege, and fed up with graft, the fare-paying public turned on its supposed benefactors. Payne became the man Milwaukeeans loved to hate, and his company emerged as the ready-made villain in a political morality play that lasted for the next forty years.

The first act in that play was the 1896 streetcar strike. When TMER&L's motor-men and conductors demanded a raise and union recognition, Henry Payne react-ed decisively, berating his employees, im-porting 1,200 replacement workers, and adamantly refusing to bargain. "Arbi-trate?," he huffed. "The company has noth-ing to arbitrate." Payne was woefully ignorant of the public mood. In an out-pouring of support that shocked even the most hopeful union leaders, local residents mounted a near-total boycott of the transit system. Hundreds of Milwaukeeans wore badges declaring, "To Ride Gives Me a Payne." Hotels refused to house the strike-breakers, forcing the company to set up cots in its carbarns. Grocers wouldn't fill TMER&L's orders, forcing Payne to buy his supplies in Chicago. When Mayor William Rauschenberger urged union members to compromise, his butcher refused to sell him meat. The strike wore on for two months and ended only after some mis-guided militants fired on a pair of passen-ger cars. TMER&L won the dispute, but the company lost every last ounce of public good will.

Motormen on the march: The streetcar strike of 1896 attracted a massive outpouring of public support.

The breadth and intensity of support for the strikers, most of it entirely spontaneous, underlined the community's discontent with the status quo. The situation was ripe for an organizer, someone who could translate public indignation into action. Henry Payne's fellow Republicans were not about to spearhead a crusade for better government in Milwaukee, and the city's Socialists were not yet a sound alternative. That left a Democrat, David Stuart Rose, to gallop in on a white horse. Born and raised in Darlington, Wisconsin, Rose was a small-town lawyer who had moved to the big city in 1886. Dapper, debonair, and blessed with a silver tongue, he was the Democratic candidate for mayor in 1898. Although he was nominally running against industrialist William Geuder, Rose made "the streetcar ring" his real opponent. He charged that Milwaukeeans were already "the humble slaves of that monopolistic power" and contended that a Republican victory "would be equivalent to the election of the officers of the streetcar company to the office of mayor." With enthusiastic support from Robert Schilling and other long-time reformers, Rose won in a walk.

David Rose on the stump and David Rose in office were two different people. The Common Council had already declared war on TMER&L, passing an ordinance that required the utility to cut its streetcar fares from a nickel to four cents. When the measure was voided by a federal court in 1898, the aldermen promptly passed it again. Rose was more conciliatory. Despite his shameless utility-bashing on the campaign trail, the new mayor quickly answered TMER&L's call for "a cessation of hostilities." In negotiations that dragged on for nearly eighteen months, he hammered

Mayor David S. Rose, the "Apollo in figure" who took Milwaukee politics to a new low.

Milwaukee Journal Sentinel

out a deal that included the four-cent fare but also extended the company's existing franchises through 1934. The mayor's erstwhile supporters were livid when the Common Council approved the agreement. The new franchise, they charged, surrendered "the rights of citizens yet unborn" and placed the utility beyond public control for more than a generation. (No one noticed, or cared, that TMER&L had agreed to freeze its transit revenues for thirty-five years.) The circumstances of the measure's passage in early 1900 – behind closed doors and despite court injunctions – fed perceptions that something unseemly had occurred. Henry Payne had been much in evidence before the voting, and it was widely assumed

City of Milwaukee

The Common Council of 1898-99 in its new City Hall chambers

than by his logic. His eloquence and force as a public speaker attracted national attention and his friends predicted a brilliant future for him.... No man in Milwaukee ever attained greater personal popularity.

Rose was an adroit politician as well as a formidable campaigner. Although he was deeply irreligious until a deathbed conversion to Catholicism, the mayor carefully cultivated the Catholic vote, particularly the Polish immigrant vote. Visits to South Side parishes were frequent, and the candidate sometimes brought more than his glib tongue: One of the stained-glass windows in St. Josaphat's Basilica was a gift from Rose and his second wife.

On the opposite end of the constituent spectrum, the mayor had an unusually warm relationship with purveyors of what most citizens regarded as vice. In his memoirs, Rose recalled the lofty ambitions of his first mayoral term: "I wanted to make mine as nearly a perfectly administered municipal government as could be wrought out of the materials that would certainly be reached or encountered." He continued the thought with a howling non sequitur: "Following this desire I went to St. Louis to study the problem of operating a red light district under strict regulations." Prostitutes had been plying their trade in Milwaukee since the frontier period, and the east bank of the river, in the morning shadow of the new City Hall, had brothels catering to a variety of tastes and clienteles. (Miss Jack Hunter piled racism on racism, running a "colored" house that refused entry to "colored gentlemen.") David Rose favored a policy of containment rather than enforcement; the denizens of River Street were unmolested as long as they stayed

that he had greased more than a few palms to ensure a favorable outcome.

Rose's conduct on the franchise issue demonstrated that he was a chameleon at heart, a political opportunist who could change his message, his demeanor, and even his wardrobe to give voters what they seemed to want. "I believe in winning," he said in 1900. "Standing up and dying for an alleged principle is all damned rot." The obvious absence of true north on his moral compass did not seem to jeopardize the mayor's political career. David Rose was a difficult man to dislike. William George Bruce, a civic activist who once ran against him, described Rose's appeal to the masses:

Mayor David S. Rose was an Apollo in figure, princely in manner, handsome, dashing, and courageous. He frequently dominated a situation by the force of his personality rather

put. His policy was rooted, Rose claimed, in a simple biological imperative:

Men are, and always have been, men. They have their natural passions which, in the great majority of cases, must and will be gratified .... If desires can be fed without turning the animal loose to destroy and ruin young girls, but confining him to the paths which have been provided for him to follow; where lust can be subdued; where diseases can be prevented; where youth may travel without encountering the fiend laying in wait to destroy, is it not better than to try to prevent what cannot be, and never has been, prevented?

The mayor took an equally broad view of two other local institutions: gambling houses and all-night saloons. Milwaukee, in fact, became a stronghold of municipally sanctioned vice during his administration. "I live to see my people at play and happy," Rose once remarked, and he was always willing to share the city's bounty with out-of-town guests. Beating the drum for "Conventions, Celebrations, and a Live Town," Rose welcomed, by his own estimate, an average of 340 state and national gatherings to Milwaukee every year. He appeared at the head of countless reception committees in full regalia – silk top hat, Prince Albert coat, striped afternoon trousers, gray silk gloves – and thousands of visitors heard him extol the virtues of "our beautiful cit-eh!"

There was a dark side to life under "All the Time Rosy." Some citizens wondered how their mayor could afford to buy an Arizona copper mine on an annual salary of $4,000, and there was a never-ending stream of rumors about the "brigade of grafters" in City Hall. The smoke finally burst into flames of indignation. On September 28, 1903, the Milwaukee Turners called a mass

Milwaukee Journal Sentinel

from Milwaukeeans as We See 'Em, 1904

meeting to protest "the general and widespread municipal corruption that has prevailed for years in the city and county of Milwaukee." The conclave drew at least 3,000 people, including industrialists, bankers, brewers, and a vocal cadre of organized Socialists. One speaker, Thomas Boggs, used a well-known public works project to suggest the answer to Milwaukee's problems: "What we want to do is to connect the flushing tunnel of politics with the lake of clear conscience and let it run through the putrid river of polluted politics, and clean out the stream."

The protest meeting helped to sustain grand jury investigations that were nearly

201

continuous between 1901 and 1909. A team led by District Attorney Francis McGovern, a Progressive Republican and future Wisconsin governor, uncovered a cesspool of abuses. Aldermen routinely sold saloon licenses for cash. Rigged bids, kickbacks, and phony purchase orders constituted business as usual. Residents who wanted exemptions from the building code generally paid for them. Officials regularly helped themselves to public supplies of hay, oats, coal, and even horses. By the end of 1905, grand juries had returned a total of 276 indictments against 83 individuals, including aldermen, county supervisors, and a bevy of bureaucrats. David Rose escaped prosecution himself, but Francis McGovern blasted the mayor as "the self-elected, self-appointed attorney general of crime in this community."

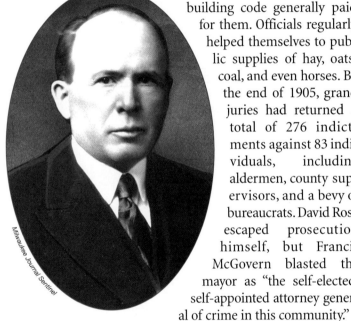

Francis McGovern, the future governor whose investigations led to 276 indictments against public officials of the Rose era

Despite the damning disclosures, Milwaukee's chief scalawag kept getting elected. David Rose spent ten years in the mayor's office between 1898 and 1910, losing only once, in 1906, to Sherburn Becker, an even more flamboyant campaigner but a thoroughly inept administrator. Rose was at all times a likable and entertaining figure, and public tolerance for his antics made it clear that reform sentiments were not yet universally shared. The fact that local Republicans were in disarray also helped the Democratic incumbent's cause. Robert La Follette,

who became Wisconsin's governor in 1900, led the Progressive wing of his party to power, shutting out Milwaukee "Stalwarts" like Henry Payne. Payne, the Republicans' chief wire-puller for decades, soon found a more congenial post, moving to Washington in 1902 as Teddy Roosevelt's postmaster general.

David Rose kept winning elections, but enough was finally enough. His share of the vote in Milwaukee's multi-party mayoral races dropped steadily, from 55 percent in 1898 (Rose's only majority) to 49.5 percent in 1902 and 37 percent in 1908. As the moral bankruptcy of the old-line politicos became more and more apparent, Milwaukeeans decided that it was time for a party that offered a genuine alternative. It was time for the Socialists.

The Sewer Socialists

If ever an American city was bound to give Socialism a fair trial, that city was Milwaukee at the turn of the twentieth century. The community was, to begin with, the most German metropolis in the United States, and Germans, their vaunted diversity notwithstanding, were inveterate supporters of liberal causes. Milwaukee's earliest residents included a group of exiled revolutionaries, the veterans of 1848, who made their new home the *Deutsch-Athen* of America. Some of the émigrés had brought a utopian socialism with them, while others shared the iconoclastic beliefs of their fellow Forty-Eighters, Karl Marx and Friedrich Engels. After decades of exposure to American life, the German community's radical impulses had been somewhat domesticated, but a left-leaning idealism persisted in the city's Turner halls, freethinker societies, and intellectual circles. These were the seedbeds of Milwaukee Socialism.

The city's enormous concentration of industrial workers was another guarantee of receptiveness. After the bloodshed of 1886 and the political adventures of the following two years, Milwaukee's workers had abandoned one-size-fits-all industrial unions like the Knights of Labor and embraced trade unions, whose members represented particular skills in particular industries. The movement thereby lost mass appeal but gained focus. In 1887 the Federated Trades Council was formed as the umbrella group for Milwaukee's skilled and semi-skilled workers. Although economic issues dominated its agenda, the Council honored the spirit of 1886, even resurrecting (with mixed results) the campaign for an eight-hour day. The FTC was also pledged to political activism on its members' behalf. The gap between workers and owners widened steadily in the late 1800s, and appeals to class-consciousness had enormous resonance. On the eve of an 1894 election, the Trades Council issued a statement that could have been written by any card-carrying Socialist:

> *Our only hope of industrial emancipation lies in alliance with the progressive political forces of the times. Our greatest error in the past has been in the support of parties pledged to the perpetuation of an industrial system which has produced an arrogant plutocracy and impoverished the common people.*

A third advantage, one open to all reformers, was supplied by David Rose himself. The general ineptitude and glaring malfeasance of his administration offered perfect examples of how *not* to govern a city, and Socialists invariably blasted Rose's reign of "personal liberty" as a blight on Milwaukee's good name.

The mayor's shortcomings were obvious, but it should be noted that the period before 1910 witnessed more progress than is commonly supposed. Milwaukee's rapid growth created a variety of problems that screamed for attention, and solutions emerged despite the prevailing level of corruption. In 1885, for instance, after endless complaints that the police force was nothing more than a patronage machine, the Fire and Police Commission was created to select applicants on the basis of merit. The result, even in David Rose's "live town," was a significantly higher standard of law enforcement. Four years later, the city (not the county) established a Park Commission to meet a crying need for public green space. In 1890-91 the Commission purchased six tracts of land for Lake, Washington, Riverside, Mitchell, Kosciuszko, and Humboldt Parks; they anchored a system that would become one of the most widely admired in the nation. Another problem proved more difficult to solve: garbage disposal. Milwaukee used every means available to get rid of its trash in the late 1800s, burying it, burning it, and even, incredibly, dumping it in the lake. "Old Michigan Gets It," read an 1887 *Sentinel* headline, and the *Daily News* (October 27, 1891) insisted that Milwaukee was lucky: "She has the broad bosom of Lake Michigan upon which the foul substances may be permitted to escape with no danger of ever being heard from again." In 1902, finally, the city opened a "crematorium" on Jones Island to burn its accumulated garbage. Although public incinerators, public parks, and a public-oriented police force were all

Milwaukee Public Museum

Milwaukee Journal Sentinel

(top)
Park development got under way in the 1890s. Free band concerts in Lake Park drew crowds of well-dressed Milwaukeeans.

(bottom)
Solid waste disposal became a critical problem in the same years. This old lumber steamer was loaded with garbage destined for the "broad bosom" of Lake Michigan.

welcome solutions to pressing urban problems, they were only incremental steps, often taken with reluctance. No one in David Rose's town was naive enough to mistake them for a civic transformation.

Milwaukee, in sum, was a heavily German, solidly working-class city governed by a band of ethically challenged political hacks. These were all promising conditions for Socialist hopefuls, but leaders of the left faced nearly as many obstacles as opportunities. Their first task was to counter the redbaiting that had been going on since the labor disturbances of 1886; Socialists had to convince voters that they didn't intend, as David Rose charged, to "substitute the red flag of anarchy for the glorious old emblem of our country." They also had to project their message beyond the ranks of German industrial workers. Other ethnic groups voted, of course, and there were other reform movements afoot; support from the Municipal League, a good-government group formed by middle-class Yankees in 1893, would have been especially welcome. The party, finally, had to overcome a definite anticlerical strain in its own history; there were still clergymen, particularly Catholic clergymen, who believed that Socialists wanted to turn every one of their churches into a Turner hall. Reversing this bundle of long-held perceptions was an uphill battle. Like the immigrants who had carried the movement across the ocean, Socialism had to shed its European associations and show that it could thrive in the New World. It needed, in other words, to become Americanized.

That was the particular role, and the particular genius, of Victor L. Berger. No individual did half as much to shape the character of Milwaukee Socialism or, in his day, the course of Milwaukee politics. As a theorist, tactician, publisher, and office-holder, Berger was the movement's Moses, the man who led it from the thickets of theory and into City Hall. Born in Austria-Hungary in 1860, Berger moved to the United States at the age of eighteen. He settled in Milwaukee three years later, working variously as a tutor, drama critic, and finally as a German teacher in the public schools. The immigrant became a fixture in the German community's liberal circles as well, serving as an officer of the Turner Society and organizing his own *Sozialistischer Verein* to debate the burning issues of the day. At the end of 1892, he decided to become a full-time Socialist. With money set aside from his teacher's salary, Berger bought the *Arbeiter Zeitung* ("Worker's Times") and renamed it *Vorwärts* ("Forward"). The paper was a leading oracle of Socialism for the next forty years.

Victor Berger quickly became Milwaukee's best-known Socialist, and he rose to prominence on the national level as well. In a legendary 1895 encounter, he visited labor leader Eugene Debs in an Illinois jail cell, bringing words of encouragement and an English version of Marx's *Das Kapital*. Debs was converted to the cause; he later called Berger "a providential instrument [who] delivered the first impassioned message of Socialism I had ever heard." In 1897 the crusader and his convert helped form the Social Democracy of America, which became the Socialist Party in 1901. (The Milwaukee branch, the party's first local unit, retained the name "Social Democrats" under its original charter; the more familiar "Socialist" is used in this narrative.) Debs was soon running for president as the party's official candidate.

Victor Berger was different from other American Socialists, including, eventually, Eugene Debs himself. One of the keys to Berger's success was his ability to sidestep the arcane ideological squabbles that were constantly cleaving the left. He shared the orthodox Marxist belief that capitalism, by divorcing the interests of owners from those of producers, had sown the seeds of its own demise, but his vision of the class struggle stopped considerably short of revolution. Berger found his place on the right side of a left-wing movement. He was a confirmed gradualist or, as one party member put it, an "evolutionary moderate." Berger believed that the cooperative commonwealth would come one day – that glorious age when workers would enjoy what he called "the collective ownership and democratic management of the social means of production and distribution" – but it would come only after a lengthy period of public education and practical experience. Berger made his views clear in a 1901 editorial:

Victor Berger, the pragmatic idealist who became the Moses of Milwaukee Socialism

Milwaukee County Historical Society

In America for the first time in history, we find an oppressed class with the same fundamental rights as the ruling class – the right of universal suffrage. It is then nonsense to talk of sudden bloody revolutions here, until the power to ballot has been at least tried.... The Socialist party in this country must be a party which will take the cooperative commonwealth as the guiding star, and by means of every kind of real, not pretended social reforms, gradually work over our present capitalist state into the socialistic society.

Meta Schlichting Berger was a power in her own right, providing leadership for the Socialist women's caucus and serving on the Milwaukee School Board for thirty years.

Berger never wavered from his core beliefs, but he was more complex than the average ideologue. A Jew by heritage and an agnostic by inclination, he married a German Lutheran, Meta Schlichting, whose father and brother were active Republicans. Berger's social relations were just as enigmatic. Although he stood for the common man, the party chieftain never developed the common touch. Frederick Olson, a leading authority on Milwaukee Socialism, summed up Berger's persona neatly: "He never quite lost the appearance of a scholar talking down to a world of intellectual inferiors." This professorly politician was affable and overbearing by turns, famously short-tempered, and inordinately fond of publicity. "I am the best-known Socialist in the country," he crowed in a 1913 letter, "and hope to remain so as long as I live." Although his fame rested

on his concern for the proletariat, Berger's life was not much different from the average bourgeois Milwaukeean's. Despite chronic financial woes, his family owned a cottage on Lake Shawano as well as a spacious home on N. Second Street, and they enjoyed a generally warm domestic life. In letters home during his frequent travels, this scourge of the ruling class typically addressed his wife and two daughters as "my Schatzl and my Schnuckies."

He may not have been the archetypal working-class hero, but Victor Berger was a matchless tactician. It was not enough, in his view, to stand up for principle; like David Rose, he wanted to win. The heart of his strategy was a hand-in-glove alliance with organized labor. Without a mass constituency, Berger concluded, the Socialists were just another band of ineffectual intellectuals, and without higher social goals, labor unions were just another economic interest group. The godfather of the alliance summarized his strategy in 1905:

We must have a two-armed labor movement – a labor movement with a political arm and with an economic arm. Each arm has its own work to do, and one arm ought not to interfere with the other, although they are parts of the same body. That is the 'Milwaukee idea.' In the personal union of the workers of both ... we find the same men, with the same thoughts, aims and ideals working in the economic and the political field, thus forming a grand army moving on two roads for the abolition of the capitalist system.

The "Milwaukee idea" bore abundant fruit. After a few years of diligent organizing, the city's leading unionists and leading Socialists were generally the same people. The Social Democratic slate was

206

Milwaukee County Historical Society

always top-heavy with union members, while trade unions provided both financial support and an army of volunteers during every Socialist campaign. The Federated Trades Council summarized the relationship succinctly in 1908: "The Social Democratic party is the political expression of the working class and is fighting our battles on the political field." The Social Democrats, in turn, scrupulously observed a pro-union code of conduct. When the city dedicated its new Auditorium with a parade in 1909, Socialist officials boycotted the procession because it was led by a non-union band.

The party that emerged from this partnership was probably the most highly structured and highly disciplined in Milwaukee's political history. Every Social Democrat had to sign a pledge affirming his or her commitment to basic principles, and every candidate for public office had to submit an undated letter of resignation as a guarantee of faithful performance. The Milwaukee County Central Committee was the seat of power, but the party's strength was in its local branches. There were dozens of them, arranged by ward, ethnic group (German, Polish, Jewish, Bohemian, Scandinavian, Italian), and gender; several branches were composed entirely of women. Beginning with Berger's own *Vorwärts*, party regulars supported several newspapers, including the English-language *Social Democratic Herald*, which debuted in 1901 under Frederic Heath. Faith in the printed word was a Socialist trademark, and it was never more

An energized, class-conscious labor movement was the key to the success of Milwaukee Socialism. Labor Day parades like this one on N. Third Street drew thousands of spectators. The Schlitz brewery is in the background.

apparent than during election time. In addition to newspapers, the party presses turned out thousands of leaflets, broadsides, and tabloids in a variety of tongues, all distributed by the famous Bundle Brigade, a corps of volunteers nearly a thousand strong. Historian Marvin Wachman described its method of operation:

> *By 1908, the organization of this Bundle Brigade had become so efficient that within forty-eight hours after it had been decided to circularize the people on any public question, the literature desired could be placed in almost every house in the city in the language best understood by its inhabitants.*

Although it took years for their strategy and structure to jell, the Socialists were ready to enter the political arena in 1898. They fielded a full slate of candidates in the spring mayoral race, all running on a platform that promised slum clearance, more public natatoria, free medical care, jobs for the unemployed, free schoolbooks, and monthly symphony concerts at popular prices. This concern for the practical details of local government was entirely typical of Berger's party. Latter-day critics on the left might charge him with serving up "Socialism lite," a pale version of Marxism watered down for American tastes, but Berger couldn't have cared less:

> *To those who regard us as being too moderate, we reply that if you demand too much at one time you are likely to get nothing.... We do not care ... whether our Socialism be Marxian or otherwise, as long as we change the present system and emancipate all the people and especially the proletariat.*

As the Milwaukeeans showed an ever-deepening interest in public works, some of their simon-pure comrades in other cities dubbed them "sewer Socialists" – a tag no one seems to have minded overmuch.

The outcome of the 1898 election was predictable. David Rose won in a landslide, and the Socialist candidate, machinist Robert Meister, took barely five percent of the vote. No matter; the Social Democrats were in it for the long haul. In 1900 they fielded a slate headed by Frederic Heath, whom Berger often introduced as "the first Milwaukee Yankee Socialist." The results were no better, but the party's 1902 mayoral candidate, union organizer Howard Tuttle, came home with fourteen percent of the vote. The tide was rising.

There is little doubt that the Socialists benefited as much from Republican dissension as David Rose himself. The struggle between La Follette Progressives and old-line Stalwarts diluted the GOP's strength, making it easier for alternative voices to be heard. But the Progressive movement also complicated life for Milwaukee Socialists. Although La Follette's base of support was different from Berger's – more rural than urban, more native than immigrant – both men headed movements that spoke to the reform impulse in the electorate. Berger felt the need to distance his cause from the governor's. He called La Follette "a half-baked reformer" whose pet issues – the direct primary and railroad regulation – addressed "merely the mechanics of government." Berger maintained that he and his comrades were different:

> *We Social-Democrats say, we are willing to accept and help on every social reform. But we also say that social reforms are but installments by which we must not allow ourselves to be bribed – that full economic freedom will only be achieved by Social-Democracy.*

And how, one might have asked, could the voters of a single Midwestern city bring about the cooperative commonwealth? Berger had a ready answer:

Now a municipal campaign is a very small and insignificant part of the grand social and economic revolution which we intend to accomplish. Yet municipal Socialism is very important. There can be no doubt that the Social-Democrats will carry cities and towns before they carry states, or before they carry a national election. Like everything else that is growing Socialism must grow from the bottom up.

Socialism's growth was self-evident in the spring election of 1904. Tainted by the ongoing grand jury investigations, David Rose saw his share of the vote fall to 39 percent, while the Socialist ticket, headed by Berger himself, captured 25 percent – not far from the Progressive Republican candidate's 29.5 percent. The Democratic rapscallion won again, but Socialists took 9 of 46 seats on the Common Council and a number of minor offices. (Not surprisingly, most of the winners were from North Side German wards.) David Rose looked to his back. "While we have slept," he intoned darkly, "an enemy, cunning and insidious, has crept into our midst to poison the vitals of our civic body." The bringer of this pestilence was, of course, the "disciple of Satan" named Victor Berger.

The Socialists who took office in 1904 proved themselves vastly superior to the hacks and grafters of the Rose regime. They were politicians the voters could trust: hard-working, well-prepared, and incorruptible. Honesty in office, said Berger, was the highest quality a Democrat or Republican could attain. "With us," he declared, "this is the first and smallest requirement." Socialists in office also faced the real-world challenges of governing a city, and the result was a further retreat from the doctrinal purity of by-the-book Marxism. Instead of deferring decisions until the arrival of some distant utopia, the aldermen were obliged to take concrete action *now* – informed by Socialist principles, perhaps, but hardly abstract.

Members of the growing Socialist bloc on the Common Council earned a reputation for honesty and diligence.

Milwaukee County Historical Society

Emil Seidel, the patternmaker who became Milwaukee's first Socialist mayor in 1910

Both David Rose and the Socialists were sidetracked in 1906, when Sherburn Becker, the "boy mayor," glad-handed his way into City Hall. When that one-term wonder stepped aside, the Socialists were on nearly even ground with the old-line parties. Their standard-bearer in 1908 was Emil Seidel, an alderman and the owner of a small pattern shop. Earnest, upright, and plain-spoken, Seidel did especially well in the working-class wards. When the results were tabulated, he had outpolled the Republican candidate and come within 2,200 votes of David Rose himself. Victory was in the air.

The traditional parties scrambled to avert a Socialist landslide in 1910. The Democrats, after deciding that David Rose had finally worn out his welcome, nominated Vincenz Schoenecker, a boot manufacturer and the city treasurer, for mayor, while the Republicans put forward John Beffel, a physician who had lived in Milwaukee for barely ten years. Emil Seidel headed the Socialist ticket again, running with candidates like Charles Whitnall for treasurer and a young labor lawyer named Daniel Hoan for city attorney. The Social Democrats pulled out all the stops on behalf of their ticket. A Polish-language weekly,

Naprzod ("Forward"), was launched to pull Polish voters away from the Democratic fold. A small army of stump speakers haunted the factory gates and union halls. The Bundle Brigade circulated nearly 750,000 pieces of literature, including copies of a platform that called for everything from a municipal stone quarry to better parks. The document closed by inviting all well-meaning voters "to join in our undertaking for the emancipation of mankind." The party spent a grand total of $5,569 on the 1910 campaign, most of it for printing.

The outcome of the contest was a resounding victory for the Socialists. Voters chose Seidel and all his running mates, along with 21 of 35 aldermen, 10 of 16 county supervisors, and 2 judges. There was more to come: Victor Berger won a congressional seat in the fall election. He viewed the rout as proof that the voting public was finally "saturated with Socialist doctrine." That was hardly the case, as later events would demonstrate, but the victory was sweet nonetheless. The workingman, and working woman, had triumphed. The ethnic industrial character of Milwaukee, so pronounced for so many years, had finally found mature political expression. For the first time in a major American city, the people had turned over their entire government to card-carrying Socialists who rose from and spoke for the working class. Eighteen of the 35 aldermen who took office in 1910 – a majority – worked with their hands.

A few, perhaps, looked back to the first week of May, 1886, as their personal and political watershed, and a few more might have felt that the ghosts of Bay View had finally been avenged. A movement baptized in blood had, under Victor Berger's careful ministrations, gained focus, discipline, and strength. The latent energy of outrage had been harnessed; the politics of protest had become the politics of electoral success. Now the Socialists looked ahead to the task of governing. After rising to a sustained ovation at the 1910 victory party, Victor Berger spoke, for once, with genuine humility:

> *Comrades, I want to ask every man and woman in this audience to stand up and with lifted hand take a pledge that we will do all in our power to help the men that the people have chosen to do their duty and to fulfill our promises. The eyes of the country will be upon us. We must make good for the faith that is in us.*

The party press pictured the Socialist landslide of 1910 as "Milwaukee Welcoming the Sunrise."

Milwaukee Public Library

Getting into line: The citizens of Milwaukee, including the Chain Belt workers in this artfully composed photograph, became more like other Americans after 1910.

Chapter 6

A Bigger, Brighter, and Blander Milwaukee, 1910 – 1930

**P**recisely when it happened is a matter of continuing debate. Some date the change to the 1860s, when the Civil War imposed a bloody consensus on America's sectional differences. Others place the transformation as late as the 1950s, when the mass media, particularly television, spawned a common national consciousness. Still others identify World War I or World War II as the critical point of convergence. Whatever the date, there is general agreement that, at some moment in American history, purely regional differences began to fade in the bright light of an emergent national identity. Slowly but inexorably, communities separated by thousands of miles felt their sharp edges melting away, and residents of Miami, Muskogee, and Milwaukee came to believe that they were different not so much in kind as in degree.

Milwaukee's experience suggests that the sea change took place between 1910 and 1930. It was during that period that the city experienced the full force of America's homogenizing influences – later than some communities and more painfully than most. Milwaukee had always reflected national trends, of course; major themes in its history – the westward movement of the frontier, mass immigration from Europe, large-scale industrialization – were major themes in American history as well. But the community had developed, over the decades, a thoroughly distinctive sense of place, a personality understood, in the national consciousness, as a blend of three related elements: Germanism, Socialism, and beer. Between 1910 and 1930, all three of those hallmarks were threatened with extinction. World War I spelled an end to self-conscious German culture. The war and its aftermath reduced Victor Berger's Socialist movement to an urban anomaly. And Prohibition shuttered the breweries that had been turning out Milwaukee's most celebrated product since the 1840s.

These and other catastrophes took place, ironically, during a time of unusual economic prosperity. World War I touched off an industrial boom that lasted through the 1920s, and Milwaukee experienced steady growth in population, land area, and ethnic diversity. The city was also practically overrun with the symbols of America's budding consumer culture: automobiles, radios, electric appliances, dance clubs, and movie theaters. The 1910-1930 period was corrosive and expansive by turns; Milwaukee moved, under significant duress, away from the singular haven of its traditions and toward the broad and forgetful waters of mass society. The immersion was never complete. In one area, in fact – municipal government – the city continued to distinguish itself from its peers. But there is no question that, by the period's end, Milwaukee was, for better or worse, edging closer to a new identity as a typically modern, typically American urban community.

Socialists at Work

Leveling influences were the last thing on Emil Seidel's mind in 1910. He and his comrades were the first Socialists to govern a major American city, and they were determined to make the most of their opportunity. In his inaugural address to the Common Council, Seidel sounded what would be the central theme of his administration:

> *The workers of our city are its most valuable asset. Your attention should be directed to the passage of such measures as will promote the well-being of this class of citizens, safeguard health, check any tendency to encroach upon such few rights as the workers still enjoy, and wherever possible extend for them the opportunity of life.*

The Socialists launched a barrage of initiatives designed to make Milwaukee a model city for the workingman and his family. The minimum wage for city laborers was raised from $1.75 to $2.00 a day. An eight-hour workday became the standard for municipal crews. Policemen were granted an extra two days off each month, and city officials took their business to union shops for everything from printing to horseshoeing.

Taxpayers who feared that Seidel and company were giving away the store needn't have worried. In keeping with an esteemed Milwaukee tradition, the Socialists took a craftsmanlike approach to government; they sought a municipal administration that was, above all, well-made. Efficiency was a Socialist watchword, and Seidel's team pursued it with a zeal that would have warmed the heart of any red-blooded capitalist. "The

Emil Seidel provided vigorous leadership as Milwaukee's first Socialist mayor, and he was surrounded (center) by an equally committed group of advisors.

Milwaukee County Historical Society

governing of our city," the mayor declared, "must become a scientific function." To that end, the city hired one of Wisconsin's leading social scientists: John R. Commons, an economist at the university in Madison. It was Victor Berger, still very much in charge of the local Socialist movement, who approached the professor. "Berger came to me," recalled Commons, "... and offered me $6,000 salary, out of which I should pay my personal expenses, if I would make an investigation of the Milwaukee city government with a view to reorganizing it on an efficiency basis." With the full support of Berger, Seidel, and a majority of the city's aldermen, John Commons organized a new agency, the Bureau of Economy and Efficiency, and began a top-to-bottom study of local government. The professor had substantial input from local Socialists, and he found their company stimulating:

> The Socialist officials and aldermen, to the number of fifty or more, held a caucus every Saturday afternoon to consider and agree upon policies. I appeared at these caucuses, with blueprints and charts, to report progress and answer criticisms. Nearly all of those present were mechanics and trade-unionists. Never before, even in England, had I met such a capable and rational body of men in charge of a city government. I soon discovered that their goal was Efficiency coupled with Service to the poor and the working classes of the city.

Commons and his crew generated a blizzard of reports and recommendations, most of which found their way into municipal practice. Voluminous line-item budgets replaced the single sheets of the Rose years. Centralized purchasing eliminated a great deal of duplication and waste. Unit cost accounting enabled department heads to gauge their spending with unprecedented

precision. The first-ever inventory of city property was completed. Voting procedures were revamped and tightened. (Seidel claimed that he removed so many dead men's names from the polling lists that he saved the city $500 in annual printing costs.) The Health Department stepped up its inspections of factories, schools, and milk plants. A municipal quarry was opened to provide crushed rock for street projects, and a beginning, at least, was made on a municipal street-lighting system. In 1912 the Milwaukee Vocational School (now Milwaukee Area Technical College) began to offer classes; it became one of the largest schools for workers in the country. These and other reforms did not bring Milwaukee appreciably closer to the cooperative commonwealth, but Socialists considered them necessary first steps. Emil

Established in 1912, the Milwaukee Vocational School (now MATC) made Milwaukee a national leader in worker's education. The present main building on Sixth and State was built in stages between 1920 and 1927.

Milwaukee Journal Sentinel

Seidel, the former patternmaker, borrowed an analogy from the skilled trades:

When a mechanic sets to work to do a job everyone understands that he first must put his tools in proper condition. A carpenter will file his saws and get an edge to his chisels. A city government is like a larger machine.

As Milwaukee's chief mechanic, Seidel was pragmatic to the core. Although he worked diligently for the triumph of Socialist ideals, the mayor avoided the dense ideological thickets that waylaid other leftists. He was, if anything, even less doctrinaire than Victor Berger himself. In his memoirs, Seidel provided a concise summary of the Socialists' here-and-now agenda:

Some eastern smarties called ours a Sewer Socialism. Yes, we wanted sewers in the workers' homes; but we wanted much, oh – so very much more than sewers. We wanted our workers to have pure air; we wanted them to have sunshine; we wanted planned homes; we wanted living wages; we wanted recreation for young and old; we wanted vocational education; we wanted a chance for every human being to be strong and live a life of happiness.

And, we wanted everything that was necessary to give them that: playgrounds, parks, lakes, beaches, clean creeks and rivers, swimming and wading pools, social centers, reading rooms, clean fun, music, dance, song and joy for all. That was our Milwaukee Social Democratic movement.

Fervent, unassuming, and transparently well-meaning, Emil Seidel was an ideal herald of municipal Socialism. He had some illustrious company. Victor Berger, as the first and only member of his party in Congress, became America's Socialist, pledged to "give expression to the hopes and ambitions of the American class-conscious proletariat." Some of Berger's proposals – abolishing the U.S. Senate and repealing the presidential veto – were rejected as ludicrous, while others, including woman's suffrage and old-age pensions, were merely premature. Closer to home, City Attorney Daniel Hoan waged a one-man war against The Milwaukee Electric Railway & Light Company. As a private monopoly providing an essential public service, TMER&L was a natural target for the Socialists, and Dan Hoan was a relentless antagonist. He and his assistants forced the company to pave and sprinkle between its streetcar tracks, to upgrade city transit service, and to cough up license fees that had gone unpaid for years. On the county level, District Attorney Winfred Zabel tried just as hard to wipe out prostitution, beginning with a house run by the queen of Milwaukee madams, Kitty Williams. In true Socialist fashion, Zabel's party assembled some compelling statistics to support the campaign. According to their estimates, Milwaukee had roughly 200 brothels with 1,000 residents, each of whom entertained 15 visitors a day at a minimum of one dollar per visit – making prostitution a $5,500,000 annual enterprise. Zabel's crusade created some highly selective unemployment and probably cost the city some convention business, but there was absolutely no public outcry. Other Socialists labored in relative obscurity. One of the unsung party faithful was Mayor Seidel's private secretary, a raw-boned Illinois native who had earned his Socialist spurs as a Wisconsin state organizer – Carl Sandburg.

This diverse cast of characters was involved in a novel urban experiment, and their work attracted national attention. In one of its periodic reports from the provinces, the *New York Times* (July 31, 1910) managed to hit all the Milwaukee stereotypes. Its tongue-in-cheek story described municipally owned babies giving "the Proletariat yell," brass bands serenading sewer workers with German tunes, and a municipal brewery as large as Buckingham Palace. "As the beer belongs to the municipality," wrote the *Times* correspondent, "it is patriotic to drink as much as possible." A few months later (November 27, 1910), the newspaper covered "a Socialist public ball" in the Milwaukee Auditorium, where admission was only twenty cents, Mayor Seidel wore "ordinary clothing," and "machinists danced with society belles."

The Socialists made good copy, but they were not about to let the mainstream press speak for them. On December 7, 1911, hoping to counter the hostility of other newspapers (particularly the hometown *Milwaukee Journal*), Socialists launched the daily *Milwaukee Leader* under Victor Berger's editorial hand. "We shall preach no class hatred," Berger decreed in the inaugural issue. "But we will preach class consciousness and class conscience six days in the week." The *Leader* was a good deal less polemical than the congressman seemed to promise. It was a paper that practically any American family could welcome into its home, with news of the day, regular features, a woman's page, a sports section, comic strips, and ads for everything from lampshades to eczema cures. Its financial problems were chronic, but the *Milwaukee Leader* became the most successful and longest-lived Socialist daily in the country.

Despite the power of the party press, their impressive organizational strength, and their obvious political savvy, the Socialists faced some imposing obstacles

Milwaukee Journal Sentinel

in their crusade to transform Milwaukee. The city was legally a creature of the state, first of all, and the absence of true home-rule powers forced Seidel and his comrades to run to Madison every time they wanted authority for a new program. Within City Hall, holdover officials did their best to frustrate the Socialist program. The most recalcitrant was Police Chief John Janssen, a hard-headed German who was virtually chief-for-life under the civil service statutes of 1885. When Emil Seidel demanded his resignation over the chief's questionable handling of a garment worker's strike, Janssen's reply was a model of

Mayor Seidel with his private secretary and left-hand man, Carl Sandburg

217

brevity: "Go to hell." Nor were the Socialists always their own best friends; some unfortunate appointments and a few injudicious statements alienated lukewarm supporters. When his party's candidates stumbled in the fall election of 1910, Victor Berger blamed "goody-goodies" and "church club men" who had defected to the Progressive side.

Milwaukee's Socialists faced any number of obstacles, but the most formidable by far was the doubled enmity of the Republican and Democratic organizations. Both parties were deeply embarrassed by the Socialist victory of 1910, and they were determined not to let it happen again. As the 1912 mayoral election approached, the erstwhile

opponents decided to join forces, just as they had against Robert Schilling's Populist ticket in 1888. The fusion ticket that emerged was a study in ethnic balance: Dr. Gerhard Bading, a German Lutheran, ran for mayor; Louis Kotecki, a Polish Catholic, for comptroller; and J.P. Carney, an Irish Catholic, for treasurer. The fusionists promised to "Redeem Milwaukee" from the supposed blot of "Red rule," and Dr. Bading, who had served with some distinction as the city's health commissioner, blasted the Socialists for allegedly ignoring the city's water problems. Milwaukee's water supply was so bad, charged Bading, that residents drew "typhoid highballs" every time they opened a tap.

Fusion itself became an issue in the 1912 campaign. Hoping to lift public discourse from the swamp of party politics, good-government groups were beating the

drum for "nonpartisan" municipal elections. The Bading forces found it convenient to endorse the nonpartisan concept, and the Socialists, for reasons just as self-interested, opposed it. Victor Berger argued that "the abolition of party responsibility" would create "political anarchy."

Facing a united front of the old parties in 1912, Milwaukee's Socialists stood on their record. Emil Seidel's administration had been the most pro-active (perhaps even hyperactive) in the city's history, and he ran for re-election promising more of the same. In a reprise of the 1910 contest, his party staged hundreds of campaign rallies, and the Bundle Brigade distributed 632,000 pieces of literature. The most ambitious piece was the *Municipal Campaign Book*, a remarkable pocket-sized document of 224 pages. It was a digest of the Seidel team's accomplishments, larded with testimonials from clergymen and professors and illustrated with photographs of the very latest in waste receptacles and street-cleaning equipment. One of the *Campaign Book's* passages reflected a deep understanding of the average Milwaukee voter: "The Social-Democratic party does not intend to curtail the few amusements and places of recreation that capitalism has left the working class. The saloon is still the proletarian's clubhouse."

When the votes were counted in 1912, Gerhard Bading had beaten Emil Seidel by the lopsided margin of 43,176 to 30,272. Other incumbents met the same fate. The Socialists lost their Common Council majority, most city-wide offices, a majority of their County Board seats, and Victor Berger's post in Congress. To make matters worse, the Wisconsin legislature passed a nonpartisan election law in 1912, blurring

John Janssen, the police chief who resisted the Socialist stampede

A Socialist campaign card urged Milwaukeeans to "Vote For Principles Rather Than Men" in the fall election of 1912.

the ideological distinctions between candidates and destroying the leverage that a strong third party generally enjoyed. Party labels have been absent from local ballots ever since.

There were multiple reasons for the Socialists' 1912 drubbing: middle-class discomfort with the party's radical rhetoric, public exhaustion after two years of frenetic activity, and the all-too-obvious willingness of the mainline parties to forsake their threadbare principles for the sake of victory. Historians Bayrd Still and Frederick Olson offer another explanation: Once the Socialists had restored good government, voters could safely return control to more familiar figures with less challenging philosophies. The party was, to some degree, a victim of its own success.

Dr. Gerhard Bading, the former city health commissioner, beat Emil Seidel handily in the 1912 mayoral race.

Milwaukee County Historical Society

Although they were trounced in 1912, Milwaukee's Socialists had no intention of leaving the battlefield. They were "the only party with the social conscience," as Victor Berger often said, and their platforms, full of highly specific proposals expressed in highly charged language, tended to dominate public discussion. Whether fused or not, the other parties had little choice but to respond to, and frequently to support, reforms proposed by Socialists. The party was also present in person. A core of Socialist aldermen kept watch in the Common Council, and one Socialist official continued to make headlines: Dan Hoan, the city attorney. As the only major officeholder with a four-year term, he escaped the purge of 1912 and continued to make life as difficult as possible for the streetcar company and other "entrenched interests." During his re-election campaign in 1914, Hoan boasted that he had "licked every big law firm in Milwaukee" and had generated enough fee revenue to pay the operating costs of his department. Emil Seidel lost his rematch with Gerhard Bading in the 1914 election, but voters kept Dan Hoan in the city attorney's office, making him the most visible Socialist (and the most viable Socialist candidate) in municipal government.

The attorney's personal history had a Lincolnesque flavor. Daniel Webster Hoan, Jr., was born in Waukesha on March 12, 1881, the youngest son of an Irish father and a German-English mother. His father was Waukesha's village radical, a man who made his living variously as a quarry laborer, omnibus driver, and well-digger. The family was relatively comfortable in most years, but Dan Hoan was forced to grow up early, first by his parents' divorce and then by his father's death. He was on his own at the age of thirteen, working as a dishwasher and then a cook in Milwaukee and Chicago. An idealist with inborn sympathy for the underdog, Hoan converted to Socialism in his teens and resolved to rise above his circumstances. In 1901, without a day of high school to his credit, he entered the University of Wisconsin as an "adult special" and proceeded to graduate as president of his class. Hoan's next stop was Chicago, where he opened a restaurant to support himself while he studied law. In 1908, fresh from the Illinois and Wisconsin bar exams, the young barrister answered Victor Berger's call to set up practice in Milwaukee. Two years later, at the tender age of twenty-nine, he entered the city attorney's office on the same Socialist landslide that carried Emil Seidel into City Hall.

Dan Hoan was the obvious choice when Milwaukee Socialists met to choose their mayoral candidate for 1916. His personal dynamism and his record as a fighter stood in marked contrast to the tepid, technocratic demeanor of Gerhard Bading, who had done little wrong but little right. The "nonpartisan" camp tried to define the 1916 race in terms of "Americanism vs. Socialism," and Bading urged voters to show the world that they would "never again allow the Red Flag to replace the Stars and Stripes" in Milwaukee. Hoan, citing the mayor's cozy relationship with TMER&L, countered that another Bading victory would put "the flag of the street car company ... over the City Hall." Voters picked the challenger. Running well ahead of his ticket, Dan Hoan beat Gerhard Bading by a margin of 33,863 to 32,206.

Milwaukee's second Socialist mayor sounded a hopeful note in his 1916 inaugural address. Hoan promised "a comprehensive, progressive and enlightened administration" that would, in time, produce "a better, bigger and brighter city." The last phrase became a mayoral mantra, repeated in dozens of speeches over the years. In true Milwaukee Socialist fashion, Hoan followed his first "brighter" pledge with calls for a better street-lighting system.

The mayor knew that success was anything but guaranteed. Although Socialists picked up a few seats in the 1916 election, they numbered only eleven of the city's thirty-seven aldermen. Milwaukee voters had chosen a Socialist chief executive and a nonpartisan Common Council – a balance they liked enough to keep for most of the next half-century.

Daniel Hoan, the Lincolnesque figure who became Milwaukee's second Socialist mayor in 1916 and stayed in office for twenty-four years

Milwaukee Journal Sentinel

The War to End Wars

By the time Dan Hoan took the oath of office, war in Europe had pushed purely local concerns off the front page. When the shooting started in the summer of 1914, local residents were quick to back what was, for many of them, the home team. As the most German city in America, Milwaukee became a principal center of support for Kaiser Wilhelm II and his expansionist German Empire – even after U-boats sank the *Lusitania*, with the loss of 128 American lives, on May 7, 1915. The support was material as well as moral. One of the biggest events of the decade was a "charity war bazaar" that packed the Milwaukee Auditorium for a full week in March, 1916. Held for the benefit of German and Austrian "war sufferers," particularly the widows and orphans of fallen soldiers, the bazaar had prominent backing from the Blatzes, Brumders, Pabsts, Trostels, Vogels, Uihleins, and other members of the German upper crust. Volunteers spent days building elaborate re-creations of a Viennese cafe, the village square in Old Nuremberg, and a Hansel-and-Gretel cottage covered with candy. Thousands of donated items were offered for sale, including a forty-acre farm, steamship tickets to Europe, and a collection of handkerchiefs once used by Bismarck himself. Zither concerts and German vaudeville acts were offered regularly, and visitors flocked to a faithful replica of a military trench in the war zone, complete with a field kitchen and working cannon. The bazaar attracted 175,000 patrons – in a city of 400,000 – and netted $150,000 for the cause. The *Milwaukee Journal* (March 5, 1916) was duly impressed:

> *It is impossible to conceive the immensity of the bazaar. The state fair and several circuses, together in one enclosure, wouldn't be in it. It is*

Nearly 175,000 people attended a 1916 charity bazaar for German "war sufferers." Its highlights included a scene from Old Nuremberg.

without doubt the biggest thing ever attempted in Milwaukee, and imagination cannot begin to conjure up the tons and tons of things on sale or the amount of dollars involved.

Such open sympathy for the Central Powers raised eyebrows elsewhere in the country. "Germany," observed the *Houston Post*, "seems to have lost all of her foreign possessions with the exception of Milwaukee, St. Louis and Cincinnati." But support for the Kaiser was permissible as long as the United States had not officially taken sides. Woodrow Wilson urged Americans to remain "neutral in fact as well as in name" when the conflict erupted, and he won re-election in 1916 on the Democratic boast that "He Kept Us Out of the War." But America was inching inexorably toward the Allied camp. As a major supplier of food and munitions for Great Britain and its partners, the United States found its national interests following its financial interests. By the summer of 1916, the country's focus had shifted from neutrality to readiness for war, and nearly 30,000 marchers turned out for a July 15 "preparedness" parade in downtown Milwaukee. When Germany lifted its ban on submarine warfare at the end of January, 1917, all bets were off. In March, barely a year after Milwaukeeans had filled the Auditorium for the war bazaar, the same building hosted a "patriotic mass meeting" that ended, amid much flag-waving, with a pledge "to protect American lives and American rights." Tensions finally rose to the boiling point, and the United States entered the fray on April 6, 1917.

America's decision to fight created special pressures for Milwaukee and the rest of Wisconsin. Most residents would gladly have sat out the conflict; nine of the state's eleven congressmen were among the fifty who voted against the declaration of war – the highest proportion in the country. But the primacy of national interests, however painfully they conflicted with emotional ties to the *Vaterland*, was beyond question. As mobilization for war proceeded, Milwaukee led the nation in military enlistments for a time, and Liberty Loan drives were routinely oversubscribed. ("Every quarter, every dollar, helps to make the Kaiser holler.") A thousand vacant lots were converted to gardens, many of them tended by schoolchildren, and local industries supplied the armed forces with everything from ship gears to chipped beef.

Milwaukee's cooperation with the war effort was impressive, but it was not always completely voluntary. A substantial number of German families continued to harbor misgivings about the conflict, and a cadre of self-appointed patriots took it upon themselves to bring these slackers

Thousands more Milwaukeeans marched in a 1916 "preparedness" parade.

223

into line. From the patriots' point of view, it was a matter of hometown pride. Milwaukee had already been castigated for its embrace of Socialism, and the community's early enthusiasm for the Kaiser made it doubly suspect in the nation's eyes. A number of local boosters felt that extraordinary measures were needed to redeem the city's good name. Determined to avoid the stigma of "disloyalty" at all costs, they mounted a campaign to search out and destroy every last vestige of support for Germany.

The *Milwaukee Journal* led the charge. The paper had reflected community sentiment at first, printing relatively unbiased news from the front and providing ample coverage of the 1916 war bazaar. (Mrs. Lucius Nieman, the editor's wife, was a prominent volunteer.) But Nieman soon changed his tune. On October 14, 1916, the *Journal* printed a diatribe against the Brumder-owned *Germania-Herold*, accusing its German-language rival of "disloyalty," "hatred for this government," and a commitment to "Germany first." The paper

translated lengthy excerpts from *Germania* stories that condemned arms sales to the Allies, justified Germany's submarine attacks, and blasted "the Britannization of America" – editorial stands that the *Journal* condemned as diabolical propaganda.

When the United States declared war in 1917, the *Germania's* editor, Emil von Schleinitz, suffered a nervous breakdown, and the *Journal* found new targets. The German-American National Alliance was denounced as little more than a front for Kaiser Wilhelm, and the teaching of German in Milwaukee's public schools, a virtually mandatory practice for years, was compared to the U-boat menace. In time, the *Journal* found the very existence of German culture seditious. On May 27, 1918, the paper printed an editorial predicting the end of *Deutschtum* (Germanism) in American society:

> *Here, in this trusting, peace-loving land of ours, Deutschtum has in truth been a hydra-headed monster. Evil, cunning, sinuous, it has worked and plotted in our schools, using its language to*

Hoping to rouse anti-German sentiment, the Milwaukee Journal *altered a photograph to help its readers visualize a Zeppelin attack on Grand Avenue.*

Milwaukee Journal Sentinel

Would You Encourage the Hope of the Hun?

inculcate moral treason in the unsuspecting minds of children; it has used the church, the temples of God, to serve its wicked purposes; it has found in the German language press, and in some other newspapers and periodicals, fit and willing tools for its silent, subterranean warfare against America, and in the German-American alliance and other organizations like it, it found in its hands as willing and efficient forces, in times of peace, as the kaiser's own army divisions are proving to be in time of war. It is the revelation of the deadly character of Deutschtum in our land that has spurred the people of America to prompt and effectual action.

In 1919, with the war over and victory secured, the *Milwaukee Journal* won a Pulitzer Prize for its efforts to save the community from the terrors of rampant Germanism.

If the *Journal's* World War I editorial stance seems strident to modern readers, it was sweet reason in comparison with other patriotic voices. As war fever degenerated to simple hysteria, "Kaiser Bill" was demonized as a butcher and his soldiers as "bloody Huns." Superpatriots, particularly those in the ranks of the Wisconsin Loyalty Legion, found it easy to transfer their hatred for Germans "over there" to Germans "over here." Families who refused to buy what the Legion considered their "fair share" of Liberty Bonds had their houses splashed with yellow paint. Teachers and other public employees deemed less than "100% American" were forced to sign loyalty oaths. Citizens caught speaking German on the sidewalk or inside stores were singled out for insult. Even history was not spared. When the Loyalty Legion discovered a 1918 Milwaukee guidebook describing the city's heyday as the "German Athens," its leaders demanded a retraction.

The combined power of the press, the superpatriots, and American public opinion was more than Milwaukee's German community could withstand. Although the rout was never complete, thousands of local Germans began a headlong flight from their heritage. Schmidts and Schneiders became Smiths and Taylors. The German-English Academy, established by Forty-Eighters in the city's infancy, was renamed Milwaukee University School. The Deutscher Club, a center of German social life for a generation, became the Wisconsin Club. When America's sauerkraut consumption fell 75 percent during America's first year at war, the old German staple was rechristened "liberty cabbage." The resident company of the Pabst Theater stayed scrupulously away from German plays during its 1918 season. The Brumders were forced to pull down the statue of Germania from atop their publishing house. The number of local schoolchildren enrolled in German classes plummeted from 30,000 in 1916 to a mere 400 in 1918. With some conspicuous

Milwaukee Journal Sentinel

As anti-German hysteria reached a fever pitch, the Brumders were forced to remove the statue of Germania from their publishing headquarters.

exceptions, the German language disappeared from the pulpit, the press, and finally from the street corners.

There is no question that the vitality of Milwaukee's German community had been waning for years, a direct result of long tenure and general prosperity. The good burghers of America's *Deutsch-Athen* were, in most cases, much less German than their tormentors supposed. It was nonetheless natural, even at a distance of one or two generations, for local Germans to feel at least some sympathy for their homeland during the war. The superpatriots magnified that sympathy to monstrous proportions and tried to stamp it out with "loyalty" crusades that were little more than witch hunts. The result was assimilation by coercion. Milwaukee's distinctly German society had been blending into the mainstream for decades, but World War I forced a brutal acceleration of the process. The German community, and with it the larger community, suffered a blow from which neither ever really recovered.

Not the least of the losses was cultural. From Polish drama to Italian music, Milwaukee had an impressive range of arts groups, but Germans had always been in the vanguard. The community's visual arts tradition was a heavily German tradition. When drama-lovers thought of the resident theater in Milwaukee, they thought of the German theater. Fine music in the city, particularly of the choral variety, was generally German music. As recently as 1911, only three years before the outbreak of war, 3,200 German singers had massed in the Auditorium for a national *Saengerfest*. That scene was never repeated. With painfully few exceptions, German arts organizations ceased to exist in the years

after World War I, and there was nothing of comparable scale to replace them. It would take the community nearly two generations to regain the cultural ground lost to the war.

The struggle in Europe was not, it should be stressed, an unqualified disaster for every Milwaukee ethnic group. The same conflict that neutralized local German culture was welcome news for thousands of immigrants from the Slavic nations of eastern and southern Europe. Poles, Czechs, Slovaks, Serbs, Croats, and Slovenes looked back to homelands that had been under foreign rule for centuries, in some cases, and the war was, from their point of view, a war of liberation. On June 9, 1918, some 20,000 Slavs of all varieties paraded through the rain to show their support for American intervention. The "United Slavs" ended their march at the Auditorium, where they sang patriotic songs, waved American flags, and heard Louis Kotecki, the city comptroller and therefore "Polish mayor," pledge the Slavs' unconditional allegiance to "our government and our matchless president, Woodrow Wilson." Wilson delivered the goods. Polish independence was one of the Fourteen Points he pursued when the fighting stopped, and in 1918 Poland became a free country for the first time since 1795. The new nations of Czechoslovakia and Yugoslavia were created at the same time. The establishment of free homelands, after so many decades of subjugation, stirred a palpable pride in the city's Slavic communities. For Milwaukee's Poles, who had labored under German rule in Europe and then played second fiddle to Germans in Milwaukee, the reversal of fortunes was especially sweet.

The Polish Women's Alliance joined a 1918 parade that demonstrated Slavic support for the war effort.

Milwaukee Public Library

Socialists at War

If World War I was good for the city's Slavs and terrible for the Germans, it was nearly catastrophic for Milwaukee Socialists. Long before America entered the strife, the party was an outspoken champion of unambiguous pacifism. Victor Berger, like most Socialists, analyzed the European conflict in economic terms, calling it "a capitalist war caused chiefly by the struggle between Great Britain and Germany for the world market." It was, in other words, a rich man's war but a poor man's fight, and Socialists endorsed any and all proposals to end the ongoing slaughter of European workers. The plan they preferred was an embargo on shipments of American food and munitions to the Allies. In 1916 a new slogan appeared on the masthead of Berger's *Milwaukee Leader*: "Starve the War and Feed America."

Although every Socialist was opposed to the war, pacifism had its limits. "The Socialist party is not for peace at any price," Berger wrote in 1916. "War may be hell, but there are some things in this world worse than 'hell.'" The editor even offered a grudging endorsement of military preparedness, arguing that "any nation, class or individual that is defenceless ... will soon be enslaved or cease to exist." Such remarks sounded suspiciously like saber-rattling to some of Berger's comrades, particularly those who didn't share his German ancestry. A split developed between radical doves and moderate doves in the party, and a national parley was called at St. Louis to resolve their differences. It convened, unfortunately, on April 7, 1917, one day after America entered the war. The horrified delegates quickly endorsed a radical pacifist platform by a margin of 140 to 36. The document blamed "predatory capitalists" for the fighting and called America's declaration of war "a crime ... against the people of the United States and against the nations of the world." The assembled delegates pledged themselves to "continuous, active and public opposition to the war, through demonstrations, mass petitions, and all other means within our power." Berger, Seidel, and other Milwaukee Socialists favored a less strident minority report, but they signed the St. Louis platform in the interests of party unity.

That platform instantly marginalized the Socialist Party. Whatever their earlier doubts, most Americans supported the war effort, and pacifism in the face of the German threat seemed perilously close to treason. A number of rising stars left the party, among them Upton Sinclair, Jack London,

A 1917 Socialist Party convention held in St. Louis adopted a strident anti-war platform, much to the dismay of Milwaukee delegates.

and Carl Sandburg, and there was a steady influx of radical pacifists, many of them foreign-born. National membership rose from 83,284 in 1916 to 104,822 in 1919, but few of the newcomers had any interest in the gradualist doctrines of a Victor Berger.

The St. Louis proclamation made life doubly difficult for Dan Hoan. As a card-carrying Socialist, he was pledged to oppose the war but, as the mayor of Milwaukee, he was obliged to coordinate his city's efforts on behalf of the Allies. Pressed to explain his position, Hoan responded, "I am a Socialist – my whole soul rebels at the thought of the war and the horrors of it," but he left no doubt that his official duties came first. A few weeks after the United States entered the conflict, Hoan organized the Milwaukee County Council of Defense to coordinate

Milwaukee Public Library

local activities. Nearly 1,500 volunteers took part in bond drives, victory garden promotions, relief efforts, and the coordination of defense work in local industries.

Faced with a wave of wartime profiteering, the mayor found a novel application for his Socialist principles. Over the vigorous objections of local retailers, the city sold government-surplus food to the public at prices well below those on the private market. By the end of 1917, the Hoan administration had supplied grateful Milwaukee families with 3 carloads of apples, 2,500 pounds of cheese, 30 carloads of potatoes, 140,000 pounds of rough fish (mostly carp and suckers), and 4,000 pounds of split peas. "I believe I have done more to lower the high cost of living," Hoan boasted, "than all the congressmen put together."

Victor Berger found accommodation more difficult. Although he was becoming a stranger in his own party, the Socialist godfather paid a steep personal price for the militancy of his comrades. In the wave of hysteria that engulfed the nation in 1917, when superpatriots were finding enemies under every plate of bratwurst, leftists were singled out for scrutiny, particularly those who spoke with a German accent. In the autumn of 1917, after printing editorials deemed seditious by postal authorities, Berger's *Milwaukee Leader* was stripped of its second-class mailing privileges. The paper instantly lost touch with its out-of-town subscribers – more than 40 percent of its base – and ceased to be the national voice of Socialism. A protest meeting at the Milwaukee Auditorium produced a washtub filled with cash and jewelry worth $4,000, but the *Leader's* financial problems soon reached the crisis point. Still the government bore down. By August, 1918, the newspaper

Dan Hoan tried to balance loyalty to his party with his legal obligations as the city's mayor.

Milwaukee Journal Sentinel

Congressman Victor Berger's anti-war views got him into trouble with everyone but his constituents.

Milwaukee Journal Sentinel

could neither send nor receive even first-class mail. Staff members resorted to posting letters in plain envelopes, and Dan Hoan let it be known that any *Leader* correspondence addressed to the mayor's office would find its way to the right people. The paper's mailing privileges were not restored until mid-1921, more than two years after the war ended.

The editor himself was the next target. On March 11, 1918, Berger and four other Socialists were indicted for violations of the Espionage Act passed nine months earlier; the Milwaukeean's particular crime was a series of anti-war editorials he had written in the summer of 1917. His trial began in December, a month *after* the Armistice, under Judge Kenesaw Mountain Landis, a man who would soon move on to greater things as America's first commissioner of baseball. Landis made little pretense to objectivity; he denied requests for a change of venue despite the fact that he had earlier characterized German Americans as "reeking with disloyalty." In three days of testimony, Berger argued that free speech itself was on trial. He articulated his party's war position and pictured himself as the voice of "sane, constitutional and conservative" Socialism. "I kept the population [of Milwaukee] exceeding law abiding," he bragged, "and we had less trouble there than in any other city." His arguments fell on deaf ears. The Chicago jury found all five defendants guilty, and Judge Landis sentenced each to twenty years in Leavenworth. When the verdict was announced, the Milwaukee Press Club terminated Berger's membership, and the American Legion pushed for his deportation.

Victor Berger had the last, bittersweet laugh. The 1918 elections gave American voters their first chance to weigh in on the European war and its domestic repercussions. There were few surprises elsewhere in the country, but Milwaukeeans made it perfectly clear that they were tired of the endless German-bashing, tired of the shackles on free speech, tired of high prices, and tired of government in general. In the April contests, they made Dan Hoan their mayor again and added one Socialist to the Common Council. In the November races, with Allied victory all but certain, Milwaukeeans elected the entire Socialist county ticket, sent a largely Socialist delegation to the state legislature and, in the most stunning development of all, elected Victor Berger to Congress – just weeks before he was convicted of sedition. When the House refused to seat the felon in 1919, voters elected him again by an even more convincing margin. When Congress still refused to seat him, the Fifth District went without a representative for an entire term.

Berger's double trial – in the courts and in Congress – generated national headlines; one of America's most famous Socialists became its most infamous after 1917. The pillars of mainstream Milwaukee were mortified. The fact that the majority of Berger's would-be constituents had German ancestors was not lost on national reporters following his case, and the city suffered through a fresh round of invective. One weekly journal, *Outlook*, described Milwaukee's support for Berger as nothing less than "secession," and the *Baltimore Sun* panned the community as "that sweet-scented city of Socialism and disloyalty." It was not until 1921 that a semblance of reason returned. Berger's conviction was voided on January 31, lifting the specter of Leavenworth from the editor's life, and he was elected to Congress again in 1922. Seated without incident, Berger served continuously until 1928.

Victor Berger's tribulations were not over. Although he remained a Socialist, Berger watched helplessly as the party he had helped to found came apart at the seams. The long-standing alliance between Socialists and unionists was one of the first casualties of World War I. In the wave of industrial prosperity that accompanied the conflict, union membership nearly doubled, both nationally and locally. A strong worker's movement might have seemed promising for the Socialist cause, but Woodrow Wilson's pro-labor policies – a limited eight-hour day, nationalization of the railroads, and an independent Department of Labor – made it easy for blue-collar voters to back the Democrats. Socialists could still count on labor's support in Milwaukee, at least, but there was no longer a "personal union" on the leadership level. In 1905 Berger had pic-

tured his party and the unions as "a grand army moving on two roads for the abolition of the capitalist system." During World War I, that army came to a parting of the ways.

Developments on the other side of the globe proved even more troublesome for the Socialists. The bloody victory of the Bolsheviks in the 1917 Russian Revolution seemed to confirm the West's most extravagant fears of the red flag. Some American Socialists were delighted with Lenin's success, but the Berger wing of the party was skeptical, particularly as the Soviet system took shape. The Milwaukeeans were, after all, Social Democrats, and they opposed the

In 1919 Berger was re-elected even after Congress had refused to seat him. The Leader *took an excessively upbeat view of his victory.*

Although the "personal union" between Socialists and laborites was dissolving fast, party organizers continued to seek blue-collar support. This group gathered at the International Harvester plant gates.

Milwaukee County Historical Society

231

dictatorship of anyone, including the proletariat. Berger himself became a staunch anti-Communist, dismissing the October Revolution as "a dubious experiment" and Soviet Communism itself as "a retrogression to a very primitive and low stage of human society." That stance did not stop old critics from tarring his brand of Socialism with the same brush they used for the Soviets. In 1920 F. Perry Olds, who had worked the anti-German beat for the *Milwaukee Journal* during the war, served up a wildly inaccurate view of Berger's views as a blend of "Bolshevism and near-anarchy" based on "the principles of Lenine and Trotsky."

The moderate wing of the Socialist Party faced an equally formidable threat from within. The party's rank and file drifted steadily leftward after the war, a trend Berger attributed to an influx of workers, many of them foreign-born, who "despaired of the possibility of solving any social question by peaceable means or through the ballot." These revolutionaries pushed the Socialist Party's membership to a peak of 104,822 in 1919, but they also created intolerable tensions within the organization. The radicals departed in September to form the Communist and Communist Labor

Milwaukee Journal Sentinel

As their party came unraveled, Socialists backed Progressive Robert La Follette in the 1924 presidential election.

Parties, and the ranks of dues-paying Socialists plummeted to 26,766 in 1920 – a decline of 75 percent in a single year.

The dramatic drop prompted Victor Berger to seek an alliance with a man some considered his ideological counterpart in Wisconsin: Robert La Follette. As governor from 1901 to 1906 and a U.S. senator thereafter, La Follette had been one of the nation's most conspicuous Progressives for two decades. Despite their different power bases and radically different views of the free-market system, Progressives and Socialists had common roots in the reform impulse that galvanized American politics in the early 1900s. The two sides worked together in the fabled 1911 state legislature, a session that gave Wisconsin the nation's first worker's compensation law. Shared opposition to World War I brought them even closer together. Bob La Follette believed that European disputes were, in essence, none of America's business, and he vehemently opposed the declaration of war as a distraction from the more important business of reform. Like Victor Berger, he was roundly condemned for his views, but the senator was never indicted, a circumstance Berger attributed to the fact that La Follette's name didn't "sound like sauerkraut." In 1924, when Berger was seeking someone to head "a new party with new ideas," "Fighting Bob" was the obvious choice. The shrunken Socialist Party vigorously backed his independent run for the presidency, with disappointing results. The senator won 5 million votes but carried only Wisconsin, and La Follette died the following June. Berger, who eulogized him as "the Great American," was fully aware that his death marked the end, for the time being, at least, of a third party united against "the autocracy of the present-day capitalism."

There would be no more alliances, but there was no end of defections. By 1927 the Socialist Party's national membership stood at a mere 7,425. Milwaukee, with Hoan in the mayor's office and Berger in Congress, was one of the party's last strongholds. Socialists would remain a force in local politics for another generation, but grandiose visions of the cooperative commonwealth vanished into the inhospitable air over postwar America.

The Pressures of Peacetime

Milwaukeeans celebrated the Armistice of November 11, 1918, with unrestrained glee. After four years of global struggle and local anxiety, life was finally returning to "normal." It soon became apparent, however, that the end of the war did not mean the advent of a golden peace. Brutalized by the horrors of modern combat and disappointed that the world had not been made "safe for democracy," Americans turned decisively inward, rejecting the League of Nations, avoiding foreign entanglements, and continuing their campaign to uproot alien elements from the body politic. Milwaukee's Germans found that they were still on the defensive. In October, 1919, nearly a year after the war ended, the Pabst Theater announced a performance of *Wilhelm Tell*, in the original German, as a benefit for its impoverished acting company. A group of war veterans placed a cannon in the square outside City Hall, aimed it at the Pabst, and announced that they would literally bring down the house if management even tried to raise the curtain. It was

These Milwaukeeans celebrated the 1918 Armistice by hanging "Kaiser Bill" in effigy.

incidents like these, comical only in hindsight, that kept Milwaukee in the news. A visiting *New York Times* reporter (December 21, 1919) declared flatly, "The German question has not died down in this Northern city since the war, as it has, for example, in Cincinnati."

Dan Hoan himself heightened tensions in another celebrated incident. In September, 1919, Hoan was asked to invite the king of Belgium, whose people had suffered terribly during the war, to visit Milwaukee on his good-will tour of the United States. The mayor adamantly refused. "I stand for the

233

man who works," he harrumphed. "To hell with the kings." The remark probably made political hay among Hoan's working-class constituents, but it certainly embarrassed the business community and did little for Milwaukee's already-blemished reputation in the national arena.

Postwar tensions touched even the Slavs, who had little time to savor the liberation of their homelands in the peace settlement. As America's retrenchment gathered strength, the nation suffered a fresh outbreak of nativism – a malady that seems to arise whenever the country temporarily loses faith in its destiny. The melting pot was already part of the national mythology, but it seemed obvious that the "industrial immigrants" from southern and eastern Europe – Italians, Greeks, and the whole family of Slavs – were refusing to melt, that they insisted on preserving their cultures, customs, and languages in the New World. Even worse, according to

Polish immigrants were among those who faced intense pressure to assimilate after World War I. John Gurda, the author's grandfather, stood outside his Lincoln Avenue hardware store in 1918.

the nativists, was their supposed receptiveness to Bolsheviks, radical unionists, and other malcontents who wanted to destroy the American way of life. Already attuned to signs of disloyalty in their German neighbors, superpatriots turned their attention to the newcomers, insisting that all subscribe to "100% Americanism." Their goal, in historian Gerd Korman's apt phrase, was "to replace the melting pot with a pressure cooker."

Much of the pressure, both nationally and locally, was supplied by Americanization programs. In 1911, as part of the "lighted schoolhouse" initiative of the Seidel administration, the city's public schools had introduced a program of evening classes for adults. Within two years, the curriculum included courses in the English language and American civics that drew thousands of immigrants. The classes provided a genuine service to the newcomers, but Americanizers wanted to speed up the process of assimilation. They focused their attention on the workplace, where the Europeans were practically a captive audience. In 1919 Pfister & Vogel, Chain Belt, International Harvester, and other leading employers began to offer language and civics classes inside their plants. P&V workers attended one-hour sessions every morning for ten weeks, earning their regular wages while they learned. Chain Belt's Polish employees were invited to a free supper twice each week, with the "dessert" consisting of lectures on civics, economics, history, and other topics. It was clear that the employers were motivated by self-interest as much as patriotism; English lessons at the Harvester plant included stock phrases like "I leave my place nice and clean" and "I hear the whistle. I must hurry."

When they had learned enough English and civics to pass the citizenship test, many immigrants "graduated" in lavish Americanization pageants. Beginning in 1918 and continuing for several years thereafter, the Auditorium was filled every spring with newcomers marching in full costume behind a red-white-and-blue figure representing Liberty. The immigrants sang their national songs, danced their national dances, and presented tableaux of their national heroes, all as "offerings" on the "altar of citizenship." At the pageant's climax, the new citizens were summoned to the altar, where they sang *Up with the Flag* and received certificates of citizenship from actors dressed as Washington, Jefferson, and Lincoln. Although the ceremony was festive, the message was clear: Preserve your customs if you like, but never forget where your first loyalties lie.

Americanization programs were, in most cases, relatively benign attempts to forge a unified national consciousness. Other attempts were anything but subtle. In 1921 a resurgent Ku Klux Klan sent one of its organizers north to establish a klavern in Milwaukee. Within three years he had found 4,400 adherents, and the local Klan was prosperous enough to set up headquarters in an old German industrialist's mansion at 2432 W. Kilbourn Avenue. Like Klansmen across the country, the Milwaukee group was pledged to "faithful maintenance of white supremacy," using an extraordinarily narrow definition of "white." The Klan's targets included all new immigrants, all Catholics, and all Jews – in addition to all African Americans. The KKK was generally non-violent in its Northern incarnation, but its rhetoric infuriated citizens who were working for tolerance, including Dan Hoan. In 1922 the mayor blasted the "hoods and nighties" set, warning them to leave his city alone: "Milwaukee will become the hottest place this side of

Back to school: an Americanization class at the Chain Belt plant in 1919

Rexnord Corporation

A resurgent Ku Klux Klan made life uncomfortable for residents who didn't share the group's definition of "white."

hell for the Ku Klux Klan if any of the Klan pounce upon one of our citizens, whether he be black or white, red or yellow, Jew or Gentile, Catholic or Protestant." The threat of Klan trouble lasted for only a few years, ending when all but the most confirmed racists grew tired of the group's adolescent rituals and empty rhetoric.

Another expression of nativism had the force of law. In the years following World War I, convinced that America's "new" immigrants were ultimately indigestible, nativists campaigned for rigid restrictions on the flow of newcomers from Europe. Otherwise responsible scholars used traits like body type and head size to argue that Slavic and Mediterranean peoples were different from earlier arrivals, and their overtly racist claims gained wide currency. In 1921 and 1924, bowing to nativist pressures, Congress passed a pair of quota laws that effectively ended free immigration from southern and eastern Europe. Forty years earlier, Emma

Lazarus had pictured the Statue of Liberty as the "Mother of Exiles," lifting a lamp of welcome "beside the golden door." In the 1920s, that door was slammed shut. The chill was felt distinctly in Milwaukee, a city that had long been a haven for "the wretched refuse of your teeming shore," as Lazarus patronizingly described the immigrants. The flood of newcomers slowed to a trickle, and existing ethnic communities came to realize that their story, at least in its European dimension, was over.

A better-known postwar law highlighted the nation's growing capacity for intolerance. Prohibition, that hardy perennial in America's garden of moral crusades, came to full flower in the wake of World War I. Milwaukee, for obvious reasons, had never been especially fertile ground for the temperance movement. When Carrie Nation came to give a speech on "Why I Smashed" in 1902, she expressed disgust at being "back again in the town where all you hear is

236

With heads bowed and tongues firmly in cheek, a group of Milwaukeeans held a funeral for John Barleycorn on the eve of Prohibition in 1919.

Milwaukee County Historical Society

beer, beer." The ax-wielder continued: "If there is any place that is hell on earth, it is Milwaukee." Some saloonkeepers might have considered that an unqualified endorsement, but no one took the Prohibitionists lightly. Milwaukee brewers provided major funding for the long-running battle against the arrayed forces of the Anti-Saloon League. Their money supported lobbyists, advertising campaigns, and a small army of orators, among them David Rose, who stumped against Prohibition in 238 American cities after retiring from the mayor's office. Even Victor Berger, mindful of the role brewery workers played in his party's success, hit the lecture circuit on behalf of the "wets."

World War I changed the balance of power in the battle between wets and drys. After years of rhetorical pounding from the Prohibitionists, Americans found it easy to make alcohol the scapegoat for all of society's ills, and beer itself acquired a reputation as downright unpatriotic. In 1918 John Strange, a Menasha papermaker who had served as Wisconsin's lieutenant governor in 1909-1910, professed to see subversives all around him: "We have German enemies across the water. We have German enemies in this country too. And the worst of all our German enemies, the most treacherous, the most menacing, are Pabst, Schlitz, Blatz and Miller."

Although they must have been legion, the defenders of a beverage dubbed "Kaiser brew" showed little inclination to stand up and be counted. The debate ended months before the last American troops had returned from overseas. "Wartime prohibition" went into effect on July 1, 1919, and the drought was rendered permanent (or so its supporters thought) by the Eighteenth Amendment and then the Volstead Act. Milwaukee took the news with relative equanimity. In the last days of June, 1919, saloons, private clubs, and liquor stores

237

sold off the last of their stock, and nearly every adult male went home, reported the *Sentinel*, "with a mysterious paper-covered package under his arm." On the night of June 30, Prohibition Eve, police arrested thirty revelers for public drunkenness, and a solitary horn-player closed the Schlitz Palm Garden with a soulful rendition of *Taps*. The *Milwaukee Journal* compared the scene downtown to New Year's Eve:

> *Long before midnight every available table was filled at the most popular cafes, where the bright lights had their last chance to be reflected in the sparkle of the cup that cheers. Orchestras and jazz bands whanged and strummed away at their peppiest, on anything but dirgeful melodies. Couples glided and dipped in the latest dance steps to strains of The Alcohol Blues.*

Prohibition's local impact was, first of all, economic. In the national consciousness, Milwaukee without beer was as unthinkable as Detroit without cars or Hartford without insurance. Brewing had never been quite that central to the city's fortunes, but it was definitely big business. In 1918 Milwaukee was the home of 9 breweries with 6,540 employees

Milwaukee's brewers improvised during the long national drought. Pabst made cheese products, and Schlitz turned out chocolate bars.

and an annual output of $35 million – fourth in value behind machinery, packed meats, and leather. Two years later, brewing had vanished from the list of leading industries, and the damage to ancillary businesses was just as serious. Cooper shops, box companies, and the makers of everything from glassware to bar fixtures found themselves in trouble, and even local government felt the pinch. Milwaukee had 1,980 saloons in 1918 (one for every 230 men, women, and children), and their demise meant the loss of nearly $500,000 in annual license fees.

Although Milwaukee's breweries did their best to stay open, Prohibition forced them to make some bizarre adjustments. Nearly all produced near beer (less than 0.5-percent alcohol), malt tonic (a favorite with nursing mothers), and malt syrup (a must for home brewers). Blatz and Miller bottled soda water "in all the popular flavors," but some of their competitors entered fields far removed from the traditions and technologies of brewing. Schlitz, owned by the Uihlein family, produced "Eline" candy bars in a new plant on Port Washington Road. Gettelman manufactured snowplows designed by the founder's son. Pabst turned out processed cheese, using milk from the family's prize-winning Holstein herd near Oconomowoc. Despite their best efforts, Milwaukee's brewers could use only a fraction of their productive capacities. State-of-the-art equipment worth millions of dollars lay idle for years, and empty floor space was rented to fledgling firms on easy terms. Small wonder that the 1921 Common Council, by a vote of twenty-nine to one, implored Congress to make beer and wine legal again.

Consumers fared better than their old suppliers. Prohibition was selectively enforced by the police and widely ignored by the general public. Milwaukee's "soft drink parlors" dispensed a great deal more than strawberry phosphates. Roadhouses just outside the city limits attracted droves of drinkers. Wealthy residents with Canadian connections husbanded stockpiles of bonded whiskey through the dry spell. Hardware stores did a brisk business in copper boilers and metal tubing, and jewelers learned to stock a large assortment of hip flasks. The late-night smells wafting over some neighborhoods, particularly the Italian Third Ward, were almost literally intoxicating. If someone wanted to find a drink, a drink could always be found.

Despite the enormous profits to be made in the illegal liquor trade, the city never became a stronghold of organized crime; the Al Capones of the era found no easy foothold in Milwaukee. Periodic visits by "sponge squads" kept owners of the speakeasies on their toes, and local officials, if not absolutely untouchable, were at least harder to reach than their counterparts ninety miles south. "Notwithstanding its proximity to Chicago," Dan Hoan crowed in 1927, "Milwaukee is the most law-abiding large city in America." The city's real loss was cultural. Breweries and beer gardens had been fixtures on the local scene since the mid-1800s, and beer had always been an indispensable ingredient of the community's fabled *Gemütlichkeit*. Prohibition meant that even social drinkers had to resort to subterfuge. The legal loss of Milwaukee's amber lubricant was deeply felt, and there was nothing, really, to replace it. For most residents, neither the rollicking atmosphere of the roadhouse nor the taste of bathtub gin behind closed doors could match a good glass of lager, freely and openly enjoyed.

Periodic raids did little to stem the flow of liquor in Milwaukee. "If I had the whole United States Army," Dan Hoan said in 1929, "I could not prevent illegal drinking.... Prohibition is a big joke."

Milwaukee County Historical Society

"The City of Diversified Industry"

By 1920, beer was illegal, Socialists were endangered, and Germans were on the run. Did any of Milwaukee's hallmarks survive the pressures of World War I and its aftermath? The resounding, one-word answer is "manufacturing." Milwaukee's industrial roots were well-established before 1914, and the war itself strengthened them significantly. Orders from the Allies sparked a business upturn as early as 1915, but the real boom came when America entered the conflict. By 1918 local employers faced a serious labor shortage, despite a steady influx of workers from rural Wisconsin and other parts of the country.

Virtually every industry was involved in the war effort. Packing plants supplied mess pork and other rations for hungry soldiers. Tanneries provided leather for the doughboys' boots and belts. Harley-Davidson equipped them with motorcycles. Even the breweries felt a temporary lift, as Milwaukee suppliers reached the South American markets that had once belonged to Germany. Scores of local machine shops took part in the effort to build a "bridge of ships" across the Atlantic. Allis-Chalmers manufactured marine engines, naval artillery, and shrapnel shells. Falk made the gear drives for 229 American warships – the highest total in the gear industry – and Cutler-Hammer equipped most of them with electrical controls. For some businesses, the war was quite literally a lifesaver. In 1914 Allen-Bradley was a hand-to-mouth enterprise occupying rented quarters in someone else's machine shop. By 1918, with war orders accounting for 70 percent of their motor-control business, the Bradley brothers had bought out their landlord and started work on a three-story addition.

The pattern was the same everywhere: triple-digit increases in sales, profits, and

Milwaukee was a major source of Allied munitions and supplies during World War I. Harnischfeger's products included mobile artillery.

Milwaukee County Historical Society

240

plant space. Between 1914 and 1919, according to the federal census, the city of Milwaukee's manufacturing output swelled from $223.56 million to $576.16 million – a staggering 158-percent increase in just five years. Needless to say, German-born industrialists and German-born workers were responsible for much of that output. There is no small irony in the fact that Milwaukee, widely viewed as a den of disloyalty elsewhere in the country, played a pivotal role in the Allied military effort.

Despite a nasty bout of war-related inflation and a short but sharp 1921 recession, the industrial boom continued after the Armistice. The city's manufacturing output rose to $700.76 million in 1929, an increase of 22 percent in a decade, and the county's output bumped against the billion-dollar mark. The metal trades were still absolutely dominant, accounting for one-third to one-half of Milwaukee's total production each year, but there was substantial movement elsewhere on the *Milwaukee Sentinel's* annual list of leading products. Brewing, of course, faded to insignificance after 1919. Tanning dropped out of the top five in 1921; shoes lasted longer in the automobile era, buggy whips and harnesses were nearing extinction, and electric motors reduced the need for heavy leather belting in the nation's factories. Old standbys – meat-packing and footwear – retained their importance, and new industries filled the vacuum left by the fallen giants. Milwaukee became a national center of the American automotive industry in the 1920s, led by A.O. Smith (car frames), the Seaman Body Company, and a relative newcomer: Briggs & Stratton. Founded in 1908, Briggs & Stratton made a variety of automotive parts in the 1920s, on its way to becoming the world's largest manufacturer

Wartime labor shortages brought large numbers of women into local industries for the first time. This group worked at the Evinrude Motor factory.

Milwaukee Public Library

241

of car locks and small gasoline engines. Knit goods entered the top five in 1921; Phoenix and Holeproof Hosiery turned out silk stockings by the millions, and both companies became leading employers of women. Agricultural equipment was another local specialty. Allis-Chalmers began to make tractors in 1914, joining the International Harvester plant opened thirty years earlier; by 1929 Milwaukee was turning out more tractors than any other city in the world.

Most Milwaukeeans had long since embraced what seemed to be their economic destiny. Otto Falk, the head of Allis-Chalmers for nearly three decades and an officer of the family-owned Falk Company, was a leading spokesman for the community's industrial interests. In 1911 he put the matter plainly: "The city of Milwaukee glories in a forest of factory chimneys rather than commercial skyscrapers. It is primarily a great manufacturing center..., a monster workshop whose products go to the four ends of the world." When Socialists suggested that the city's industrial valleys would have seen better use as public parks, Falk took vigorous exception:

> *If Milwaukee had no factories it would have little use for its parks. Let us regard our factory districts as blessings rather than nuisances. We ought to have more Menomonie and Kinnickinnic valleys and more factories and more railroads. We need more blazing furnaces and smoking chimneys. That would mean more work, more wages, more thrift and more prosperity.*

Pollution problems aside, Milwaukee's pride in its resident manufacturers was even more evident after the war. Stripped of its fame as the *Deutsch-Athen* of America and the Beer Capital of the World, the community tried to build a new national reputation on its industrial prowess. In 1925 the First Wisconsin Bank proclaimed Milwaukee "The City of Diversified Industry," a slogan that was widely circulated during the decade. (An earlier campaign for "Monarch of the Sausage Kingdom" failed to generate much

The Allis-Chalmers tractor plant helped make Milwaukee a world center of farm machinery production.

Milwaukee County Historical Society

sizzle.) Milwaukee turned out so many different products, asserted the boosters, that it was virtually recession-proof; if one company faltered, another was sure to take up the slack. The roster of leading industries was indeed impressive. In 1925 the *Milwaukee Journal* surveyed the field and found that Milwaukee County had America's largest manufacturers of heavy machinery (Allis-Chalmers), cranes and hoists (Harnischfeger), motorcycles (Harley-Davidson), steam shovels and dredges (Bucyrus, a prime contractor on the Panama Canal), electrical controls (Cutler-Hammer), outboard motors (Evinrude), automobile frames (A.O. Smith), enamelware (National Enameling & Stamping, better known as Nesco), temperature regulators (Johnson Controls), refrigeration machinery (Vilter), herringbone gears (Falk), silk hosiery (Phoenix and Holeproof), mine hoists (Nordberg), cement machinery (Koehring), and even wheelbarrows (Sterling). These giants and hundreds of smaller plants were

the economic lifeblood of the community. In 1920 manufacturing provided jobs for 88,861 city residents – a remarkable 58 percent of Milwaukee's labor force.

None of those workers failed to notice a dramatic shift in the tenor of labor relations after the Armistice. The war years had been good for factory hands; unemployment was nearly nonexistent, and the eight-hour day was mandatory in military plants. In 1918 Milwaukee's unions launched a "Labor Forward" movement to protect their wartime gains and advance their campaign for the closed shop. Management promptly counterattacked. In 1919 the Milwaukee Employers Council was organized to make sure that local shops remained open to non-union workers. Within two years, the Council's membership had grown to 600 companies, and they employed more than half the area's work force. Management had nearly all the weapons in the struggle that followed; lockouts, injunctions, labor spies, and boycotts were used so aggressively that the state

(left)
Foundry hands posed with an oversized gear at the Maynard Steel plant.

(below)
William Davidson and William Harley took one of their creations on a highly productive fishing trip in the early 1920s.

legislature felt compelled to limit their legality. The determined resistance of Milwaukee's employers made the Twenties a dismal decade for organized labor. By 1930, despite steady growth in the work force, union membership had subsided to prewar levels.

Many employers used the carrot as well as the stick in their attempts to avoid industrial conflict. All-plant picnics, employee publications, Christmas parties, and bowling leagues became standard practice during the postwar period, and some firms went considerably farther. In 1928 Allen-Bradley dedicated a seven-story addition that included marble washrooms, a reading room with beamed ceilings and a huge fireplace, and a rooftop deck featuring badminton courts, a boxing ring, and six nets to catch the practice shots of aspiring golfers. The Bradleys even hired a golf pro to give lessons once a week. Cutler-Hammer started a drill team, a drum corps, a band, a glee club, and a horseshoe-pitching club just

after the war. E.P. Allis had supported a mutual aid society for shop workers back in 1883, and his successors at Allis-Chalmers added a two-week paid vacation and a company hospital in the 1920s. Milwaukee's white-collar workers were not forgotten. In 1915, one year after moving into its monumental home office on E. Wisconsin Avenue, Northwestern Mutual Life began to offer a hearty free lunch to all workers – a practice that continues to the present.

The era's most ambitious industrial program was probably the Employees' Mutual Benefit Association, an organization launched by The Milwaukee Electric Railway & Light Company in 1912. The EMBA began as a health-care plan, but its umbrella spread during and after World War I to include sports leagues (indoor baseball was a favorite), after-work classes (from blueprint reading to poultry breeding), a dramatic society, a band and chorus, marriage and financial counseling, and

More than one firm strived to develop a "family" atmosphere in the 1920s. When Allen-Bradley finished a major addition in 1928 (left), the rooftop deck (right) included room for dancing, badminton, boxing, and even golf practice. Lynde Bradley looked on paternally from the upper terrace.

even collective bargaining. By 1920 the EMBA had become a poor man's Masons, with its own initiation rituals, handshake, logo, password, and song: *On, Electric*, sung to the tune of *On, Wisconsin*. The Association was literally a cradle-to-grave society; a member could come into the world with the help of an EMBA doctor, work for the utility under EMBA auspices until retirement, and go to his or her grave escorted by an EMBA color guard.

The various employee programs of the war and postwar years made Milwaukee a center of "welfare capitalism," usually defined as the provision of amenities beyond a job and a paycheck. Most employers were motivated by the same force that underlay their Americanization efforts: self-interest. Welfare activities helped them attract and retain workers in a tight labor market, fostered a healthier and more productive work force and, not least of all, kept union organizers at bay. In TMER&L's case, EMBA

activities gave employees of the chronically embattled utility a sense of shared purpose in the face of a skeptical public and spiteful politicians. But something more was at work in Milwaukee's home-grown industrial plants. Entrepreneurs like Herman Falk,

Northwestern Mutual Life built a monumental home office in 1914. Its amenities included a daily free lunch, served family-style.

Milwaukee County Historical Society

Indoor baseball, played with an oversized ball and an undersized bat, was a favorite employee activity at The Milwaukee Electric Railway & Light Company.

We Energies

Henry Harnischfeger, Bruno Nordberg, and Lynde and Harry Bradley took an intensely personal interest in the companies they had created. The founders were a constant presence on the shop floors, and most were on intimate terms with workers in every department. In such an atmosphere, the analogy to family was more than a press agent's pipe dream. No one had to ask who sat at the head of the table. Louis Allis, one of E.P. Allis's younger sons, owned an electric motor company with a particularly cohesive corporate culture. When his employees threw a birthday party for "the old man" one year, Allis responded simply, "God bless you, my children." Paternalism was implicit in the relationship, but there was also a personalism, a mutual regard between owners and employees, that would have been impossible in any other setting.

The turbine room of the massive Lakeside power plant expressed the "Industrial Moderne" spirit of the 1920s.

We Energies

Growing Up, Growing Out

In the World War I era, as in earlier years, an industrial boom touched off a population boom. The number of Milwaukee residents swelled from 373,857 in 1910 to 457,147 in 1920 and 578,249 in 1930, an increase of 22 percent in the first decade and 26.5 percent in the second. The gain of the Twenties alone – 121,102 people – was the greatest absolute increase in the city's entire history. Double-digit growth might have been taken for granted in the frontier period, but it was a sign of impressive strength in a community already past the quarter-million mark.

Other cities were demonstrating the same strength. As America became a predominantly urban society after World War I, Milwaukee could do little more than hold its own, slipping from twelfth place to thirteenth among the nation's cities in 1920 and then climbing back to twelfth in 1930. The national rankings revealed a strong westerly drift in America's urban geography. In 1920 Milwaukee fell behind Los Angeles – a clear sign of the Sunbelt's future – and ten years later moved ahead of Buffalo, the historic point of entry for the entire upper Midwest.

Rapid population growth aggravated one of Milwaukee's oldest problems: overcrowding. The immigrant's habit of thrift and the developer's desire for profit had created a city of narrow lots, compact housing, and precious little private green space. The rowhouse developments of Eastern cities were practically absent, but the prevalence of duplexes and Polish flats had virtually the same effect. In 1920 Milwaukee's population density peaked at 18,213 persons per square mile – second only to New York City's.

An assortment of suburbs stood ready to relieve the pressures on their larger neighbor. Two new villages were incorporated during the period: Fox Point in 1926 and River Hills in 1930. Both North Shore communities had begun as summer retreats for well-to-do East Siders, and both relied on strict zoning ordinances to maintain their upper-crust characters. The future of River Hills was implicit in its origins. The community's leading (in fact, its only) institution was the Milwaukee Country Club, whose board decided in 1929 "to effect the organization of a village comprising certain properties including and surrounding the Milwaukee Country Club, with the understanding that this village be organized and incorporated in the interests of the Milwaukee Country Club." The golf group's elegant new clubhouse served as River Hills' first polling place, the green-keeper's cottage became the first village hall, and club leaders rotated the village presidency for years.

Fox Point and River Hills were, by design, communities of large homes on large lots; neither housed more than a minuscule fraction of the county's population. Older suburbs, both industrial and residential, experienced phenomenal growth during the period. The population of West Allis, Milwaukee's largest satellite, increased fivefold between 1910 and 1930, and Wauwatosa grew by a factor of six. Gains on the South Shore, in Cudahy and South Milwaukee, were

"What? Another one?" The steady procession of suburbs drew the attention of Ross Lewis, the Milwaukee Journal's *cartoonist.*

Riding to hounds on Range Line Road was still a possibility in 1930, when River Hills was incorporated at the behest of the Milwaukee Country Club.

247

somewhat less spectacular, but the North Shore communities of Shorewood and Whitefish Bay, after years of relative stagnation, registered huge proportional gains in the 1920s. By 1930 the suburban population of Milwaukee County was 17.5 percent of the city's – up from just 7 percent in 1910.

Milwaukee and Its Suburbs, 1910-1930

Population	1910	1920	1930	% change, 1910-1930
Milwaukee	373,857	457,147	578,249	55%
Wauwatosa	3,346	5,818	21,194	533%
South Milwaukee	6,092	7,598	10,706	76%
Whitefish Bay	542	882	5,362	889%
Cudahy	3,691	6,725	10,631	188%
North Milwaukee	1,860	3,047	—	—
Shorewood	707	2,650	13,479	1,807%
West Allis	6,645	13,745	34,671	422%
West Milwaukee	1,458	2,101	4,168	186%
Fox Point	—	—	474	—
River Hills	—	—	280	—

With suburbs springing up around it, the city of Milwaukee came to resemble a large dog surrounded by a pack of rambunctious puppies, all nipping at its flanks and helping themselves to its food. The municipality began to bite back during Dan Hoan's administration. Hoping to stem a steady erosion of tax base, bring a semblance of order to metropolitan growth, and perhaps even garner a few more Socialist votes, Hoan's team launched an aggressive annexation campaign in 1920. Their immediate target was the developed but unincorporated zone lying just beyond Milwaukee's borders. Arthur Werba, the campaign's field general, described the effort in humanitarian terms:

Milwaukee owes a duty to its citizens, and a moral obligation to people of outlying communities, to annex these built-up areas, extend its facilities and thus by promoting the growth of the city make the new districts safer and more desirable for human habitation. The people of the outlying districts will gladly pay their share of the cost because they will get, dollar for dollar, more city services and conveniences than any other municipality could give them.

Annexation was always voluntary; no area came into the city unless a majority of its residents endorsed the move. Although agreement was seldom unanimous, thousands of outlying residents found Milwaukee's arguments compelling. Between 1920 and 1930, the city's land area swelled from 26.089 square miles to 43.109 – an increase of 65 percent in a single decade – and its population density shrank from 18,213 persons per square mile to 13,867. The annexations took in established neighborhoods like Pigsville on the West Side (named for an adjoining pig farm) and Silver City on the South Side, but the city added even more territory on its developing fringe, where communities like Sherman Park, Rufus King, and Layton Park were taking shape. Steady expansion helped Dan Hoan honor his often-repeated pledge to create a "bigger, better and brighter Milwaukee."

Hoan's annexation specialists were interested in much more than piecemeal growth. Their ultimate goal was one big city, a metropolitan government operating under the auspices of the community that, in their view, governed best: the city of Milwaukee. The one-government vision was a natural outgrowth of the Socialists' demonstrated interest in economy, efficiency, and municipal coherence, and it roused some natural enemies, beginning with the suburbs themselves. Art Werba blasted the "suburban blockade" that nearly surrounded Milwaukee, stifling the city's economic potential and needlessly complicating life for all residents. Although he faced entrenched resistance, there was one substantial breach in the "blockade." On January 1, 1929, after years of rancorous debate, the industrial suburb of North Milwaukee joined the city of Milwaukee. Tired of higher taxes, higher water rates, and inferior public services, voters had approved consolidation by a margin of more than two to one. North Milwaukee thereby joined Bay View as one of only two independent suburbs in Milwaukee's history that became city neighborhoods. Art Werba found the move heartening:

> Now there remains the task of consolidating the other incorporated suburbs with Milwaukee, namely: West Allis, Wauwatosa, Shorewood, Whitefish Bay, West Milwaukee, Cudahy and South Milwaukee. If Milwaukee is to grow in an orderly way these barriers to its progress will gradually have to be removed, but the power to do so rests with the people of the suburbs.

Dreams of metropolitan government never died but, needless to say, the suburban surrender that Werba so ardently anticipated never came to pass.

As North Milwaukeeans beat the drum for consolidation, the once-independent village became a unique Milwaukee neighborhood.

Milwaukee Public Library

"Where All Is New"

Whether it took place on the city's fringe or in nearby suburbs, geographic expansion was a predictable outcome of rapid population growth. The outward-bound impulse signified, at the same time, a pronounced shift in public tastes. Milwaukeeans, like most Americans, developed a disdain for the old and a desire for novelty after the war. That desire, honed to a razor's edge by mass advertising, extended to home and neighborhood. "Live Where All Is New!," urged an ad for a Sherman Park subdivision in 1919. Hoping to lure customers to the open fields near Forty-ninth and Center Streets, the developer hired "Browne's Aeroplane" to perform acrobatic tricks and drop coupons good for a twenty-five-dollar discount on any lot. Such high-flying stunts marked a new and more aggressive stage in local real-estate advertising. Other Milwaukee-area developers offered picnics, concerts, fireworks, and free ice cream in an effort to pull urbanites out to the city's edge.

The houses that sprang up on the fringe may have been brand-new, but the people who built them were only one step removed from much older neighborhoods; the centrifugal pattern of earlier decades still applied. As South Siders moved south and North Siders moved north, their new communities absorbed the ethnic flavors of the old. Thousands of Polish families settled in the blocks south of Oklahoma Avenue. Irish West Siders were an appreciable element in suburban Wauwatosa. Remnants of the Yankee elite migrated from the East Side to the North Shore suburbs. North Milwaukee was a heavily German community, and Sherman Park reflected the German, Czech, and later the Jewish character of its source neighborhoods on the North Side. Newly minted community institutions – churches, schools, and hospitals – were usually updated versions of those left behind in the old neighborhood.

For nearly every home-buyer, the move out was also a move up. The post-World War I period saw the emergence of a genuine middle class in Milwaukee, a new economic stratum between industrialists and industrial laborers. Many of its members were Irish, Polish, and Italian Americans, historically impoverished groups who rode

The steam shovel and horse-drawn wagons worked in tandem on a subdivision at Twenty-second Street and Concordia Avenue.

Milwaukee Public Library

their jobs as skilled tradesmen, office workers, and small-scale entrepreneurs to new economic heights. Their homes reflected their rise in status. Just as the Polish flat and the duplex had been the signature houses of the previous generation, the Milwaukee bungalow typified the city of the 1920s. Local versions of the bungalow ranged from simple frame homes to elaborate brick structures, but the average specimen featured a highly efficient floor plan, an attic easily converted to living space, and amenities like hardwood moldings and stained-glass window lights. Compact, convenient, and surprisingly spacious, Milwaukee bungalows embodied a feeling of substance that flowed naturally from the prosperity of the Twenties.

Behind the typical bungalow stood a small frame structure that would have puzzled Milwaukeeans of the 1800s: a garage. The automobile it sheltered was an entirely new force in the local landscape. Streetcar and interurban lines had long been the region's growth corridors, but it was the private automobile that fueled Milwaukee's outward expansion after the

The bungalow was the house of choice in the 1920s. This specimen was among the first on S. Thirteenth Street.

Milwaukee Historic Preservation Commission

war. From River Hills to Elm Grove to Hales Corners, as well as in the city itself, bedroom communities filled up with commuters who traveled back to the heart of town on rubber tires. The automobile's dominion began earlier than might be supposed. In 1910 there was only one car for every eighty-four families in Wisconsin. By 1920 there was one for every two families, and in 1930 the ratio was one to one; a luxury became a necessity in less than twenty years. Milwaukee, the state's urban center, was its automotive center as well. In 1926 the number of cars registered in Milwaukee County passed the 100,000 mark, roughly 20 percent of all the automobiles in Wisconsin.

The new vehicles were inescapable in the Teens and Twenties. Collisions between automobiles and streetcars rose 140 percent between 1914 and 1915. Milwaukee's wooden wagon industry, a million-dollar business in

A luxury in 1910, the automobile was a necessity by 1930, and its impact on American life was pervasive. This 1924 Dodge was stopped at Lincoln and Kinnickinnic Avenues.

Milwaukee Public Library

1915, practically disappeared in the next decade. Cars outnumbered horses on the city's streets for the first time in 1916, and six years later public officials found it necessary to install the first automatic traffic signals. Motorists were enthralled by the freedom and mobility the car gave them. Sunday newspapers featured thick automobile sections during the summer "touring season," and in 1921 Milwaukee established tourist camps for itinerant motorists in Grant, Estabrook, and Currie Parks. Whether purchased for camping or commuting, the vehicle of choice after World War I was the Model T. Available for as little as $260 in 1925 (roughly $2,100 in current dollars), Mr. Ford's marvelous invention was within the means of even working-class families.

The automobile's runaway popularity signaled a new stage in America's evolution as a consumer society. There had always been a demand for products that promised

Automobiles and streetcars were evenly matched in this 1926 view of W. Wisconsin Avenue.

We Energies

to make life easier, but never before the 1920s had the world witnessed the uniquely American phenomenon of mass-produced goods sold on the mass market with the help of mass advertising. Automobiles were just the beginning. With the growth of electricity in the Twenties, there was a surge in demand for all kinds of new appliances. In 1910 only the most affluent tenth of Milwaukee households could afford electricity. By 1920 the proportion of "electric homes" in the metropolitan area had reached 35 percent, and it continued climbing to 67 percent in 1923 and 97 percent in 1927. Milwaukee was almost completely electrified, creating an enormous appetite for toasters and roasters, nightlights and floor lamps, egg-cookers and cigar-lighters. In 1927, 45 percent of Milwaukee-area households had washing machines and 66 percent owned vacuum cleaners.

National chain stores popped up to sell these and other consumer goods. The homegrown Schuster's department stores remained Milwaukee's largest, but they faced stiff competition from the downtown Gimbels as well as from Sears Roebuck, which opened huge emporiums on North Avenue and just off Mitchell Street in the 1920s. Walgreen's made its debut in 1925, and A&P had 140 Milwaukee outlets by 1932. The advent of mass merchandising sent a chill through the local retail establishment. Frank Schuster, a long-time Bay View grocer, penned a bit of doggerel in protest:

Oh, yes, their stores are pretty,
And their windows have a flash;
But they never know a person
If he hasn't got the cash.
For their bosses live in Wall Street,
And we are a bunch of fools
If we think these fellows give a hoot
For our churches and our schools....

As the Milwaukee area was almost completely wired in the 1920s, "electric living" became the vogue. The huge devices on the far right and left are a dishwasher and a mixer.

We Energies

> *Let's patronize our local stores,*
> *And keep the cash at home,*
> *And let the doggone chain stores*
> *Start a Bay View of their own!*

Both chain stores and independent retailers carried one of the period's most popular "appliances": the radio. From the day Pittsburgh's KDKA went on the air in 1920, the medium's growth was nothing less than explosive. Milwaukee's first entrant was WAAK, a 100-watt wonder that began to broadcast from Gimbels department store on April 26, 1922. Programming was limited to a few hours each week and consisted of live local performances and speeches by public figures like Dan Hoan. Most of the early receivers were homemade. In 1924 only 9 percent of Milwaukee-area families owned radios, and two-thirds of them were crystal sets built by ambitious amateurs. Giants like Westinghouse, GE, and RCA transformed the industry almost

overnight. By 1927, 44 percent of the area's households owned radios, and nearly all were factory-built models. Networks were the next logical step. With the debut of NBC in 1926 and CBS a year later, millions of Americans huddled around their consoles to hear the *A&P Gypsies*, *The Eveready Hour*, *Grand Ole Opry*, and *Amos 'n' Andy*. Milwaukee's leading stations at the decade's end were both owned by newspapers: WTMJ (*The Milwaukee Journal*, 1927) and WISN (*WISconsin News*, 1928).

The radio encouraged Milwaukeeans to stay home, but there was no shortage of opportunities for more active nightlife. As the Twenties began to roar, the younger set met at venues like the Riverview Dancing Palace on North Avenue (capacity 5,000), the ballroom of the new Eagles Club on Twenty-fourth and Grand or, most novel of all, the Wisconsin Roof. Opened in 1924 atop a new building at Sixth and Grand, "the Roof" featured open-air dancing to the music of live orchestras; promoter George Devine billed his creation as "The World's Wonder Ballroom." Whether they were mixing with "the better crowd" promised by Devine or meeting old friends at the neighborhood hall, Milwaukee's young people danced to the same tunes that were moving their peers across the country, including *Charleston, Ain't We Got Fun?, Stardust, Makin' Whoopee,* and *I Wish I Could Shimmy Like My Sister Kate.*

Theaters attracted more sedentary citizens of all ages. Vaudeville was still thriving after World War I, but motion pictures were already the leading medium of mass entertainment. Milwaukeeans of 1929 could watch the latest films at any of ninety-four movie theaters, from the Alhambra downtown to the Zenith on N. Hopkins Street. Until 1927, when Al Jolson's *The Jazz Singer* ushered in the era of the "talkies," moviegoers followed the action with the help of a pit orchestra, a theater organ or, at the very least, an out-of-tune piano. The names on the marquees, like the songs in the dance halls and the programs on the radio, transcended regional differences; stars like Douglas Fairbanks, Greta Garbo, Charlie Chaplin, and Mary Pickford developed loyal followings throughout the country. These larger-than-life figures were often showcased in larger-than-life settings. The Twenties were the heyday of the "movie palace," an outlandishly original form of architecture that survives in gems like the Oriental (1927), the Avalon (1929), the Riverside (1929), and the Modjeska (1924). The appeal was the same in every case: escape. "Come out of your humdrum existence," coaxed a 1921 ad for the Butterfly Theater. "Live in the land of mystery and romance."

Milwaukee County Historical Society

Completed in 1925, the Eagles Club gave younger Milwaukeeans a new place to swing.

We Energies

The Butterfly was one of the city's more ornate movie theaters. It lit up the corner of Second Street and Wisconsin Avenue from 1911 to 1930.

courtesy Joan Cummings

courtesy John Duggan

courtesy Meta Lawrie

Milwaukee at home, 1910-1930:
(clockwise from top) the Cummings boys of
the Third Ward, the Gardner kids of Merrill
Park, a bevy of priests at St. Francis
Seminary, and swinging in the hammock
in Humboldt Park

Milwaukee Public Library

New Neighbors

Even in their "humdrum" everyday lives, local residents could see the evidence of modernity all around them. New houses, new cars, new appliances, new radios, and new movies made Milwaukee as up-to-date as any American city, and the trends were especially apparent on the urban fringe. There was a complementary shift in the heart of the city. As older, upwardly mobile groups moved to the edge of town, newer and poorer groups settled around the central business district. The pattern was familiar; new groups had been relegated to old houses for most of Milwaukee's history. But the newcomers of the postwar era were different from their predecessors in one important particular: They were no longer European immigrants. World War I had slowed transatlantic immigration to a trickle, and the quota laws of the early 1920s kept the faucet tightly closed. For the country as a whole, the number of new European arrivals plummeted from 1,058,391 in 1914 to 148,366 in 1925.

The unforeseen result was a critical shortage of unskilled workers. Like their counterparts elsewhere in America, Milwaukee industrialists had long relied on Europeans, particularly southern and eastern Europeans, to take their entry-level jobs. With that source of supply cut off and the economy in high gear, manufacturers were virtually forced to find help closer to home. Thus began the first large-scale movement of African Americans and Latinos to Milwaukee. Few of the newcomers saw the inside of a new bungalow or owned a new car, but their presence was even more a foretaste of the modern city than any shift in material culture.

The city's black population showed the most dramatic growth, rising from 980 in 1910 to 2,229 in 1920 and then jumping to 7,501 in 1930 – a 665-percent increase in twenty years. Thousands of African Americans were recruited by labor agents who roamed the South in search of workers for Milwaukee's packing plants, tanneries, foundries, and construction crews. Those workers transformed the existing black community. Historian Joe Trotter calculated that only 19 percent of Milwaukee's black males held industrial jobs in 1919; by 1930 the proportion had risen to 80 percent. The *Milwaukee Journal* (August 19, 1917) noted their presence even before the war ended:

One who knew Milwaukee a half-dozen years ago, or even twelve months ago, and who knows it today, will be surprised if he stops to note the number of colored people he meets on the streets now as compared with preceding years. So silently have they slipped into the city that few of us have noted their coming. They are but part, however, of the general exodus from the south, which has been

The promise of jobs brought thousands of African Americans to Milwaukee in the 1920s. This asphalt crew worked for The Milwaukee Electric Railway & Light Company.

We Energies

bemoaning for months the loss of the colored laboring class.

The colored man has come to live among the 'yankees' without solicitation from the people of the north. He will be received and welcomed as an addition to the community. Nothing of the class hatred that has so much marred his living in the watermelon country will be evident here. He will be given an opportunity to do his best. Every door of every field of work is open. Men are needed everywhere.

As long as the black community was small enough to be viewed as a curiosity, there was little overt racism in Milwaukee, but the welcome mat was never as wide as the *Journal* indicated. African Americans were invariably the first to be fired in economic downturns, and many experienced discrimination in theaters, restaurants, and the housing market. Like newcomers of every background and every generation, blacks lived together by choice, but the choice of neighborhoods was not entirely theirs. By 1930 nearly every African American in Milwaukee could be found in an area bordered by State Street and North Avenue between Third and Twelfth Streets – a neighborhood they shared with Jews, Grecks, Germans, Slovaks, and Croats.

An impressive range of institutions developed within that neighborhood: the local branch of the NAACP in 1915, the *Milwaukee Enterprise* newspaper (later the *Enterprise Blade*) in 1916, the Milwaukee Urban League in 1919, the Negro Business League in 1925, and Columbia Building and Loan in the same year. (Dan Hoan provided crucial early support for Columbia.) But the African-American community's leading institutions were the same as those at the

heart of Milwaukee's European neighborhoods: places of worship. St. Mark AME, founded in 1869, remained a cornerstone, and it was joined by Calvary Baptist in 1895, St. Benedict the Moor Catholic in 1908, and Greater Galilee and Mt. Zion Baptist, both organized in 1919. By the late 1920s, there were more than a dozen black clergymen in Milwaukee, among them Earl Little, a footloose Baptist preacher whose young son, Malcolm, would one day change his last name to X.

The city's African-American community was firmly established before 1930, but Milwaukee was not by any measure a leading center of black settlement. Of the million-plus Southern blacks who came north in the Great Migration of 1910-1930, the 7,500 who found their way to the former *Deutsch-Athen* were a handful indeed. Chicago, by contrast, was a primary destination, its black population growing from 44,103 in 1910 to 233,903 in 1930. African

Americans made up 4 percent of the Windy City's population in 1920 and 7 percent in 1930; the comparable figures for Milwaukee were 0.5 percent and 1.3 percent. The disparity may help to explain why Chicago endured nearly a week of barbarous race riots in the summer of 1919, while black-white relations ninety miles north were generally pacific.

Latinos, most of them Mexicans, came to Milwaukee at the same time and for the same reasons as African Americans. *Los primeros* – the pioneers – arrived in 1920, when labor agents for Pfister & Vogel recruited nearly 100 young Mexican males

Milwaukee Journal Sentinel

(above)
In 1925 Wilbur Halyard founded Columbia Building and Loan, the city's first African-American financial institution.

St. Benedict the Moor Catholic Mission operated a boarding school whose alumni included Harold Washington and Redd Foxx.

Milwaukee County Historical Society

to work in the company's South Side tannery. Sleeping on "sanitary cots" in a tannery annex and taking their meals in the P&V dining room, the newcomers were completely isolated at first. Some took advantage of the company's English classes, but their chief diversion was the "recreational evenings" offered three times a week by the YMCA. As steel plants, foundries, and other tanneries established their own Mexican connections, hundreds of other newcomers made the long journey north. Social clubs, businesses, and even a short-lived newspaper appeared in the 1920s, but the leading Latino institution was the Mission of Our Lady of Guadalupe, established in a S. Fifth Street storefront in 1926. The Catholic mission served as the spiritual and social anchor for a community on the rise. In 1930 the federal census tallied 1,479 Mexicans in the city, almost certainly an undercount; a YWCA study in the same year placed the number at 4,000. Then as now, the center of the Latino community was the old Walker's Point neighborhood on the near South Side.

The growth of the black and Latino populations marked a new chapter in Milwaukee's ethnic history, a shift away from Europe alone toward Africa and Latin America as cultural headwaters for the community. Both groups were, in a statistical sense, minorities, but "minority" was a slippery term in the World War I era. In 1914 the *Milwaukee Journal* described the city's Greeks as a "little colony of aliens," and other late-arriving Europeans were singled out in similar fashion. In an era of vivid distinctions, however, none were more vivid than those defining people of color. Older residents couldn't help but notice that their city was becoming black and brown as well as white. The broader significance of the shift was evident only in hindsight: After decades as a European enclave, Milwaukee was finally approaching the full range of ethnic diversity that characterizes the community today.

(left)

Jobs in tanneries and other industries brought hundreds of Mexicans to Milwaukee after World War I.

(right)

The community's anchor was the Mission of Our Lady of Guadalupe, a storefront church on S. Fifth Street near National Avenue.

courtesy Arnoldo Sevilla

courtesy Arnoldo Sevilla

Municipal Enterprise

The forces of modernism were universal. New modes of transportation, novel forms of entertainment, the rise of mass marketing, and the arrival of new minorities were all part of a twentieth-century tide that engulfed urban America during the postwar period. Year after year, Milwaukee looked and behaved more like other cities. Even as the tide rose, however, the community was developing another quality that became, in time, a genuine hallmark: good government. Long after the reform impulse had spent itself in other cities, Milwaukee was animated by a spirit of municipal enterprise that established new standards of honesty, efficiency, and creativity in public affairs. In a period of major cultural losses, that spirit represented a significant gain.

The Socialist victory of 1910 was the Big Bang in the evolution of good government.

Presented with a clear mandate, Emil Seidel gave Milwaukee a program that was, if anything, overly ambitious. Although Gerhard Bading defeated Seidel in 1912, the nonpartisan doctor made no serious attempt to derail the reform movement. Socialism returned four years later in the person of Dan Hoan, but the energies of local government were bent to the war effort during his first term. With victory finally secured in 1918, there was an explosion of municipal activity. The times were certainly propitious; the economic prosperity and social fluidity of the Twenties made it easier to try new ideas than might have been the case in quieter times. But activism was also a basic Socialist instinct. In his twenty-four years at the city's helm, Dan Hoan proved to be just as aggressive as Emil Seidel.

Hoan was handicapped by the absence of a Socialist majority on the Common Council. "Do not elevate me to a place of honor," he pleaded with voters in 1918, "and

City Hall remained the focal point of Milwaukee's continuing experiment in municipal government.

Milwaukee Journal Sentinel

Milwaukee County Historical Society

Dan Hoan at home: The Socialist mayor won praise for his fresh approach to public administration.

reactive, if not a reactionary, posture. The mayor lost more often than he won, but the net impact was steady growth in the character and capacity of city government.

Hoan's view of his job was, on one level, entirely pragmatic. "The objective," he told a reporter in 1927, "is to give the best government possible, and, though not necessarily at a low tax rate, at the lowest cost that can be paid." Throughout his tenure, the mayor demonstrated a fiscal conservatism that meshed perfectly with the local tradition of frugality; the city, like its citizens, paid cash whenever possible. In an effort to keep Milwaukee out of "bondage" to the banking interests, first Seidel and then Hoan moved to put all municipal departments on a pay-as-you-go basis. Bonds were still issued, but in 1923 the city established its debt amortization fund, a civic savings account meant to reduce and finally eliminate every last nickel of public indebtedness.

Although Milwaukee paid cash, the city was not afraid to spend money. The growth of the 1920s created problems as well as opportunities, and a growing tax base supplied the revenue necessary to deal with both. Water quality remained a critical issue. In 1910 the city began to chlorinate the lake water piped to its homes and businesses, a move that sharply reduced the incidence of typhoid. When a breakdown in the system led to a massive outbreak of diarrhea in 1916, voters decided that it was finally time to stop mixing raw sewage with their drinking water. In 1925 Milwaukee's present sewage treatment plant went into operation on the northern end of Jones Island. "Sewer Socialism" took on a literal meaning, and the worst of the community's water problems seemed to be over. In a particularly imaginative case of civic recycling,

then put shackles on my hands, hobbles on my feet, and a millstone around my neck." The public generally ignored his appeals, electing Hoan by ever-wider margins but holding the Socialist bloc to about 45 percent of the Council's strength. The advent of woman's suffrage in 1920 changed little. Although they were more apt to support pet Hoan projects like public marketing, women voted for Socialists in roughly the same proportion as men.

Even without a Council majority (except on occasions when a group of Polish mavericks took their side), there is no question that Milwaukee's Social Democrats shaped the municipal agenda. "The Socialists are the only people on earth who are purposeful," Victor Berger once declared, "... the only people who present a clear-cut, definite solution." As Hoan proposed and the aldermen disposed, the motley nonpartisan majority was forced into a

Milwaukee sold its dried sewage sludge as fertilizer. By 1931 Milorganite sales had added nearly $1 million to the city's coffers, and demand for the product continued to grow.

Jones Island was the site of another municipal development in the 1920s. Although trains and, increasingly, motor trucks moved most of Milwaukee's freight, lake ships still carried the bulk cargoes, including coal, grain, salt, and stone. As the ships grew larger, the narrow, bridge-choked Milwaukee River was practically useless as a harbor. In 1920, convinced that the city still needed water transport, the Common Council approved plans for an up-to-date outer harbor on Jones Island. That meant, of course, the removal of the Kaszubs and other fishing families who had been braving Lake Michigan storms since the 1870s. The last Islander, Capt. Felix Struck, held out until 1943, but his neighbors dispersed quickly, and with them vanished one of the most colorful communities in Milwaukee's history. Construction crews practically remade Jones Island in their wake. The inner harbor was dredged for use as a winter mooring basin, and muck from the river side was deposited behind a seawall on the lake side, swelling the peninsula's land area by a factor of four or five. A few hundred yards east, the Corps of Engineers completed the present outer breakwater in 1929, creating a genuine harbor of refuge. A carferry terminal was finished on Jones Island in the same year, and cargo slips and terminals sprouted on the landfill in the 1930s. It was fondly hoped, even in the World War I era, that Milwaukee would one day become an ocean port, linked to the Atlantic by way of the St. Lawrence River, and no one championed that cause with more vigor than Dan Hoan.

Milwaukee Journal Sentinel

The new sewage treatment plant on Jones Island solved the worst of Milwaukee's water woes.

Milwaukee County Historical Society

The plant and related developments erased the Jones Island fishing village, an unusually colorful community established in the 1870s.

Massive landfill activities created a genuine outer harbor on Jones Island.

With the completion of new port facilities and the federal breakwater, Milwaukee took one long step away from its geographic roots. In the schooner days of the 1830s, it was the deep blue river and the broad, sheltering bay that had drawn speculators to the site; Milwaukee's urban future depended absolutely on its potential as a port. The breakwater, not the bay, provided shelter after 1929, and the docks on Jones Island ended the Milwaukee River's days as a major transportation artery. With its commercial importance fading by the year, the polluted stream was so derelict that some planners actually suggested paving it over to create "a great boulevard."

Several miles inland, Dan Hoan launched another project that had a definite Socialist flavor. In 1921, as part of the city's larger effort to ease a severe postwar housing shortage, Milwaukee broke ground for a cooperative development called Garden Homes. It was the first municipally sponsored public housing project in the country. Located just beyond the city limits near the crossing of Teutonia and Atkinson Avenues, Garden Homes consisted of ninety-three houses (including twelve duplexes) laid out on curvilinear streets around a central park. The houses were all simplified versions of the English cottage – a conscious bow to the project's roots in England's "garden city" movement. Completed in 1923, Garden Homes quickly filled in with working-class families (all of them white) who wanted sound housing, ample green space, and a good deal. In lieu of rent, they made monthly payments toward stock in a non-profit corporation, but most members quickly lost interest in the cooperative aspect of the plan. As property values soared, residents wanted the potential profits for themselves, and they voted to terminate the cooperative in 1925. Dan Hoan must have been disappointed – he had drafted the bylaws and tenancy agreements

Milwaukee County Historical Society

himself – but Garden Homes was a trail-blazing success in the field of affordable working-class housing. The project's best-known resident was Emil Seidel, who finished his public career as the district's alderman and spent his final days trying to capture with brush and paint the changing scene outside his bedroom windows.

The spirit of municipal enterprise was not always expressed in bricks and mortar. Milwaukee Socialists were devout believers in "scientific city planning," and a concern for orderly development was one of the Hoan administration's hallmarks. In 1920 the city adopted its first zoning ordinance, a step that Dan Hoan praised as "perhaps the greatest single advancement ever made by Milwaukee." Uniform heights, setbacks, and patterns of land use meant the loss of some visual variety in the landscape, but the regulations also ended the days when a tannery could locate down the street from a townhouse. City officials were just as interested in

public health. Hoping to reduce appalling rates of child mortality, the Health Department developed a neighborhood-based, prevention-oriented outreach program that included vaccination against killers like smallpox. The campaign helped to raise the average Milwaukeean's life expectancy at birth from a meager 27.6 years in 1900 to 38.7 years in 1920 and 52.6 in 1932.

City government led the way, but neither the city nor the Socialists had a monopoly on good ideas. As people sprawled beyond the city limits by the tens of thousands, Milwaukee County took on new stature and new responsibilities. The 1873 courthouse on Yankee Hill was overcrowded even before World War I, and officials began to plan for a replacement that would reflect the county's rising fortunes. The planning process soon involved something much larger: a civic center that would encompass all future government buildings, both city and county. Elaborate civic

Garden Homes, a worker's cooperative, typified the Hoan administration's blend of idealism and pragmatism.

265

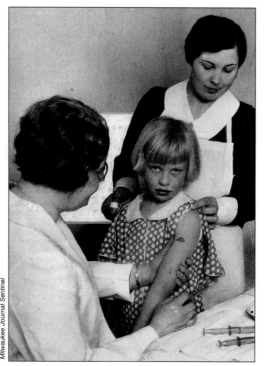

Milwaukee Journal Sentinel

centers were a trademark of the City Beautiful movement, a turn-of-the-century crusade whose leaders showed an inordinate fondness for neoclassical buildings, broad plazas, and grand boulevards. Alfred Clas, a prominent, public-spirited local architect, developed a Milwaukee version of the City Beautiful in 1909. He proposed a civic center for the entire area bordered by Fourth and Ninth Streets between State and Wells, with a new courthouse crowning the hilltop near Ninth. Clas sketched Kilbourn Avenue as a wide, tree-lined boulevard providing a visual connection between the courthouse and City Hall and then running eastward to the bluff above Lake Michigan. Later consultants made significant revisions, but it was the Clas plan that defined the terms of the civic center debate.

That debate lasted for nearly twenty years. Officials argued about the type and placement of buildings, the scope of the city's condemnation powers, and the proper roles of the city and county governments, but the most divisive question was also the oldest: Which side of the river would get the civic center? The East Side, as the seat of county government since 1836, was not about to give up the courthouse without a fight. The West Side, despite its growing importance as a retail and entertainment center, wanted to be a governmental center as well. No one wished to repeat the Bridge War of 1845, but entrenched resistance from both sides delayed action for what seemed an eternity. Inertia, compromise, and a growing need to address blighted conditions on the West Side finally forced a resolution; in the late 1920s, the civic center came to rest on roughly the same site Alfred Clas had suggested in 1909. The University of Wisconsin put up a building for its Extension program in 1928. The Safety Building, a joint city-county project, followed one year later, and work on the center's focal point – the Milwaukee County Courthouse – began in June, 1929, after a nationwide design competition. The winning entry was a gigantic Roman temple, a ponderous composition of limestone blocks and Corinthian columns. Completed in 1931, the new building drew mixed reviews. Frank Lloyd Wright, no lover of recycled designs, called it "a million-dollar rockpile" and "a pseudo-classic horror." Hometown observers, including county officials, were more charitable. The Courthouse may have lacked the appealing airiness of City Hall or the studied elegance of the library-museum building, but no one could deny that it was a monumental expression of Milwaukee County's new role in urban society.

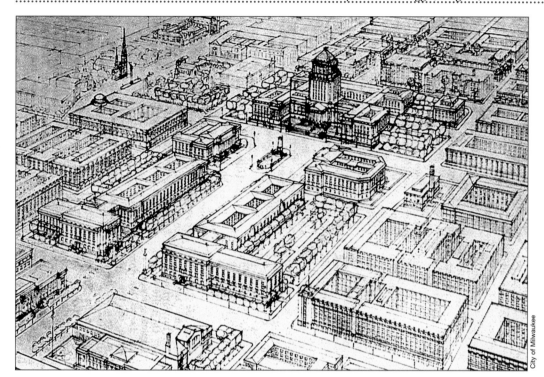

Architect Alfred Clas's plans for a downtown civic center reflected the classical spirit of the City Beautiful movement.

Completed in 1931, the new County Courthouse loomed over the western end of downtown like an apparition from ancient Greece.

Parks for the People

The physical impact of the 1920s is still apparent in Milwaukee; landmarks like the Courthouse, the Safety Building, Garden Homes, the outer harbor, and the sewage treatment plant still figure prominently in the local landscape. But one more development of the decade has had a deeper, more durable impact than all of those combined: the public park system. When Milwaukee's first major parks were purchased in 1890, urban planners promoted them as "lungs of the city" – breathing spots open to every citizen, regardless of age, color, gender, or income. That egalitarian concept had enormous appeal to local Socialists. Emil Seidel made park planning a priority of his administration, with special emphasis on the upper Milwaukee River. Seidel and Victor Berger secured options on nearly five miles of riverfront land between the Locust Street bridge and what is now Lincoln Park. That corridor might have become a spectacular public parkway, but nonpartisans balked at the $900,000 price tag. Criticism of Seidel's "million-dollar park" prompted the Common Council to deny funding for the river project.

It fell to another Socialist to carry park planning to the next level: Charles B. Whitnall. He was uniquely qualified for the task. Whitnall was, first of all, a trained horticulturist. His father, Frank, operated the largest floral business in Milwaukee, and "Charlie" was practically raised in the family greenhouses overlooking the Milwaukee River at

Charles Whitnall: Socialist, florist, banker, and godfather of Milwaukee's renowned park system

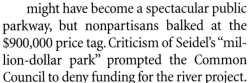

Locust Street. There he developed an unshakable belief in the formative influence of nature. "We have come to realize," he wrote in 1920, "that environmental influences determine largely what we shall be," and nature, in his view, provided the perfect environment. Whitnall lamented that Americans were "suffering by waste of physical and mental vigor, caused by too many of us being in discord and not within reach of those essential natural influences." As a florist and "landscape artist," he did much to cultivate natural influences. Following his father's lead, Whitnall became a figure of national prominence in the floral industry, creating and then managing the familiar FTD (Florist Telegraph Delivery) system. By 1905, however, he had developed an even more compelling interest in applied economics. Whitnall leased the family greenhouses and went to work for a local trust company, learning capitalism from the inside. He accepted the Socialist nomination for city treasurer in 1910 and was swept into office on the Seidel landslide. When the nonpartisan wave washed him out again in 1912, Whitnall founded the Commonwealth Mutual Savings Bank, "a cooperative savings bank, designated to benefit the wage earner, whether he became a depositor or a borrower." In his oxymoronic role as a Socialist banker, Whitnall tried to put capital to work for the workingman.

Although he remained a Commonwealth executive for the rest of his life, Charles Whitnall was every bit as committed to his second, largely unsalaried career as a planner. He was a charter member of the city's Public Land Commission and the county's Park Commission (both organized in 1907) and served as secretary of both in the 1920s. Whitnall was thus the leader of

Milwaukee's two most important planning bodies and virtually the only person with power on both the city and the county levels. By virtue of his position, his passion, and his obvious gift for long-range thinking, Whitnall was the dominant figure in regional planning for an entire generation.

The key to his vision was a concept borrowed from urban geography: the "conurbation." Although he was born before the Civil War, Whitnall was entirely at home in the automobile age. He foresaw the day when Milwaukee would become a decentralized "regional city" consisting of a specialized commercial core ringed by a host of "subsidiary centers" spreading fifteen or twenty miles out into the countryside. It was a prospect that Whitnall welcomed. He hated apartment buildings, skyscrapers, and all other high-density developments that isolated people from the natural world. But the conurbation would not work, he argued, without two major improvements. The first was a system of "major thoroughfares" designed to keep the city from choking on its automobile traffic. In 1926 Whitnall drew a box around the older part of town – using Capitol Drive on the north, Sixtieth Street on the west, Oklahoma Avenue on the south, and Humboldt/Clement Avenues on the east – and identified those streets as Milwaukee's "cordon." He envisioned the cordon as a regional beltway, "a by-pass for reaching many objectives without entering older developed areas." Whitnall was planning, in essence, an expressway system. Instead of fenced-in, high-speed turnpikes, however, he proposed "broad, comfortable roadways" created by "the heroic widening of the county arteries."

The second vital improvement, and ultimately the more important, was a

coherent system of parks and parkways designed to preserve the influence of nature in the Milwaukee conurbation. Whitnall's master plan, released in 1923, called for eighty-four miles of "parked driveways" following the county's rivers, creeks, and lakeshore. From the Root River in Franklin

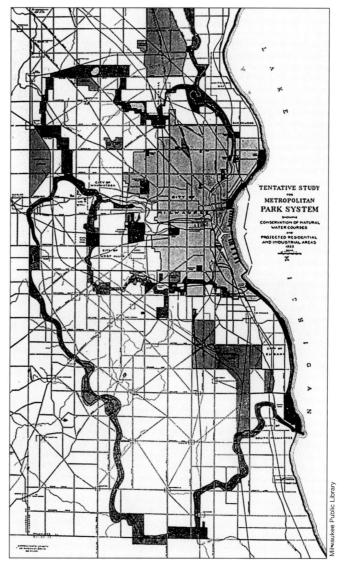

Whitnall's 1923 plan showed eighty-four miles of parkway along the county's watercourses. It became the official template for all future development.

to the upper Milwaukee in River Hills, the proposed system formed an irregular double loop that touched virtually every suburb and dozens of city neighborhoods. But the parkway loop was the skeleton of a much more ambitious plan. In Whitnall's scheme, selected wetlands along the corridor would become lakes, miles of degraded streambanks would be reforested, and major regional parks would grow at specific points on the loop—much like pearls on a necklace. The plan had multiple dimensions, including flood control, public recreation, and sanitation, but its author was after something even grander. He hoped that the parkway system would aid the cause of civilization by "conserving those environmental influences which park experts recognize as essential to wholesome living conditions." Nature was the ultimate teacher, in other words, and the park loop would literally surround Milwaukeeans with nature.

Whitnall's highway and park maps became, with very little revision, the official guides for all local land-use planning. Thanks in no small part to his own persistence and political skills, key elements of the plans became realities before the period's end. In 1927 Milwaukee County adopted America's first county zoning ordinance, bringing a semblance of order to exurban development, and both city and county officials worked to fill in the blank spaces on Whitnall's park map. Milwaukee County was the more aggressive partner, purchasing some 2,173 acres of parkland by 1930, including gems like Grant, Estabrook, Brown Deer, Greenfield and, of course, Whitnall. The city system was considerably smaller at 1,405 acres, but it featured two of the region's leading tourist attractions: the Washington Park Zoo, where animals had been displayed since 1892; and the Mitchell Park Horticultural Conservatory, a glass palace built in 1898.

Two of Milwaukee's most-visited green spaces in the early 1900s were the zoo in Washington Park ...

The city also owned what many considered the most spectacular pearl in the necklace of parks: Lincoln Memorial Drive. Completed in 1929 after years of landfill activity, the three-mile parkway gave Milwaukee one of the finest stretches of urban lakefront on the entire Great Lakes.

Milwaukee might have had ample green space even if Charles Whitnall had been a plumber instead of a planner; pillars of the system like Lake and Washington Parks predate his involvement by more than fifteen years. But Whitnall's plan had inestimable value as a blueprint. It provided a well-reasoned and highly specific guide to development in outlying areas of the county, and it established two policies that influenced land-use planners for decades: Buy well in advance of need, and develop land with utmost respect for native contours and vegetation. Whitnall's most important contribution may have been perceptual; no one did more to convince voters and elect-

ed officials that public parks were absolutely vital to the public welfare. The lasting result was a park system acknowledged as world-class by any standard.

Elsewhere in America, the Twenties were generally considered a low point in the nation's moral development. Social critics deplored the easy credit, rampant speculation, flagrant law-breaking, and ethical malaise that seemed to characterize the decade. Milwaukee had its share of flappers and moonshine, but there was a countervailing sense, especially in the public sector, that the community was doing the right thing, and doing it rather well. The expanding park system typified the larger trend. In his report for 1926, Dan Hoan declared that "our city is experiencing its golden age of progress." Two years later, the *Milwaukee Journal*, normally skeptical on all matters concerning Hoan, offered grudging praise: "Milwaukee has had pretty good government for some years and seems to like it.

... and the horticultural conservatory in Mitchell Park.

Milwaukee Journal Sentinel

Milwaukee Journal Sentinel

Milwaukee's lakefront was relatively quiet (top) until the 1920s, when extensive landfill and the construction of Lincoln Memorial Drive (right) made it the city's most beloved public green space.

Milwaukee Journal Sentinel

Mayor Hoan gets a good deal of the credit for this." As public officials honed their administrative skills, outsiders began to take notice. Between 1925 and 1940, Milwaukee won numerous awards as the healthiest, safest, and best-policed big city in the United States.

Underlying Milwaukee's success was a characteristic attitude toward government. There was undoubtedly more than a hint of "Father knows best" in the outlooks of men like Berger, Seidel, Hoan, and Whitnall – Socialists never ran short of Answers – but there was also an unwavering faith that every problem had a solution, and that it was government's particular obligation to find it. That faith was shared by many non-Socialists as well. Local government had a quasi-religious dimension in the Twenties, a highly developed sense of mission that has since gone out of style. Architect Alfred Clas advanced his civic center plans as "Civic Art," designed to uplift the public mind. "A good picture cultivates the taste of a family circle," he wrote, "[but] a grand boulevard educates the minds of millions." Dan Hoan considered municipal office an exalted calling: "Local government, next to family life itself, is the very foundation of our nation." Charles Whitnall believed that civic planners aspired to an even higher plane: "We are seeking to conserve not only God's country but Humanity." Such attitudes may seem hopelessly romantic, even naive, to modern readers, but it was precisely those attitudes that made Milwaukee such a vibrant center of municipal enterprise in the 1920s.

✶✶✶✶✶

In some respects, the 1910-1930 period in Milwaukee's history ended as it had begun. A Socialist was in the mayor's office, a pro-active government was breaking new municipal ground, and the local economy seemed generally healthy. In other respects, practically everything had changed. Milwaukee entered the period as the nation's capital of Socialism, Germanism, and beer. By 1930, Dan Hoan headed a splinter party, chest-thumping Germanism was practically dead, and beer had all but disappeared. The mayor continued to promise voters "a bigger, brighter and better Milwaukee" but, in the wake of World War I, he might have said "blander" as well. Gone was the hint of danger implied in the city's radical politics, "alien" traditions, and proud intemperance. "Milwaukee may have been disreputably distinctive," lamented Ruben Levin in 1929, "yet it is today becoming respectably obscure." In a facetious monograph titled *Milwaukee: The Bier of Beer*, Levin described the shift as "a tragic decline from eminence":

> *The once apologetic representative of a Milwaukee industry, traveling beyond Wisconsin, need no longer defend his home town. Today, he walks into the Kiwanis club of any hamlet and boasts of Milwaukee's civic spirit. He points with pride to its great industries (not beer). He rejoices in its home-loving citizens, its stable and satisfied workers, its outer harbor project, its modern sewage plant, and, above all, its civic service clubs.*
>
> *You may shed a bitter, briny tear, who loved the old Milwaukee. It is gone, a vanished city. It is now as Procrustean as any of the Americanized, boosterized cities that sprawl over this fair and powerful realm. Prohibition, Americanization, the World War, Rotarianism and prosperity have spelled its ruin.*

Milwaukeeans did not awaken one morning to find their town crawling with Babbitts, but Levin had a point. Between 1910 and 1930, the community moved materially from its base. Responding to forces close to the heart of the American experience, local residents retreated from one set of identifications and embraced, however selectively, another. By the period's end, the outlines of the modern city were apparent – in the physical landscape, in the increasingly heady mixture of local ethnic groups, and in the overwhelming power of mass culture.

Milwaukee did not, however, surrender its individuality. The city's oldest traditions proved hardier than many had supposed, and newer qualities, including a talent for manufacturing and a penchant for creative government, continued to set the community apart from its peers. But Milwaukee moved closer to the American middle between 1910 and 1930, and events of the next period, dominated by a spectacular economic collapse and an equally momentous global conflict, would only hasten that movement.

Of all the events that might be cited to mark the passing of an era, the death of

Hats off to municipal enterprise: Victor Berger's death in 1929 marked the end of an era.

Milwaukee Journal Sentinel

Victor Berger on August 7, 1929, was perhaps the most pointed. There was brutal irony in the circumstances. After decades of berating The Milwaukee Electric Railway & Light Company as a money-grubbing monopoly, Berger died from injuries suffered when he was struck by a streetcar on N. Third Street. He was mourned by friends and foes alike. Proud German and proud American, tireless intellect and pragmatic idealist, Victor Berger was the patriarch of a movement that caused a brief stir on the national scene and sparked a more enduring transformation in his adopted city. After a simple funeral service, the Socialist's body was cremated. Berger's long journey ended on Lincoln Memorial Drive, where his ashes were spread along the new lakefront Milwaukee had created for all its people.

Chapter 7

Hard Times and Wartime, 1930 – 1945

Les Greget left Mayville for Milwaukee in 1922. Good with his hands and comfortable with machinery, the young man was seeking opportunities beyond anything his Dodge County hometown had to offer. He found them at the Falk Company. Greget became an apprentice machinist in the Menomonee Valley plant and, after four years of work and study, graduated to a job at the boring bar, a gargantuan machine tool used to drill high-precision holes in marine gear casings. "I thought I had it made," he recalled. Greget and his wife purchased a $12,500 brick duplex on the Northwest Side and proceeded to live the 1920s version of the good life.

The Depression rudely interrupted their blue-collar idyll. As business in the Falk shops dwindled to the vanishing point, Les Greget lost his job, then his savings, and finally his home. When the lender foreclosed, he and his wife were forced to move into a $45-a-month upper flat. As the bad times got even worse, they prevailed upon their landlord to lower the rent to just $20.

Then came World War II. Greget went back to his boring bar even before the Japanese attack on Pearl Harbor, turning

The Falk plant in the Menomonee Valley during World War II

Milwaukee Journal-Sentinel

out marine gear drives for a Navy trying desperately to ease its shortage of ships. Falk was swamped with orders for the duration of the war. As the fighting intensified, Greget found himself working ten hours a day, seven days a week, for four-and-a-half years – more than 1,600 consecutive days without a single break!

Les Greget's story, multiplied by thousands, is the story of Milwaukee between 1930 and 1945: a disjointed chronicle of crash and recovery, privation and patriotism, events moving too slowly and then too fast. The community lurched from one extreme to another in fifteen years, but the period was dominated by a single emotion: anxiety. America faced a monetary crisis that became a military crisis with practically no intermediate stage, generating enormous social and psychological pressures. The roar of the Twenties subsided quickly, and the struggle for success became a struggle for survival.

The community as a whole found its options limited during the period. National developments crowded strictly local concerns off the stage, and civic isolation was no longer a possibility. Developments of the previous decades – Prohibition, the anti-German juggernaut, the decline of Socialism – had moved Milwaukee materially away from its traditional base. By 1945, despite some impressive survivals, the community was even more thoroughly immersed in the American mainstream.

Slipping into Darkness

The stock market crash of October 24, 1929, produced barely a ripple in the calm waters of the Milwaukee economy. Order rates dipped in the following month or two, but local leaders closed their books on 1929 with a general feeling of satisfaction. "We haven't noticed any drop in business," said Herman Falk, "and are going ahead as ever."

Downtown Milwaukee in 1932

Milwaukee Public Library

Walter Kasten, head of the First Wisconsin Bank, seemed almost grateful that the crash had driven speculators out of the market. "Agreement is general," he wrote, "that business will be the sounder for removal of this unnatural factor in demand." Daniel Hoan blithely predicted at year's end that Milwaukee "will continue to grow with constantly accelerated pace, notably free from spasmodic booms and disastrous slumps." Even a year later, the *Milwaukee Journal* could afford to look on the sunny side: "During 1930, Milwaukee was one of the few bright spots on the nation's business map. Here is a market immune from peaks and panics. Industrial diversification is a sure stabilizer of steady progress."

The same errant optimism infected local government. As other cities defaulted on their bonds and observed "payless paydays" for their employees, Milwaukee seemed to be an island of sanity and solvency. Even when the local economy began to show signs of stress, the Hoan administration's penchant for saving drew national attention. "The city of Milwaukee," reported the *New York Times* (December 19, 1931), "has paid its bills, expended hundreds of thousands of dollars in unemployment relief and at the end of the year will have about $4,000,000 in the bank." The debt amortization fund established in 1923 was a major reason for the apparent surplus. As news of the city's prosperity spread, Milwaukee was hailed as a shining example of municipal government at its best. The *Literary Digest* (January 30, 1932) concluded that the community had finally found something to replace beer: "A new fame comes to Milwaukee as a model city, and debt-curst, politics-ridden sister municipalities are turning to it in their anguish in the hope of finding a cure for their ills."

The "Milwaukee miracle" ended soon enough. The community's vaunted diversity may have delayed the onset of hard times, but the impact of the Depression, when it finally arrived, was horrifyingly complete. City officials acknowledged an "unemployment crisis" in the autumn of 1930, and the downward slide was just beginning. As factory layoffs reached epidemic proportions, the number of wage-earners in Milwaukee County plummeted from 117,658 in 1929 to 66,010 in 1933 – a 44-percent decline in just four years. Those who managed to keep their jobs faced smaller paychecks and diminished hours. The sum total of wages paid in

A Detroit News cartoon highlighted the "Milwaukee miracle" in 1931.

As the "miracle" gave way to massive unemployment, homeless Milwaukeeans developed a "Hooverville" (below) in Lincoln Park.

An elderly Yugoslavian immigrant foraged for coal in the Menomonee Valley freightyards.

Milwaukee Journal Sentinel

Milwaukee's black community was especially hard-hit. Jobless men gathered outside a storefront church on N. Eighth Street in the late 1930s.

Wisconsin Historical Society

Milwaukee County dropped 64.6 percent during the same four-year period, and value added in manufacture – a key measure of industrial output – slumped 61.4 percent. In every case, Milwaukee's numbers were roughly ten percentage points worse than those for the nation as a whole. Spared in the early rounds, Milwaukee ultimately absorbed more than its share of the pounding dished out in the 1930s.

The community's suffering was palpable. For Les Greget and thousands like him, the 1930s were a decade of deepening darkness, a nightmarish descent into a totally unforeseen state of worry and want. After years of working to get ahead, they were suddenly struggling to get by. Having no choice, Milwaukee tightened its collective belt. Neck bones and spareribs replaced more expensive cuts on the dinner table, and "one-meatball casseroles" became a popular staple. Medical care was deferred as long as possible and dental care ignored entirely. Women wore the same dresses and men the same shoes until they were literally worn out. As the unemployed lost their homes, it was not unusual for three or four households to share a single living unit. Some older Americans look back on the Depression with a kind of skewed nostalgia, recalling it as a time of family togetherness and courageous self-denial, but few would trade their present comforts for the physical hardships and gnawing anxieties of the 1930s.

It was hardly surprising, given the circumstances, that many citizens began to question the fundamental tenets of the American economic system; a strong back and a sturdy work ethic were patently not enough to ensure anyone's survival in the free market. The dream of upward mobility died hard, particularly for those who had crossed an ocean in its pursuit, and what rose in its wake was a profound sense of disappointment. In too many cases, that disappointment hardened into disillusionment and finally bitterness. Families who had lost their savings to bank failures and their homes to foreclosure concluded that something systemic had gone wrong, that the entire economy was built on a foundation of sand. Milwaukee's Socialists, of course, had been saying precisely that for decades, and the Depression gave their arguments a new cogency. Dan Hoan pulled out all the rhetorical stops in 1932:

> *We are in the midst of a world-wide economic and social revolution that will not cease until the present industrial system, called capitalism, is entirely replaced by the next stage of human development, which is called Socialism. The causes and effects which shake the very foundation of the present order are but the death agonies of a dying system, and the birth pains of the building of a new and better world.*

His constituents had heard it all before, but more of them were inclined to listen during the Depression. Given up for dead in some quarters, the Socialist Party roared back to life. Mayor Hoan won a landslide re-election victory in 1932, and Socialists captured the city attorney's post, the city treasurer's office, and twelve of twenty-seven aldermanic seats. With the addition of two Polish mavericks to the bloc, Hoan had a working majority on the Common Council for the first and only time in his long tenure.

That majority could do little to change existing conditions. City government, in fact, faced the same basic handicap that was crippling city residents: a lethal combination of soaring needs and shrinking resources. The economy sank like a stone through 1932 and dropped to its absolute nadir in the spring of 1933. More than 53 percent of the city's property taxes went unpaid during the latter year. With its primary source of revenue slashed, Milwaukee

Unemployed workers found it easy to believe that American capitalism was shattered beyond repair. Communists organized this demonstration at the haymarket on Fifth and Vliet Streets in 1930.

Milwaukee Journal Sentinel

was forced to cut municipal services. City crews paved 52.7 miles of streets in 1929 and only 0.63 miles in 1933. Park lighting was reduced by a third in 1933. With no money to buy new materials, resourceful public librarians created "books" by clipping serialized novels from popular magazines. There was even talk of slaughtering some of the heavier eaters in the Washington Park Zoo.

Dan Hoan was not about to see elephant steaks added to local soup-kitchen menus. Even in the depths of the Depression, he insisted that the city take a pro-active role in dealing with the crisis. "A business may quit," he said. "Your city can't." Hoan argued that it was false economy to cut municipal spending to the bone. "The only solution for unemployment," he said in 1931, "is shorter working hours and no cut in wages to maintain the purchasing power of the worker." The mayor resisted attempts to reduce the municipal payroll and supported efforts to create jobs for those idled by factory clos-

Mayor Dan Hoan provided Milwaukee with sure-handed leadership in the depths of Depression.

ings. In 1930, using local milkmen as their distribution network, city officials passed out 100,000 cards soliciting odd jobs for the unemployed. (They reported "substantial results.") The Common Council launched the area's first work-relief program in the same year and expanded it as conditions deteriorated. Funded in part by a voluntary 10-percent cut in city paychecks (including Dan Hoan's), the program provided jobs for 14,144 men in the winter of 1931-1932, most working ten-day shifts for sixty cents an hour. The city's annual report for 1931 described the initiative:

> *The work furnished to these men is for the most part pick-and-shovel work, and is largely concerned with the development of new parks and playgrounds. While some of this work could be more economically done by machinery than by hand, the great majority of the men have taken their employment seriously and have striven to give real value for their wages.*

One evidence of the project's "real value" was the Jackson Park lagoon, which was excavated entirely by hand.

Not everyone appreciated the Hoan administration's hands-on response to the Depression. Although voters elected a Socialist slate in April, 1932, they also approved a November referendum that held the city's tax rate to its 1926 level, well below the figure for 1931. Hoan himself, who called the referendum "foolhardy," was the target of an abortive recall effort in 1933. Despite the fiscal handcuffs and the presence of spirited opposition, the mayor continued to look for ways out of the city's fiscal crisis. One of the most creative was the introduction of "baby bonds" in 1933. Other cities on the brink of bankruptcy had already begun to pay their employees

Milwaukee Journal Sentinel

in scrip – promissory notes based on nothing more than the good faith of the municipality. Milwaukee carried the idea one large step further. The city became the "unwitting and unwilling" owner of tax-delinquent property worth millions of dollars during the Depression, most of it vacant lots platted during the real estate boom of the 1920s and then abandoned. The municipality thawed this frozen asset by pledging it as collateral for negotiable bonds paying 5-percent interest. The first baby bonds were issued in denominations of $10 and $100, and non-interest-bearing notes of $1 and $5 followed shortly, all redeemable for the larger certificates. In July, 1933, Milwaukee began to pay its 10,600 employees, including public school-teachers, with a blend of baby bonds and cash. Some workers promptly turned in the securities as payment for their city property taxes, while others used them to buy clothes and groceries in the open market.

The glut led to steep discounts at first, but the bonds were considered "as good as currency" by the end of 1934, and some investors were buying them at a premium. Circulated many times in the local economy, the baby bonds provided a welcome transfusion of capital for a community in dire need of new blood.

courtesy Tom Casper

The city used interest-bearing "baby bonds" to pay its employees when tax collections lagged.

Home-grown bonds were only one indication of Milwaukee's fresh approach to municipal financing. Despite a precipitous drop in revenue, the city never missed a bond payment, and Milwaukee was even able to make some financial headway. Doggedly pursuing its pay-as-you-go policy, the municipality stopped issuing general-obligation bonds in 1932. That step, coupled with the growth of its untouchable debt amortization fund, led to predictions

Milwaukee also provided relief work for jobless residents, including this crew sprucing up Jackson Park.

Milwaukee Journal Sentinel

that Milwaukee would be entirely debt-free as early as 1955. The city had no illusions that it could stop spending money on streets, schools, and sewers. In 1936 the Common Council created a permanent improvement fund for capital projects, setting aside an amount equal to the city's annual savings on bond interest. All these measures were practically unheard-of in the 1930s. At a time when other large cities were virtually drowning in red ink, Milwaukee won praise in the national press as "an American legend" and "a by-word of perfection in the United States."

Milwaukee County, on the other hand, found it impossible to make comparable progress, for one very simple reason: Care of the indigent was a county responsibility. Ever since 1835, when Solomon Juneau served as a "superintendent of the poor," the county had been supporting its neediest residents with "outdoor relief." In the nineteenth century, that meant food, firewood,

and sometimes lodging. In the 1930s, outdoor relief supplied the destitute with bulk quantities of flour, cereal, potatoes, milk, oatmeal, cheap cuts of meat, and occasional oddities like figs and herring. The program also provided low-grade coal and vouchers for rent and utilities. The foodstuffs were dispensed through a network of relief stations scattered across the county, and clients typically carried the goods home in coaster wagons. Outdoor relief was the last resort for most families, and "pulling the coaster" involved a certain amount of swallowed pride. The fact that poverty was so widely shared helped to dispel the sense of shame. The number of Milwaukee County households on outdoor relief skyrocketed from 2,580 in 1929 to 20,839 in 1931 and a peak of 40,176 in 1935. The last figure represented 140,000 individuals – nearly a fifth of the county's population.

The expenses of direct relief, coupled with programs for the infirm and a modest

Milwaukee County operated dozens of "outdoor relief" stations that provided needy families with bulk food supplies.

MILWAUKEE COUNTY
DEP'T. OF OUTDOOR RELIEF
STATION № 13

public works effort, threatened to bankrupt the county. No sooner had officials moved into their colossal new courthouse in 1931 than the roof figuratively caved in. As unemployment soared, relief costs rose to absorb more than half of Milwaukee County's budget. The county's tax rate doubled between 1928 and 1932, and still it was necessary to issue millions of dollars in bonds to keep the needy from freezing or starving.

It was natural for taxpayer groups, business leaders, and public officials themselves to look for operating efficiencies during the Depression, and one of the first places they looked was the relationship between Milwaukee County and the city of Milwaukee. It made little sense for one branch of government to dispense aid to the needy of another, particularly when they served largely the same population, and there were some obvious redundancies in areas like parks and planning. Talk of consolidation, a warmly debated topic since the mid-1800s, generated new heat in the 1930s. Dan Hoan himself spoke in favor of "a single consolidated government for all of Milwaukee County" with "a single executive head," and a 1936 referendum showed overwhelming support for the idea. (The fact that 80 percent of the county's residents were also city residents shaped the outcome.) The debate did not end there. Consolidation was the prerogative of state government, and the Wisconsin legislature, apparently wary of the big city's intentions, rejected the proposal.

All the state would allow was a consolidation of specific city and county functions, and attention quickly turned to the community's dual park systems. With larger holdings, more aggressive management, and a larger population base, Milwaukee County appeared to be the stronger steward

of public land. City taxpayers also found it odd that they owned some units, including Doctors, Lincoln, and Wilson Parks, that lay beyond the city limits. With surprisingly little debate, voters chose to consolidate the systems. The move was expected to save money, but more important, in the view of planners like Charles Whitnall, was the potential for growth under one coherent management and a single master plan. At the stroke of midnight on December 31, 1936, the city park system was absorbed – trees, rocks, and policemen – by Milwaukee County.

Charles Whitnall, chief architect of Milwaukee's park system, lived to see work-relief crews make dramatic progress on his master plan.

Milwaukee Journal Sentinel

Alphabet Soup

Even the liveliest, most creative local governments could do nothing to halt the American economy's downward slide in the 1930s. It became painfully obvious that national problems required national intervention, and the election of Franklin Roosevelt in November, 1932, marked the beginning of a coordinated federal response. Within weeks of his inauguration, Roosevelt began to replace the ineffectual policies of the Hoover administration with a blizzard of new programs constituting a "New Deal" for the American people. Ranging from the experimental to the unconstitutional, their only common bond was pragmatism; Roosevelt's team was willing to try anything to get the economy moving again. Re-employment was their first priority. With the private sector in a state of advanced collapse, New Dealers launched a multitude of public-sector employment programs between 1933 and 1935, including the Civilian Conservation Corps (CCC), Civil Works Administration (CWA), Federal Employment Relief Administration (FERA), National Youth Administration (NYA), and Works Progress (later Projects) Administration (WPA).

Milwaukee used them all. From the morning the first CCC camps opened in July, 1933, to the day WPA workers cashed their last paychecks almost exactly a decade later, tens of thousands of Milwaukeeans earned their daily bread through federal work-relief programs. They performed an amazing variety of tasks. Local residents hired by the WPA – the largest and longest-lived of the programs – might have spent their days building exhibits for the Public Museum, compiling a central fingerprint file for the city's Police Department, serving as tour guides at the Washington Park Zoo, staging historical pageants, tending wildflowers in the county greenhouse, or preparing a comprehensive index of the *Milwaukee Sentinel* for the 1837-1891 period – to name just a few assignments. Some WPA projects were especially imaginative. A handicrafts program trained nearly 5,000 Milwaukeeans, most of them women, to produce artfully designed dolls, drapes, quilts, costumes, and furniture; and a WPA toy loan program circulated more than 75,000 refurbished bicycles, bears, and board games through twenty toy "libraries" in Milwaukee County.

These "indoor" programs kept a small army of the unemployed busy, but federal relief guidelines favored projects that could absorb large numbers of able-bodied men, many of them unskilled, for extended periods of time. In virtually every American community, that meant parks. Thanks to Charles Whitnall and his fellow visionaries, Milwaukee was ideally positioned to use the federal programs. Not only were there thousands of acres of public green space in the county, but park officials had drawers full of detailed plans for its development. When CWA money became available in November, 1933, Milwaukee County was able to put 4,000 men to work on two days' notice. With the advent of WPA support in 1935, the corps of park workers climbed to more than 8,000. Most were assigned to "made work," either sprucing up the old city parcels or developing new properties, including some acquired from bankrupt developers. One of the Depression's silver linings was the transformation of tax-delinquent real estate into neighborhood parks like Dineen, Cooper, Lindsay, Madison, Nash, and La Follette. Milwaukee County also bought new parcels, generally at bargain-basement prices.

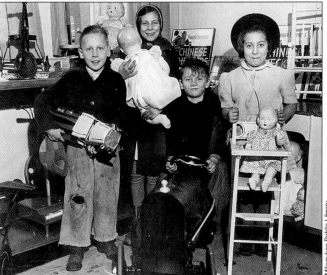

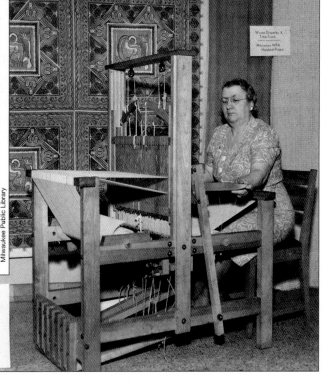

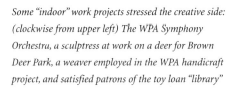

Some "indoor" work projects stressed the creative side: (clockwise from upper left) The WPA Symphony Orchestra, a sculptress at work on a deer for Brown Deer Park, a weaver employed in the WPA handicraft project, and satisfied patrons of the toy loan "library"

Outdoor projects were the backbone of federal work-relief efforts: (clockwise from top) Redirecting the flow of the Milwaukee River in Lincoln Park, trimming stone at the county quarry, resetting cobblestones on a city street, and making a waterfall by hand in Whitnall Park

Milwaukee Journal Sentinel

Milwaukee Journal Sentinel

Milwaukee County Historical Society

Milwaukee Public Library

Whitnall Park became the county's largest during the 1930s, and relief workers turned it into a mile-square showplace, with a chain of picturesque lagoons and waterfalls, a challenging eighteen-hole golf course, and a botanical garden that remains one of Milwaukee's favorite destinations.

By the time the Depression was over, virtually every park in the county had been improved in some way. Relief crews spent countless hours digging, dredging, grading, and planting, and they tackled more concrete projects as well. WPA workers installed full-sized swimming pools in six parks and erected a full range of bathhouses, pavilions, and shelters in styles ranging from "modern Colonial" at Grant to "Swiss chalet" at Kletzsch. Smaller jobs included footbridges in the county's parkways and a new hippo tank at the zoo. The building program reflected the comprehensive nature of the relief effort: WPA architects developed the plans, WPA crews provided the physical labor, and WPA artists and artisans decorated the finished products with furniture, carvings, and murals.

The program's only serious handicap was a critical shortage of building materials. Federal officials wanted to spend tax dollars on people, not supplies, and local authorities were often forced to improvise. The rustic fieldhouse at Hawthorn Glen, a nature center for local schoolchildren, was a composite of salvaged materials, including oak timbers from the deck of the old Twenty-seventh Street viaduct, lumber from demolished homes, and brick from an East Side playground. One building material was available in quantity: a buff-colored dolomite supplied by the county quarry in Currie Park. Opened with a blast in 1933, the quarry provided more than 25,000 cubic yards of stone for bridges, walkways, retaining walls, and public buildings spread throughout the community.

Park work, by its nature, was geographically diffuse and oriented to the outdoors. The Roosevelt administration also sponsored highly focused, heavily capitalized projects that represented another dimension of the federal relief effort. Milwaukee won three big-ticket projects, all of them still prominent in the local landscape. The first, and probably the most welcome, was the Linnwood Avenue water purification plant. Frequent outbreaks of "intestinal flu" (the latest in 1936) finally came to an end in 1939, when the fortress-like facility opened on the north lakefront. Funded by a loan and grant from the Public Works Administration (PWA), the $5 million project engaged 1,700 men, many of them skilled union workers, for at least a year. Their efforts gave Milwaukee, in the words of one happy bureaucrat, "a quality of water

The Linnwood Avenue purification plant, a PWA project, improved Milwaukee's water quality dramatically.

287

uniformly good throughout the year, free from turbidity and unpleasant tastes."

A second PWA project helped to alleviate a critical shortage of low-income housing in Milwaukee. Public housing was perennially controversial, but any city that could design and build a development like Garden Homes entirely on its own was at least open to the idea. In 1935 New Deal administrators announced plans for a $2.8 million project on the emerging Northwest Side. Parklawn, covering forty acres west of Sherman Boulevard at Lincoln (then Mud) Creek, ultimately consisted of 518 housing units, most of them in two-story brick rowhouses. "Moving-in day" was June 1, 1937. "The fact that the buildings are alike brought grief to some young children who strayed and then couldn't find the right house," reported the *Milwaukee Journal*, but Parklawn residents were generally delighted with their new homes. By 1938 there were 1,400 families on the waiting list.

Parklawn was operated by the federal government until 1950, when it was transferred to the Milwaukee Housing Authority.

The third and boldest big-ticket project made Milwaukee the focus of a novel experiment in social engineering. In 1935 the planners of the U.S. Resettlement Administration decided to relocate a number of urban industrial workers to "greenbelt towns" on the outskirts of major cities. Their thinking mirrored Charles B. Whitnall's: If you take workers away from the blight and congestion of the central city, if you surround them with the beneficent influence of nature, they will inevitably rise to higher levels of both morality and democracy. The living laboratory for this experiment was the new town of Greendale, one of three greenbelt communities in the nation. (The others were outside Washington, D.C. and Cincinnati, Ohio.) By mid-1936, the New Dealers had purchased 3,500 acres – more than five square miles – in the old Town of Greenfield,

Hundreds of Milwaukeeans "window shopped" at Parklawn before the housing project opened in 1937.

Milwaukee Journal Sentinel

just a few miles southwest of Milwaukee, and started work on a compact village of simple cinder-block homes. Nearly 2,000 men, both skilled tradesmen and unskilled WPA workers, labored on the project at its high point. (CCC crews developed nearby Root River Parkway at the same time.) Eleanor Roosevelt visited the site in late 1936, pronouncing the village "absolutely wonderful" but lamenting that it was not open to blacks. "We must not permit discrimination to creep in," she scolded. Greendale's first residents moved in on April 30, 1938, and before long the community's 572 homes supported a population of nearly 2,500, most of them young families with blue-collar backgrounds. Although it has long since been overwhelmed by more prosaic developments, the original Greendale, with its curving streets, cul-de-sacs, and picturesque town center, remains a much-admired example of Depression-era urban planning.

From the gardens of Greendale to the heroic murals in the Milwaukee County Courthouse, the fruits of federal relief efforts seemed to be everywhere in the 1930s. Their limitations were just as obvious. Relief jobs failed to provide more than the most rudimentary standard of living for unemployed workers. In 1934 the *Milwaukee Journal* reported that FERA crews were putting in "a full six-hour day" – a term that would have been an oxymoron just a few years earlier – and the prevailing wage rates barely reached subsistence levels. Unskilled workers on the WPA rolls earned just seventy cents an hour (for eighty-six hours a month) in the early years, and the rate was slashed to forty cents in 1939, a "security wage" so low it had to be supplemented with outdoor relief. Nor did federal aid slow the decay of America's urban infrastructure.

Despite massive infusions of dollars from Washington, public-works spending actually fell sharply during the Depression. In Milwaukee and elsewhere, crumbling streets, sidewalks, and sewers were problems left for the next generation to address. There was political controversy as well. The WPA was known as "We Poke Along" in some communities, and conservatives criticized Roosevelt's relief programs as "boondoggles" that were bleeding the taxpayers dry. On the leftward end of the political spectrum, Socialists and others dismissed

With its distinctive homes and forward-looking street layout, the village of Greendale was a national showcase for New Deal urban planning efforts.

the programs as "mere palliatives" that only masked the need for systemic change.

Although critics on both sides derided the jumble of New Deal agencies as "alphabet soup," no one could deny that it was nourishing. Despite the meager wages, the limited hours, and the potshots from both right and left, federal relief efforts played a pivotal role in the 1930s. For the unemployed, they were sometimes the last defense against starvation, and the programs' emphasis on productive labor helped to preserve at least a modicum of pride. "The desire of the clients to work was so great," reported a local FERA official in 1934, "that it became a privilege to work on such a plan." For local governments, the New Deal programs were a godsend. The advent of federal relief saved Milwaukee County from ruinous debt or even bankruptcy, and the breathtaking progress of the county park system was probably the high point of a low period. It is doubtful that showplaces like Whitnall Park would exist at all in their current forms without the WPA, the CCC, and all the other acronyms in FDR's anti-Depression broth. In 1936, long before the work programs had ended, county officials estimated that development of the park system was already ten to fifteen years ahead of schedule. In its report for 1942, the County Park Commission looked back with gratitude on a decade of New Deal work relief:

> *Yes, it cost money, but it also opened thousands of acres of desirable home districts, with several millions of assessable values created along the parkways, and a future well ordered home environment, in the open country away from congestion – besides, it gave, and is giving, employment to thousands of men who otherwise would be supported in relief ....*

Solidarity Forever

It is sometimes forgotten that a majority of Americans were still working in the 1930s, although generally at reduced hours and wages. Even full-time workers, however, felt the impact of the New Deal; factory hands who never had to "pull the coaster" or join the WPA were every bit as affected by the Roosevelt administration's policies as their unemployed brethren. In his continuing campaign to revive the economy, Franklin Roosevelt offered a variety of incentives to American business, but he balanced the management carrots with concessions to organized labor. One of the most important was the National Industrial Recovery Act (NIRA) of 1933, which guaranteed the right of workers "to organize and bargain collectively through representatives of their own choosing." The NIRA's impact was electric. Unions suddenly had a powerful new weapon in their drive to organize American workers, and they used it aggressively to reverse the steep declines of the business-dominated 1920s. The field was certainly ready for harvest. Nonstop layoffs, wage cuts, and reductions in hours had created a feeling of powerlessness in the labor force, and workers embraced any and all organizations that promised to give them some control over their destinies. The American Federation of Labor claimed 50,000 members in Milwaukee County by the end of 1934 – at least triple its pre-Depression total – and the union's greatest growth period was still ahead.

Conflict was probably inevitable in the charged atmosphere of the Thirties. Workers wanted to flex their muscles after more than a decade of quiescence, and employers, unaccustomed to sharing power with anyone, were equally determined to resist. There were 107 strikes in Milwaukee during 1934, and they involved 27,000 workers in tanneries, tailor shops, garment factories, glove plants, steel foundries, and sausage factories. More people were voluntarily on the streets than at any time since the general strike for the eight-hour day in 1886. The wave of walkouts affected even schoolchildren; in October the student body of Bay View's Dover Street School struck for shorter schooldays, longer recesses, and no homework. (The kids may have undermined their cause by carrying picket signs that read "Unfare to Children.")

Other strikes were deadly serious. The worst disturbance of 1934 involved the Electric Company, whose president, S.B. Way, was adamantly opposed to an independent union. Way went so far as to fire eight union activists – an unfair labor practice that forced the government to remove his company's name from the list of firms "cooperating for recovery." Faced with an intractable management, union members walked out on June 26, 1934. The public's reaction brought back memories of the great streetcar strike of 1896. Like their parents and grandparents almost forty years earlier, thousands of Milwaukeeans turned out in support of the strikers, and the demonstrations outside the company's carbarns reached riot proportions. As the Electric Company posted extra guards and covered its streetcars with wire mesh, S.B. Way informed Dan Hoan that he would hold the city responsible for any and all damage to the utility's property. The mayor's reply showed a man struggling to control his outrage:

I now notify you ... that you alone are solely responsible for the riots that have so far blotched the good name of the city.... Your attitude toward your employees, our people, our city, our federal government, is more arrogant than that of any ruler in the

Thousands of pro-union Milwaukeeans took to the streets during the 1934 Electric Company strike. This crowd gathered at the Kinnickinnic Avenue car station.

We Energies

world. Not since the days of King George III of England has any such ruler successfully defied our nation.... You are now harvesting the pent-up public indignation you yourself have aroused.

Way was finally forced to negotiate on June 29, the morning after a demonstrator was fatally electrocuted during a charge on the Lakeside power plant. The settlement was a total victory for organized labor, and the Electric Company has been a union firm ever since.

The drive to organize unrepresented workers suffered a setback in May, 1935, when the Supreme Court struck down the National Industrial Recovery Act, but passage of the Wagner Act two months later affirmed and broadened labor's right to organize. As both sides gradually adjusted to the new environment, the high tide of labor disturbances passed; the number of Milwaukee strikes dropped from 107 in 1934 to 31 in 1935. The union tide swept in some real gains for Milwaukee's working class. A combination of labor activism and better economic times boosted the average industrial worker's weekly paycheck from $16.14 in 1932 to $24.11 in 1936, and benefits like paid vacations became standard features in local labor agreements.

Despite their dramatic progress, the unions of the 1930s were hardly one happy family. In the 1880s, the Knights of Labor had enjoyed spectacular success by opening their ranks to all workers within a given industry, regardless of skill levels or job duties. Mirroring national trends, Milwaukee had moved away from the industrial model and toward trade unionism after the Bay View shootings of 1886. Organized labor in Milwaukee thereafter meant organized craftsmen, and workers with fewer skills were left to fend for themselves. The old arguments were rekindled in the 1930s. Not only had the New Deal given labor the green light, but the rise of mass production had created a huge class of workers who didn't fall into well-defined craft categories. In 1935 the Committee for Industrial Organization was established within the American Federation of Labor to pursue unionization on an industrial basis. Complicated by issues of status, income, and personality, the relationship between trade and industrial unionists descended from uneasy to acrimonious. The two groups split in 1936, and the former Committee became the Congress of Industrial Organizations in 1938. The AFL and CIO remained at odds for the next twenty years.

Milwaukee was an especially active battleground in the fratricidal conflict. An all-out CIO drive led to the formation of new locals at Bucyrus-Erie, Harnischfeger, Heil, Harley-Davidson, and Briggs & Stratton, but

Jubilant workers greeted the news that the Electric Company had agreed to a settlement.

Milwaukee Journal Sentinel

the group's biggest coup was convincing nearly 6,000 shop workers at Allis-Chalmers to switch their allegiance from the AFL to the United Auto Workers of the CIO. Local 248, representing the majority of workers at the West Allis plant, was by far the largest of the seventy young CIO unions that formed the Milwaukee County Industrial Union Council in 1937. AFL organizers were busy at the same time and often in the same plants. Although the AFL-CIO rivalry probably pushed both sides to greater heights than either would have reached alone, it also tended to confuse workers, multiply organizing costs, and alienate the general public.

Labor faced another internal problem during the 1930s: the specter of Communist infiltration. When the first signs of economic distress appeared, local Communists launched a campaign of nonstop agitation, organizing marches of the unemployed, contesting for union leadership, and fomenting revolution at every opportunity.

Although they benefited from the same leftward shift that revitalized Milwaukee's Socialist Party, the two groups were mortal enemies. The Communists denounced Socialists as "yellow servants of the capitalist class," and the *Milwaukee Leader* responded by describing Communism as "the method of making social changes by violent revolution, dictatorship and terror." It could flourish, stated Dan Hoan, only in places "where opportunity for the individual is lacking and gross injustices are perpetrated." (The defection of Meta Berger, Victor's widow, to the Communist cause in the mid-1930s was no small embarrassment for her old comrades.) The Communists' philosophy may have been anathema to the moderate left as well as to the right, but no one could deny the near-fanatical zeal that the party faithful brought to their task. Working skillfully and usually under cover, they rose to positions of dominance in several unions, particularly on the CIO side. Although he never acknowledged

A 1941 CIO walkout at Allis-Chalmers led to angry confrontations between workers and police, punctuated by volleys of tear gas.

Milwaukee Journal Sentinel

membership in the party, Milwaukee's most prominent Communist confederate was Harold Christoffel. As head of both the huge Allis-Chalmers local and the county's Industrial Union Council, Christoffel tried to craft a labor policy that served the interests of the Soviet Union as well as his own membership. A number of CIO locals and CIO leaders were intensely patriotic, but the presence of known and suspected Communists within the ranks of the labor movement did little to improve its credibility with the average Milwaukee citizen.

Although endless organizational and ideological warfare made the ideal of solidarity seem like a distant mirage, there is no question that Milwaukee's labor movement came of age in the 1930s. The number of union members in the county, of all affiliations, skyrocketed from 15,000 in 1929 to more than 100,000 in 1939. By the end of the decade, open shops had become a rarity, and union agreements determined wage levels and working conditions for employees in virtually every plant. After decades as a stronghold of industry, Milwaukee became a stronghold of organized industrial workers as well.

Who's Afraid of the Big Bad Wolf?

The 1930s were not a period of unrelieved strife, strike, and struggle. One of the paradoxical "benefits" of the Depression was a dramatic increase in leisure time, and thousands of Milwaukeeans used it to their advantage. The unforeseen result was a steady rise in the prevailing levels of education and culture. Teenagers were most immediately affected. With virtually no demand for their services in the market-place, young people who might have entered the work force at fourteen decided to stay in school. Between 1924 and 1934, the number of students attending city high schools increased by 12,850, and graduation rates soared. Adults showed similar interest in self-improvement. As idled workers spent more time with books, the public library's circulation rose from 5,103,509 volumes in 1929 to 6,320,933 in 1932 – a 24-percent gain in three years. More Milwaukeeans also made use of the school system's thirty-two social centers, which offered classes in sketching, photography, clay modeling, woodcarving, public speaking, needlecraft, china painting, dressmaking, radio, aeronautics, and four varieties of dance – tap, folk, ballroom, and "creative." Parents hard-pressed to find the money for Christmas presents were especially grateful for the "Santa Claus toy shops" that opened in the social centers each December.

There was also an abundance of free recreational opportunities for those with time on their hands. Sandlot baseball was a local passion in the Thirties, with as many as 23,000 fans turning out to watch teams like the Milwaukee Valves take on the Ryczek Morticians at the Mitchell Park diamond. Droves of homemakers descended on the Electric Company's downtown auditorium for free demonstrations of "electric health cooking," followed by coffee cake and canasta. Recreation centers in the county parks offered a full schedule of athletic activities, concerts, and dances. At the start of the jitterbug craze in the late 1930s, several park pavilions were open for dancing until 10:30 every evening. The music was provided by an "orthophonic phonograph" (at a nickel per tune), and proud park officials called the jitterbug sessions "an innovation that took the youngsters by storm." A more permanent musical attraction appealed to a somewhat older audience. In 1938 Milwaukee County dedicated its Temple of Music, a $100,000 bandshell and amphitheater in Washington Park. Donated by brewer Emil Blatz, the facility became the home of Music under the Stars, one of the longest-running cultural series in the community's history. Although a south wind sometimes brought the ripe smell of elephants from the nearby zoo, tens of thousands came to the Temple of Music for concerts headlined by Lily Pons, Andre Kostelanetz, Jeanette MacDonald, and other stars of the era. A smaller number heard groups like Heinie and the Grenadiers perform at the Humboldt Park bandshell, some paying for seats inside the fence, a greater number sprawled on blankets and lawn chairs for free. The concerts at both parks have continued in modified form to the present day.

For those with a little money to spend, the entertainment options multiplied. Motion pictures were hugely popular, with stars like Greta Garbo and Clark Gable offering viewers a momentary escape from the rigors of the Depression. Young adults still flocked to local ballrooms on weekends, packing places like the Modernistic at State Fair Park and George Devine's at the Eagles Club. Baseball fans who tired of the sandlot leagues could pay to watch professionals at Borchert Field on Eighth and Chambers, home of the (minor-league) Milwaukee Brewers since 1902. Borchert's first night game was played on June 6, 1935, and 4,747 fans turned out to see their heroes compete under the new electric lights. Other diversions were more occasional: circus performances, symphony concerts and, in the summer of 1935, dirigible rides at the lakefront. (More than a thousand sightseers went aloft over a four-day period.) Entertainment of all kinds was a good deal cheaper than it had been only a few years before. The cost of living in America actually dropped 24 percent between 1929 and 1933,

Sandlot baseball drew thousands of entertainment-starved spectators to Mitchell Park in the 1930s.

Milwaukee Public Library

Depression-era diversions:
(from top) Free cooking
demonstrations at the
Electric Company, evening
concerts at the new Blatz
bandshell in Washington
Park, and minor-league
baseball in the cramped
confines of Borchert Field

We Energies

Milwaukee Journal Sentinel

Milwaukee Journal Sentinel

Milwaukee Journal Sentinel

a rare round of deflation that produced ground beef for ten cents a pound, eggs for sixteen cents a dozen, and straw hats for less than a dollar. Bargains were everywhere in the 1930s – for those who could afford them.

Milwaukeeans who had once been able to afford anything found that they were not immune to hardship. Business failures and bank closings forced a number of Lake Drive residents to put their mansions on the block, and the Milwaukee Country Club's roster dropped 15 percent in the 1930s. (One thrifty member avoided paying dues by putting his gardener to work on the golf course.) Even those who escaped catastrophe lowered their expectations, postponing foreign travel, putting off the purchase of new cars, and living inconspicuously. An exceptional few carried on the spirit of the Roaring Twenties. When the father of one North Shore bride agreed to host a wedding reception for 750 guests in 1934, he puzzled over how to mix drinks for the multitude. The problem was solved by purchasing two brand-new washing machines: one for Manhattans, the other for martinis.

A few Depression-era diversions brought cheer to Milwaukeeans on all economic levels. The most notable was the end of Prohibition on April 7, 1933. Only 3.2-percent beer was available at first, but that was close enough for people who had been waiting nearly fourteen years for legal alcohol of any description. Milwaukee's seven breweries hopped back into production, cooper shops and bottle plants dusted off their equipment, and the city's 1,776 taverns (no longer saloons) were suddenly operating within the law again. There was an impromptu celebration on the night of April 6 but, at the request of Christian clergy leaders, the official party

was postponed until the end of Lent. On April 17, the day after Easter, nearly 15,000 hungry, thirsty Milwaukeeans jammed the Auditorium for an old-fashioned *Volksfest*, and 5,000 more were turned away at the doors. The *Milwaukee Sentinel* (April 18, 1933), described the event as a rebirth of pre-World War Germanism:

> *"Blue Danube" and "Trinklieder" and "Bier Waltzen" rang out in three halls, and a Bavarian yodeler, his white plume bobbing, danced through all of them with a puffing, pear-shaped gray haired frau. Glasses clinked; "Prosits!" echoed; Nuernberger bratwurst, kalter aufschnit, sauerkraut and frankfurters swam past on trays.... Accordions whined; pretzels crunched; dancers eddied; feet stamped; the din grew; and eight bars dripped beer. Who said Milwaukee is living in memory?*

By the time the night was over, revelers had consumed 500 pounds of frankfurters, 300 pounds of potato salad, 250 pounds of

Happy Milwaukeeans accompanied the first trainload of beer that left the Schlitz brewery after Prohibition's repeal in 1933.

Milwaukee Public Library

A Third Street bartender proved that he could still handle ten steins of Milwaukee's finest even after years of drought.

Milwaukee Public Library

sauerkraut, and enough beer to wash away, if only for an evening, distasteful memories of the long national drought.

The April 17 *Volksfest* was such enormous fun that Milwaukeeans decided to do it again on a regular basis. Dan Hoan had been promoting a civic festival ever since a 1931 trip to Europe, and he knew precisely where to stage it: the lakefront. "Let us have a huge spectacle there every year," he said upon his return, "like the Mardi Gras in New Orleans, like the festivals in Versailles, for our own people and for others." Milwaukee happened to be the site of the national Elks Club convention in 1933. Using the *Volksfest* of the previous April as his inspiration, the mayor decreed a "civic homecoming celebration" and welcomed both Elks and local residents to a full week of activities on the downtown lakeshore. They included boat races, band concerts, carnival rides, and a well-patronized "Bavarian beer

garden," all free and open to the public. Nearly 500,000 entertainment-starved citizens attended, and that was all Hoan and company needed to make the celebration an annual event.

The Midsummer Festival, as organizers called the bash, was the high point of Milwaukee's warm-weather season for the next eight years. Co-sponsored by the city and the county, it was a low-budget, almost no-budget, affair; public spending never topped $40,000. The Festival depended on free local talent, including accordion orchestras, high school bands, theater troupes (including one with a Shakespearean repertoire), opera companies, church choirs, and gymnastic groups. True to its roots in the community, the event had a pronounced ethnic dimension; the annual Festival of Many Nations, foreshadowing the current line-up of lakefront fests, featured hundreds of folk dancers in full costume. Then as now, fireworks were a major draw. Ground displays depicted major events in the life of the community, including the Third Ward Fire and the Return of Beer, and in 1938 one mile of the outer breakwater was illuminated with flares and Roman candles.

Some of the Midsummer Festival's attractions seem to have no modern counterparts: motorcycle hill climbs above Bradford Beach, swimming races in the frigid waters of Milwaukee Bay (including an event for dogs), and demonstrations of "group and solo clubswinging" by the Milwaukee Turners. Most unusual of all were the elaborate pageants written, produced, and presented by relief workers of the WPA. These annual spectacles were typically organized around historical or allegorical themes, some more high-flown than others.

The Midsummer Festival drew huge crowds to the lakefront every year between 1933 and 1941, foreshadowing the later development of Summerfest.

Milwaukee Public Library

The 1937 production, for instance, featured a "symbolic nature wedding" of Lake Michigan and the land. The "bride" approached by water, escorted by Father Neptune and four sprites representing the other Great Lakes. The "groom" approached by land, flanked by attendants representing the Fields, the Forests, the Mountains, and the Snows. The nuptials took place on a lakefront platform, where the happy couple was surrounded by "a host of girls and women dressed in white and blue, whose movements simulate the shoreline."

The Midsummer Festival mixed eclectic entertainment with parades, a midway, and plenty of beer. That was a powerful combination in the best of times, but the firm free-admission policy made it unbeatable during the Depression. Reported attendance for Festival week neared the one-million mark by the end of the decade, and local officials couldn't have been happier. In 1939 Dan Hoan called the Festival throngs "one large, happy family, playing together as we work together for the greater glory of the city we all love." The mayor expressed a fervent desire that the Midsummer Festival would "in time ... become recognized as a national institution." Almost thirty years later, his wish would come true, and with no change in venue, as Summerfest.

Free festivals, legal beer, blimp rides, and ballgames were all welcome diversions, but they were no substitutes for prosperity. As years passed with no sign of lasting recovery, Milwaukeeans found it hard to see the silver lining in the thick clouds of the Depression. There were a few glimmers of light. The return of beer, for instance, provided an economic as well as a psychological boost; by the end of 1934, local breweries employed more than 4,000 workers, up from 500 during Prohibition. New Deal capital spending also brought a modest stream of orders into Milwaukee's machine shops; Harnischfeger, Falk, and Allis-Chalmers were among the firms that called back laid-off employees to work on equipment for the Hoover Dam. In 1936, with better times apparently around the corner, Milwaukee County decided to close a few of its outdoor relief stations.

Then the bottom fell out – again. After posting modest gains in the previous year or two, the economy suffered a brutal relapse in late 1937. Public relief spending reached a Depression-era high in the next year, when one of every five Milwaukee County residents depended on some form of government aid. The 1938 outlay exceeded $26 million, making relief programs the largest "industry" in the county. Economic recovery resumed by the end of 1938; Harnischfeger had orders for thirty-two cranes from the Navy, Nordberg was working on diesel engines for cargo ships, and local hosiery firms were experimenting with a

Milwaukee's industrial pace began to quicken in the late 1930s, as orders came in for everything from mine hoists at Nordberg (left) to nylon stockings at Phoenix Hosiery (right).

new synthetic fiber called nylon. Workers in these and other shops were putting in abundant overtime, but a hard core of the jobless remained; in 1940 more than 16 percent of the county's labor force was either unemployed or working for the WPA.

Mayor Hoan and Mr. Zeidler

By the beginning of 1940, the Depression had been under way for a full ten years. Beleaguered Milwaukeeans who looked back on the decade must have felt that they had been living in a state of suspended animation. After double-digit gains in the Twenties, the city's population grew a scant 1.6 percent between 1930 and 1940, rising from 578,249 to 587,472. That 9,223 gain was entirely the result of natural increase. Births exceeded deaths in Milwaukee by a margin of 45,415 during the decade, leading to the inescapable conclusion that the

city had suffered a major out-migration of residents. Other urban centers fared no better. Despite its poor showing, Milwaukee slipped only one notch in the national population rankings, dropping from twelfth to thirteenth. (It was Washington, D.C., swollen with New Dealers, that moved ahead.)

Although natural increase was (barely) sufficient to keep the community growing, Milwaukeeans had put off starting families as soon as they sensed danger in the economy. The number of weddings in the city dropped from 5,442 in 1929 to 3,300 in 1932 – a decline of nearly 40 percent in three years. Fewer marriages meant fewer children; Milwaukee's birth rate dipped from 21.9 per 1,000 in 1929 to a low of 14.5 in 1933. Fewer families, in turn, meant fewer new homes and fewer new businesses. The value of building construction in the city plummeted from $46,930,686 in 1929 to a paltry $3,123,765 in 1933. The numbers in every category began to rebound by the middle of the decade, but it took years for them to regain the levels of the 1920s. By the time prosperity returned, a majority of local residents had been forced to go on the dole. Describing conditions a decade after the stock market crash, the *Milwaukee Journal* (May 27, 1939) concluded that "more than one-half of the families in Milwaukee county have been on relief at some time in the last ten years."

It was a dismal decade, but Milwaukeeans could look back on the 1930s with pride in at least one area: the performance of their local government. Worker-oriented administrations on the city and county levels had made the best of a bad situation. Both had launched work relief programs at the start of the crisis, and both had put federal aid to creative use when it became available. The city's fiscal innovations and continuing solvency were practically without parallel in urban America. Milwaukee County used the 1930s to develop one of the finest park systems in the country. Officials on both levels resisted attempts to slash public services, opting instead to provide their hard-pressed citizens with libraries, social centers, athletic leagues, recreation programs, and inexpensive entertainment. Dan Hoan looked back on the municipal initiatives with pride:

> Let it be said that Milwaukee County led every other community in the country not only in the promptness in which it assumed the job, not only in the efficiency and dispatch of its efforts, but in the adequacy and generosity of the relief measures themselves.

Daniel W. Hoan was without question the representative figure of the period. Few individuals have ever been so closely identified with Milwaukee, and no official has represented the city more effectively. As a founder and early president of the U.S. Conference of Mayors, Hoan was a prominent spokesman for the nation's cities and a regular guest at the Roosevelt White House. As the author of *City Government*, a well-received 1936 book about the "Milwaukee experiment," he was a much-quoted authority on municipal administration. As head of the city, it was Hoan who accepted

Dan Hoan considered public service an exalted calling, and he made Milwaukee, according to Time, "perhaps the best-governed city in the U.S."

Milwaukee Journal Sentinel

more than a dozen first-place awards for Milwaukee in public health, fire prevention, and traffic safety contests during the 1930s. (The city was periodically barred from the health contest to give other communities a chance for recognition.) Hoan was also one of the few big-city mayors in American history whose face appeared on the cover of *Time*. The magazine (April 6, 1936) was lavish in its praise: "Daniel Webster Hoan remains one of the nation's ablest public servants, and under him Milwaukee has become perhaps the best-governed city in the U.S."

The adulation of the national press must have been gratifying, but Hoan kept his eyes fixed on the local scene. In 1935 he marked the completion of twenty-five years in public office, six as Milwaukee's city attorney and nineteen as mayor. Nearly 400 allies and admirers attended a May 16 banquet in his honor, and they heard Hoan wax eloquent on his favorite subject:

We are all proud of Milwaukee. Stable in its industries, sound in its government, healthful in environment, beautiful in location, we have done our best to make it an inspiration for the sisterhood of cities.... We have given Milwaukee a civic heart, a civic soul and a civic mind.

The mayor was always careful to give a full measure of credit for Milwaukee's success to the Socialist Party. The city's accomplishments, Hoan wrote in 1931, "were attained under our leadership and the influence of our movement." Without the Socialists, he argued, Milwaukee "would still be wallowing in the cesspool of graft, crime and corruption" that had engulfed it before 1910. But the city had not become a worker's utopia. Although glimmers of the cooperative commonwealth were apparent in municipal ownership of the waterworks, the sewage treatment plant, the streetlighting system, the garbage incinerator, and port facilities, voters were unwilling to go much further. In 1936 they narrowly rejected a proposal to take over the electric utility – a goal Socialists had been seeking for nearly forty years.

Faced with fixed limits on their programs, local Socialists stressed instead their principles. Hoan and company made honesty, efficiency, and innovation Milwaukee trademarks, and they worked to instill something even larger in the populace: a sense that the welfare of one was vital to the welfare of all. Although it was frequently couched in radical rhetoric, the heart of their message was a compassionate communality. Hoan stressed the point at the 1935 banquet in his honor:

Up to about 1910 our people were ranged in a large number of groups rather than organized in one great civic consciousness. Then came a gradual

Socialism remained viable in Milwaukee long after its peak had passed elsewhere. This billboard was posted for a 1932 election.

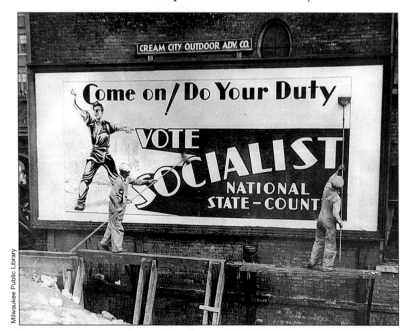

CREAM CITY OUTDOOR ADV. CO.

Come on/Do Your Duty

VOTE SOCIALIST
NATIONAL
STATE – COUNT

Milwaukee Public Library

development of a genuine local civic spirit, the rallying principle of which may best be described by one expressive word – service.

Their commitment to public service made Hoan and his comrades the most successful Socialists in American municipal history. It did not, however, guarantee that they would govern forever. After the resurgence of 1932, the news for Milwaukee Socialism was all bad. The national party was split between "militants" and the "old guard." Communists were chipping away on the far left. The Progressive Party, launched by the La Follette brothers in 1934, siphoned off moderate supporters. Most significantly, Franklin Roosevelt's Democratic Party was making dramatic inroads among labor unions and liberal groups. As New Dealers appropriated their ideas, their supporters, and even their rhetoric, Socialists found their political turf shrinking by the day. Faced with a smaller constituency but unwilling (yet) to surrender to the Democrats, they sought an alliance with others on the left. In 1935 Wisconsin's Socialists helped to found the Farmer-Labor Progressive Federation, a coalition designed to merge the rural clout of the Progressives with the urban strength of the Socialists and their union allies. The results were disastrous. With the illusory scent of economic recovery in the wind, voters decided to reverse their leftward drift in the 1936 election. Running under the Federation banner, Dan Hoan won re-election with 54 percent of the vote, but nonpartisans surged to a 22-5 majority on the Common Council.

The next four years were difficult for Hoan. Not only did he have to deal with the economic relapse of 1937-1938, but the mayor also faced a group of intractable aldermen who rejected his proposals, overrode his vetoes, and refused to confirm his appointments. Still the mayor was in no apparent trouble as the 1940 election approached. His challenger was Carl Zeidler, a political neophyte who worked as an assistant city attorney in Hoan's former office. Born on January 4, 1908, Zeidler was a barber's son and native West Sider who had already won some notoriety as Milwaukee's "No. 1 extrovert." Blessed with Teutonic good looks and a golden singing voice, the young man belonged to dozens of groups, from the Liederkranz Chorus to the Sunday Morning Breakfast Club. Zeidler was giving 300 speeches a year even before he entered the mayoral race, and his baritone was familiar to thousands. (*God Bless America* and *On the Road to Mandalay* were standards in his repertoire.) When asked why he spent so much time in the company of others, he said, "I am Carl Zeidler, that is why. I gravitate toward people. I love my fellow man. I am intensely interested in people."

Carl Zeidler, the tireless extrovert who challenged Hoan in the 1940 mayoral election

Milwaukee Journal Sentinel

This Type A extrovert's 1940 campaign helped to set the standard for all that have followed. Innocent of ideology, Zeidler concentrated instead on image. His key advisors, a circle of callow newcomers with few traditions to impede them, approached the election with all the gusto of advertising men. "See 'em, tell 'em, sell 'em" was the group's motto, and their chief product was Zeidler himself. Young, dynamic, and glamorous, he strode into campaign gatherings with brass bands blaring, balloons descending, and a pretty girl on each arm. (Zeidler's status as Milwaukee's leading bachelor wasn't lost on half the electorate.) The emphasis on presentation extended to the candidate's platform. There were no manifestos from the Zeidler camp; in contrast to the epic scale of most Socialist platforms, the challenger's document was short, sweet, and vague. It called for lower taxes, new industries, a city plan, labor peace, and a program to rehabilitate young people

Dan Hoan stood proudly on his record in 1940...

Milwaukee Journal Sentinel

"caught by the depression years." These and other ideas were offered as antidotes to the supposed lethargy of the Hoan administration. In his campaign kickoff at the South Side Armory, Zeidler attacked the mayor as a tired has-been:

> *Milwaukee has changed but only one thing remains unchanged, and that's your platform. For 24 years Milwaukee has been the victim of pernicious inertia and chronic inactivity. A new idea hasn't been permitted the light of day for years in the city hall, which is like a cavern of darkness into which new ideas are flung to perish, or to be devoured by the serpents of bureaucratic red tape.*

Dan Hoan failed to take Zeidler seriously at first, apparently considering him a lightweight. The challenger's assertion that "Milwaukee has no city plan" must have seemed especially ludicrous to the mayor and his department heads. Hoan won the primary handily and turned up the heat only in the last month of the campaign. To Zeidler's assertion that his was a do-nothing administration, the mayor replied, "Give me a Common Council with vision and intelligence instead of a gang of 'no' men, and I will do something." Of Zeidler's plan to make a "clean sweep" of department heads and replace them with newcomers, Hoan charged, "Now he glorifies inexperience as a positive asset in a public official." In a campaign article written for the *Milwaukee Evening Post* (March 21, 1940), the incumbent stoutly defended the status quo, surely an ironic position for a Socialist:

> *The things that are most important in the history of Milwaukee's government are the things that don't happen. The epidemics we don't have, the burglaries that are not committed, the gangsters who don't come to town, the fires that don't*

break out, the graft that is not handed out – these are among the things that make Milwaukee the finest city in the country.

And these things that don't happen are the result of a clear and definite philosophy of government. We believe in removing the causes of tragedy and misfortune, rather than in working to cure evils after they are here.... Prevention rather than cure has always been our watchword. And we have done such a good job over the years that our opponents can't even imagine the host of evils we have kept out of Milwaukee.

Thousands of Milwaukeeans found it just as hard to imagine a day when Dan Hoan hadn't been mayor, and they were apparently ready for a change. The charismatic Zeidler made them notice, many for the first time, that Hoan sometimes wore shiny suits, that his voice could be shrill on occasion, that his rhetoric hadn't changed in decades. When the votes were counted on April 2, 1940, the challenger had won by a margin of 111,957 to 99,798. After twenty-four years, the Hoan era was over, and with it passed the high tide of municipal Socialism in America.

When the initial shock had worn off, comment poured in from all quarters. The *New York Times* called Zeidler's victory proof of "music's power to soothe the elector's breast," and added, "Here is a young man who actually sings for his votes, and the people apparently love it." Frank Zeidler, Carl's younger brother and a prominent Socialist Party official, offered a more trenchant analysis: "Organized business in Milwaukee has been gunning for Socialists ever since they first appeared, and finally organized business 'got' the Socialist mayor." The *Milwaukee Sentinel*, despite its historically strained relations with Hoan,

looked back on a quarter-century of good government with fondness:

Before 1910, Milwaukee was famous for its beer; in the three decades that followed it was to become famous also for its city government.... No one can say precisely at what point notoriety gave way to celebrity, infamy to fame. But somewhere along the line America began to discover that Milwaukee, where socialism ran rampant and the mayor said "To hell with kings," was unique in respect to the efficiency and honesty of its government, its enforcement of the laws, its handling of traffic, the preservation of its municipal credit, its long range planning.

Hoan himself departed gracefully. "One of my great ambitions when assuming the position of mayor," he said a few days after the election, "was that when I left the office it could honestly be said that I contributed something to enhance the reputation of this city as a better place in which to live." After

... but the public's desire for change and his golden singing voice carried the day for Carl Zeidler.

Milwaukee Journal Sentinel

twenty-four years, even his harshest critics would have given Hoan credit for all that and much more. But the stage now belonged to Carl Zeidler. In the same flamboyant style that had marked his campaign, the victor held his inauguration ceremony in the Auditorium rather than the Common Council chambers. Nearly 8,000 supporters heard Zeidler promise to revamp city government, restore sagging public morale, and regain ground lost to the Depression. He closed with a ringing declaration: "Hats off to the past, coats off to the future!"

The new mayor was as energetic as his word. Although his reorganization plans amounted to very little (even a modest tax cut proved difficult), Carl Zeidler was practically everywhere in the early 1940s. He welcomed every foreign ship that called on Milwaukee, greeted scores of visiting celebrities (particularly singers), and regaled hundreds of luncheon audiences. Zeidler made no secret of his interest in higher office, an ambition that found him crowning the Cherry Blossom Queen in Sturgeon Bay and leading an informal songfest at the Waupun state prison. Even vacation time was no occasion for rest; during a 1941 trip to Mexico City, members of a DAR group from Washington, D.C. were startled to find themselves being addressed by the irrepressible mayor of Milwaukee. Although his pace was always frenetic, Zeidler may have reached a personal pinnacle during 1940's Fourth of July observance. In a burst of energy that spanned 12 hours and covered 95 miles, he visited every park celebration in the city, giving 15 speeches on democracy and leading the multitudes in song: *God Bless America* 5 times and *John Brown's Body* and *Old Mill Stream* ("with gestures") once each. By the

time his marathon day was over, the mayor had entertained nearly 85,000 people. If mayoral energy were municipal wealth, Carl Zeidler could have pulled Milwaukee out of the Depression single-handed.

Milwaukee at War

In a different decade, under different circumstances, Carl Zeidler might well have realized his dreams of higher office; he was an attractive candidate and a tireless campaigner with a malleable political philosophy. But Zeidler began his political career in 1940, and 1940 was the first full year of World War II. An obvious turning point in the city's political history was completely overshadowed by a much more ominous period of transition in world history. However dynamic their new mayor, Milwaukeeans traded one set of anxieties for another with barely enough time to catch their collective breath. After calling the roll of countries that had fallen to the Nazis and their allies in the preceding twelve months – France, Belgium, Holland, Luxembourg, Norway, Denmark, Finland, and Hungary – the *Milwaukee Journal* (December 31, 1940) solemnly concluded, "We have come to the end of the darkest year that anyone now living has known." Considering the trauma of the previous decade, that was saying something.

The clouds of war had been gathering over Europe since Adolf Hitler's rise to power in 1933. Emerging only fifteen years after the end of World War I, Hitler's militarism was shocking to some, but the *Führer* was not universally despised. A Milwaukee chapter of the Friends of New Germany was founded in late 1933 to rally support for the Nazis. The group sponsored a 1934 meeting that drew a reported 600, and a Midwest regional gathering in November of the next year attracted 2,000. As a phalanx of storm troopers stood watch, national leaders gave incendiary speeches and silver-shirted children pledged allegiance to a huge swastika mounted on the Auditorium stage. The Friends group was soon renamed the German-American *Volksbund*, more familiarly known as "the Bund." Most of its members were post-World War I immigrants whose Germany had been emasculated and embittered by the Treaty of Versailles; Hitler's defiant chauvinism struck a definite chord. But his depredations sparked intense local resistance to the Bund, particularly among Milwaukee's Communists, Jews and, most tellingly, other Germans. In 1937 the Bund had established Camp Hindenburg in Grafton as a place to drill and practice the Nazi salute. In 1939 the Federation of German-American Societies, an umbrella organization representing sixty Teutonic groups, leased the camp from under the Bund's nose and renamed it for Carl Schurz, the famed Forty-Eighter who had begun his American career in Wisconsin.

Despite the embarrassment of the Bund, Milwaukee generally avoided the ethnic factionalism that had caused such heartbreak during World War I. There were no witch hunts, no loyalty oaths, and few name changes. The overwhelming majority of local Germans considered Hitler a diabolical menace, and support for the Allies grew with each Nazi incursion into neutral territory. The invasion of Poland in September, 1939, clinched it. Although the United States remained officially neutral in the ensuing bloodbath, Franklin Roosevelt pledged "all aid short of war" to the Allies and cast his nation in a new role as "the great arsenal of democracy." As military orders streamed into Milwaukee, industrial plants that had been idle for years were suddenly bursting with life.

Then came Pearl Harbor. Smoke finally erupted into flame on December 7, 1941, and life changed practically overnight. Guards were posted at the region's electric power plants. A fence went up around the municipal waterworks. Construction projects in the county parks were enclosed as quickly as possible and abandoned for the duration. As a state of emergency gripped the nation, Milwaukeeans experienced new levels of both prosperity and anxiety. Plants already operating in high gear shifted into overdrive, and the Depression soon became a fading memory. At the same time, residents who had been worried about the survival of their families began to fear for the future of their civilization.

Milwaukee was in a unique position to do something about it. As a stronghold of heavy industry, the community was poised

Marine recruits were all smiles when they lined up for fingerprinting on December 8, 1941 — the day after Pearl Harbor was bombed.

307

to become a major "arsenal of democracy," and defense planners were quick to make Milwaukee a federal priority area. Haltingly at first, they coordinated a massive outpouring of ordnance and materiel for the Allied war effort. The move required surprisingly few adjustments. There were practically no "war babies" in the region, no plants conceived and brought to life solely for the defense effort. In roughly 70 percent of all cases, existing industries used their existing technologies to turn out their standard products for the Allies. Kearney & Trecker machine tools, after all, could be used to produce tanks as easily as toasters, and the same flexibility applied to Allis-Chalmers turbines, Harnischfeger cranes, Koehring construction equipment, Harley-Davidson motorcycles, and electrical controls from Allen-Bradley, Cutler-Hammer, and Square D.

The war did create new uses for old products, of course. Allen-Bradley had developed a full line of molded carbon resistors during the radio craze of the 1920s; twenty years later, the company's resistors went directly to war in radar sets, walkie-talkies, and aircraft instruments. Small engines from Briggs & Stratton were used to power field generators on the front lines, and the firm's ignition systems were standard equipment on Thunderbolts, Invaders, and other warplanes. At the Falk plant, an inflatable clutch developed for the barge industry became a vital component in LSTs and other Navy landing craft. In these and hundreds of other cases, peacetime products found military applications.

Some companies applied their old technologies to products that were more obviously military. Hosiery firms turned out parachute silk. Pabst introduced a camouflaged beer can for troops at the front. Tanneries supplied leather for boots, holsters, rifle straps, and belts. Other adaptations required a little more ingenuity. A.O. Smith, the nation's top producer of car frames, had become a leader in welded steel tubing as well. With the help of forge hammers that pounded out the tail and nose sections, Smith turned lengths of tubing into bombshells. The massive North Side complex ultimately produced 5 million bomb casings – 80 percent of America's wartime supply.

In a minority of cases, local manufacturers took on products that had nothing to do with their peacetime lines. Vilter, normally a refrigeration specialist, made howitzers. Nordberg, famous for its diesel engines, turned out torpedo tubes. Heil, a leading producer of truck bodies, manufactured water tanks, gun turrets, and smoke generators. Upholding Milwaukee's reputation as "Machine Shop of the World," these companies and many others adopted new lines simply because they had the equipment and the expertise to do so.

There were also a few built-from-scratch industries. Milwaukee had not been a shipbuilding center of any importance since the 1800s, but Froemming Brothers, a highway contractor in peacetime, opened a sizable yard on the Kinnickinnic River near First Street. By war's end, eight tugboats, four naval corvettes, and fourteen cargo ships had begun their careers on the muddy Kinnickinnic. Allis-Chalmers pioneered on a much larger scale. The sprawling West Allis factory was the largest war employer in the state, providing jobs for 20,000 people at flood tide, but its most singular contribution to the Allied cause was the atomic bomb. As a primary contractor on the Manhattan Project, Allis-Chalmers produced more nuclear equipment, by weight, than any company in America. When the *Enola Gay* dropped the finished product on

Milwaukee was a leading "arsenal of democracy" during World War II: (clockwise from top left) Machine tool production at Kearney & Trecker, the Harley-Davidson school for Army mechanics, A.O. Smith bomb casings, the mammoth Allis-Chalmers complex in West Allis, and the 1944 launching of a warship in the Kinnickinnic River

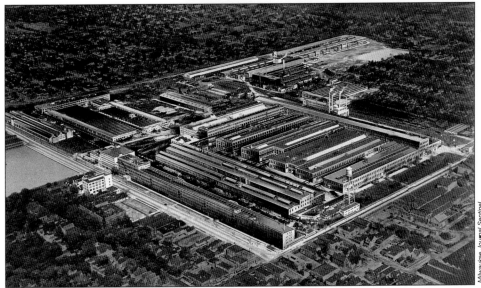

Hiroshima in 1945, Milwaukee could claim an important measure of responsibility.

The cumulative impact of all this war work on Milwaukee's economy was staggering. As their outputs doubled, tripled, and quadrupled, local industries were hard-pressed to keep up with demand. They were perennially short of machinery and starved for space, but federal officials provided substantial help, authorizing nearly $270 million for plant expansions during the war. The greater challenge was finding workers to fill those plants. With enlistments on the rise and the draft operating at full blast, the armed forces grew at the expense of the local labor force. Roughly 70,000 Milwaukee men and women signed on with Uncle Sam for the duration of the conflict. Although workers in defense-vital industries were exempt from the draft, a horrendous shortage of manpower was apparent by the latter part of 1942.

The most prominent Milwaukeean to trade civilian garb for a military uniform was Carl Zeidler. In 1942, after less than two years in office, the mayor decided that he could better serve America by entering the service than running a major city. Although his maritime experience was limited to a single trip on a Lake Michigan excursion steamer, Zeidler chose the high seas. Too old (at thirty-four) to enlist in the regular Navy, he accepted a lieutenant's commission and took command of the gunnery crew aboard an American merchant vessel. Just before his departure in April, 1942, the guileless romantic explained his actions to the *Milwaukee Sentinel*:

> *I have decided that my life is not my own – it belongs to my country. This is a different kind of war than any we have fought before. It requires everyone in service to win. What does my life matter when the life of my country is at stake? The future without liberty would be meaningless.*

In December, 1942, Zeidler's ship, the *La Salle*, was reported missing with all hands in the south Atlantic, the apparent victim of a U-boat attack. John Bohn, a South Side alderman and Common Council president, had become acting mayor when Zeidler enlisted. Seventy-five years old when the *La Salle* went down, Bohn led a caretaker administration with enough vigor to earn a full term of his own in 1944.

War work built to a fever pitch in the months following Carl Zeidler's disappearance. Industrial employment in the metropolitan area soared from 110,000 in 1940 to a peak of nearly 200,000 in the autumn of 1943 – a gain of more than 80 percent in four years. That was significantly more workers than Milwaukee's traditional labor market could begin to supply; the gain reflected a host of innovations and adjustments. Thousands of factory hands moved into town from the farms and villages of rural Wisconsin, including some who had gone home when the Depression claimed their jobs a decade earlier. African Americans were finally in demand again. As the last hired in the 1920s and the first fired in the 1930s, they had suffered acutely during

Mayor Zeidler became Lieut. Zeidler in 1942, going to war on a merchant vessel and perishing in the south Atlantic.

the Depression; in 1940, 51 percent of the city's black adults were still either unemployed or on work relief. They faced a double-edged sword of discrimination from both employers and unions, particularly AFL trade unions, but a combination of civil rights protests, federal pressure, and market demand finally disarmed those who wanted to bar the door. In 1943 the Milwaukee Urban League reported a sea change: "For the first time in over a decade Negro labor was actually sought by heavy industry. Today there is hardly a Negro man in Milwaukee who is physically able and willing to work who is not employed."

Rural migrants and urban minorities helped to keep the war plants humming, but there were simply not enough of them to ease the labor shortage that materialized in late 1942. A sign of things to come appeared in October, when the Falk Company's board allocated $50,000 to build washrooms "for possible women shop employees." By the end of 1943, after an intensive recruiting drive that included door-to-door solicitation, women filled more than one-fourth of Milwaukee County's industrial jobs. Rosie the Riveter had found her niche. Although they were paid less for the same work than their male counterparts, women were prized for their dexterity and attention to detail. In a profile of Cutler-Hammer, *Fortune* (August, 1942) offered backhanded praise for the females who turned out electrical controls by the ton:

> *The company is up against the fact that women frequently make better assemblers than men, and there will be every reason to keep them on when the men return.... Cutler-Hammer has also discovered that even highly educated and intelligent women, generally believed to be bored*

with assembly work, take to it well. Once they master the operation to the point where it is automatic, they can do a flawless job and yet be free to think about other things.

Even after women had come to the rescue, the labor shortage persisted. Perhaps the most novel expedient was the importation, under federal auspices, of more than a thousand black workers from Barbados and Jamaica. They were housed in barracks at the Mitchell Field airport, the same barracks used later, ironically, to house German prisoners of war. Although the islanders helped to boost foundry production and saved the 1944 season for local canneries, they were ill-prepared for Wisconsin's winters. By the middle of 1945, most had gone home.

Thousands of women answered the call to keep Milwaukee's war plants humming. They included Theresa Langolf, a welder at Chain Belt, who said, "I can do as much work as any man, and I can do it just as well or better." Her supervisor concurred.

Milwaukee Journal Sentinel

311

Milwaukee Public Library

Whatever their race, gender, or national origin, Milwaukee's war workers had generally similar experiences. Overtime was constant; like Les Greget hunched over his boring bar at Falk, the typical employee's life was work and little else. Security was extraordinarily tight. Uniformed soldiers stood guard at the entrances to most defense plants, and employees were generally denied access to all but their own work areas. Factory hands working on the Manhattan Project at Allis-Chalmers were instructed not to talk to each other. The Vilter howitzer factory included a machine-gun turret (still extant) overlooking the corner of First and Becher; armed soldiers were ready to open fire on any subversives who tried to invade the South Side. It is no exaggeration to state that the average defense plant was a quasi-military installation for the duration of the war.

The Home Front

The federal penchant for regulation and regimentation carried over into civilian life. The long arm of the government reached into nearly every corner of American society, shaping, none too gently, a sense of national purpose. Citizens who had grown familiar with the WPA, CCC, NYA, NLRB, and FERA during the Depression were forced to learn an entirely new set of acronyms, including the OPA (Office of Price Administration), WPB (War Production Board), OWI (Office of War Information), and WLB (War Labor Board) – not to mention military agencies like the SSS (Selective Service System).

Civil defense was the primary focus early in the war. Milwaukee staged a series of "practice blackouts" in 1942, and 12,149 air raid wardens were trained to identify incendiary bombs and administer first aid by year's end. Every defense plant had its designated "light wardens" and "roof watchers" as well as fire brigades. Such precautions began to seem faintly silly in a community separated from the front lines by two oceans and thousands of miles of land. Interest tapered off in 1943, but a faithful core of volunteer wardens stood ready to help in any emergency.

The advent of rationing in 1942 was taken far more seriously. Some of life's necessities were in critically short supply during the war, among them meat, metal, sugar, shoes, butter, coffee, canned goods, tires, and gasoline. As production was diverted to military channels, access to these and other items was subject to a truly Byzantine system of ration books and stamps. In an effort to help their readers navigate the maze, local newspapers published reminders that might seem arcane to a modern reader: "Eight No. 3 stamps in basic A books good for purchase of 32 gallons of gasoline through Jan. 21" or "Stamp No. 10 good for purchase of three pounds of sugar to Jan. 31." Holding the proper stamps was no guarantee that stores would have the desired goods. Meat supplies were often limited to liver, brains, pig's feet, sausage and – a wartime special – "Porterhorse steak." Defense workers at A.O. Smith reported in 1943 that 63 percent of their lunches lacked butter and 43 percent lacked meat or cheese; peanut butter and jelly became a staple for thousands. Iron and steel were equally scarce. As the fighting intensified, sewer pipe in some of the failed subdivisions of the 1920s was torn up for use in the war effort.

Wartime rationing also cooled America's torrid love affair with the automobile. New cars were not to be had for any price, and supplies of gasoline and tires for old

Milwaukee Public Library

Homemakers from the Italian Third Ward signed up for ration tickets in 1942.

vehicles were limited. After spiking up briefly in 1940-1941, car registrations in Wisconsin actually sank back to their pre-Depression levels for the balance of the war. Grocers stopped making deliveries, several florists shared a single truck, and brewers brought back horse-drawn wagons to distribute their product. Milwaukeeans also returned in droves to the trolleys and buses they had forsaken years earlier. The flood of war workers created such enormous pressures on the public transit system that downtown employers (including City Hall) adopted a system of staggered working hours in 1942. The innovation reduced peak demand by 25 percent, but strap-hanging was still more the rule than the exception. Despite outmoded equipment and a scarcity of motormen, transit ridership in Milwaukee climbed to an all-time high of 428 million in 1944, roughly nine times the level of the 1990s.

courtesy Irwin Scroggins

With automobiles in short supply, most people walked or took the streetcar. Downtown Milwaukee, shown here in December, 1944, was busier than it has been at any time in its history.

schools turned out airplane models for the military, ping-pong paddles for the Red Cross, and crutches for veterans' hospitals. For the city's adult learners, the Milwaukee Vocational School offered three full shifts of classes in mechanics, welding, foundry work, and engine repair.

Nearly 200,000 Milwaukeeans made their most valuable contributions on the job. War workers were vitally aware of the decisive role that manufacturing played in the larger military effort, and they had the earnest support of their fellow citizens. A number of Catholic parishes introduced midnight Masses on Saturday for the convenience of factory hands who had to be on the job Sunday morning. Athletic events and movie screenings were scheduled at odd hours for the convenience of night-shift workers. The Milwaukee Brewers played a number of early-morning games at Borchert Field; ushers dressed in nightgowns passed out cereal and doughnuts, and a pajama-clad band entertained between innings. Such gestures were good business, but they also conveyed the message that defense work was crucially important. For those who needed reminding, the government sponsored a never-ending series of rallies, good-will tours, and expositions. In 1944 a delegation of soldiers from the front visited Milwaukee to describe how an ammunition shortage had reduced their artillery batteries to "priority shelling." Reduced absenteeism, it was hinted, would help bring the war to a prompt conclusion. A few months later, a show dubbed "Here's Your Infantry" came to the lakefront. Nearly 40,000 Milwaukeeans turned out to watch an Army platoon crawl through the mud to storm a "Japanese pillbox" with rifle fire, bayonets, and flame throwers.

The shortages were aggravating and the regulations irksome, but morale on the home front remained high. The nonstop bond drives were always successful; virtually every Milwaukee household had a sizable stockpile of government securities by war's end. Local residents were equally supportive of blood drives, scrap metal campaigns, and special appeals like the American Legion's "smokes for Yanks" – an effort to provide GIs overseas with cigarettes. Victory gardens were another sign of spontaneous patriotism. The proportion of Milwaukee-area households growing their own vegetables jumped from 30.2 percent in 1942 to 54.8 percent in 1943. Milwaukee County opened ninety acres of parkland to gardeners without yards of their own, and a group of patriotic policemen raised tomatoes and cucumbers behind the precinct station on Forty-seventh and Vliet. Even schoolchildren did their part for the war effort. Students at Boys' Technical High School actually manufactured machine-tool parts under a subcontract with Kearney & Trecker, and shop classes in other

Milwaukee Journal Sentinel

(top)

*Victory gardens at
Fifty-Third and Roosevelt*

(bottom)

*Boys' Tech students making
parts for Kearney & Trecker*

Milwaukee Public Library

Milwaukee Journal Sentinel

Milwaukee Public Library

(top)

The Klopotek family showed off its war bonds.

(bottom)

*A group of West Allis Victory Midlines
(kid Marines) displayed the results of their scrap drive.*

For many in the crowd, it was an uncomfortably close look at what their sons and husbands, fathers and brothers were experiencing on the other side of the world.

Patriotism may well have been its own reward, but there were more tangible compensations for Milwaukee's war workers. With rising wages and abundant overtime, the average industrial worker's weekly paycheck swelled from $29.50 in 1940 to $52.52 in 1945. The burning question was how to spend the windfall. If the 1930s were a decade of no money but plenty of time, the 1940s brought no time but plenty of money. Leisure was limited, goods were scarce, and vacations were out of the question. There were still, however, diversions to be found. The golden age of cinema continued through World War II, and the big band era was in full swing. Downtown, as the home of the grandest theaters and some of the best-known ballrooms, was busier than it has been at any time before or since. Stars like Woody Her-

man and Spencer Tracy (both hometown boys) passed through on occasion, but downtown's best-known entertainer had nothing to do with music or the movies. In April, 1945, a mallard laid a clutch of eggs on a piling below the Wisconsin Avenue bridge. Dubbed "Gertie the Duck" by a local journalist, she became an overnight celebrity. The saga of her family's tribulations (a fall into the river, a dramatic rescue, a drenching storm) and their final deliverance to the peaceful waters of the Juneau Park lagoon captivated readers from coast to coast. In the waning days of World War II, Gertie demonstrated just how starved the public was for distractions of any kind.

Reading tales of downtown ducks, swinging to the strains of *The Chattanooga Choo Choo*, or simply watching *Casablanca* were all welcome diversions, but nothing short of victory could end a period of painfully high anxiety. Everyone had friends, relatives, or neighbors at the front, and news

War-weary Milwaukeeans embraced the saga of Gertie the Duck as a welcome diversion.

Milwaukee Journal Sentinel

of battlefield casualties came with distressing frequency. World War II, everyone knew, was a struggle to the death. The fighting in Europe ended on May 7, 1945, but millions were still in harm's way. With Japan's surrender on August 14, the joy was general. Tens of thousands filled the streets of downtown Milwaukee, drunk on legal beer and victory. By the next morning, however, the celebration was over. Jubilant but subdued, local residents looked ahead to the awesome task of rebuilding the lives they had left behind when the shooting started.

★ ★ ★ ★ ★

The years between 1930 and 1945 were some of the most distinctly abnormal in American history. The nation as a whole swung from one extreme to another without pausing in any sort of recognizable middle. Milwaukee swung with the rest of the country, moving from self-doubt and dissension in the Thirties to life-or-death solidarity in the Forties. Any lingering sense of local autonomy vanished utterly, but Milwaukee was by no means interchangeable with other American cities. A humane, focused, and creative municipal government remained one of its distinguishing features, and the community's industrial might, humbled in the Thirties and harnessed in the Forties, helped to win a global war. Without the guns and gears, boots and bombs produced on the home front, Allied soldiers would have been forced to fight the enemy with their bare hands.

Some of the changes of the 1930-1945 period are apparently permanent. The ubiquity of the federal government, born of a double emergency, has yet to recede in any significant way, and America's role in world

Milwaukee Journal Sentinel

Joy in the streets: V-J Day, August 14, 1945

affairs was utterly transformed. In a broader view of the century, however, the period can be viewed as an interruption, a long, anxiety-filled time-out. The United States had been heading somewhere in the 1920s; it was becoming a mass society oriented to the suburbs, to the automobile, to the media and consumer goods. Those trends were disrupted by an economic collapse and a world military crisis that produced fifteen years of disequilibrium. The trends of the Twenties would return with a vengeance after V-J Day, and Milwaukee would be remade once again.

Chapter 8

The Exploding Metropolis, 1945 – 1967

When John and Florence Bruno moved to 8120 W. Clovernook Street in 1957, the scent of new-mown hay was still in the air. Black-and-white Holsteins grazed in a pasture south of Mill Road. Forest wildflowers bloomed in a woodlot on the old Herman Kuphal farm, soon to become Noyes Park. Seventy-sixth Street, the main-traveled highway into town, was only a two-lane turnpike. At its crossing with Good Hope Road – less than a mile from Clovernook – lingered two mainstays of the rural regime: the Granville town hall and a one-room country schoolhouse. Still farther north on Seventy-sixth, near Brown Deer Road, the Batzler family tended a herd of Brown Swiss cows known for their chocolate-colored coats and gentle dispositions.

All these icons of the agrarian past were about to topple in 1957. The Brunos were in the shock wave of an explosion that would utterly transform the landscape around Milwaukee and replace an older farming culture with one that had barely begun to evolve. The process was familiar. Developers purchased several farms northwest of town, reassembled them as the Menomonee River Hills subdivision, and petitioned the city for annexation. When the streets, sewer lines, and water mains were completed, the developers went looking for customers. The people they found were typically residents of older neighborhoods on the North Side,

many with German surnames, most with young children, and all with at least a tentative hold on places in the middle class. John Bruno was a Milwaukee firefighter (one of three on Clovernook), and his neighbors included a bus driver, a machinist, an insurance clerk, a tool-and-die-maker from Briggs & Stratton, and an electrician at the Harnischfeger plant. Each paid approximately $12,000 for a home just like the Brunos': a small, two-bedroom ranch with brick veneer and an attached garage, set on a 60-by-130-foot lot totally devoid of vegetation. The grass and the trees would come later; it was enough, in 1957, to drive up Clovernook after a day's work and feel the stirrings of a new way of life.

Another transformation, different in kind but not in scope, enveloped the neighborhood the Brunos left behind. John and Florence moved from the upper unit of an aging duplex at 2021 N. Twenty-second Street, near the heart of the old German North Side. When the Brunos headed northwest to greener pastures, Samuel and Stella Davis took over their flat. Both were natives of Tennessee who had traveled north after World War II in search of work. They found it in Milwaukee, Sam as a laborer at the Seaman (later American Motors) body plant on Richards Street, Stella as a maid. The Davises were among the first African Americans on their block. They were in the shock wave of an explosion that would remake the

John and Florence Bruno bought this modest ranch house on the Northwest Side in 1957, leaving behind a duplex on N. Twenty-second Street (right) that became the home of Sam and Stella Davis, two of the first African Americans on the block.

demographic face of Milwaukee's central city and replace an older European culture with one rooted in Africa and shaped by harsh experience in the rural South. The transformation of the inner city was every bit as rapid as the revolution occurring on the urban fringe. In 1960, three years after the Davises moved to Twenty-second Street, blacks made up just 8.2 percent of the surrounding census tract's population. By 1970 their proportion had risen to 82.4 percent.

Stella Davis would remain at 2021 N. Twenty-second for forty years, losing Sam to a heart attack in 1963, buying the duplex and moving downstairs, and staying until ill health forced her to enter a nursing home in 1997. During her long reign as the matriarch of the block, Stella witnessed dramatic change, all of it for the worse. Although she and a handful of neighbors took meticulous care of their properties, blight ultimately claimed nearly a third of the homes on the street. As the houses came down, poverty rates went up; unemployment and underemployment were distressingly familiar problems. Crime rates rose at the same time; wire mesh eventually hid the white curtains on Stella's windows.

The process of decay was well under way by the late 1960s. In the charged social climate of the decade, conditions in the North Side ghetto generated a potent mixture of unfocused frustration and self-righteous anger. Touched off by nothing in particular, that mixture resulted in a different kind of explosion: the riot of July 30 and 31, 1967. For the first time since the eight-hour disturbances of 1886, a confrontation between angry residents and civil authorities had mortal consequences. The final toll was three dead, scores injured, and a blow to the community's confidence that remained fresh a generation later. Milwaukee had developed, over the years, a self-image as "the biggest small town in America." It was a low-key community, a place described by travel writer Eli Waldron in 1949 as "the most comfortable city in the land, ... the city of the overstuffed chair and the big bosom, the unhurried pedestrian and the easygoing cop." By the end of 1967, that image was fading fast, replaced by a growing awareness that Milwaukee had all the problems as well as the attractions that typified life in big-city America.

The Road to Clovernook

The combination of outward sprawl represented by the Brunos and inner decay witnessed by the Davises might appear to be a uniquely post-World War II phenomenon. It is not. The twin themes of decentralization and deterioration are nearly as old as America's cities, and Milwaukee is hardly an exception. Older groups have always moved out as they moved up, leaving their homes behind, somewhat the worse for wear, to more recent arrivals. What changed over the years, and changed radically, was the severity of decay in the city's historic core and the distance between the center and the urban fringe. The gap between old and new, between have-nots and haves, grew steadily wider with time, and the story of most urban areas in postwar America is a tale of two cities. The inner-city side of Milwaukee's story is told later in this chapter; the subject here is the road that led to Clovernook Street.

Americans have always been ambivalent about their big cities. Since the days of Thomas Jefferson, there has been a strong impulse to live elsewhere, preferably in the soul-renewing quiet of the countryside. In Milwaukee, ironically, that impulse was brought to life by the same force that brought the region's modern economy to life: industrialization. The fouled rivers and fetid air of the late 1800s were hardly conducive to pleasant living. The typical worker's neighborhood – a jumble of small, tightly spaced houses teeming with people and plagued by smoke and smells from nearby factories and packing plants – was an environment that more affluent residents fled at their earliest opportunity.

Milwaukee Journal Sentinel

Air pollution had long been one of the drawbacks of city living, particularly in the days of coal-burning furnaces and locomotives.

The outward-bound impulse was given official sanction by city planners. Leading figures of the Socialist period, notably Charles Whitnall, revealed a frankly anti-urban bias in their visions of the future metropolis. Nature was the all-nourishing mother, Whitnall believed, and he designed an extensive park system around the county's natural waterways. His goal was to pull residents away from the denatured squalor of the central city and into the maternal shelter of woods and water. "There remains no plausible excuse for a congested city," Whitnall wrote. "Every home should feel the environmental influence of natural shores with the essential forest support."

Technology imposed some definite limits on that vision. In the horsecar era, thirty minutes was considered the maximum commuting time for city workers; development was limited to neighborhoods within a three-mile radius of downtown. The coming of the streetcar in 1890 pushed the borders back dramatically, and the private automobile practically erased them; thirty minutes was enough time to reach the next county in a Model T. Common after 1910 and nearly universal by 1930, automobiles

The postwar housing crisis led to some novel expedients, including Wingfoot homes in Glendale (center) and trailers at McKinley Beach. The sameness of such developments (top) occasionally caused confusion.

Milwaukee Journal, June 1, 1946

VETERANS' QUONSET HUT HOUSING PROJECT

POLICE

'Now Just Tell Us Where You Live, Joe'

Milwaukee County Historical Society

Milwaukee County Historical Society

drove the building frenzy of the 1920s, a decade that witnessed a 65-percent increase in Milwaukee's land area and runaway growth in the suburbs.

The genie of urban sprawl was loose – until the Depression put the cork back in the bottle. World War II kept it there. Practically nothing was built for fifteen years, creating enormous pressure on the city's existing housing stock. In the late 1930s, with a pre-war industrial boom swelling local payrolls, adequate housing was hard to find, and the supply grew even tighter during the war. Deprived of its usual outlets, the outward-bound impulse built up like water behind a dam. When the *Milwaukee Journal* conducted its annual survey of consumers in 1945, 48.2 percent expressed a desire to buy or build new homes. Of that number, 62.2 percent intended to relocate beyond the city limits. Consumers, concluded the *Journal*, were showing "a marked intention to get away from urban areas."

The postwar exodus was eminently predictable. It was, at root, simply a resumption of trends that had surfaced decades earlier. But a rare constellation of forces pushed the mid-century explosion to heights that no one could have foreseen. The first was a housing crisis. The shortage was bad enough in wartime, but hordes of veterans, many on the verge of starting families, came home after V-J Day to find that adequate shelter was not to be had at any price. Until contractors caught up with demand, municipal governments had little choice but to improvise. Building codes were relaxed to permit doubling up in private homes, and vacant schools were converted to makeshift apartments. City and county officials put up more than 2,500 temporary units wherever they could find room: trailers at McKinley Beach, Quonset huts and Wingfoot cabins in the parks, even barracks on the front lawn of the courthouse. The county's largest "development" was in Wilson Park, where veterans occupied 374 prefabricated homes made by Milwaukee's own Harnischfeger Corporation. Some of the housing projects were little more than campgrounds; ice-cold floors and sweating walls were common complaints during the winter months, and hundreds of families were forced to share bathroom, recreation, and laundry facilities. But even temporary housing was preferable to no housing at all.

Economic prosperity was the second force fueling the explosion. Fears that the American economy would relapse into recession without the artificial stimulus of war proved groundless. Milwaukee, in fact, missed barely a beat in retooling for peacetime. There were nearly 30,000 layoffs in the wake of Japan's surrender, but many of the furloughed workers were married women who had assumed their jobs were temporary. Despite some anxious moments, their returning husbands had little trouble finding work; Milwaukee's unemployment rate was barely 2 percent in 1946. The community's relief was evident in the Common Council's report for the year:

> The anticipated postwar slump in employment did not materialize in Milwaukee. Work openings were well in excess of applicants, particularly in the skilled worker field; and, by early summer, the only sizeable pool of new workers were returning veterans. Of the 67,000 veterans returned to Milwaukee, only a few hundred were without jobs or not in school at the end of the year.

Milwaukee's national image was still inextricably linked with beer, an obvious outcome of nonstop advertising campaigns. But Schlitz, Pabst, Miller, and their counterparts employed only 7,130 workers in 1948, barely 2 percent of the county's labor force. As in earlier years, durable goods were Milwaukee's mainstay, particularly heavy machinery, engines, electrical equipment, castings, and other products of the metal-bending trades. With giants like Allis-Chalmers, A.O. Smith, Cutler-Hammer, Allen-Bradley, Ladish, and Globe-Union leading the way, Milwaukee County's industrial output more than doubled in the

Milwaukee Journal Sentinel

Milwaukee Journal Sentinel

Whether the product was beer at Pabst or a gargantuan mining shovel at Bucyrus-Erie, Milwaukee industries adjusted to peacetime without missing a beat.

immediate postwar period, soaring from $1.5 billion in 1946 to $3.1 billion in 1953.

At least 56 percent of the work force was engaged in manufacturing during the same years, one of the highest concentrations in America, and the vast majority of workers belonged to labor unions. With the end of the war came the end of the no-strike pledge that most unions had honored for the duration of the conflict. In the wave of work stoppages that followed, the most serious was a walkout at Allis-Chalmers that dragged on for 329 days in 1946 and 1947. Marred by periodic violence, it ended with the purge of Local 248's left-leaning leadership by UAW moderates under Walter Reuther. Harold Christoffel, the local's most prominent leader, went to jail for perjury after a congressional inquiry into the Allis-Chalmers union. Communist infiltration ceased to be a major source of controversy within the labor movement, and the merger of the AFL and the CIO in 1955 further enhanced a sense of solidarity. As

The 1946-47 Allis-Chalmers walkout went on for 329 days, some marked by confrontations between strikers and strike-breakers.

Milwaukee Journal Sentinel

assertive unions pressed affluent corporations, Milwaukee wages rose to record heights. The average industrial worker's weekly paycheck swelled from $47 in 1946 to $67 in 1950 and $93 in 1956, growing at more than double the rate of inflation.

Government loan programs helped workers put that new money into new homes. The Federal Housing Administration and the Veterans Administration both encouraged homeownership on unbelievably easy terms: as little as nothing down, 4-percent interest, and thirty years to pay. There was a catch, however: FHA and VA guarantees were available only on "conventional" homes in "harmonious, attractive neighborhoods" free from the threat of "incompatible racial or social groups." The federal government, in other words, became the nation's leading practitioner of "red-lining." Tax dollars subsidized the existing bias against central-city development, adding significant momentum to the outward migration.

Another, more ominous force hastened the exodus. As the physical horrors of World War II gave way to the gnawing anxieties of the Cold War, it was obvious that major cities, particularly industrial centers like Milwaukee, were prime military targets. Visions of a nuclear holocaust lent a sinister undertone to a period usually remembered for its innocence and optimism. Milwaukee was ringed with Nike anti-aircraft missile installations in the mid-1950s, including a battery on the present Summerfest grounds. In 1955 the Common Council designated St. John's Military Academy in Delafield as the emergency site for city government and adopted a succession plan ranking more than forty municipal officials. Evacuation route signs went up in the same year, and in 1956 nearly 180,000 schoolchildren received bracelets to identify them in case they were separated from their families during an enemy attack. Civil Defense preparations intensified with the Cuban missile crisis of 1962. By the end of the year, Milwaukee had nearly 400 public fallout shelters stocked with 1,000 tons of disaster supplies. The appropriate response to the Cold War was clear: Leave town, because your chances of survival are better on the edge.

Milwaukeeans, then, had both a critical need for new housing and the money to pay for it. Federal loan programs subsidized their flight to the outskirts, and Cold War tensions encouraged it. That combination of forces would have been more than enough to fuel a boom on the fringe, but another factor played an equally decisive role: the lingering psychological impact of the Depression and World War II. When Milwaukeeans looked around them after V-J Day, everything seemed worn-out. Most automobiles were working antiques. The transit system's newest streetcar dated from 1929. A lack of money in the 1930s and a lack of time in the 1940s had forced most residents to defer maintenance on their homes. The city's streets, bridges, and public buildings showed signs of similar neglect. Words like "tired" and "dingy" appear frequently in descriptions of postwar Milwaukee.

It could not have been otherwise, given the prevailing national emergencies, but the fifteen-year famine in building, buying, and births had left Milwaukeeans sick of the old and starved for the new. Neighborhoods now cherished as historic were scorned as used-up. Homes that had once seemed cozy were cramped, and blocks that had always been comfortable began to

feel crowded. After years of getting by, people wanted to get ahead again. They wanted new families; with privation and war no longer providing "birth control," the city of Milwaukee's birth rate jumped from 17.2 per 1,000 in 1947 to 27.9 per 1,000 in 1957. They wanted new consumer goods; the demand for appliances, paint, power equipment, and clothing constantly outstripped supply. They wanted new cars; buyers had to wait a full year for even a no-frills sedan in mid-1947. And they wanted new homes; practically all the metropolitan area's postwar growth took place outside the central city. What Milwaukeeans wanted, in short, was new lives, and they found them, more often than not, on the urban fringe.

With so many forces at work, the explosion on the fringe was absolutely predictable, but its intensity was still a shock. As fifteen years of pressure built to the breaking point, the dam holding back pent-up demand groaned, cracked, and finally

As the Cold War intensified, Nike anti-aircraft missiles were installed to protect Milwaukee from enemy attack. This battery was located on the present Summerfest grounds.

burst wide open, unleashing the greatest wave of building activity in Milwaukee's history. The resulting flood overwhelmed the construction industry, severely taxed the resources of local governments, and buried thousands of acres under new homes, new lawns, and new swingsets. Between 1940 and 1970, the number of housing units in the four-county metropolitan area almost doubled, rising from 238,514 to 449,044. At the crest of the wave in the 1950s, new homes were popping up at the rate of nearly 1,000 a month. Still there were not enough. Some veterans' families were waiting in line for "temporary" housing as late as 1953, and it took until mid-decade for supply to catch up with demand. The explosion's impact was most evident in Milwaukee County: By the end of 1960, more than one-third of the county's 327,736 housing units had been built since World War II.

Cape Cods, many with "doghouse dormers," were the most popular housing style in the years just after World War II.

Living on the Edge

Life was different on the edge of town. Whether they were city residents moving into newly annexed subdivisions or suburbanites whose communities had just incorporated, the edge-dwellers shared a distinctive physical environment. Just as earlier generations had favored characteristic housing types – duplexes at the turn of the century, bungalows in the 1920s – postwar Milwaukeeans built signature homes of their own. The simple Cape Cod, with its shed roof, square floor plan, and often "doghouse dormers," was the design of choice just after the war. By the 1950s, builders had shifted to the more capacious ranch house – a somewhat ironic term for shelter on the "crabgrass frontier." Split-levels appeared soon after, rounding out the rather narrow mix of styles that identified postwar developments from coast to coast.

Subdivisions like this one at Seventy-sixth and Hampton sprawled across thousands of acres of farmland.

Milwaukee Public Library

326

Social expectations were different as well. Tracts like Menomonee River Hills – John and Florence Bruno's new address – marked a profound shift in orientation. Allegiance to the group, whether ethnic or religious, had been expressed geographically in the old neighborhoods; each had its own blend of steeples, stores, and taverns that served as anchors of community. On the edge, by contrast, and within clear racial limits, neighbors were little more than an afterthought; the emphasis was on the progress of the individual and the prosperity of his or her family. The old patterns never disappeared, but they certainly diminished with distance; no Catholic parish would ever again be as Polish as St. Josaphat's on the South Side, no neighborhood as Jewish as the Haymarket section of the North Side.

Places like Bentgrass Hills, Golden Gate, and Cloverland reflected, much more tangibly, the influence of technologies that came to the fore after World War II. Many edge-dwellers displayed a helpless infatuation with anything new, from Formica to Naugahyde. The ranch houses and split-levels on the fringe were filled with transistor radios, hi-fi systems, air conditioners, power mowers, and a stunning array of kitchen appliances. Between 1946 and 1965, as consumers heeded the call to "Live Better ... Electrically," power usage per household more than tripled. There was, during the same period, a striking shift in the seasonal balance of power. The Wisconsin Electric system's annual peak had always occurred in late December, when the days were short, the lights were on, and streetcars were filled with Christmas shoppers. The demise of electrified transit and the dramatic growth of air conditioning changed all that; the summer peak rose steadily against the winter high point, overtaking it permanently in 1968.

The most popular electrical "appliance" of the postwar period was undoubtedly television. Although the technology had been available since 1929, the Depression and World War II delayed the commercial advent of the new medium. Milwaukee's first station was WTMJ-TV, which signed on during the evening hours of December 3, 1947. The premiere broadcast included a fashion show, a golf demonstration, nightclub acts, Marquette University football highlights and, of course, beer commercials. There were fewer than 1,000 sets in Milwaukee at the time. WTMJ-TV had thoughtfully placed one in the lobby of the Central Library, where nearly 500 people craned their necks for a better view of the eight-by-ten-inch screen.

Like most new technologies, the first TV sets were exorbitantly expensive. In 1949 department stores charged $269.50 for a low-end RCA Victor with a fifty-two-inch screen – fifty-two *square* inches, that is, or roughly six by nine. That price was equivalent to nearly $2,000 in current dollars, and the stores demanded an old radio in trade. People still lined up to buy the new sets. Americans have always been quick to embrace new inventions, from the telephone to "talkies," but it is doubtful that any enjoyed quite the same reception as television. According to the *Milwaukee Journal's* annual consumer survey, the proportion of Milwaukee-area households who owned a TV set skyrocketed from 0.4 percent in 1948 to 54.6 percent in 1951 and 97.2 percent in 1957. The next breakthrough – color television – debuted on January 1, 1954, when NBC broadcast the

A 1947 demonstration
of television in the
Boston Store window
drew a crowd of
interested Milwaukeeans.
Early sets (below) were
extraordinarily small
by later standards.

Milwaukee Journal Sentinel

Milwaukee Journal Sentinel

Rose Bowl parade in "living color"; by 1967 nearly 17 percent of Milwaukee households had made the switch from black-and-white.

The urban edge provided a home for new technologies, but it also encouraged absolute dependence on a somewhat older invention: the private automobile. The number of motor vehicles registered in Milwaukee County soared from 177,969 in 1945 to 319,071 in 1955 – a 79-percent increase in ten years – and kept rising to 419,638 in 1965. Most households had at least one car after the war, and the proportion of two-vehicle families in the greater Milwaukee area jumped from 4.2 percent in 1950 to 29 percent in 1965. The dominance of the automobile was not the result of some technological curse or corporate conspiracy; people wanted cars because nothing else could match their convenience, their comfort, and their flexibility. The automobile's drawbacks would be apparent

soon enough, but its postwar appeal could be summed up in a single word: freedom.

As cars took over the streets, older forms of transportation were pushed to extinction. The city's horse population plummeted from 12,192 in 1907 to fewer than 200 in 1950, most of them hitched to wagons that hauled trash to the municipal incinerator in the Third Ward. When garbage collection was motorized in the early Fifties, only a handful remained; the last city-owned steed, a draft horse named Dolly, was sold for fifty dollars in 1957 and put out to pasture. Streetcars joined them in oblivion. One of the finest electric interurban systems in the nation – a network that linked Milwaukee with Sheboygan, Watertown, East Troy, Burlington, and Kenosha – was dismantled between 1938 and 1946. The first motor buses appeared on city routes in 1920, and they were joined in the late 1930s by "trackless trolleys," rubber-tired vehicles tethered to the overhead electric lines. Although conventional trolleys continued to anchor the system through World War II, they became an increasingly endangered species; the last streetcar made its farewell run in 1958. Bus service continued, of course, but mass transit struggled to maintain its position in an automobile-saturated society.

It was the private automobile that determined the physical scale of the postwar housing explosion. By removing artificial constraints on distance, the car made sprawl possible in the first place, and it inflated lot sizes just as predictably. After generations in close quarters, people apparently wanted to see less of each other, and the automobile gave them their wish. The thirty-foot lots of the central city became sixty-foot parcels in even the entry-level subdivisions, and "lots" in the more affluent developments were practically the size of small farms.

The automobile's influence on local shopping patterns was just as revolutionary. On September 20, 1951, traffic was snarled for blocks as 60,000 people came to celebrate the opening of a new Milwaukee landmark: Southgate Shopping Center. Located on S. Twenty-seventh Street at Morgan Avenue, Southgate was little more than a strip mall by modern standards – 20 stores, 105,000 square feet of retail space, and parking for 2,000 cars – but the *Milwaukee Journal* hailed this "modernistic milestone" as the ultimate in convenience:

> *The variety of merchandise offered in the block would permit a family to buy a complete outfit for each of its members, toys for all the children, paint for the house, a television set, a gift, a card and a box of candy for Aunt Minnie's birthday, groceries for the week and carpeting for the living room. Mother could have her hair set while*

> *father had his shoes half soled and the children dropped off the cleaning. Then everybody could have a soda to celebrate.*

Southgate was only the first of many centers that catered to automobile traffic. Others followed in short order, each larger and more complete than the last: Bayshore in 1954, Capitol Court in 1956, and Mayfair (originally Westgate) in 1958. As the centers proliferated, older commercial districts began to feel the pressure. Downtown, ironically, celebrated the grand reopening of Wisconsin Avenue (minus its streetcar tracks) in the same month that Southgate

(top)

Dobbin's last stand: Horses were used to haul Milwaukee's garbage until the early 1950s.

(bottom)

In a scene that would bring tears to the eyes of any rail buff, retired streetcars were hauled to a Waukesha quarry and unceremoniously burned.

Milwaukee Journal Sentinel

Milwaukee County Transit System

Southgate, Milwaukee's first shopping center, opened for business in 1951.

Milwaukee Journal Sentinel

North Third Street was one neighborhood "downtown" that lost customers to the new centers. Schuster's is on the right in this 1939 view.

Milwaukee Journal Sentinel

debuted in 1951. Merchants hopefully dubbed their avenue the "Magnificent Mile," and newspaper advertisements trumpeted the appeal of "DOWNTOWN ... the magic hub of the city that offers you every service, every convenience, every amusement you could wish."

The sheer mass of establishments in the central business district assured its vitality for a time, but neighborhood shopping centers were more vulnerable. One of the anomalies of Milwaukee's retail trade had always been the strength of retailers in the city's neighborhoods. Schuster's, for instance, had become the largest department store chain in the state – without a single downtown location. All of Schuster's business was done at stores on Third and Garfield, Twelfth and Vliet, and Eleventh and Mitchell. The rise of automobile-oriented shopping centers changed the pecking order significantly. When Schuster's opened a new store as the anchor of Capitol

Court, shoppers deserted N. Third Street in droves. Merchants watched in dismay as business on Third, once the "downtown" of Milwaukee's North Side, fell 37 percent between 1955 and 1959. One well-established clothing store, Bitker-Gerner, saw its volume drop by half in the first fifteen months that Capitol Court was open.

The automobile was responsible for the shopping center, but its greatest physical impact was probably the host of alterations forced by its very presence. Milwaukee's streets were built for wagons and streetcars, not Ramblers and Buicks; a nineteenth-century network was practically overwhelmed by a twentieth-century technology. The result was a condition approaching gridlock. The *Milwaukee Journal* (October 7, 1951) was unequivocal: "The toughest problem facing Milwaukee, one which must be solved swiftly lest the metropolitan area strangle in its own prosperity, is the automobile." Public officials had little choice but to deal with the growing crisis. A multi-million-dollar program of street reconstruction eased congestion to some extent, and the wholesale removal of trolley tracks and safety islands helped. In 1947 a system of paired one-way streets (Sixteenth/Seventeenth, State/Highland, Seventh/Eighth) was adopted to speed the flow of traffic in and around downtown. The city's first 548 parking meters were installed east of the Milwaukee River two years later; by 1952 an expanded system was adding nearly $350,000 to the city's coffers annually. Parking remained a major complaint; the first public structure, a concrete monolith at Michigan and Milwaukee Streets, was dedicated with considerable fanfare in 1957. Still conditions deteriorated. For anyone who had to sit through three lights just to cross

Milwaukee Journal Sentinel

Wisconsin Avenue every morning, the supposed freedom of the private car began to seem more than a little illusory.

A more radical solution was already in the works. In 1944 the State Highway Commission launched a study that proved to be a seminal document of the freeway era. The final report, published in 1946, recommended two major expressway corridors intersecting in the heart of the city, one following Sixteenth Street and the other Highland Avenue and Clybourn Street. Support for the plan was instantaneous and unconditional. Politicians, editors, business leaders, and motorists viewed freeways as the concrete answer to their prayers, and voters expressed a willingness to pay for them. City residents approved a $5 million bond issue for "a system of express highways" in a 1948 referendum. By 1951 that system was the largest item in the city's capital budget, and the *Milwaukee Journal* promised its readers that deliverance was at hand:

The postwar automobile boom overwhelmed Milwaukee's street system. Traffic jams like this 1950 tangle on the Sixth Street viaduct convinced most residents that freeways were absolutely necessary.

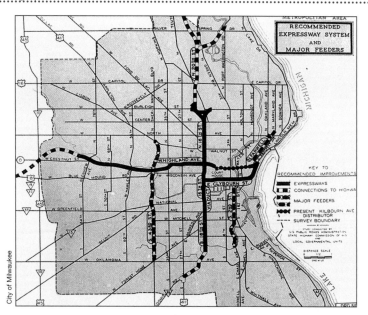

Milwaukee's first expressway plan was published in 1946.

While you are circling block after block hunting a parking space, while you're creeping to work at maybe 15 miles an hour, try to vision what's in your future. It may be hard to see as your blood pressure rises, but some day you will speed downtown at 50 or 60 miles an hour (even without jet, rocket or atomic engines).... There will be smooth, wide expressways splitting the city from north to south and east to west.

Cold War concerns hastened the arrival of the freeway era; six-lane highways would obviously speed evacuation in the event of a Soviet attack, and the corridors themselves were promoted, somewhat macabrely, as firebreaks. After a long series of revisions and expansions, the construction phase finally began on March 17, 1952, when city officials broke ground for the Stadium South expressway. It was apparent by that time that traffic problems, and their ultimate solutions, reached well beyond the city's borders. In a rare instance of intergovernmental cooperation, city and county officials prevailed upon the Wisconsin legislature to

create the Milwaukee County Expressway Commission in 1953. Responsibility for the system moved to a more appropriate level of government, and city taxpayers were reimbursed for the $2.5 million they had already invested in the project. (The move also helped to save the County Sheriff's Department from oblivion: As rural towns became suburban villages and formed their own police departments, the sheriffs were reassigned to freeway patrol.) Higher authorities were also involved in the effort. State and federal tax dollars provided the lion's share of the original freeway budget, and in 1956 the federal portion soared to 90 percent – a provision designed to ensure completion of the Interstate Highway System. Milwaukee was already hard at work on its own portion of that system, but extra federal funding was welcomed with open arms.

Milwaukee County's expressway system proved to be the largest public works project in the community's history. Not since the prodigious landfill activities of the pioneer period had there been, relatively speaking, such a wholesale rearrangement of the landscape. As the engineers tinkered with old routes and added new ones, the project developed an irresistible momentum. From the first 24 miles approved in 1952, the planned system grew to 45 miles in 1955, 54 in 1963, and 80.3 in 1967. Actual construction nearly kept pace with planning. The first segment of the county system was formally dedicated on January 27, 1962, when the barricades came down on a 4.86-mile stretch that included Interstate 94 between Thirteenth and Sixty-eighth Streets and the Stadium Freeway between Wisconsin and National Avenues. The east-west route instantly became the busiest highway in the state, creating enormous pressure to speed

From clearance (left) through grading (lower left) to paving (below), freeway construction proceeded with all due speed. The scenes pictured are in the corridors of I-94 at Thirty-fifth Street and I-43 at Capitol Drive and at Bender Road.

Milwaukee Journal Sentinel

Milwaukee Journal Sentinel

Milwaukee Journal Sentinel

In September, 1958, with a little help from Miss Concrete and Miss Black Top, Gov. Vernon Thomson opened Wisconsin's first freeway, a seven-mile segment of Interstate 94 in Waukesha County. Milwaukee County's first link followed in January, 1962.

Casualties were abundant, including Our Lady of Pompeii Church, spiritual center of the Third Ward's "Little Italy."

up construction. The Expressway Commission was spending money at the rate of $25 million a year through the 1960s, and by decade's end the planners had 63.9 miles of completed roadway to show for it. In 1966 alone – the high-water mark of the entire project – 22.5 miles of freeway entered the system.

Despite ample funding and an army of construction workers, the Commission encountered any number of setbacks: steel strikes, weather delays, tardy subcontractors, and a desperate shortage of engineers. The freeway project also generated an unusual number of casualties. Thousands of people were uprooted to make room for the roads, a problem that was handled with a shrug in the early years. "The displacement of families and business activities is a time-consuming process," reported the Commission in 1959. "A certain amount of extended litigation is inevitable." The more obvious casualties included some of Milwaukee's most cherished

The Marquette Interchange, linchpin of Milwaukee's freeway system, neared completion in April, 1968.

landmarks: Our Lady of Pompeii, the "little pink church" that anchored the Third Ward Italian community; St. Joseph's Church, a comparable hub for the North Side's German Catholics; Brisbane Hall, home of the Socialist Party and leading labor unions since 1911; Grand Avenue Methodist Church; and the Layton School of Art's new building on Prospect Avenue. A later generation would find the destruction of these icons unforgivable, but the freeway-builders believed that their cause was just. Bridge columns, in their view, were "pillars of progress," and bulldozers were agents of community improvement. Using a standard industry formula, the Expressway Commission asserted that, in 1965 alone, freeways "saved" 14 lives and spared motorists nearly $12 million in time, gasoline, and maintenance costs.

A milestone of sorts was reached in 1964, when work began on the Marquette Interchange. It was the largest single construction project ever undertaken in Wisconsin and, as the Expressway Commission put it, the "critical hub for the entire Interstate System in Milwaukee County." Demolition crews cleared more than 500 buildings from a 35-acre site for the grand junction, obliterating the old Tory Hill neighborhood and an adjacent industrial district. (Cutler-Hammer was the major casualty.) When the interchange was finally completed in late 1968, more than 3.5 miles of road were piled in a mound of concrete spaghetti visible from outer space.

Opposition to the freeways had begun to surface by that time. Critics viewed the stack as a monument to folly, a triumph of engineering that had destroyed part of the city's soul and a significant portion of its tax base. For a larger number of people – the tens of thousands who used the Marquette Interchange every day – expressways were viewed as a costly convenience, not without their drawbacks but certainly preferable to the gridlock of the previous period.

Expressways, of course, affected everyone in the metropolitan area, as did television, shopping centers, and new appliances. But the changes were most pronounced on the urban fringe. Life was different there after World War II, both physically and socially. Thousands of edge-dwellers whizzed to work in streamlined vehicles on six-lane roads every morning and returned every night to new homes packed with the latest technological marvels. Transportation, commerce, and entertainment had all been revolutionized, and their particular shapes varied not at all from Sacramento to Savannah. Milwaukeeans who moved to the edge were therefore moving to the middle as well – a characteristically American middle, filled with the creature comforts of postwar prosperity.

An aerial view of downtown in the mid-1960s showed how much land had been taken for expressways, parking lots, and urban renewal projects.

Milwaukee Public Library

City vs. Suburbs

Viewed from the air, metropolitan Milwaukee was all one world. A modest central business district lay at its heart, surrounded by gridwork neighborhoods in the older section that gave way to curvilinear subdivisions and open fields on the urban fringe. The fringe zone, whether within or beyond the city limits, was especially uniform: an accretion of new homes, new streets, and new stores that were practically indistinguishable from one end of the region to the other. This apparent coherence vanished at the political level. City and suburbs entered a no-holds-barred struggle for territory after World War II, turning the urban fringe into a battle zone. When the fighting was over, the four-county metropolitan area had been splintered into one central city and more than two dozen suburbs, separated by a tracery of municipal borders more complex than the average jigsaw puzzle.

City residents elected a new leader in 1948. When Mayor John Bohn decided, at the age of eighty, to close out his caretaker administration, a field of fifteen hopefuls lined up to replace him. They included later luminaries like Henry Reuss and Henry Maier, but the winner was Frank Zeidler. Born on Milwaukee's West Side on September 20, 1912, Frank was the younger brother of Carl Zeidler, the blond baritone who had won the 1940 mayoral race and perished at sea two years later. Although name recognition was a major factor in the race, it would be hard to imagine a more dissimilar pair of siblings. Frank was a surveyor by trade, not a lawyer, and his interest in electoral politics actually preceded his brother's. The younger Zeidler had run for office eight times before 1948, winning two terms (and some favorable notice) as a member of the Milwaukee School Board. The brothers' personal differences were even more pronounced. Carl was the ultimate extrovert, while Frank seemed born to attract terms like "bookish" and "bespectacled." Where Carl was Milwaukee's most eligible bachelor, Frank and Agnes Zeidler had six small children in 1948.

The greatest difference between the brothers was philosophical. Carl had no discernible ideology, and Frank, by contrast, was a devout Socialist. Coming of age during the Depression, he had devoured every political treatise on the shelves of the Merrill Park branch library, finally deciding that the cooperative commonwealth of Socialist theory was a worthy ideal. In 1937, just after his twenty-fifth birthday, Zeidler became secretary of the state and county units of the Socialist Party. Weakened by New Deal defections, the party was in steep decline at the time; Dan Hoan himself became a Democrat in the early 1940s. When Zeidler opened his mayoral campaign in 1948, he ran under the banner of the Municipal Enterprise Committee, an ad hoc group of assorted liberals, rather than the party Victor Berger had brought to life. Other candidates tried to make an issue of his politics but, after twenty-four years under Hoan, the Socialist label held no particular terrors for Milwaukee voters. Earnest, thoughtful, and a self-described "crusading type," Frank Zeidler beat attorney Henry Reuss in the general election with 56 percent of the vote.

Zeidler in office was, in some respects, a throwback to Hoan: reflexively honest, personally forthright, and frequently at odds with the Common Council. Thirteen of Milwaukee's twenty-seven aldermen were

Frank Zeidler, Milwaukee's mayor from 1948 to 1960, continued the Socialist tradition of honesty, efficiency, and concern for the underdog.

Milwaukee Journal Sentinel

The new mayor, shown with his family in 1948, didn't quite fit the picture of the radical revolutionary called up by anti-Socialist rhetoric.

Milwaukee Journal Sentinel

newcomers in 1948, and there was not a single Socialist in the bunch; disagreements regarding city policy were frequent. But Zeidler, unlike Hoan, was not contentious by nature. He based his stands on a highly developed sense of what he believed was right, and an unmistakable moral tone permeated his administration. "We participate in local government," the mayor said in 1957, "in order that by our participation there may emerge nobler beings with enlarged concepts of liberty, truth, justice, co-operation, peace and righteousness."

Although he generally staked out the higher moral ground, Frank Zeidler was also one of the most innately curious figures who ever occupied the mayor's office. Like many another self-taught intellectual, he was interested in practically everything – sometimes with unusual results. The mayor's off-duty projects included a piano with alternating black and white keys, a book of philosophical poetry, and – most novel of all – an attempt to translate Shakespeare's plays into "more modern speech." When one of his daughters struggled with *Macbeth*, Zeidler decided to simplify the bard's language, and he went on to "Zeidlerize" several other works. It was easy enough to change "Aroint thee, witch!" to "Get on, you witch!," but Zeidler confessed to rhyming problems every time he turned "thrice" into "three times." Critical reaction was less than encouraging.

This singular figure inherited a swollen agenda when he took office in 1948. The housing shortage and central-city blight led the list, but urban growth was not far from the top. It was obvious that a boom was under way, and Zeidler, like Dan Hoan before him, believed that Milwaukee had two choices: Grow or die. The annexation

effort, suspended during the Depression and war years, had resumed in 1946, and Zeidler's team pursued it with military efficiency, posting land, circulating petitions, and recruiting supporters in a broad arc around Milwaukee. Annexation remained completely voluntary, a condition that called for hard-sell tactics on the city's part. Milwaukee's most important weapon in the war for territory was water. As homeowners faced the growing expense of private wells and growing uncertainty about ground-water supplies, the municipality's promises of cold, clear water from Lake Michigan convinced many to join Milwaukee. When residents of a given area agreed to annexation, the city promptly supplied them with water, streets and sidewalks, sewer service, garbage pick-up, and police and fire protection. Schools, branch libraries, and other urban amenities followed as soon as threshold densities were reached.

It was an expensive policy. Because they required so many services, newly annexed parcels were a drain on the municipal treasury for at least a decade after they came into the city. Between 1950 and 1955, the developing outer wards absorbed 34.62 percent of the city's spending and provided only 27.56 percent of its tax revenue. The extension of city water service caused special problems. Lake Michigan was a virtually inexhaustible resource, but Milwaukee's water distribution system was not. In 1948, as the system neared capacity, the city began to restrict lawn-sprinkling to alternate nights; violators were subject to fifty-dollar fines and thirty days in jail. It was not until 1962, when a second filtration plant opened on the South Side, that Milwaukee's distribution problems were solved. There was also grumbling that annexation made it too

Milwaukee Journal Sentinel

easy for developers to sell homes. In 1949 a local builder estimated that it cost him $975 per lot to drill a well and install a septic tank; the comparable assessment for municipal water and sewer service was only $200. Small wonder that most requests for annexation were coming from real estate developers by the mid-1950s.

Spending inequities, water problems, and apparent developer subsidies were of little concern to Milwaukee's annexation officials. What mattered was bringing in territory, and they pursued that goal with a passion unsurpassed among the cities of the North. Between 1948 and 1956, the busiest years of the campaign, Milwaukee annexed an average of 33 parcels and 1,338 acres annually. A peak was reached in 1956, when the city took in 2,926 acres of land – more than 4.5 square miles. An urban variant of manifest destiny was at work. Frank Zeidler and his lieutenants believed that it was natural, even inevitable, for the city to

grow beyond its old borders, and they saw any impediment to that growth as a threat to the integrity of the urban organism. Annexation also served Zeidler's larger interest in civil defense. Certain that global tensions would touch off a nuclear holocaust in the foreseeable future, the mayor believed that "planned decentralization" was vital, and he envisioned "ribbon-shaped developments" reaching far into the countryside. "The atomic bomb era," Zeidler said in 1952, "has sealed the doom of the massed globular metropolitan community as we know it today."

Survival of a different sort provided an even more compelling rationale for annexation. As its most prosperous residents moved to the edge and the most impoverished stayed behind, Milwaukee seemed destined for trouble. In his political memoir, *A Liberal in City Government*, Frank Zeidler described how annexation helped to soften the impact of some ominous trends:

Mayor Zeidler presided over a civil defense meeting in 1950. Downtown Milwaukee is at ground zero on the map behind him.

Milwaukee itself would have been a ghetto of the poor and nothing else. Instead it had room for people to move to for new industry and for commercial centers, and it provided the living space so that an attack could be made on the slums without tearing down houses of people who had no place to go.

Although it made eminent sense from the city's point of view, Milwaukee encountered stout resistance at every stage of its annexation campaign, both from existing suburbs who coveted the same territory and, even more frequently, from would-be suburbanites. Residents of unincorporated areas generally had a choice of governments after World War II – to join older communities or to start new ones – and their decisions reflected both geographic circumstance and the zeal of leaders on both sides of the issue. In most cases, the contest was closely fought. Thousands wanted the first-rate services and administrative efficiency of the city, despite its usually higher tax rates. Suburban advocates countered that incorporation would pro-

vide independence, local control and, not least of all, a tax break. The state returned half the income tax dollars it collected to their communities of origin, making incorporation almost irresistible for areas with large industrial plants or concentrations of upper-income residents. Thus Glendale, whose railroad corridors were lined with industries, became a city in 1950, and a rash of incorporations followed: St. Francis in 1951, Hales Corners in 1952, Bayside in 1953, and Brown Deer in 1955.

Suburbanization received a huge boost in 1955, when a rural-oriented state legislature passed the famous Oak Creek Law. Incorporation had once been an option reserved for communities that met a common-sense definition of "urban place," with minimum population and density levels. The Oak Creek Law extended the privilege to any town adjoining Milwaukee that had at least 5,000 people and property valued at $20 million. "Piecemeal" annexation suddenly came to an end, and wholesale incorporation followed. The Town of Oak Creek, the site of a huge power plant development, became a fourth-class city in 1955; Franklin, its neighbor to the west, followed a year later. Both were rural in everything but name. At the time of their incorporation, Milwaukee County's two southernmost suburbs had a combined population of barely 15,000 people scattered across 63 square miles; less than 2 percent of the county's population occupied more than a quarter of its land area.

There was some movement in the opposite direction. Civic leaders in St. Francis had been trying for decades to create a village around Wisconsin Electric's massive Lakeside power plant. When they finally succeeded in 1951, the remaining residents

Tax revenue from the gigantic Oak Creek electric plant gave town residents a powerful incentive to incorporate.

We Energies

of the Town of Lake were saddled with the highest property tax rates in the county. Voters decided that consolidation with the city was the only reasonable alternative. In 1954 the Town of Lake ceased to exist, and Milwaukee grew overnight by 13,000 people and 9.35 square miles.

The more typical relationship between Milwaukee and its younger siblings was open warfare. City officials, led by Frank Zeidler, tended to view the suburbs as incorporated selfishness. They railed against the political fragmentation of the county as illogical, unnecessary, and even unnatural. "This city consults with suburban governments," said Zeidler in 1958, "but we do not believe they have a reason for existing." Most galling was the suburbs' obvious desire for city resources, particularly water, and their equally transparent unwillingness to share responsibility for city problems, particularly those associated with poverty. But comfort, not conscience, was the deciding factor in the move to the edge; most newcomers were quite willing to leave the city's problems behind as they pursued fresher lives in more contemporary surroundings. The result was a curious transformation. Many new suburbanites had been urbanites all their lives, but they found it surprisingly easy to trade their ancestral loyalties for an attitude of outright hostility to the city – particularly if they took an active part in annexation fights. Suburban residents tended to view Milwaukee as a "rapacious plunderer," intent on gobbling up territory until it was the only government left standing.

City-suburban tensions came to a memorable head in the battle for the Town of Granville. Milwaukee had been nibbling at the unincorporated town to its northwest for years, and in 1956, after a lengthy courtship, a majority of Granville's remaining residents and property-owners voted to consolidate with their larger neighbor. The brand-new village of Brown Deer, in the meantime, had posted much of the same area for annexation. The upshot was a David-and-Goliath legal battle that lasted for six years and caused enormous

The semi-rural Town of Granville was the focus of a prolonged tug-of-war between the city of Milwaukee and the village of Brown Deer. The view is southeast from Forty-third and Good Hope.

Years of confusion about their legal status led some Granville homeowners to declare "independence" in 1962. They were about to become Milwaukee residents.

confusion regarding everything from school assignments to garbage pick-up. Goliath won. In 1962, citing a technical glitch in the village's annexation papers, the Wisconsin Supreme Court awarded nearly all of the contested 16.5 square miles to Milwaukee; Brown Deer got the Tripoli Country Club. The Granville consolidation was the largest single addition to Milwaukee's land area in the history of the city.

It was also the last addition of any significance; the territorial wars had virtually ended by the time the court issued its ruling. The last battles were fought in the Town of Greenfield, where Milwaukee had been busily annexing territory since the end of World War II. Some of the town's leaders had been just as busy trying to incorporate their community. When Greenfield finally be-

The battle line in Milwaukee's border war with Greenfield was frozen when the suburb incorporated in 1957, producing a hopelessly tangled municipal boundary.

came a city in 1957, the battle lines were frozen, creating one of the most jagged municipal boundaries imaginable; some residents literally ate in Greenfield and slept in Milwaukee, without leaving their homes. But there was an even broader significance in the creation of Greenfield: It eliminated the last block of unincorporated land in Milwaukee County. The old town form of government, a Milwaukee staple since the pioneer period, was instantly extinct, and the "iron ring" of suburbs around the city of Milwaukee was complete. It had taken forty-six years for the county's first eleven suburbs to emerge, beginning with South Milwaukee in 1892 and ending with Greendale in 1938. The next eight – Glendale, St. Francis, Hales Corners, Bayside, Brown Deer, Oak Creek, Franklin, and Greenfield – appeared in a single burst between 1950 and 1957. The *Milwaukee Journal* (February 18, 1957) called the creation of the county's last suburb "another minor tragedy in municipal administration":

> *Greenfield's incorporation merely writes the last chapter in the planless and chaotic urbanization of government in the metropolitan county. The whole picture is indeed tragic in the sense that it is frustrating, inefficient, expensive and unintelligent.... Every last acre of Milwaukee County is now incorporated, in a jumble of ten cities and nine villages, all being one community, really.*

With Milwaukee County's political fragmentation complete, the suburban wave surged outward to neighboring counties. Mequon, on Milwaukee's northern border in Ozaukee County, became a city in 1957, taking in an unimaginable forty-eight square miles of land – nearly half the city of Milwaukee's present size. The four original townships on the eastern edge of

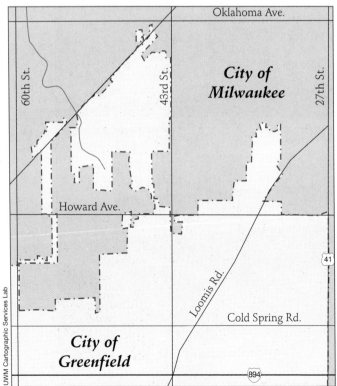

UWM Cartographic Services Lab

Waukesha County were transformed during the same period. In 1958 the tiny village of Menomonee Falls expanded to cover more than thirty-two square miles in the surrounding Town of Menomonee. Brookfield incorporated as a city in 1954, and Elm Grove, an enclave of affluence since the 1920s, became a village one year later. To the south, New Berlin received its city charter in 1959, and Muskego followed in 1964.

The proliferation of governments in the region obscured the fact that historic urban patterns continued to shape the course of settlement. The suburban explosion was centrifugal. Although time and distance certainly diluted the old associations, new communities tended to absorb the qualities of neighborhoods one step closer to downtown. Settlement patterns on the greater South Side were so well-established that they seemed carved in the bedrock. Ever since Green Bay speculators jumped George Walker's claim in the 1830s, the South Side had developed more slowly than the settlements to the north. By the late 1800s, there was only one person living south of the Menomonee Valley for every two to the north – a ratio that has held, in both city and county, ever since. The pattern extended to the eastern tier of Waukesha County suburbs. In 2000 Menomonee Falls, the northernmost suburb, had 50 percent more people than Muskego on the southern end, although they were practically the same size. Ethnic patterns displayed similar staying power. In 2000, as South Siders moved southwest and North Siders moved northwest, Polish Americans were more than twice as numerous in Muskego as they were in Menomonee Falls.

Although the old patterns showed remarkable persistence, the cumulative effect of the postwar annexations, consolidations, and incorporations was a radical remaking of metropolitan Milwaukee. The city's showing was spectacular. As urban communities elsewhere stagnated, Milwaukee's land area more than doubled, growing from 44.33 square miles in 1946 to 96.54 in 1967. The Granville addition made Milwaukee one of the few big cities in America that could claim to have working farms within its limits. Dairying ended when the Batzler family sold its Brown Swiss herd in 1965, but corn and soybeans were still being cultivated in the early twenty-first century. Milwaukee's population followed the same upward curve as its land area, rising from 587,472 in 1940 to 637,392 in 1950 and an all-time high of 741,324 in 1960. The city ranked eleventh nationally in 1960, and there may have been a brief moment in the early Sixties when it cracked the ranks of the fabled Top Ten.

It was obvious, during the same years, that Milwaukee's weight was shifting to the edge, first to new neighborhoods ringing the central city and then to the outer ring of suburbs. In 1920, before the suburban boom of the Roaring Twenties, city residents had accounted for 85.3 percent of Milwaukee County's population. That proportion dropped to 76.6 percent in 1940 and, despite wholesale annexations, to 71.6 percent in 1960. Journalists noted with some wonder that the population of greater Milwaukee, both city and suburban, topped the one-million mark in the mid-1950s. It was clear, as that growth continued, that the balance of power was tipping slowly but steadily toward the suburbs.

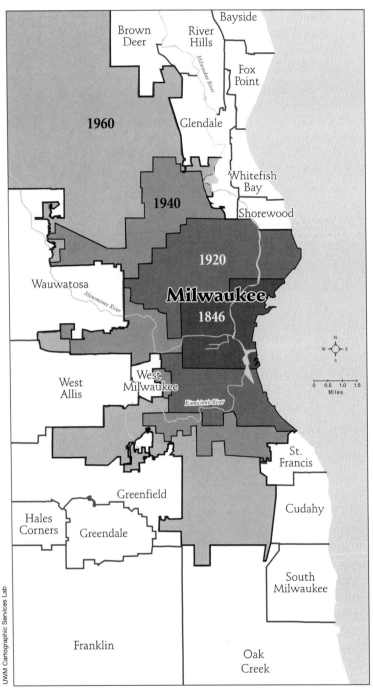

Brown
Deer

River
Hills

Bayside

1960

Fox
Point

Glendale

Milwaukee River

Whitefish
Bay

1940

Shorewood

1920

Wauwatosa

Menomonee River

Milwaukee

1846

West
Allis

West
Milwaukee

Kinnicinnic River

St.
Francis

Greenfield

Cudahy

Hales
Corners

Greendale

Franklin

Oak
Creek

South
Milwaukee

0   0.5   1.0   1.5
Miles

UWM Cartographic Services Lab

Milwaukee County in its modern configuration. Between 1945 and 1960, the city of Milwaukee more than doubled its land area, taking in thousands of acres of farmland.

As the postwar explosion remade the metropolis, it had a profound impact on one more level of government: Milwaukee County. Once a collection of seven rural towns wrapped around an urban core, the county became a blend of urban and suburban communities in the 1950s. As its population grew, so did its responsibilities. The county's job description had always been set by a combination of statute and circumstance. Some activities – welfare, health care, the courts – were part of its original charter, but others were anything but preordained. When Milwaukee County took over the park system at the end of 1936, it also assumed responsibility for the zoo in Washington Park and the conservatory in Mitchell Park. A primitive landing strip established in Currie Park in 1919 got the county into the aviation business; Mitchell Field, purchased in 1926, became one of the nation's leading civilian airports even before World War II. Milwaukee County took on more tasks after the war. With typical foresight, the Park Commission tried to ensure that practically every resident lived within walking distance of a park; the system expanded from 5,377 acres in 1946 to 12,928 in 1967, with the greatest growth occurring during the building boom of the 1950s. As the metropolitan area continued to expand, there was serious talk of shifting tax collection, library services, the museum, and even garbage pickup from the city to the county.

The steady enlargement of Milwaukee County's jurisdiction was evident in its budget, which ballooned from $22 million in 1946 to $175 million in 1967. The city still spent more money in a typical year, but county allocations, like the county's

A board of part-time supervisors found it hard to keep pace with the growth of Milwaukee County government after World War II.

Milwaukee Journal Sentinel

The election of John Doyne as Milwaukee's first county executive in 1960 led to greater efficiency and accountability.

Milwaukee Journal Sentinel

population, showed a faster rate of increase, rising from 52 percent of the city's budget in 1946 to 76 percent in 1967. The governmental structure that oversaw this spending – a board of part-time elected supervisors and a group of nearly autonomous department heads – began to seem anachronistic as the county grew. In 1959, finally, the state legislature created the post of county executive as a sort of mayor for Milwaukee County. The position was new, but its first two occupants showed the persistence of some time-honored political traditions; John Doyne (1960-1976) and William O'Donnell (1976 1988) were both proud Irishmen with close ties to Milwaukee's Merrill Park neighborhood.

Meanwhile, Back in the City...

As the urban fringe, both city and suburban, looked newer and newer, the heart of Milwaukee looked more and more decrepit. There was general agreement, in the wake of World War II, that downtown and the neighborhoods around it had seen better days. Milwaukee's only convention center, the Auditorium, dated to 1909. The minor-league Brewers had been playing in the same shoebox of a stadium, Borchert Field, since 1902. No building of any significance had risen on the local skyline since the beginning of the Depression, and decades of coal smoke from locomotives, furnaces, and factories had given older structures, particularly those faced with Cream City brick, a dingy patina. Sidewalks were crumbling, streets were showing their age, and much of downtown had succumbed to the automobile. The *Saturday*

Milwaukee's skyline in 1948 was something less than overwhelming.

Milwaukee County Historical Society

Evening Post (September 15, 1951) was less then complimentary:

> *Milwaukee, though more than a century old, has a look of being half-finished. Parking lots and filling stations make ugly gaps, like missing teeth, in the downtown business district. Block on block of run-down frame houses blights the center of the city.*

The local passion for civic beauty had not died out; one of Frank Zeidler's first acts as mayor was to donate a thousand tulip bulbs that were promptly planted around City Hall. But the desire for beauty collided head-on with another Milwaukee trademark: civic frugality. In late 1943, after years of scrimping and saving, Milwaukee had become the only big city in America to achieve freedom from debt. Its amortization fund finally exceeded its outstanding bond obligations, and the city's capital improvement account had swollen to nearly $20 million. It had not, however, swollen enough; estimates of the outlay required to bring Milwaukee up to date ranged as high as $250 million. Voters faced a stark choice between forging ahead on a cash basis and going into debt.

They chose both. In 1948 Milwaukeeans elected Frank Zeidler, who had campaigned on a no-debt platform and, in the same month, approved borrowing $13 million for veterans' housing, blight clearance, off-street parking, and expressways. The upshot was a cautious departure from past practice. Zeidler held the line on municipal debt, vetoing long-term bonds when he thought short-term issues would suffice, but the city did borrow extensively for schools, streets, sewers, and other urban necessities. Although Milwaukee maintained a gilt-edged credit rating, its general-obligation debt rose from less than $1 million in 1948 to $55 million in 1956 and $144 million in 1967.

Support for borrowing, particularly on behalf of big-ticket projects, was centered in the business community. In 1945 a group of executives held a lunch meeting to discuss "their mutual alarm over what they considered the degeneration of Greater Milwaukee." That alarm led directly to the establishment of the 1948 Corporation, a "non-partisan, non-political, non-sectional" group advocating "a program of community improvement" keyed to Wisconsin's centennial in 1948. The leaders of the effort, many with German surnames, drew part of their inspiration from the Forty-Eighters of the previous century. Although no one had the slightest interest in resurrecting Milwaukee's reputation as America's *Deutsch-Athen*, the 1948 Corporation did focus its attention on quality-of-life projects, including a sports arena, an outdoor stadium, a new museum, an expanded library, a relocated zoo, new concert stages, and an art gallery. After surviving the Depression and putting in overtime to help win the war, it was obvious that Milwaukee had been working too hard; the community was ready to reclaim some of its traditional *Gemütlichkeit*. As the effort progressed, banker William Brumder expressed a sentiment that Forty-Eighters of the nineteenth century would have found congenial:

> *Milwaukee's challenge is to strive constantly for the Good Life. By the Good Life we mean to include and emphasize things of the spirit – culture, beauty, friendship....*
>
> *Milwaukee can't be the biggest city in America or the richest. But Milwaukee can be the ideal city in which to live, to truly live.*

When it became apparent that the work of building a livable metropolis would extend well beyond the 1948 centennial, the group adopted its present name: the Greater Milwaukee Committee. The GMC's abiding role was motivational rather than financial. Building its campaigns around forward-looking slogans – "It Can Be Done," "Turn the Turtle Over" – the group tried to convince Milwaukeeans to trade their pay-as-you-go policy for a "pay-as-you-benefit" philosophy. Some public officials, notably Frank Zeidler, were deeply suspicious of the GMC's motives, but the Committee's clout was indisputable. Although its roster was limited to 150 members, they owned or managed at least a quarter of the business property in the city, with a concentration on the larger end of the scale.

The Greater Milwaukee Committee was a powerful catalyst for civic projects. In the skit pictured below, "Mr. Greater Milwaukee" forsakes "Procrastination" and "Stalling" for "Miss Progress," all played by business executives in drag.

Milwaukee County Historical Society

As local officials recognized the need and the GMC supplied the motivational muscle, Milwaukee began to rebuild its cultural infrastructure. The Arena opened as a companion to the Auditorium in 1950. Distinguished by the telescoped arches of its roofline, the $5 million structure more than doubled the city's convention space and opened the door to professional basketball, hockey, and other sports. One of the Arena's first large events was, fittingly, the 1952 American Bowling Congress tournament. The floor of the building was lined with 40 lanes for 85 days, and attendance topped the 300,000 mark.

Progress on a memorial to Milwaukee's war dead was considerably slower. In 1946, hoping to "honor the dead by serving the living," civic leaders announced plans for a $5 million memorial complex consisting of "a community art gallery, a veterans' center and a music hall-theater at one location." Volunteer fund-raisers went door-to-door in the next year, accompanied by drill teams and Legionnaires. Major donors stepped forward as well, but the campaign soon bogged down. Arguments about site consumed the next six years, and financial shortfalls forced postponement of the music hall-theater component until the late 1960s. Although planners considered their work only half-finished, the memorial building they dedicated in 1957 was a standout. Designed by Eero Saarinen, best-known as creator of the Gateway Arch in St. Louis, the War Memorial Center was cantilevered over the downtown lake bluff like a seagull in flight. With space for veterans' and civic groups on the upper floors and the Milwaukee Art Center below, the building was completely functional, but it was also the most striking piece of local architecture in at least a generation. A reporter for the *New Republic* (October 7, 1957) described the Saarinen structure as a symbol of "Resurrection in Milwaukee."

Signs of resurrection, or at least significant change, were evident elsewhere in Milwaukee by the time the War Memorial Center opened. Ground for the freeway system was broken in 1952. (At the luncheon following, Frank Zeidler described the new road as "a citizens' highway, a people's highway" that would "make our streets safer" and "restore property values that are now depressed by traffic.") The Vocational School dedicated a block-square addition to its original building at Sixth and Highland in 1953. A new terminal was completed at Mitchell Field in 1955 to serve the soaring population of air travelers. After jostling for space in the same neoclassical building since 1898, the Central Library and the Public Museum began to part company in the 1950s. The library completed a utilitarian annex in 1957, and work on a new museum across Wells Street began three years later. The Washington Park Zoo, criticized as "an overgrown circus display" and "a mere collection of cages," was also scheduled for replacement. Milwaukee County began to assemble a 175-acre parcel at the extreme western limits of the city shortly after World War II, and the first contracts for a new zoo on the site were let in 1956. In the field of higher education, the 1956 merger of the old State Teachers College and the University Extension created a school that would become one of the largest and most comprehensive in the state: the University of Wisconsin-Milwaukee.

Another noteworthy project helped to bolster the local economy. In 1959, after decades of nonstop agitation, political

The Arena doubled Milwaukee's convention space and opened the door to professional indoor sports.

Eero Saarinen's War Memorial Center was Milwaukee's first significant piece of modern architecture. Early plans (lower right) called for a "music hall-theater" on the same site.

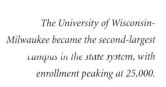

A $3.5 million terminal dedicated in 1955 enlarged Mitchell Field's capacity as an air hub.

The University of Wisconsin-Milwaukee became the second-largest campus in the state system, with enrollment peaking at 25,000.

intrigue, and heroic construction efforts, the St. Lawrence Seaway was finally finished. Although dreams of parity with America's ocean ports proved overly optimistic, the volume of cargo shipped through the rebuilt port of Milwaukee climbed from 67,000 tons in 1958 to 230,000 in 1960 and 686,000 in 1961. One of the port's specialties underlined the central importance of manufacturing: More than a third of the 1961 season's tonnage consisted of scrap metal produced by the region's booming industries.

Of all the developments completed in the 1950s, none had a greater impact on the community than Milwaukee County Stadium. After a brief flirtation with major-league baseball at the turn of the century,

In an unprecedented leap of faith, Milwaukee built County Stadium with no assurance of landing a major-league baseball team.

Milwaukee Journal Sentinel

Milwaukee had lapsed into the ranks of the minors. Although the hometown Brewers gave their fans eight American Association titles and introduced such memorable characters as Bill Veeck and Casey Stengel, few residents relished the town's status as one of the biggest minor-league cities in the country. Milwaukee's hunger for big-league ball was almost palpable, but the community lacked an adequate stadium. Whatever its value as an object of nostalgia, Borchert Field was an ancient, undersized firetrap shoehorned into a single city block at Eighth and Chambers. Talk of a replacement had begun as early as 1909, when Charles Whitnall suggested a sports stadium adjacent to the planned Menomonee River parkway. World War I intervened, but the stadium resurfaced in the 1920s as a proposed memorial to Milwaukee's veterans. The usual arguments about location and funding delayed meaningful action. By the time the idea surfaced again, the stadium was discussed as a memorial to World War II soldiers. In 1950, after a few more years of bickering, ground for Milwaukee County Stadium was broken on a parcel of land adjoining the Veterans Administration Center. The architects designed an open-air ballpark with 36,000 seats, and Milwaukee's freeway planners cooperated by moving the Stadium South segment to the very top of their construction list.

The decision to build County Stadium was a staggering leap of faith for a community that no one has ever mistaken for impetuous. Although the Brewers were nominally the stadium's major tenants, Milwaukee was obviously angling for a big-league team, without the slightest assurance that one was available. The long-awaited news finally came on March 13, 1953: The

Boston Braves, parent team of the Brewers, would move to Milwaukee in time for the upcoming season. The reaction of Wisconsin residents, whether urban, suburban, or rural, bordered on hysteria. On the Sunday after the announcement, nearly 60,000 people drove out to County Stadium just to peer over the third-base fence and watch the grass grow. The first game, an April exhibition match between the Braves and the Boston Red Sox, was sold out instantly, and the pandemonium continued through the regular season. As many as 15,000 fans showed up before games just to cheer infield practice. Comparable crowds formed at Union Station or Mitchell Field to welcome the team back from routine road trips. The players were showered with free beer, cheese, sausage, clothing, pens, jewelry, outboard motors, and assorted other gifts; pitcher Warren Spahn, an Oklahoma rancher in the off-season, received a $5,000 tractor from the Federation of German-American Societies.

The hometown heroes closed their inaugural season with a second-place finish and an attendance mark of 1,826,397 – a new National League record. The Braves were clearly a dream team in a dream town, and they attracted an enormous amount of national publicity. "Have you noticed?," the Greater Milwaukee Committee asked in its report for 1954. "We now live not in 'Milwaukee (Wis.).' WE LIVE IN MILWAUKEE!" The fact that media coverage usually reinforced the city's image as a "big small town" was accepted as part of the package. A profile in the *New York Times* (July 5, 1953) was typical:

> By and large, Milwaukeeans are a gentle, ruminative lot, physically prepossessing in the Wagnerian manner, expansively hospitable in a Polish-Germanic way, polite to policemen (and vice versa), partial to Socialist Mayors and rarely moved by anything other than the remote prospect of owing anybody money.... The advent of the Braves aroused in Milwaukee a vernal passion (coupled with a willingness to spend money, at least on baseball)."

Comparing the city with another baseball hotbed, the *Times* called Milwaukee "more Brooklyn than Brooklyn."

Milwaukeeans didn't mind the caricatures, if only because the Braves story, already the stuff of legend, was getting even better. In 1957, behind the pitching of Warren Spahn and Lew Burdette and the hitting of Henry Aaron and Eddie Mathews, the team won the National League pennant and prepared to face the New York Yankees in the World Series. It was a classic match-up: David vs. Goliath, a crew of Midwestern upstarts against the East Coast's pinstriped dynasty. When one of the Yankees offhandedly described Milwaukee fans as "bush-league," the contest became something even greater: small-city virtue against big-city vice, right vs. might. It took a full seven games, but right finally prevailed. "Bushville Wins," proclaimed a famous homemade sign, and there was literally dancing in the streets of downtown Milwaukee. No single event in the community's history – not V-J Day or the end of World War I or even the return of legal beer – has ever caused such a spontaneous outpouring of joy.

The 1957 World Series proved to be the high point of the Braves' tenure in Milwaukee. The team lost its rematch with the Yankees in 1958 and then slowly faded from contention, but baseball remained a

Pitching ace Warren Spahn of the hometown Braves prepared to face down a Yankee batter in the 1957 World Series. The contest ended in a hugely gratifying victory for "Bushville" and a dizzying whirl in the national spotlight.

summertime staple for tens of thousands of Milwaukeeans. The team's early success seemed to reflect the fortunes of the community as a whole. For a few years on either side of 1960, Milwaukee was at a pinnacle, a civic summit that seems all the more imposing in hindsight. Riding a wave of unprecedented prosperity, the city rose to new heights as an industrial powerhouse, surged to an all-time population peak, entered and then conquered the big leagues, rebuilt much of its civic infrastructure, and welcomed new institutions ranging from an urban university to an ultra-modern Memorial Center. Consigned for decades to a position in the second tier of America's cities, Milwaukee was clearly aspiring to higher things. The community's ascent continued through the early 1960s, but some of the more perceptive observers of the local scene were finding it hard to ignore the effects of gravity.

Change at the Helm

If 1960 was a historic high point for Milwaukee, it was also a turning point, particularly in local politics. John Doyne, Milwaukee's first county executive, took office in 1960 and brought unaccustomed rigor to a layer of government where casual oversight had long been the rule. City residents elected a new mayor in the same year. Frank Zeidler had won re-election rather handily in 1952 (spending a total of $14,138) and again in 1956, but twelve years of unrelenting pressure had left him worn-out and ready to pursue other interests. Zeidler's successor was a man who would serve longer than any big-city mayor in modern American history: Henry W. Maier. Born Henry Nelke on February 7, 1918, the future mayor was raised by his maternal grandparents in Springfield, Ohio. His father, a photographer by trade, had died when Henry was an infant,

Henry Maier served as Milwaukee's mayor from 1960 to 1988, a tenure so long that "Mayor" and "Maier" eventually became synonymous.

Milwaukee Journal Sentinel

and his mother had moved to Milwaukee, where she eventually married a contractor named Charles Maier. Henry joined them after high school and took his stepfather's surname. Following graduation from the University of Wisconsin in 1940 and service in the Pacific during World War II, Maier returned to Milwaukee as an insurance agent, but his real calling was politics.

The candidate's debut was auspicious. As one of fifteen mayoral hopefuls in 1948, Maier opened his campaign with an elaborate rally that featured marching bands, a drum majorette, and a thousand screaming "delegates" of the "New Milwaukee Committee." They heard their man excoriate the political status quo in Milwaukee:

> *This is a declaration of war. War against the cross-breed Common Council – a cross-breed of drifting dunces and bumbling buzzards.... The City Hall is an old haunted house, inhabited by ghouls, ghosts, bats, bugs and mice for 100 years.*

> *The dull, heavy, smoke-laden air will have to be blown away. We'll have to throw open the windows, sweep out the corridors, take the heel marks off the desks, and air condition the whole structure.*

"Let's quit the circus stuff," admonished the *Milwaukee Journal*, and voters were equally unimpressed; Maier finished a poor sixth in the 1948 primary. He did not, however, lose any of his flair for bombastic rhetoric and spirited campaigning. Closely aligned with a resurgent Democratic Party, Maier won a state Senate seat in 1950. He spent a full decade in Madison, serving multiple terms as minority leader and earning a reputation for parliamentary skill and general contentiousness. When Frank Zeidler declined to run again in 1960, Maier jumped into the race with both feet, defeating Congressman Henry Reuss in the general election with 58 percent of the vote.

In the months after his inauguration, Mayor Maier (the two words would soon meld into one) emerged as a tireless technocrat who took an engineer's delight in the mechanics of municipal government. One of his first steps was to group all city departments into "development operation units" for greater efficiency. In 1961 he combined Milwaukee's planning, housing, and redevelopment functions into a single Department of City Development, which eventually became an important source of patronage as well as ideas. "Performance budgeting" and Form M-25 ("a formal guide to decision-making") were unveiled in the same period. The mayor's viewpoint was apparent in a passage from *Challenge to the Cities,* a 1966 book he wrote as a how-to guide for municipal executives: "One of the mayor's tasks of institutional leadership is to see that he has developmental centers from which recommendations can flow around a rational plan of priorities matched with resources."

As Henry Maier tinkered with the nuts and bolts of local government, Milwaukee continued to move forward on the momentum of the 1950s. A correspondent for the *New Yorker* (April 9, 1960) commented sardonically (and accurately) that much remained to be done at the heart of the city:

> *No new large office building has been put*
> *up in downtown Milwaukee in more than twenty*
> *years, and the skyline, if approached from Lake*
> *Michigan, gives the impression of a city that had*
> *its picture taken around 1920 and liked the results*
> *so much that it decided to leave matters alone.*

Continued development, both private and public, helped to soften, if not erase, that impression. In 1962, with help from a controversial city tax freeze, the Marine Bank completed its high-rise headquarters on the banks of the Milwaukee River at Wisconsin Avenue. Designed by the same firm that created the United Nations building, the green glass monolith was the first significant piece of commercial architecture in central Milwaukee since the Depression. A few blocks west, the Public Museum began moving into its new home on Wells Street in 1962 and completed the relocation five years later. With exhibits depicting everything from a Crow Indian bison hunt to the great beasts of Africa, the museum steadily enlarged its reputation as one of North America's leading interpreters of cultural and natural history. The Milwaukee County Zoo finished its move from Washington Park to 100th and Blue Mound in 1963. The new facility was an eloquent expression of the latest trends in zoo design; barless enclosures outside and glass walls inside created what park publicists called, with perhaps a touch of hyperbole, a "wonderland of nature as close to its actual appearance as man can make it." Comparable innovation was on display in Mitchell Park, where three beehive-shaped glass domes replaced the old horticultural conservatory between 1964 and 1967. The domes constituted a sort of zoo for plants: one for tropical species, another for desert specimens, and a temperate-zone dome featuring shows that changed with the seasons.

The museum, the zoo, and the conservatory – each defining the state of its respective art – signified a community looking to the future with unbounded confidence. Taken with similarly expansive developments in the private sector, they prompted talk of a civic "renaissance." A number of smaller projects reinforced the impression. One of the community's most striking postwar buildings – Annunciation

Milwaukee Journal Sentinel

Milwaukee County Historical Society

Milwaukee County Historical Society

Milwaukee Journal Sentinel

New landmarks of the 1960s:
(clockwise from above) Marine Plaza, the
Milwaukee Public Museum, the polar bear
"habitat" in the Milwaukee County Zoo, and the
Mitchell Park Horticultural Conservatory. The
domes were compared by one visiting journalist
to "a brassiere manufacturer's model."

Annunciation Greek Orthodox Church, one of Frank Lloyd Wright's last designs, was an icon of modernism.

The Great Circus Parade, which debuted in 1963, brought back the spirit of Old Milwaukee.

Greek Orthodox Church – rose from perhaps its least expected quarter. Greeks were among the smallest, the poorest, and the last European immigrant groups who made their homes in Milwaukee. In the 1950s, with the downtown neighborhood around their original church in a state of advanced decay, the immigrants and their children decided to rebuild on the northwestern edge of the city. Their architect, chosen after considerable debate, was an American original: Frank Lloyd Wright. The legendary designer married the cross and the circle in his plans for the church. A shallow dome rested on a gently curved bowl, which rested, in turn, on a concrete cradle that took the shape of an equilateral Greek cross. Although he drew his inspiration from ancient Byzantine forms, Wright described his design as "contributing to Tradition instead of living upon it." Just as St. Josaphat's Basilica had symbolized the determination of early Polish immigrants to make their presence known, Annunciation Church was an unmistakable sign of ethnic arrival. Dedicated in 1961 (more than two years after the architect's death), it was also Wright's only public building in the metropolis of his home state.

Milwaukee was looking ahead in the first years of Henry Maier's mayoralty, but there were also the first faint stirrings of concern for the past. In 1960 the city preserved a priceless piece of its German heritage by purchasing the Pabst Theater. The Milwaukee Landmarks Commission was established four years later. Although the group had no enforcement powers, it did focus public attention on buildings of "historical or architectural value." The past was also increasingly a cause for celebration. One of the most popular exhibits in the new museum was the Streets of Old Milwaukee, an imagined replica of the city's downtown in the late 1800s. History came alive even more tangibly in the Great Circus Parade, which rolled off to its first start in 1963. Sponsored by Schlitz Brewing, the parade highlighted Wisconsin's proud heritage as home of the Ringling Brothers and other circus legends. As newly restored wagons were added every year and attendance crowded the 800,000 mark, visiting journalists nearly exhausted the circus lexicon in describing the colossal, stupendous, and gigantic scale of the event.

Just as Milwaukee seemed to be scaling new civic heights, a number of countervailing trends asserted themselves. The community was beset in the years around 1960 by a variety of problems that tended to diminish its quality of life and sap its self-confidence. Some were entirely beyond local control. In most of the city's older neighborhoods, elm trees planted early in the century turned residential streets into green cathedrals during the summer months. Those cathedrals began to crumble in 1956, when Dutch elm disease was discovered on the East Side. The epidemic rose to a peak in 1967, when city crews cut down 19,000 trees – nearly 15 percent of the original total. Venerable neighborhoods suddenly looked as naked as the newest subdivision in Waukesha County. Milwaukee's beloved lakefront suffered similar indignities. Beginning in 1959 and continuing through the 1960s, millions of alewives, a type of herring, died off near shore and piled up in putrefying windrows on every beach. Like the Dutch elm beetle, the alewife was an unwanted immigrant, in this case an oceangoing interloper that migrated to Lake Michigan through the St. Lawrence Seaway. It was not

Milwaukee Journal / Sentinel

Piles of dead alewives made Milwaukee's beaches virtually unusable for weeks at a time in the 1960s.

until Pacific salmon were introduced that the die-off ceased to be a major problem. The alewife infestation demonstrated just how thoroughly human activity had upset the ecological balance of the big lake: A non-native predator was imported to control a non-native pest.

Developments on the baseball front smelled even worse. As the heroes of 1957 moved on and the novelty of the game wore off, Milwaukee's support for the Braves dropped from hysterical to merely above-average. Things began to change in 1962, when a group of Chicago investors bought the team. Although fans remained blissfully ignorant of the impending catastrophe, the new owners promptly entered negotiations with Atlanta, a city that was just as hungry for baseball as Milwaukee had been a decade earlier. Rumors began to swirl in 1963. Despite desperate measures to boost attendance and a number of last-ditch legal maneuvers, the Braves moved south at the end of the 1965 season. From rage to humiliation to simple heartbreak, Milwaukeeans felt all the emotions of a faithful spouse abandoned for a younger lover after thirteen years of marriage.

Crisis in the Inner Core

Dying trees, dead fish, and a departed baseball team were only short-term problems in comparison with a crisis that had been developing for decades: the deterioration of Milwaukee's inner city and the poverty of the people who lived there. No amount of construction in the downtown area could mask the blight that was enveloping the surrounding residential neighborhoods. The trend had been apparent since the 1920s, when the exodus to the city's edge began in earnest. Conditions worsened during the Depression, and the prosperity created by World War II left central-city neighborhoods untouched. A study of building permits for 1941 and 1945 showed that inspectors had approved $4,518,020 in new construction for a single ward on the Northwest Side, compared with $112,900 for the *twelve* wards closest to downtown. The authors of the study reached an ominous conclusion: "The city was found to be dying at its core." It was in this light that

Frank Zeidler's postwar annexation campaign made the most sense. The urgency of the mayor's grow-or-die strategy was underscored by a pair of rather stark statistics: Between 1950 and 1960, Milwaukee gained a total of 123,870 people within its newly annexed holdings and suffered a net loss of 19,938 inside its 1950 borders. It was annexation, not internal growth, that carried the city to its 1960 population peak.

Milwaukee's core may have been dying, but not all sections were dying at the same rate. As late as 1959, the city's renewal coordinator reported that he was "unable to find any large deteriorated South Side area," an observation that Frank Zeidler called "a great compliment to the people of the South Side." The point might have been argued by the rural whites and Latinos huddled in hand-me-down housing around Walker's Point, but no one could deny that things were much worse on the north side of the Menomonee Valley. The problems were most severe in the square mile bordered roughly by Third and Twelfth Streets between Juneau and North Avenues, a section widely referred to after World War II as "the inner core." Although the area had housed dozens of groups since the city's infancy, three had been dominant: Germans in the mid-1800s, eastern European Jews at the turn of the century, and African Americans in the 1920s and later. The area's housing stock was old by the time the Jews moved in, and it did not improve with age. The city's annual report for 1933 sounded an alarm:

> *Conditions in the negro district constitute a menace to health, morals, and public welfare which call for immediate remedial action. Poor housing is a most important factor in contagious diseases of children and tuberculosis and a contributing factor to delinquency, crime, and other*

Blight had claimed scores of buildings in the Sicilian Third Ward even before World War II. This scene is from St. Paul Avenue in 1935.

Milwaukee Public Library

social irregularities which require tremendous public and private expenditures for care and cure.

The situation was no better in 1946, when the Citizens' Governmental Research Bureau released its landmark study of a substantially enlarged African-American district. Researchers found that, relative to the white population, Milwaukee's blacks had dramatically higher rates of infant mortality, welfare dependence, and criminal convictions, and lower rates of employment, homeownership, and educational attainment. (The same patterns could be reported with as much accuracy sixty years later.) The CGRB study focused particular attention on housing conditions. More than 67 percent of the city's African Americans lived in homes that were either "unfit for use" or "in need of major repair," compared with 34 percent in Detroit and 36 percent in Buffalo. Other observers noted the same deterioration. In 1950 the *Milwaukee Journal* called the near North Side a "dilapidated, overcrowded tinder box," and in 1953 Frank Zeidler declared that 10,000 housing

units north of the Menomonee Valley should be torn down "tomorrow." A grim joke made the rounds of the North Side: Blight was claiming so many homes that there was getting to be a shortage of blacks to live in them.

Milwaukee's record in addressing these problems was abysmal. Despite a favorable referendum vote in 1948 and drawers full of plans, only nine square blocks of residential blight were cleared by the end of 1955 – nine blocks in eight years. Public housing fared no better. In 1944 the city's newly established Housing Authority announced plans to replace two blocks of North Side slums with "permanent housing" for war workers. Political infighting delayed construction until the war was over, and Hillside Terrace was finally completed in 1950 as a low-income housing project – the city's first. Progress thereafter was slow. Public housing for military veterans and senior citizens encountered only token opposition, but projects for low-income families invariably faced an uphill battle.

Conditions were far worse in the North Side black community. For many African Americans newly arrived from the South, Milwaukee was just as poor and a great deal colder.

After years of wrangling, Hillside Terrace was completed in 1950 as Milwaukee's first low-income housing project.

Milwaukee Journal Sentinel

Why the resistance, particularly in a city that prided itself on clean streets and solid neighborhoods? Inertia played a role, as did the vocal opposition of Milwaukee's real-estate interests, but the lack of action also reflected some profound misgivings about the community's newest residents. "To many people," Frank Zeidler told a labor group in 1957, "urban renewal means only public housing, and to them public housing means housing for migrant Negro families, so they are against the whole program." Racism, in other words, was rearing its ugly head. It provided an important measure of the dark energy that carried white families out to the suburbs, and it was imbedded in everything from hiring practices to housing covenants.

Milwaukee was not markedly different from other American cities in these respects; blacks encountered unreasoning fear and irrational hatred wherever they settled in the urban North. But specific factors on both sides of the color line tended to aggravate Milwaukee's racial problems. The first was the late start and relative youth of the local black community. Although Joe Oliver had planted the flag in 1835 and a cluster of key institutions had emerged in the next century, Milwaukee was hardly an African-American stronghold. Of the fifteen largest cities in America, it generally ranked dead-last in percentage of black population until 1970. (San Francisco was slightly lower in 1930 and 1940.) The community's geographic position helps to explain its relative scarcity of blacks. Chicago historically absorbed the major share of migrants entering the region from the South; Milwaukee, lying squarely in the bigger city's shadow, was a secondary destination at best. African Americans made up only 0.5 percent of the community's population in 1920 and 3.4 percent in 1950. The comparable figures for Chicago were 4.1 and 13.6 percent.

As long as the black population remained relatively small, other residents could afford to feel magnanimous. Wasn't Milwaukee famous for its progressive political tradition? Hadn't a 1950 study ranked it the third-most-livable city in America? Didn't civic leaders brag about its "freedom from intolerance and bigotry"? The explosive growth of the black community after World War II severely tested that self-image. Pushed by economic dislocations in the South and pulled by job opportunities in Milwaukee, thousands of African Americans moved to the city, among them Sam and Stella Davis, the couple who helped open this chapter. Milwaukee's black population mushroomed from roughly 13,000 in 1945 to 21,772 in 1950, 62,458 in 1960, and 105,088 in 1970 – an increase of more than 700 percent in 25 years. During the same quarter-century, African Americans rose from approximately 2 percent of the city's population in 1945 to 3.4 percent in 1950, 8.4 percent in 1960, and 14.7 percent in 1970.

These triple-digit increases transformed the social geography of Milwaukee's North Side. Following the same corridors used by earlier German families, African Americans moved north and west from the original inner core, and neighborhoods changed with astonishing speed. It was not unusual for census tracts that had been 90-percent white in one decennial census to reappear as 90-percent black in the next. The community's more affluent residents showed the way. African Americans began to cross Capitol Drive in the late 1950s (Henry Aaron was among the first), and by the mid-1960s "the Negro commu-

nity" extended from Juneau Avenue to Capitol Drive between Holton and Twenty-seventh Streets – an area six times larger than the mile-square ghetto of 1950.

Not since the peak of Polish immigration at the turn of the century had a single group grown so rapidly, and the new arrivals resembled their European predecessors in another respect: their youth. In 1960 the median age of Milwaukee's nonwhite males was only 20.3 years, compared with 28.5 years for the city's whites and 24.6 for nonwhites in Chicago. Milwaukee's black population was extraordinarily young, and its fertility rates were correspondingly high. Natural increase exceeded the rate of in-migration by 1957, and the population explosion continued.

Whether they were born in Mississippi or on Walnut Street, Milwaukee's African Americans formed one of the newest and youngest ghettoes in America. The attendant social problems were painfully obvious. Existing institutions were overwhelmed, experienced leadership was spread far too thin, and social disorganization was a constant concern. Progress in the political arena – the customary route to group recognition – was exceptionally slow. Vel Phillips, the city's first black (and first female) alderman, was not elected until 1956, and she was the Common Council's only African American for the next twelve years. Milwaukee, in summary, felt the impact of race a full generation later than some of its Northern neighbors. The result was a transition both more abrupt and more painful than those experienced by other cities.

Specific conditions in the white community made the transition even more difficult. In a labor market dominated by factory workers, competition for jobs was intense,

Milwaukee Journal Sentinel

Elected to the Common Council in 1956, Vel Phillips was the city's only African-American alderman for twelve years.

unprincipled real estate agents widened racial divisions. As the "tipping point" was reached – generally about 30 percent – older North Siders moved out in a state approaching panic. Their hostility was often palpable.

The resentment apparent on the North Side transcended specific ethnic and geographic communities. Although cultural conflict had been a Milwaukee mainstay since the very beginning – Irish vs. Germans, Germans vs. Poles, Yankees vs. everyone – residents of European ancestry could generally agree on one thing: their whiteness. As the years passed, some of the sharper group distinctions had weathered to a sort of panethnic attitude best expressed by the German word *Gemütlichkeit.* The emphasis in Milwaukee was on domestic tranquility: a warm hearth and a pleasant home, flowers in the front yard and tomato plants in the back. From South Side to North Side, from Glendale to Greendale, white Milwaukeeans shared a common set of expectations.

African Americans represented change of a different order of magnitude. Their culture was so unfamiliar, and their living conditions were so patently *un*pleasant, that there was no room for the North Side ghetto in the inherited picture of *gemütlich* Milwaukee. As that ghetto grew and its problems became more apparent, many whites simply could not make the necessary perceptual adjustment. Despite vivid memories, or at least poignant stories, of the poverty and prejudice their own people had suffered, they found it impossible to see "the me in thee." Too many children and grandchildren of immigrants wrapped themselves in the myth of an Old Milwaukee that was supposedly warmer, less contentious, and more wholesome than the present. African Americans were viewed,

particularly during recessions; blacks were often perceived as an economic threat in blue-collar households. In a city known for its European ethnic neighborhoods, resistance to black in-migration was frequently fierce. Despite the massive exodus of the postwar years, the old ethnic shorthand still applied: Germans on the North Side, Poles on the South Side, and Italians in the Third Ward. As African Americans in search of housing followed the old corridors to the north and west, they entered heavily German neighborhoods that retained a significant measure of their original vitality. Where the races met, the encounter quickly assumed the oil-and-water character that typified the urban North. Neighborhoods, it seemed, could be either black or white, but rarely both, and the blockbusting tactics of

from this frankly racist perspective, as gate-crashers. Small wonder, then, that issues like blight clearance and public housing generated so much controversy. In 1952 Edward Plantz, president of the Milwaukee County Property Owners Association, came right out and said it: "The only thing that has kept 10,000 – aye, 20,000 – Negroes from coming up here is the lack of housing." Plantz conceded that all Americans had the right to live where they chose, but he favored strict limits on Milwaukee's supply of low-rent public housing. Ignore them, in other words, and maybe they'll go away.

The point here is not to rationalize racism, but rather to explain the roots of racial tension in Milwaukee. Two specific conditions – the relative youth of the black community and the relative brittleness of the white community – combined to make a problem that was bad enough in most cities even worse in Milwaukee. It is just as important to note the North Side was not an irredeemable sinkhole. Had they bothered to look more closely, Edward Plantz and his fellow landlords would have seen that most blacks were just as interested in hearth, home, and other pillars of Milwaukee *Gemütlichkeit* as any Schultz or Kowalski. Particularly in the 1950s, when the ghetto was still fairly small and self-contained, Milwaukee's North Side was an impressively complete community. The residents of "Bronzeville" ranged from doctors and lawyers to the proprietors of late-night gambling parlors, often living on the same blocks. Third Street was the neighborhood's shopping district, Walnut Street its entertainment center, and an eclectic mix of institutions developed in the interior; a 1959 survey turned up thirty-five

churches and thirty-five taverns in the same seven-by-seven-block area. High-school basketball teams, especially the championship squads from Lincoln and North Division, were cheered with the rabid enthusiasm usually associated with small towns. Although it was achieved under extreme duress, Milwaukee's black community developed much of the same cohesiveness that had marked the long procession of earlier ethnic neighborhoods.

The effort to build on the community's strengths and work on its obvious problems brought together a biracial group of church leaders, social workers, and other interested Milwaukeeans, including a handful of public officials. Frank Zeidler's name topped the official list. In his twelve years as mayor, Zeidler fought tirelessly for slum clearance and public housing as basic obligations of a civil society; justice, not pity or politics, was his motivation. When an addition to the Hillside Terrace housing project was dedicated in 1955, the mayor urged, "Let's give these people who are to live here a chance to really mean it when they sing, 'God Bless America.'" Five years later, at a farewell dinner in his honor, Zeidler said, "That city is greatest which cares best for its submerged people. Some have said that this has been of too much concern to me, but I think not." The mayor's concern for the inner city was not widely shared. One highly public reaction to his crusade provided irrefutable evidence of Milwaukee's racial tensions. In 1952 and even more viciously during the 1956 mayoral race, Zeidler's opponents spread rumors that he had blanketed the South with billboards inviting blacks to move to his city. *Time* (April 2, 1956) described the whispering campaign as "The Shame of Milwaukee."

Milwaukee Journal Sentinel

Despite high levels of both poverty and prejudice, Milwaukee's black community developed a robust organizational life. Some of its better-known institutions were Greater Galilee Baptist Church...

... the Near North Side Businessmen's Advancement Association ...

Milwaukee Journal Sentinel

Milwaukee Journal Sentinel

... and championship basketball teams at North Division High School.

By the twilight of Frank Zeidler's administration, the problems of the inner core had become too serious for anyone to ignore. In the summer of 1959, one violent crime and a series of near-riots at juvenile arrest scenes produced a wave of worried indignation in the white community. A September conference at City Hall led nowhere – one North Side alderman blasted it as a "smokescreen" for the mayor's urban renewal program – but Zeidler ordered yet another study of the inner city's problems. His own conclusions stressed the importance of environment. "Good leadership," said the mayor, "could not come out of bad housing." If the North Side's problems were getting out of hand, Zeidler argued, the entire community shared the blame for its prolonged tolerance of wretched living conditions.

Mayor Maier and Father Groppi

The Inner Core Report commissioned in 1959 was on Henry Maier's desk when he took office in 1960. The new mayor was hardly a firebrand on social issues – he dismissed the Zeidler study as "an incontrovertible (and almost indigestible) mass of facts, figures, statistics, and bleak reports" – but conditions in the inner city cried out for attention. Maier was convinced that they cried out to authorities far beyond the municipal level. He took a consistently narrow view of what Milwaukee could accomplish on its own, and calls for help from higher layers of government became a hallmark of his administration. Maier's first victory on that front was a genuine breakthrough for the inner city. It came at the midpoint of his inaugural term, when he

convinced Milwaukee County, the Milwaukee School Board, the Milwaukee Vocational School, and the local United Way agency to join the city in forming the Social Development Commission. Established in 1963, SDC became an important channel for public and private efforts to assist "underprivileged and underdeveloped areas of the community."

In one of the supreme ironies of the period, the Social Development Commission, a supposed beacon of hope for Milwaukee's minorities, became the flash point for the city's accumulated racial tensions. The American civil rights movement was well under way by 1963 – sit-ins and freedom rides were already old news – but Milwaukee activists were just beginning to open a local front. Their first issue appeared in the person of Fred Lins, a North Side sausage-maker who was one of the county's charter appointees to SDC. In an unguarded moment, Lins referred to poor blacks who had "an IQ of nothing" and looked "so much alike that you can't identify the ones that

Sausage-maker Fred Lins ran a gauntlet of CORE members demanding his resignation from the Social Development Commission for racial insensitivity.

Milwaukee Journal Sentinel

committed the crime." That was enough for the newly formed chapter of the Congress of Racial Equality. On August 28, 1963 – the same day that Martin Luther King delivered his "I Have a Dream" speech in Washington – CORE staged a sit-in at the Milwaukee County Courthouse, demanding that Lins resign. Picket lines, a "phone-in," and a brief occupation of Mayor Maier's office followed. The civil rights movement had come to Milwaukee.

Responding to community pressures, local officials began to give the central city an unprecedented amount of attention. The Lins controversy had died down by the time the sausage-maker resigned at year's end, but SDC remained in the news. Lyndon Johnson launched his War on Poverty in 1964, and the Commission became, somewhat serendipitously, the conduit for millions of dollars in federal aid for inner-city social programs. Henry Maier also took a fresh interest in the area's physical problems.

Although he generally ignored calls for new public housing, the mayor did step up the city's urban renewal efforts. "We will establish a blight line in Milwaukee," Maier said hopefully in 1964, "and halt the cancerous spread of municipal decay." Projects hatched during the Zeidler years – Hillside and the Third Ward – were pushed to completion, and a variety of new efforts transformed sizable sections of the central city. One cleared the way for Juneau Village, downtown Milwaukee's first luxury high-rise apartment complex. Another eliminated most nonconforming uses on the Marquette University campus. Still another opened the old Haymarket area on the North Side to industrial and commercial redevelopment.

The urban renewal program had plenty of critics. Some viewed Milwaukee's activities as pitifully modest in comparison with those in other cities, where renewal projects covered square miles rather than square blocks. Milwaukee redeveloped just

Urban renewal and expressway construction hit the black community particularly hard. This couple lost their home to the Park West Freeway, a road that was never built.

Milwaukee Journal Sentinel

over 250 acres between 1956 and 1975 – a tiny fraction of the 7,300 originally proposed by the Housing Authority and barely 10 percent of the acreage cleared for the county expressway system. But the residents most directly affected complained that the city was going too far. The first attempts at urban renewal were heavy-handed by later standards. Like loggers clear-cutting a forest, city officials insisted on reducing every project area to rubble and then starting over from scratch. There was little or no input from the community, an approach that led to fierce conflict with fledgling preservationists on the West Side and Sicilian grandmothers in the Third Ward. Urban renewal, they charged, was nothing more than urban removal. The program caused genuine hardship for some residents, but there is little doubt that Milwaukee's renewal efforts eliminated sizable pockets of decay that had advanced well beyond the possibility of repair.

The civil rights movement gathered steam as bulldozers rumbled through the central city, but its focus shifted from sausage-makers to schools. It was no secret that Milwaukee's public schools were racially segregated, if only because Milwaukee's neighborhoods were segregated. White children went to white schools, black children went to black schools and, where the lines blurred, authorities kept the races separate. When inner-city schools became overcrowded, as was often the case, officials went so far as to bus intact classes of black students to empty rooms in all-white buildings, bring them back to the core for lunch, and then bus them out to finish their days in total segregation. In late 1963, nine years after the Supreme Court outlawed separate-but-equal education, an interra-cial group of Milwaukeeans began to push for desegregation of the Milwaukee Public Schools. Separating the races, they argued, deprived both groups of an equal education. The group's leader was Lloyd Barbee, a Memphis-born, Wisconsin-trained lawyer who headed the state chapter of the NAACP. His opening arguments fell on deaf ears. Harold Story, a prominent school board member (and Allis-Chalmers executive), declared that desegregation "would abolish the neighborhood school system as it operates here." Well, yes, responded Barbee and company.

When school officials refused to change their policies, the integrationists attacked on two other fronts. In 1965 Lloyd Barbee, by this time a state assemblyman, filed suit on

Lloyd Barbee, the lawyer and state legislator who led the desegregation suit against the Milwaukee Public Schools

Milwaukee Journal Sentinel

behalf of black and white students, alleging a pattern of illegal segregation in Milwaukee's public school system. The lawsuit lit a long fuse that would produce an educational explosion a decade later. More immediately, the activists formed a group called MUSIC (Milwaukeeans United for School Integration Committee) and organized a boycott of the MPS system at the end of the 1964 spring term. As many as 15,000 students (more than 10 percent of city enrollment) stayed away from their assigned buildings, learning instead at thirty-one "Freedom Schools" established in North Side churches. The boycotts, marches, and demonstrations continued intermittently for the next two years, with little visible effect on school authorities. (Superintendent Harold Vincent called desegregation "administratively unfeasible.") Although the group's short-term impact was muted, MUSIC sounded an urgent and unmistakable call for official Milwaukee to change its tune.

MUSIC also marked the debut of one of the most improbable civil rights leaders in America: Father James Groppi. His early years gave only the slightest hints of future controversy. Groppi was a native son, the eleventh of twelve children born to Italian immigrants who ran a general store in Bay View. Italians were among the last ethnic groups who gravitated to jobs in the old Bay View iron mill before it closed in 1929. Although they were Catholic to the core, the newcomers were not especially welcome at Immaculate Conception, the neighborhood's Irish church. The Groppi children were baptized at Our Lady of Pompeii in the Third Ward, and the family regularly joined an Italian priest for Mass in the little cobbler shop across from their store.

Whether or not these early experiences as an outsider influenced his later career, a single-minded interest in social justice pervaded James Groppi's priesthood. In 1963 he was an assistant at St. Boniface, an

Members of MUSIC protested the forced busing of black children to other neighborhoods in 1965.

Milwaukee Journal Sentinel

old German parish in the heart of the inner core. The young priest had already demonstrated an interest in the civil rights movement, but his interest became a passion during a trip to Selma, Alabama, in early 1965. Marching with Martin Luther King and other giants of the era, Groppi was struck by the hypocrisy of Northern liberals who traveled hundreds of miles to confront Southern racism but ignored the prejudice in their own backyards. Soon after returning to Milwaukee, he joined MUSIC and logged his first arrest. By the end of the year, Groppi was the advisor to Milwaukee's NAACP Youth Council and on the brink of national notoriety.

The sheer novelty of a white priest leading a group of young blacks in civil rights protests was bound to attract the media's attention, but James Groppi was a difficult man to ignore under any circumstances. Quick to anger and slow to compromise, Groppi was confrontation personified. Although he later distanced himself from such tactics as overly divisive, the priest's basic strategy was to flush racial hatred into the open and thereby force white society to confront the dark emotions that lay beneath the rhetorical sheen of most public discourse on race. Groppi's identification with the African-American cause was so complete that he generally used "we" in referring to the community, and he did not necessarily preach non-violence. "If black people tore up this city," he once told a visiting reporter, "it would simply be dynamic revolution." For whites who grew up with a more sedate notion of the priesthood, such comments fell somewhere between scandal and heresy.

In the early months of 1966, Father Groppi and the Youth Council chose their first target: the Eagles Club. It was a fraternal

An unlikely leader in an explosive period, Father James Groppi crystallized emerging civil-rights sentiment in Milwaukee.

Milwaukee Journal Sentinel

Groppi was most visible in his role as advisor to the NAACP Youth Council.

Milwaukee Journal Sentinel

Milwaukee Journal Sentinel

group whose members included scores of Milwaukee judges, politicians, and business leaders – all of them, by club rules, Caucasians. Picketing the Eagles headquarters on Wisconsin Avenue failed to change the club's whites-only policy or attract much media interest, prompting a change in tactics. In August, the protests began to hit the Eagles where they lived. For eleven straight nights, Youth Council members and their supporters demonstrated in front of Judge Robert Cannon's home in the quiet enclave of Wauwatosa. Hecklers gathered almost immediately, some threatening violence. When crowd levels neared the 2,000 mark, Gov. Warren Knowles called out the National Guard. Young people from the inner core marched behind a phalanx of soldiers with bayonets at the ready, and *Time* and *Newsweek* sent reporters. The *Time* story (September 9, 1966) featured Father Groppi ("rhymes with puppy") and described the Wauwatosa confrontation as "The Pulpit vs. the Bench."

After more demonstrations and three failed attempts at mediation, the Eagles controversy died down with no appreciable change in the group's policies. Groppi and the Youth Council soon moved on to a meatier issue: open housing. Although a relatively innocuous state law was already on the books, most forms of housing discrimination were not prohibited in Milwaukee. Vel Phillips had tried and failed four times since 1962 to push an openhousing ordinance through the Common Council, casting the lone affirmative vote each time. Henry Maier was not about to lend his support. The mayor, who made no secret of his disdain for Groppi, followed his customary practice of deflecting criticism to other levels of government. The "real battle," he argued, was with Milwaukee's suburbs, "the most segregated ... of any metropolitan area in the country." Until they opened their doors to people of color, said the mayor, it was pointless for Milwaukee to enact tougher legislation.

The city obviously housed a disproportionate share of the region's minorities, agreed civil rights activists, but that was no excuse for official inaction. In June, 1967, Father Groppi and the Youth Council began to march on the homes of city aldermen, demanding that they declare their support for an open-housing ordinance.

The marches were interrupted by a riot. In the summer of 1967, there was almost no possibility that Milwaukee could have escaped a racial explosion – with or without James Groppi. Since August, 1965, when the Watts section of Los Angeles went up in smoke, a wave of urban violence had been spreading across the country, and it crested in 1967. There were 164 separate disturbances in the first nine months of the year, ranging from minor confrontations in small cities to cataclysms in Newark (July 12 to 17) and Detroit (July 23 to 28). Milwaukee's riot began like most of the others: at night, in the heart of the ghetto, and without much warning. At about 9 P.M. on Sunday, July 30, while the ruins of Detroit's West Side were still smoldering, a crowd of young African Americans gathered at Third Street and North Avenue, the commercial crossroads of Milwaukee's inner core. One stone sailed through one store window, and the situation quickly spun out of control. Passing cars ran a gauntlet of bottles and bricks. Arsonists set fires throughout the neighborhood. Sporadic gunfire and the wail of sirens shattered the customary silence of Sunday night. When the spreading chaos threatened to overwhelm local authorities, Mayor Maier and Police Chief Harold Breier asked Gov. Knowles to call out the National Guard. By 3 A.M. on Monday, July 31, with timely help from a rainstorm, the streets of the inner core were quiet again, and the arrival of Guardsmen in the morning kept them that way. The entire Third Street corridor was blockaded from Burleigh to State Streets between First and Fifth – a distance of more than two miles. Although tensions remained high for several days, the worst of the violence ended within a matter of six hours. The final toll included 1,740 arrests, nearly 100 injuries, and 3 deaths: a police officer, an elderly woman, and a young man suspected of looting.

Without diminishing the individual losses or the collective tragedy of July 30 and 31, Milwaukee's "civil disturbance" was a relatively tame affair. (*Time* went so far as to call it "abortive.") Police estimated that no more than 300 persons took an active part in the violence, and the number of inner-city residents trying to put out fires was equal to the number trying to start them. Compared with 43 deaths in Detroit and 26 in Newark, Milwaukee got off easy. But its relative good fortune did not keep the community from feeling traumatized to its bones. Not since the labor disturbances of May, 1886, had local authorities faced such chaos in the streets, and not since 1886 had a civil disturbance cost people their lives. The connections between the Polish and German workers of 1886 and the African Americans of 1967 are admittedly tenuous; black rioters had no Knights of Labor to focus their discontent, and African Americans had grievances that extended well beyond their working hours. But there are connections nonetheless. In both cases, conditions perceived as oppressive drove groups of angry residents to the streets, and in both cases, the ensuing violence signaled that something was terribly wrong with the status quo.

Milwaukee Journal Sentinel

Milwaukee Journal Sentinel

Milwaukee Public Library

Scenes from the riot of July, 1967: A policeman with shotgun at the ready on Second and Center, a looted storefront on Third Street, and a mother's grief. Clifford McKissick's mother broke down at the funeral of her son, a suspected looter shot by police.

There was one more parallel between the disturbances of 1886 and 1967: the speed and scale of the official response. Henry Maier played the role of Gov. Jeremiah Rusk. Using emergency powers granted during a terrible blizzard in 1947, Maier declared the municipal equivalent of martial law. Less than five hours after the first reports of trouble, he imposed a round-the-clock curfew on the entire city. Taverns and filling stations were closed. Bus service and mail delivery were suspended. Streets were barred to all but emergency traffic. As Milwaukee's suburbs followed suit, an eerie silence settled over the entire metropolitan area. Commuters who tried to go to work on Monday morning were turned back at roadblocks by rifle-toting officers in riot gear. The blanket curfew was lifted after twenty-six hours, but nighttime restrictions remained in effect for another eight days.

No other big-city mayor responded so swiftly and with such sweeping measures to the racial unrest of the 1960s. Although Maier acknowledged that "guns and nightsticks aren't going to solve the problems of the central city," his first objective was to regain control. With the enthusiastic cooperation of Harold Breier, the city's tough-as-nails police chief, that mission was accomplished quickly. Did Maier overreact? There is no doubt that Milwaukee's self-

imposed paralysis helped to keep the violence from spreading, but it is equally certain that, by shutting down the entire metropolis rather than the neighborhoods most directly affected, the mayor magnified the impact of the disturbance. Kept from work, kept from play, kept from even their neighborhood taverns, many city and suburban residents developed a siege mentality, fed by nonstop rumors. Revolution seemed imminent, and worried whites hauled any number of deer rifles and target pistols out of storage, just in case crazed blacks decided to attack communities miles from the inner core. Extraordinary levels of fear were still evident months

later. Planners of the Great Circus Parade decided to cancel the 1968 spectacle because they "could not assure the safety of viewers in the event of a civil disturbance."

In the immediate aftermath of the crisis, there was the same round of impassioned pleas and lukewarm official responses that followed inner-city violence virtually everywhere in the North. On August 5, Henry Maier unveiled his 39-Point Program "to help alleviate racial and social problems in Milwaukee." When civil rights activists noticed that thirty-five of the points involved county, state, or federal assistance, they ceased to pay serious attention. But Maier felt no particular need to

Mayor Maier (far left) acted quickly to quell the violence, imposing a twenty-four-hour curfew on the city. Milwaukee's freeways, normally jammed with commuters, were absolutely empty on the Monday morning following the riot.

build rapport with activists of any description. Whatever its long-term impact, his swift, decisive handling of the riot enhanced his reputation enormously, and the mayor basked in the glow of resoundingly positive press coverage. The *New York Times* (August 2, 1967) published a sidebar profile of Maier ("rhymes with higher"), describing him as "a methodical, intelligent, and somewhat authoritarian executive" – as well as a good sheepshead player. The adulation of his constituents, black as well as white, was even more gratifying. In the 1968 mayoral election, Maier captured 86 percent of the popular vote – the greatest landslide in Milwaukee's history.

Standing firm had obvious political rewards, but there were some less conspicuous hazards. The riot was perceived as a mortal threat, not a wake-up call, and the city's swift quelling of the violence was widely seen as a victory, not a prelude to remedial action. For most white residents, the story ended when the status quo had been restored. The result was that Milwaukee's racial divide grew even wider, and some menacing long-term trends gained considerable energy. Henry Maier's resounding win at the polls could not mask an accelerating pattern of white flight. North Third Street, already in steep decline, became a commercial ghost town after the riot, and the number of whites still living on the North Side dropped at an unprecedented rate.

The riot of late July, 1967, provided a fitting capstone to a tumultuous period, but the drama was not over yet. The same season that brought violent unrest to Milwaukee was known, ironically, as the "summer of love" in other cultural circles. A youth movement that had taken root on the coasts was rapidly spreading its tendrils to the Mid-west; Milwaukee's first protest against the Vietnam War dated from the previous November, and the first "be-in" at Lake Park took place at the end of April, 1967.

The counterculture was an increasingly visible presence, particularly on the East Side, but civil rights activities continued to hold center stage. In late August, less than a month after violence erupted at Third and North, Father James Groppi and the NAACP Youth Council resumed their marches in support of open housing. This time, however, they visited neighborhoods where they expected to find resistance rather than the homes of individual aldermen. The Youth Council's first destination was an overwhelmingly white, overwhelmingly blue-collar section of the South Side. On the evening of August 28, roughly 200 marchers crossed the Sixteenth Street viaduct from the North Side and walked all the way to Kosciuszko Park, in the shadow of St. Josaphat's Basilica. They were greeted along the route by more than 5,000 whites, none of them sympathetic. The confrontation was even more intense the next night; marchers were greeted with effigies and epithets, bottles and bricks, and tempers on both sides rose to the boiling point. Mayor Maier banned nighttime assemblies on August 30, but the protest walks continued. Despite dire predictions that the demonstrations would touch off a Detroit-scale riot, incidents of violence were sporadic and generally confined to the line of march.

The marathon marches continued, in various directions, for 200 consecutive days, attracting civil rights celebrities like Dick Gregory and a gaggle of national reporters. A foray to City Hall resulted in major damage to the mayor's office, but the South Side remained a favorite destination.

Milwaukee Journal Sentinel

Less than a month after Milwaukee's "civil disturbance," the NAACP Youth Council resumed its open-housing marches. The demonstrations provoked a hateful response on the South Side, but Father Groppi remained a defiant leader.

Milwaukee Journal Sentinel

Milwaukee Journal Sentinel

"We're going to keep marching here," Father Groppi told *U.S. News & World Report*, "until we get fair housing, so we can move in here with these white bigots or wherever we want." The last march was held on March 21, 1968. Within a month or two, Milwaukee and most of its suburbs passed open-housing laws that matched or exceeded new federal mandates. By that time, of course, Milwaukee was famous for something more than beer.

✶✶✶✶✶

"Explosive" is an appropriate word for the 1945-1967 period. In the years immediately following World War II, Milwaukee experienced any number of booms: in industrial output, population growth, construction activity, suburban expansion, and downtown redevelopment. Records were set in every category, and the arrival of the Braves simply confirmed that Mil-

waukee's big-league aspirations had been well-founded. As those multiple explosions lit up the civic firmament, however, pressures of another sort were building. Years of neglect, indifference, and open hostility had set the inner core smoldering, and smoke finally exploded into flame at the end of July, 1967. The riot's casualties were counted in more than arrests and fatalities. With the coming of violence died the sense of civic innocence that an earlier generation had cherished, the feeling that Milwaukee was somehow set apart in immaculate isolation from its neighbors. The tumult of 1967 demonstrated that the community was truly in the major leagues of urban America, for worse as well as for better. "Milwaukee for years," wrote Henry Maier in 1966, "regarded herself somewhat complacently as more fortunate than her sister cities." The summer of 1967 exploded that illusion forever.

Chapter 9
Shifting Currents, 1967-

AK-Mart rises from the rubble of the old Allis-Chalmers brass foundry. The company's Hawley works, center of production for the Manhattan Project during World War II, is now an office complex. Where Machine Shops 1 through 4 once hummed with the sounds of turret lathes and boring mills, you can fill a prescription, order a pizza, pick out a greeting card, or rent a video. In the long row of buildings that housed the Allis-Chalmers offices, more than forty different organizations have found homes, from PJ's Dental Lab to the Presbytery of Milwaukee. The company maintained a presence in the row after declaring bankruptcy in 1987, but its West Allis work force, once a virtual army, finally dwindled to a single individual housed in a single, rented office. He retired in 1999, and an industrial epoch ended with barely a whimper.

Many Milwaukeeans still find it hard to believe that Allis-Chalmers is gone. The firm was, after all, the largest corporation in Wisconsin and the region's leading private employer. Nearly 15,000 people came to work in West Allis every day in the late 1950s, swarming through a complex of shops and offices that turned out an unmatched variety of turbines, tractors, engines, pumps, mills, and other heavy equipment. But the company suffered a breathtaking crash in the 1980s, and its 130-acre complex has been adapted to other uses, most of them distinctly non-industrial.

Machine Shop 1 of the Allis-Chalmers complex now anchors a strip mall. The shop's original overhead crane, a Harnischfeger model, is still visible behind the glass wall.

The enormity of its collapse may set Allis-Chalmers apart, but evidence of a similar devolution is easy to find in Milwaukee. The Blatz brewery has been converted to upscale condominiums. The Schlitz brewery, home of "the beer that made Milwaukee famous," is an office park whose tenants include two health insurance firms and a public middle school. The old Pfister & Vogel tannery in the Menomonee Valley provides space for businesses dealing in everything from software to cell phones. Milwaukeeans can get their annual physicals on the site of the old Mueller Furnace factory, shop for fine art in the Phoenix Hosiery plant, and buy lumber or lawn mowers where the Caterpillar Tractor factory once stood. Year by year, the local economy has shifted from its base in manufacturing to a reliance on jobs that fall under the amorphous rubric of "service."

Perhaps the most telling sign of Milwaukee's economic transformation rises from the heart of the South Side. In 1908 the Heil Company moved into a new factory

Health-care giant Aurora has taken over the old Heil plant on Milwaukee's South Side.

complex on the Kinnickinnic River near Twenty-seventh Street. The firm became a major manufacturer of truck bodies, metal tanks, and other heavy equipment, providing jobs for as many as 1,800 workers at one point, but its days in Milwaukee were numbered. In the late 1980s, after moving much of its work to lower-wage plants in the South, Heil relocated to Chattanooga, and Aurora Health Care, a flourishing hospital network, took over the South Side property. Heil's red brick office building at 3000 W. Montana became Aurora's "corporate center," and the machine shops across the street were converted to conference rooms, a computer center, hospital laundry facilities, and the Tiny Town Day Care Center. With a 2008 payroll approaching 27,000 people, Aurora Health Care has long since replaced Allis-Chalmers as the largest private employer in the Milwaukee area.

"Deindustrialization" is the force behind this epidemic of re-use and replacement. In the closing decades of the twentieth century, the process was nearly as pervasive, and its influence nearly as profound, as the industrialization that transformed Milwaukee 100 years earlier. The metropolitan area lost more than 50,000 manufacturing jobs between 1979 and 1983 – a quarter of the total – and most have not returned. Although the transformation is hardly complete, the community's rapid fade as an industrial powerhouse has upset ancient expectations, challenged Milwaukee's traditional self-image, and caused untold social havoc.

If deindustrialization is a hallmark of the post-1967 period, it is also one of the very few trends that can be clearly discerned in the flux of recent events. The problem is chiefly one of perspective. Pivotal events of the distant past – wars and revolutions, breakthroughs and breakdowns – practically announce themselves; epochs and eras stand out obligingly in the evolving timescape. There are no such signposts in the recent past; it is simply too early to see them. But the search for patterns is further hampered by the ambiguous nature of the period itself. The years since 1967 have been decidedly mixed for Milwaukee, a melange of light and darkness, boom and bust, spectacular cultural advances and exasperatingly slow racial progress. Some old neighborhoods have been reborn while others have practically disintegrated. The fortunes of downtown have ebbed and flowed through two major rebuildings. Industrial collapse has given way to record prosperity for some and catastrophic unemployment for others. It has been, in the old phrase, the best and worst of times, generating an almost-Dickensian tale of two cities. This chapter, perched on the border between history and current events, carries the story into the first decade of the twenty-first century. The years have flowed past in a stream of shifting currents and many channels, converging, always converging, in the turbulent waters of the present.

The Ongoing Explosion

Milwaukee remained an explosive metropolis after 1967. Three trends that shaped the previous period – social unrest, suburban expansion, and the growth of minorities – continued into the next without losing a fraction of their power. Distinct but related, these movements overlapped and intersected to transform the face of the community, socially, physically, and politically.

Social unrest remained at a rolling boil through the late 1960s, fueled by a generalized discontent that seemed to touch everyone in the city. Despite widespread fears of renewed bloodshed, however, the watershed racial violence of July 30 and 31, 1967, was not repeated. African Americans sought other outlets to express and redress their grievances, whether through the separatist rhetoric of the local Black Panther militia or the emerging bureaucracy of federal anti-poverty programs. Although the black community was fast developing its own leaders, Father James Groppi remained a conspicuous figure. In 1969, with the open-housing

Continuing his earlier crusade, Father James Groppi led a march from Milwaukee to Madison to protest welfare cuts in 1969.

Milwaukee Journal Sentinel

379

campaign behind him, Groppi organized a group of welfare mothers to march on the state capitol in Madison. Nearly a thousand protesters occupied the Assembly chamber, leading to yet another confrontation with authorities and another arrest for Groppi. It was the latest step in a personal odyssey that would take the firebrand to law school, marriage, an Episcopal seminary, and finally the driver's seat of a Milwaukee County bus. Before his final illness in 1985, Groppi served as president of the county's transit union.

Although African Americans remained Milwaukee's most outspoken minority, other voices were heard in the late Sixties. Latino activism began in 1968 with calls for more liberal hiring practices in local factories and bilingual/bicultural programs in the public schools. Both calls were heard, however selectively. The national grape boycott initiated by Cesar Chavez in 1968 was another focal point for Latino organizing activities. *"Viva la Raza!"* ("Long live the people")

became the rallying cry of the moment, particularly among the young. Native Americans were the next group to step forward. Between 1960 and 1980, the proportion of Wisconsin Indians living in urban areas soared from 21 to 46 percent, and they were increasingly restless. In August, 1971, members of the American Indian Movement seized an abandoned Coast Guard station on Milwaukee's lakefront. The station provided a picturesque but primitive home for the Indian Community School, a venture started by a group of Indian mothers one year earlier. Although AIM eventually departed the scene, the Community School has remained, in different quarters, a cultural mainstay of native Milwaukee. It was the school's search for a stable source of revenue that brought Potawatomi Bingo to town in 1991.

The counterculture came to full flower during the same period. Drawn by its supply of relatively cheap housing and its proximity to the University of Wisconsin-Milwaukee,

(left)
Puerto Ricans were among the Latino groups flexing their political muscles after 1967.

(right)
A member of AIM kept watch at the Coast Guard station seized by Indian militants in 1971.

Milwaukee Public Library

Milwaukee Journal Sentinel

"hippies" turned the Lower East Side into Milwaukee's echo of Haight-Ashbury. Head shops, record stores, and newsstands sprouted among the Italian and Polish businesses on Brady Street, and Water Tower Park, with its new fountain, became the tie-dyed set's favored gathering spot – much to the dismay of the park's affluent neighbors. When the city imposed a curfew at Water Tower in July, 1970, the park's regulars resisted, sparking an ugly three-night confrontation with local police. Deeply earnest and baldly sybaritic by turns, the young people of the counterculture vibrated wildly between extremes of pleasure and protest. Milwaukee had its share of love-ins, rock concerts, and non-prescription drug use, but opposition to the Vietnam War was just as universal as long hair. Organized resistance reached its first peak on September 24, 1968, when fourteen activists, including five Catholic priests, seized draft records from the downtown Selective Service office and burned them in the small park at Second and Wells Streets. As anti-war sentiment continued to swell, a student strike virtually shut down the UWM campus in May of 1970.

A distinct women's movement emerged from the shadow of the larger crusade during the same years. A growing number of women observed that they were treated as second-class citizens, not least of all by the young men of the counterculture, and "sisterhood" became a powerful point of convergence for those who wanted to challenge the prevailing order. Local feminists formed a Milwaukee chapter of the National Organization for Women in 1967. True to the spirit of the era, the group proceeded directly to confrontation. In 1968 NOW chose the "men's grill" of the downtown Heinemann's restaurant as the site for its first sit-in, and protests against bridal fairs and beauty contests followed. As the movement matured, its attention shifted from symbolic street theater

A Lake Park "love-in" attracted crowds of young people in the late 1960s.

Milwaukee County Historical Society

The Milwaukee 14, five of them priests, sang as they waited for police to arrest them for burning Selective Service records in 1968.

to a concern for broader issues of work, worth, and women's health.

Feminism showed a capacity to reinvent itself, but calls for the several other varieties of power – Black, Brown, Red, and Flower – were heard less and less often by the mid-1970s. Incipient adulthood, the end of the Vietnam War, and simple fatigue tended to mute the cry for change, and leadership of the various movements fell to a committed core of activists working through more traditional channels. Social protest did not, however, grind to a halt. Long after the shouting was over, Milwaukee's school system faced the period's quietest but ultimately most potent expression of discontent with the status quo: the desegregation lawsuit filed by Lloyd Barbee and associates in 1965. It took until 1973 for the case to reach the top of the federal court calendar, and another three years passed before Judge John Reynolds issued his final ruling. On January 19, 1976, after reviewing months of

testimony and scores of documents, Reynolds found that the Milwaukee Public Schools had maintained "a consistent and deliberate policy of racial isolation and segregation for a period of twenty years."

The judge's order to desegregate the system did not end the wrangling, but MPS took its first tentative steps toward a new structure in the 1976-77 school year. The heart of its plan was an array of voluntary magnet schools with specialties so attractive that racial balance, it was hoped, would practically take care of itself. Legal challenges delayed full implementation for another three years. Under the terms of a consent decree finally signed on March 27, 1979, at least 75 percent of MPS students were required to attend racially balanced schools, and a smorgasbord of choices was ready for the following school year, including Montessori, open classroom, arts, language immersion, computer, college preparatory, and a variety of other programs. The magnet idea

Milwaukee Journal Sentinel

was so popular that, within two years, 120 of the system's 143 schools met the court's desegregation criteria, up from 12 in 1976. Milwaukee's program was also one of the very few in the nation with a suburban component; state financial aid made it possible for a limited number of students (3,843 in 1986) to cross the border in both directions. Although black parents were disturbed to find that their children bore the brunt of the busing, the program was successful, for a time, in meeting its primary goal, peacefully and without coercion. In 1981 Deputy Superintendent David Bennett declared that Milwaukee had "probably the most racially balanced urban school system in the North."

As the various movements of the 1960s and '70s continued to reshape Milwaukee's social and political landscape, a different kind of movement continued to transform the land itself: the wholesale conversion of farms to subdivisions in an ever-widening

arc around the city. This ongoing explosion, whose first tremors were felt in the 1920s, probably did more to alter Milwaukee's character than all the confrontations and conflagrations of the period combined. Its most obvious impact was a dramatic redistribution of population. In 1920 Mayor Dan Hoan had blithely predicted that his city would house two million residents by 1967. As late as 1966, Mayor Henry Maier forecast a population of one million by 1986. Both estimates were hopelessly generous. The city's population dropped from 741,324 in 1960 to 596,974 in 2000 – a 19-percent loss – and Milwaukee County as a whole experienced a similar seepage. During the same forty-year period, the rest of the metropolitan area (Waukesha, Washington, and Ozaukee Counties) experienced a 131-percent population increase, from 242,809 to 560,577. Waukesha, which had more people than Ozaukee and Washington together, was Wisconsin's fastest-growing county

The cornerstone of Milwaukee's desegregation effort was a system of magnet schools designed to attract students of all backgrounds. Montessori programs (above) were among the most popular.

throughout the period. As the population of one-time farm towns like Merton and Mukwonago doubled and then tripled, "Cow County, USA" became better-known for housing developments than Holsteins, and the rural way of life faded with the sunset over the western hills. The regional shift, it should be noted, took place during a period of general demographic stability; the population of the four-county metro area grew only 17 percent between 1960 and 2000, from 1,278,850 residents to 1,500,741. Roughly the same number of people, in other words, occupied a much larger land area: the classic definition of sprawl.

As the continuing exodus to the retreating edge devoured thousands of acres of farmland, something quite different was happening in Milwaukee's older suburbs: the slow but steady process of maturation. "Communities" that had consisted of little more than tract houses in cornfields after World War II began to take on a full range of quasi-urban characteristics after 1967. Maturing trees and shrubbery helped to soften the raw edges of suburban cul-de-sacs. Libraries, parks, community centers, and other cultural necessities joined the schools that had gone up in the first wave of settlement. Some communities even courted industry – provided it was "clean" industry. New Berlin was one of the more entrepreneurial suburbs. In 1965 the city opened a mile-square industrial park on the west side of Moorland Road; within a decade, it housed 114 businesses dealing in everything from meat to machine tools. By 1984 there were industrial parks in seventeen of Milwaukee's thirty-three suburbs, covering a total of 5,384 acres.

Commerce followed the same path to the fringe. The region's first shopping centers – Southgate, Capitol Court, and Mayfair – lay fairly close to the historic edge of Milwaukee. The next generation of centers – Brookfield Square (1967), Southridge (1970), and

From soybean fields to subdivisions: Rapid residential growth transformed old rural settlements like Mukwonago.

Milwaukee Journal Sentinel

Northridge (1972) – reflected the progressive unbundling of the city. Not only were they miles farther removed from the center of town, but they were also significantly larger than their predecessors. Southgate opened in 1951 with 20 stores, 105,000 square feet of retail space, and room for 2,000 cars. Southridge, the state's largest center, followed in 1970 with 125 stores, 1,400,000 square feet of space, and nearly 7,000 parking spots – not to mention such amenities as a 30-foot waterfall and a two-story aviary. Built literally across the street from the first homes in Greendale, Southridge overwhelmed the greenbelt character of the original New Deal community, but most residents seemed quite willing to accept the mall's help with their property tax bills.

As former bedroom suburbs became free-standing centers of commerce and industry, people traveled to them from all parts of the metropolitan area. The result was a colossally inefficient but thoroughly American traffic pattern, one more typically associated with Los Angeles than the urban Midwest. The average work commute in the metropolitan area increased from 6.7 miles in 1963 to 9.1 miles in 1991, and the movement was multi-directional; an Elm Grove lawyer heading to his downtown office might have crossed paths with a Milwaukee millwright driving to work in New Berlin's industrial park. In the 1960s, an observer standing on the glacial ridge in eastern Brookfield would have witnessed a tide of commuters flooding into the city on Interstate 94 each morning and ebbing out again at night. Thirty years later, the volume of traffic in both directions, morning and evening, was practically the same.

As Milwaukee's suburbs grew up, their residents tended to grow away from the city. Many came into town only for special events, and their ties to the region's metropolis became more and more attenuated.

Southridge, the state's largest shopping center, featured 125 stores covering 1,400,000 square feet of retail space.

Milwaukee Journal Sentinel

The unforeseen consequence was a dramatic increase in social distance. Like most American cities, Milwaukee had always been a stratified community, beginning in the days when Irish maids walked up from the swamp-ridden Third Ward to the mansions of Yankee Hill. Some neighborhoods housed the movers and shakers, while others housed the moved and shaken. But social distance had been leavened by physical proximity; Milwaukeeans of all stations tended to know the lives of their neighbors, great and small, in general outline if not in detail. That familiarity vanished with the suburban exodus following World War II. Droves of Milwaukeeans moved miles away from the patchwork quilt of urban neighborhoods, and an entire generation of children grew up with no memory of city life. What was lost in the process was a certain urban fluency, a working knowledge of the conditions of other ethnic and economic groups. The loss, in truth, was not sharply felt, but it tended to shape public perceptions of the metropolis, and ultimately public policy.

The city, in turn, grew away from its suburbs. The third continuing explosion of the period – the growth of minority communities – changed Milwaukee's demographic face so thoroughly that many suburbanites had difficulty recognizing their old neighborhoods. The city's population loss was relatively modest – only 19 percent from 1960 to 2000 – but that figure masked the racial dimensions of the shift. The wave of families leaving Milwaukee in the post-World War II years was overwhelmingly, almost exclusively, white. The community's white population plummeted from 675,572 in 1960 to 298,379 in 2000 – a decline of 56 percent. There is no doubt that many were fleeing what they felt

to be the incursions of minority groups; the fact that nearly half the flight took place in the 1970s, the first census decade after the 1967 riot, must have been more than coincidental. Paradoxically, it was the growth of those same minority groups that kept Milwaukee from showing a cataclysmic population loss.

The minorities of the post-1967 period represented an increasing variety of cultures. Latinos – primarily Mexicans but also Puerto Ricans and a full complement of Central and South Americans – grew from less than 2 percent of the city's population in 1960 to more than 12 percent in 2000, when the community numbered over 70,000 people. By 1980 Latinos made up half the population of Walker's Point, and the near South Side became a much-visited center of Latin American culture and cuisine. Asian Milwaukeeans were multiplying even faster. Their population quintupled in twenty years, rising from 3,600 in 1980 to 17,571 in 2000. The majority were Southeast Asians, particularly Hmong, Laotian, and Vietnamese refugees who had fought on the American side during the Vietnam War and suffered exile for their troubles. Often resettled by church groups, they formed distinctive and close-knit communities in the old immigrant neighborhoods on the South, West, and North Sides. The Hmong were also linked to outstate communities that made Wisconsin, its climate notwithstanding, a leading center of Hmong settlement in the United States.

The largest minority community in Milwaukee was also the oldest: African Americans. Their numbers exploded from 62,458 in 1960 to 222,933 in 2000, and their share of the city's population swelled accordingly, from 8.4 percent in 1960 to 23.1 percent in 1980 and 37.3 percent in 2000. In the four-county area, the corresponding 2000 figure for

blacks was only 15.7 percent, leading to the in-escapable conclusion that Milwaukee was a highly segregated metropolis. Racism un-doubtedly played a role, but the severity of segregation in metropolitan Milwaukee has an important geographic qualifier. The whole-sale annexations of the postwar years gave the city thousands of acres of prime land open for development, and the largest tracts lay on the Northwest Side – squarely in the path of the expanding North Side. Germans and other Milwaukeeans of European lineage had been moving steadily north and west from the heart of town for decades, and African Ame-ricans followed precisely the same routes as their numbers grew. In cities with less gener-ous borders, they would soon have reached the suburbs. In Milwaukee, thousands of African Americans found suburban-style housing well within the city limits. The fact that Milwaukee has always housed more than 95 percent of the metropolitan area's blacks is therefore a somewhat misleading gauge of residential segregation. It should not be

Milwaukee's fastest-growing minorities were Latinos and Hmongs (top left and right), but African Americans (above) remained the city's largest minority group, making up more than 37 percent of the population in 2000.

assumed, on the other hand, that Milwaukee had much to teach the rest of American society about racial harmony. Far from it. More revealing than city-suburban comparisons was the degree of racial clustering *within* the city. Study after study of big-city residential segregation placed Milwaukee in the same company as Detroit, St. Louis, Cleveland, and Chicago.

The growing concentration of African Americans in the city had profound implications for the Milwaukee Public Schools. In 1970, when Lloyd Barbee's desegregation suit was still awaiting a court date, black students made up 26 percent of MPS enrollment. As whites left Milwaukee in droves and the black birth rate remained high, the African-American presence in the public schools climbed to 52.6 percent in 1985 – a clear majority – and finally leveled off at about 60 percent. The system's specialty programs continued to grow, but "racial balance" became a matter of attracting enough white children to achieve a roughly representative student population.

Specialty programs like the dance major at Milwaukee High School of the Arts remained strong as African-American students made up the majority of MPS enrollment.

Milwaukee Journal Sentinel

Life at MPS was further complicated by the rise of educational alternatives. Wisconsin became a closely watched center of reform efforts in the 1990s, some of which strained traditional concepts of education to the breaking point. Charter schools, operating under public auspices but functionally independent, ranged from military-style boot camps for chronic truants to academies for budding entrepreneurs. "Open enrollment" allowed students to cross into neighboring districts regardless of ethnic background. But the most important initiative, and by far the most controversial, was the Milwaukee Parental Choice Program, better known as School Choice. Created by the state legislature in 1990 and steadily expanded, School Choice applied public funding – a stipulated amount per child, paid by voucher – to private and parochial institutions. The program was a godsend for Milwaukee's faith-based schools, but its impact on MPS was the subject of vigorous debate. Some praised School Choice as a long-overdue prod to better performance, while others panned it as a financial blow at a time when the tide of special-needs and at-risk children was on the rise. The district, in the meantime, broadened its own reform efforts, with an emphasis on smaller high schools and neighborhood-based elementary schools. The proliferation of programs on every front reached bewildering proportions, but the ultimate goal – uniformly effective education – remained as elusive as ever.

Problems associated with low income were another challenge facing MPS and virtually every other public agency. Despite some genuine progress in the 1970s, nearly 30 percent of Milwaukee's African Americans were living in poverty at the decade's end – more than three times the rate for the metropolitan area as a whole. Poverty was not exclusively a black phenomenon – other minorities and numerous whites faced similar problems – but the growing prevalence of low-income households in Milwaukee tended to aggravate the social distance developing in the region. The city's median household income was 72 percent of the suburban figure in 1970; it fell to 58 percent in 1980 and just under half in 1990. "We are part of a deepening trend," Mayor Henry Maier told the *New York Times* in 1975. "That trend is toward an ever-growing concentration of the poor and the relatively poor in the central cities of America." Conditions in Milwaukee reflected a truism about life in a capitalist society: The essence of free enterprise is competition, and the result of competition is always winners and losers. In Milwaukee and elsewhere, the losers were increasingly concentrated in the city, and they were increasingly people of color.

It was at this point that the continuing explosions of the post-1967 period converged to create an urban vortex. Political antagonism between city and suburbs, which rose to a peak during the Maier years, reflected the nonstop exodus of whites to the urban fringe, the nonstop growth of minorities inside the city limits, and the widening social gap between the two. Never one to speak timidly of trends affecting his city, Henry Maier used the term "urban apartheid" to describe the situation. Within the city itself, the growing concentration of poverty claimed an increasing share of local government's decreasing financial resources, and growing concerns about schools, crime, and taxes gave middle-class whites even more reasons to leave. Milwaukee, many observers believed, was trapped in a vicious circle with no end in sight.

Back to the City

America's big cities were widely viewed as an endangered species after 1967. The same juggernaut of forces – racial, economic, and political – that clouded Milwaukee's future confronted scores of other communities, and scholars were quick to predict an apocalypse. Virtually every "urban studies" text of the period was an unrelieved exercise in urban pathology; the academic presses churned out one bleak chronicle after another of impoverished minorities trapped in the city, privileged whites ensconced in the suburbs, and practically nothing in between.

The end of the urban world did not come. Despite the community's manifold problems, the view from Milwaukee, at least, was considerably more complex, and considerably more hopeful, than the preliminary evidence seemed to warrant. The contrast between city and suburbs, first of all, was less extreme than it may have appeared. Older residential satellites like Whitefish Bay and Shorewood experienced population losses similar to Milwaukee's, and some industrial suburbs were hit even harder. West Milwaukee was the extreme case. Incorporated as a tax island in 1906, the village received a triple dose of bad news after 1967. In the late 1960s, hundreds of homes on the eastern edge of the community were demolished to make room for a freeway that was never built. West Milwaukee lost another major source of revenue in 1973, when the state legislature, hoping to stimulate business growth, exempted industrial machinery and equipment from the property tax. The coup de grace came in the 1980s, when deindustrialization reduced the community's tax base by 40 percent in six years. West Milwaukee's population dropped from 5,043 in 1960 to 3,973 in 1990 – a 21-percent loss – and taxes rose accordingly. The village had levied no property tax at all until 1956; by 1986 its property tax rate was the highest in the entire metropolitan area.

If the suburban news was not all good, reports from the city were not all bad. Milwaukee, in fact, fared relatively well among its peers in the urban North. Of the fourteen "Frostbelt" communities studied in 1998 by UWM's Marc Levine, the Milwaukee area ranked third in its proportion of residents who lived in the city proper. Although the city's population fell 15 percent between 1960 and 1990, some of Milwaukee's counterparts were practically hemorrhaging. St. Louis lost close to half its residents in the same period, and Cleveland and Detroit lost more than a third. The city's "secret," once again, was the vast expanse of farmland it had annexed after World War II – a legacy of Frank Zeidler's administration.

The largest single acquisition was the Granville tract on the Northwest Side, which supported developments that were suburban in all but name. Granville pro-

vided room on the urban edge for thousands of North Siders, both white and black, who were moving up economically, but it was not entirely residential. In 1964, long before most suburbs joined the parade, Milwaukee began to develop a sprawling industrial park just west of Seventy-sixth Street; it was the first of several that would eventually cover nearly a thousand acres in several locations. Farther north, near the county line, the Kohl family began to develop Northridge in 1969. It was planned as both a regional shopping center and a comprehensive residential community, with housing for 20,000 people, three artificial lakes, schools, a library, and assorted places of worship. Although the Kohls' dreams of a community as large as Shorewood were scaled down in execution, Northridge did become a highly distinctive "city within the city."

Even more important than these new city developments was a sea change in public attitudes toward what constituted "progress." Ever since the days of Juneau, Kilbourn, and Walker, Milwaukee's civic leaders had

Northridge, a community planned for 20,000 people, developed at the city's northern limits in the 1970s.

Milwaukee Journal Sentinel

labored to provide the community with every material advantage. Citizens applauded as their hometown moved from dirt trails to plank roads to railroads in the nineteenth century and to automobiles in the twentieth. Each stage was an obvious step forward, an advance in the state of the art, an accession of the next best thing. But progress lost its halo after 1967. A new generation looked around the city and saw old buildings being demolished, old neighborhoods being devalued, and old traditions being discarded. Convinced that post-World War II developments had undone much of the city's historic fabric, they resolved to undo the undoing.

Historic preservation was the first fruit of this wholesale inversion of attitudes, and the movement's clarion call was probably the demolition of the North Western Railroad depot. The graceful Romanesque tower had dominated Milwaukee's lakefront since 1889, but passenger trains fell on hard times after World War II; in 1960 the railroad offered the building and its adjoining acreage to the city of Milwaukee. The North Western depot was precisely the kind of building that other communities, including Indianapolis and St. Louis, would later bring back to life as shrines of commerce, but Milwaukeeans of the 1960s weren't interested. (The Greater Milwaukee Committee thought the parcel, cleared of its buildings, had great potential as a freeway corridor.) The depot ultimately became a vacant, vandalized hulk looming over the east end of Wisconsin Avenue. It was torn down in 1968 to make way for nothing at all.

"Never again," vowed a group of fledgling preservationists. Convinced that the loss of the North Western depot was a tragically missed opportunity, they stepped up

The loss of the North Western Railroad depot in 1968 convinced fledgling preservationists that it was time to speak up. One of their early successes was the Pabst Mansion (below), a gracious relic from Grand Avenue's heyday that became a popular house museum.

Milwaukee Journal Sentinel

Milwaukee Journal Sentinel

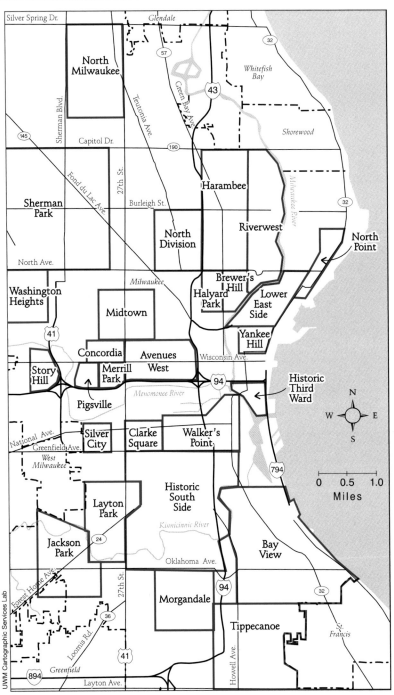

Milwaukee's neighborhoods, long the primary building blocks of the city, were discovered by a new generation of residents after 1967.

their vigilance of any and all developments that threatened historic structures. It soon became apparent that Milwaukee's innate conservatism was, at least in this context, an asset. However unintentionally, the go-slow attitude of the 1950s and '60s had spared a surprising number of buildings that would have been lost in a more aggressive prosecution of urban renewal. Milwaukee, relatively speaking, had more structures worth saving than other cities of its size, and preservationists tried to save them all. They lost more battles than they won, but there were some notable victories, including the opulent mansion brewer Frederick Pabst built for himself on Grand Avenue in 1892. It had served as the Catholic archbishop's residence from 1908 until 1975, when the home was sold and slated for demolition. Before the wreckers arrived, a non-profit group called Wisconsin Heritages was formed to save the building, and its members have operated the Pabst Mansion as the region's favorite house museum ever since.

Milwaukee's new taste for the old reached beyond historic buildings. As the suburban exodus continued without interruption, there was a countercurrent of home-seekers who were discovering, or rediscovering, a taste for city life. They were an extraordinarily eclectic group: young and middle-aged, gay and straight, Democratic and Republican, largely white but by no means all, architects and bricklayers, suburban matrons and countercultural dropouts. The only traits they shared were an aversion to the architectural blandness and social homogeneity of most postwar suburbs and a desire for character, color, authenticity, and diversity – cultural as well as architectural. They found those qualities in any number of Milwaukee neighborhoods. Bay View offered spectacular

Milwaukee Journal Sentinel

Milwaukee Journal Sentinel

From ready-for-company condos in the Third Ward (left) to sweat-equity specials in Brewer's Hill (right), there was ample evidence of vitality in Milwaukee's oldest neighborhoods.

lakefront scenery in the historic confines of a one-time mill town. Walker's Point and Brewer's Hill featured the city's oldest housing in a comprehensive range of sizes and styles. The Third Ward had dozens of warehouses and small factories awaiting conversion to condominiums, loft apartments, galleries, and specialty shops. (As late as 1977, the district was proposed as a "combat zone" for adult-oriented businesses.) Riverwest, originally a working-class Polish neighborhood, attracted hundreds of refugees from the high-rent East Side. Sherman Park offered Craftsman bungalows and gracious Period Revival homes in a racially mixed setting. The homes of Washington Heights, Concordia, Story Hill, and parts of the Lower East Side were filled with natural fireplaces, hardwood floors, built-in china cabinets, leaded-glass windows, and a builder's catalog of other architectural amenities.

In the middle- to upper-income neighborhoods, like Washington Heights, homes were generally in good repair; houses in antique communities like Walker's Point and Brewer's Hill often required enormous infusions of "sweat equity." In either case, the new owners were interested in restoration, not remodeling, and in virtually all cases, neighborhood organizations sprang up to protect and promote the interests of their residents. From Historic Walker's Point to the Sherman Park Community Association to ESHAC in Riverwest, the city's neighborhoods added some articulate new voices to the ongoing discussion of Milwaukee's future.

After some initial hesitation, public officials actively abetted the back-to-the-city movement. Urban renewal projects still followed, for a time, the knock-it-all-down policy of earlier years; the sites of East Side "A,"

Milwaukee Journal Sentinel

The suburban ideal was the inspiration for Halyard Park (above), a new neighborhood that attracted scores of middle-income blacks, but Milwaukee's growing regard for its heritage also led to restoration of old landmarks like the Pabst Theater (right).

Milwaukee Journal Sentinel

in the shadow of City Hall, and Kilbourn-town No. 3, northwest of downtown, were both reduced to rubble in the late 1960s and early 1970s. In "renewed" residential areas, federal policies encouraged a "suburb in the city" approach, which produced the rather anomalous sight of ranch houses and split-levels on curvilinear streets in the heart of the inner city. Two of those subdivisions – Halyard Park and Parkview – became enor-mously popular havens for Milwaukee's small but growing African-American mid-dle class. They also added a new element to the inner city's sociological mix. As black families built bright new ranches in Halyard Park, a mixed group of preservationists was busy restoring pre-1900 homes in Brewer's Hill – only a few blocks east.

Although the suburban ideal remained powerful, the city's focus shifted steadily from redevelopment to preservation over the years. In 1969 the Midtown Conserva-tion Project, covering the neighborhood west of Twentieth Street between State and Vliet, became the first to seek a balance between fixing homes up and tearing them down. The search for that balance dis-solved into a battle between city officials and local residents, but scores of homes were spared the wrecking ball. Midtown proved to be the transitional project; by 1976 Milwaukee's policy was all preser-vation, all the time. Urban renewal gave way to an array of tool loan centers, home improvement loans, tax incentives, and programs designed to shore up neighborhood business districts. The city even became a hands-on leader in preservation efforts. In 1976 the elegant-ly restored Pabst Theater reopened under city auspices, and in 1981 the Historic Preservation Commission was chartered with power to impose (subject to Common Council review) strict design standards on work affecting Milwaukee's most historic buildings.

With or without support from the public sector, historic preservationists and neighborhood activists were passionately in favor of anything that promised to restore the fabric and reclaim the flavor of the pre-automobile city. Most had no desire to re-create a lost world. They favored restoration because the pre-automobile city was a human-scale community that worked for its residents, not its residents' cars. Conversely, the new traditionalists were passionately opposed to anything that threatened a further distortion of that human scale, and nothing aroused their ire more than freeways. To describe the shift in public attitudes toward expressways as a reversal would be an understatement. In the 1950s, superroads were viewed as Milwaukee's salvation, bringing freedom to a gridlocked metropolis. By the 1970s, they were viewed as clear-cut evidence of a municipal death-wish. Opponents argued that, whatever their value as movers of traffic, expressways uprooted residents, divided neighborhoods, wiped out millions of dollars of tax base, and hastened the flight to the suburbs. Resistance began to surface in 1966, primarily over the issue of relocation. (Between 1959 and 1971, Milwaukee County's freeway program eliminated 6,334 housing units and displaced nearly 20,000 people.) By the time its annual report for 1969 was published, even the Expressway Commission had to admit that the climate had changed:

In the early 1960's, the Commission heard vocal and strident demands for accelerated freeway design and construction.

In 1969, equally loud voices were heard, only this time directed toward other goals – design the freeway elsewhere, don't design it at all, build a mass transit system instead, call a moratorium on all construction, provide good housing before a single additional person displacement is made.

While acknowledging that 1969 was "a difficult year," the Commission pressed on, only to meet hostility from practically every quarter, including City Hall. "The time has come," declared Henry Maier in 1972, "to throttle the concrete monster which gulps up huge blocks of housing each year." Opponents of the Stadium South Freeway tied ribbons around every tree the road would have taken in Jackson

Milwaukee Journal Sentinel

By the late 1960s, freeways were no longer viewed as the symbols of progress they had appeared to be earlier in the decade.

Opposition from neighborhood and environmental groups stopped the freeway in its tracks at Milwaukee's lakefront.

Milwaukee Journal Sentinel

Park, effectively stalling construction. Foes of the Park West Freeway succeeded in stopping the highway in its tracks at Sherman Boulevard. But the most virulent opposition was reserved for the Park East and Lake Freeways. Engineers designed a road that would have cut through the Lower East Side at Ogden Avenue, descended the lake bluff in Juneau Park, crossed the harbor on a high-rise bridge, and then continued to Mitchell Airport through Bay View, St. Francis, and Cudahy. The bridge, because it had no impact on residential areas, was built first; crews finished their work in 1974. (The span was named, with abysmally poor judgment, for Mayor Daniel Hoan, whose opposition to lakefront development of any kind was so keen that he questioned even the landmark War Me-

morial Center.) Completing the segments to the north and south was not so easy. Residents of the South Shore communities objected to the prospect of losing more than 500 homes to six lanes of concrete. East Siders, joined by lovers of green space from throughout the region, objected to the prospect of losing a major portion of Juneau Park. Freeway planners tried valiantly to appease their adversaries, promising "a truly environmental design" that would produce "the most beautiful urban freeway in America." Where they saw "a lakefront that was imaginative and bold," however, critics saw only acres of concrete swallowing Milwaukee's most hallowed ground. Opponents on both sides of the bridge launched a continuing barrage of lawsuits, petition drives, and

The Hoan Bridge was a conspicuous symbol of the shift in public attitudes. The span was Milwaukee's "bridge to nowhere" for three long years before it was finally connected to surface streets in 1977. By the time it opened, the freeway era was virtually over.

Milwaukee Journal Sentinel

demonstrations that brought construction to a standstill. Portions of the land already cleared for the Park East and Park West Freeways were converted to community gardens and playgrounds, and the Hoan Bridge became Milwaukee's celebrated "bridge to nowhere." It stood in magnificent isolation for three long years, prompting suggestions for its use as a tourist promenade or a skateboard park. In 1977, finally, the Expressway Commission added on- and off-ramps that connected the span to the city's surface streets. Bay View was suddenly five minutes away from downtown, and demand for housing in the neighborhood soared accordingly.

The Hoan Bridge saga marked the effective end of the freeway era in Milwaukee County. A few odds and ends of road were completed (notably the Airport Spur), but Milwaukee County began to remove long segments from its official expressway map in 1978. Engineering contracts were canceled, plans for additional corridors (the Bay, the Belt) were quietly shelved, and homes acquired along old rights-of-way were put back on the market. The process of redeveloping cleared corridors proved to be excruciatingly slow. An upscale housing project called East Pointe Commons healed the scar of the uncompleted Park East Freeway, and there was comparable activity along the route of the Stadium South in West Milwaukee. Elsewhere in the system, large tracts of land were still covered with weeds nearly forty years after they had been removed from the tax rolls.

The Performing Arts Center, shown a few months before its completion in 1969, marked a giant step forward in Milwaukee's cultural development.

Milwaukee Journal Sentinel

Fighting freeways, reclaiming old neighborhoods, and preserving historic buildings were all activities that expressed a new ethic, a new aesthetic, a new way of looking at urban life. After decades of neglect, Milwaukeeans began to value their city again, to rediscover the nooks and crannies, quirks and qualities that had always made the community unique. The struggle to "undo the undoing" and bring the city's native potential to light was never finished. The forces of blight and renewal were almost evenly matched in some neighborhoods, and Sherman Park residents found that racial equilibrium was a particularly difficult quality to maintain. Nor did the back-to-the-city movement have sufficient weight to counterbalance the suburban exodus. Those who valued the city in all its gritty glory were undoubtedly a minority, but they were a significant minority, and their activism added a powerful new stream to the shifting currents of the post-1967 period.

Of Ballet, Beer Gardens, and Baseball

Another new stream ushered in a cultural renaissance. Milwaukee's prominence as a capital of the fine arts had ended during World War I, when anti-Hun hysteria killed or crippled German music and theater in the city. The death of the *Deutsch-Athen* had left local residents without many choices in the performing arts, and they turned instinctively to Chicago. Beginning in 1915, the Chicago Symphony Orchestra played ten concerts each year in Milwaukee. They were invariably high points of the local aristocracy's social season, but many resisted the notion that the Cream City had become a cultural satellite of the Windy City. Slowly, by degrees, they nurtured home-grown arts organizations to meet the need for first-class music, theater, and dance in Milwaukee.

It was not until 1969, when the Performing Arts Center opened, that the community's aspirations to the artistic big leagues

Culture meets counterculture: Youthful protesters disrupted opening night at the PAC.

Milwaukee Public Library

Sweet harmony prevailed as the Milwaukee Symphony, the building's major tenant, grew into its new home.

Milwaukee Journal Sentinel

were realized. The building was a long time coming. A "music hall-theater" was part of the Milwaukee County war memorial that civic leaders had been discussing for generations. Funding shortfalls limited the project's first phase to the Saarinen-designed War Memorial Center, but the idea of a music hall remained alive. In 1966, after the familiar arguments about site, money, and control had been exhausted, ground for the Performing Arts Center was broken on the banks of the Milwaukee River, diagonally across the street from City Hall. The final product, paid for with a combination of private donations and county funds, was worth the wait. Architect Harry Weese designed a marble-clad temple to the arts, an all-in-one complex of theaters, halls, and pavilions that provided venues for everything from Berlioz to Beckett to Balanchine.

Opening night – September 17, 1969 – turned into a confrontation between culture and counterculture. Nearly 600 young people staged a demonstration outside the PAC, rubbing balloons, blowing soap bubbles, and launching rolls of toilet paper to protest the "arrogance" of $100-a-seat cultural events at a time when poverty was so prevalent. The initial controversy notwithstanding, the Performing Arts Center was a resounding success on all levels. *Architectural Record* (November, 1969) called the $12 million structure "elegant and glamorous as befits its role as a catalyst for the growth of downtown Milwaukee and as a center of civic life," adding that it was "certainly one of the best performing arts centers built in the United States or Canada since the postwar building-for-culture boom began." No single structure said half as much about Milwaukee's cultural coming of age.

The PAC (later the Marcus Center for the Performing Arts) did not bring any new arts groups into existence. The Milwaukee Symphony Orchestra, its anchor tenant, was organized in 1959, after a series of abortive attempts dating back to 1890. The Milwaukee Repertory Theater, another mainstay, had come to life in 1954, when the Fred Miller Theater took over an old movie house on Oakland Avenue near Locust. The amateur ensembles housed at the PAC were even older than the two professional companies. The Bel Canto Chorus was founded as an *a cappella* singing society in 1947 and graduated to oratorios in 1959 under James Keeley's direction. The Florentine Opera began in 1932, when Third Ward residents, most of them Sicilians, formed an Italian opera chorus at a neighborhood social center. Under the ubiquitous John Anello, the Florentine became a highly respected regional company. One more professional troupe joined the fold after the PAC opened: the Milwaukee Ballet Company, which started in 1970 with a corps of seven paid dancers and fifteen college students.

For all these groups, and for others who used the building only occasionally, the Performing Arts Center provided first-class technical facilities, access to a huge regional audience, and the synergy of a shared venue, shared promotion, and sometimes even shared performances. The United Performing Arts Fund, whose first campaign began in 1967, helped just as tangibly by providing a firm financial foundation for the always-struggling arts groups. (One charter UPAF member, the Skylight Comic Opera, maintained its own, highly distinctive performance space on Cathedral Square.) The result of all this activity was growth, both economic and artistic. The Repertory Theater's season ticket sales nearly doubled after the move to the PAC. *Dance Magazine* commented on the Milwaukee Ballet's "remarkable transformation" from "a handful of young dancers [to] a well-directed ensemble of sensitive technicians with serious aspirations," and the *New York Times* called the Milwaukee Symphony "a shiny young example of America's virtuoso orchestra tradition." Milwaukee earned its place on the cultural map in the post-1967 period, and the community has never looked back.

Although the performing arts took center stage, the visual arts were not forgotten. Milwaukee had at least one art collector of national standing: Peg Bradley, whose husband, Harry, headed the Allen-Bradley Company. In a "career" that began in the 1940s, Mrs. Bradley had acquired nearly 600 works by modern artists ranging from Picasso to Kandinsky and from Chagall to Warhol. In 1970 she shocked and delighted her fellow Milwaukeeans by announcing plans to donate the bulk of her collection to the Milwaukee Art Center. The works were valued at $11 million, and Peg Bradley and Allen-Bradley pledged another $1 million in seed money to build an addition to house them. The gift, in other words, was equal in value to the Performing Arts Center. The Bradley Wing, a low-profile addition to the original Saarinen landmark, was dedicated in April, 1975, and the collection it housed marked a quantum leap forward for both the institution and the community. In 1980, reflecting its new place in the aesthetic firmament, the Milwaukee Art Center became the Milwaukee Art Museum.

The cultural renaissance was not limited to art, music, theater, and dance. During the city's heyday as the *Deutsch-Athen* of America, the differences between highbrow activities and more plebeian pursuits were muted; many Germans were equally fond of Bach and bowling, and some beer gardens featured opera and light classics on their concert stages. The same egalitarianism applied after 1967. Milwaukee's achievements in high culture were matched by new developments in popular culture, and Summerfest topped the list. It was an idea whose time had been coming for decades. Dan Hoan viewed Milwaukee's Midsummer Festival, the free lakefront extravaganza that ran from 1933 to 1941, as the prototype for something much larger. In 1939 he expressed hope that the event would become "a national institution," drawing as many visitors as the Mardi Gras in New Orleans and the Kentucky Derby in Louisville. Carl Zeidler seconded the motion, suggesting in his 1940 inaugural address that the event had room to grow in its present location: "With this unequaled facility for a beautiful festival, certainly more use should be made of our lake front." It was Henry Maier who finally brought the idea to fruition.

Early in his tenure, Maier returned from a visit to Munich's Oktoberfest with plans for a "Milwaukee World Festival." The concept became, in the mayor's vision, "a series of subfestivals – jazz, music, art, folk, and so on – grouped into a package with a number of existing tourist events in Milwaukee." Henry Maier confidently predicted attendance of one million and an economic impact of $10 million.

More pressing concerns, including the riot of 1967, delayed implementation of the mayor's plans, but Milwaukee held its inaugural Summerfest in 1968. The event bore almost no resemblance to its more recent incarnations. It consisted, first of all, of literally dozens of smaller events: a folk festival at the Arena, clay-court tennis playoffs at the Town Club, stock car races at State Fair Park, German band concerts in what is now Zeidler Union

Peg Bradley donated a highly regarded collection of modern art to the Milwaukee Art Center. She is shown with Tracy Atkinson, the Center's director, at the dedication of the Bradley Wing in 1975.

Summerfest weathered downpours and uproars in its early years to become America's largest outdoor music festival. The spacious lakefront grounds, shown in 1999, often drew more than 900,000 patrons during the event's eleven-day run.

Square, a seminar on "Women's Progress" at Mount Mary College, a national polka festival, the Miss Milwaukee pageant, and a "Negro musical and cultural show," not to mention parachute-jumping, a midway, and fireworks. Although a portion of the lakefront became a "tent city" for youth-oriented activities, Summerfest '68 had no single center of attention. Bob Hope appeared at County Stadium, Ferrante and Teicher played their twin pianos at South Shore Park, and drum and bugle corps filled the streets of South Milwaukee with joyful noise. The festival's unintended highlight was provided by the Flying Indians of Acapulco, a folkloric troupe who stripped a female cast member to the waist before "sacrificing" her to the rain gods at every show. She was arrested repeatedly, and the resulting publicity pushed ticket sales through the roof. One Summerfest official attempted to dismiss the controversy as "a tempest in a C cup."

402

The festival faced more than its share of growing pains – fickle weather, fiscal shortfalls, tardy performers, and disruptive fans among them. Henry Maier remained the picture of confidence, even taking pen in hand to write the lyrics to the *Summerfest Polka* in 1969:

> *Go to Milwaukee!*
> *How humming a city you'll see.*
> *Sing in Milwaukee!*
>   *Trah, lah, lah, lah, lee.*
> *Prosit Milwaukee!*
>   *Toast gaily and so free.*
> *Milwaukee, Milwaukee, Milwaukee!*
>   *A happy place to be.*

The mayor's sunny outlook was eventually justified. Summerfest's focus began to sharpen after 1970, when the various events were consolidated at the abandoned Nike missile site on the lakefront. Popular music became the festival's theme, and the first stages – wooden platforms perched on concrete blocks – were gradually replaced with permanent facilities, each devoted to a particular type of music: jazz, rock, oldies, country, blues, and a growing list of others. With completion of the Marcus Amphitheater in 1987, some of the largest national acts began to make Summerfest a regular stop on their tours. Local restaurateurs turned the eleven-day festival into a culinary event as well, and beer was consumed in prodigious quantities. With the passage of time, in fact, the Summerfest grounds came to bear more than a passing resemblance to an old-fashioned beer garden. Milwaukee was reclaiming its heritage of *Gemütlichkeit*, and the public response was overwhelming. By 1977, with annual attendance crowding the 700,000 mark, Summerfest claimed to be "the world's largest music festival," and no one took serious exception. Henry Maier, for whom the festival park was named in 1986, put the event in its proper perspective: "Truly, in these days of struggles against blight, prejudice, and poverty, it is a pleasure to have at least one goal which involves joy."

Just as the Performing Arts Center encouraged a wide range of artistic endeavors, the emergence of a full-fledged festival park on the lakefront opened the door to a wide range of civic celebrations. In 1978 a group of Italians from the Third Ward, still grieving the loss of their church and neighborhood to urban renewal, decided to hold a reunion on the Summerfest grounds and invite the general public. The result was Festa Italiana, the first and for

The Summerfest grounds provided an ideal home for ethnic festivals, beginning with Festa Italiana in 1978. The Sunday morning procession has always been one of Festa's emotional highlights.

Milwaukee Journal Sentinel

many years the largest of Milwaukee's lakefront ethnic festivals. The public's response was so enthusiastic that other ethnic groups quickly followed suit. Mexican Fiesta debuted in 1978, followed by German Fest and Irish Fest in 1981, Polish Fest in 1982, African World Festival in 1983, Indian Summer in 1987, Asian Moon in 1994, and Arabian Fest in 1998. (PrideFest, a celebration of gay and lesbian culture, moved to the lakefront in 1995.) The ethnic festivals served up *Gemütlichkeit* in several languages. Each was, in essence, a party that members of one group threw for everyone else and, with nine events to choose from, Milwaukeeans could spend most of their summer weekends absorbing the food, music, and culture of a different ethnic group. The combined attendance at the festivals passed the 400,000 mark in 1984 and exceeded 600,000 in 1995. Those figures, combined with Summerfest attendance, made Maier Festival Park the most-visited

entertainment venue in the metropolitan area, and they underpinned Milwaukee's reputation as the "City of Festivals." The celebrations also worked wonders for several of the ethnic groups. Irish Fest became the largest showcase of Celtic music and culture on the planet, and proceeds from Festa Italiana supported construction of the Italian Community Center just west of the grounds in the old Third Ward. Completed in 1990, the ICC marked, quite literally, a homecoming.

There was a vital connection between the success of the ethnic festivals and the rediscovery of Milwaukee's historic neighborhoods. The same link was apparent in one of the Public Museum's most popular new exhibits: the European Village. Dedicated in 1979, the Village recreated typical homes of the community's major (and some minor) European groups at the time they left the Old World. An older event found new audiences during the same period.

Since its inception in 1944, the Holiday Folk Fair has showcased a staggering variety of cultures, costumes, and cuisines, not to mention folk dance troupes like these Serbian performers.

International Institute of Wisconsin

Attendance at the Holiday Folk Fair, a celebration of diversity launched by the International Institute in 1944, reached the 70,000 mark in the 1970s, making it the largest indoor multi-ethnic festival in the country. What all these attractions had in common was a rediscovered interest in heritage. Milwaukeeans, like most Americans, had spent much of the post-World War II period running away from the past toward a future that proved to be less glamorous than expected. After 1967, the past resumed its rightful place in the context of the present.

Milwaukee made notable progress in one more area of leisure activities: professional athletics. Although it could boast major-league cultural facilities and major-league festivals after 1967, the community was, curiously, one of the few in its size class without a major-league sports team. The Green Bay Packers played half their "home" games at County Stadium, but Milwaukee had no franchise to call its own after the Braves moved to Atlanta in 1965. That deficiency was remedied in 1968, when the expansion Milwaukee Bucks became the newest members of the National Basketball Association. The team finished last in its inaugural season, earning it the right to draft a soft-spoken giant from UCLA named Lew Alcindor. Alcindor, who changed his name to Kareem Abdul-Jabbar after converting to Islam, recalled in his memoirs that the change of address was not particularly welcome. The only cities he knew were New York and Los Angeles, and Milwaukee, he soon discovered, was neither:

Milwaukee was then a quiet, conservative factory town. I felt transplanted into a completely foreign environment. I felt like I was living in a place that was on the edge, the periphery, of everything, and that made me extremely uncomfortable. In the beginning, I wasn't mature enough to handle it. I used to drive ninety miles south to Chicago just to sit in a friend's living room for an hour and a half.

This self-described "city man among farmers" found it difficult to relate to his new fans, but Abdul-Jabbar's adjustment on the basketball floor lacked nothing. The combination of Kareem at center and Oscar Robertson in the backcourt proved virtually unstoppable. The Milwaukee Bucks soared from a 27-55 record in their first season to 66-16 in their third, sweeping the Baltimore Bullets in the playoffs and winning the 1971 NBA championship. It was Milwaukee's first sports title since the Braves won the World Series in 1957.

Memories of the Braves' graceless departure remained an open wound for many local sports fans, one that refused to heal until big-league baseball returned. That day arrived in 1970, when the expansion Seattle Pilots became the Milwaukee

Kareem Abdul-Jabbar, shown in the tender embrace of Wilt Chamberlain, carried the Milwaukee Bucks to an NBA championship in 1971.

Milwaukee Journal Sentinel

405

Milwaukee Journal Sentinel

The balletic grace of shortstop Robin Yount, shown here in the 1982 World Series, was a major reason for the success of "Harvey's Wallbangers."

Brewers. The announcement was made barely a week before opening day, but 7,000 fans flocked to the airport to greet their new team on April 5. Their enthusiasm was obvious, but the community's reaction was notably devoid of hysteria. *Sports Illustrated* (April 27, 1970) observed that "Milwaukee is falling in love quietly this time":

> *To old hands who remembered long lines of snake dancers weaving down Wisconsin Avenue celebrating the arrival of the Braves in 1953, the welcome for the Brewers seemed remarkably subdued, but the reticence seemed to indicate greater sophistication rather than less enthusiasm.*

Bud Selig, who led the effort to land the Brewers, agreed: "There is something of a long-range, healthier feeling.... The town is going to have to grow with the team."

That growth took longer than even Selig could have anticipated. The Brewers were perennial contenders for the cellar in their early years, finishing thirty-two games out of first place in 1971 and thirty-three behind in 1977. The drought finally ended in 1982, when manager Harvey Kuenn took "Harvey's Wallbangers" to the World Series against the St. Louis Cardinals. The fact that the contest involved two beer capitals was not lost on sportswriters, who delighted in reporting the "wicked hops" and "stouthearted performances" that characterized this "Oktoberfest of a World Series." Despite red-hot hitting from Robin Yount and Paul Molitor and solid pitching from Mike Caldwell, the Brewers lost in seven games. The miracle of 1957 was not repeated, but there was jubilation in Milwaukee nonetheless.

New Life at the Center

The various booms of the post-1967 period – athletic, ethnic, and cultural – coincided with a building boom that transformed the face of downtown Milwaukee. Compared with communities of roughly the same size and age, Milwaukee had always had a minor-league skyline – a condition that reflected the regional magnetism of Chicago and the importance of neighborhood "downtowns" like Third Street and Mitchell Street. The city may not have joined the architectural big leagues after 1967, but a renaissance was apparent in the central business district. Developers asserted downtown's place at the heart of the region, and the result was a skyline more commensurate with what might have been expected of a metropolitan area with 1.5 million residents.

The boom did not occur overnight. For several years, the green glass walls of the Marine Bank (finished in 1962) provided the only hint that the modern age had ever touched the heart of downtown. The Performing Arts Center (1969) added new evidence of modernism, and the inverted pyramid of the Mortgage Guaranty Insurance Corporation (1973), on the opposite side of Water Street, made an even bolder statement. Another 1973 building carried downtown development to new heights: the First Wisconsin (later US Bank) Center. It was, in essence, an upright box clad in glass and white aluminum. At forty-two stories (601 feet), the Center wouldn't have turned many heads in Chicago's Loop, but it was easily the tallest building in Wisconsin. Its most arresting interior feature was the forest of towering ficus trees that filled the bank lobby – a horticultural innovation in 1973. Another building of note, or at least

At forty-two stories, the First Wisconsin (later US Bank) Center was easily the state's tallest building when it opened in 1973.

Milwaukee Journal Sentinel

MECCA, Milwaukee's convention center, earned generally low marks for architectural distinction.

Milwaukee Journal Sentinel

notoriety, was completed a year later: the convention hall of the Milwaukee Exposition and Convention Center and Arena. (The facility's acronym, MECCA, was considered blasphemous in some quarters). The center was as plain as a shoebox, with no exterior embellishment and few windows, and it covered a monumental two square blocks at the heart of the city. Critics have generally panned MECCA's main hall as one of the most regrettable buildings of the 1970s.

Anchored by the historic Plankinton Arcade, the Grand Avenue retail mall helped to boost the commercial fortunes of Milwaukee's downtown.

LANG HOMES

Milwaukee Journal Sentinel

Downtown's pace slowed to a crawl in the second half of the decade. Hopelessly out of scale with its neighbors, the First Wisconsin Center was a solitary spike on Milwaukee's horizon for more than ten years. The central business district, in the meantime, showed unmistakable signs of decline. The first-run movie theaters closed, the first vacant storefronts began to appear, and the city's commercial lifeblood seemed to be ebbing away to the suburbs. An otherwise positive 1978 story in the *Boston Globe* described Milwaukee's downtown as "a dreary and underused melange that includes more than its share of Kung-fu movies and adult bookstores."

That picture changed dramatically in the 1980s, which proved to be the Decade of Downtown in urban America. The decade's signature project in Milwaukee was undoubtedly the Grand Avenue retail mall. Determined to bring the city's commercial core back to life, an adventurous group of public officials and private investors made plans for an enclosed mall linking Gimbels, on the Milwaukee River, with Boston Store on Fourth Street – a distance of nearly four blocks. The visual anchor of the project was the Plankinton Arcade. Built by meat-packer John Plankinton's family in 1916, the Arcade was a glass-enclosed galleria in the grand European style. It had been, appropriately enough, Milwaukee's first shopping center, providing room for nearly 130 small stores. A 1916 *Milwaukee Journal* account described it as "a great business home, complete in appointment and thoroughly modern, which gives to the firms housed under one roof all the advantages of individual trade quarters and at the same time the advantages of exchange that come from close proximity." While the Plankinton Arcade was being restored to its original glory as a "great business home," a brand-new galleria went up in the next block west. Its focal point was the Grand Court, an atrium rising three levels to the Speisegarten (German for "garden of eating"), where an array of small restaurants served, predictably, ethnic cuisine. The Grand Avenue mall ultimately housed 160 stores, linked by skywalks, served by adjoining parking structures, and selling everything from shoes to chocolate. The entire ensemble was dedicated with much fanfare in August, 1982 – a few weeks before the Brewers clinched the American League pennant.

For Northwestern Mutual Life, which supplied $30 million of the project's $35 million in private capital, the Grand Avenue mall was an act of civic faith. NML and its fellow investors were pleasantly surprised when the mall opened to a land-office business. It seemed that shoppers couldn't get enough of the Grand Avenue's distinctive old/new character, and they came back to downtown in droves. The *Milwaukee Journal's* annual consumer survey recorded a striking change in a single year: The proportion of metro-area shoppers who had visited downtown in the previous thirty days jumped from 23.6 percent in 1982 to 35 percent in 1983. The central business district was the region's most popular "shopping center" until 1989, when Mayfair regained the lead.

The success of the Grand Avenue, coupled with more generous federal depreciation schedules and historic preservation credits, was the catalyst for nearly $1 billion in downtown construction during the 1980s. Office buildings led the way. The First Wisconsin Center finally got some company on Milwaukee's skyline, including the 100 East Building (549 feet) in 1989, 411 E. Wisconsin

(385 feet) in 1985, and the Northwestern Mutual Data Center (350 feet) in 1990. The 100 East tower, Milwaukee's second-tallest structure, rose from the site of the Pabst Building, Milwaukee's first "skyscraper"; its postmodern design owed more than a little to the lines of its predecessor. Another new landmark was built to house government workers: the Reuss Federal Plaza (1983), finished in a blue so bold that it was dubbed the "Milk of Magnesia building." One more was

Milwaukee Journal Sentinel

The 100 East Building, Wisconsin's second-tallest, rose from the site of Solomon Juneau's trading post in 1989.

Milwaukee Journal Sentinel

The Bradley Center, Milwaukee's major venue for indoor sports, was built by Jane Pettit (right) as a memorial to her father, Harry Bradley.

an outright gift: the Bradley Center (1988), donated by Jane Pettit as a memorial to her father, Harry Bradley. With a distinctive octagonal footprint based on the Allen-Bradley trademark, the Center provided a new home for the Milwaukee Bucks, the Marquette Warriors (later Golden Eagles) basketball team, the Milwaukee Admirals hockey squad, and the Milwaukee Wave indoor soccer team. Other projects rescued (or resurrected) historic spaces that had been given up for dead: the Grain Exchange Room (1983), the Riverside Theater (1984), the Iron Block office building (1984), and the Blatz Brewery apartments (1988). The Grain Exchange was a lavish re-creation of the trading room that had been Milwaukee's nerve center during its years as a world wheat capital.

One of the decade's most unusual projects married culture and commerce. The Milwaukee Repertory Theater was growing restless after a decade in the Performing Arts Center; there was simply not enough room for offices, storage and, above all, scenery and paint shops. After a diligent search, the MRT decided that its ideal new address was literally across the street, in Wisconsin Electric's historic East Wells Power Plant. The Rep's managers began to dream of a new theater in the plant's cavernous interior and, to make the project financially viable, a contributing commercial development on the rest of the property. After years of hard work and happy accidents, that is precisely what happened. Wisconsin Electric closed the plant and donated the riverfront site to the Rep in 1984, and Texas developer Trammell Crow paid the MRT more than $4 million for the northern portion of the parcel. The aptly named Powerhouse Theater made its debut in 1987, and two private developments opened next door in 1988: the twenty-eight-story Milwaukee Center office tower, and the 221-room Wyndham Hotel. These disparate structures were

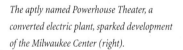

The aptly named Powerhouse Theater, a converted electric plant, sparked development of the Milwaukee Center (right).

New landmarks towered above the old Milwaukee skyline in this 1990 view.

connected by a boldly patterned central rotunda that rose two stories to a skylit dome. The historic Pabst Theater filled the southeast corner of the block, and the PAC stood immediately north. The result was a critical mass, architectural as well as cultural, that brought people downtown and helped make N. Water Street the city's newest nightclub district.

"Critical mass" is an appropriate term for Milwaukee's downtown in the 1980s. A wave of pride and optimism crested over the heart of the city during the decade, reshaping its face and making it a regional destination for work, shopping, culture, and nightlife. There were times, in the Eighties, when a long-time resident who came downtown only once a month would have seen a familiar sight replaced by something new at every visit. Momentum, however, is notoriously difficult to maintain in most endeavors, including real estate development. An oversupply of office space led to ownership

changes in several downtown buildings during the 1990s, and the Grand Avenue mall lost market share to burgeoning suburban centers. The 1997 closing of Marshall Field's, in the original Gimbels building, prompted a new look at the mall's future.

Despite renewed concerns about its long-term viability, the central business district demonstrated impressive resilience at the turn of the twenty-first century. A second wave of development, less spectacular but also less speculative than the first, began to reshape the heart of Milwaukee once again. Several older landmarks underwent major makeovers. The Milwaukee Auditorium was reborn as the elegant Milwaukee Theatre in 2003, the Grand Avenue Mall became the Shops of Grand Avenue in 2004, and the vacant Marshall Field's building filled up with offices, shops, and a boutique hotel. Other projects involved new construction. The Midwest Airlines Center became Milwaukee's latest

Two signature projects from the turn of the twenty-first century added a new dynamism to Milwaukee's landscape. Miller Park, the new home of the Brewers, featured a retractable roof that opened to the stars …

convention facility in 1998, replacing the much-maligned MECCA convention hall. Like several other postmodern buildings in the immediate vicinity, the Center pays stylistic homage to some distinguished forebears, particularly City Hall. The Milwaukee Public Market opened in 2006 as an updated version of the market halls that once supplied local hausfraus with the freshest in meats and produce. Located in the Third Ward, the Public Market became a key destination along the city's new Riverwalk, a waterside promenade that turned a long-neglected resource into a sparkling urban amenity.

The two signature projects of the period, both completed in 2001, were even grander reincarnations of old institutions. The largest addition to Milwaukee's landscape emerged two miles west of downtown: Miller Park, the new home of the Milwaukee Brewers. Rising from the parking lot of the old County Stadium, the ball-

park blends a nostalgic facade with the ultimate in high-tech amenities: a retractable roof. Far less nostalgic but just as kinetic, the bold new addition to the Milwaukee Art Museum earned critical raves for Spanish architect Santiago Calatrava. As much a work of art as an arts facility, the building rests under a large, movable sun-screen that resembles a bird in flight. Just as the adjoining War Memorial Center brought Milwaukee into the architectural modern age in 1957, the wings of Calatrava's bird spread to carry the community into the next millennium.

As the Calatrava addition grew into its unanticipated role as Milwaukee's civic symbol, a neighboring complex reconnected the city with its most important natural resource: Lake Michigan. Pier Wisconsin, completed in 2006, provided a berth for the *Denis Sullivan*, a graceful re-creation of an early Milwaukee lake schooner; a new home for Discovery World, a hands-on science

... while Santiago Calatrava's Art Museum addition spread its wings to a new millennium. The schooner Denis Sullivan *sails serenely by in the background.*

and technology museum; and a variety of freshwater educational exhibits. With the growth of the nearby Betty Brinn Children's Museum, the development of Lakeshore State Park on a seventeen-acre island just offshore, and continuing improvements to the Summerfest grounds, the downtown lakefront came to resemble an enormous cultural theme park.

There was more to come. Milwaukee was one of the few cities in America with ample land to develop at its very core – a situation all the more unusual because much of it was once covered with a freeway. The Park East spur, a mile-long stub completed in 1971, came down by degrees in the early 2000s, opening sixty-four acres on the northern perimeter of downtown to development. A potpourri of projects began to transform both the cleared corridor and the vacant Pabst Brewing complex overlooking its western end. An even greater opportunity materialized on the southern edge of downtown: the Menomonee Valley. Once a wetland of vital importance to the early Indian tribes and then a center of industry just as vital to later white residents, the Valley had lost most of its employers in the economic restructuring of the post-World War II era. Beginning in 1998, a public-private coalition developed plans to reclaim hundreds of acres of vacant land for industry, green space, and a mixture of other uses, including recreation. The Potawatomi Casino drew more than two million visitors every year after a major 2000 expansion, and the Harley-Davidson Museum at the Valley's eastern end promised to become another five-star destination.

With so much happening in the heart of town, it was hardly surprising that people wanted to live there again. A condominium craze gathered momentum in the 1990s, fueled by demand from younger singles and older empty-nesters. The skylines of several central communities – the Third Ward, Yankee Hill, Commerce Street, Walker's Point, and the business district itself – practically bristled with cranes for months at a time. The finished products ranged from converted warehouses overlooking freeways to rapier-like towers overlooking Lake Michigan, but they shared an unmistakable urban sensibility. By 2005, a decade of development had yielded nearly 5,000 new units – hardly sufficient to counterbalance the continuing suburban exodus, but enough to make much of downtown feel like a neighborhood again for the first time in fifty years or more.

Blue-Collar Blues

The complex, even contradictory, nature of the post-1967 period is best captured in three events that took place during 1982: The Grand Avenue mall opened, the Brewers won the American League pennant, and unemployment spiked to its highest level since the Depression. Of all the bad news in this good news/bad news period, the worst was undoubtedly the beating that Milwaukee manufacturers took in the recession of the early 1980s. Tens of thousands of blue-collar families had to scramble to make ends meet, and the community as a whole faced a seismic shift in its economic underpinnings and a disturbing challenge to its historic self-image.

There was no hint of danger in the years before 1967. Ever since the Depression, Milwaukee had been known as a high-skill, high-wage town, where no job was too tough to tackle and few shops were without at least one union. The community was particularly famous for its metal-working industries. Although their products were sold all over the world, Milwaukee's metal-benders formed a chain of production that was impressively local. Kearney & Trecker machine tools installed by Harnischfeger overhead cranes might have produced parts for Allis-Chalmers turbines used to generate electricity that passed through Allen-Bradley or Cutler-Hammer controls to Louis Allis motors equipped with Falk speed-reducers to drive Chain Belt conveyors in the Kearney & Trecker plant. The circle of mutual dependence was reinforced, on the personal level, by intermarriage and interlocking directorates. Allises, Vogels, Pabsts, Strattons, Falks, and Harnischfegers saw each other at family gatherings and board meetings as well as at the city's finest private clubs.

This cozy corporate circle came completely undone after 1967. One agent of its destruction was, ironically, the same high wage rates that had enabled thousands of blue-collar workers to claim their share of the American Dream. Companies with less specialized product lines and stiffer price competition had long found the wage expectations set by the metal-working industries a source of unwelcome pressure. As early as the mid-1930s, Holeproof Hosiery was subcontracting work to Southern textile mills, and two local shoe companies – Weyenberg and Weinbrenner – were moving much of their production to lower-wage communities in rural Wisconsin. The geographic shift accelerated after World War II. As machines did more of the work that had once been the province of human hands, and as price competition intensified, even the metal-benders began to build plants elsewhere, and non-union Sunbelt communities welcomed them with open arms. Dallas, San Diego, San Antonio, Phoenix, and Memphis all passed Milwaukee in population between

Although it was slowly beginning to crumble, heavy industry remained the cornerstone of Milwaukee's economy. Allis-Chalmers workers posed with the crankshaft of a 43,200-horsepower marine diesel engine in 1980.

Milwaukee Journal Sentinel

415

1960 and 1980 – dropping the city from eleventh to sixteenth place in the national rankings – and they did so with substantial help from Northern manufacturers who were moving work to the South and West. By 1970 very few of Milwaukee's old-line manufacturers had all their eggs in the local basket, and many had multiple plants overseas as well as in the Sunbelt.

Some chief executives were particularly eager to decentralize. David Scott, who became the head of Allis-Chalmers in 1968, spoke plainly of his distaste for Milwaukee's labor climate at the company's 1980 annual meeting:

> *We have an enormous investment in West Allis, and good people, but we are completely non-competitive on wage rates. We have a very serious problem with our cost of production in West Allis. You can't make a loaf of bread for a dollar and sell it for eighty cents. We've built a new plant each year for the last ten years somewhere in the world, but not here.... We've either got to get away from the UAW or get out of the business.*

David Scott was an avid decentralizer who led Allis-Chalmers as the company moved from record profits to ruin.

Milwaukee Journal Sentinel

The West Allis complex provided jobs for 11,000 workers in 1965, three years before Scott's arrival. By 1969 Allis-Chalmers' local work force had shrunk to 8,000, and in 1980 it stood at 5,500. Deindustrialization was under way.

The circle of Milwaukee manufacturers was also threatened by its own advancing age. In the 1950s and '60s, some of the community's largest firms entered their second or third generation of family leadership, and the gene pool had not always grown deeper with talent. Even the best-managed family firms fit a predictable profile: conservatively managed, cash-rich, and undervalued in the marketplace. They were, in other words, irresistible acquisition targets. The case of the Falk Corporation was typical. By the early 1960s, ownership of the gear-making giant was spread among dozens of nieces, nephews, cousins, and relatives-by-marriage of founder Herman Falk, and some of them had a fervent desire to liquidate their holdings. In 1961 they forced an initial public stock offering that brought the company some unwanted attention. Suitors began to line up at its door but, rather than waiting passively to be bought, Falk decided to do some buying of its own. The firm asked several New York investment bankers to suggest acquisition candidates, a strategy that backfired. As Harold Falk, Jr., Herman's great-nephew and successor at the helm, recalled, "It turned out that some of these bankers we were dealing with had bigger clients who wanted to acquire *us*." In 1968 the Sundstrand Corporation, an aerospace company based in Rockford, Illinois, made the Falk board an offer it couldn't refuse: a stock exchange worth $78 million. After seventy-six years of independence, the home-grown enterprise became a wholly owned subsidiary.

The Falk transaction was among the first in a wave of mergers and acquisitions that profoundly altered Milwaukee's corporate landscape after 1967. A similar set of circumstances led to the purchase of Miller Brewing by Philip Morris in 1969, and dozens of other deals followed. Two of the largest produced cross-town combinations; in 1970 Rex Chainbelt (chain drives and conveyors) bought Nordberg (diesel engines and mining machinery) to form Rexnord, and in 1978 Johnson Controls (building control systems) acquired Globe-Union (automotive batteries). These local mergers were exceptions to the rule; most purchases were made by firms based in other states or even other countries.

Not all such deals were bad news for the community. Some of the acquirers saved struggling companies from ruin and, in Miller's case, Philip Morris supplied the marketing muscle necessary to make it the second-largest brewer in the country, passing old rival Schlitz. Nonetheless, loss of the power and prestige associated with local ownership – not to mention the profits – was deeply felt. What workers missed most was the personalism of the old regime: a Herman Falk forgiving all employee debts accumulated during the Depression, a Fred Miller working to ensure that his hometown had both major-league baseball and major-league theater. However skilled or well-intentioned, no hired executive could hope to duplicate the emotional investment of someone whose name appeared on every product that went out the door.

By the early 1970s, a process of slow bleeding was apparent. The local manufacturing establishment was losing mass to locations in the Sunbelt and overseas, and it was losing control to out-of-state ownership. Those changes did not signal an end to blue-collar prosperity – not yet, at least. The metropolitan area's industrial output, as measured by value added in manufacture, jumped from $2.98 billion in 1967 to $8.5 billion in 1980 – a 185-percent increase that outpaced, however narrowly, the period's 147-percent inflation rate. Even the 1973-1975 recession did only minimal damage to the local economy. The crisis sparked by the Arab oil embargo led to changes in behavior – the Allen-Bradley clock was left dark for a time – but it did not derail the community's industrial expansion. Mining-equipment specialists, including Bucyrus-Erie and Harnischfeger, even found new business as America tried to squeeze more out of its coal reserves. The 1973-75 downturn may have left other communities reeling, but Milwaukee was, in the *Wall Street Journal's* often-quoted phrase, a "Cold Belt Star."

The recession of the early 1980s was a different animal entirely. It was, to oversimplify, the product of a chain reaction: Interest rates rose to record highs, which encouraged foreign investment in the United States, which created an unusually strong dollar. That combination of events acted like a highly selective virus, one that devastated America's manufacturing sector but left other areas of the economy largely intact. High interest rates made it more expensive to produce goods, while the strong dollar crippled export sales and opened the door to a flood of relatively inexpensive foreign products. American manufacturers had to charge more, in other words, while their global

The last tractor rolled off the Allis-Chalmers assembly line (top) in December, 1985, and the factory buildings on Greenfield Avenue came down less than a year later.

and International Harvester sold more tractors, General Electric and Westinghouse were miles ahead in electrical machinery, and Caterpillar was dominant in construction equipment. The company relied on volume and diversity for its success, a strategy that worked for generations. By 1980 annual sales had risen to a peak of $2 billion, and profits approached $50 million. That banner year proved to be the last that Allis-Chalmers would spend in the black. A gathering depression in American agriculture dampened the demand for tractors, and a pall soon settled over the company's other markets. Allis-Chalmers lost $28.8 million in 1981, $207 million in 1982 (a state record at the time), and $261 million in 1984. Management tried everything to stop the bleeding: closing plants, laying off workers, selling divisions, even razing part of the West Allis complex for a shopping center in 1985. Nothing worked. The price of Allis-Chalmers stock sagged from $38.625 a share in 1979 to $3.125 in 1985, and the company was so broke that it dumped its entire pension plan in the lap of the federal government. Local employment, in the meantime, dipped to fewer than 500 people. Bowing to the inevitable, Allis-Chalmers filed for bankruptcy on June 29, 1987. Its most valuable surviving "asset" was more than $300 million in tax-loss carry-forwards.

Allis-Chalmers was a conspicuous fatality, but virtually every major manufacturer was ravaged by the same economic cancer. Falk's employment dropped from 3,412 to 1,975 during 1982. The work force in the Ladish forge shop in Cudahy fell from 4,850 in 1981 to 2,300 in 1985. Harnischfeger's payroll plummeted from 8,000 people in 1979 to 3,800 in 1982. The story was the same everywhere, and its cumulative ending

competitors were charging less. The inevitable result was a steep decline in the market for American capital goods.

As Milwaukee's largest capital-goods manufacturer, Allis-Chalmers was hit particularly hard. Otto Falk, who headed the firm from 1912 to 1940, once observed that A-C was "a sleeping giant," a company that manufactured 1,600 different products and led the field in none of them. John Deere

was a staggering loss of jobs. Manufacturing employment in the four-county area sank from 220,200 in 1979 (its all-time high) to 164,200 in 1983 – a drop of 56,000 workers. That was more jobs, in absolute numbers, than Milwaukee lost during the Depression. As the unemployment rate reached 13.3 percent in the autumn of 1982, thousands of local families felt the crisis personally.

The community soon began to lose real economic size. In 1980, eleven Milwaukee firms were listed on the Fortune 500: Allis-Chalmers, Clark Oil, Johnson Controls, Rexnord, Schlitz, A.O. Smith, Pabst, Briggs & Stratton, Harnischfeger, Bucyrus-Erie, and Koehring. By 1989 the Milwaukee contingent had shrunk to six. Johnson Controls, Harnischfeger, A.O. Smith, and Briggs & Stratton held their positions, and Harley-Davidson and Universal Foods were added to the list. The other 1980 powerhouses had been wiped out, sold, or dramatically reduced in scale.

The recession of the 1980s nearly leveled Milwaukee's largest manufacturers, but hard times also hit a smaller industry that was virtually synonymous with the city: brewing. Although Miller prospered under Philip Morris, particularly after the 1975 introduction of Lite beer, the firm's hometown counterparts were not so fortunate. Schlitz shortened and cheapened its brewing process in the 1970s, producing a beverage that few self-respecting Milwaukeeans could bring themselves to drink; the company's share of the local bottled-beer market shrank from 18 percent in 1970 to 4 percent in 1978. The unexpected death of Robert Uihlein, Jr. in 1976 created leadership problems, and a 1981 strike caused a "temporary" shutdown of the brewery. The end came in 1982, when Stroh's, a much

Miller Brewing posted record earnings after Philip Morris purchased the company in 1969, but it was destined to become the last of Milwaukee's major brewers.

Milwaukee Journal Sentinel

smaller brewer based in Detroit, purchased the shrinking giant and closed its plant. Stroh's sold the Schlitz complex to a group of local investors who eventually turned it into an office park. Pabst was another "troubled" Milwaukee brewery, operating without a clear sense of direction until 1985, when it was acquired by a California investor. The new owner's directions were clear enough: Cut costs, defer capital investment, and rely on past momentum to generate profits. The result was a steady decline in sales that led to the closing of Pabst's Milwaukee plant in 1996. The demise of two local icons was felt more psychologically than economically; beer, after all, had not been the city's most important product since 1890. It was, however, Milwaukee's best-known consumer product, and the departure of Schlitz and Pabst was widely viewed as a fall from grace.

The economic dislocations of the 1980s created a mood of general uncertainty, to say the least. Industry had been Milwaukee's bedrock for more than a century, and now local residents could feel the earth shifting beneath their feet. The most common reaction was stunned disbelief. Generations of Milwaukeeans had grown up with the expectation that they could finish high school, enter an apprenticeship program, and work for one employer until retirement. That expectation vanished utterly. As the number of metro-area workers engaged in manufacturing shrank from 40.5 percent of the total in 1960 to 24.1 percent in 1990, the number of job openings shrank accordingly, and not one held the promise of lifetime tenure.

When the implications of the change sank in, Milwaukee was gripped by what might be described as a collective midlife crisis. Divorced from its past but uncertain of its future, trusting in neither its accumulated skills nor its long-term prospects, the community engaged in a great deal of anxious soul-searching. "Who are we now?," asked the community's leaders, and issues of image and identity came to the fore. In 1984 the Convention Bureau sought suggestions for a new community slogan, finally embracing "A Great Place on a Great Lake." (Among the rejected proposals: "Come Up By Us Once, Hey.") More than half the respondents to a 1989 survey believed that Milwaukee needed a new image, something that went beyond bratwurst, beer, and bowling. There was a growing consensus that suds and sausage no longer represented the urban reality, that Brew City had lost some of its head.

Schlitz Brewing fell victim to problems involving labor, leadership, and product quality. The end came in 1982.

Milwaukee Journal Sentinel

Whether it seemed poignant or faintly silly, Milwaukee's civic navel-gazing was the merest diversion in comparison with the real-world adjustments forced on local families. Breadwinners who lost high-paying factory jobs found it virtually impossible to locate comparable employment. A 1988 study by Sammis White of UWM reported that the ten fastest-shrinking manufacturing industries paid wages averaging $30,552 a year, while the ten fastest-growing service industries paid $16,225. Machinists in the old Allis-Chalmers plant earned at least $11.60 an hour; clerks in the shopping center that replaced much of that plant in 1987 earned $5.23. In the straitened circumstances of the 1980s, blue-collar workers faced some stark choices: retire, retrain, or put in more hours to maintain the same standard of living. Many took second jobs, and most households discovered

that two incomes were absolutely necessary. Although women had already entered the work force in droves, economic pressures gave their movement additional momentum. The number of metro-area females over sixteen who were gainfully employed rose from 45.9 percent of the total in 1970 to 60.3 percent in 1990. Even more telling was the participation rate of women with children under six, which soared from 28.9 percent in 1970 to 46 percent in 1980 and 62.4 percent in 1990. The stay-at-home mom, once an American institution, was becoming an endangered species.

The economic upheaval of the 1980s made life harder for thousands of Milwaukee families, but there is no doubt that the burden fell most heavily on residents of the inner city, particularly African Americans. In the years following World War II, blacks had made significant inroads in local

In 1983, with industrial jobs evaporating by the day, nearly 20,000 people showed up at State Fair Park to apply for a mere 200 openings at the A.O. Smith Corporation.

Milwaukee Journal Sentinel

Thousands of African Americans found high-paying industrial jobs in the 1960s and '70s, only to lose them in the recession of the 1980s.

industry, finding work as machinists and welders as well as foundry hands. In 1980, 49.7 percent of Milwaukee's employed black males were engaged in manufacturing, compared with 40.9 percent of all male workers. Many African Americans, in other words, had finally found family-supporting jobs, but they had found them in the most rapidly declining sector of the economy. When the ax began to fall in the 1980s,

blacks bore a disproportionate share of the cuts; deindustrialization reversed what had been a heartening development. To make matters worse, the jobs that vanished in the recession were overwhelmingly urban. Between 1979 and 1987, according to another UWM study, the city of Milwaukee suffered a net loss of 28,386 jobs, most of them in manufacturing, while the suburbs posted a net gain of 33,672. "In short," concluded principal author Sammis White, "job generation is basically a suburban phenomenon." For urban workers without cars who faced a trek to areas without convenient public transportation, many of the new jobs might as well have been in Idaho.

As old jobs disappeared and new ones moved beyond easy reach, parts of the inner city came perilously close to collapse. Milwaukee's black unemployment rate approached 26 percent in 1986, more than triple the metropolitan figure, and the proportion of African Americans living in poverty climbed from 28.4 percent in 1980 to an astounding 41.9 percent in 1990. The mid-decade arrival of crack cocaine, relatively cheap and highly addictive, offered the worst possible diversion at the worst possible time; between 1984 and 1990, drug-related shootings fueled a 253-percent increase in Milwaukee's homicide rate. Although the community did not self-destruct – thousands of lives continued to go well – many African Americans had less and less in common with other groups in the metropolis. In Marc Levine's 1998 study of fourteen Frostbelt cities, Milwaukee had the unhappy distinction of leading the field in black poverty, and the community trailed only Detroit and Cleveland in the disparity between city and suburban income.

Although the Milwaukee story was becoming a tale of two cities, the worst of times finally seemed to pass. Metropolitan employment began to grow again in 1984 – nearly two years after economists had declared the recession officially over. Manufacturing rebounded modestly from the trough of 1983, but no one predicted another boom. A pair of relatively mild recessions, in fact – the first in 1990-1991, the second in 2001 – ravaged the manufacturing sector once again, helping to bring down some storied names in Milwaukee industry. Evinrude, Louis Allis, Nordberg, Harnischfeger (in its original form), and Pelton Casteel all ceased production, but the highest-profile fatality was the A.O. Smith complex, once the largest producer of automobile frames in the world. In 1997, after American carmakers had abandoned steel frames for less costly (and less reliable) unibody construction, A.O. Smith sold its frame business to Tower Automotive, a Michigan-based conglomerate. Unable to recover lost momentum, Tower cut wages, laid off workers, and finally closed the sprawling Milwaukee facility in 2006. A plant that had once employed 9,000 people – many of them African Americans – became a 140-acre ghost town. Manufacturing employment, in the meantime, plunged from 56.9 percent of the Milwaukee area's work force in 1951 to 15.4 percent in 2007. For local workers, the evidence was overwhelming: A strong back and a willing attitude were no longer enough to secure a foothold in American industry. As family-supporting jobs dried up, neighborhoods that had long depended on factory wages stood in bleak contrast to the bright new developments downtown.

The local experience was shaped increasingly by global forces. It was no longer the lower-wage locales of rural Wisconsin, the Sunbelt states, or even the Mexican border that gave Milwaukee industry its stiffest competition; the entire world was open for business. Manufacturers could make their products virtually anywhere, and China, aggressively reshaping its economy to become "the factory floor of the world," exerted an almost-irresistible pull. European peasants had once bettered themselves by taking industrial jobs in America. In the twenty-first century, their Chinese counterparts advanced by taking industrial jobs *from* America, often with the help of American capital. Earning less in one month than a skilled Milwaukee machinist could make in a single day, Chinese workers were unbeatable on the basis of cost; even the venerable Nesco roaster, a Milwaukee mainstay for decades, moved to the far side of the Pacific. The depth of America's deindustrialization is evident in one telling statistic: In 2007, even though the proportion of its work force engaged in manufacturing had dwindled to 15.4 percent, Milwaukee still had the second-highest concentration of industrial workers in the country, trailing only San Jose.

However diminished, manufacturing remained an integral part of Milwaukee's economy, and there was always, despite the deluge of bad news, a countercurrent of success stories. Harley-Davidson, one of the city's most venerable metal-benders, roared ahead as demand for "Milwaukee Iron" soared to new heights; company-sponsored reunions were practically pilgrimages for the legions of devout Harley riders. Johnson Controls broadened its focus from building controls to automotive batteries and car seats, becoming Milwaukee's only Fortune 100 company. Allen-Bradley, purchased by Rockwell International in 1985, traded the click-clack of electromechanical devices for the hum of computers, rising to a position of global leadership in factory automation equipment. None of the firms that survived the sea change of the late 1900s did so by pursuing business as usual; virtually all downsized, outsourced, re-engineered, automated, or adopted "quality" programs. The result of all these buzzwords was a healthier bottom line, but not necessarily expanded employment; even as Allen-Bradley (Rockwell Automation) sold more equipment, its shop force on S. Second Street shrank from 5,500 in 1980 to 1,850 in 1990 and barely 300 in 2008. Nor did blue-collar paychecks show much growth. After 1980, in fact, the average hourly wage for all Milwaukee-area production workers grew at substantially less than the rate of inflation.

Milwaukee's modern economy eventually reached a state of what might be termed ambiguous prosperity. Employment rates generally exceeded the national average, as losses on the industrial side were more than balanced by gains in the service sector – a category elastic enough to cover tax attorneys, teachers, telemarketers, and X-ray technicians as well as teenaged burger-flippers. The number of service jobs in the Milwaukee area exceeded manufacturing employment for the first time in 1986, and the balance continued to shift inexorably away from blue-collar work. Areas of specific growth included temporary help agencies (Milwaukee-based Manpower is the world's largest "employer"), health care (led by the giant Aurora), and eating and drinking establishments. Northwestern Mutual, with more than $1 trillion of life insurance in force, made Milwaukee an insurance center by its very presence. Younger companies like Quad/Graphics (printing) and GE Mar-

As other manufacturers fell by the wayside, Harley-Davidson roared to new heights of prosperity. Its 2003 centennial celebration drew 250,000 loyal riders to the birthplace of "Milwaukee Iron."

Milwaukee Journal Sentinel

quette Medical Systems (imaging equipment) rose to national leadership in their fields. Fiserv and Metavante turned Milwaukee into a world capital of data processing for banks, and the community showed surprising strength as a headquarters for everything from department store chains (Kohl's) to mortgage insurance (MGIC). What this motley group of enterprises had in common was an emphasis on knowledge rather than physical strength, on information rather than mechanical ability. The implications for workers with an older, less informed understanding of the workplace were chilling.

Urban geographers observe a useful distinction between two types of economic activity: city-forming and city-serving. The first brings new money into the community from outside, while the second simply circulates the dollars already there. Manufacturing, tourism, and wholesale trade are examples of city-forming activities; health care, education, and retail trade generally fall into the city-serving category. When a Home Depot replaces the Caterpillar factory or Aurora takes over the Heil plant, the local economy has moved by degrees from city-forming to city-serving. It was manufacturing, specifically capital-goods manufacturing, that "made" Milwaukee in its modern form. The dollars that customers from around the world paid for turbines and tractors, cranes and controls became the economic lifeblood of the community. As manufacturing loses its dominant role, what activities will make the Milwaukee of the twenty-first century? The answer is unknown and probably unknowable, but there is little doubt that the economic dislocations of the late 1900s will be remembered as the fulcrum on which Milwaukee turned from past to future.

Milwaukee Journal Sentinel

Milwaukee Journal Sentinel

Newer companies rode high technology to positions of leadership in their industries. The success stories included Quad/Graphics (left) and GE Marquette Medical Systems (right).

The Politics of Change

Change in the outside world generally produces change in local government; periods of volatility often prompt voters to try new leaders and leaders to try new ideas. Given the sweeping changes of the post-1967 period, both economic and social, it might seem logical to assume that there was frequent turnover in Milwaukee's political leadership and constant turmoil on the policy level. Just the opposite was true. Under Henry Maier, the city's virtual mayor-for-life, Milwaukee was an oasis of political stability in urban America. Maier's twenty-eight-year tenure, stretching from 1960 to 1988, was the longest of any big-city mayor's in the twentieth century, and it was not until he left the scene that there were perceptible signs of change in municipal governance.

Henry Maier will forever remain an enigmatic figure in Milwaukee's political history. He was creative and contentious by turns, a cool theoretician but notoriously thin-skinned, deeply committed to his city but just as demanding of personal loyalty. Maier was capable of both measured statesmanship and petty petulance, sometimes on the same issue, and he was as famous for his feuds as for his command of the local bureaucracy. There were some notable high points in his administration of the city's affairs. Maier was the father of Summerfest. He oversaw a systematic reorganization of city government, without jeopardizing the tradition of honesty, efficiency, and municipal solvency he had inherited from Socialists Dan Hoan and Frank Zeidler. Maier took a pro-active approach to industrial development and, despite a generally combative relationship with neighborhood groups, used the city's clout to advance redevelopment projects both downtown and in outlying sections of Milwaukee.

Mayor Maier was also a figure of national standing. As president of the National League of Cities (1964-1965) and the U.S. Conference of Mayors (1971-1972), he was a tireless spokesman for urban interests, demanding "a reordering of national priorities" to stem the decline of America's central cities. Maier found a friend in Lyndon Johnson and a philosophical home in the president's Great Society. As a field lieutenant in Johnson's War on Poverty, the mayor became a past master at bringing federal dollars home to his community. Although some critics blasted his "tin cup" approach, Maier was unapologetic; he once bragged that he "carted a washtub, not a tin cup, to get some of Milwaukee's money back from Washington." The mayor continued to beat the drum for government aid long after federal priorities had shifted elsewhere.

There was no shortage of substance in Maier's approach to municipal affairs, but matters of style attracted considerably more attention. There was an operatic quality to his administration. Where ordinary bureaucrats might have been content with policy directives and position papers, the mayor wrapped his favorite initiatives in rhetorical grandiloquence. Maier's campaign for expanded state and federal aid became the "Great City Crusade for Resources." His industrial development program was dubbed "Operation Bootstrap," and his proposals for the inner city constituted a "Little Marshall Plan." The mayor was a tireless proponent of the "Milwaukee Idea," which he defined, not very helpfully, as the "coming together of various segments of the community to work for a common cause." Maier's fondness for the grand gesture and the rhetorical flourish was most apparent in his response to the economic shifts of the 1980s. As manufacturing faded and brewing declined, he was determined to keep his community on the map. "We need a unique, striking symbol for the city," Maier told the Common Council in 1987. "Whatever it is, it must be a giant." The mayor had something as memorable as the Eiffel Tower or the Golden Gate Bridge in mind, but most suggestions fell somewhat short of the mark: an immense badger, a solar-heated geodesic dome over the city, and a towering statue of Maier himself holding a beer and a brat. The mayor favored a 600-foot fountain on the lakefront as "a symbol of this city's vibrancy and its abundance of fresh water." His second choice was a panoply of huge, colorful pennants flying from Milwaukee's tallest buildings during the summer months, all bearing letters that stood for presumed local virtues, including "O" for opportunity, "P" for productivity, and "C" for cleanliness. Maier opined that the pennants would lend his city "the aura of Camelot." The fountain was a statement of civic virility whose time had not yet come, but the mayor's flags, minus their symbolic letters, flew over downtown Milwaukee until the early twenty-first century.

Henry Maier's flair for the dramatic extended to his treatment of enemies. The mayor was a relentless suburb-basher, and Milwaukee's relations with its neighbors sank to a new low during his tenure. Despite evidence that demographic trends and economic shifts played the larger role, Maier blamed the collapse of his city's inner core on the "iron ring" of "lily-white suburbs" whose residents wanted Milwaukee water and Milwaukee jobs "but not our housing problems, not the problems of our poor." Blaming the suburbs tended to absolve the

Milwaukee Journal Sentinel

city of responsibility for the inner core's distress. Although he fought for Milwaukee's fair share of anti-poverty funds, Maier studiously avoided dealing with the larger issues of prejudice and inequality; the city's racial sores continued to fester with only the most cursory official attention.

Maier might have damned the suburbs to perdition, but the hottest place in his personal hell was reserved for the *Milwaukee Journal*. Convinced early in his tenure that the newspaper wanted to "preside as mayor without being elected," Maier maintained perhaps the longest-running media feud in American municipal history. Most big-city mayors have had difficult relationships with the local press at one time or another, but relatively few threatened antitrust action or filed complaints

Henry Maier was the combative chief executive who served as Milwaukee's mayor from 1960 to 1988 — a record that may never be broken.

Mayor Maier struck an imperial pose during a 1982 parade marking the opening of the Grand Avenue mall.

with the Federal Communications Commission. Fewer still refused to answer questions from reporters for one news organization, as Maier did with the *Journal* in the 1970s, and it is doubtful that anyone blamed a newspaper for fomenting racial strife. In his 1993 political autobiography, *The Mayor Who Made Milwaukee Famous,* Maier commented on Father Groppi's open-housing marches in a passage that combines some of his favorite themes:

> As for Groppi and the Journal, I believe both were guilty of spiritual violence at a time when the city needed peace after the civil disorders. Groppi was the newspaper's tool to avert calling upon the suburbs for any significant effort to ameliorate central city problems in the aftermath of the riots. The newspaper took refuge behind Groppi's central-city-only housing marches.

Maier never resolved his differences with the *Journal* and its affiliates. "His anger has seemed bottomless," wrote editor Sig Gissler in 1988, and the mayor carried it with him into retirement. Nearly 60 percent of the pages in his 1993 memoirs contain some reference to his one-sided war with the local media.

For most of his constituents, Maier's feud with the *Milwaukee Journal* was little more than a sideshow, entertaining to some and intensely embarrassing to others. What voters liked about Maier, and the reason they kept re-electing him by wide margins for more than a quarter-century, was his enormous affinity for the status quo. In a time of pervasive change, Henry Maier represented a firm hand on the tiller; whatever his personal foibles, voters trusted him to keep their city on an even keel. Maier was an efficient administrator, a scrapper in the Dan Hoan tradition, and anything but a revolutionary. Although he amassed huge reserves of political capital, the mayor's reluctance to use it, particularly in support of social initiatives, was legendary. The Milwaukee he spoke for was becoming an anachronism as his term wore on, but as long as Henry Maier was in office, voters could afford the perception that nothing of real import had changed.

For those who governed Milwaukee County, such stability was neither possible nor especially desirable. John Doyne, who became the first county executive in 1960, relished his role as a trailblazer. Doyne's aim was to create "a dynamic and responsive organization out of a heterogeneous collection of unrelated departmental units," and he made substantial progress toward that goal, through the force of his own personality as well as his canny use of budget and veto powers. Bill O'Donnell, who followed Doyne in 1976, was somewhat less assertive, but he advanced the cause of modernization, particularly after Wisconsin's legislature gave him the power to hire and fire department heads in 1977.

Both of these proud Milwaukee Irishmen governed during a time of unusual volatility. Milwaukee County was legally responsible for public medical care and public welfare programs, and costs for both services skyrocketed as the problems of low-income residents multiplied. Health and welfare spending, which generally accounted for at least half the county's budget, soared from $68.5 million in 1967 to $364.6 million in 1980 and $637.3 million in 1995 – rising at more than twice the rate of inflation. The County Institutions in suburban Wauwatosa became a "service center" of daunting complexity, and there was a related rise in spending for courts and correctional facilities. At the same time, voters endorsed the county's continuing expansion into other spheres of activity. In 1975, with major help from the federal government, Milwaukee County took over the ailing private bus system, and in 1977, after surveys showed that fewer than half its patrons were city residents, the city-owned Public Museum became a county facility.

With these and other additions, Milwaukee County cemented its identity as a sort of super-agency whose role was to provide county residents with an array of vital but unrelated services and amenities, including parks, welfare, courts, medical care, the airport, expressways, the zoo, mass transit, and the museum. The city of Milwaukee and its eighteen suburbs were by nature more organic; each constituted "home" for its residents. Defined by its functions rather than geographic borders, Milwaukee County's

John Doyne, Milwaukee's first county executive, was an aggressive but savvy leader who set the parameters of the office for all who have followed.

Milwaukee Journal Sentinel

Bill O'Donnell, who succeeded Doyne in 1976, continued the trend toward modernization in county government.

Milwaukee Journal Sentinel

government lacked such coherence, but it was definitely big business. In 1988 the county budget totaled nearly $732 million, exceeding, for the first time in its modern form, the city of Milwaukee's planned expenditures. Five years later, the County Board adopted its first billion-dollar budget.

On both the city and county levels, and later than some observers might have predicted, Milwaukee's political guard finally changed. The turning point came in 1987, when Henry Maier, nearing the age of seventy, decided that twenty-eight years in office was long enough. "I did the best I could with the job," he told the *New York Times*, "and now it's time to go." A number of hopefuls lined up to replace him, but the field soon narrowed to two prominent Democrats: Martin Schreiber and John Norquist. Schreiber was a high-profile product of Milwaukee's mainstream, a North Side German Lutheran whose father had spent thirty-two years on the Common Council, including twelve as its president.

The County Institutions, already Milwaukee's largest health and social services complex, grew to mammoth proportions after 1967.

The younger Schreiber had pursued a career in state government, serving in the Wisconsin Senate and then as lieutenant governor under Patrick Lucey. In 1977, when Lucey was named ambassador to Mexico, Schreiber stepped into the state's top job for eighteen months. John Olof Norquist, by contrast, was a relative outsider: a Swedish Presbyterian born in Princeton, New Jersey, and raised in a succession of Midwestern towns where his father had followed his calling as a Presbyterian minister. The younger Norquist was eighteen when his father took charge of a small congregation on Milwaukee's near South Side. He graduated from UW-Madison in 1971, one year after anti-war activists shut down the campus, and soon launched his own career in state government, winning election to the Assembly in 1974 and the Senate in 1982. Although he was only ten years younger than his rival, Norquist represented a new generation.

The 1988 county executive's race was strikingly similar to the mayoral match-up. William O'Donnell, the three-term incumbent, was tradition personified: sixty-six years old, a County Board member since 1948, and the ultimate stay-at-home Milwaukeean. Responding to a pre-election newspaper questionnaire, O'Donnell stated, without a hint of affectation, that his favorite vacation spot was his front porch and his favorite restaurant was his wife's kitchen. The challenger was David Schulz, a Milwaukee native who had served as Chicago's budget director in the groundbreaking administration of Mayor Harold Washington. Schulz came home in 1984 to work for O'Donnell, first as the county's budget director and then as head of the park system, which he promoted with considerable flair. Schulz briefly considered making his own run for the mayor's seat, but ultimately threw his support to Norquist. Bill O'Donnell promptly fired him, charging that his activism would politicize the parks, and Schulz just as promptly declared his intention to run for his boss's job. Bright, flamboyant, and endlessly articulate, Dave Schulz proved to be a formidable opponent.

The 1988 election was widely viewed as a referendum on change. Despite some notable bright spots, Milwaukee had been through the wringer in the previous decade; layoffs, plant closings, and rising poverty rates were all depressingly familiar news stories. The four candidates gave voters a clear choice. Norquist and Schulz positioned themselves as the more dynamic contenders, independent spirits who weren't afraid, in Norquist's words, "to shake things up a little bit." Although they were hardly running mates, the two were frequently paired in the popular imagination. Born within a month of each other in 1949, they were the first representatives of the baby-boom generation to run for Milwaukee's highest offices, and their physical characteristics were certainly striking. Norquist, at six feet seven inches, may have been the tallest candidate for any office in Milwaukee's history, and Schulz, at 375 pounds, was probably the heaviest, out-weighing even genial George Walker. Schreiber and O'Donnell were the more traditional choices, physically as well as philosophically. Both were men of middle height, middle weight, and moderate views – steady, experienced leaders who could be counted on to preserve the status quo. When the votes were counted, change had won in a walk. Schulz handed O'Donnell a two-to-

one drubbing, and Norquist beat Schreiber by a 55-to-45 margin. At his victory party, Dave Schulz recalled that he had hoped to "ignite a new spirit" in his campaign for county executive. "Tonight," he exulted, "we celebrate that this new spirit burns blindingly bright." Bill O'Donnell spoke more bluntly: "I guess we just couldn't buck the change."

The election of 1988 marked a watershed in Milwaukee's political history. The mayoral contest (top) pitted Martin Schreiber (with chart) against John Norquist, and the county executive's race was fought between David Schulz (standing) and Bill O'Donnell.

Milwaukee Journal Sentinel

Milwaukee Journal Sentinel

Change was the clear victor in 1988. Representing a new generation, John Norquist and Dave Schulz promised a fresh approach to municipal government.

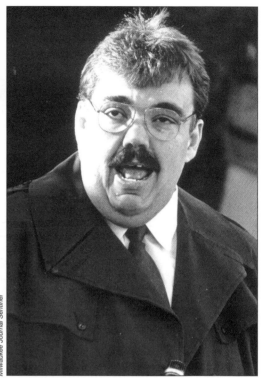

Milwaukee Journal Sentinel

The pair's physical characteristics inspired a memorable cartoon from the Milwaukee Sentinel's *Stuart Carlson. Schulz's honeymoon proved to be brief.*

THE HONEYMOONERS

Although 1988 was a watershed year in Milwaukee's political history, Schulz's bright light proved to be a flash in the pan. Unaccustomed to the demands of elective office and unable to get along with the county supervisors, he stepped down after a single unremarkable term. His successor, Thomas Ament, seemed to mark a return to tradition. A courthouse veteran with twenty-four years of service on the County Board and sixteen as its chairman, Ament was also a member of the mythical (but still powerful) "3M Club," a cadre of Milwaukee leaders who had graduated from Marquette High School, Marquette University, and Marquette Law School. Tom Ament's ten years in office were a transitional period for county government. As voter impatience with rising taxes grew more and more pronounced, Milwaukee County was gripped by the same zeal for economy that was transforming corporate Milwaukee. What that meant in practice was "privatizing." The Milwaukee Brewers assumed responsibility for the old County Stadium in early 1992. A few months later, the county turned over operation of its Public Museum to a private board, retaining title to the collections and providing a base of financial support. An even larger step was taken in 1995, when Milwaukee County sold Doyne Hospital to its privately funded neighbor, Froedtert Memorial. The county got out of the hospital business entirely, contracting instead with private facilities to provide health care for its low-income residents. Although the sale of Doyne caused an overnight drop of 20 percent in the county budget, pressures still mounted in other areas, particularly social services and criminal justice. As the fiscal balancing act continued, spending for quality-of-life resources like Milwaukee's beloved park system declined sharply.

On the city level, John Norquist continued Milwaukee's penchant for long mayoral terms, presiding over City Hall for nearly sixteen years. Although he came of age during the leftward swing of the late 1960s, anyone who expected the new mayor to lead Milwaukee back to the days of municipal Socialism was sorely disappointed. As his tenure lengthened, Norquist developed an ever-firmer belief in "the magic of the marketplace." Cities, in his view, were highly efficient, highly organic centers for the creation of wealth, and it was government's job to remove all but the most essential impediments to the free markets that create that wealth. Norquist singled out two obstacles for particular attention: crime and taxes. As spending for public safety rose every year,

Milwaukee Journal Sentinel

Thomas Ament, who became county executive in 1992, presided during a time of extreme volatility in county government. His decade-long tenure ended in an uproar over pension benefits in 2002.

Milwaukee boasted one of the highest proportions of police officers per capita in the country, but the Police Department was virtually the only unit of city government exempt from downsizing. John Norquist was evangelical, even obsessive, in his desire to keep municipal spending within the rate of inflation, and his administration, with Common Council approval, actually reduced the city's tax rate every year for a full decade. Milwaukee's rate dropped from first place among metro-area municipalities in 1983 to fifth in 1994 and thirteenth in 1995. Although he was less than adept at the ceremonial small talk typically associated with his post, Norquist could speak with genuine passion about cross-training forestry workers for greater efficiency or forcing city departments to compete with private vendors who provided the same services.

433

There were definite limits on how far Norquist could go in his attempts to restructure the city – a lesson brought home forcefully by a comparison of his neoliberal leanings with Henry Maier's passionate pragmatism. Maier repeatedly accused the federal government of gross neglect in its treatment of the nation's central cities, and he described his attempts to shake the federal money tree as a matter of simple justice. In John Norquist's view, federal funding for freeways, public housing, and public welfare amounted to a frontal assault on America's cities, and he took a decidedly dim view of federal aid in any form, dismissing it as destructive interference. "You can't build a city on pity," he wrote. The mayors' viewpoints could hardly have been more divergent, and yet neither was able to halt suburban flight, reverse the concentration of poverty in the central city, or create a basic level of family-supporting jobs. Governing a city in the modern era came to resemble steering a canoe through nonstop rapids: Speed and direction could be altered meaningfully, but the boat's ultimate course was set by forces far more powerful than the people holding the paddles.

John Norquist had a much more tangible impact on the city's physical landscape. A tireless exponent of the "new urbanism," he insisted that all projects within the city's control (and some that were not) flow from plans that evoked the spirit of an older America: sensitive to the human scale and friendly to pedestrians. In *The Wealth of Cities*, his 1998 book on urban life, Norquist described his backward-looking approach as aesthetic pragmatism: "People realize, on some level, that traditional forms work. And that's what's important for cities – not hailing back to some amber-hued days of a nostalgic past, but resurrecting what works." The mayor took the lead on several high-profile projects, including the downtown Riverwalk, removal of the Park East freeway spur, redevelopment of the Menomonee Valley, and the rows of condos on Commerce Street. Norquist made a visible difference in the look and feel of his adopted hometown, and his passion for urban design may prove to be his most enduring legacy.

John Norquist, Tom Ament, and the governments they led were, to all appearances, rooted in the very substance of Milwaukee: stable, more frugal than flashy, and deeply concerned with making things work. Scandal was the last thing anyone saw on the horizon. Then, in a period of barely two years, the wheels seemed to fall off the bus. In December, 2000, John Norquist admitted a "consensual sexual relationship" with a female staff member. The disclosure, if not the behavior, was a Milwaukee first. In the early weeks of 2002, public outrage at a stunningly generous Milwaukee County pension plan began to boil over. In October, 2002, a Milwaukee alderman was indicted for misuse of federal funds – the first of three Common Council members who would ultimately go to prison. Days later, two Wisconsin legislative leaders were charged with putting state employees to work on partisan political campaigns – a prelude to deeper investigations and more jail time. The individual incidents built to a perfect storm, an unprecedented political cyclone that overturned the status quo on the city, county, and state levels, without the slightest regard for party or race. Not since the Bennett Law flap of 1890 had Milwaukeeans exhibited such a well-developed sense of moral indignation. Not since the excesses of the David Rose era had there been such a rash of indictments and convictions.

It was the pension scandal that generated the most heat. Poorly understood even by those who had approved it, the plan promised six-figure payouts to the county's most senior employees – in addition to their regular pensions. The wrath of the citizenry knew no bounds, demonstrating the truth of Frank Zeidler's trenchant observation: "Milwaukeeans want their representatives to come into office poor and to leave office penniless." Seven county supervisors were unseated in recall elections – a revolution that attracted national attention – and Tom Ament, facing more than 180,000 signatures on recall petitions, resigned as county executive in February, 2002. Scott Walker, a state legislator from Wauwatosa, won the special election to succeed him and earned a full term in 2004. A conservative Republican in a seat once considered safely Democratic, Walker's strategy for dealing with Milwaukee County's mounting budget woes was crystal-clear: Cut where you can and at least freeze where you can't.

John Norquist's exit was less dramatic than Tom Ament's but just as humbling. Torpedoed by his libido, the mayor was forced to empty his campaign treasury – a total of $276,000 – and add $99,000 of his own money to settle a sexual harassment suit in 2002. Norquist's mayoral career was effectively over. He left office at the end of 2003, a few months before his final term expired, for a tailor-made job as head of the Congress for the New Urbanism in Chicago.

Norquist had won his first term in an election determined, in part, by generational differences. The contest to succeed him turned, in equal measure, on race. The 2004 primary field was evenly split – five blacks and five whites – and the two finalists maintained the same balance. The top

After nearly sixteen years in office, Mayor John Norquist stepped down at the end of 2003, his last term tarnished by an affair with a female staff member.

finisher was Marvin Pratt, an African American who had served as an alderman since 1987 and Common Council president since 2000. As acting mayor after Norquist's departure, Pratt was a highly visible candidate. "It's time," he declared, and no one missed his point. Pratt's opponent in the general election was Tom Barrett, a Milwaukee-born, Wisconsin-trained attorney who had launched his political career as a state assemblyman in 1984. Barrett moved up to the Wisconsin Senate in 1989 and then on to Washington in

"Reform Now": In the wake of the 2002 pension scandal, Scott Walker became the first Republican to hold the county executive's seat.

Milwaukee Journal Sentinel

Milwaukee Journal Sentinel

1992, representing the northern half of Milwaukee County in Congress. Stressing his broader experience, Tom Barrett beat Marvin Pratt in the 2004 mayoral election by a margin of 54 to 46. Some of Pratt's sup-

porters painted the outcome as painful evidence of Milwaukee's continuing racial divide. Their voices were muted after November, when Gwen Moore, an African American with long tenure in the state legislature, won the race to represent Milwaukee in Congress. Moore, who had once been a single mother on welfare, scored a landslide victory in a district whose voting-age population was predominantly white.

After two or three years of general chaos, equilibrium finally returned to Milwaukee's political scene. Tom Barrett restored a sense of calm (and an understated Irish presence) to City Hall, and conditions in the County Courthouse, if still unsettled, were at least less volatile. The perfect storm had stripped Milwaukee down to its political bedrock. Most of the transgressions that made the local headlines, including the pension flap, wouldn't have raised many eyebrows in Chicago or Providence. In a community with a sterner conception of civic integrity, however, they were viewed as capital offenses; the height of public outrage mirrored the height of public expectations. That made the meltdown all the more corrosive. Misdeeds and misjudgments destroyed a number of political careers, but the real casualty of the perfect storm was the public's confidence in its own government. Raised on a tradition of reflexive honesty and tangible results, an earlier generation of Milwaukeeans had viewed municipal government as a fundamentally collaborative "us." In the early 2000s, as a minority of miscreants used public office for private gain or raw political advantage, too many voters came to think of government as a predatory "them." Trust once lost is notoriously difficult to regain; the future of local government depends in part on the ability of elected officials to find their way back to the higher ground that once sustained a proud tradition of civic enterprise.

"A Substantial, Agreeable, and Well-ordered Way of Life"

The recent past is uncertain terrain, best left to journalists. Some trends – emerging political patterns, fundamental economic shifts – are transparent enough, but there are many more developments, including welfare reform and changes in public education, whose ultimate significance is open to only the crudest form of guesswork. The way back is clearer. Milwaukee began where a deep wilderness river created a passage between lake and land. It prospered first as a classic port city, a point of exchange between farm products headed east and finished goods coming west. It became a haven for immigrants, particularly Germans and Poles, whose muscle and ambition fueled an industrial revolution. Milwaukee suffered through calamities like the bloodshed that ended the clamor for the eight-hour day in 1886 and the anti-Hun hysteria that virtually wiped out German culture during World War I. The city also weathered bouts of political malfeasance to become, under the Socialists, a stronghold of sound government, and it experienced the cyclonic leveling influences of the Depression and World War II.

The urban "universe" was hurtling outward all the while, as it had been since the first population explosion of the 1830s. Development reached the county line before World War II and surged far beyond in the 1950s and '60s. As the children and grandchildren of immigrants moved to the edge, their old neighborhoods were remade by relative newcomers who were uniformly poor and overwhelmingly black. Discontent with the status quo boiled over into violence again in July, 1967. Milwaukee weathered that disturbance and then a recession that hollowed out its industrial establishment in the 1980s, finally settling into a period of uneasy prosperity that left a yawning gap between winners and losers.

Through this long and often painful procession of turning points, Milwaukee developed a character, first fluid and then fixed, that made it different from any other place in urban America. In the mid-nineteenth century, the city was a scrappy upstart that kept on growing despite its place in the deep shade of Chicago. Although Milwaukee's shoulders were considerably narrower than its neighbor's, the city was just as aggressive, and its political atmosphere every bit as rank. But Milwaukee chose a different path in the late 1800s, when immigrant values finally triumphed. Under the social influence of the home-loving Germans, *Gemütlichkeit* became the community's normative state; the desire for a leisurely pace, pleasant parks, and meat and

potatoes for dinner translated easily into any language. Under the influence of heavy industries and industrial unions, Milwaukee developed some representative blue-collar values: pragmatism, a strong work ethic, and an insistence that the price charged reflect the value received. Under the guidance of the "sewer Socialists" of the early 1900s, local government earned a national reputation for probity, efficiency, and concern for the underdog.

Chicago, too, played a continuing role. Milwaukee was to Chicago what Canada was to the United States: a place with a culture and character all its own, but perennially overshadowed by its larger neighbor to the south. The result was, if not an inferiority complex, then at least a dearth of illusions and a bare minimum of self-importance. Milwaukeeans learned early to keep their feet on the ground. Bayrd Still offered a succinct summary of the community's character in his comprehensive 1948 history. The city, he wrote, was dominated by "a fundamentally worker-

A portrait of urban change: Wisconsin Avenue looking west from the Milwaukee River over a period of 130 years

1870s

1890s

1910-192

minded citizenry" whose primary desire was "a substantial, agreeable, and well-ordered way of life." Simply put, Milwaukeeans wanted things to work.

That expectation still applies. Just as surely as the downtown bridges continue to cross the river at an angle and Germanic gables grace the rooflines of landmarks new and old, the industrial immigrant's outlook still shapes life in Milwaukee. But the city's character grew more complex as the twentieth century wore on. In the late 1930s and early 1940s, local officials began to call Milwaukee "a big small town" – a characterization that was partly the truth, partly an acknowledgment that the city would never enter the demographic big leagues, and partly a means of distancing it from problems that had begun to plague larger urban centers. *Milwaukee Journal* columnist Richard Davis captured much of the local ambience in "Old Lady Thrift," a profile of Milwaukee published in the 1947 book *Our Fair City:*

Small town is the word for Old Lady Thrift. Her hundredth anniversary came in 1946 and found her with a population of about six hundred thousand, but she remains essentially a small town. A great majority of her people want to keep her that way. Everything has been so comfortable, so pleasantly Old World, so free of false pretentions and the travails of ambition that only the vain, the restless, and the conscience-stricken want to change things.

That bucolic self-image grew more and more nostalgic in the years after Davis's essay was published. As Milwaukee developed some obvious big-city problems of its own, local residents looked back wistfully to a time they viewed as simpler, when ethnic diversity was not so daunting, when conflicts were fewer and poverty not so prevalent. The community remained "a big small town," but it became something more: a reluctant metropolis.

Milwaukee has moved even farther from its traditional base in the recent past – far too rapidly, in fact, for its self-image to

1930   *1960*   *2006*

adjust. The shift reflects, to some degree, changes in American society. In an age described by some pundits as both post-religious and post-industrial, a city whose skyline still bristles with steeples and smokestacks might be expected to feel at least a twinge of insecurity. But the dissonance between past image and present reality is not limited to the skyline. Milwaukee is no longer an industrial powerhouse populated by blue-collar ethnics who go to the neighborhood tavern on Saturday night and church on Sunday morning. The ethnics, the taverns, and the churches are all still present in abundance, but they are a smaller part of a larger whole than ever before. The metropolitan area is diversifying, unbundling, perhaps even fragmenting. Milwaukee became a "majority minority" city in the late 1990s, and diversity is coming to suburban communities as well. From the Russian Jewish families in Shorewood to the Hmong clans on the near West Side, Milwaukee's character increasingly reflects the character of the world. Between the pseudo-Victorian trophy houses going up in Mequon and the aged duplexes coming down in the inner city, there yawns an all-but-unbridgeable gap in social status and economic well-being. An incipient regionalism looms on the horizon,

evident in closer economic and transportation ties to Chicago. As the last open lots are sold in Oak Creek and Franklin and the first subdivisions go up in once-rural Jefferson County, Milwaukee is fast becoming one node in a megalopolis sprawling from northern Indiana to Madison. What suffers in this stretched-out urban world is something that has been notoriously fragile from the start: a community of interest.

Traditionalists might be inclined to view the recent changes as Milwaukee's death-knell. They should consult Ezra Pound's wicked parody of melancholic English poet A.E. Housman:

> *O woe, woe,*
> *People are born and die,*
> *We also shall be dead pretty soon*
> *Therefore let us act as if we were*
> *dead already.*

It is much too early for an urban obituary, and it will always be too early, simply because change is the one inescapable fact of urban life. The Milwaukee of the early twenty-first century would be nearly as incomprehensible to Emil Seidel as the Milwaukee of 1900 would have been to Solomon Juneau or the Milwaukee of 2100 will be to anyone alive today. Current residents face the future

with no more certainty than their ancestors; their sole assurance is that change will continue. Milwaukee's present problems are obvious and the long-term trends seem ominous, but the community remains a work in progress, evolving toward new forms, new crises, and new opportunities that are presently beyond imagination.

At the same time, change never takes place in a vacuum. It is impossible, for better or worse, to shed the accumulated weight of the past, to truly reinvent the character of either an individual or a community. History serves as both ballast and bedrock, shaping the present in ways that are largely subconscious. In Milwaukee's case, not all gifts from the past are equally useful. The community's progress on racial issues has been glacially slow. A learned conservatism has created a social climate that can be toxic to new ideas. Milwaukeeans share an inherent complacency, a stubborn insistence that things are basically all right and don't need fixing until they are broken beyond repair.

But history has also produced that relative rarity: a major American city that is still eminently livable. Milwaukee is built at the human scale. It has all the resources of a much larger city, but it has preserved the easy pace and even the intimacy of a much smaller community. This characteristic blend of big and small has spawned amenities that few other urban centers can match: a manageable streetscape, abundant cultural opportunities, short commutes, fine restaurants, world-class festivals, an assortment of tranquil neighborhoods, and ready access to the natural world. History has also given Milwaukee a heritage of ethnic diversity that, despite its obvious potential for conflict, remains a cause for celebration, not simply tolerance. But the most endearing legacy of Milwaukee's past – and the most endangered – is its ideal of mutual responsibility. Rooted in European traditions and brought to life by municipal Socialists, visions of the common wealth are still alive in Milwaukee. There remains, however tenuous, a sense of collective ownership, a concern for the public good that other communities have long since left behind. Although it may seem imperiled in an age of shrinking government and endemic selfishness, that quality offers Milwaukee its best prospect for the future. Conflict will not cease and the way ahead will never be clear, but a sense of civic possibility endures. At the turn of the millennium, poised between echoes of the Old World and stirrings of a new age, Milwaukee has reason to look ahead with hope.

Bibliography

General

Aderman, Ralph M., ed. *Trading Post to Metropolis: Milwaukee County's First 150 Years.* Milwaukee: Milwaukee County Historical Society, 1987.

Anderson, Harry H., and Frederick I. Olson. *Milwaukee: At the Gathering of the Waters.* Tulsa, OK: Continental Heritage Press, 1981.

Austin, Russell H. *The Milwaukee Story.* Milwaukee: The Journal Co., 1946.

Bruce, William G. *History of Milwaukee City and County.* Chicago-Milwaukee: S.J. Clarke Publishing Co., 1922.

_____. *Builders of Milwaukee.* Milwaukee: Bruce Publishing Co., 1946.

City directories, 1847-1997.

Common Council, City of Milwaukee. Annual reports, 1921-1998.

Conard, Howard L., ed. *History of Milwaukee from Its First Settlement to the Year 1895.* Chicago and New York: American Biographical Publishing Co., 1895.

Flower, Frank A. *History of Milwaukee, Wisconsin.* Chicago: Western Historical Co., 1881.

Gavett, Thomas W. *Development of the Labor Movement in Milwaukee.* Madison: University of Wisconsin Press, 1965.

Gregory, John G. *History of Milwaukee, Wisconsin.* Chicago-Milwaukee: S.J. Clarke Publishing Co., 1931.

"History of Milwaukee." Milwaukee: WPA Writers Program, 1947.

Holli, Melvin G., and Peter D. Jones. *Biographical Dictionary of American Mayors, 1820-1980.* Westport, CT: Greenwood Press, 1981.

Lamers, William M. *Our Roots Grow Deep.* Milwaukee: Board of School Directors, 1974.

Landscape Research. *Built in Milwaukee: An Architectural View of the City.* City of Milwaukee, 1980.

Lankevich, George J. *Milwaukee: A Chronological & Documentary History.* Dobbs Ferry, NY: Oceana Publications, 1977.

Latus, Mark A., and Mary Ellen Young. *Downtown Milwaukee: Seven Walking Tours of Historic Buildings and Places.* Milwaukee: Bicentennial Commission, 1978.

McBride, Genevieve G. *On Wisconsin Women.* Madison: University of Wisconsin Press, 1993.

Milwaukee Journal. Consumer Analysis surveys, 1922-1998.

Milwaukee Sentinel. Indexed 1837-1891, Milwaukee Public Library.

Nesbit, Robert C. *Wisconsin: A History.* Madison: University of Wisconsin Press, 1973.

Perrin, Richard W.E. *Milwaukee Landmarks.* Milwaukee: Milwaukee Public Museum, 1968.

Schafer, Joseph. *Four Wisconsin Counties: Prairie and Forest.* Madison: State Historical Society of Wisconsin, 1927.

Still, Bayrd. *Milwaukee: The History of a City.* Madison: State Historical Society of Wisconsin, 1965.

United States census materials, 1840-1990.

Watrous, Jerome A., ed. *Memoirs of Milwaukee County.* Madison: Western Historical Association, 1909.

Wells, Robert W. *This Is Milwaukee.* Garden City, NY: Doubleday & Co., 1970.

Wisconsin Highways, 1835-1945. Madison: State Highway Commission of Wisconsin, 1947.

Zimmermann, H. Russell. *The Heritage Guidebook,* 2nd edition. Milwaukee: Harry W. Schwartz, 1989.

Chapter 1: Native Milwaukee

Aspects of the Fur Trade: Selected Papers of the 1965 North American Fur Trade Conference. St. Paul: Minnesota Historical Society, 1967.

Bieder, Robert E. *Native American Communities in Wisconsin, 1600-1960.* Madison: University of Wisconsin Press, 1995.

Birmingham, Robert, and Leslie E. Eisenberg. *Indian Mounds of Wisconsin.* Madison: University of Wisconsin Press, 2000.

Brown, Charles E. "Archaeological History of Milwaukee County." *Wisconsin Archeologist.* July, 1916.

Clifton, James A. *The Potawatomi.* New York: Chelsea House Publishers, 1987.

_____. "The Potawatomi." *Handbook of North American Indians.* Washington: Smithsonian Institution, 1978.

Collections of the State Historical Society of Wisconsin.
Vol. 1, 1855 — "Lt. James Gorrell's Journal, 1761-63"
Vol. 3, 1857 — "Augustus Grignon's Recollections"
Vol. 5, 1868 — "Early Reminiscences of Wisconsin," John Fonda
Vol. 7, 1876 — "The Fur Trade and Factory System at Green Bay, 1816-21"
Vol. 15, 1900 — "Narrative of Andrew J. Vieau, Sr.," 1887
"Antoine le Clair's Statement," 1868
"Narrative of Alexis Clermont," 1888
"Narrative of Morgan L. Martin," 1887
"Narrative of Peter J. Vieau," 1889
Vol. 20, 1911 — Jean Baptiste Jacobs letter to John Lawe

Crow, Lois. Personal interview. June 16, 1994.

Daniels, Billy. Personal interview. June 17, 1994.

Edmunds, R. David. *The Potawatomis: Keepers of the Fire.* University of Oklahoma Press, 1978.

Feest, Johanna and Christian. "The Ottawa." *Handbook of North American Indians.* Washington: Smithsonian Institution, 1978.

Haeger, John Denis. *Jacob Astor: Business and Finance in the Early Republic.* Detroit: Wayne State University Press, 1991.

Juneau, Solomon. Papers. Milwaukee County Historical Society.

Kellogg, Louise Phelps. *The French Regime in Wisconsin and the Old Northwest.* Madison: State Historical Society of Wisconsin, 1925.

Lapham, Increase A. *The Antiquities of Wisconsin.* Washington: Smithsonian Institution, 1855. Reprinted, University of Wisconsin Press, 2001.

Lavender, David. *Fist in the Wilderness.* Garden City: Doubleday & Co., 1964.

Lawson, Publius. "The Potawatomi." *Wisconsin Archaeologist.* April, 1920.

Loew, Patty. *Indian Nations of Wisconsin.* Madison: Wisconsin Historical Society Press, 2001.

Lurie, Nancy O. "The Winnebago Indians: A Study in Cultural Change." Ph.D. dissertation. Northwestern University, 1952.

_____. *Wisconsin Indians.* Madison: State Historical Society of Wisconsin, 1987.

Martin, Calvin. *Keepers of the Game: Indian-Animal Relationships and the Fur Trade.* Berkeley: University of California Press, 1978.

Mason, Carol I. *Introduction to Wisconsin Indians.* Salem, WI: Sheffield Publishing Co., 1988

O'Brien, Dean W., ed. *Historic Northeast Wisconsin: A Voyageur Guidebook.* Green Bay: Brown County Historical Society, 1994.

Ourada, Patricia K. *The Menominee.* New York: Chelsea House Publishers, 1990.

Ritzenthaler, Robert E. and Goldstein, Lynne. *Prehistoric Indians of Wisconsin.* Milwaukee Public Museum, 1985.

Rowe, Chandler. *The Effigy Mound Culture of Wisconsin.* Milwaukee Public Museum, 1956.

Royce, Charles C. *Indian Land Cessions in the United States.* U.S. Bureau of American Ethnology, 1899.

Salamun, Peter J. "Milwaukee's Plants and Trees 120 Years Ago." *Historical Messenger of the Milwaukee County Historical Society.* December, 1957.

Tanner, Helen Hornbeck, ed. *Atlas of Great Lakes Indian History.* University of Oklahoma Press, 1987.

Thwaites, Reuben Gold, ed. *Travels and Explorations of the Jesuit Missionaries in New France, 1610-1791.* Cleveland: Burrows Brothers Co., 1940.

Vieau family papers. Milwaukee County Historical Society.

Vogel, Virgil J. *Indian Names on Wisconsin's Map.* Madison: University of Wisconsin Press, 1991.

White, Richard. *The Middle Ground: Indians, Empires, and Republics in the Great Lakes Region, 1650-1815.* Cambridge University Press, 1991.

Whitford, Philip and Kathryn. "An Ecological History of Milwaukee County." *Historical Messenger of the Milwaukee County Historical Society.* Summer, 1972.

Chapter 2: City on the Swamp, 1835-1846

Berquist, Goodwin F. *Byron Kilbourn and the Development of Milwaukee.* Milwaukee: Milwaukee County Historical Society, 2001.

Buck, James S. *Pioneer History of Milwaukee.* Milwaukee: Swain & Tate, 1890.

Collections of the State Historical Society of Wisconsin.
    Vol. 1, 1855 — "Alexander F. Pratt's Memoir"
    Vol. 4, 1859 — addresses at opening of Chamber of Commerce, 1858
    Vol. 13, 1895 — "Significance of the Lead and Shot Trade in Early Wisconsin History," Orin Grant Libby

Ellis, David M. et al. *A History of New York State.* Ithaca: Cornell University Press, 1967.

Juneau, Solomon. Papers. Milwaukee County Historical Society.

Kilbourn, Byron. Papers. Milwaukee County Historical Society.

Lapham, Increase A. *A Documentary History of the Milwaukee and Rock River Canal.* Milwaukee: The Advertiser, 1840.

_____. *Wisconsin: Its Geography and Topography*, 2nd edition. Milwaukee: I.A. Hopkins, 1846.

Martin, Morgan. Papers. Neville Public Museum of Brown County (Green Bay).

Milwaukee Advertiser, 1837-41.

"Milwaukee Fifty Years Ago." *Milwaukee Sentinel.* Dec. 9, 1894.

Old Settlers' Club of Milwaukee County. *Early Milwaukee: Papers from the Archives.* Self-published, 1916.

Olson, Frederick I. "Juneau and the Postmastership." *Historical Messenger of the Milwaukee County Historical Society.* September, 1953.

Pierce, Bessie L. *A History of Chicago.* Chicago: University of Chicago Press, 1937.

Smith, Alice E. *The History of Wisconsin.* Vol. 1, *From Exploration to Statehood.* Madison: State Historical Society of Wisconsin, 1973.

Whalen, Barbara. "The Lawyer and the Fur Trader: Morgan Martin and Solomon Juneau." *Milwaukee History.* Spring-Summer, 1988.

Wheeler, A.C. *The Chronicles of Milwaukee.* Milwaukee: Jermain & Brightman, 1861.

Wisconsin Democrat (Green Bay), 1836-38.

Wisconsin Enquirer (Madison), 1838.

Chapter 3: Here Come the Germans, 1846-1865

Anderson, Harry H. "Early Scandinavian Settlement in Milwaukee County." *Historical Messenger of the Milwaukee County Historical Society.* March, 1969.

_____, ed. *German-American Pioneers in Wisconsin and Michigan: The Frank-Kerler Letters, 1849-1864.* Milwaukee: Milwaukee County Historical Society, 1989.

Behling, Reis. "The Watertown Plank Road." *Historical Messenger of the Milwaukee County Historical Society.* June, 1954.

Buck, James S. *Milwaukee under the Charter.* Milwaukee: Symes, Swain & Co., 1884.

Butler, Diane S. "The Public Life and Private Affairs of Sherman S. Booth." *Wisconsin Magazine of History.* Spring, 1999.

Collections of the State Historical Society of Wisconsin.

Vol. 12, 1892 — "How Wisconsin Came by Its Large German Element," Kate Asaphine Everest.

Vol. 14, 1898 — "Geographical Origin of German Immigration to Wisconsin," Kate Everest Levi.

Conzen, Kathleen Neils. *Immigrant Milwaukee, 1836-1860.* Cambridge: Harvard University Press, 1976.

_____. "Precocious Reformers." *Historical Messenger of the Milwaukee County Historical Society.* Summer, 1977.

Current, Richard N. *The History of Wisconsin.* Vol. 2, *The Civil War Era, 1848-1873.* Madison: State Historical Society of Wisconsin, 1976.

De Haas, Carl. *North America Wisconsin: Hints for Emigrants.* Elberfeld (Germany): Julius Badecker, 1848. Translated and republished, 1943.

Everest, Kate A. "Early Lutheran Immigration to Wisconsin." *Transactions of the Wisconsin Academy of Sciences, Arts and Letters.* Vol. 8 (1892).

Haight, Theron W., ed. *Memoirs of Waukesha County.* Madison: Western Historical Association, 1907.

Hesse-Jensen, Wilhelm, and Ernst Bruncken. *Wisconsin's Deutsch-Americaner.* Published 1902. Translated by Joseph Schafer and republished by State Historical Society of Wisconsin, 1939.

History of Washington and Ozaukee Counties. Chicago: Western Historical Company, 1881.

Journey of the John Fr. Diederichs Family from Elberfeld to Manitowoc in North America. Manitowoc: Manitowoc County Historical Society, 1983.

Kamphoefner, Walter D. et al., eds. *News from the Land of Freedom.* Ithaca: Cornell University Press, 1988.

Koss, Rudolf A. *Milwaukee.* Milwaukee: Milwaukee Herold, 1871. Translated by Hans Ibsen for WPA, 1930s.

Krause, Lebrecht. *The Chronicle of Rev. L.F.E. Krause.* Translated and edited by Roy A. Suelflow. Trinity Lutheran Church of Freistadt. No date.

Lacher, J.H.U. *The German Element in Wisconsin.* Milwaukee: Steuben Society of America, 1925.

Lucas, Henry S. *Netherlanders in America.* Grand Rapids, MI: William B. Eerdmans Publishing Co., 1955.

McDonald, Grace. *History of the Irish in Wisconsin in the Nineteenth Century.* New York: Arno Press, 1976.

Miter, John J. *The Patriot's Duty.* Milwaukie: Edward Hopkins, 1845.

Mueller, Theodore. "Milwaukee's German Heritage." *Historical Messenger of the Milwaukee County Historical Society.* September, 1968.

Overmoehle, Sister M. Hedwigis. "The Anti-Clerical Activities of the Forty-Eighters in Wisconsin, 1848-1860." Ph.D. dissertation, St. Louis University, 1941.

Report of the Joint Select Committee Appointed to Investigate into Alleged Frauds and Corruption in the Disposition of the Land Grant by the Legislature of 1856, and for Other Purposes. Madison, 1858.

Rice, Herbert W. "Early History of the Chicago, Milwaukee and St. Paul Railway Company." Ph.D. dissertation, University of Iowa, 1938.

Wheeler, A.C. *The Chronicles of Milwaukee.* Milwaukee: Jermain & Brightman, 1861.

Chapter 4: Wheat, Iron, Beer, and Bloodshed, 1865-1886

Alexander Mitchell Reception and Banquet. Milwaukee Chamber of Commerce, 1884.

Casson, Robert N. *The Romance of Steel: The Story of a Thousand Millionaires.* New York: A.S. Barnes & Co., 1907.

Chamber of Commerce of Milwaukee. *Annual Statement of the Trade and Commerce of Milwaukee.* 1855-1886.

Cochran, Thomas C. *The Pabst Brewing Company: The History of an American Business.* New York: New York University Press, 1948

"Commerce" and "Manufactures." *Transactions of the Wisconsin State Agricultural Society.* Vol. 8, 1869.

Cooper, Jerry M. "The Wisconsin National Guard in the Milwaukee Riots of 1886." *Wisconsin Magazine of History.* Autumn, 1971.

Cudahy, Patrick. *My Life.* Milwaukee: Burdick & Allen, 1912.

Current, Richard N. *The Typewriter and the Men Who Made It.* Urbana: University of Illinois Press, 1954.

Derby, William E. "A History of the Port of Milwaukee, 1835-1910." Ph.D. dissertation, University of Wisconsin, 1963.

Flower, Frank. *Second Biennial Report of the Bureau of Labor and Industrial Statistics.* Madison, 1886.

Frederick, George G. *When Iron Was King in Dodge County, Wisconsin, 1845-1928.* Mayville: Mayville Historical Society, 1993.

Geib, Paul. "'Everything but the Squeal': The Milwaukee Stockyards and Meat-packing Industry, 1840-1930." *Wisconsin Magazine of History.* Autumn, 1994.

Glazier, Willard. *Peculiarities of American Cities.* Philadelphia: Hubbard Brothers, 1884.

Heming, Harry. *The Catholic Church in Wisconsin.* Milwaukee: Catholic Historical Publishing Co., 1897.

Howard, Leora M. "Changes in Home Life in Milwaukee from 1865 to 1900." Master's thesis, University of Wisconsin, 1923.

In Memoriam: John Lendrum Mitchell, 1842-1904. Milwaukee, 1906.

Korman, Gerd. *Industrialization, Immigrants and Americanizers: The View from Milwaukee, 1866-1921.* Madison: State Historical Society of Wisconsin, 1967.

Korn, Bernhard C. "Eber Brock Ward: Pathfinder of American Industry." Ph.D. dissertation, Marquette University, 1942.

_____. *The Story of Bay View.* Milwaukee: Milwaukee County Historical Society, 1980.

Kriehn, Ruth. *The Fisherfolk of Jones Island.* Milwaukee: Milwaukee County Historical Society, 1988.

Kruszka, Waclaw. *A History of the Poles in America to 1908.* Edited by James S. Pula, translated by Krystyna Jankowski. Washington: Catholic University of America Press, 1993.

Kuzniewski, Anthony J. "Milwaukee's Poles, 1866-1918: The Rise and Fall of a Model Community." *Milwaukee History.* Spring/Summer, 1978.

Lapham, Increase A. et al. *Report on the Disastrous Effects of the Destruction of Forest Trees Now Going on So Rapidly in the State of Wisconsin.* Madison: Atwood & Rublee, 1867.

Leonard, David B. "A Biography of Alexander Mitchell." M.S. thesis, University of Wisconsin, 1951.

Mariner, Mary A. *Woman's Club of Wisconsin, 1876-1923.*

Merk, Frederick. *Economic History of Wisconsin during the Civil War Decade.* Madison: State Historical Society of Wisconsin, 1916.

Merritt, Raymond H., and Carol L. Snook. *Milwaukee Menomonee Valley: An Inventory of Historic Engineering and Industrial Sites.* U.S. Department of the Interior: National Architectural and Engineering Record, 1980.

Milwaukee Industrial Exposition Association. Annual reports, 1882-1904.

Nesbit, Robert C. *The History of Wisconsin.* Vol. 3, *Urbanization and Industrialization, 1873-1893.* Madison: State Historical Society of Wisconsin, 1985.

Peterson, Walter F. *An Industrial Heritage: Allis-Chalmers Corporation.* Milwaukee: Milwaukee County Historical Society, 1978.

Simon, Roger. "Foundations for Industrialization, 1835-1880." *Milwaukee History.* Spring/Summer, 1978.

Small, Milton M. "The Biography of Robert Schilling." Master's thesis, University of Wisconsin, 1953.

Smith, Alice E. *George Smith's Money.* Madison: State Historical Society of Wisconsin, 1966.

Swank, James M. *History of the Manufacture of Iron in All Ages.* Philadelphia: American Iron and Steel Association, 1892.

Walsh, Margaret. "Industrial Opportunity on the Urban Frontier: 'Rags to Riches' and Milwaukee Clothing Manufacturers, 1840-1880." *Wisconsin Magazine of History.* Spring, 1974.

_____. *The Manufacturing Frontier: Pioneer Industry in Antebellum Wisconsin, 1830-1860.* Madison: State Historical Society of Wisconsin, 1972.

Warren, Kenneth. *The American Steel Industry, 1850-1970: A Geographical Interpretation.* Oxford: Clarendon Press, 1973.

Zarob, Virginia M. "The Family in an Expanding Industrial Economy: Economic, Occupational, Social, and Residential Mobility in Milwaukee, Wisconsin, 1860-1880." Ph.D. dissertation, Marquette University, 1978.

Chapter 5: Triumph of the Workingman, 1886-1910

After the Fire: 18 Photogravures and Descriptive Text Illustrating the Great Fire at Milwaukee, Friday Night, October 28, 1892. Milwaukee: Art Gravure & Etching Co., 1892.

Anderson, W.J. and Julius Bleyer, eds. *Milwaukee's Great Industries.* Milwaukee: Association for the Advancement of Milwaukee, 1892.

Andreozzi, John. "Contadini and Pescatori in Milwaukee." Master's thesis, University of Wisconsin-Milwaukee, 1974.

Beck, Elmer A. *The Sewer Socialists: A History of the Socialist Party of Wisconsin, 1897-1940.* Fennimore, WI: Westburg Associates Publishers, 1982.

Berger, Victor. "What is the Matter with Milwaukee?" *Independent.* Apr. 21, 1910.

Bird, Miriam. *The Village of Whitefish Bay, 1892-1992.*

The Book of Milwaukee. Milwaukee: Evening Wisconsin Co., 1901.

Borun, Thaddeus, ed. *We, the Milwaukee Poles.* Milwaukee: Nowiny Publishing Co., 1946.

Bruce, William George. *The Auditorium.* Milwaukee: Auditorium Governing Board, 1909.

_____. *I Was Born in America.* Milwaukee: Bruce Publishing Co., 1937.

Burbach, J.H. *Historical Review of West Allis.* 1927.

Carini, Mario. *Milwaukee's Italians: The Early Years.* Milwaukee: Italian Community Center, 1984.

Carlin, Kathleen M. "Chief Janssen and the 'Thirty-Three Year War.'" M.S. thesis, University of Wisconsin-Milwaukee, 1961.

Chamber of Commerce of Milwaukee. *Annual Statement of the Trade and Commerce of Milwaukee.* 1889-1910.

Commons, John R. et al. *History of Labour in the United States.* New York: Macmillan Co., 1918.

Cudahy, Wisconsin: A 50-Year Review. 1956.

1888: Frederick Layton and His World. Milwaukee: Milwaukee Art Museum, 1988.

Fabishak, Mary Clare. "The Rhetoric of Urban Reform: Milwaukee during the Progressive Era." Master's thesis, University of Wisconsin-Milwaukee, 1974.

Founding Industries of Wisconsin collection. Urban Archives, University of Wisconsin-Milwaukee Library.

Frank, Louis F. *Musical Reminiscences and Reflections on the Cultural Life of Old Milwaukee.* Milwaukee: Milwaukee County Historical Society, 1979.

"The German Theatre in Milwaukee." *Theatre Arts.* August, 1944.

Goff, Charles D. "The Politics of Governmental Integration in Metropolitan Milwaukee." Ph.D. dissertation, Northwestern University, 1952.

Greene, Victor R. *For God and Country: The Rise of Polish and Lithuanian Ethnic Consciousness in America, 1860-1910.* Madison: State Historical Society of Wisconsin, 1975.

Herzog, Lewis W. "The Beginnings of Radio in Milwaukee." *Historical Messenger of the Milwaukee County Historical Society.* December, 1955.

_____. "Radio in Milwaukee, 1929-1955." *Historical Messenger of the Milwaukee County Historical Society.* March, 1956.

Howard, William W. "Milwaukee." *Harper's Weekly.* July 18, 1891.

An Illustrated Description of Milwaukee. Milwaukee: Milwaukee Sentinel, 1890.

King, Charles. "The Cream City." *Cosmopolitan.* March, 1891.

_____. "Milwaukee." *New England Magazine.* March, 1892.

Kuzniewski, Anthony J. *Faith and Fatherland: The Polish Church War in Wisconsin, 1896-1918.* South Bend: Notre Dame University Press, 1980.

La Piana, George. *The Italians in Milwaukee, Wisconsin.* Milwaukee: Associated Charities, 1915.

Leavitt, Judith Walzer. *The Healthiest City: Milwaukee and the Politics of Health Reform.* Princeton: Princeton University Press, 1982.

Litzow, Joseph A. "The Poles in Milwaukee, 1906 to 1909." Master's thesis, St. Francis Seminary, 1943.

McDonald, Forrest. *Let There Be Light: The Electric Utility Industry in Wisconsin, 1881-1955.* Madison: American History Research Center, 1957.

McShane, Clay. *Technology and Reform: Street Railways and the Growth of Milwaukee, 1887-1900.* Madison: State Historical Society of Wisconsin, 1974.

Meir, Golda. *My Life.* New York: Putnam, 1975.

Meloni, Alberto C. "Italy Invades the Bloody Third: Milwaukee Italians, 1900-1910." *Historical Messenger of the Milwaukee County Historical Society.* March, 1969.

Milwaukee: A Half-Century's Progress, 1846-1896. Milwaukee: Consolidated Illustrating Co., 1896.

Mowry, Duane. "The Reign of Graft in Milwaukee." *Arena.* December, 1905.

Nailen, R.L., and James S. Haight. *Beertown Blazes: A Century of Milwaukee Firefighting.* Milwaukee, 1971.

Olson, Frederick I. "The Milwaukee Socialists, 1897-1941." Ph.D. dissertation, Harvard University, 1952.

Pappas, Theodore. "George W. Peck and the Political Revolution of 1890." Master's thesis, University of Wisconsin-Milwaukee, 1965.

Paras, Frank G. "The Assimilation of the Greek Population in Milwaukee." Master's thesis, Marquette University, 1945.

Peterson, Walter F. *An Industrial Heritage: Allis-Chalmers Corporation.* Milwaukee: Milwaukee County Historical Society, 1978.

Pienkos, Donald. "The Polish Americans in Milwaukee Politics." *Ethnic Politics in Urban America.* Chicago: Polish American Historical Association, 1978.

_____. "Politics, Religion, and Change in Polish Milwaukee, 1900-1930." *Wisconsin Magazine of History.* Spring, 1978.

Ranney, Joseph A. "The Political Campaigns of Mayor David S. Rose." *Milwaukee History.* Spring, 1981.

Reagan, Ann B. "Art Music in Milwaukee in the Late Nineteenth Century, 1850-1900." Ph.D. dissertation, University of Wisconsin, 1980.

Report of the Committee on Construction of the New Court House. Milwaukee County, 1913.

Rose, David S. "Paradise and Hell! Saints and Hypocrites! Politics, Parties, and Leaders of Past and Present! Fifty Years in Political Life. Travels and Experiences in China and South America." Unpublished memoirs, 1929-30. Milwaukee Public Library.

Saloutos, Theodore. "Growing Up in the Greek Community." *Milwaukee History.* Winter, 1992.

Simon Roger D. *The City-Building Process: Housing and Services in New Milwaukee Neighborhoods, 1880-1910.* Philadelphia: American Philosophical Society, 1978.

_____. "The Bay View Incident and the People's Party in Milwaukee." Unpublished paper, 1967.

Stevens, Michael E., ed. *The Family Letters of Victor and Meta Berger, 1894-1929.* Madison: State Historical Society of Wisconsin, 1995.

Swichkow, Louis J. and Lloyd P. Gartner. *The History of the Jews in Milwaukee.* Philadelphia: Jewish Publication Society of America, 1963.

The Sporting and Club House Guide to Milwaukee. Rochester & Taylor, 1889.

Thibaudeau, May Murphy. *For the Good of Others: The Life and Times of Frederick Layton.* University of Wisconsin-River Falls Press, 1984.

Through the Years. South Milwaukee Centennial, Inc., 1935.

Wachman, Marvin. *History of the Social-Democratic Party of Milwaukee, 1897-1910.* Urbana: University of Illinois Press, 1945.

The Wauwatosa Story. 1961.

West Milwaukee Diamond Anniversary, 1906-1981.

Chapter 6: A Bigger, Brighter, and Blander Milwaukee, 1910-1930

Ameringer, Oscar. *If You Don't Weaken: The Autobiography of Oscar Ameringer.* Norman: University of Oklahoma Press, 1983.

Beck, Elmer A. *The Sewer Socialists: A History of the Socialist Party of Wisconsin, 1897-1940.* Fennimore, WI: Westburg Associates Publishers, 1982.

Bedford, Henry F. "A Case Study in Hysteria: Victor L. Berger, 1917-1921." Master's thesis, University of Wisconsin, 1953.

Buchanan, Thomas R. "Black Milwaukee, 1890-1915." Master's thesis, University of Wisconsin-Milwaukee, 1973.

Chamber of Commerce of Milwaukee. *Annual Statement of the Trade and Commerce of Milwaukee.* 1911-1930.

"A Collection of Newspaper and Magazine Articles on Daniel W. Hoan." Milwaukee Public Library, 1969.

Crepeau, Richard C. "Prohibition in Milwaukee." Master's thesis, Marquette University, 1967.

Falk, Otto. Papers. Milwaukee County Historical Society.

Fenton, Agnes M. *The Mexicans of the City of Milwaukee, Wisconsin.* Milwaukee: YWCA, 1930.

Glad, Paul W. *The History of Wisconsin.* Vol. 5, *War, a New Era, and Depression, 1914-1940.* Madison: State Historical Society of Wisconsin, 1990.

Hackett, Francis. "How Milwaukee Takes the War." *New Republic.* July 17, 1915.

Hoan, Daniel. *Socialism and the City.* Girard, KS: Haldeman-Julius Publications, 1931.

Howard, Eugene A. "Personal Recollections of the Milwaukee County Park System, 1924-1960." *Milwaukee History.* Spring-Summer, 1982.

_____. "Planning for Milwaukee County." *City Planning.* October, 1929.

Jackson, Kenneth T. *The Ku Klux Klan in the City, 1915-1930.* New York: Oxford University Press, 1967.

Kerstein, Edward S. *Milwaukee's All-American Mayor: Portrait of Daniel Webster Hoan.* Englewood Cliffs, NJ: Prentice-Hall, 1966.

Korman, Gerd. *Industrialization, Immigrants and Americanizers: The View from Milwaukee, 1866-1921.* Madison: State Historical Society of Wisconsin, 1967.

Levin, Ruben. *Milwaukee — the Bier of Beer.* Girard, KS: Haldeman-Julius Publications, 1929.

Miller, Sally M. *Victor Berger and the Promise of Constructive Socialism.* Westport, CT: Greenwood Press, 1973.

Milwaukee: Its Industrial Advantages. Milwaukee Association of Commerce, 1931.

Municipal Campaign Book. Milwaukee County Central Committee, Social-Democratic Party, 1912.

Niven, Penelope. *Carl Sandburg: A Biography.* New York: Scribner's Sons, 1991.

Olds, Frank Perry. "Milwaukee's Secession." *Outlook.* January, 1920.

Olson, Frederick I. "The Milwaukee Socialists, 1897-1941." Ph.D. dissertation, Harvard University, 1952.

Reinders, Robert C. "The Early Career of Daniel W. Hoan: A Study of Socialism in the Progressive Era." Master's thesis, University of Notre Dame, 1948.

Seidel, Emil. "Sketches from My Life." Unpublished autobiography, 1938. Urban Archives, University of Wisconsin-Milwaukee Library.

Stachowski, Floyd J. "The Political Career of Daniel Webster Hoan." Ph.D. dissertation, Northwestern University, 1966.

Trotter, Joe William, Jr. *Black Milwaukee: The Making of an Industrial Proletariat, 1915-1945.* Urbana: University of Illinois Press, 1988.

Valdovinos, Salvador. "The Mexican in Milwaukee." Unpublished paper, 1950. Milwaukee Public Library.

Ward, Charles A. "The Serbian and Croatian Communities in Milwaukee." *General Linguistics.* Vol. 16, Nos. 2 and 3, 1976.

Washington, R.O., and John Oliver. *A Historical Account of Blacks in Milwaukee.* Milwaukee: Urban Observatory, 1976,

Weaver, Norman F. "The Knights of the Ku Klux Klan in Wisconsin, Indiana, Ohio and Michigan." Ph.D. dissertation, University of Wisconsin, 1954.

Werba, Arthur W. *Making Milwaukee Mightier: A Record of Annexation and Consolidation and a Study of Unification of Government Here and Elsewhere.* Milwaukee: Board of Public Land Commissioners, 1929.

Widen, Larry, and Judi Anderson. *Milwaukee Movie Palaces.* Milwaukee: Milwaukee County Historical Society, 1986.

Whitnall, Charles B. "How a Lecture Course Saved the Shores of Milwaukee County." *American City.* August, 1941.

_____. "Milwaukee's efforts in City and Regional Planning." *City Planning.* October, 1929.

_____. *Open Letter to Our Honorable Mayor and Common Council of Milwaukee.* Milwaukee, 1924-1929.

Chapter 7: Hard Times and Wartime, 1930-1945

Alanen, Arnold R., and Joseph A. Eden. *Main Street Ready-Made: The New Deal Community of Greendale, Wisconsin.* Madison: State Historical Society of Wisconsin, 1987.

"A.O. Smith at War." *Fortune.* October, 1941.

Bennett, Charles. "Milwaukee's Lake-Front Accomplishments." *American City.* August, 1937.

"Carl Zeidler: Clippings from the *Milwaukee Journal* and *Milwaukee Sentinel.*" Milwaukee Public Library.

"A Collection of Newspaper and Magazine Articles on Daniel W. Hoan." Milwaukee Public Library, 1969.

Cowley, Betty. *Stalag Wisconsin: Inside WWII Prisoner-of-War Camps.* Oregon, WI: Badger Books, 2002.

"Duration of Public Relief in Milwaukee County." *Monthly Labor Review.* April, 1939.

"Everything's under Control." (Cutler-Hammer.) *Fortune.* August, 1942.

Friske, Leo J. "Roosevelt and Depression Days in Milwaukee." *Milwaukee History.* Summer/Autumn, 1985.

Hallagren, Mauritz A. "The Milwaukee Miracle." *Nation.* July 13, 1932.

Hoan, Daniel. *City Government.* New York: Harcourt, Brace and Co., 1936.

Holter, Darryl. "Sit-down Strikes in Milwaukee, 1937-1938." *Milwaukee History.* Summer, 1986.

Koprowski-Kraut, Gayle. "The Depression's Effects on a Milwaukee Family." *Milwaukee History.* Autumn, 1980.

Levin, Ruben. "Milwaukee Stays Socialist." *Nation.* Nov. 1, 1933.

Milwaukee County Park Commission. Reports, 1937, 1939-42, 1951.

Pifer, Richard L. "A Social History of the Home Front: Milwaukee Labor during World War II. Ph.D. dissertation, University of Wisconsin, 1983.

Quinn, Lois M., John Pawasarat, and Laura Serebin. *Jobs for Workers on Relief in Milwaukee County, 1930-1944.* Employment Training Institute, University of Wisconsin-Milwaukee, 1995.

Raskin, Max. "Milwaukee and Its Baby Bonds." *Milwaukee History.* Spring, 1985.

Relief Costs in Milwaukee. Milwaukee: Citizens' Bureau of Milwaukee, 1937.

Report of the Commission on the Economic Study of Milwaukee. Milwaukee: City of Milwaukee, 1948.

Schulson, Florence. *Manufacturing in Milwaukee City, Milwaukee County, the Milwaukee Industrial Area, Wisconsin, the East North Central Division and the United States, 1919-1939 compared with 1947.* Milwaukee: Board of Public Land Commissioners, 1950.

Slayton, William L., and Robert L. Filtzer. *Manufacturing in the Milwaukee Industrial Area Compared to Five Comparable Industrial Areas, 1929, 1931, 1933, 1935, 1937, 1939.* Milwaukee: Board of Public Land Commissioners, 1944.

Zeidel, Robert F. "Beer Returns to Cream City." *Milwaukee History.* Spring, 1981.

Chapter 8: The Exploding Metropolis, 1945-1967

Aicher, Joseph R., Jr. "The Brown Deer Annexation: A Case Study in the City of Milwaukee's Consolidation Activity." Master's thesis, Marquette University, 1968.

Ammann & Whitney, Consulting Engineers. *Preliminary Plan for Milwaukee Expressways.* Milwaukee, 1952.

Aukofer, Frank A. *City with a Chance.* Milwaukee: Bruce Publishing Co., 1968.

Bernard, Richard M., ed. *Snowbelt Cities: Metropolitan Politics in the Northeast and Midwest since World War II.* Bloomington: Indiana University Press, 1990.

Cutler, Richard W. *Greater Milwaukee's Growing Pains, 1950-2000: An Insider's View.* Milwaukee County Historical Society, 2001.

Davis, Richard S. "Milwaukee: Old Lady Thrift." In *Our Fair City,* ed. Robert S. Allen. New York: Vanguard Press, 1947.

Final Report to Mayor Zeidler. Milwaukee: Mayor's Study Committee on Social Problems in the Inner Core Area of the City. Apr. 15, 1960.

Flaming, Karl H. "The 1967 Milwaukee Riot: A Historical and Comparative Analysis." Ph.D. dissertation, Syracuse University, 1970.

Fleischmann, Arnold P. "The Politics of Annexation and Urban Development: A Clash of Two Paradigms." Ph.D. dissertation, University of Texas, 1984.

Fox, C.P. *America's Great Circus Parade.* Milwaukee: Reiman Publications, 1993.

"Frank Zeidler: Clippings from the *Milwaukee Journal,* 1944-1969." Milwaukee Public Library.

Greater Milwaukee Committee. Annual reports, 1951-1963.

Hansbury, Patricia C. "Miracle in Milwaukee: A Study of the Impact of Major League Baseball." Master's thesis, University of Wisconsin-Milwaukee, 1972.

Hardie, George A., Jr. *Milwaukee County's General Mitchell International Airport.* Milwaukee: Friends of the Mitchell Gallery of Flight, 1996.

Lurie, Nancy O. *A Special Style: The Milwaukee Public Museum, 1882-1982.* Milwaukee: Milwaukee Public Museum, 1983.

"Made in Milwaukee." *Fortune.* November, 1950.

Maier, Henry W. *Challenge to the Cities: An Approach to a Theory of Urban Leadership.* New York: Random House, 1966.

Mason, Jerry. "Fighting the Postwar Blues." *This Week.* Mar. 30, 1947.

Meyer, Stephen. *"Stalin over Wisconsin": The Making and Unmaking of Militant Unionism, 1900-1950.* New Brunswick: Rutgers University Press, 1992.

"Milwaukee Centurama: Clippings from the *Milwaukee Journal* and *Milwaukee Sentinel,*" 1946. Milwaukee Public Library.

Milwaukee County Expressway Commission. Annual reports, 1954-1978.

Milwaukee County Government Report, 1962.

"Milwaukee: More than Beer Makes It Famous." *Business Week.* Nov. 8, 1952.

Milwaukee's Negro Community. Milwaukee: Citizens' Governmental Research Bureau, 1946.

"Miracle in Milwaukee." *Ebony.* November, 1967.

The Negro in Milwaukee: Progress and Portent, 1863-1963. Milwaukee: Commission on Community Relations, 1963.

O'Reilly, Charles T. *The Inner Core North: A Study of Milwaukee's Negro Community.* Milwaukee: University of Wisconsin-Milwaukee, 1963.

Origin-Destination Traffic Survey: Milwaukee Metropolitan Area. Madison: State Highway Commission of Wisconsin, 1946.

Thompson, William F. *The History of Wisconsin.* Vol. 6, *Continuity and Change, 1940-1965.* Madison: State Historical Society of Wisconsin, 1988.

Wilde, Harold R. "Milwaukee's National Media Riot." In *Cities under Siege: An Anatomy of the Ghetto Riots, 1964-1968,* ed. David Boesel and Peter H. Rossi. New York: Basic Books, 1971.

Zeidler, Frank P. "A Liberal in City Government: My Experiences as Mayor of Milwaukee." Unpublished memoir. Milwaukee Public Library.

Chapter 9: Shifting Currents, 1967-

Abdul-Jabbar, Kareem. *Kareem.* New York: Random House, 1990.

Berry-Caban, Cristobal. *Hispanics in Wisconsin: A Bibliography of Resource Materials.* Madison: State Historical Society of Wisconsin, 1981.

Chute, James. *Milwaukee Symphony Orchestra 25th Anniversary.* Milwaukee Journal, 1984.

The Economic Future of Metropolitan Milwaukee. Hearings before the Joint Economic Committee, Oct. 8-9, 1981. Washington: U.S. Congress, 1981.

Eggers, William D. "America's Boldest Mayors." *Policy Review.* Summer, 1993.

"Florentine Opera Company: A Series of Articles from the *Milwaukee Journal* and *Milwaukee Sentinel,* Feb. 3, 1942-Nov. 16, 1970."Milwaukee Public Library.

Groppi, James. Papers. Urban Archives, University of Wisconsin-Milwaukee Library.

Gruberg, Martin. *A Case Study in U.S. Urban Leadership: The Incumbency of Milwaukee Mayor Henry Maier.* Aldershot (England): Avebury, 1996.

A History of the Counterculture in Milwaukee (1960-1975). Milwaukee: Bugle American, 1975.

Levine, Marc et al. *The Economic State of Milwaukee: The City and the Region, 1998.* Center for Economic Development, University of Wisconsin-Milwaukee, 1998.

Maier, Henry W. *The Mayor Who Made Milwaukee Famous: An Autobiography.* Lanham, MD: Madison Books, 1993.

McNeely, R.L., and Melvin Kinlow. *Milwaukee Today: A Racial Gap Study.* Milwaukee: Milwaukee Urban League, 1987.

Metropolitan Milwaukee Association of Commerce. Periodic statistical reports.

Milwaukee County. Periodic reports, 1967-1993.

Milwaukee in Focus. Milwaukee: Department of City Development, 1992.

The Milwaukee Repertory Theater Company: Our First Twenty Years. Milwaukee: Milwaukee Repertory Theater, 1974.

Milwaukee, Wisconsin Metropolitan Area ... Today. Urban Land Institute, 1987.

Norquist, John O. *The Wealth of Cities.* Reading, MA: Addison-Wesley, 1998.

Nussbaum, David, and Sammis B. White. *What Has Happened to Unemployed Manufacturing Workers in Milwaukee?* Urban Research Center, University of Wisconsin-Milwaukee, 1988.

O'Connor, Sara, and Sherrill Myers. *Working Space: The Milwaukee Repertory Theater Builds a Home.* New York: Theater Communications Group, 1992.

Osborne, David. "John Norquist and the Milwaukee Experiment." *Governing.* November, 1992.

Public Policy Forum (formerly Citizens' Governmental Research Bureau). Various reports, 1967-1998.

Rury, John L., and Frank A. Cassell, eds. *Seeds of Crisis: Public Schooling in Milwaukee since 1920.* Madison: University of Wisconsin Press, 1993.

von Kaas, William K. *Wisconsin: One Decade, Two Recessions.* Madison: Wisconsin Department of Industry, Labor and Human Relations, 1983.

White, Sammis et al. *The Changing Milwaukee Industrial Structure, 1979-1988.* Urban Research Center, University of Wisconsin-Milwaukee, 1988.

_____ et al. *City and Suburban Impacts of the Industrial Changes in Milwaukee, 1979-1987.* Urban Research Center, University of Wisconsin-Milwaukee, 1989.

Related Works by John Gurda

Bay View, Wis. University of Wisconsin Board of Regents, 1979.

The Bradley Legacy: Lynde and Harry Bradley, Their Company, and Their Foundation. Lynde and Harry Bradley Foundation, 1992.

Centennial of Faith. Basilica of St. Josaphat, 1989.

"Change at the River Mouth: Ethnic Succession on Milwaukee's Jones Island, 1700 to 1922." Master's thesis, University of Wisconsin-Milwaukee, 1978.

"The Church and the Neighborhood." In *Milwaukee Catholicism,* ed. Steven Avella. Knights of Columbus, 1992.

Cream City Chronicles: Stories of Milwaukee's Past. Wisconsin Historical Society, 2006.

Discover Milwaukee Catalog. City of Milwaukee, 1986. Reprinted 1987, 1989.

Forging Ahead: A Centennial History of Ladish Co. Ladish Company, Inc., 2005.

Keeping Faith in the City: A 150th-Anniversary History of Immanuel Presbyterian Church. Immanuel Church, 1987.

The Latin Community on Milwaukee's Near South Side. Urban Observatory, University of Wisconsin-Milwaukee, 1976.

The Making of "A Good Name in Industry": A History of the Falk Corporation, 1892-1992. Falk Corporation, 1991.

Miller Time: A History of Miller Brewing Company, 1855-2005. Miller Brewing Company, 2005.

New World Odyssey: Annunciation Greek Orthodox Church and Frank Lloyd Wright. Annunciation Church, 1986.

Path of a Pioneer: A Centennial History of the Wisconsin Electric Power Company. Wisconsin Electric Power Company, 1996.

"Profits and Patriotism: Milwaukee Industry in World War II." *Wisconsin Magazine of History.* Spring, 1994.

The Quiet Company: A Modern History of Northwestern Mutual Life. Northwestern Mutual, 1983.

A Sense of Tradition: The Centennial History of the Milwaukee Country Club. Milwaukee Country Club, 1993.

Silent City: A History of Forest Home Cemetery. Forest Home Cemetery, 2000.

The West End: Merrill Park, Pigsville, Concordia. University of Wisconsin Board of Regents, 1980.

The Will to Succeed: A Centennial History of the Harnischfeger Corporation (with Henry Harnischfeger). Harnischfeger Corporation, 1984.

Index